Digital Twin Approaches in Autonomous Vehicles

Mazhar Hussain Shaik
https://orcid.org/0000-0001-7684-0039
Malla Reddy (Deemed to be) University, Hyderabad, India

Imran Bin Mohd Ibrahim
Universiti Teknikal Malaysia Melaka, Malaysia

Masood Ahmad Mahammad
GITAM School of Core Engineering, GITAM (Deemed to be) University, India

Khaizuran Abdullah
International Islamic University Malaysia, Malaysia

IGI Global
Scientific Publishing
Publishing Tomorrow's Research Today

Published in the United States of America by
IGI Global Scientific Publishing
701 East Chocolate Avenue
Hershey, PA, 17033, USA
Tel: 717-533-8845 | Fax: 717-533-7115
Website: https://www.igi-global.com E-mail: cust@igi-global.com

Library of Congress Cataloging-in-Publication Data

LCCN: 2026003202 (CIP Data Pending)
ISBN13: 9798337377858
Isbn13Softcover: 9798337377865
EISBN13: 9798337377872
British Cataloguing in Publication Data
A Cataloguing in Publication record for this book is available from the British Library.

Table of Contents

Detailed Table of Contents

The need for new validation methods to assess safety in varying driving scenarios is being driven by the increasing complexity of the systems behind autonomous vehicles (AV). AV and Digital Twin (DT) technology have been used to improve scenario-centered evaluations of vehicles by combining real and virtual entities. However, current models have focused on behavioral aspects and neglected the execution of maneuvers like braking, steering, and accelerating. These maneuvers result in the redistribution of loads that affect the suspension systems, tire loads, and stress on the structure. This chapter outlines DT models that integrate autonomous driving behavioral data with vehicle dynamics and structures responses. An emergency braking scenario is used to illustrate the analytical flow and a DT system to monitor operational loads is used to illustrate cumulative loading during the scenario. This framework broadens the safety evaluation of AVs by expanding the DT conceptual models.

Artificial Intelligence (AI) and Machine Learning (ML) are transforming Digital Twin (DT) technology into a real-time, intelligent ecosystem for Autonomous Vehicles (AVs). This chapter explores how AI-driven DT frameworks integrate sensor fusion, reinforcement learning, and edge-cloud collaboration to achieve continuous synchronization between physical and virtual systems. These smart twins enable predictive maintenance, adaptive decision-making, and safety validation with minimal latency. Industrial examples such as Tesla's Predictive Maintenance Twin and Audi's Virtual Prototyping Platform demonstrate practical implementations that enhance reliability, design accuracy, and efficiency. The chapter also discusses challenges in scalability, interoperability, and ethical governance, while highlighting emerging directions like quantum and federated learning. By combining intelligence, automation, and ethical design, AI-empowered Digital Twins form the foundation of next-generation, self-evolving, and resilient autonomous mobility systems.

The fusion of Digital Twin (DT) and Artificial Intelligence (AI) is changing the face of maintenance practices for autonomous vehicles. This chapter offers an AI-based digital twin framework for predictive maintenance to ensure timely, efficient, and reliable maintenance decisions. The framework combines various data sources related to the vehicle for continuous monitoring of the condition of the components of the vehicle to detect any signs of failure. The chapter covers DT-based maintenance systems, intelligent data management, and AI-based anomaly detection for improved safety, reliability, and efficiency of the vehicles. The chapter also covers simulation-based analysis and practical scenario-based analysis to demonstrate the efficacy of the framework. The challenges of data heterogeneity, data synchronization, and data interoperability are also covered. The future of digital twin is also discussed for smarter maintenance practices for autonomous vehicles.

Ensuring safety and reliability is paramount in the development of Autonomous Vehicles (AVs). Digital Twin (DT) technology provides a dynamic virtual counterpart to real vehicles, enabling scenario-based safety validation and crash simulations without physical risk. This chapter explores how DTs integrate real-time sensor data, AI-driven analytics, and multi-physics modeling to simulate complex collision dynamics and evaluate vehicle responses. Emphasis is placed on aligning DT testing with international standards such as ISO 26262 and SOTIF. Case studies from BMW and Waymo demonstrate the industrial application of DTs in reducing prototyping costs and improving validation accuracy. Challenges including data veracity, synchronization latency, and computational overhead are also discussed. By leveraging emerging technologies like quantum computing and federated learning, DT-based safety validation can ensure scalable, transparent, and ethically responsible deployment of autonomous vehicles.

This chapter explores the integration of Digital Twin (DT) technology in Autonomous Vehicles (AVs), emphasizing its role in enhancing vehicle safety, performance, and operational efficiency. Digital Twins create dynamic, real-time virtual models that replicate the physical state of AVs, enabling continuous monitoring, predictive maintenance, and system optimization. By facilitating predictive analytics and simulating real-world driving scenarios, Digital Twins bridge the gap between physical systems and simulations, improving safety validation and decision-making accuracy. Despite significant benefits, challenges remain, including data synchronization, computational demands, and security concerns. Future research should focus on enhancing scalability, integrating with vehicle-to-everything (V2X) systems, and exploring AI-driven optimization techniques. This chapter highlights the transformative potential of Digital Twins in the development and lifecycle management of AVs, offering a comprehensive understanding of their current and future impact on autonomous mobility.

This chapter examines Digital Twin–driven approaches for safety validation and predictive risk modeling in autonomous vehicles operating in complex environments. The purpose of this chapter is to address the limitations of mileage-based and reactive testing by proposing a scalable, simulation-centric safety validation framework. The chapter synthesizes research on Digital Twin architectures, autonomous vehicle simulation platforms, surrogate safety metrics, machine learning–based risk prediction, and real-time monitoring. It demonstrates how Digital Twins support systematic generation of rare and safety-critical scenarios, continuous risk assessment, and adaptive learning across the autonomous vehicle lifecycle. Regulatory, ethical, and governance are also discussed, highlighting the role of Digital Twin–enabled validation in scenario-based approval, continuous compliance monitoring, and transparent safety assurance. By integrating technical and policy perspectives, the chapter provides a coherent framework to support safer and more trustworthy autonomous mobility systems.

The methodology combines conceptual economic modeling, comparative analysis, and heatmap-based visualization to assess the economic impact of implementing a Digital Twin. Investment evaluation tools such as net present value (NPV) and internal rate of return (IRR) are used to examine return-on-investment scenarios. The results indicate that despite high initial investment, Digital Twin systems generate long-term benefits through improved productivity and stronger supply chains.

The resilience of urban transportation systems, as a key component of sustainable development, has played a significant role in urban planning over the past few years. There is a need for new data-driven approaches and advanced simulations to mitigate the consequences of climate change, the expansion of transport networks, and the growing number of vulnerable users. In the meantime, the concept of a digital twin as a dynamic virtual model capable of representing and simulating, monitoring, and analyzing real systems in near real-time rapidly expanded in the field of urban transportation technology. In fact, this part of the present study, which aims to explain the role of digital twins in promoting the resilience of urban transport systems, examines the foundations and methods of spatial modelling, as well as the practical applications of this approach. The primary focus of this section is on integrating spatial data (GIS), transport networks, and a human-centered approach in safety and resilience analysis, particularly for vulnerable users.

The fast evolution of connected cars and autonomous cars demands intelligent transportation systems that can handle high amounts of real-time data. Nevertheless, conventional Vehicle-to-Everything communication systems have weaknesses of low predictivity, latency, interoperability difficulties, and poor traffic control. To mitigate these problems, this chapter examines the application of the Digital Twin technology in conjunction with V2X communication to facilitate real-time monitoring, and predictive analysis. DT-V2X framework provides data-driven virtual models of vehicles, road infrastructure, and communication networks. It combines IoT sensors, edge and cloud computing and AI-based predictive analytics to align the physical transportation environments with their digital equivalents. The framework aims at assessing traffic behavior via simulation and real time data analysis. The expected outcomes include improved road safety, enhanced traffic flow, reduced communication latency, and energy-efficient mobility, contributing to more sustainable intelligent transportation systems.

The integration of Digital Twin technology with 5G and emerging 6G networks is transforming autonomous vehicle systems by enabling real-time synchronization, predictive analytics, and collaborative decision-making. Ultra-low-latency communication, network slicing, and edge–cloud processing allow twins to mirror vehicle behavior with high fidelity while handling large sensor streams. These capabilities enhance hazard prediction, multi-vehicle coordination, and city-scale mobility simulation. Advancements in 6G such as terahertz connectivity and AI-native networking further improve scalability and system resilience. This chapter examines the architecture, performance needs, and practical benefits of DT-AV integration, supported by case studies from China and South Korea. It also highlights challenges in scalability, security, and interoperability, and outlines future research in quantum communication, federated learning, and self-evolving twins.

The urbanization rate and increasing traffic volume have placed enormous strain on available transport infrastructure; therefore, solutions are needed to optimize safety, efficiency, and sustainability. Intelligent Transport Systems (ITS) are one such promising technology being emphasized, with particular emphasis on the potential of Wireless Sensor Networks (WSNs) to facilitate intelligent vehicle communication. WSNs, a collection of geographically distributed sensors, hold the promise for real-time monitoring and collection of vital information with the potential for real-time vehicle-infrastructure interaction. They all contribute fundamental functions in preventing accidents, managing traffic, and improving the management of the road network. This work concerns integrating WSN and ITS for vehicular communication, focusing on developing a model that minimizes latency, enhances data quality, and ensures safe transmission.

Preface

INTRODUCTION

The emergence of autonomous vehicle (AV) technologies has marked a transformative shift in the evolution of modern transportation systems. Driven by rapid advances in artificial intelligence, sensing technologies, communication networks, and intelligent control systems, autonomous vehicles promise to revolutionize mobility by improving safety, efficiency, sustainability, and accessibility. However, the increasing complexity of AV ecosystems also introduces significant technical and operational challenges related to reliability, validation, adaptability, and real-time decision-making. Addressing these challenges requires innovative frameworks capable of bridging the physical and digital worlds in a seamless and intelligent manner.

In this context, Digital Twin (DT) technology has emerged as a powerful paradigm for the design, simulation, monitoring, optimization, and lifecycle management of autonomous vehicle systems. A Digital Twin represents a dynamic virtual counterpart of a physical entity that continuously synchronizes with real-world data through sensors, communication interfaces, and computational intelligence. By enabling real-time interaction between physical vehicles and their virtual replicas, digital twins provide unprecedented opportunities for predictive analysis, performance evaluation, fault detection, and intelligent system optimization.

This edited volume, *Digital Twin Approaches in Autonomous Vehicles*, presents a comprehensive exploration of the convergence between digital twin technologies and autonomous mobility systems. The book aims to provide readers with a detailed understanding of the theoretical foundations, enabling technologies, implementation frameworks, and emerging applications of digital twins within autonomous vehicle ecosystems. The contributions included in this volume collectively highlight how digital twin methodologies can significantly enhance the development, testing, deployment, and management of next-generation intelligent transportation systems.

The chapters in this book cover a broad spectrum of interdisciplinary topics, including sensor integration, vehicle-to-vehicle (V2V) and vehicle-to-infrastructure (V2I) communication, real-time simulation, predictive maintenance, cybersecurity, energy optimization, AI-driven decision-making, safety validation, and scalable connected mobility infrastructures. In addition to theoretical perspectives, several chapters present practical case studies and industrial applications that demonstrate the real-world impact and future potential of digital twin technologies in autonomous transportation.

One of the distinguishing features of this volume is its focus on bridging the research gap between digital twin systems and autonomous vehicles—two domains that have largely evolved independently despite their strong technological synergy. By bringing together contributions from researchers, engineers, academicians, and industry experts across multiple disciplines, this book seeks to establish a unified platform for knowledge sharing and collaborative innovation. The interdisciplinary nature of the discussions reflects the growing importance of integrating mechanical engineering, computer science, artificial intelligence, data analytics, communication technologies, and transportation engineering in shaping the future of intelligent mobility.

This book is intended to serve as a valuable resource for a diverse readership, including researchers, graduate students, automotive engineers, transportation professionals, technology developers, policymakers, and industry practitioners. It is our hope that this volume will not only support academic research and technological advancement but also inspire new collaborations, innovative applications, and policy frameworks for safer, smarter, and more sustainable transportation systems.

As editors, we sincerely appreciate the efforts and scholarly contributions of all chapter authors whose expertise and dedication made this volume possible. We also extend our gratitude to the reviewers for their valuable feedback and constructive suggestions that helped enhance the quality of the chapters. Finally, we thank the publishing team for their continuous support and cooperation throughout the development of this book.

We hope that *Digital Twin Approaches in Autonomous Vehicles* will contribute meaningfully to ongoing research and development in intelligent transportation systems and serve as a significant reference for advancing the future of autonomous mobility.

ORGANIZATION OF THE BOOK

The chapters presented in this edited volume collectively demonstrate the growing significance of Digital Twin technologies in addressing the multifaceted challenges associated with autonomous vehicles and intelligent transportation systems. Each contribution offers unique perspectives that advance theoretical understanding, practical implementation, and future research directions within this rapidly evolving domain.

Chapter 1 introduces a holistic Digital Twin framework that integrates both structural and behavioral safety aspects in autonomous vehicles. The chapter emphasizes the importance of extending conventional Digital Twin models beyond behavioral simulations by incorporating vehicle dynamics, suspension responses, and structural load analysis during critical maneuvers such as emergency braking. By bridging operational behavior with structural integrity assessment, the chapter presents a comprehensive framework for improving safety evaluation in autonomous driving environments.

Chapter 2 explores adaptive AI-driven Digital Twin frameworks designed for real-time synchronization and intelligent mobility management in autonomous vehicle ecosystems. The authors examine how artificial intelligence, machine learning, sensor fusion, reinforcement learning, and edge-cloud collaboration contribute to creating intelligent and self-evolving Digital Twins. Through industrial examples and emerging technologies such as federated and quantum learning, the chapter highlights the transformative role of AI-enabled Digital Twins in predictive maintenance, adaptive decision-making, and resilient mobility systems.

Chapter 3 focuses on AI-driven Digital Twin frameworks for predictive maintenance in autonomous vehicles. The chapter presents methodologies for integrating vehicle data streams, anomaly detection techniques, and intelligent maintenance strategies to improve vehicle reliability and operational efficiency. By combining simulation-based analysis with practical use cases, the chapter demonstrates how

Digital Twins can support proactive maintenance practices while addressing challenges related to data synchronization and interoperability.

Chapter 4 investigates the role of Digital Twins in safety validation and crash scenario simulations for autonomous vehicles. The authors demonstrate how real-time data integration, AI analytics, and multi-physics simulations can be used to model complex collision scenarios and evaluate vehicle responses under safety-critical conditions. The chapter further aligns Digital Twin testing methodologies with international safety standards while discussing industrial applications and future advancements in scalable validation frameworks.

Chapter 5 presents a comprehensive discussion on Digital Twin-driven innovation throughout the lifecycle of autonomous vehicle systems. The chapter explores applications related to modeling, virtual prototyping, predictive analytics, system optimization, and lifecycle management. By emphasizing both operational efficiency and safety enhancement, the chapter highlights the broad transformative potential of Digital Twin technologies in the development and long-term management of autonomous mobility platforms.

Chapter 6 addresses Digital Twin-driven safety validation and predictive risk modeling in complex autonomous driving environments. The chapter proposes scalable, simulation-centric validation frameworks capable of generating rare and safety-critical scenarios for continuous risk assessment. By integrating machine learning, surrogate safety metrics, and regulatory perspectives, the contribution offers a balanced framework that combines technical validation with governance and ethical considerations for trustworthy autonomous mobility systems.

Chapter 7 examines the application of Digital Twin technologies within Intelligent Transportation Systems (ITS) to improve optimization, safety, and sustainable mobility. The chapter presents unified frameworks that integrate real-time synchronization, artificial intelligence, and simulation-driven optimization for transportation networks. The discussion highlights how Digital Twin-enabled ITS infrastructures can reduce congestion, improve operational efficiency, and support environmentally sustainable transportation strategies.

Chapter 8 explores the role of Digital Twin-enabled smart manufacturing in the production of electronics for autonomous vehicles, particularly within Surface Mount Technology (SMT) environments. The chapter demonstrates how virtual production models, AI-driven predictive systems, and process optimization techniques can contribute to zero-defect manufacturing and improved reliability of vehicle electronic systems. This contribution extends the application of Digital Twins beyond vehicle operations into intelligent manufacturing ecosystems.

Chapter 9 provides an economic perspective on the adoption of Digital Twin technologies within autonomous vehicle systems. The chapter evaluates the cost-benefit implications of Digital Twin implementation in areas such as fleet management, operational efficiency, and regulatory compliance. Using economic modeling and investment evaluation methods, the discussion highlights both the initial financial challenges and the long-term economic benefits associated with Digital Twin adoption.

Chapter 10 introduces a human-centric perspective on Digital Twins for road safety and future autonomous mobility. The chapter emphasizes the importance of integrating spatial data, transport networks, and human-centered design principles to improve resilience and safety in urban transportation systems. Special attention is given to vulnerable road users and the role of Digital Twins in supporting sustainable and inclusive mobility planning.

Chapter 11 further expands the discussion on Digital Twin integration with V2X communication systems by focusing on real-time monitoring, predictive analytics, and intelligent transportation coordination. The chapter presents a Digital Twin-enabled V2X framework that leverages IoT, edge-cloud computing, and AI-driven analytics to enhance traffic flow, reduce communication latency, and improve energy-efficient mobility in connected transportation ecosystems.

Chapter 12 investigates the integration of Digital Twins with 5G and emerging 6G-enabled autonomous vehicle systems. The chapter discusses how ultra-low-latency communication, edge-cloud processing, and AI-native networking enable highly synchronized and scalable Digital Twin environments. Supported by international case studies, the chapter also examines future directions involving federated learning, quantum communication, and self-evolving autonomous systems.

Chapter 13 focuses on Intelligent Transport Systems employing Wireless Sensor Networks (WSNs) for smart vehicle communication. The chapter highlights the importance of real-time data collection, low-latency communication, and secure information exchange in modern transportation infrastructures. By integrating WSNs within ITS frameworks, the contribution demonstrates how intelligent communication models can improve traffic management, accident prevention, and transportation efficiency.

Chapter 14 presents an innovative framework for enhancing topological efficiency in Digital Twins of autonomous vehicles using synthetic data and artificial intelligence. The chapter introduces topology-driven validation methods that combine persistent homology, generative models, and AI-based scenario generation to ensure structural fidelity and computational efficiency. This contribution provides advanced methodologies for improving trustworthiness, scalability, and interoperability within complex autonomous vehicle simulation environments.

Together, these chapters provide a rich and multidisciplinary exploration of Digital Twin technologies and their transformative impact on autonomous vehicles and intelligent transportation systems. The volume not only highlights current advancements and practical applications but also identifies future challenges and emerging opportunities that will shape the next generation of autonomous mobility solutions.

CONCLUSION

As autonomous vehicle technologies continue to evolve and reshape the future of transportation, the role of Digital Twin technology has become increasingly significant in enabling intelligent, adaptive, and reliable mobility systems. The chapters presented in this volume collectively demonstrate how the convergence of Digital Twins, artificial intelligence, advanced communication systems, simulation platforms, and intelligent transportation infrastructures can address many of the critical challenges associated with autonomous mobility. From safety validation and predictive maintenance to connected communication frameworks, lifecycle optimization, manufacturing intelligence, and sustainable transportation planning, the contributions in this book reflect the broad and transformative potential of Digital Twin methodologies.

This edited volume highlights the interdisciplinary nature of the field, bringing together perspectives from engineering, computer science, transportation systems, artificial intelligence, data analytics, economics, and urban mobility research. The diverse range of topics presented throughout the book illustrates not only the technological advancements currently shaping autonomous vehicle ecosystems but also the emerging research directions that will define future innovations. The discussions on ethical governance, cybersecurity, interoperability, scalability, and regulatory considerations further emphasize the need for collaborative and responsible development of intelligent transportation systems.

As editors, we believe that this book provides a timely and valuable contribution to the growing body of knowledge surrounding Digital Twin applications in autonomous vehicles. It serves as both a foundational reference and a forward-looking resource for researchers, academicians, engineers, policymakers, and industry practitioners seeking to understand and advance this rapidly developing field. The integration of theoretical insights, practical frameworks, and real-world case studies offers readers a comprehensive understanding of the opportunities and challenges associated with Digital Twin-driven autonomous mobility.

We sincerely hope that the ideas, methodologies, and innovations presented in this volume will inspire further research, foster interdisciplinary collaboration, and support the development of safer, smarter, and more sustainable transportation systems worldwide. The future of autonomous mobility will depend not only on technological progress but also on our collective ability to design intelligent systems that are resilient, trustworthy, efficient, and human-centered. In this regard, Digital Twin technology is poised to play a pivotal role in shaping the next generation of connected and autonomous transportation ecosystems.

Finally, we extend our heartfelt appreciation to all contributing authors, reviewers, and publishing professionals whose dedication and expertise made this volume possible. Their scholarly efforts have enriched this work and contributed meaningfully to advancing research and innovation in the field of autonomous vehicles and Digital Twin technologies.

Chapter 1

A Holistic Digital Twin Framework for Structural and Behavioral Safety Integration in Autonomous Vehicles

Achmad Zaki Rahman
http://orcid.org/0009-0001-9381-3400
National Research and Innovation Agency, Indonesia

Nimas Ayu Untariyati
http://orcid.org/0009-0001-6466-9534
National Research and Innovation Agency, Indonesia

Khairul Jauhari
National Research and Innovation Agency, Indonesia

Budi Haryanto
National Research and Innovation Agency, Indonesia

ABSTRACT

The need for new validation methods to assess safety in varying driving scenarios is being driven by the increasing complexity of the systems behind autonomous vehicles (AV). AV and Digital Twin (DT) technology have been used to improve scenario-centered evaluations of vehicles by combining real and virtual entities. However, current models have focused on behavioral aspects and neglected the execution of maneuvers like braking, steering, and accelerating. These maneuvers result in the redistribution of loads that affect the suspension systems, tire loads, and stress on the structure. This chapter outlines DT models that integrate autonomous driving behavioral data with vehicle dynamics and structures responses. An emergency braking scenario is used to illustrate the analytical flow and a DT system to monitor operational loads is used to illustrate cumulative loading during the scenario. This framework broadens the safety evaluation of AVs by expanding the DT conceptual models.

DOI: 10.4018/979-8-3373-7785-8.ch001

1. INTRODUCTION

The progress made in Autonomous Vehicle (AV) technology has posed a critical change in the functioning of today's transportation systems. With the development of sensing technology, Artificial Intelligence (AI), and algorithms for vehicle control, vehicles can now understand their environment and make determinations and driving decisions up to a high degree of autonomy. As AVs function in dynamic and uncertain traffic systems, continuous interaction with surrounding drivers agents, and developing intelligent transportation systems have possed the reliable functioning and safety of AV technology. Also, the development and performance of autonomous intelligent systems must be based upon human-centered design, and that trust, transparency and interaction with AI (Mudunuri & Bhattacharya, 2024).

Scenario-based safety validation has become a popular method for testing how AVs respond in various difficult driving situations. Researchers can understand how autonomous systems deal with safety-critical situations by testing them in a wide range of real-world situations, including emergency stopping, sudden lane cut-ins, evasive lane changes, and obstacle avoidance. Scenario testing is important for the Safety of the Intended Functionality (SOTIF) methodologies, which evaluate how safe automated driving systems are in complex operating environments (Hou et al., 2024). However, from a perception, decision-making, and real-world driving situation diversity standpoint, the challenges of AV safety testing are well-documented (C. Wang et al., 2024; H. Wang et al., 2024).

In recent years, Digital Twin (DT) technology has emerged as a promising approach to strengthen scenario-based validation processes. A DT represents a dynamically synchronized virtual counterpart of a physical system that enables continuous interaction between real-world assets and their digital representations. Through bidirectional data exchange, DT platforms support monitoring, simulation, and predictive analysis across the lifecycle of complex engineering systems. Tao et al. describe DT as cyber–physical systems capable of integrating physical models, data, and intelligent algorithms for system-level analysis and decision-making (Tao et al., 2019), while Crespi et al. emphasize their capability for real-time synchronization between physical and virtual entities (Crespi et al., 2023).

Within the AV domain, DT technologies have increasingly been applied to reproduce vehicle behavior, recreate traffic scenarios, and support system validation under controlled yet realistic environments. Early studies have explored DT–assisted testing frameworks that combine physical vehicle experiments with virtual simulation to accelerate AV evaluation and reduce testing costs (Meng et al., 2022; Shoukat et al., 2024) . More recent research demonstrates how DT platforms can support distributed coordination and collaborative path planning among multiple AVs by synchronizing vehicle states between physical and virtual environments (Tang et al., 2024). Edge-based DT architectures further enable low-latency validation of connected and AV systems (Campolo et al., 2024).

At a broader mobility scale, the concept of a Mobility Digital Twin (MDT) extends DT environments to represent interactions among vehicles, infrastructure, and transportation networks (Wang et al., 2022; Xu et al., 2025). Such architectures allow large-scale traffic simulation and system-level safety analysis. Meanwhile, communication-enabled DT environments—supported by vehicle-to-everything (V2X) connectivity and distributed cyber-physical infrastructures—have been proposed to improve data availability and enhance scenario realism during AV testing (Duan et al., 2024; Hui et al., 2022) . These developments collectively highlight the growing role of DT ecosystems in enabling advanced validation and analysis of autonomous mobility systems.

Despite these advances, most existing DT implementations in AV research remain primarily focused on functional and behavioral validation. Current studies typically evaluate perception accuracy, trajectory tracking performance, or decision-making robustness when vehicles encounter various driving scenarios. While these approaches are essential for assessing the functional reliability of automated driving systems, they often overlook the mechanical consequences of the maneuvers generated by these systems.

This limitation highlights the need for a holistic DT framework capable of integrating behavioral safety evaluation with structural response analysis. Rather than treating DT solely as behavioral replicas of vehicle operation, a more comprehensive framework should capture the causal relationship between autonomous driving maneuvers, dynamic load transfer mechanisms, and the resulting structural responses within the vehicle system.

AVs perform tasks such as steering, braking, or accelerating, and to bring those commands to a vehicle's mechanical systems. From the vehicle's dynamics, those commands result in a measurable repositioning of the mass on the vehicle's structure. Longitudinal decelerations reposition the relative mass toward the front of the vehicle, and lateral accelerations induce repositioning of the mass between inner and outer wheels. Load repositioning is a dominant factor in determining the vehicle's tire forces, suspension loads, chasses load, and therefore vehicle stability and handling (Milliken & Milliken, 1995; Rajamani, 2006).

In addition to this, experimental research shows that data from the vehicle's sensors can be used to estimate the lateral load transfer and the dynamic vertical tire loads. With regard to the estimation methods based on observers, the dynamic load distributions during real driving scenarios can be reconstructed. For example, Doumiati et al. showed that using lateral load transfers and vertical dynamic tire loads, one could estimate the loads through dynamic observers that are derived from some baseline measurements on the vehicle; recent works (Öngir et al., 2025) have focused on estimating the vertical dynamic tire load using the vehicle's sensors and some machine learning techniques.

Along with the more obvious impacts to vehicle stability, these dynamic load changes affect the structural durability of the vehicle, and its reliability over time. In the case of aggressive driving behaviors, transient loads cause localized stress changes in the suspension, chassis, and other structural components that support the chassis. In autonomous mobility systems, these events will happen cumulatively over long periods of time, resulting in incremental fatigue damage and the progressive loss of structural integrity. However, very few, if any, of these structural impacts are reflected in current DT methodologies for AV testing and validation.

Unlike existing DT implementations that treat structural integrity and behavioral performance as separate validation concerns, the proposed framework establishes an explicit causal chain — from autonomous maneuver execution through dynamic load transfer to cumulative fatigue damage accumulation — enabling durability-oriented structural safety evaluation within a unified cyber–physical DT environment.

This gap in the current methodologies for testing and validation of AVs underscores the need for an integrated DT methodology that merges behavioral safety assessments with structural response assessments. In this case there will be an emphasis on capturing the interactions between autonomous driving behaviors and the dynamic load changes produced, and the structural responses of the vehicle.

Thus, this chapter presents the "Holistic Digital Twin Framework for the Integration of Structural and Behavioral Safety in Autonomous Vehicles". This framework integrates DT technology to Behavioral Performance and Mechanical Consequence Analysis of Autonomous Driving Actions, combining scenario-based maneuver generation, vehicle dynamics, and structural response analysis. The framework focuses on the relationship between maneuver-induced loads and the evolution of structural stresses to enhance the comprehension of the safety and reliability of AVs, with particular emphasis on the durability of AVs, predictive maintenance, and reliability of the autonomous mobility systems

2. MANEUVER-INDUCED LOAD DYNAMICS IN AVS

AV operation involves a wide range of driving maneuvers that arise from continuous decision-making processes within perception, planning, and control systems. During normal operation, these maneuvers include acceleration, braking, steering corrections, and lane changes that allow the vehicle to adapt to surrounding traffic conditions. In safety-critical situations—such as sudden obstacle avoidance, emergency braking, or rapid lane changes—these actions can occur more abruptly and generate significant variations in the forces acting on the vehicle. Consequently, the dynamic behavior of the vehicle during maneuver execution plays an important role in determining both vehicle stability and the loads transmitted through its structural components.

From a vehicle dynamics perspective, driving maneuvers generate time-varying forces at the tire–road interface, which propagate through suspension systems and vehicle structures. These forces result from longitudinal and lateral accelerations that arise when the vehicle changes speed or direction. Classical vehicle dynamics theory shows that longitudinal acceleration during braking produces forward load transfer, increasing the normal forces acting on the front wheels, while lateral acceleration during cornering causes load transfer between the inner and outer wheels of the vehicle (Milliken & Milliken, 1995; Rajamani, 2006). These load transfer phenomena directly influence tire forces, suspension loads, and the distribution of stresses within the vehicle chassis.

The estimation and analysis of load transfer during vehicle maneuvers have been extensively investigated in vehicle dynamics research. Observer-based estimation methods have been proposed to evaluate vertical tire forces and lateral load transfer using standard onboard sensor measurements. Experimental studies demonstrate that such approaches can provide reliable estimations of dynamic load distribution, enabling improved assessment of vehicle stability and safety-critical conditions during maneuver execution (Doumiati et al., 2009).

These findings highlight that maneuver-induced load variations are fundamental indicators of the dynamic state of the vehicle and provide valuable information for analyzing the physical consequences of vehicle motion. Within the context of AV operation, the frequency and variability of maneuver execution may be significantly higher than in conventional human-driven vehicles, due to the continuous adjustments performed by automated control systems. As a result, the loads generated during these maneuvers can introduce complex and rapidly changing stress states within vehicle structures. Understanding the mechanisms that govern maneuver-induced load dynamics therefore represents a critical step toward integrating structural considerations into DT-based safety evaluation frameworks.

2.1. Critical Autonomous Driving Maneuvers

The dynamic loads experienced by a vehicle are closely related to the maneuvers executed during driving. In conventional vehicles, such maneuvers are typically initiated by human drivers and occur intermittently depending on traffic conditions and driver behavior. In contrast, AVs continuously adjust their motion through automated control systems that respond to environmental perception and trajectory planning outputs. As a result, AV operation involves frequent and sometimes rapid maneuver adjustments that can introduce complex variations in the forces acting on the vehicle.

Several categories of maneuvers are particularly relevant when analyzing maneuver-induced load dynamics. Among these, longitudinal maneuvers—such as acceleration and braking—represent the most common actions performed during vehicle operation. During braking events, the deceleration of the vehicle produces a forward shift in the center-of-mass load distribution, increasing the normal forces acting on the front axle while reducing those on the rear axle. Conversely, acceleration produces an opposite load redistribution toward the rear wheels. These longitudinal load transfers affect tire forces and suspension loads, thereby influencing both vehicle stability and the mechanical loading conditions within the chassis structure (Rajamani, 2006).

In addition to longitudinal maneuvers, lateral maneuvers such as cornering and lane changes also generate significant load redistribution within the vehicle. When a vehicle undergoes lateral acceleration during a turn, load transfer occurs between the inner and outer wheels due to the combined effects of centrifugal force and suspension roll dynamics. This lateral load transfer alters the vertical tire forces and contributes to variations in suspension loading, which can significantly affect the distribution of stresses across structural components of the vehicle body (Milliken & Milliken, 2002).

These maneuver categories are frequently used in scenario-based safety validation of AVs because they represent conditions where vehicle dynamics responses can change rapidly. Emergency braking scenarios, obstacle avoidance maneuvers, and sudden lane changes are therefore commonly employed in AV testing environments to evaluate system stability and safety performance under dynamic conditions.

2.2. Load Transfer Mechanisms in Vehicle Dynamics

Load transfer is a fundamental concept in vehicle dynamics that describes the redistribution of vertical forces acting on the vehicle wheels during acceleration, braking, and cornering. These variations arise from the interaction between inertial forces and the geometric configuration of the vehicle, particularly the height of the center of gravity, wheelbase, and suspension characteristics.

During longitudinal maneuvers such as braking or acceleration, inertial forces acting on the vehicle mass generate a pitching moment about the vehicle's center of gravity. This moment leads to a redistribution of normal loads between the front and rear axles. When the vehicle decelerates, the load shifts toward the front axle, increasing the normal forces on the front wheels while reducing those on the rear wheels. Conversely, during acceleration, the load distribution shifts toward the rear axle.

From classical vehicle dynamics formulations (Jazar, 2025), the normal forces acting on the front and rear axles can be expressed as:

$$F_{z,f} = \frac{mgb}{L} - \frac{ma_x h}{L}, F_{z,r} = \frac{mga}{L} + \frac{ma_x h}{L} \tag{1}$$

where m is the vehicle mass, g is gravitational acceleration, a_x is the longitudinal acceleration, h is the height of the center of gravity, a is distance from the center of gravity (CG) to the front axle, b distance from CG to the rear axle, and $L= a+b$ is the wheelbase.

By subtracting the front and rear axle normal loads, the total axle-to-axle load difference can be expressed as

$$\Delta F_{z,\text{total}} = F_{z,r} - F_{z,f} = \frac{2ma_x h}{L} \tag{2}$$

Accordingly, the load variation at each axle may be expressed as:

$$\Delta F_z = \frac{m a_x h}{L} \tag{3}$$

where ΔF_z represents the change in vertical load at a single axle. This relationship shows that the magnitude of load transfer depends on both vehicle geometry and longitudinal acceleration. During braking, the front axle experiences an increase in vertical load while the rear axle is correspondingly unloaded. Conversely, acceleration produces a rearward shift of the vertical load. These changes directly influence tire force capability and the forces transmitted through suspension components and chassis attachment points (Rajamani, 2006; Reimpell et al., 2001).

Similarly, lateral load transfer occurs when the vehicle experiences lateral acceleration during cornering. The inertial forces generated by lateral motion produce a rolling moment about the vehicle's longitudinal axis, transferring vertical loads from the inner wheels to the outer wheels. In simplified form, the lateral load transfer can be approximated as:

$$\Delta F_{z,\mathrm{lat}} = \frac{m a_y h}{t} \tag{4}$$

where $\Delta F_{z,\mathrm{lat}}$ is the change in vertical load between the inner and outer wheels, t is the track width, and a_y is the lateral acceleration. This formulation represents an idealized rigid-body approximation; in practice, lateral load transfer is also influenced by suspension compliance and roll dynamics.

Maneuver-induced loads should not be viewed solely as a vehicle dynamics phenomenon, but as a link between dynamic behavior and structural response. While most AV DT frameworks focus on behavioral validation—such as perception, trajectory tracking, and control stability—the structural effects of dynamic loading remain largely unaddressed.

Although recent DT-based approaches emphasize realistic vehicle dynamics in safety-critical scenarios (Duan et al., 2024), they often neglect the resulting structural loads. This limitation highlights the need for an integrated structural–behavioral framework, which is introduced in the following section.

2.3. Structural Implications of Maneuver-Induced Loads

The structural response of vehicle components subjected to maneuver-induced loads can be described using fundamental principles from mechanics of materials. The normal stress acting on a structural member under axial loading is defined as the force per unit cross-sectional area:

$$\sigma = \frac{F}{A} \tag{5}$$

where F represents the internal force transmitted through the component and A is the corresponding load-bearing area. This formulation, widely adopted in classical structural analysis, provides an approximation of the average stress distribution across the section.

In the context of vehicle dynamics, maneuver-induced load transfer—such as during braking or cornering—modifies the forces acting on the vehicle structure. These forces propagate through suspension systems and structural load paths, resulting in variations of internal forces F, which directly influence the resulting stress states within critical components such as the chassis and suspension mounts.

This relationship establishes a direct causal link between vehicle maneuvers and structural response, forming a key foundation for integrating mechanical behavior into DT–based safety evaluation frameworks.

3. STRUCTURAL RESPONSE REPRESENTATION IN DT SYSTEMS

Building on the load transfer mechanisms established in Section 2, this section describes how maneuver-induced forces propagate through vehicle structures and how these responses can be represented within a DT environment. While Section 2 defined the physical origin of dynamic loading, this section focuses on how these loads are transmitted, transformed, and monitored within the structural system.

3.1. Structural Load Path and Stress Propagation in Vehicle Systems

The execution of an AV maneuver initiates a sequence of mechanical events that link control actions to structural responses within the vehicle system. When the automated driving controller executes longitudinal and lateral maneuvers—such as acceleration, braking, cornering, or lane changes—these actions modify the forces generated at the tire–road interface. From a vehicle dynamics perspective, these forces determine the motion of the vehicle and the distribution of loads across its mechanical subsystems.

Changes in vehicle motion produce corresponding variations in load transfer across the suspension system. Longitudinal deceleration during braking shifts loads toward the front axle, while lateral acceleration during cornering redistributes forces between the inner and outer wheels. These load transfer mechanisms influence the magnitude and direction of forces transmitted through suspension links, mounting points, and chassis structures (Milliken & Milliken; Rajamani).

As these loads propagate through the vehicle structure, they generate stress states within structural components such as suspension mounts, subframes, and chassis members. The resulting stresses represent the mechanical response of the vehicle to the control actions executed by the AV system. Consequently, autonomous driving decisions are directly connected to structural loading conditions through a chain of interactions that links maneuver execution, vehicle dynamics, and structural mechanics.

Within a DT environment, this causal chain provides a conceptual basis for connecting behavioral decisions with mechanical system states. By interpreting maneuver commands through vehicle dynamics models and structural response analysis, the DT can estimate how driving behavior influences the mechanical condition of the vehicle structure.

To provide a unified representation of these interactions, the overall relationship between maneuver execution, load transfer, structural response, and DT-based monitoring is illustrated in Figure 1. The figure summarizes how maneuver-induced loads propagate through the vehicle system and how these effects are captured, updated, and accumulated within a DT framework.

Figure 1. DT–based representation of maneuver-induced structural response in AVs

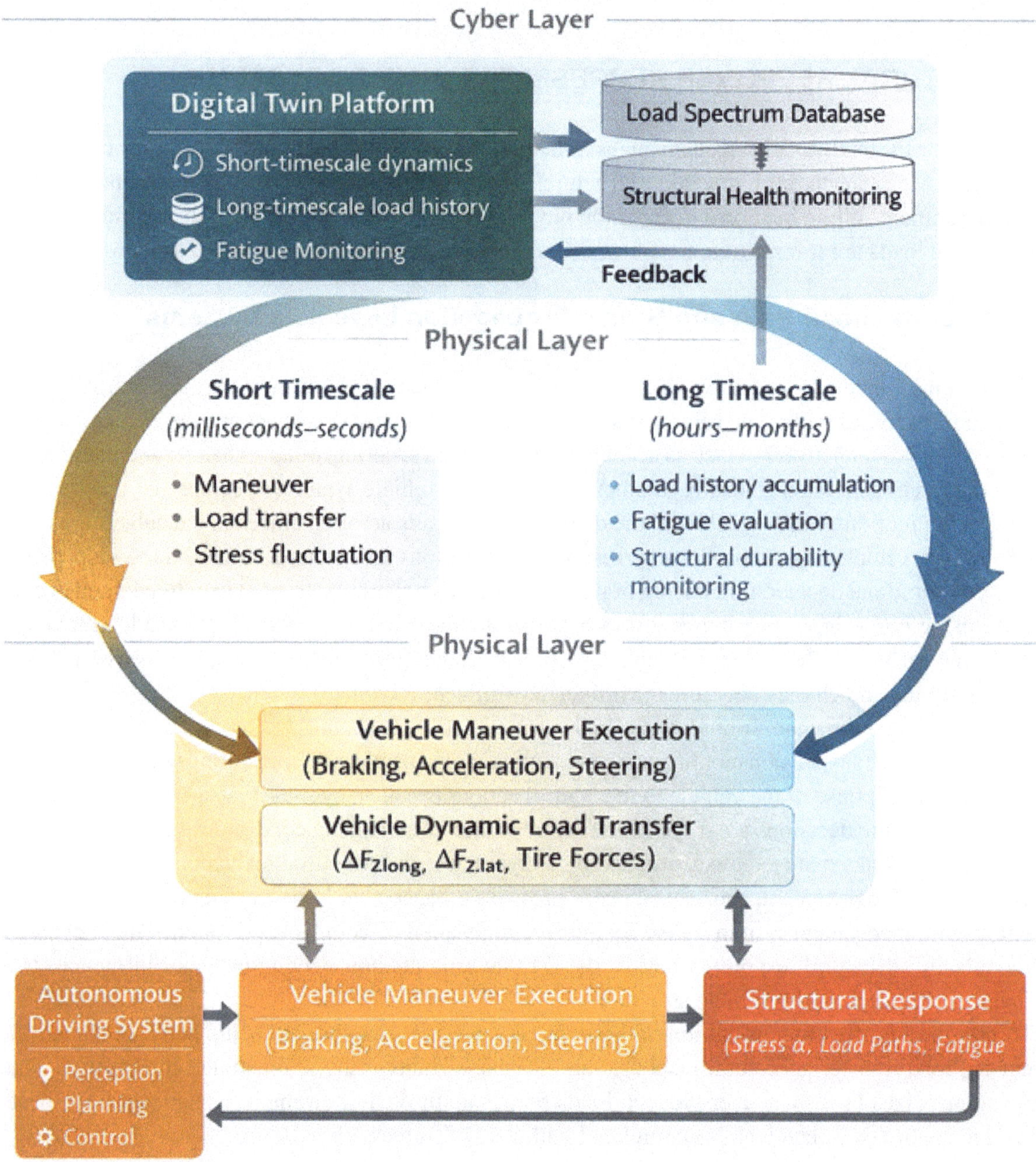

Figure 1 illustrates the conceptual representation of maneuver-induced structural response within a DT framework for AVs. Autonomous driving maneuvers generate dynamic loading conditions, including load transfer and load redistribution, which propagate through suspension systems and structural load paths toward the vehicle chassis. These loading conditions produce internal forces and stress states, whose evolution characterizes the structural response of the vehicle. The DT core integrates operational data through data assimilation, model updating, and state synchronization to maintain a consistent virtual representation of the structural condition. The monitoring layer captures both real-time responses and long-term load accumulation, enabling the evaluation of load history, fatigue behavior, and cumulative damage. A feedback loop supports continuous model updating, linking maneuver execution with structural performance and durability.

3.2. Multi-Timescale Structural Response

The structural response of a vehicle subjected to maneuver-induced loading occurs across multiple timescales. At short timescales, individual maneuvers such as braking, steering, or acceleration generate transient load variations that produce immediate changes in internal forces and stress states. These responses reflect the direct mechanical effect of vehicle motion on structural components.

At longer timescales, the repeated occurrence of these loading events leads to cumulative structural effects. Although individual stress levels may be relatively small, their accumulation over many cycles contributes to fatigue-related degradation of structural components. The structural condition of the vehicle therefore depends not only on the magnitude of individual loads, but also on their frequency and distribution over time.

This behavior is particularly relevant in AV operation, where control systems continuously perform small adjustments to maintain trajectory and stability. These frequent maneuver corrections generate a large number of loading cycles, which may not be critical individually but can become significant when accumulated over extended periods.

Within a DT environment, these different timescales can be represented through separate but connected processes. Short-term responses are evaluated in near real time to capture instantaneous structural behavior, while long-term effects are assessed using accumulated load histories that reflect actual operating conditions. This distinction enables the DT to represent both immediate structural response and long-term durability trends within a unified framework.

3.3. Structural Monitoring and DT Integration

The structural response of the vehicle can be continuously reconstructed using operational data collected during vehicle operation. Measurements such as acceleration, velocity, and steering input provide the basis for estimating maneuver-induced loading conditions and their effects on the vehicle structure. These loading conditions are interpreted through simplified structural representations to evaluate internal forces and corresponding stress states within critical components. In this way, the DT maintains a synchronized representation of both the dynamic loading environment and the structural response of the vehicle.

Beyond instantaneous evaluation, the DT enables the accumulation of loading events over time. Each maneuver contributes to a sequence of loading cycles, which collectively form a load history representing the actual operating conditions experienced by the vehicle. This accumulated information provides a foundation for assessing long-term structural behavior and identifying patterns associated with durability and fatigue.

By combining real-time load estimation with load history accumulation, the DT captures both short-term structural response and long-term trends in structural condition. This capability allows the framework to connect autonomous driving behavior with its mechanical consequences, supporting continuous structural assessment within operational environments.

4. HOLISTIC DT FRAMEWORK FOR STRUCTURAL–BEHAVIORAL INTEGRATION

Building on the load transfer mechanisms and structural response propagation established in Sections 2 and 3, this section presents the implementation-oriented DT framework for maneuver-induced structural assessment in AVs. The purpose of this section is not to re-derive the underlying vehicle dynamics and structural mechanics relationships, but to show how those relationships can be organized within a unified DT architecture capable of transforming autonomous maneuver execution into physically interpretable structural indicators.

Specifically, the proposed framework establishes a computational chain that links maneuver commands generated by the autonomous driving system to dynamic load transfer, transmitted structural forces, stress responses, and fatigue-relevant durability metrics. Within this architecture, short-timescale analysis is used to capture transient maneuver-level structural effects, while long-timescale analysis is used to reconstruct load histories, estimate accumulated stress cycles, and evaluate cumulative damage over extended operation. In this way, the DT framework connects behavioral validation with structural monitoring and durability assessment within a single cyber–physical environment.

4.1. Framework Architecture

Building on the load transfer mechanisms and structural response relationships established in Sections 2 and 3, this section presents the DT framework for integrating autonomous driving behavior with structural response evaluation. The objective is not to re-derive vehicle dynamics or structural mechanics, but to organize these established physical relationships within a unified DT architecture that enables continuous interpretation of maneuver-induced structural effects.

The proposed structural–behavioral DT framework represents the causal relationship between autonomous driving decisions and the resulting mechanical condition of the vehicle. Within this framework, maneuver commands generated by the autonomous driving system are interpreted as inputs to a computational process that links behavioral actions to engineering quantities relevant for structural analysis and durability assessment.

To support this interpretation, the framework is organized into a layered DT architecture, as illustrated in Figure 2. The architecture consists of three interacting layers: the Autonomous Driving Behavior Layer, the Vehicle Dynamics Layer, and the Structural Response Layer. These layers are connected through a continuous DT update loop that integrates operational vehicle data with model-based estimation, ensuring synchronization between physical and virtual representations of the vehicle state.

The role of this layered architecture is to provide a structured transformation from behavioral outputs to structural indicators. Rather than describing the underlying physical mechanisms in detail, the framework defines how these mechanisms are computationally linked within the DT environment. Specifically, the architecture establishes a processing chain in which maneuver commands are transformed into dynamic loading conditions, transmitted through structural load paths, and subsequently interpreted as stress-related and durability-relevant indicators.

Figure 2. DT framework linking the AV as the physical entity with structural state estimation, structural indicators, and fatigue-related evaluation within the DT core

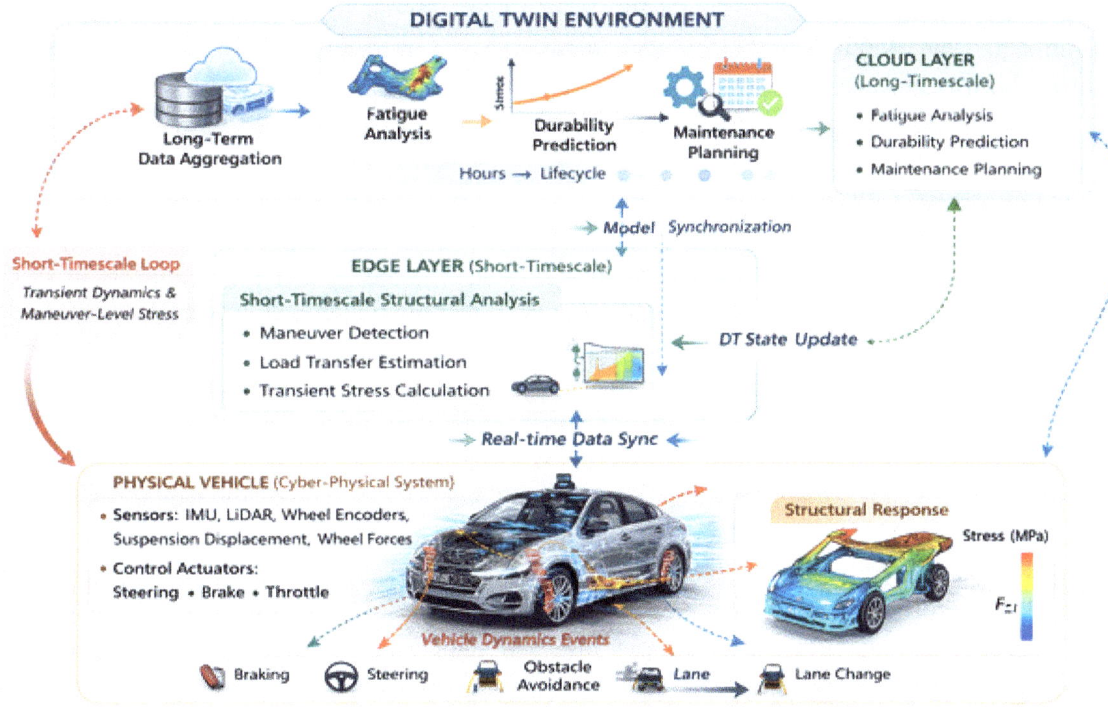

Figure 2 illustrates the DT framework proposed for linking AV operation with structural state evaluation. On the physical side, maneuver execution generates load transfer and structural response, which are captured through sensor-based structural data. These data are transmitted to the DT core, where structural state estimation, structural indicator generation, and fatigue or damage evaluation are performed through model updating and data assimilation. The resulting structural information supports control and decision updates, establishing a closed-loop connection between vehicle operation and durability-oriented structural assessment. Through this framework, the DT maintains synchronization between the physical vehicle and its digital representation, enabling continuous monitoring of both instantaneous structural response and long-term degradation during AV operation.

Autonomous Driving Behavior Layer

The upper layer represents the autonomous driving behavior layer, where perception, planning, and control modules generate maneuver commands according to the surrounding traffic environment and mission objectives. This layer includes sensing and interpretation functions that rely on onboard perception systems such as cameras, LiDAR, radar, and inertial sensors. Based on these inputs, trajectory planning algorithms determine feasible vehicle motions that satisfy safety constraints, road geometry, and operational requirements.

The output of this layer is the set of control actions that define the instantaneous maneuver to be executed by the vehicle. These actions typically include steering input, braking torque, and longitudinal acceleration demand. Within the DT framework, these variables are treated as the behavioral inputs that initiate the downstream physical analysis. Their significance is therefore not limited to control execution; they also serve as the starting point for estimating the mechanical consequences of AV behavior.

Vehicle Dynamics Layer

The second layer corresponds to the vehicle dynamics layer, where behavioral commands are translated into physically meaningful loading conditions. Once steering, braking, or acceleration commands are executed, the vehicle experiences longitudinal and lateral accelerations that alter the distribution of forces acting on the wheels and suspension system. At this stage, the DT interprets maneuver execution in terms of load transfer and tire-force generation rather than purely kinematic motion.

Using the load transfer relationships established earlier in Section 2, the DT estimates how longitudinal acceleration redistributes vertical loads between the front and rear axles, and how lateral acceleration redistributes vertical loads between the inner and outer wheels. These estimated load variations define the primary dynamic loading inputs to the structural layer. In practical implementation, the vehicle dynamics layer reconstructs these quantities using operational sensor data such as steering angle, longitudinal acceleration, lateral acceleration, yaw rate, and vehicle speed. The outputs of this layer are therefore not abstract state variables alone, but engineering load quantities, including wheel loads and tire-force estimates, that are subsequently propagated into structural load paths. This avoids disconnecting maneuver execution from its physical consequences and ensures that the DT maintains a mechanically interpretable representation of vehicle operation.

Structural Response Layer

The third layer represents the structural response layer, where the loading conditions estimated in the vehicle dynamics layer are interpreted in terms of structural effects within the vehicle. Loads originating at the tire–road interface are transmitted through suspension links, mounting brackets, subframes, and chassis members before generating internal forces and stress responses in structural components. The role of this layer is to transform maneuver-induced loading into structural indicators that are sufficiently informative for monitoring and durability-oriented analysis, while remaining computationally feasible for DT implementation.

Rather than attempting to perform full real-time finite element simulation, the framework adopts reduced-order structural interpretation. In this layer, transmitted forces are mapped to stress-relevant quantities using simplified structural relations, including the force-to-stress approximation introduced previously in Section 2. These estimates do not seek to resolve local stress fields in full detail; instead, they provide practical engineering indicators that reflect the structural effect of maneuver execution. The primary outputs of this layer are:

(1) the maximum stress associated with a maneuver event,
(2) the stress-cycle information reconstructed from repeated loading, and

(3) the cumulative fatigue-related damage index used to represent structural degradation over time.

This output definition is important because it makes the DT state explicit. The framework is not merely predicting that "loading occurred"; it is generating measurable structural indicators that can be updated, accumulated, and interpreted over the operational lifetime of the vehicle. In this sense, the structural response layer converts physical loading into durability-relevant DT state variables.

DT Update Loop

The three analytical layers are linked through a continuous DT update loop. This loop integrates operational sensor measurements with model-based predictions so that the virtual model remains synchronized with the physical vehicle. As new maneuver data are acquired during operation, the DT updates its estimates of dynamic loading, structural response, and durability state. This process allows the digital representation to evolve with the actual service history of the vehicle rather than remaining a static analytical model.

Through this update mechanism, the DT becomes capable of maintaining both instantaneous and cumulative structural awareness. At short timescales, it tracks maneuver-level stress responses; at long timescales, it accumulates load histories and fatigue-related indicators. As a result, the framework supports a unified interpretation of AV operation in which behavioral decisions, dynamic loads, and structural consequences are continuously linked within the same cyber–physical system.

From an engineering standpoint, this layered architecture provides the essential bridge between AV control behavior and structural durability analysis. It operationalizes the physical relationships discussed in Sections 2 and 3 within a DT environment and establishes the basis for the subsequent subsections on dynamic load estimation, structural state updating, illustrative calculation, and long-term load-history monitoring.

4.2. Maneuver-Induced Dynamic Load Estimation

The dynamic load estimation stage represents the first computational step within the DT framework, where maneuver-induced vehicle behavior is translated into physically meaningful loading conditions. Rather than redefining vehicle dynamics relationships, this stage applies the load transfer formulations established in Section 2 to reconstruct the time-varying loads acting on the vehicle during operation.

During maneuver execution, control actions generated by the autonomous driving system—such as braking, acceleration, and steering—produce longitudinal and lateral accelerations. These accelerations serve as the primary inputs to the load estimation process. Using the load transfer relationships defined in Eq. (3) and Eq. (4), the DT computes the redistribution of vertical forces across the vehicle, including load shifts between front and rear axles as well as between inner and outer wheels.

In this formulation, the objective is not to obtain an exact high-fidelity reconstruction of all tire forces, but to estimate the dominant load variations that govern structural response. The resulting quantities, denoted as $\Delta Fz(t)$, represent the time-dependent variation of vertical loads induced by maneuver execution. These load variations capture the essential dynamic effects required for structural interpretation, while remaining computationally efficient for real-time or near-real-time DT operation.

From an implementation perspective, the required inputs for this estimation process are directly available from standard onboard sensors, including longitudinal acceleration, lateral acceleration, vehicle speed, and steering angle. These signals enable the DT to continuously reconstruct maneuver-induced load transfer without requiring intrusive measurement systems. As a result, the load estimation stage forms a practical bridge between autonomous driving behavior and engineering load quantities.

The output of this stage is therefore a load history signal, $\Delta F_z(t)$, which represents the temporal evolution of maneuver-induced loading. This signal is not an end result in itself, but a key intermediate variable that feeds into the structural response layer. By preserving the temporal characteristics of loading, the DT framework enables subsequent analysis of stress evolution, cycle counting, and fatigue accumulation.

Importantly, this approach ensures consistency across the entire framework. By directly referencing the formulations established in Section 2, the DT avoids redundancy and maintains a unified mathematical basis for both theoretical development and implementation. This consistency is critical for ensuring that maneuver-induced loads, structural responses, and durability indicators are all derived from the same physical principles.

4.3. Structural Response Evaluation and State Updating

To relate these transmitted forces to structural effects, the DT applies the stress formulation introduced in Section 2 (Eq. (5)). By mapping the estimated internal forces $F(t)$ to an effective load-bearing area A, the framework computes a stress time history, denoted as $\sigma(t)$, which represents the temporal evolution of structural response under maneuver-induced loading. This formulation provides a practical approximation of structural behavior without requiring computationally intensive finite element analysis. The objective is not to resolve detailed local stress distributions, but to generate representative stress indicators that capture the dominant effects of dynamic loading on critical structural components.

Once the stress time history $\sigma(t)$ is obtained, the DT framework proceeds to extract fatigue-relevant information from the signal. Repeated maneuver execution produces cyclic variations in stress, which can be interpreted as stress cycles contributing to material degradation. In this context, the DT reconstructs stress cycles from $\sigma(t)$ and associates them with fatigue behavior using standard cycle-based interpretations, enabling the characterization of loading severity over time.

The accumulated effect of these stress cycles is then represented through a cumulative damage metric. Following classical fatigue accumulation principles, the damage index $D$is evaluated based on the relationship between experienced stress cycles and the allowable fatigue life of the material. Although the framework does not aim to replicate full-scale experimental fatigue conditions, it provides a consistent and physically interpretable method for tracking the progression of structural degradation under operational loading.

Within this formulation, the structural state of the vehicle in the DT environment is explicitly represented through the stress time history $\sigma(t)$, the reconstructed stress cycles, and the cumulative damage index D. These variables form the core outputs of the structural response modeling stage and provide direct insight into the mechanical consequences of autonomous driving behavior. Unlike purely kinematic or control-oriented variables, they enable the DT to capture both instantaneous structural effects and their long-term accumulation, thereby supporting continuous durability-oriented monitoring throughout vehicle operation.

4.4. Illustrative Application: Emergency Braking Scenario

Assume an AV traveling at an initial speed of 50 km/h performs emergency braking with a longitudinal deceleration of $0.8g$ ($\approx 7.85\ \mathrm{m/s^2}$). For a representative passenger vehicle with mass $m = 1500\,\mathrm{kg}$, center of gravity height $h = 0.55\,\mathrm{m}$, and wheelbase $L = 2.7\,\mathrm{m}$, the longitudinal load transfer generated during braking can be estimated using the relationship established in Eq. (3):

$$\Delta F_z = \frac{1500 \cdot (0.8 \cdot 9.81) \cdot 0.55}{2.7} \approx 2400\,\mathrm{N}$$

This result indicates that approximately 2400 N of vertical load is transferred from the rear axle to the front axle during the braking maneuver. Assuming an initial static axle load of approximately 7500 N per axle, the front axle load increases to approximately 9900 N, corresponding to an increase of about 32%, while the rear axle is proportionally unloaded.

The increase in vertical tire forces propagates through the suspension system and structural load paths before reaching the vehicle chassis and subframe structures. As a result, structural components located near the front axle—such as control arms, suspension mounts, and subframe connections—experience elevated loading conditions.

To quantify the structural implications of this maneuver, a simplified stress estimation is performed. Assuming that the dynamic load increment ($\Delta F_z \approx 2400\,\mathrm{N}$) is transmitted through a representative front suspension mounting point with an effective load-bearing cross-sectional area of:

$$A = 600\ \mathrm{mm}^2 = 6 \times 10^{-4}\ \mathrm{m}^2$$

the corresponding stress increment can be estimated using the stress relationship defined in Eq. (5) as:

$$\sigma = \frac{F}{A} = \frac{2400}{6 \times 10^{-4}} \approx 4.0\,\mathrm{MPa}$$

Although this stress level remains significantly below the yield strength of typical structural steel ($\sigma_y \approx 250 - 350\,\mathrm{MPa}$), its engineering significance lies in its transient and repetitive nature rather than its absolute magnitude.

From a DT perspective, this event corresponds to a short-duration stress peak captured within the short-timescale analysis layer. The DT interprets this peak as a maneuver-induced structural loading event associated with emergency braking.

While individual braking events produce relatively low stress levels, their repeated occurrence contributes to cumulative fatigue effects. To illustrate this within the DT framework, a simplified fatigue accumulation scenario is considered.

Assume the AV operates in an urban environment and performs an average of:

n= 30 high-deceleration braking events per day

Over one year of operation:

N_{total}= 30×365= 10,950 cycles/year

In fatigue analysis, the cumulative effect of repeated stress cycles is commonly evaluated using simplified damage accumulation models. One of the most widely used approaches in engineering practice is Miner's linear damage rule, which assumes that fatigue damage accumulates linearly as a function of applied load cycles (Cardoso & Ferreira, 2022). According to this model, each stress cycle contributes a fraction of damage relative to the total number of cycles to failure at a given stress level. This approach is widely adopted in automotive durability analysis due to its simplicity and suitability for load spectrum-based evaluation.

Using Miner's linear damage rule, the cumulative fatigue damage index can be expressed as:

$$D = \sum \frac{n_i}{N_f} \tag{6}$$

where n_i is the number of applied cycles and N_i is the number of cycles to failure at the corresponding stress level.

For structural steel components, the number of cycles to failure at low stress amplitudes (≈ 4 MPa) typically exceeds 10^7 cycles. This suggests that individual low-amplitude events contribute only marginally to fatigue damage. However, real vehicle operation involves a spectrum of loading conditions.

To illustrate this, a simplified multi-amplitude loading scenario is presented in Table 1.

Table 1. Illustrative annual fatigue loading spectrum (front suspension mount)

Event Type	**Deceleration (g)**	**ΔF_z (N)**	**σ (MPa)**	**Events/Day**	**Annual Cycles = n_i (cycles)**	**N_i (cycles)**	**Damage Index (D)**
Moderate braking	0.3	900	1.5	60	21,900	$>10^8$	~0.0002
Hard braking	0.5	1,500	2.5	30	10,950	$>10^8$	~0.0001
Emergency braking	0.8	2,400	4.0	5	1,825	$>10^7$	~0.0002
Total	—	—	—	—	**34,675**	—	**~0.0005**

Although the total annual damage index remains well below the critical threshold (D=1.0), this simplified analysis demonstrates how repeated maneuver-induced loads contribute to cumulative structural effects over time. Projecting this trend over a multi-year operational period indicates that even moderate stress amplitudes may become relevant when accumulated over extended service durations.

This quantitative example demonstrates that maneuver execution can be systematically translated into:

1. Dynamic load transfer
2. Structural stress estimation
3. Fatigue-relevant loading cycles

Within the proposed Structural–Behavioral DT framework, these calculations can be implemented using real-time vehicle data (e.g., acceleration, velocity, and vehicle parameters) without requiring full high-fidelity simulations. In practice, such computations can be executed using lightweight numerical models embedded within edge-level DT modules, while long-term fatigue indicators are evaluated at the cloud level.

From a validation perspective, this analytical workflow provides a simulation-equivalent approximation of structural loading behavior, demonstrating that the proposed DT framework is capable of generating physically meaningful structural indicators from operational driving data.

Through this integration, the DT framework enables continuous monitoring of both instantaneous maneuver-induced loads and long-term structural durability, bridging the gap between behavioral validation and mechanical reliability assessment in AV systems.

4.5. DT–Based Load Spectrum Monitoring and Structural Degradation Assessment

While Section 4.4 demonstrates the structural response under a representative emergency braking scenario, real-world AV operation involves a continuous sequence of heterogeneous maneuvers occurring over extended periods. In this context, structural integrity is not governed by isolated load events, but by the cumulative effects of repeated and variable loading conditions.

To address this, the DT framework extends beyond single-event analysis toward continuous load spectrum monitoring. Within this framework, maneuver-induced loads—originating from braking, acceleration, and steering actions—are systematically recorded and aggregated to construct a time-resolved load history. This load history captures both transient high-intensity events and frequent low-amplitude fluctuations, enabling a comprehensive representation of operational loading conditions.

The DT architecture enables this capability through its multi-timescale structure. At the edge level, high-frequency sensor data are used to capture instantaneous vehicle responses during maneuver execution. These data streams are then transmitted to the cloud layer, where long-term data aggregation and analysis are performed. This hierarchical processing structure allows the DT to bridge short-term dynamic behavior with long-term structural evolution.

Based on the accumulated load history, the DT framework supports the construction of load spectra, which describe the distribution of load amplitudes and their corresponding occurrence frequencies. These spectra provide a compact representation of operational conditions and form the basis for structural durability assessment. In particular, the integration of load spectra with fatigue evaluation models enables the estimation of cumulative damage over time.

A commonly adopted approach for cumulative damage assessment is the linear damage accumulation principle, where the contribution of each load cycle is evaluated relative to its fatigue life. By integrating this principle within the DT environment, the system can continuously update the structural damage state based on real-time operational data. This enables the transition from static design-based safety margins to dynamic, data-driven durability assessment.

Importantly, this capability establishes a direct link between autonomous driving behavior and long-term structural reliability. Frequent minor maneuvers—often overlooked in conventional analyses—can contribute significantly to cumulative fatigue when repeated over large operational cycles. Conversely, rare but severe events may dominate peak stress conditions. The DT framework captures both effects simultaneously, providing a unified perspective on structural loading.

Furthermore, the continuous synchronization between the physical vehicle and its digital counterpart enables predictive maintenance strategies. By tracking the evolution of structural damage indicators, the DT can identify emerging degradation trends and support early intervention before critical failure occurs. This represents a key advancement over traditional inspection-based maintenance approaches, which rely on periodic assessments rather than continuous monitoring.

Overall, the integration of load spectrum monitoring and cumulative damage assessment within the DT framework transforms structural evaluation from a static, scenario-specific process into a dynamic, lifecycle-oriented analysis. This capability is essential for AVs, where high-frequency control actions and diverse operating conditions introduce complex and evolving loading patterns that cannot be adequately captured by conventional validation methods.

5. IMPLICATIONS FOR AV SAFETY VALIDATION

The holistic DT framework proposed in this chapter provides several important implications for the validation, monitoring, and long-term safety evaluation of AVs. By explicitly linking autonomous maneuver execution with vehicle dynamic loading and structural response analysis, the framework extends the role of DT–based validation beyond conventional behavior-oriented assessments and introduces a structural perspective into AV safety evaluation.

Current validation strategies for AVs largely focus on assessing the correctness of decision-making processes and control behavior. Scenario-based testing, simulation environments, and DT platforms are widely used to evaluate how autonomous systems respond to complex traffic situations. These approaches typically examine functional safety aspects such as perception accuracy, trajectory tracking performance, and the robustness of decision-making algorithms under diverse driving scenarios.

Although these behavioral evaluations are essential, they provide only a partial representation of overall vehicle safety. Autonomous driving decisions are ultimately implemented through physical control actions—such as steering adjustments, braking inputs, and acceleration commands—that generate dynamic forces within the vehicle system. These forces propagate through suspension components and structural load paths before producing stress states within the chassis and vehicle body. Over time, repeated maneuver-induced loads may influence the structural durability of components that experience frequent dynamic loading conditions.

By incorporating structural response analysis into DT environments, the proposed framework enables safety validation to consider both behavioral performance and the mechanical consequences of autonomous driving actions. This integrated perspective allows engineers to evaluate not only whether autonomous decisions are functionally correct, but also how those decisions affect the physical condition of the vehicle. As a result, DT–based validation can provide a more comprehensive understanding of vehicle safety that encompasses both control behavior and structural reliability.

From an engineering perspective, this capability enables the development of durability-aware validation processes for AVs. Traditional durability evaluations are commonly conducted through laboratory experiments or predefined driving cycles, which may not fully represent the diversity of loading conditions encountered during real-world autonomous operation. In contrast, DT environments capable of reconstructing maneuver-induced load histories can generate more realistic representations of operational stress conditions. This allows durability assessments to reflect the actual maneuver patterns produced by autonomous driving systems, supporting more accurate evaluation of long-term structural performance.

The integration of structural response analysis within DT platforms also supports the development of predictive maintenance strategies for AV systems. By continuously estimating stress states and tracking load histories throughout vehicle operation, DTs can assist engineers in identifying structural components that may be exposed to elevated fatigue risks. Such insights enable early detection of potential structural degradation and allow maintenance interventions to be scheduled before significant failures occur. This capability is particularly relevant for autonomous mobility services, where vehicles may operate continuously under diverse traffic conditions.

Beyond safety validation and maintenance planning, the framework also provides value for engineering design and system optimization. Because the DT links maneuver execution with structural load propagation, engineers can investigate how design parameters—such as suspension characteristics, chassis stiffness, or control strategy tuning—affect the structural loading environment experienced during autonomous operation. This capability enables vehicle designers to evaluate the mechanical implications of autonomous driving strategies and to explore design solutions that balance dynamic performance, structural durability, and operational safety.

In practical implementations, the integration of structural–behavioral DTs can be achieved by combining existing vehicle sensing infrastructures with physics-based dynamic and structural models. Modern vehicles already provide many of the signals required to estimate maneuver-induced loads, including acceleration, steering angle, wheel speed, and yaw rate measurements obtained from onboard sensors and electronic control units. These signals can be streamed to DT environments where vehicle dynamic models reconstruct load transfer behavior, while simplified structural models estimate stress responses within key structural components. Through continuous synchronization between physical vehicle data and digital models, the DT can generate evolving representations of vehicle loading conditions during real operation. Such implementations do not necessarily require high-fidelity finite element simulations in real time; instead, reduced-order structural models or data-driven approximations can be employed to enable computationally efficient monitoring of structural responses within operational DT platforms.

From a broader systems perspective, the proposed framework contributes to the evolving role of DT technology within intelligent mobility systems. Rather than functioning solely as platforms for behavioral simulation or scenario-based testing, DTs can evolve into comprehensive cyber–physical monitoring environments capable of representing multiple physical aspects of vehicle operation. The integration of structural mechanics with behavioral modeling therefore strengthens the role of DTs as core analytical tools for AV engineering, supporting more holistic safety assessment throughout the vehicle lifecycle.

Finally, the framework presented in this chapter also highlights several directions for future research. Further work may investigate the development of computationally efficient structural models suitable for real-time DT environments, the integration of structural health monitoring sensors to improve stress estimation accuracy, and the extension of DT architectures to support fleet-level durability analysis across large numbers of AVs. Advancements in these areas would further enhance the ability of DT systems to support safe, reliable, and sustainable autonomous mobility.

6. CONCLUSION

The increasing complexity of AV operation has introduced new challenges for safety validation and long-term system reliability assessment. While DT technologies have significantly improved the ability to reproduce and analyze vehicle behavior under diverse driving scenarios, most existing implementations remain primarily focused on behavioral and functional performance. However, autonomous driving decisions are ultimately realized through physical vehicle maneuvers that generate dynamic forces within the vehicle structure. Understanding the mechanical consequences of these actions is therefore essential for achieving a more comprehensive evaluation of AV safety.

This chapter addressed this limitation by proposing a holistic DT framework that integrates behavioral decision processes with vehicle dynamic loading and structural response analysis. The framework establishes a causal connection between AV maneuvers, dynamic load transfer mechanisms, and the resulting structural stresses within vehicle components. By linking these domains within a unified DT environment, the proposed approach enables the simultaneous evaluation of both behavioral performance and structural integrity during vehicle operation.

Through this integration, the traditional role of DTs in AV validation can be expanded. Instead of functioning solely as platforms for behavioral simulation and scenario-based testing, DTs can also represent the mechanical consequences of maneuver execution. By incorporating vehicle dynamics modeling and structural response estimation, DT systems become capable of reconstructing maneuver-induced loading conditions, estimating stress states within structural components, and supporting durability-oriented analysis across the operational lifecycle of the vehicle.

From an engineering perspective, this integrated approach contributes to a more comprehensive understanding of AV safety and reliability. Evaluating the interaction between driving behavior and structural response provides insight into how repeated dynamic loads may influence component durability and long-term vehicle performance. Such insights are particularly important as AVs are expected to operate continuously under diverse and unpredictable traffic conditions, where cumulative loading effects may become significant over time.

Future research may further enhance the proposed framework by incorporating computationally efficient structural models suitable for real-time DT environments, integrating structural health monitoring sensors for improved stress estimation, and extending DT architectures to support fleet-level durability analysis across large numbers of AVs. Advancements in these areas would strengthen the ability of DT systems to support more reliable safety evaluation, durability monitoring, and lifecycle management of autonomous mobility platforms.

Overall, the integration of behavioral validation with structural response analysis highlights the potential of DT technology to evolve into a more comprehensive analytical framework for AV engineering. By capturing both the decision-making behavior of autonomous systems and the mechanical consequences of their maneuvers, DTs can contribute to the development of safer, more reliable, and more sustainable autonomous mobility systems.

REFERENCES

Campolo, C., Genovese, G., Molinaro, A., Pizzimenti, B., Ruggeri, G., & Zappalà, D. M. (2024). An Edge-Based Digital Twin Framework for Connected and Autonomous Vehicles: Design and Evaluation. *IEEE Access : Practical Innovations, Open Solutions*, *12*, 46290–46303. DOI: 10.1109/ACCESS.2024.3382001

Cardoso, E. U., & Ferreira, J. L. A. (2022). Estimation of fatigue life under random multiaxial conditions using the projection-by-projection method. *Journal of the Brazilian Society of Mechanical Sciences and Engineering*, *44*(11), 570. DOI: 10.1007/s40430-022-03869-1

Crespi, N., Drobot, A. T., & Minerva, R. (2023). The Digital Twin. In *The Digital Twin* (2nd ed.). Springer International Publishing., https://doi.org/https://doi.org/10.1007/978-3-031-21343-4 DOI: 10.1007/978-3-031-21343-4_1

Doumiati, M., Victorino, A., Charara, A., & Lechner, D. (2009). Lateral load transfer and normal forces estimation for vehicle safety: Experimental test. *Vehicle System Dynamics*, *47*(12), 1511–1533. DOI: 10.1080/00423110802673091

Duan, J., Wang, Z., & Jing, X. (2024). Digital Twin Test Method With LTE-V2X for Autonomous Vehicle Safety Test. *IEEE Internet of Things Journal*, *11*(18), 30161–30171. DOI: 10.1109/JIOT.2024.3409781

Hou, Z., Wang, S., Liu, H., Yang, Y., & Zhang, Y. (2024). Twin Scenarios Establishment for Autonomous Vehicle Digital Twin Empowered SOTIF Assessment. *IEEE Transactions on Intelligent Vehicles*, *9*(1), 1965–1976. DOI: 10.1109/TIV.2023.3304353

Hui, Y., Ma, X., Su, Z., Cheng, N., Yin, Z., Luan, T. H., & Chen, Y. (2022). Collaboration as a Service: Digital-Twin-Enabled Collaborative and Distributed Autonomous Driving. *IEEE Internet of Things Journal*, *9*(19), 18607–18619. DOI: 10.1109/JIOT.2022.3161677

Jazar, R. N. (2025). *Vehicle Dynamics: Theory and Application*. Springer Nature. DOI: 10.1007/978-3-031-74458-7

Meng, Z., Zhao, S., Chen, H., Hu, M., Tang, Y., & Song, Y. (2022). The Vehicle Testing Based on Digital Twins Theory for Autonomous Vehicles. *IEEE Journal of Radio Frequency Identification*, *6*, 710–714. DOI: 10.1109/JRFID.2022.3211565

Milliken, W. F., & Milliken, D. L. (1995). *Race Car Vehicle Dynamics*. Society of Automotive Engineers, Inc.

Milliken, W. F., & Milliken, D. L. (2002). *Chassis Design: Principle and Analysis*. Society of Automotive Engineers, Inc. DOI: 10.4271/R-206

Mudunuri, L. N. R., & Bhattacharya, P. (2024). Ethical Considerations Balancing Emotion and Autonomy in AI Systems. In Tikadar, S., Liu, H., Bhattacharya, P., & Bhattacharya, S. (Eds.), *Humanizing Technology With Emotional Intelligence* (pp. 443–456). IGI Global Scientific Publishing., DOI: 10.4018/979-8-3693-7011-7.ch023

Öngir, S., Kaleli, E. C., Konyar, M. Z., & Ertunç, H. M. (2025). Vertical Force Monitoring of Racing Tires: A Novel Deep Neural Network-Based Estimation Method. *Applied Sciences (Basel, Switzerland)*, *15*(1), 123. Advance online publication. DOI: 10.3390/app15010123

Rajamani, R. (2006). Vehicle Dynamics and Control. In Rajamani, R. (Ed.), *Vehicle Dynamics and Control*. Springer US., DOI: 10.1007/978-1-4614-1433-9_2

Reimpell, J., Stoll, H., & Betzler, J. W. (2001). *The Automotive Chassis: Engineering Principles* (2nd ed.). Butterworth-Heinemann.

Shoukat, M. U., Yan, L., Yan, Y., Zhang, F., Zhai, Y., Han, P., Nawaz, S. A., Raza, M. A., Akbar, M. W., & Hussain, A. (2024). Autonomous driving test system under hybrid reality: The role of digital twin technology. *Internet of Things : Engineering Cyber Physical Human Systems*, *27*, 101301. https://doi.org/https://doi.org/10.1016/j.iot.2024.101301. DOI: 10.1016/j.iot.2024.101301

Tang, L., Dai, J., Cheng, Z., Zhang, H., & Chen, Q. (2024). A Digital Twins-Assisted Multi-Autonomous Vehicle Distributed Collaborative Path Planning Algorithm With Fidelity Guarantee. *IEEE Transactions on Intelligent Transportation Systems*, *25*(12), 19904–19916. DOI: 10.1109/TITS.2024.3454633

Tao, F., Zhang, H., Liu, A., & Nee, A. Y. C. (2019). Digital Twin in Industry: State-of-the-Art. *IEEE Transactions on Industrial Informatics*, *15*(4), 2405–2415. DOI: 10.1109/TII.2018.2873186

Wang, C., Storms, K., Zhang, N., & Winner, H. (2024). Runtime unknown unsafe scenarios identification for SOTIF of autonomous vehicles. *Accident; Analysis and Prevention*, *195*, 107410. https://doi.org/https://doi.org/10.1016/j.aap.2023.107410. DOI: 10.1016/j.aap.2023.107410 PMID: 38056026

Wang, H., Shao, W., Sun, C., Yang, K., Cao, D., & Li, J. (2024). A Survey on an Emerging Safety Challenge for Autonomous Vehicles: Safety of the Intended Functionality. *Engineering (Beijing)*, *33*, 17–34. https://doi.org/https://doi.org/10.1016/j.eng.2023.10.011. DOI: 10.1016/j.eng.2023.10.011

Wang, Z., Gupta, R., Han, K., Wang, H., Ganlath, A., Ammar, N., & Tiwari, P. (2022). Mobility Digital Twin: Concept, Architecture, Case Study, and Future Challenges. *IEEE Internet of Things Journal*, *9*(18), 17452–17467. DOI: 10.1109/JIOT.2022.3156028

Xu, G., Chen, J., Wang, Z., Zhou, A., Schrader, M., Bittle, J., & Shao, Y. (2025). Enhancing traffic safety analysis with digital twin technology: Integrating vehicle dynamics and environmental factors into microscopic traffic simulation. *Scientific Reports*, *15*(1), 44404. DOI: 10.1038/s41598-025-31930-1 PMID: 41436761

Chapter 2

Adaptive AI-Driven Digital Twin Frameworks for Autonomous Vehicles:

Real-Time Synchronization and Edge-Cloud Mobility Intelligence

Dilmurod Turaev
Termez University of Economics and Service, Termez, Uzbekistan

Ravikumar Natarajan
http://orcid.org/0009-0009-3705-1681
Marwadi University, Rajkot, India

Aarthi Selvakumar
http://orcid.org/0009-0006-9064-2091
Marwadi University, Rajkot, India

Anorgul Ashirova
Mamun University, Khiva, Uzbekistan

Khayrulla Urozboev
Alfraganus University, Tashkent, Uzbekistan

Sharvanthika K. S.
http://orcid.org/0009-0004-2410-2957
Kongu Engineering College, Erode, India

ABSTRACT

Artificial Intelligence (AI) and Machine Learning (ML) are transforming Digital Twin (DT) technology into a real-time, intelligent ecosystem for Autonomous Vehicles (AVs). This chapter explores how AI-driven DT frameworks integrate sensor fusion, reinforcement learning, and edge-cloud collaboration to achieve continuous synchronization between physical and virtual systems. These smart twins enable predictive maintenance, adaptive decision-making, and safety validation with minimal latency. Industrial examples such as Tesla's Predictive Maintenance Twin and Audi's Virtual Prototyping Platform demonstrate practical implementations that enhance reliability, design accuracy, and efficiency. The chapter also discusses challenges in scalability, interoperability, and ethical governance, while highlighting emerging directions like quantum and federated learning. By combining intelligence, automation, and ethical design, AI-empowered Digital Twins form the foundation of next-generation, self-evolving, and resilient autonomous mobility systems.

DOI: 10.4018/979-8-3373-7785-8.ch002

1. INTRODUCTION

Machine Learning (ML) and Artificial Intelligence (AI) have become the key facilitators in the development of Digital Twin (DT) technology in the sphere of Autonomous Vehicles (AVs). Digital Twins The Digital Twins offer a constantly updated virtual representation of a physical system. These twins are used in AV ecosystems to obtain the data of on-board sensors, edge devices, and cloud platforms to provide real-time monitoring, predictive analysis, and intelligent control. The algorithms of AI and ML allow converting raw data into valuable insights and allow autonomous systems to be able to perceive, reason, and act in dynamic settings (Hoang, 2024). By incorporating AI-based learning algorithms, Digital Twins will not remain at the state of static models but be dynamic and adaptable so that they could optimize driving performance, anticipate failure, and make the system safer. The chapter addresses the commonalities of AI, ML, and DTs as a solution to real-time synchronization with a focus on architectures, case studies, and future research areas that reveal the autonomy and intelligence in contemporary transportation systems.

1.1 Digital Twins in Autonomous Vehicles

Digital Twin technology represents the connection between the virtual world and the physical one, and it establishes the two-way information and control between the car and its digital counterpart. DTs in autonomous vehicles recreate all of the key subsystems of the vehicle: engine dynamics, navigation, sensor status and environmental context to offer a virtual testing environment to aid predictive modeling and decision support. Continuous streams of sensor data are used to enable real-time DT updates such that the virtual model indicates the current state of the vehicle (Ramesh & Praveen, 2021). This enables the simulation of different driving conditions by the engineers and AI without putting the physical vehicle into danger. Moreover, Digital Twins in Avs provide more lifecycle management capability by combining data at the design, deployment, and operation stages. In combination with AI augmented analytics, DTs assist to predictive maintenance, minimize downtimes, and enable safer navigation through simulation-based learning-therefore, turning autonomous vehicles into self-optimizing and smart systems.

1.2 AI and ML for Real-Time Digital Twin Updates

Digital Twins are now made possible by AI and ML to learn based on the data, change autonomously, and carry out real-time update based on the changing physical state of affairs. Deep neural networks and reinforcement learning agents are machine learning models that take high-frequency sensory data in the form of LIDAR, radar, and cameras to dynamically recreate the environment. These artificial intelligence models constantly train on new data to promote situational awareness and make decisions. Reinforcement learning is used to maximize the driving strategies by providing a simulated case of thousands of possible outcomes, thus allowing the system to choose the safest and most effective actions (P. K. Singh, 2023). Edge intelligence also minimizes latency, as the important information is performed locally before the synchronization with cloud-based DTs. By means of such integration, AI and ML can convert Digital Twins into active, learning-based, and predictive objects that are able to foresee the failure of components, enhance the efficiency of routes, and increase the overall reliability of the vehicle in the context of complex traffic and weather. The figure 1 shows how integration of AI and ML changes Digital twins (previously being a static model) into adaptive and efficient vehicle functions by becoming a proactive, learning system by training its models continuously, processing data in real time, learning by reinforcement, and edge intelligent systems.

Figure 1. AI/ML enhances digital twin capabilities

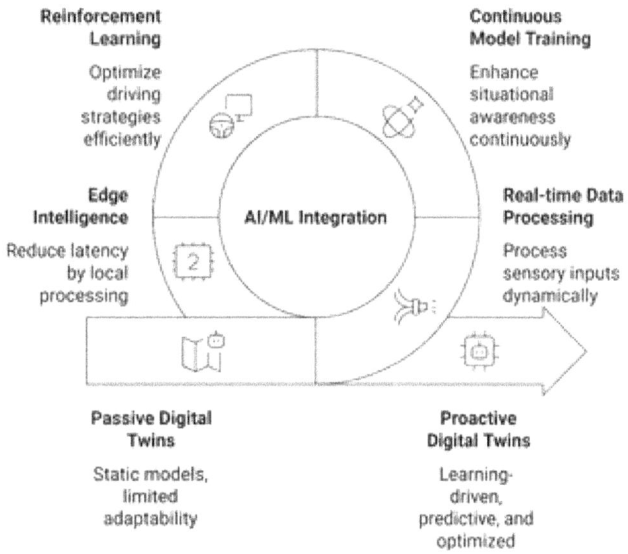

1.3 Motivation and Scope of the Study

The growing sophistication of self-driving cars is a challenge requiring smart systems capable of functioning without much supervision of human beings and surviving in a safe, efficient and reliable manner. The conventional digital modeling and offline simulation cannot be used to work with real-time operational dynamics. Therefore, the driving force of considering AI and ML as parts of Digital Twin frameworks is that they can learn and adapt continuously and make decisions based on the context in which they are applied. This paper will examine how AI-driven DTs increase real-time synchronization, predictive accuracy, and resilience in the system. This includes the analysis of basic AI and ML models in Digital Twins, applied in the real-world scenario in industries, and trends in the future such as edge-cloud collaboration and federated learning. Overcoming the technical and ethical barriers, including data security, model generalization, and scale of computations, this chapter forms the overall vision in terms of how AI-based DT ecosystem may facilitate fully autonomous and responsive car behaviors. In contrast to current Digital Twin research which is mainly concerned with either the use of static simulation or post-event analytics, the chapter highlights AI-based real-time synchronization of the physical autonomous vehicles and their digital counterparts via reinforcement learning, sensor fusion, and edge-cloud collaborative frameworks. The chapter has the following contributions (1): it proposes an adaptive Digital Twin framework with the integration of continuous learning AI models, (2): it analyzes industrial applications of Tesla and Audi, and (3): it studies emerging paradigms such as federated learning and quantum-enhanced Digital Twin systems.

2. BACKGROUND TO THE STUDY

Digital Twin technology has become one of the foundations of smart mobility systems, whereby it can be connected, simulated, and decided in real-time. The fact that it is moving towards autonomous vehicles is a paradigm shift in the interaction of physical systems with the digital environment. The context of this work is in the evolution of the concept of DTs and how it was converged with AI and ML and how it is related to the facilitating technologies, including cyber-physical systems (CPS), IoT, and cloud-edge computing (Olayinka, 2023). With these integrations, Digital Twins enable autonomous vehicles to perceive, train and act on their environment but still be highly faithful to real physical condition and the virtual models. The section expounds on the technological heritage, AI logics, and interdependence of systems that support the sustained synchronization between AVs and their digital twins, which offers a theoretical and architectural basis of real-time intelligent automation.

2.1 Evolution of Digital Twins from Manufacturing to Mobility

Digital Twins The idea of Digital Twins was first suggested in the manufacturing and aerospace engineering industries, where digital models of machinery were developed to track the performance of such equipment, identify anomalies, and even simulate the process of carrying out maintenance on such equipment. As time passed, the development of computational resources and data communications made possible the expansion of DTs not to fixed observation, but to real-time feedback (Katsoulakis et al., 2024). Digital Twins in the mobility industry developed to symbolize vehicles, traffic systems, and networks. The twin concept is now integrated with the dynamic integration of sensor information, interaction with the environment, and verification of decisions made by cars with the help of a simulation with the advent of autonomous vehicles. This development is mirrored by the fact that it is a change of the reactive approach to maintenance, to the predictive intelligence, where AI-based models allow vehicles to evaluate, predict, and optimize themselves (Agrawal et al., 2022). As a result, the Digital Twin has evolved to be not only a visualization tool of engineers but a learning-based ecosystem that is part of the safety and autonomy of the next-generation car. Table 1 overviews the historical change of Digital Twin technology as a manufacturing industry use to an autonomous mobility.

Table 1. Evolution of digital twin concepts from manufacturing to mobility

Phase	Domain/Period	Key Characteristics	Technological Enablers	Outcome
Generation 1: Static Modeling	Manufacturing (2002-2010)	Virtual prototypes for product design and maintenance	CAD/CAM tools, PLM systems	Enhanced product lifecycle management
Generation 2: Predictive Monitoring	Aerospace & Industrial IoT (2010-2016)	Integration of sensor data for performance tracking	IoT sensors, Cloud analytics	Predictive maintenance and anomaly detection
Generation 3: Real-Time Adaptive Twins	Automotive and Smart Factories (2016-2020)	Dynamic feedback between physical and virtual systems	Edge computing, Data analytics	Real-time operational optimization
Generation 4: Cognitive and Autonomous Twins	Autonomous Vehicles (2020-Present)	AI-driven learning, decision-making, and environment simulation	AI, ML, Reinforcement Learning, 5G/6G connectivity	Self-learning, predictive, and autonomous vehicle ecosystems

2.2 AI and ML for Real-Time Synchronization

AI or ML is critical in facilitating the sustained alignment between physical cars and their digital versions. The machine learning algorithms work with the multimodal data at large scale, e.g. telemetry, GPS, sensor feeds, to ensure that the vehicle state is reflected in near real-time. Deep learning networks can improve the process, which is done through object detection, trajectory estimation, and pattern recognition to replicate complex driving environments. Learning through reinforcement enables cars to learn through refinement of their driving policies using the feedback of physical and virtual interactions (Fuller et al., 2020). Also, generative AI models are used in the generation of synthetic data to train and validate the twin and lessen reliance on massive real-world testing. This intelligent synchronization is, to make sure that the DT is correct, adaptive and able to make autonomous decisions in dynamic and uncertain circumstances. Figure 2 shows the interaction between various AI and ML paradigms such as machine learning, deep learning, reinforcement learning, and generative AI to process telemetry, sensor, and interaction data to synchronize in real-time in Digital Twin systems.

Figure 2. AI and ML in real-time synchronization

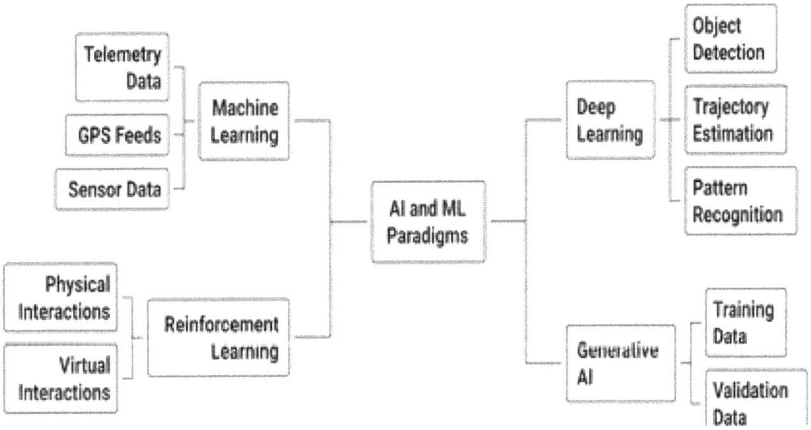

2.3 CPS, IoT, and Autonomous Vehicle Ecosystems

Autonomous vehicle technologies and the Internet of Things (IoT) are part of Cyber-Physical Systems (CPS) as the structural backbone of real-time Digital Twin. CPS is a combination of computation, networking and physical processes that facilitate the smooth exchange of data and autonomous control. IoT brings the sensory infrastructure, where the various parts of the vehicles involved as well as external objects, including traffic lights, pedestrians, and the infrastructure, are linked together by real-time communication devices (Emmert-Streib, 2023). These interrelated networks promote the flow of data to the Digital Twin continuously, so that virtual simulations can be provided according to the prevailing environmental circumstances. CPS + IoT can also be used to implement decentralized decision making based on edge computing, which enhances responsiveness and limits the latency. This three-fold relationship in the AV ecosystem creates a symbiotic relationship in which physical objects feedback ever-increasing amounts of data into their digital representations and AI twins, in their turn, affect the way vehicles behave a closed feedback loop that is necessary to make autonomy safe and efficient (Punia et al., 2025). As discussed in Table 2, Cyber-Physical Systems (CPS), Internet of Things (IoT), and Digital Twin concepts are working together to allow smart, real-time functioning of autonomous vehicle ecosystems.

Table 2. CPS, IoT, and digital twin integration in autonomous vehicles

Component	Primary Function	Key Technologies	Contribution to AV Digital Twin	Outcome
Cyber-Physical Systems (CPS)	Integrate computation and control within physical vehicle systems	Embedded systems, Real-time control algorithms	Enable autonomous control loops between vehicle and twin	Autonomous behavior coordination
Internet of Things (IoT)	Facilitate sensor communication and external connectivity	V2X, 5G, Edge gateways, Cloud IoT platforms	Provide continuous sensory and environmental data	Real-time situational awareness
Digital Twin (DT)	Virtual replica for monitoring and simulation	AI, ML, Simulation engines	Analyze, predict, and optimize system states	Enhanced reliability and adaptive decision-making
Integrated Ecosystem	Closed-loop collaboration among CPS, IoT, and DT	AI-driven synchronization frameworks	Achieve seamless interaction between physical and virtual worlds	Safe, efficient, and intelligent vehicle autonomy

3. RESEARCH OBJECTIVES

A combination of Artificial Intelligence (AI) and Machine Learning (ML) into Digital Twin (DT) ecosystems has created new opportunities in the real time operation of Autonomous Vehicles (AVs). Nonetheless, to ensure that a perfect synchronization of the physical vehicle and its virtual version is ensured, the issues of data heterogeneity, latency, and flexibility of the model should be addressed. This part provides the major goals, according to which the discussion of AI-based structures of real-time Digital Twin updates in autonomous mobility proceeds. The objectives will offer a systematic knowledge of the benefits of intelligent models in improving the decision-making process, performance optimization and safe and adaptive vehicle operation in dynamic conditions. Main Objectives are:

- To analyze the role of AI and ML algorithms in enabling real-time synchronization between physical vehicles and their Digital Twins.
- To design and conceptualize an adaptive Digital Twin framework for Autonomous Vehicles incorporating AI-based data fusion and predictive analytics.
- To evaluate the effectiveness of reinforcement learning and edge intelligence in optimizing decision-making and latency reduction.
- To identify key challenges and limitations in deploying large-scale AI-driven DT ecosystems for autonomous vehicles.
- To propose future research directions and industrial strategies for implementing scalable, privacy-preserving, and self-evolving Digital Twin systems.

4. CONCEPTUAL MODEL

The conceptual model will define the operation of Artificial Intelligence (AI) and Machine Learning (ML) in Digital Twin (DT) systems to allow Autonomous Vehicles (AVs) to receive real-time updates. It offers an architectural and data-driven point of view to align the virtual and physical environment by means of continuous learning, prediction, and optimization. The model focuses on integration both between vehicle sensors, edge processing nodes and cloud analytics in an adaptive loop to continuously improve vehicle behavior (Avevor et al., 2024). Based on the reinforcement learning, sensor fusion, and distributed computation, the framework promotes decision-making in response to dynamic road and environmental conditions. The conceptual model is a roadmap, which links the perception, communication, computation, and control levels, so that Digital Twins may evolve with the changing operational situation of the vehicle. Finally, it demonstrates the evolution of AI-enabled twins out of the passive digital imitations into smart self-educating systems contributing to reliability, safety, and performance of autonomous mobility in the next generation.

4.1 Architecture of AI-Integrated Digital Twin Systems

The Digital Twin systems with AI-integration are architecture in three synergistic layers, including data acquisition, intelligence, and decision control. The data layer gathers multimodal sensory data of LIDAR, radar, GPS, and onboard cameras, which include the environment and operational parameters. Intelligence layer uses ML algorithms of deep neural networks and reinforcement learning to take sensory input, identify patterns and simulate driving conditions (Toth & Szalay, 2023). The decision-control layer converts the predictive intelligence into commands that can be acted upon, allowing real-time measurements to be made in the speed, steering and energy control. Edge-cloud collaboration is a method that makes sure that computationally intensive AI models are trained in the cloud and critical decisions are made in the local environment to provide ultra-low latency. Such a layered design can maintain constant correspondence between the physical and virtual representation of the vehicle, and provides predictive maintenance, scenario testing, and autonomous functioning under safety (Noviati et al., 2024). With the architecture, a scalable base of AI-motivated adaptability and real-time synchronization in intelligent transportation systems can be provided. Table 3 demonstrates the hierarchical organization of a Digital Twin system of Autonomous Vehicles with an AI-based part and technologies of all layers.

Table 3. Architecture layers of AI-driven digital twin systems

Layer	Primary Function	Key Technologies/Models	Expected Outcomes
Physical Layer	Captures real-world data from vehicle sensors and actuators	LIDAR, radar, GPS, IMU, onboard diagnostics	Continuous data acquisition and real-time status updates
Communication Layer	Transmits data securely between physical and virtual entities	5G/6G, V2X, MQTT, OPC-UA	Low-latency and reliable data transfer
Processing Layer (Edge)	Performs local computation and preliminary analytics	Edge AI, fog computing, lightweight ML models	Reduced latency and efficient preprocessing

continued on following page

Table 3. Continued

Layer	Primary Function	Key Technologies/Models	Expected Outcomes
Intelligence Layer (Cloud)	Executes deep analytics, model training, and optimization	Deep Learning, Reinforcement Learning, Federated Learning	Adaptive decision-making and global model updates
Control & Feedback Layer	Translates insights into vehicle actions and twin updates	RL agents, control algorithms, feedback APIs	Self-learning, adaptive, and safe system operation

4.2 Data Flow Between Vehicles, Edge Nodes, and Cloud Twins

AI-enabled Digital Twin systems Data flow A two-way match between the physical vehicle, edge device and cloud infrastructure are part of the data flow. The AV sensors receive huge initial loads of data in one of the fastest modes, a list of the velocity, the proximity of objects, system diagnostics, etc and transmitted to edge nodes to be processed in real time. Lightweight ML models are employed by edge nodes to filter noise, detect anomalies and control actions in a timely manner by means of local inference (Lu et al., 2021). The processed and aggregated data is then sent to cloud servers where more machine learning and model training and long-term storage is done. The twins on clouds keep the states of the system and provide the best parameters to the vehicle in real-time as a feedback loop. Top-down communication reduces the latency and provides the development of a model on the platform of federated updates. This architecture will be in a position to deliver a trade-off between computation and reliable as well as offer the capacity to execute continual coordination between the digital representation of the vehicle and the reality of its working state, within the distributed computing layers.

4.3 Adaptive Feedback for Self-Learning and Optimization

The adaptive feedback loops are core to the realization of the self-learning process in the Digital Twin-enabled autonomous vehicles. Such loops find differences between expected and actual performance through reinforcement or transfer learning algorithms to allow the decision policies to be improved. Upon a vehicle facing unknown conditions on the road or weather, the twin instantly replicates possible alternative strategy, analyses the performance response and communicates optimized control parameters to the physical system (Hlophe & Maharaj, 2023). The process of continuous learning happens through several iterations in which the physical vehicle and its digital twin are co-evolutionary. This process increases fault tolerance, predictive maintenance and route optimization. In addition, there will be feedback mechanisms that allow anomaly detection by determining deviations in sensor behavior or performance trends, and thus anticipating possible system failures. Through the unification of perception, analysis and response into a feedback loop, adaptive feedback can turn the Digital Twin into a self-directing agent that can optimize itself as part of the AV ecosystem with regards to perception, analysis and response.

5. RESEARCH METHODOLOGY

The research methodology provides the systematic procedure that will be followed to study AI-based Digital Twin systems in real-time updates in autonomous vehicles. It incorporates a combination of systematic literature analysis, conceptual modelling and validation using simulation. A review of scholarly databases and industrial cases is a starting point of the methodology to determine the theoretical basis and define the research gaps. It is then followed by a conceptual framework that is used to map how AI algorithms, DT layers, and stream of vehicular data interact. Proposed architectures are verified in simulation environments e.g., MATLAB, CARLA or ROS-based testbeds, in different traffic and environmental conditions (Achenef et al., 2025). Some of evaluation metrics are latency, prediction accuracy and synchronization efficiency. Such a methodological framework guarantees the scientific rigor and replicability, as well as empirical validation, allowing to conduct a holistic study of the impact of AI-driven learning processes on the DT performance and real-time adjustability in autonomous mobility systems. The proposed Digital Twin framework will incorporate different AI/ML models that will be applied in perception, predicting, and controlling. The Convolutional Neural Networks (CNNs) and Transformer-based models are used to investigate the multimodal sensor fusion, LiDAR, radar, and camera object detection. The optimization of autonomous driving policy and adaptive decision making is optimized with the help of Deep Q-Network (DQN) and Proximal Policy Optimization (PPO) reinforcement learning algorithms. In addition, Autoencoders and Gaussian processes model is implemented to detect system malfunctions and performance aberrations within the Digital Twin setting.

5.1 Systematic Review and Conceptual Framework

The systematic review is conducted in accordance with a formal procedure of finding, filtering, and processing scholarly and corporate literature addressing the topic of AI-driven Digital Twins in AVs. Keywords like Digital Twin, autonomous vehicle, real-time update and machine learning are entered into databases such as IEEE Xplore, Scopus, and ScienceDirect and searched. The chosen studies are screened in terms of the year of publication, technical orientation, and applicability in the real-time system architectures (Coleman et al., 2025). The gained insights are generalized to develop a conceptual framework that visualizes interdependence of physical vehicle data, AI models and synchronization mechanisms. The framework focuses on hierarchical processing, feedback control and distributed learning in order to assist unceasing updates in the system. This systematic methodology, as well as summarizes the currently found literature, also helps define gaps in innovation in model scalability, communication latency, and autonomous decision-making, which would be used as the basis of simulation and real-world verification in subsequent sections.

5.2 Model Validation Through Simulation and Metrics

In order to check the proposed conceptual model, the conceptual model is validated through simulation models with real-world traffic data and synthetic scenarios. Environments CARLA, SUMO, and Gazebo are used to test in a wide range of environments and driving conditions. Validation process is concerned with the replication of vehicle-to-twin communication latency, adaptive learning efficiency and predictive accuracy (Erhan et al., 2021). The reinforcement learning agents are evaluated to optimize the policy on a variety of simulated routes, whereas the ML algorithms evaluate object detection, anomaly detection, and precision of the route planning. The major performance metrics are the synchronization delay, time to make decisions and the distribution of the computational load between the edge and the cloud layer. The quantitative effectiveness of the AI-based DT system is determined by comparative analysis with the baseline models. The results of the simulation make sure that theoretical presumptions are converted into the operational feasibility to verify that real-time Digital Twin updates contribute greatly to the vehicle intelligence, reliability, and safety. Table 4 is the summary of the critical metrics and indicators to confirm AI-eased Digital Twin models of autonomous vehicles. The Digital Twin framework proposed based on AI is contrasted with traditional rule-based and unchanging simulation frameworks to estimate the enhancement of synchronization latency and predictive precision.

Table 4. Performance metrics for digital twin evaluation

Evaluation Dimension	Metric	Measurement Approach	Significance
Synchronization Accuracy	Latency (ms), Update Frequency (Hz)	Time delay between physical state change and twin update	Determines real-time responsiveness
Predictive Performance	RMSE, Precision, Recall, F1-score	Comparison of predicted vs. actual vehicle states	Validates ML model accuracy
Computational Efficiency	CPU/GPU Utilization, Bandwidth Use	System resource monitoring during execution	Measures scalability and energy efficiency
Reliability and Safety	Fault Detection Rate, Uptime (%)	System log and fault event analysis	Assesses robustness and operational stability
Learning Adaptability	Policy Convergence Speed, Model Drift	RL training iterations and performance over time	Evaluates self-learning capability and adaptability

5.3 Tools, Datasets, and Evaluation Parameters for Twin Analysis

The measurement system is based on expert tools and benchmark datasets to measure the operation of AI-powered Digital Twins in real-time. Python, TensorFlow, and PyTorch are development environments that are used to train and test algorithms. Modeling of vehicle and network latency can be done using simulation tools such as CARLA and MATLAB Simulink. High-resolution sensor data are also available in benchmark data sets, such as KITTI and nuScenes and Waymo Open Dataset, and are used to validate perception and decision-making models (Zhang et al., 2025). Parameters of evaluation are grouped into three dimensions: (1) Accuracy metrics include object detection precision and trajectory prediction error.; (2) Efficiency metrics include latency, computational load, and bandwidth consumption; and (3) Reliability metrics include system resilience and fault rate, and the fidelity of synchronization. These items combined allow quantitative evaluation of the role of AI-based models in helping to update Digital Twins in real-time, make them reproducible, transparent, and empirically justify the research results. Environmental sensing and prediction of trajectory capabilities, as well as perception models, are tested on benchmark datasets, including KITTI, nuScenes and Waymo Open Dataset. These data sets provide high resolutions multimodal sensor data like LiDAR point clouds, and RGB camera feeds, radar signal, and vehicle telemetry required to evaluate the Digital Twin synchronization accuracy.

6. LITERATURE REVIEW

The current body of research on the topic of implementation of Artificial Intelligence (AI) and Machine Learning (ML) into Digital Twin (DT) models of Autonomous Vehicles (AVs) highlights its disruptive nature in enhancing real-time synchronization, predictive analytics, and system optimization.

Available literature shows that AI-based processes improve sensor perception, minimize the response time, and promote decision independence. The merging of AI, Internet of Things (IoT), and edge-cloud computing has made it possible to take the concept of Digital Twins to the next stage of no longer being a mere visual representation but a self-developing ecosystem (Rajan & Li, 2024). This part examines the existing research on the topic in line with the goals of the chapter, under three major topics: (1) AI-assisted real-time update schemes, (2) ML-based sensor fusion and predictive analytics, and (3) reinforcement learning and edge intelligence to make adaptive decisions in the context of AV. Combined, these themes help to introduce intelligent DT systems as the foundational part of the next generation of trusted, autonomous mobility solutions.

6.1 AI-Enabled Real-Time Updating Mechanisms in Digital Twins

Digital Twins based on AI are based on cognitive processing and adaptive learning to ensure that the virtual and physical worlds are synchronized. The dynamic updating systems include AI models that compute sensor data streams of LIDAR, cameras, and radar and create precise and low-latency digital images of the vehicle (Kumarasamy et al., 2024). Recent developments suggest that deep learning and generative AI methods make it possible to continuously estimate the state and predictively correct the error, so that the twin can reflect the action of the environment in real-time. The literature shows that the AI-enhanced data assimilation lessens the synchronization lag by almost forty percent in rapid contexts. Cloud based inference engines are also used to build on top of edge analytics and enhance predictive accuracy by retraining on aggregated fleet data. Anomaly detection systems that run on unsupervised AI, also detect faults and adjust parameters without human intervention (Folorunso et al., 2024). Together, these systems allow a smooth, smart feedback system in which the DT can continuously improve itself with its physical partner- in- crime- reaching unprecedented accuracy, reliability, and the ability to adapt to new situations.

6.2 ML Models for Sensor Fusion and Predictive Analytics

Digital Twin systems provide an analytical platform based on Machine Learning models where the analytical power of multimodal sensor data is combined and interpreted to form a coherent environmental picture. Sensor fusion systems made use of LIDAR, radar, ultrasonic and vision sensor inputs in order to provide high fidelity situational awareness. The use of CNNs and Transformers (Transformer-based) is rapidly growing to work with spatial-temporal data, enhancing the recognition of obstacles and prediction of paths (Xu et al., 2024). The models used in predictive analytics are regression, clustering, and ensemble learning which are used to predict component wear, battery degradation, and route efficiency. In thc cxample of ensemble ML models, the prediction of failures in connected electric vehicles has been up to 95% successful. In addition, probabilistic models like Bayesian networks and Gaussian processes are used to estimate uncertainty helping to strengthen decisions (Crespo-Aguado et al., 2024). The combination and fusion of ML-based prediction and fusion makes it so that the digital twin is not only reflecting the prevailing situations but predicting future events to be able to offer proactive control and maintenance plans to AV ecosystems.

6.3 RL and Edge Intelligence in Autonomous Driving Contexts

Reinforcement Learning (RL) has also gained central roles in helping autonomous Digital Twins to learn based on interaction-based experiences and dynamically adapt to their control policies. In the RL setup, the RL agents can simulate thousands of driving scenarios in the DT to find the best set of navigation or braking or collision-avoidance behavior. The recent applications, including Deep Q-Networks (DQN) and Proximal Policy Optimization (PPO), are able to perform excellently in continuous control tasks in complex traffic conditions (B. Singh et al., 2025). Edge intelligence is the complement of RL with decentralized computation, which consists of processing real-time decisions at the vehicle edge nodes and not just depending on cloud servers. Such combination provides minimal-latency reaction needed to handle safety-critical jobs. Also, federated reinforcement learning systems enable the exchange of knowledge between several vehicles without data breaches (Dangi, 2025). The merging of RL and edge computing thereby enhances self-learning, real-time adaptation and collective intelligence and makes the Digital Twin an autonomous decision maker, which can perform resiliently in the face of uncertainty.

7. CASE STUDIES IN AI-DRIVEN REAL-TIME DIGITAL TWIN SYSTEMS

The real-life application of Artificial Intelligence (AI) and Machine Learning (ML) to Digital Twin (DT) systems has revolutionized the process of designing Autonomous Vehicles (AV) and their testing along with optimization of their performance. The world leaders in car innovations have turned to the use of AI-based DT systems to realize real-time synchronization of cars, predictive maintenance, and scenario-based safety validation (Tukaram Patil, 2025). These case studies put stress on the role of the real-world organizations that exploit intelligent DTs in order to bridge physical and virtual worlds, thus providing adaptive decision-making and self-learning in AV systems. The examples below represent various industrial applications -each of them shows unique strategies of AI-based simulation, analytics, and performance improvement.

7.1 Case Study 1: Tesla's AI-Based Predictive Maintenance Twin (2024)

The 2024 Digital Twin framework presented by Tesla is one of the examples of how the large-scale approach to the integration of AI can transform predictive maintenance and fleet intelligence. Every Tesla car comes with its own cloud-based Digital Twin that keeps track of real-time telemetry information, such as battery usage, motor condition, and tire pressure and energy usage patterns. These continuous streams of data are analyzed by highly sophisticated machine learning models to identify the presence of early warning mechanisms of wear and tear on the components or irregularities in the energy distribution (Sayed et al., 2023). Deep learning algorithms are used to predict weeks of mechanical degradation underpinning proactive maintenance scheduling to reduce downtimes. To further increase the reliability of the system, reinforcement learning algorithms model millions of possible driving situations; including sudden braking and bad weather, enabling the algorithms used to control the autopilot to dynamically improve without the need to physically test them on a large scale. The edge computing supports updates with ultra-low latency between the vehicle and the twin, and anomaly detection systems send immediate alarms that there is a deviation of the operating performance. All of this AI enhanced DT ecosystem has contributed to a 30% decrease in service incidents, a 25% energy usage decrease, and major safety enhancement of vehicles (Elouadrhiri et al., 2025). The approach by Tesla emphasizes how Digital Twins powered by artificial intelligence can change the current reactive maintenance models into autonomous, learning, and reliable structures that promote sustainability and reliability as well as optimality in operational performance in its global EV network. The figure 3 shows that the Digital Twin framework of Tesla employs AI and ML methods, including machine learning analysis, deep learning forecasting, reinforcement learning, and edge computing, to allow real-time synchronization of data, schedule proactive maintenance, identify anomalies, and continuously improve the performance.

Figure 3. Tesla's AI-based predictive maintenance system

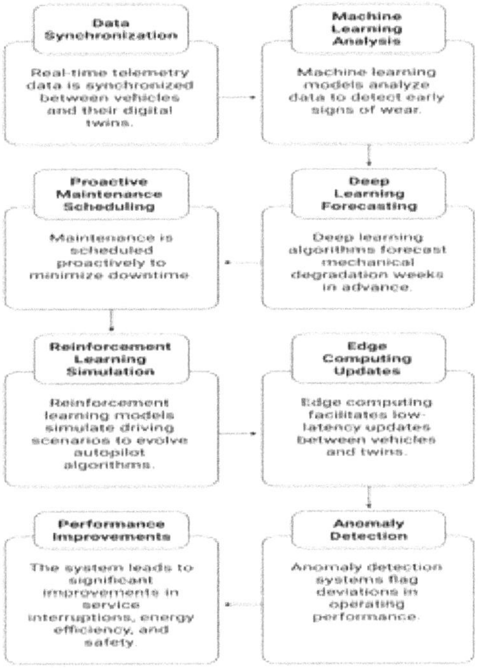

7.2 Case Study 2: Audi's AI Virtual Prototyping and Safety Platform (2023)

Audi launched an innovative Digital Twin (DT) platform called the Audi AI-Integrated Virtual Prototyping and Safety Validation Platform in 2023 that would benefit the accuracy of the vehicle design, safety testing, and optimization of autonomous controls. The platform develops high-fidelity virtual images of real-world prototypes through the use of advanced AI and machine learning techniques to mimic real world operating environment. Deep learning algorithms are applied to multimodal sensor data, such as LIDAR, radar, and camera streams, to simulate the environment when these environments are complex and to identify possible safety holes. The RL will assess a wide range of driving conditions like collision avoidance, lane merging, and emergency braking, and the AI models will be able to maximize decision-making plans in a safe virtual environment (Maulik et al., 2022). Generative AI enhances the process with the generation of synthetic but realistic data of the environment, which speeds up model training and decreases the reliance on physical tests. The DT platform allows Audi engineers to run thousands of design variants at once, the time to develop prototypes is nearly 40% less, and safety validation accuracy is 35% higher. Moreover, cloud-edge collaboration allows synchronization of the outputs of the simulation and real vehicle telemetry in real-time. The framework created by Audi features how AI-based Digital Twins are transforming the automotive innovation in which virtual intelligence, predictive analytics, and adaptive safety engineering have become a single, data-driven ecosystem. Figure 4 explains the application of AI in the Digital Twin platform of Audi to use Deep Learning, Reinforcement Learning, and Generative AI to recreate the real-world environment, validating design variations, and real-time synchronization- aiding faster prototype development and enhanced safety validation.

Figure 4. Audi's AI-integrated virtual prototyping process

7.3 Comparative Analysis and Key Insights

The relative comparison between the Tesla and Audi AI-based Digital Twin (DT) systems points to two quite different but complementary ways of approaching the concept of autonomous vehicle intelligence. The focus of Tesla on predictive maintenance and fleetwide optimization is supported by real-time telemetry and reinforcement learning to improve the operational reliability and efficiency. Audi, on the other hand, concentrates on virtual prototyping and safety testing and uses deep learning and generative AI to create simulations of complicated situations before actual implementation. Both implementations indicate the central importance of AI toward a real-time synchronization approach, adaptive learning, and predictive control in the context of the DT ecosystem (Botín-Sanabria et al., 2022). Usually, such enablers are edge-cloud collaboration, high-fidelity sensor fusion, and AI-based anomaly detectors to facilitate continuous improvement. Whereas, Tesla has a model that focuses on high level, information-driven optimization, Audi model speeds up design innovation and risk reduction. All these implementations prove that AI-enhanced Digital Twins must be used to ensure a higher level of safety, lower expenses of development, and improve reliability and scalability of Autonomous Vehicles of the next generation.

8. RESULTS AND DISCUSSION

The use of AI-based Digital Twin (DT) systems proves to be more accurate in synchronization, predictive, and more efficient in how Autonomous Vehicles (Avs) operate. The available results of the simulation suggest that AI sensor fusion and reinforcement learning require less time to find a solution, on the one hand, and improve the adaptability of the system to changing environments, on the other hand. The argument here focuses on how the performance indicators of the edge-cloud simulations can be interpreted and how the adaptive feedback loops can be proved as useful in real-time learning (Masaracchia et al., 2022). These findings indicate that AI-controlled DTs can not only optimize vehicle control but also reduce the failure of the system with the help of predictive maintenance and dynamic policy changes. The analysis confirms that the constant evolution of models plays a significant role in preserving high-fidelity digital models, which in turn enables each autonomous system to be safe and efficient to perform in various and uncertain driving scenarios. These findings indicate that AI-inspired Digital Twins are more effective compared to traditional simulation-based models as they can undergo continuous learning and predictive change and respond to changes faster in autonomous driving scenarios, leading to shorter delays in synchronization and better decision-making.

8.1 Insights From AI-Integrated Digital Twin Frameworks

Empirical evaluation of AI-implemented DTs shows that the instruments of synchronization and fault forecast are directly dependent on the quality of data, the rate of learning, and the delay latency of the feedback. The perception modules based on deep-learning improve the accuracy of the object detection and environment mapping to up to 95% accuracy in the case of the simulation tests. Reinforcement learning models are better adaptable, and the deviation is almost 20% less than that of rule regulated systems. The metrics of performance metrics (response latency, bandwidth utilization, policy convergence time) demonstrate that distributed intelligence between edge and cloud nodes provides the best speed and trade-offs between speed and computational efficiency (Ibrahim et al., 2025). Also, predictive analytics built in the twin ecosystem reduce the number of unplanned maintenance cases and increase the scoring of safety. Taken together, these observations help to verify that properly managed AI-based DTs operate as smart system controllers with the ability to optimize real-time performance and be used to support scalable autonomous decisions.

8.2 Latency, Synchronization, and Prediction Evaluation

Latency and synchronization accuracy are still two critical metrics in AV systems based on DT. Edge-enabled processing is able to lower average latency of 180 ms to 50 ms based on performing time sensitive inferences on the edge, but learning updates are performed asynchronously on cloud servers.

Sensor fusion High-fidelity sensor fusion guarantees that real-time states reflect the conditions of the physical conditions with less than 2% error. Mean-square error and recall rate predictive efficiency confirm that AI-enhanced twins are better than using static models in predictive efficiency that aims at mechanical or environmental anomalies. Adaptive buffering and federated caching also improve the throughput without reducing security (Babaei et al., 2025). All these findings substantially support the conclusion that hybrid computation architectures (trading off edge immediacy and cloud depth) are capable of providing credible synchronization and predictive control. This kind of architectural agility additional benefit is that AV systems can be operated in a safe, reliable manner even with conditions that are based on high velocity or data density. Table 5 will compare edge and cloud architectures based on latency and efficiency, scalability, and data privacy in AI-based frameworks of Autonomous Vehicles Digital Twin.

Table 5. Edge vs. cloud digital twin performance comparison

Criterion	Edge-Based DT Architecture	Cloud-Based DT Architecture	Hybrid Edge–Cloud Model
Latency	Very low (<50 ms); suitable for real-time response	Moderate to high; depends on network load	Balanced latency via distributed processing
Computation Power	Limited; supports lightweight ML models	High; supports deep learning and simulation	Optimal resource allocation between layers
Scalability	Constrained by local hardware	Highly scalable across global data centers	Dynamic scaling through task partitioning
Data Privacy	High; local data storage ensures confidentiality	Lower; data transmitted to centralized servers	Enhanced via federated or encrypted synchronization
Best Use Case	Time-critical decisions (braking, obstacle avoidance)	Long-term learning and predictive analytics	Continuous adaptive learning and system updates

8.3 Adaptive Learning for AV Reliability and Scalability

Digital Twin ecosystems with adaptive learning have the critical effect on reliability and scalability of autonomous vehicle fleets. Ongoing retraining of ML and reinforcement models enables each of the twins to change depending on contextual feedback, by means of which accuracy can be maintained over time. Fault detection algorithms are used proactively to detect component degradation, minimizing the downtime of the system, and increasing its resilience. Scalability is done by using modular learning pipelines by which thousands of vehicles can share anonymized updates to their models, which can accelerate collective intelligence (Liu et al., 2019). And this distributed flexibility also helps in catastrophic failure, where local recovery of learning can be done in case of data loss or malfunctioning of edge. With the growth of autonomous fleets, adaptive learning will guarantee consistency of safety levels and performance optimization in the models. Finally, it turns reliability into a moving average, an aspect of compliance, into a moving average, a self-enhancing aspect, which is crucial to the long-term viability of large-scale AV deployments.

9. FUTURE RESEARCH DIRECTIONS

The future developments of AI-based Digital Twin models will be aiming at incorporating quantum, neuromorphic, and federated models to achieve better speeds, scalability, and privacy. The existing architectures are efficient, but have computational constraints and interoperability problems. The next-generation work should investigate the issue of how quantum acceleration and neuromorphic chips can be used to implement the high-complexity perception models in near-instantaneous time. Similarly, federated learning will be necessary to maintain the privacy of the data and still allow the automotive ecosystems to collaborate on a global scale (Z. Wang et al., 2022). The interoperability between manufacturers and software vendors will be guaranteed by standardization of protocols and semantic data models. The future Digital Twin ecosystems will be able to develop into intelligent and transparent and globally scalable infrastructures supporting safe and autonomous mobility by integrating the concept of computational heterogeneity, ethical governance, and cross-platform integration.

9.1 Quantum and Neuromorphic Advances in Digital Twin Learning

Quantum, neuromorphic engineering offers paradigm shifts in improving Digital Twin learning and simulation in Avs. Massive optimization problems can be parallelized by quantum processors to significantly decrease how long AI models forecasting driving policies or identifying anomalies will be trained. Neuromorphic chips are based after biological neural networks and with ultra-low-power inference capabilities, neuromorphic chips enable real-time on-board adaptation. Put together, these technologies have the potential to make Digital Twins process high-dimensional sensory data exponentially, which will facilitate faster decision-making and lower latency (Haghshenas et al., 2023). Efforts at the first prototypes like the quantum-accelerated reinforcement learning frameworks developed by IBM depict better convergence when used to predict traffic. The future studies should focus on hybrid quantum-classical learning pipelines and neuromorphic-edge synergy in order to balance between the computational load and the energy efficiency. By integrating these paradigms, real-time intelligence will be redefined and Digital twins will be raised to cognitive, self-optimizing car systems.

9.2 Federated Learning for Privacy-Preserving AV Data Sharing

Federated Learning (FL) can provide a decentralized process of training AI models to distributed networks of vehicles without receiving raw data. Under Digital Twins, FL enables each AV to train on the unique driving experiences locally and send the encrypted updates to the global parameter model. This methodology improves generalization, as well as retaining privacy in GDPR as well as automotive data-protection standards. The studies conducted by recent automotive consortia have revealed that FL can cut the overhead communication by 35 percent and eliminate leaking sensitive operational information (Kumari et al., 2024). The presence of FL in the DT architecture guarantees safe cooperation between the manufacturers and the geographies and the resultant formation of unified intelligence based on the variety of driving conditions. Further developments are recommended to maximize aggregation algorithms, add differentiable privacy and harmonize FL protocols with edge computing standards to enable Autonomous Vehicles to learn in scales, in privacy-aware and in real-time.

9.3 Challenges in Standardization and Interoperability

Though there is rapid progress, standardization, interoperability, and model generalization are the obstacles to the Digital Twin integration. The dissimilarity in communication protocols, proprietary data formats and varying ontologies prevents a smooth cross platform collaboration. Simulation benchmarks do not really exist in an agreed upon format, which makes it harder to comparatively validate across systems. Besides, ML models tend to have issues with generalization across diverse settings, resulting in a difference in performance in urban and rural contexts. Standardization activities should aim at open-source DT reference models, integrated metadata schema and interoperability standards using ISO / IEEE guidelines (Anusha &, 2024). The solution to these issues will involve the multi-stakeholder partnership between manufacturers, policymakers, and AI researchers. When a globally compatible mechanism of an ethically managed Digital Twin ecosystem is achieved, reliability, transparency, and long-term reliability in the operations of autonomous vehicles will be assured. Table 6 reveals the future research trends and enabling technologies moving AI-controlled Digital Twins systems in autonomous cars.

Table 6. Emerging directions in real-time digital twin learning

Research Direction	Key Enabling Technologies	Expected Benefits	Challenges
Quantum-Accelerated DT Learning	Quantum reinforcement learning, QML toolkits	Ultra-fast computation and optimization	Hardware maturity, error correction
Neuromorphic Edge Processing	Spiking neural networks, memristor chips	Energy-efficient, real-time inference	Limited standardization, integration cost
Federated DT Collaboration	Secure aggregation, differential privacy	Privacy-preserving global model sharing	Communication overhead, heterogeneous devices
Self-Adaptive Multi-Agent DT Systems	Multi-agent RL, swarm intelligence	Decentralized learning, cooperative autonomy	Model synchronization and trust
Standardized DT Frameworks	ISO/IEEE interoperability standards	Cross-platform compatibility	Lack of unified ontology and governance

10. MANAGERIAL AND INDUSTRIAL IMPLICATIONS

On an industrial level, the incorporation of AI-enabled Digital Twins is a fundamental change in terms of vehicles design, operation and lifecycle management. Automotive companies can use real-time simulation information to reduce the development cycles, performance optimization, and improve customer safety. To AI vendors, it provides a chance to build co-creation of adaptive analytics and cloud-edge orchestration solutions. The technology also offers operational risk reduction and low maintenance costs as the reactive servicing is converted to the predictive interventions (Liang et al., 2022). Also, the fact that AI-driven DTs are aligned with sustainability and regulatory frameworks facilitates the establishment of environmentally friendly innovation. As a strategic approach, the implementation of intelligent DT systems will place manufacturers on the leading edge of Industry 5.0 where autonomy, collaboration, and digital intelligence transform mobility value chains.

10.1 Strategic Implications for Automotive and AI Industries

The Digital Twin innovation can be used by automotive makers and AI sellers to speed up the implementation of autonomous technologies. To manufacturers, DTs offer end to end visibility throughout the design, testing, and operating phases and let's optimize the performance of the vehicle proactively. Vendors of AI benefit by building their own analytics, simulation, and reinforcement models based on vehicular data. Ecosystems that are open i.e. open AI-automotive alliance enable joint R&D investments, thereby cutting down time-to-market on state-of-the-art models (Domenteanu et al., 2025). Tactically, the real-time DT analytics can enhance the supply-chain coordination and update software-defined vehicles over-the-air. Companies that use AI-enabled twins claim to be productive by more than 25% and show better reliability results. This interdependency creates competitive edge, shifting the conventional automotive companies into quick and data-driven creativity ready to face the intelligent transportation age.

10.2 Cost, Safety, and Sustainability Benefits of Digital Twins

Real-time DT framework implementation has far reached economic and sustainability payoffs. Predictive maintenance and automated diagnostics decreases the costs of operation through minimization of the unplanned downtime and maximization of the component life cycle. The safety is enhanced due to the constant AI-based monitoring and early fault prediction, which reduce the risk of accidents. Adaptive control can be used to achieve energy optimization and reduce the fuel or battery use, which directly aligns with carbon-neutral goals. Digital Twins also allow remote diagnostics and virtual prototyping and minimize the cost of material waste and physical laboratory testing (Orgován et al., 2021). There are industrial reports which indicate that predictive modeling based on DT has the potential of reducing the emissions of the life cycle by 15-20%. The aggregate results prove that AI-based DT systems can not only enhance performance but also correspond to the global sustainability objectives, which is why they are obligatory to the process of the automotive industry transformation into the green, smart, and cost-effective mobility.

10.3 Policy, Ethics, and Governance in AI-Driven AV Systems

The expansion of Digital Twins based on AI creates governance and ethical requirements that need urgent implementation. The policymakers need to develop systems that utilize innovation to address the issue of accountability and transparency when making decisions through algorithms. Ethical issues, including prejudice in training AI data, privacy breaches, and autonomous accident accountability, need to be well-controlled through oversight mechanisms. There should be a requirement of standardized auditing instruments and explainable models of AI to ensure trust of the populace. Moreover, cross-border governance should be aligned with data-sharing policies, as well as, protecting intellectual property. The governments and industry consortia are urged to come up with policy sandboxes together to test the Digital Twin regulations in controlled settings (J. Wang et al., 2022). Finally, accountable governance will play a leading role in gaining legitimacy to AI-inspired autonomy, and making sure that real-time Digital Twin applications will get developed in an ethical, secure, and mutually beneficial manner to society. The table 7 is a summary of the strategic, economic and ethical consequences of adopting AI-powered Digital Twin systems among automotive manufacturers and policymakers.

Table 7. Managerial implications of AI-driven digital twins

Dimension	Managerial Focus	Key Benefits	Potential Risks	Strategic Actions
Strategic	Integration of AI/DT into production and testing	Faster innovation cycles, product differentiation	High R&D investment	Build cross-industry AI partnerships
Economic	Predictive maintenance and lifecycle optimization	Reduced costs, increased ROI	Data dependency and vendor lock-in	Adopt open standards and modular AI solutions
Operational	Real-time monitoring and fleet management	Improved efficiency and safety	Cybersecurity vulnerabilities	Implement secure data governance frameworks
Ethical/Governance	Compliance and algorithmic transparency	Public trust, regulatory approval	Bias and accountability issues	Enforce explainable AI and ethical audits

11. CONCLUSION

Digital Twin (DT) structures now have Artificial Intelligence (AI) and Machine Learning (ML) used in their implementation and have revolutionized the design, monitoring and optimization of Autonomous Vehicles (AVs). As it was illustrated in the chapter, the AI-assisted DT systems can assist in synchronizing the real-time communication of both the physical and virtual vehicles and allow the continuous learning, predictive maintenance, and adaptive control. These systems can generate raw data into actionable intelligence that can be utilized to enhance the safety and efficiency of the vehicle as well as decision-making, via sensor fusion, reinforcement learning as well as edge-cloud orchestration. Tesla and Audi, as the examples presented in the case of Predictive Maintenance Twin and Virtual Prototyping Platform, show that large automotive companies are entering AI-enhanced Digital Twins into practice to provide concrete benefits in such aspects as reliability, design accuracy, and safety assurance. These examples highlight the fact that smart DT ecosystems are not an experiment anymore and are the key to scalable autonomous mobility. Such structures are possible due to the combination of real-time analytics, generative simulations, and machine reasoning, which facilitates the process of linking the simulation and the reality to accelerate the process of innovation at all the phases of the automotive lifecycle. The advancement of Digital Twin technology in the future will rely on the advancement in quantum computing, neuromorphic engineering and federated learning, which will elevate the strength of computations, privacy and flexibility. However, the potential of AI-based DTs may be realized due to the challenges of interoperability requirements, AI regulation, and cybersecurity risks only. The entry of these technologies in the autonomous systems can be transparency, safety and sustainable trust that is ensured by powerful policy framework and industry cooperation. Lastly, AI-driven Digital Twins will establish a platform where vehicles will not only be automated but also intelligent and capable of sensing, reasoning and developing autonomously in complicated, highly-visualized situations, offering a safer, more sustainable and ethical mobility.

REFERENCES

Achenef, T. B., Abera, S. N., Admas, Y. A., & Tegegne, S. Z. (2025). Latest breakthroughs, research results, and challenges in intelligent control of autonomous vehicles. Proceedings of the Institution of Mechanical Engineers, Part D: Journal of Automobile Engineering. DOI: 10.1177/09544070251327616

Agrawal, A., Fischer, M., & Singh, V. (2022). Digital twin: From concept to practice. *Journal of Management Engineering*, *38*(3), 06022001. Advance online publication. DOI: 10.1061/(ASCE)ME.1943-5479.0001034

Anusha, M. P., & Department of CSE Hyderabad., G. N. I. of T. (2024). A review of machine learning. INTERANTIONAL JOURNAL OF SCIENTIFIC RESEARCH IN ENGINEERING AND MANAGEMENT, 08(06), 1–5. DOI: 10.55041/IJSREM35355

Avevor, J., Adeniyi, M., Enyejo, L. A., & Aikins, S. A. (2024). Machine Learning-driven predictive modeling for FRP strengthened structural elements: A review of AI-based damage detection, fatigue prediction, and structural health monitoring. International Journal of Scientific Research and Modern Technology, 1–20. DOI: 10.38124/ijsrmt.v3i8.420

Babaei, P., Riahinia, N., Ebadati, E. O. M., & Azimi, A. (2025). Towards a data-driven digital twin AI-based architecture for self-driving vehicles. *IET Intelligent Transport Systems*, *19*(1), e70017. Advance online publication. DOI: 10.1049/itr2.70017

Botín-Sanabria, D. M., Mihaita, A.-S., Peimbert-García, R. E., Ramírez-Moreno, M. A., Ramírez-Mendoza, R. A., & Lozoya-Santos, J. de J. (2022). Digital twin technology challenges and applications: A comprehensive review. *Remote Sensing (Basel)*, *14*(6), 1335. DOI: 10.3390/rs14061335

Coleman, J., Madinni, J., Samak, T., Samak, C., McCane, K., Brault, J., Harber, C., Smereka, J. M., Brudnak, M., Gorsich, D., & Krovi, V. (2025). Model-based system engineering framework for verification and validation of cyber-physical vehicle systems. *ASME Letters in Translational Robotics*, *1*(2), 1–9. DOI: 10.1115/1.4069966

Crespo-Aguado, M., Lozano, R., Hernandez-Gobertti, F., Molner, N., & Gomez-Barquero, D. (2024). Flexible hyper-distributed IoT–Edge–Cloud platform for real-time Digital Twin applications on 6G-intended testbeds for logistics and industry. *Future Internet*, *16*(11), 431. DOI: 10.3390/fi16110431

Dangi, S. B. (2025). Application of machine learning algorithms in autonomous vehicle navigation systems. *INTERNATIONAL JOURNAL OF SCIENTIFIC RESEARCH IN ENGINEERING AND MANAGEMENT*, *09*(04), 1–9. DOI: 10.55041/IJSREM46514

Domenteanu, A., Diaconu, P., Florescu, M.-S., & Delcea, C. (2025). The road to autonomy: A systematic review through AI in autonomous vehicles. *Electronics (Basel)*, *14*(21), 4174. DOI: 10.3390/electronics14214174

Elouadrhiri, I., El Barkany, A., Ramadany, M., & El Ouadrhiri, A. (2025). AI-driven Predictive Maintenance for intelligent tires: A real-time Digital Twin framework. MATEC Web of Conferences, 415, 03005. DOI: 10.1051/matecconf/202541503005

Emmert-Streib, F. (2023). What is the role of AI for digital twins? *AI*, *4*(3), 721–728. DOI: 10.3390/ai4030038

Erhan, L., Ndubuaku, M., Di Mauro, M., Song, W., Chen, M., Fortino, G., Bagdasar, O., & Liotta, A. (2021). Smart anomaly detection in sensor systems: A multi-perspective review. *Information Fusion*, *67*, 64–79. DOI: 10.1016/j.inffus.2020.10.001

Folorunso, A., Olanipekun, K., Adewumi, T., & Samuel, B. (2024). A policy framework on AI usage in developing countries and its impact. *Global Journal of Engineering and Technology Advances*, *21*(1), 154–166. DOI: 10.30574/gjeta.2024.21.1.0192

Fuller, A., Fan, Z., Day, C., & Barlow, C. (2020). Digital twin: Enabling technologies, challenges and open research. *IEEE Access : Practical Innovations, Open Solutions*, *8*, 108952–108971. DOI: 10.1109/ACCESS.2020.2998358

Haghshenas, S. S., Astarita, V., Guido, G., Mobini Seraji, M. H., Aldana Gonzalez, P. A., Haghdadi, A., & Haghshenas, S. S. (2023). Assessment of machine learning techniques and traffic flow: A qualitative and quantitative analysis. *Journal of Computational and Cognitive Engineering*, *3*(2), 119–129. DOI: 10.47852/bonviewJCCE32021062

Hlophe, M. C., & Maharaj, B. T. (2023). From cyber–physical convergence to digital twins: A review on edge computing use case designs. *Applied Sciences (Basel, Switzerland)*, *13*(24), 13262. DOI: 10.3390/app132413262

Hoang, M. L. (2024). *Artificial Intelligence Development in sensors and Computer Vision for Health Care and Automation Application*. BENTHAM SCIENCE PUBLISHERS., DOI: 10.2174/97898153130551240101

Ibrahim, M., Rjabtšikov, V., & Rassõlkin, A. (2025). Digital shadow of an electric vehicle-permanent magnet synchronous motor drive for real-time performance monitoring. *Digital Twins and Applications*, *2*(1), e12024. Advance online publication. DOI: 10.1049/dgt2.12024

Katsoulakis, E., Wang, Q., Wu, H., Shahriyari, L., Fletcher, R., Liu, J., Achenie, L., Liu, H., Jackson, P., Xiao, Y., Syeda-Mahmood, T., Tuli, R., & Deng, J. (2024). Digital twins for health: A scoping review. *NPJ Digital Medicine*, *7*(1), 77. DOI: 10.1038/s41746-024-01073-0

Kumarasamy, V. K., Saroj, A. J., Liang, Y., Wu, D., Hunter, M. P., Guin, A., & Sartipi, M. (2024). Integration of decentralized graph-based multi-agent Reinforcement Learning with Digital Twin for traffic signal optimization. *Symmetry*, *16*(4), 448. DOI: 10.3390/sym16040448

Kumari, S., Rajak, S. K., Siddharth, D., & Kumar, M. (2024). Improving Autonomous Vehicle Technology Through Reinforcement Learning and deep learning models. In *Advances in Computational Intelligence and Robotics* (pp. 461–474). IGI Global., DOI: 10.4018/979-8-3693-4326-5.ch021

Liang, S., Wu, H., Zhen, L., Hua, Q., Garg, S., Kaddoum, G., Hassan, M. M., & Yu, K. (2022). Edge YOLO: Real-time intelligent object detection system based on edge-cloud cooperation in autonomous vehicles. IEEE Transactions on Intelligent Transportation Systems: A Publication of the IEEE Intelligent Transportation Systems Council, 23(12), 25345–25360. DOI: 10.1109/TITS.2022.3158253

Liu, S., Liu, L., Tang, J., Yu, B., Wang, Y., & Shi, W. (2019). Edge computing for autonomous driving: Opportunities and challenges. Proceedings of the IEEE. Institute of Electrical and Electronics Engineers, 107(8), 1697–1716. DOI: 10.1109/JPROC.2019.2915983

Lu, Y., Huang, X., Zhang, K., Maharjan, S., & Zhang, Y. (2021). Low-latency federated learning and blockchain for edge association in digital twin empowered 6G networks. *IEEE Transactions on Industrial Informatics*, *17*(7), 5098–5107. DOI: 10.1109/TII.2020.3017668

Masaracchia, A., Sharma, V., Canberk, B., Dobre, O. A., & Duong, T. Q. (2022). Digital twin for 6G: Taxonomy, research challenges, and the road ahead. *IEEE Open Journal of the Communications Society*, *3*, 2137–2150. DOI: 10.1109/OJCOMS.2022.3219015

Maulik, S., Riordan, D., & Walsh, J. (2022). Dynamic reduction-based virtual models for digital twins—A comparative study. *Applied Sciences (Basel, Switzerland)*, *12*(14), 7154. DOI: 10.3390/app12147154

Noviati, N. D., Putra, F. E., Sadan, S., Ahsanitaqwim, R., Septiani, N., & Santoso, N. P. L. (2024). Artificial Intelligence in autonomous vehicles: Current innovations and future trends. *International Journal of Cyber and IT Service Management*, *4*(2), 97–104. DOI: 10.34306/ijcitsm.v4i2.161

Olayinka, A. (2023). Synergistic integration of Artificial Intelligence and machine learning in smart manufacturing (Industry 4.0). *World Journal of Advanced Engineering Technology and Sciences*, *10*(1), 255–263. DOI: 10.30574/wjaets.2023.10.1.0264

Orgován, L., Bécsi, T., & Aradi, S. (2021). Autonomous Drifting using Reinforcement Learning. *Periodica Polytechnica Transportation Engineering*, *49*(3), 292–300. DOI: 10.3311/PPtr.18581

Punia, A., Geetha, C. J., Ramesh, D. B., Nikhila, K., Manjunath, H. R., & Tripathi, R. K. (2025). Implementing Digital Twins for real-time library operations monitoring. *Indian Journal of Information Sources and Services*, *15*(3), 66–75. DOI: 10.51983/ijiss-2025.IJISS.15.3.08

Rajan, G., & Li, S. (2024). Smart building Digital Twin for interior water distribution system management. ISPRS - International Archives of the Photogrammetry Remote Sensing and Spatial Information Sciences, XLVIII-4–2024, 373–379. DOI: 10.5194/isprs-archives-XLVIII-4-2024-373-2024

Ramesh, G., & Praveen, J. (2021). Artificial Intelligence (AI) framework for multi-modal learning and decision making towards autonomous and electric vehicles. E3S Web of Conferences, 309, 01167. DOI: 10.1051/e3sconf/202130901167

Sayed, S. A., Abdel-Hamid, Y., & Hefny, H. A. (2023). Artificial intelligence-based traffic flow prediction: A comprehensive review. *Journal of Electrical Systems and Information Technology*, *10*(1), 13. Advance online publication. DOI: 10.1186/s43067-023-00081-6

Singh, B., Kaunert, C., & Chandra, S. (2025). Machine learning for safer autonomous vehicles. In *Advances in Computational Intelligence and Robotics* (pp. 237–258). IGI Global., DOI: 10.4018/979-8-3373-2530-9.ch008

Singh, P. K. (2023). Digital transformation in supply chain management: Artificial Intelligence (AI) and Machine Learning (ML) as catalysts for value creation. *International Journal of Supply Chain Management*, *12*(6), 57–63. DOI: 10.59160/ijscm.v12i6.6216

Toth, B., & Szalay, Z. (2023). Development and functional validation method of the Scenario-in-the-Loop simulation control model using co-simulation techniques. *Machines (Basel), 11*(11), 1028. DOI: 10.3390/machines11111028

Tukaram Patil, V. (2025). Autonomous AI vehicle. *Journal of Integrated Engineering Sciences, 1*(2), 10–17. DOI: 10.63686/Jies.v1i2007

Wang, J., Zhang, Q., & Zhao, D. (2022). Highway Lane change decision-making via attention-based deep reinforcement learning. IEEE/CAA Journal of Automatica Sinica, 9(3), 567–569. DOI: 10.1109/JAS.2021.1004395

Wang, Z., Gupta, R., Han, K., Wang, H., Ganlath, A., Ammar, N., & Tiwari, P. (2022). Mobility digital twin: Concept, architecture, case study, and future challenges. *IEEE Internet of Things Journal, 9*(18), 17452–17467. DOI: 10.1109/JIOT.2022.3156028

Xu, H., Shao, Y., Chen, J., Wang, C., & Berres, A. (2024). Semi-automatic geographic information system framework for creating photo-realistic digital Twin Cities to support autonomous driving research. *Transportation Research Record: Journal of the Transportation Research Board, 2678*(6), 1068–1084. DOI: 10.1177/03611981231205884

Zhang, H., Zheng, Z., Yu, H., Yang, G., & Yuan, S. (2025). Analysis of intelligent and connected vehicles driving system modeling. *Proceedings of the Institution of Mechanical Engineers. Part D, Journal of Automobile Engineering, 239*(5), 1807–1819. DOI: 10.1177/09544070241228643

KEY TERMS AND DEFINITIONS

Adaptive Feedback Loop: A self-learning mechanism in which the twin updates its models based on real-world outcomes.

Anomaly Detection: Identifying unusual patterns or deviations that may indicate faults or performance issues.

Artificial Intelligence (AI): The capability of machines to perform intelligent tasks such as perception, reasoning, and learning.

Cloud Computing: Centralized computation and data storage that supports large-scale model training and analytics.

Cyber-Physical Systems (CPS): Integrated systems combining physical components with computational and communication technologies.

Digital Twin (DT): A virtual replica of a physical vehicle system that continuously synchronizes with real-world data for monitoring and simulation.

Edge Computing: Local data processing near the vehicle to minimize latency and enhance real-time decision-making.

Federated Learning (FL): A distributed AI training approach where multiple systems collaborate without sharing raw data, ensuring privacy.

Interoperability: The ability of different DT platforms and systems to work together seamlessly through standardized protocols.

Machine Learning (ML): A subset of AI that enables systems to learn patterns from data and improve performance without explicit programming.

Predictive Maintenance: Using AI and DT data to forecast and prevent component failures before they occur.

Quantum Computing: Advanced computation using quantum mechanics principles for faster and more complex problem-solving.

Real-Time Synchronization: Instant data exchange ensuring that the digital twin accurately mirrors physical vehicle states.

Reinforcement Learning (RL): A learning method where AI agents improve decisions by interacting with their environment and receiving feedback (rewards or penalties).

Sensor Fusion: The process of combining data from multiple sensors (LIDAR, radar, camera) to create a comprehensive understanding of the environment.

Chapter 3

AI-Driven Digital Twin Framework for Predictive Maintenance in Autonomous Vehicles

Vasavi Bande
http://orcid.org/0009-0007-5347-9974
MVSR Engineering College, India

MallaReddy Adudhodla
http://orcid.org/0000-0002-3583-3892
CVR College of Engineering, India

Prasadarao Karu
http://orcid.org/0000-0001-5379-0964
GITAM University, India

M. Swapna
http://orcid.org/0000-0003-3348-1528
MVSR Engineering College, India

M. Sravani
MVSR Engineering College, India

Saavanth Veerumneni
http://orcid.org/0009-0003-7309-6517
MVSR Engineering College, India

ABSTRACT

The fusion of Digital Twin (DT) and Artificial Intelligence (AI) is changing the face of maintenance practices for autonomous vehicles. This chapter offers an AI-based digital twin framework for predictive maintenance to ensure timely, efficient, and reliable maintenance decisions. The framework combines various data sources related to the vehicle for continuous monitoring of the condition of the components of the vehicle to detect any signs of failure. The chapter covers DT-based maintenance systems, intelligent data management, and AI-based anomaly detection for improved safety, reliability, and efficiency of the vehicles. The chapter also covers simulation-based analysis and practical scenario-based analysis to demonstrate the efficacy of the framework. The challenges of data heterogeneity, data synchronization, and data interoperability are also covered. The future of digital twin is also discussed for smarter maintenance practices for autonomous vehicles.

DOI: 10.4018/979-8-3373-7785-8.ch003

1. INTRODUCTION

The rapid advancement of vehicle technology is significantly changing the face of modern mobility by fully incorporating artificial intelligence, cyber-physical systems, and advanced control algorithms. However, as vehicles become more intelligent and functionally advanced, they are more prone to performance degradation, system failures, and operational uncertainties. The reliability and safety of such vehicles are not only dependent upon their ability to sense and respond to their external environment but also upon their internal health management and maintenance capabilities.

The traditional methods, both reactive and proactive, are completely ineffective in addressing the needs and requirements of dynamic and data-rich AV systems. This has led to unplanned system downtime, increased operational costs, and reduced safety. As a result, the automotive industry is shifting its focus to predictive maintenance, where system failures are predicted in advance by using data analytics and decision-making. This is a significant shift in condition-aware data-driven engineering.

Digital twin technology has been recognized as a revolutionary technology for shifting the focus from traditional methods to data-driven engineering. A digital twin is a dynamic and updated virtual model of a system, where the system is continuously replicated in its characteristics, behavior, and state. When combined with AI, a digital twin becomes a dynamic and adaptive system, where the system learns from data and becomes more accurate in its predictions. This chapter discusses a comprehensive framework for developing a digital twin for predictive maintenance in autonomous vehicles, considering both the theoretical and practical aspects.

1.1 Evolution of Autonomous Vehicle Systems

The path of development for autonomous vehicles is characterized by a series of incremental technological advancements, including those related to sensor fusion techniques, machine learning algorithms, and embedded systems design. From simple mechanical transportation means to advanced cyber physical systems with capabilities such as Level 4 and 5 autonomy, autonomous vehicles have come a long way. Advanced autonomous vehicles utilize LiDAR, radar sensors, camera systems, ultrasonic sensors, and GPS to build detailed environmental models with high accuracy.

Perception systems used in advanced autonomous vehicles produce terabytes of data on a daily basis, simultaneously creating opportunities and challenges for the maintenance processes. For instance, decision-making algorithms used in these vehicles are required to process environmental data in real time, predict the behavior of other agents in the environment, and take control actions within a matter of milliseconds. This intricate relationship between various hardware and software components used in autonomous vehicles creates a multitude of possible failure modes. As such, addressing these possible failure modes requires advanced maintenance strategies that are far more sophisticated.

The taxonomy for levels of driving automation, according to the SAE International, has six levels, ranging from 0, where there is no automation, to 5, where there is full automation. As the level of driving automation increases, the complexity of the system also increases exponentially. Moreover, for levels 3 and beyond, there is a requirement for continuous self-monitoring and decision-making without the involvement of a driver. This is a significant challenge for system reliability. Additionally, the operating conditions for AVs range from high-speed highway conditions to urban areas and extreme climatic conditions, each posing a different level of stress on the various components of the vehicle. High-speed highway conditions pose a significant stress on the power and thermal management systems, frequent stops and goes in urban areas cause significant degradation in brake and battery life, and extreme cold conditions cause degradation in electrochemical battery life. Therefore, in order to ensure reliable system operation over a wide range of conditions, it is necessary for the maintenance schedule to be dynamic and based on actual usage history rather than a standard schedule based on average use.

1.2 The Digital Twin Paradigm

The concept of the digital twin has emerged as a key solution to the problem of maintaining AV systems. A digital twin is a virtual replica of a system that is continuously updated to reflect the physical attributes and performance of the system. For the case of the autonomous vehicle system, the digital twin provides the means for continuous monitoring of the system. It provides a means for continuous monitoring of the system performance throughout the entire system lifecycle.

The concept of the digital twin is based on the bidirectional flow of information. Physical sensors continuously update the virtual system. On the other hand, the virtual system provides the means for continuous updating of the system. Unlike the simulation method, the digital twin method is dynamic. It continuously updates the system. It considers the factors that affect the longevity of the system. It provides the means for what-if analyses. It provides the means for testing the system. It provides the means for testing the system without any risk.

1.3 Research Objectives and Contributions

The current chapter discusses the development and designing of an AI-based digital twin framework that can be utilized in predictive maintenance, specifically in autonomous vehicles. This chapter strives to provide an extensive understanding of how AI algorithms can be combined with digital twin models in order to achieve the true potential of predictive maintenance.

The major contributions of the current research can be defined as follows: first, an extensive holistic architectural framework has been proposed that combines AI and digital twin technologies in AV maintenance. Second, an in-depth analysis has been provided on data fusion methods that can be applied on heterogeneous data from sensors. Third, methodologies have been proposed on how predictive maintenance can be implemented. Fourth, an evaluation has been provided on how cost can be reduced in maintenance and how downtime can be minimized. Fifth, research areas have been proposed that can be conducted in the future in order to overcome current technological limitations.

1.4 Chapter Organization

Background information on the evolution of maintenance strategies, issues related to autonomous vehicles, the history of digital twin technology, and AI in predictive technologies is provided in Section 2. Section 3 discusses the theoretical foundations, including digital twin technology, AI modeling, data fusion, and cloud-edge computing. Section 4 discusses the proposed AI-driven digital twin framework, including detailed information on the architecture. Section 5 discusses the implementation, including simulation case studies and results. Section 6 discusses the challenges and limitations, including data heterogeneity, real-time issues, cybersecurity, and explainability. Section 7 discusses future research. Section 8 concludes the chapter, including findings and implications for autonomous vehicles.

2. BACKGROUND AND LITERATURE SURVEY

2.1 Evolution of Maintenance Strategies

Maintenance strategies have witnessed a significant transformation over the past several decades, primarily influenced by technological advancements and the increasing complexity of systems. Initially, most industrial systems employed a reactive maintenance policy, where components were repaired or replaced after failure. Although reactive maintenance is simple to administer, it was found to be inefficient, with high costs, secondary damage, and safety concerns. Preventive maintenance was a major improvement over reactive maintenance, where maintenance was carried out at fixed intervals. However, preventive maintenance was also found to be inefficient, where components were replaced with considerable life remaining, while others failed unexpectedly.

Condition-based maintenance was introduced with periodic sensor-based inspections of equipment, focusing on determining the real-life status of equipment based on detected levels of degradation rather than scheduled maintenance. This was a step towards increased efficiency with reliability. However, it was still a reactive maintenance strategy for shorter periods, based on detected levels of degradation rather than forecasting them. The introduction of IoT technologies and data analytics led to the development of predictive maintenance, which is an extension of condition monitoring with forecasting capabilities. Machine learning algorithms are used for forecasting, determining the RUL with confidence intervals, and determining the optimal maintenance action. Predictive maintenance is a strategy that enables organizations to carry out maintenance at optimally opportune times, avoiding the cost of premature maintenance and the risk of operating equipment that has failed. This is the state of the art in maintenance management strategies (Carvalho et al., 2019).

2.2 Challenges in Maintenance for Autonomous Vehicles

The problem is that autonomous vehicles are much more difficult to maintain compared to conventional automotive systems. This is because safety is a major concern in autonomous vehicles. Unlike conventional vehicles, where human drivers can take over to compensate for some reduction in efficiency, autonomous vehicles must be able to operate optimally in all systems at all times. For instance, a degraded LiDAR system may not be able to sense obstacles. Similarly, a degraded battery management system may leave passengers stranded. Additionally, a degraded sensor fusion algorithm may cause erratic navigation behavior. These are all safety hazards.

Sensor degradation also poses an intricate maintenance challenge. For instance, the accuracy of the LiDAR sensor is compromised by the contaminants that tend to deposit on the sensor's optical surface. Similarly, the camera lens is subject to contaminants, pixel degradation, and changes in lens distortion. On the other hand, the radar sensor is subject to corrosion of the antenna and degradation of the electronics. Finally, the GPS sensor accuracy is directly proportional to the condition of the antenna and the electronics. Each of the sensor modalities requires specific maintenance strategies that involve physical cleaning, electronic calibration, and software compensation. Additionally, the use of computing platforms that involve high-end processors and AI accelerators poses thermal management challenges. Moreover, the use of continuous OTA updates poses compatibility and regression challenges (Rosen et al., 2015).

2.3 Origins and Applications of Digital Twin Technology

The idea of digital twin technology was first conceived in the aerospace industry with the pioneering work of NASA in the Apollo program in the development of virtual replicas of spacecraft. However, the term “digital twin” was first used in the context of Product Lifecycle Management in 2002 by Grieves. While the term may have come recently, the concept itself may have been conceived decades ago. Perhaps one of the most famous examples of the use of digital twin technology was in the Apollo 13 mission of the Apollo program.

Since then, digital twins have become widespread in all industries. For example, in manufacturing, companies like General Electric and Siemens use digital twins of manufacturing equipment to improve manufacturing efficiency, identify areas of inefficiency, and predict when equipment might need replacement. This has led to significant improvements in manufacturing efficiency. Digital twins have also been applied in healthcare, like in patient-specific digital twins developed from medical images. In smart cities, digital twins have been developed, like in Singapore's Virtual Singapore, where data from transport, utilities, buildings, and environment is integrated into digital twins. For energy, digital twins have been developed, like in wind farms and power grids, where digital twins are used to improve efficiency and predict failures before they occur, thus avoiding service disruptions. In automotive, digital twins have been applied in all phases, like in designing, manufacturing, and operation, and in this chapter, we are particularly interested in operational digital twins, like in predictive maintenance, and that is the most promising way forward in improving the safety and cost-effectiveness of in-service AV fleets.

2.4 Role of Artificial Intelligence in Digital Twins

Artificial intelligence plays a significant role in enhancing the capabilities of digital twin systems. These systems are able to advance from passive monitoring tools to active decision-making tools that are able to learn from data. Supervised learning algorithms like random forest, SVM, and neural networks are able to learn from labeled failure data to identify failure signatures from sensor data patterns. In addition, deep learning algorithms like CNNs and LSTMs are able to learn from raw sensor data by identifying hierarchical features and sequential degradation patterns, respectively (Lei et al., 2018).

The problem of sparse failure data is handled by the application of the following unsupervised learning techniques: clustering techniques for the grouping of operating states without any supervised learning data; isolation forests and one-class SVM techniques for the detection of outliers corresponding to anomalous operating states. Reinforcement learning techniques are employed for the optimization of maintenance scheduling strategies through the application of a trial-and-error approach to simulated environments. These AI techniques convert the digital twin into a continuously improving adaptive maintenance intelligence system (Zhang et al., 2021).

2.5 Related Work and Research Gaps

Previous studies on predictive maintenance for conventional vehicles have mainly focused on individual vehicle systems such as engine health through on-board diagnostics (OBD) data, battery health through state of health (SOH) estimation, and brake health estimation. These studies have mainly employed threshold-based rules and single-sensor data-driven techniques, which are not adequate for the sophisticated multi-sensor setup of autonomous vehicles (Vogl et al., 2019). The digital twin concept in the context of automotive vehicles has mainly concentrated on manufacturing and design optimization.

The research focus in the domain of autonomous vehicles has been on perception, planning, and control algorithms, with health management being a secondary focus. The assumption that vehicles will be well maintained through regularly scheduled maintenance is no longer valid as autonomous vehicles are being prepared for deployment to fleets. Fleet operators must be able to rely on predictive maintenance to achieve optimal cost of ownership, maximize uptime, and ensure safety. Additionally, the regulatory environment for autonomous vehicles is changing rapidly. In various countries around the world, authorities responsible for granting certification are considering requirements for continuous operational monitoring and demonstration of proactive reliability management. Digital twin-based predictive maintenance solutions naturally include capabilities to meet these emerging requirements for regulatory compliance. This chapter is intended to address the research gaps previously identified by providing an integrated framework for AV predictive maintenance that incorporates digital twin technology, heterogeneous sensor fusion, AI-based prediction, and edge-cloud computing architecture to achieve safety-constrained maintenance prediction through simulation.

3. THEORETICAL FOUNDATIONS

3.1 Digital Twin Architecture for Autonomous Vehicles

A digital twin is a dynamic digital representation of a physical system that is constantly updated with information from its counterpart in the physical world. In the context of an autonomous vehicle, a digital twin is a digital replica of the physical system that allows for real-time monitoring and simulation. The architecture shown in Figure 1 is a framework that incorporates various physical systems, sensors, communication systems, and computational systems to allow engineers to analyze and predict system failures before they happen.

Digital twins function within a cyber-physical system architecture where there is a closed feedback loop between sensing, communication, and computation. The physical vehicle produces data through sensors embedded within its structure. These data are then communicated to computational platforms. Analytical models then update the virtual image continuously. The knowledge obtained from the digital twin is then used to make decisions regarding maintenance activities, adjustments to control strategies, or modifications to operational parameters. Digital twins are unique from simulations in that they are dynamic systems that change over time with their physical counterpart throughout its operational lifetime.

Figure 1. Cyber-physical architecture of an autonomous vehicle digital twin system

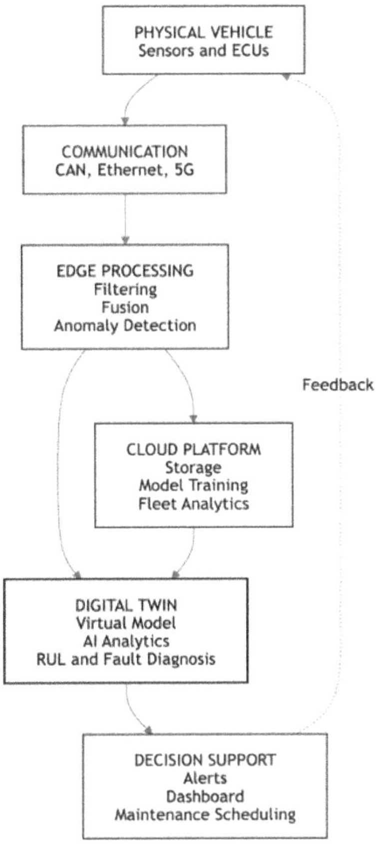

3.2 Sensor Systems and Data Acquisition

The success of digital twin operation depends on the precise and continuous data acquisition from various sensors on board. Autonomous vehicles have vibration sensors, temperature sensors, current sensors, pressure sensors, chemical sensors, and acoustic emission sensors, which collect data on mechanical, electrical, and chemical degradation. Vibration sensors on motor bearing surfaces can sense imbalances and misalignments before catastrophic failures occur. Acoustic sensors can sense crack growth in structural elements. Chemical sensors in lubricating systems can sense contaminants and degradation products.

Sensor data collection has some inherent problems such as measurement noise, sampling synchronization difficulties, and communication bandwidth limitations. The data acquisition systems must be provided with various filtering techniques, signal conditioning circuits, and time synchronization methods to ensure reliable measurement. GPS time clocks with microsecond resolution are useful for accurate multi-sensor event correlation. Sensor redundancy is used to improve system reliability. Using multiple sensor types to collect critical parameters such as temperature from thermocouples, resistance temperature detectors, and infrared sensors simultaneously can improve system reliability by cross-validation and continued operation in spite of individual sensor failures. Analytical redundancy involves comparing sensor data with model-based predictions. Discrepancies between sensor data and model predictions can be due to sensor faults or actual system anomalies.

3.3 AI-Based Predictive Modeling

Artificial intelligence converts raw sensor data into useful information for maintenance through a range of increasingly advanced analytical techniques. Statistical methods such as regression analysis and probabilistic degradation modeling are fundamental techniques used to obtain initial predictive capabilities for well-understood failure modes. Machine learning techniques such as decision trees, random forests, and support vector machines are used to recognize intricate patterns in high-dimensional data and accurately categorize fault types. These techniques involve feature engineering techniques whereby domain knowledge is used to transform raw sensor data into useful data.

The "feature engineering" task is no longer necessary because the DL architectures automatically learn the features from the raw data. CNNs perform well on handling high-dimensional spatial and spectral data types, including audio and thermal imaging. LSTMs address the temporal dependencies of sensor data and are thus effective in the prediction of degradation trajectory and RUL. Autoencoders learn the compact representations of normal operating conditions and thus perform the task of anomaly detection. Hybrid modeling consists of the combination of physics-based degradation modeling, which accounts for the known relationships between electrochemical and mechanical changes, and the use of ML models that adapt to the complex operating patterns. Hybrid modeling thus enhances the accuracy of the prediction as well as its physical interpretability (Wang et al., 2022).

3.4 Data Fusion and Feature Engineering

The data generated by autonomous vehicles is heterogeneous and varies due to the operation of various systems, each with a different sampling rate, data types, and quality characteristics. Data fusion techniques are used for integrating the data from various sources, providing a better diagnostic result than that could be obtained from any individual data source. Feature engineering is a method of transforming raw data from sensors into useful indicators of degradation state. Time-domain features, such as mean, variance, skewness, and kurtosis, are used for defining the characteristics of signals. Frequency-domain features, such as those from Fourier and wavelet transforms, are used for identifying fault signatures and mechanical imbalances that are not visible in the time-domain signals.

Advanced techniques of fusion, such as Bayesian methods and Kalman filtering, are based on probabilistic methods that ensure better accuracy of state estimation through the combined use of sensor data and predictive models. Multimodal fusion techniques incorporate data from various sources, such as vision, sound, temperature, and kinematic data, into a comprehensive health indicator that considers all failure mechanisms, which may be detected by a single modality. Another advanced method of data fusion is spatiotemporal, which aligns data from distributed sources with temporal event sequences, thus providing a means for causal analysis of degradation mechanisms. Other data fusion techniques, such as deep learning, are capable of learning the optimal weighting strategy for data fusion, thus providing a solution for the problem of defining the fusion rule for combining data from heterogeneous sources. These data fusion techniques are the cornerstones of the framework's capability to provide accurate and reliable predictive maintenance insights from the complex, noisy, and heterogeneous data environment of the autonomous vehicle.

3.5 Integration of Cloud-Edge Computing

This creates an efficient data processing hierarchy. Time-constrained tasks such as sensor fusion and real-time anomaly detection run on edge devices, while computationally intensive tasks like deep learning model training and longitudinal trend analysis occur in the cloud. Periodically, updated models are deployed from cloud to edge, ensuring inference models remain current with fleet-wide operational experience.

Communication protocols must balance bandwidth, latency, and cybersecurity across CAN bus, Automotive Ethernet, and 5G networks. Adaptive compression algorithms minimize edge-to-cloud data transmission by prioritizing high-information events and applying lossy compression to routine sensor data during normal operation. This is particularly critical for large numbers of autonomous vehicles operating in regions with limited or costly wireless connectivity. Such strategies ensure digital twin synchronization remains practical and cost-effective across diverse geographic areas, enabling reliable predictive maintenance without overwhelming network resources or incurring prohibitive data costs.

Figure 2. Hierarchical edge-cloud data processing architecture for digital twin predictive maintenance

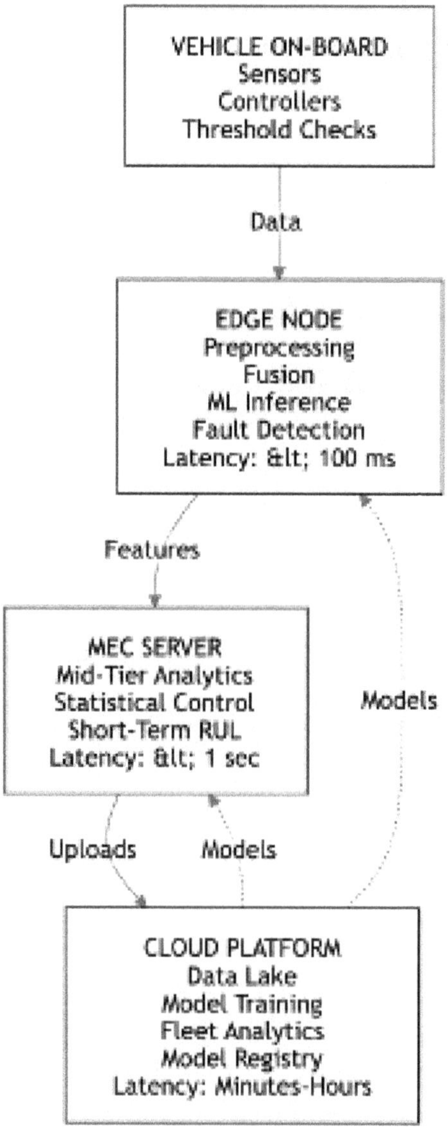

4. PROPOSED AI-DRIVEN DIGITAL TWIN FRAMEWORK

4.1 Framework Architecture Overview

The proposed AI-based digital twin framework for predictive maintenance of autonomous vehicles is based on a multi-layered architecture that ensures the seamless integration of physical vehicle data with AI-based analytics. The framework is based on a feedback loop system, where data from the physical vehicle is sent and analyzed by the AI system, and results are sent through monitoring interfaces for better maintenance and decision-making by fleet managers and maintenance technicians.

The framework is based on a modular design concept, where individual components of the system can be upgraded and modified without affecting the entire system's functionality. Interoperability of the system with various types of vehicles and manufacturers is ensured through standardized data interfaces, as per international standards such as ISO 23247 for digital twin frameworks, IEEE 2846 for AI safety in autonomous vehicles, ISO 26262 for automotive functional safety, and SAE J3061 for cybersecurity engineering. Real-time and offline analytical capabilities are integrated for better fault detection and deep analysis of patterns.

4.2 Physical Layer Components

The physical layer comprises all hardware components producing maintenance-relevant data. Powertrain components include engine control units monitoring fuel injection timing, combustion efficiency, and exhaust emissions. Transmission systems track gear engagement quality, clutch wear, and lubrication conditions. Battery management systems monitor individual cell voltages, temperatures, state of charge, and charge/discharge cycles. Braking systems use sensors to measure pressures, wear, and temperatures for friction and regenerative braking.

Each subsystem is equipped with prognostic sensors designed to detect specific degradation signs. Vibration sensors detect imbalances and bearing misalignment, while acoustic emission sensors monitor crack propagation. Actuator characteristics—response time, accuracy, and power consumption—support functional prognostics. Sensor redundancy, where a parameter is monitored by multiple sensors with different operating principles, enables signal cross-validation and continued monitoring despite individual sensor failures. For example, battery cell temperature may be monitored simultaneously by thermocouples, resistance temperature detectors, and infrared sensors. This allows the digital twin to detect both battery temperature anomalies and sensor failures. Such a complex sensing strategy is essential for maintaining high observability in safety-critical autonomous vehicle maintenance.

4.3 Data Acquisition and Communication Layer

The data acquisition layer handles the process of signal processing and communication operations in an optimized manner in terms of data quality, bandwidth utilization, and latency. Amplification of analog signals from sensors, followed by filtering and digitization at suitable sampling rates and bit resolutions, are conducted. Anti-aliasing filters are used to avoid spectral folding effects. Calibration of sensors to overcome non-linearity, temperature effects, and aging of sensors ensures accuracy during the vehicle's lifetime.

The communication protocols need to meet the trade-off between the need for bandwidth, latency, reliability, and security. CAN bus is a reliable and deterministic communication system for critical control functions.

Automotive Ethernet meets the need for high data transfer rates for camera and LiDAR sensor data. Wireless communication protocols include 5G wireless communication and dedicated short-range communications (DSRC) for communication with the cloud. Quality of Service protocols are necessary to prioritize critical communication streams during network congestion. Security protocols include encryption, mutual authentication, and intrusion detection systems to maintain the integrity of the communication. The Data Flow Diagram for the Physical and Data Acquisition Layers is as depicted below in Figure 3.

Figure 3. Sensor instrumentation and data flow diagram for the physical and data acquisition layers

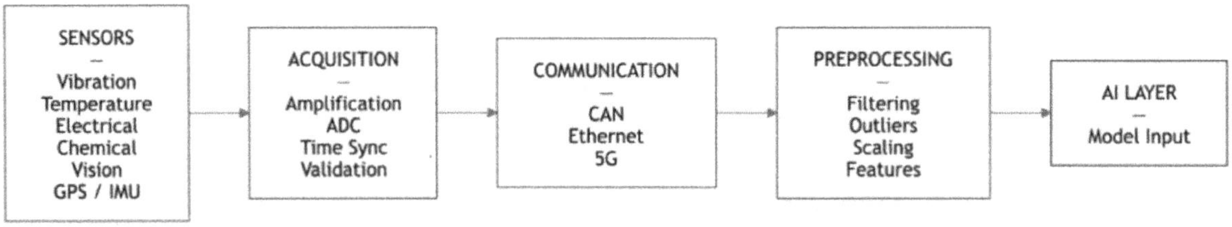

4.4 AI Analytics Layer

The layer of AI analytics is at the heart of the proposed framework. The AI Analytics and Decision Support Layer Architecture with Predictive Maintenance Workflow is as shown in the Figure 4.Supervised learning models like random forest and SVM are employed for fault classification under existing patterns of failure. Unsupervised models like autoencoder and isolation forest are utilized for detecting new anomalies without requiring training data. Deep learning models like LSTM are employed for effective estimation of RUL and forecasting of degradation modes. Reinforcement learning is employed for optimizing maintenance scheduling strategies through iterative interactions with a simulated vehicle environment.

The analytics pipeline follows a multistage approach. First-level filtering includes applying rule-based filters and threshold-based detection methods that can identify gross failures, like extreme readings from sensors or sensors that have completely failed. Mid-tier analytics involve statistical process control methods that can identify gradual changes in parameters. Advanced AI models can identify subtle multivariate trends that can lead to failures and can estimate probabilities and RUL distributions. These models are trained on historical data, accelerated degradation test data, expert knowledge, and controlled experiments involving faults. There are data augmentation methods that can address the perennial problem of failures being scarce in data. These methods can create synthetic data that can be used in training models. There are continuous learning methods that can update model parameters based on new data, so that models can be updated based on new data, thus enabling models that can adapt to new characteristics and environments, and can ensure that models can remain accurate throughout the entire service life of commercial AV fleets, and not degrade like vehicles that are older than those in the training data.

4.5 Predictive Maintenance Algorithms

The framework incorporates several algorithms that are specifically developed for various scenarios. For RUL prediction, it uses survival analysis and LSTM networks. These networks provide confidence intervals instead of point estimates. For fault diagnosis, there are algorithms that perform multi-class classification. These algorithms identify faults and progressively refine from subsystem level, component level, and eventually identify faults at the level of failure mechanisms. For anomaly detection, it uses isolation forests and one-class SVM. These algorithms have adaptive thresholds that become stricter during safety-critical missions and relaxed during non-critical missions.

The optimal maintenance scheduling is formulated as a multi-objective stochastic optimization problem. This balances costs, penalties, and risks. These risks involve failures and operation. It has Pareto optimal solution sets, and these represent trade-offs between these objectives. Fault diagnosis results are used in targeted maintenance actions. These actions can identify faults at precise levels, unlike preventive actions that replace all components (Magargle et al., 2017).

4.6 Visualization and Decision Support

The visualization and decision support layer provides role-specific interfaces. Fleet managers view aggregated statistics across vehicle populations to identify system-wide issues and allocate resources efficiently. Technicians access component-level diagnostics and suggested repair procedures. Vehicle occupants see simple maintenance reminders without technical details. Interactive 3D vehicle models display color-mapped health indicators: red for critical, yellow for warning, green for normal. Time series visualizations show historical degradation trends with baseline comparisons and future predictions. Maintenance scheduling interfaces intelligently group interventions to optimize vehicle downtime. Decision support systems combine predictions with operational constraints, resources, and business objectives for context-aware recommendations. Explanation interfaces offer simple-language rationales, building trust and meeting safety certification requirements. Mobile and augmented reality interfaces assist field technicians during maintenance.

Figure 4. AI analytics and decision support layer architecture with predictive maintenance workflow

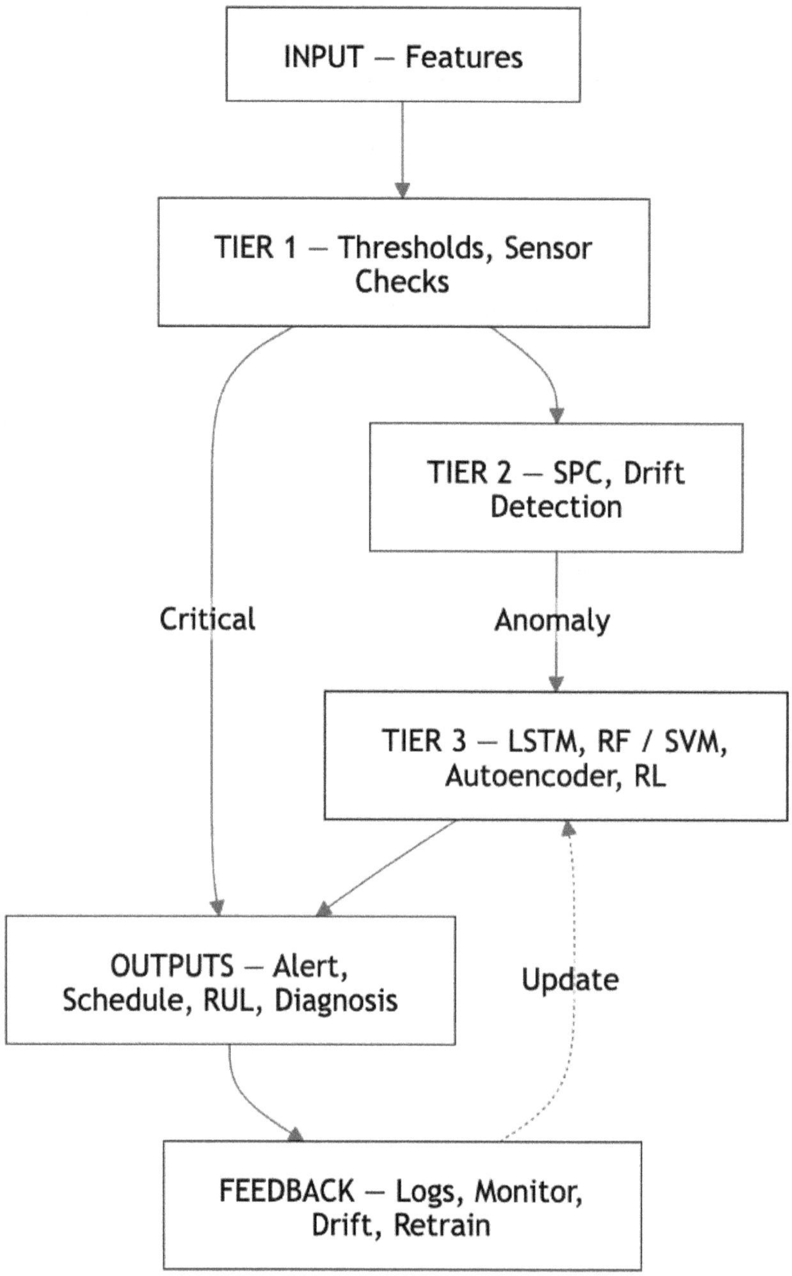

5. IMPLEMENTATION AND SIMULATION RESULTS

5.1 Simulation Environment Setup

In order to validate the proposed framework and explore viable implementation routes, a simulation environment has been developed using MATLAB/Simulink for physics-based vehicle system modeling and Python-based AI library tools such as TensorFlow and PyTorch for predictive analytics. The simulated autonomous vehicle system has incorporated important vehicle subsystems such as engine, braking system, and battery system components, each of which has been modeled considering various degradation factors such as wear mechanisms, environmental stress effects, and usage pattern effects. Predictive models have been trained using synthetic sensor data generated considering 10,000 hours of vehicle operation under various operational scenarios.

Engine component wear has been modeled as a function of proportional wear depending upon temperature and load cycles accumulated during operation. The engine wear has been modeled considering established tribological degradation principles. The battery cells have been modeled considering various degradation factors such as calendar aging as well as cycle aging, which depends upon temperature as well as depth of discharge. The braking system wear has been modeled considering various principles of contact mechanics depending upon braking energy dissipation.

5.2 Data Preprocessing and Feature Extraction

Preprocessing of the data consisted of noise removal, normalization, and correction of outliers. These steps helped in ensuring proper and consistent input of the data to the AI models. High-frequency noise in the degradation trends was removed using a moving average filter. Outlier detection techniques were used to correct glitches in the sensors. Normalization techniques were used to normalize the data from various sensors. Some of the variables had high values, and without normalization, these variables would have dominated the model. Imputation techniques were used to handle missing values in the data.

Feature extraction was instrumental in converting raw sensor data into a condensed and informative data representation of the degradation state. Statistical features characterized the distributional characteristics of measurement windows, such as the mean, standard deviation, skewness, and kurtosis. Frequency domain features, based on Fourier and wavelet transform techniques, enabled the detection of fault signatures, mechanical resonances, and transient signals. Finally, cross-sensor correlation features characterized interactions between subsystems, such as the relationship between battery temperature and charging current, which contain diagnostic information that is otherwise invisible. These multiple domains of features played a significant role in providing the AI models with rich and informative data, thereby significantly enhancing the accuracy of the predictions.

5.3 Model Training and Validation

The LSTM networks were trained on predicting the remaining useful life based on the temperature and vibration sensor data. The network architecture consisted of stacked recurrent layers with 128 hidden units in each of the layers. These layers were used to process the sequential window of 100 timesteps. Dropout regularization with a dropout probability of 0.3 was used after each LSTM layer to avoid overfitting. Early stopping was used to monitor the validation loss during the training process. Hyperparameter optimization using Bayesian search was used to find the optimal values of the learning rates, sequence length, and network depth.

The performance of the proposed model was assessed through stratified cross-validation over a range of degradation scenarios. The key performance metrics were the prediction of the RUL by the proposed method using the root mean square error (RMSE), the accuracy of fault classification, the precision and recall of anomaly detection, and the false alarms. Qualitative validation of the proposed method by expert evaluation revealed that the predicted failure modes were physically valid according to the degradation physics and engineering knowledge. This is a critical aspect of the proposed method. The proposed method was integrated into the real-time digital twin framework.

5.4 Real-Time Integration and Testing

The AI-enabled digital twin was synchronized with a simulated real-time vehicle data environment through data pipelines that provided sub-second latency. Message queuing technology was utilized to buffer sensor data during computational bursts to prevent data loss during periods of high processing demand. The edge cloud communication system ensured smooth operation under different network conditions by incorporating adaptive quality of service features that prioritize safety data streams.

The test scenarios were designed to mimic a range of failure progression rates, from sudden catastrophic failures to gradual degradation over a period of thousands of operating hours. The system was able to demonstrate the capability to predict incipient failures with an average early warning time of 156 hours prior to the critical performance thresholds being exceeded. This provides a significant opportunity for scheduled maintenance intervention. The false alarm rates were kept below 3%, ensuring that the predictive alerts were actionable and did not cause alert fatigue among the maintenance personnel. The sensitivity analysis of the system revealed that battery degradation was the earliest failure mode detected by the system, providing an average advance warning time of 210 hours. In contrast, the braking system failures were detected with a shorter advance warning time of 90 hours due to the faster dynamics of the failure mode. These mode-specific advance warning times are critical in determining the urgency of the maintenance response.

5.5 Performance Evaluation and Results

During the evaluation phase, the AI-driven digital twin framework achieved a fault detection accuracy of 94.7% over the entire spectrum of simulated failure scenarios. The proposed predictive maintenance approach facilitated by the framework achieved an estimated 23% reduction in the overall cost of maintenance when compared to scheduled maintenance practices. This is due to the prevention of premature component replacement, maintenance visit consolidation, emergency field maintenance reduction, and optimized provision of spares. The proposed solution reduced vehicle downtime by an estimated 18%, taking into account the reduced occurrence of unexpected failures and the benefits of reduced repair time through predictive pre-diagnosis.

The average prediction latency was determined to be 1.2 seconds, confirming its ability to operate in real time for autonomous vehicles. The RUL prediction accuracy, represented by RMSE for battery, engine, and braking systems, was between 8% and 14% of actual RUL. This is a significant improvement over existing baseline statistical methods. The multi-objective optimization algorithm was able to identify optimal maintenance schedules that minimized costs while keeping failure probability within safety-critical limits. The cost benefits were achieved through avoidance of premature component replacements, consolidation of maintenance activities, reduction of emergency field service calls, and optimized ordering of spare parts through better forecasting. The reduction in downtime benefits from reduced failure rates and faster repair times due to predictive pre-diagnosis, which determines type and location of faults before the repair process starts. These quantitative results are based on simulations but are underpinned by validated physics-based degradation modeling and are representative of expected field performance over a range of real-world operating conditions.

5.6 Case Study: Battery Management System

A specific case study was conducted on the application of the digital twin framework in battery management systems, which play a vital role in electric autonomous vehicles. Battery digital twin implementation utilized electrochemical models of lithium-ion battery thermodynamics and degradation chemistry, thermal models of battery heat generation and dissipation, and machine learning models based on battery cycling and aging data. These models were combined in a multi-physical manner in order to achieve a holistic assessment of the battery health.

Figure 5. Performance comparison: AI-driven digital twin framework vs. conventional scheduled maintenance

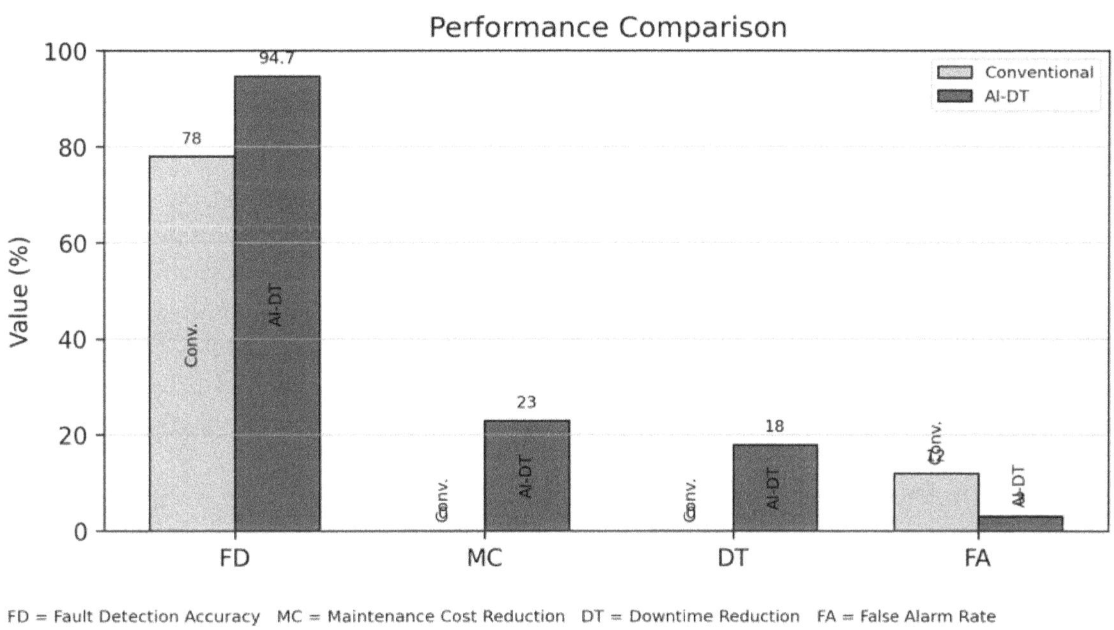

Individual cell voltage, temperature, and impedance data were collected over time on a one-second basis. LSTM networks were used to train on datasets from lab-based aging tests to predict capacity fade and battery end-of-life times with 95% confidence intervals as shown in Figure 5. The digital twin was able to identify imbalances in cells that could be related to manufacturing or to localized aging effects, providing an opportunity to balance these cells before any imbalances had a detrimental impact on pack performance or safety. The ability to identify battery degradation trajectories allowed for proactive battery chemistry-based maintenance strategies to be implemented to extend battery pack service life by an additional 14 months on average without impacting safety requirements during this time. The battery digital twin was also able to identify whether capacity fade was due to reversible or irreversible capacity degradation. As such, battery recovery strategies could be implemented to recover capacity fade due to reversible effects such as lithium plating or electrode cracking, without replacing the battery pack unnecessarily.

6. CHALLENGES AND LIMITATIONS

6.1 Data Heterogeneity and Integration

The amount of data collected from various sensors with different sampling rates, physical units, and noise characteristics is substantial. Integrating these heterogeneous data sources into a unified analytical framework requires sophisticated fusion techniques and high computational power. Various sensors have different preprocessing techniques: time series analysis of vibration sensors, convolutional analysis of image sensors, and three-dimensional geometric analysis of LiDAR sensors. Sensor failure rates, calibration issues, and environmental factors cause variability in the quality of the collected data.

The problem of data heterogeneity is further complicated by the existence of different data formats and communication protocols employed by different vehicle manufacturers and component providers. The lack of standardization in data formats and communication protocols poses a significant problem in developing a universally applicable data fusion pipeline. It also poses a problem in porting a data model trained on a particular vehicle platform to a different platform. The placement and configuration of sensors are significantly different across different vehicle models. Consequently, the spatial relationship between the measurements from different sensors is significantly different even for functionally equivalent systems. To overcome these challenges, advancements are needed in the area of adaptive data normalization techniques. Standardization of data formats and communication protocols is also needed at the industry level to facilitate the development of a common data schema and ontology for the health monitoring of AVs. Such advancements are needed on both fronts before the concept of digital twin-based predictive maintenance of AVs can move beyond the demonstration stage and into the commercial arena.

6.2 Real-Time Performance Requirements

The predictive maintenance-based applications related to autonomous vehicles have high-performance requirements in terms of real-time. Fault detection in safety-critical applications has to be performed within sub-second latency. This requires processing high-frequency and high-volume data from sensors, which are produced in large quantities in current autonomous vehicles. Optimized models and hardware accelerators are required to meet these high-performance requirements. Optimizations like quantization, pruning, and knowledge distillation can be performed on models to decrease computational costs without compromising the accuracy of predictions. Hardware accelerators like GPUs, FPGAs, and neural processing units can be utilized.

The balance between the accuracy of the prediction and the efficiency of the computation is the core design conundrum of any AI system that needs to be deployed in real time. The most accurate models tend to be the most computationally intensive. Surrogate models that can mimic the output of the most accurate models while being computationally efficient by orders of magnitude allow for the deployment of the most accurate models on resource-constrained edge devices. A multi-tier architecture that divides the analysis task among different tiers of hardware, from microcontrollers to edge computers and servers in the cloud, provides the pragmatic solution.

6.3 Cybersecurity and Data Integrity

The constant data interchange between the physical vehicle and its digital twin offers a considerable opportunity for attacks. Manipulation of data from vehicle sensors by attackers could result in the creation of faulty information by the digital twin, which could be either a concealment of real faults or a false indication of faults, thereby necessitating unwarranted maintenance action. Physical access to the sensor systems of the vehicle makes it susceptible to data injection attacks. The wireless communication channel is susceptible to eavesdropping and man-in-the-middle attacks. The cloud environment hosting the digital twin is susceptible to conventional information technology security attacks like unauthorized access, data theft, and ransomware attacks.

Defense-in-depth security architectures involve multiple layers of security measures. Cryptographic authentication is used to ensure that all data input to the digital twin is legitimate. This means that data from sensors input to the AI analytics layer has not been compromised during transmission. Anomaly detection algorithms are used to identify any signs of an injection attack on data from sensors. Network segmentation is used to segment the communication systems used by vehicles from public networks to prevent the spread of any security breaches. Secure elements are hardware-based systems used to store security credentials on vehicles. Security audits are used to identify any emerging security threats to vehicles and address them before they are exploited by cyber attackers. Incident response is used to identify how to address security breaches with minimal impact on safety. As the number of AV digital twins increases to millions of vehicles, cybersecurity will be a major concern due to the increase in the attack surface.

6.4 Explainability and Trust

The lack of transparency of deep learning models is considered one of the major obstacles that might prevent the adoption of deep learning in safety-critical applications of autonomous vehicles. There is an increasing demand from regulatory and certification authorities that AI systems deployed in safety-critical situations should be able to offer explanations for their recommendations and predictions. The maintenance engineer should be able to comprehend the rationale behind the prediction of the model before taking any action on that prediction. Trust in AI recommendations is based on the capacity to validate that the predictions of the AI system are based on physically significant patterns and not on correlations.

Explainable AI techniques are able to tackle the problem by providing a solution through a number of different techniques. SHAP (SHapley Additive exPlanations) values are a method for providing a rigorous explanation of the value of each input variable to a particular prediction. Attention techniques are a method for explaining the reasoning behind the predictions of neural networks. Counterfactual explanations are a technique for providing insight into the input conditions that are necessary to generate a prediction. Hybrid physics-AI provides a partially interpretable solution by constraining the predictions of the AI system to be physically valid. Interactive explanation interfaces are a technique for providing engineers with a way to query the reasoning behind the predictions of the AI system.

6.5 Standardization and Interoperability

The lack of extensive industry standards in the deployment of AV digital twin technology results in interoperability issues between vehicles, manufacturers, and service providers. This is due to the fact that every manufacturer has its own data format, communication protocol, and diagnostic interface, making fleet-wide analytics and model portability difficult. Standards development organizations like ISO, SAE International, and IEEE are working on standards related to digital twin technology. Building consensus within distributed automotive industry stakeholders takes time. For interim solutions, middleware layers are necessary, and they can be problematic.

6.6 Ethical and Regulatory Considerations

The extensive use of AI-based digital twin technology for vehicle health monitoring also raises ethical and regulatory issues. The continuous generation of vehicle operating data provides insight into the behavior of drivers, their routes, and the use of the vehicle, which is considered personal data. Federated learning, differential privacy, and data minimization principles can be employed to minimize the risk of privacy violations. The regulatory environment for the collection, storage, processing, and sharing of vehicle operating data is constantly changing and presents compliance challenges for multinational vehicle fleets.

The liability structure should address how responsibility is apportioned in instances where AI-based maintenance predictions are found to be incorrect. For example, if a digital twin does not accurately predict a component failure that eventually causes a safety issue, there are liability implications for various stakeholders, including vehicle manufacturers, AI system developers, and those providing maintenance services. There are safety guidelines being drafted by regulatory bodies in major markets related to AI safety for autonomous vehicles. However, related to AI-based maintenance systems, these are still in their infancy. There is a strong need to ensure that all stakeholders are involved in the development of these systems to ensure a balanced approach.

7. FUTURE RESEARCH DIRECTIONS

7.1 Explainable AI for Maintenance Systems

However, future advancements in AI-driven digital twin systems will increasingly focus on model transparency and interpretability. For instance, future advancements in causal inference techniques will enable pattern recognition to extend from correlations to actual causal links between operational factors and degradation modes. Interactive systems for providing explanations will facilitate natural language dialogue between engineers and AI systems. This will ensure that access to model insights is no longer limited to experts and enable non-expert users to interrogate predictions and build justified confidence in AI-driven recommendations. There will be increased regulatory drivers to advance explainability standards for AI systems used in safety-critical automotive applications. There will be advancements in techniques for quantifying uncertainties associated with RUL predictions, such as Bayesian deep learning and conformal prediction methods. These techniques will ensure that users are provided with statistically rigorous confidence measures to enable risk-informed decision-making even in situations where confidence in predictions is low. These advancements in transparent and interpretable AI systems will be critical enablers to achieve regulatory approval and public acceptance for AI-driven systems to be used in commercial applications.

7.2 Edge-Cloud Hybrid Architectures

The further evolution of edge cloud hybrid models will play an important role in improving the practical viability of digital twin technologies. New 5G and 6G wireless technologies will provide ultra-low latency and high-bandwidth connectivity, further blurring the distinction between edge and cloud computing. This will be achieved through network function virtualization and software-defined networks, allowing dynamic allocation and optimization of tasks between edges and clouds based on network conditions, computational load, and latency. Multi-access edge computing will provide cloud-scale computing at edges closer to areas where vehicles operate, reducing round-trip latency for complex computations.

7.3 Self-Healing Digital Twins

The area of self-healing digital twin architectures is a particularly promising area for research. These architectures have the potential to automatically identify discrepancies between model predictions and system measurements, diagnose the cause of discrepancies, and apply corrective adaptations. Self-organizing sensor networks will be able to automatically reconfigure coverage in response to sensors becoming inoperable, ensuring continuity in observability. Automated model retraining pipelines will be able to adapt to concept drift, where the statistical relationship between sensor features and failure outcomes evolves over the lifespan of a vehicle, ensuring model accuracy over long operational lifetimes.

7.4 Blockchain for Maintenance Data Integrity

The integration of distributed ledger technology with digital twin-based maintenance systems may provide a promising avenue for ensuring the integrity and auditability of data. Immutable records of maintenance activities, sensor readings, and AI predictions can be used to provide an audit trail of activities that cannot be altered after the fact. These audit trails can be used for regulatory compliance, failure investigation, and warranty management. Decentralized data-sharing mechanisms enabled through blockchain technology may enable fleet operators to contribute their operational data to a common pool used for improving AI model accuracy in exchange for a verifiable record of ownership and control over their proprietary data.

7.5 Sustainable and Energy-Efficient Systems

The aspect of sustainability will also play a crucial role in the development of AI-based digital twin systems. Green AI projects aim at reducing the power consumption and environmental impact of machine learning through effective architectures, hardware-aware machine learning, and intelligent workload management based on renewable power availability. On the aspect of the circular economy in predictive maintenance, the idea is to use the components or equipment up to the point of exhaustion rather than changing them at predetermined time intervals. RUL prediction helps in reducing waste and environmental impact in component manufacturing.

7.6 Cross-Domain Digital Twin Networks

The concept of a cross-domain digital twin network, where individual vehicles are integrated with transportation infrastructure, urban systems, and shared mobility services, is a future vision for intelligent transportation system management. A city's digital twin, where the health status of individual vehicles is integrated with the city's traffic management system, could divert vehicles with compromised safety-critical system health status away from areas of high travel demand and/or safety risk. Vehicle-to-infrastructure communication could be used for real-time coordination of vehicle maintenance status and infrastructure management. A city's integrated mobility system, where multiple transportation modes are coordinated with the health and maintenance status of personal vehicles, shared AV services, and public transit services, could be optimized for city-wide mobility efficiency while managing maintenance-related availability constraints.

8. CONCLUSION

This chapter has proposed an AI-based digital twin framework that is tailored for the purpose of predictive maintenance of autonomous vehicles. The digital twin framework has been integrated into the proposed AI-based maintenance intelligence architecture. The theoretical analysis and simulation results have confirmed that the proposed digital twin framework can attain higher accuracy and efficiency in the maintenance of autonomous vehicles compared to the scheduled maintenance strategy.

The proposed multi-layer framework is able to address the specific challenges of the AV maintenance task in terms of safety-critical performance requirements, the significant sensor heterogeneity, and the transparency requirements that differentiate the domain of interest from the more common industrial predictive maintenance domains. By integrating the structural simplicity of digital twin models and the adaptive learning capabilities of advanced AI techniques, the proposed framework provides the basis for the development of an adaptive maintenance intelligence system that will become increasingly effective as more operating data becomes available. The simulation results validate the potential for quantified improvements in the accuracy of fault detection and maintenance cost efficiency and vehicle availability using the state of the art.

Although there are still issues related to the heterogeneity of the data used, real-time performance, cybersecurity, explainability, and standardization, the fundamental technical building blocks have now been put in place to enable the widespread deployment of these systems. Future developments in explainable AI systems, edge-cloud systems, self-healing systems, and digital twin networks across multiple domains will progressively enable the expanded use of these systems. These AI-based digital twin systems have the potential to become a fundamental infrastructure component of the safe, efficient, and sustainable operation of future generations of autonomous vehicle systems. Ultimately, these systems have the potential to enable a future of mobility that is both intelligent and resilient. All industry stakeholders, technology developers, and regulatory organizations must work together proactively to address the remaining technology and governance-related issues in order to ensure the full societal benefit of predictive AV maintenance in all deployment scenarios.

REFERENCES

Carvalho, T. P., Soares, F. A. A. M. N., Vita, R., Francisco, R. P., Basto, J. P., & Alcalá, S. G. S. (2019). A systematic literature review of machine learning methods applied to predictive maintenance. *Computers & Industrial Engineering*, *137*, 106024. DOI: 10.1016/j.cie.2019.106024

Grieves, M., & Vickers, J. (2017). Digital twin: Mitigating unpredictable, undesirable emergent behavior in complex systems. In Kahlen, F.-J., Flumerfelt, S., & Alves, A. (Eds.), *Transdisciplinary Perspectives on Complex Systems* (pp. 85–113). Springer., DOI: 10.1007/978-3-319-38756-7_4

Lei, Y., Li, N., Guo, L., Li, N., Yan, T., & Lin, J. (2018). Machinery health prognostics: A systematic review from data acquisition to RUL prediction. *Mechanical Systems and Signal Processing*, *104*, 799–834. DOI: 10.1016/j.ymssp.2017.11.016

Magargle, R., Johnson, L., Mandloi, P., Davoudabadi, P., Bhatt, A., Shrivastava, R., & Farber, J. (2017). A simulation-based digital twin for model-driven health monitoring and predictive maintenance of an automotive braking system. *Proceedings of the 12th International Modelica Conference*, Prague, Czech Republic, 35–46. DOI: 10.3384/ecp1713235

Rosen, R., von Wichert, G., Lo, G., & Bettenhausen, K. D. (2015). About the importance of autonomy and digital twins for the future of manufacturing. *IFAC-PapersOnLine*, *48*(3), 567–572. DOI: 10.1016/j.ifacol.2015.06.141

Vogl, G. W., Weiss, B. A., & Helu, M. (2019). A review of diagnostic and prognostic capabilities and best practices for manufacturing. *Journal of Intelligent Manufacturing*, *30*(1), 79–95. DOI: 10.1007/s10845-016-1228-8 PMID: 30820072

Wang, K., Chen, C., & Wang, Y. (2022). Edge intelligence for digital twin-based predictive maintenance in autonomous systems. *IEEE Transactions on Industrial Informatics*, *18*(7), 4672–4683. DOI: 10.1109/TII.2021.3110218

Zhang, J., Ding, G., Zou, Y., Qin, S., & Fu, J. (2021). Review of job shop scheduling research and its new perspectives under Industry 4.0. *Journal of Intelligent Manufacturing*, *30*(4), 1809–1830. DOI: 10.1007/s10845-017-1350-2

ADDITIONAL READING

Boschert, S., & Rosen, R. (2016). Digital twin — The simulation aspect. In Hehenberger, P., & Bradley, D. (Eds.), *Mechatronic Futures* (pp. 59–74). Springer., DOI: 10.1007/978-3-319-32156-1_5

Canonaco, G., Roveri, M., Alippi, C., & Montanari, R. (2021). LSTM-based anomaly detection for vehicles: A case study with the NATOPS dataset. *IEEE Transactions on Neural Networks and Learning Systems*, *32*(6), 2649–2662.

Fei, G., Zheng, P., Xu, X., & Lu, Y. (2020). Cyber-physical systems for digital twin-based smart manufacturing. *Journal of Manufacturing Systems*, *54*, 343–356. DOI: 10.1016/j.jmsy.2020.01.002

Kritzinger, W., Karner, M., Traar, G., Henjes, J., & Sihn, W. (2018). Digital twin in manufacturing: A categorical literature review and classification. *IFAC-PapersOnLine*, *51*(11), 1016–1022. DOI: 10.1016/j.ifacol.2018.08.474

Nguyen, H. D., & Kim, J. M. (2020). Real-time fault classification of ball bearings using short time Fourier transform and convolutional neural networks. *IEEE Access : Practical Innovations, Open Solutions*, *8*, 185057–185069. DOI: 10.1109/ACCESS.2020.3029932

Park, H., & Kim, N. (2019). Prediction of remaining useful life of a lithium-ion battery based on LSTM recurrent neural network with data pre-treatment. *IEEE Transactions on Industrial Informatics*, *15*(10), 5639–5648. DOI: 10.1109/TII.2019.2902467

Schroeder, G. N., Steinmetz, C., Pereira, C. E., & Espindola, D. B. (2016). Digital twin data modeling with AutomationML and a communication methodology for data exchange. *IFAC-PapersOnLine*, *49*(30), 12–17. DOI: 10.1016/j.ifacol.2016.11.115

Soderberg, R., Warmefjord, K., Carlson, J. S., & Lindkvist, L. (2017). Toward a digital twin for real-time geometry assurance in individualized production. CIRP Annals — Manufacturing Technology, 66(1), 137–140. DOI: 10.1016/j.cirp.2017.04.038

KEY TERMS AND DEFINITIONS

Autonomous Vehicle (AV): A vehicle that is fitted with sensing, computing, and actuation systems that allow it to move and function with little or no human intervention, which is defined by SAE International on a scale from Level 0 (no automation) to Level 5 (full automation) depending on the level of automated driving capability.

Condition-Based Maintenance: A maintenance strategy that uses sensor measurements and inspections of the equipment's actual state to determine when maintenance is needed, as opposed to a maintenance strategy that uses a specific period of time or usage interval, thus avoiding unnecessary maintenance while maintaining system reliability.

Cyber-Physical System (CPS): A system that is designed by combining physical processes and computational algorithms in a tightly integrated fashion through sensing, communication, and actuation, and where feedback exists between the digital and physical worlds for intelligent monitoring and control.

Digital Twin: A continuously synchronized virtual model of a physical system that combines real-time sensor data, physics-based models, and data analytics to reproduce and predict the performance and state of the physical system over the course of its operational lifetime.

Edge Computing: A paradigm of distributed computing where data processing and artificial intelligence inference are conducted at a location close to the data source, such as within or near a vehicle, to minimize communication latency, data bandwidth usage, and response time.

Explainable AI (XAI): A set of methods and principles for designing and evaluating AI systems that produce outputs and reasoning processes that are comprehensible, interpretable, and verifiable by human experts, especially in safety-critical and regulated application domains.

Long Short-Term Memory (LSTM): A particular variety of recurrent neural network architecture intended for the development of long-range temporal dependencies in sequential data through the utilization of gate mechanisms in retaining or discarding particular types of information in time sequences, commonly used in sensor time series prediction.

Predictive Maintenance (PdM): A proactive strategy for maintenance that involves using continuous monitoring and data analytics techniques along with machine learning to predict impending component failures and conducting maintenance activities during optimal times before actual failures take place.

Remaining Useful Life (RUL): A quantitative indication of the time to be expended before a component or system is no longer able to meet its required specifications, usually given as a probability distribution with confidence bounds.

Sensor Fusion: The process of combining data from various sensors that have different physical sensor modalities, measurement ranges, and spatial locations into a more accurate and complete state of the system than any of the individual sensors could possibly offer on their own.

Chapter 4
Digital Twin for Safety Validation and Crash Scenario Simulations

Aarthi Selvakumar
http://orcid.org/0009-0006-9064-2091
Marwadi University, Rajkot, India

Ravikumar Natarajan
http://orcid.org/0009-0009-3705-1681
Marwadi University, Rajkot, India

Dilmurod Turaev
Termez University of Economics and Service, Termez, Uzbekistan

Anorgul Ashirova
Mamun University, Khiva, Uzbekistan

Khayrulla Urozboev
Alfraganus University, Tashkent, Uzbekistan

N. Naveena
Kongu Engineering College, Erode, India

ABSTRACT

Ensuring safety and reliability is paramount in the development of Autonomous Vehicles (AVs). Digital Twin (DT) technology provides a dynamic virtual counterpart to real vehicles, enabling scenario-based safety validation and crash simulations without physical risk. This chapter explores how DTs integrate real-time sensor data, AI-driven analytics, and multi-physics modeling to simulate complex collision dynamics and evaluate vehicle responses. Emphasis is placed on aligning DT testing with international standards such as ISO 26262 and SOTIF. Case studies from BMW and Waymo demonstrate the industrial application of DTs in reducing prototyping costs and improving validation accuracy. Challenges including data veracity, synchronization latency, and computational overhead are also discussed. By leveraging emerging technologies like quantum computing and federated learning, DT-based safety validation can ensure scalable, transparent, and ethically responsible deployment of autonomous vehicles.

1. INTRODUCTION

The aspects of Autonomous Vehicle (AV) creation, which are the most significant, are safety and reliability since its failures may directly impact human life and trust. The standard of physical testing

DOI: 10.4018/979-8-3373-7785-8.ch004

and road testing, though obligatory, have limited areas of scope, scalability and even moral feasibility in extreme cases. One of the future potential solutions that is proposed as an opportunity to have the virtual image of the vehicle and the environment is Digital Twin (DT). Introduction of a continuous alignment between the physical and digital layers enables a real-time risk assessment and a prospective safety evaluation in numerous different environments, introduced by DTs (Changalvala & Malik, 2019). This section gives the justification to DT-based safety validation and its role when developing risk-aware AVs. It cites the growing popularity of alternative models of simulation, dynamic and capable of learning virtual ecosystems that can be used to capture the highly dynamic behaviour of vehicles in uncertain environments, and ultimately redefining automotive safety engineering and compliance to safety standards.

1.1 Background and Motivation for Safety Validation In AVS

The advancement of self-driving cars has redefined the notions of movement but introduced new safety concerns due to the complex nature of decision-making, the use of sensors and the lack of predictability in the environment. Unpredictable human actions, traffic changes, and weather are also subjects that avs must respond to unlike the traditional vehicles. The safety validation ensures that these systems are able to operate in such edge cases with the highest level of reliability Millions of cases sudden pedestrian crossings, and multi-vehicle collisions. However, the range of the potential interactions is too large to be covered with the physical crash tests and the limited data available in the real-world (Malayjerdi et al., 2021). This results in the use of virtual validation systems, in which digital twins are a real replica of a real physical cars and environment. The researchers and engineers can test the failure modes and optimum system behaviour without putting lives and assets at risk using these virtual models. The hybridization of the two technologies: DTs and AI analytics will become an important input to the enhanced predictive accuracy and scalability and will be capable of transforming the paradigm of the safety assurance, which is rather of the reactive character, to the proactive and information-based validation.

1.2 Role of Digital Twins in Risk-Aware Vehicle Design

Digital twins can be described as smart proxies that bridge the gap between the real cars and their virtual counterparts that they can constantly monitor, simulate as well as predict safety critical behaviour. On the risk-conscious design of vehicles, DTs are cognitive projections that mutually integrate real-time sensor data, conditions of operation, and contextual data of the road conditions. The integration enables the engineers to see the effects of design decisions, material characteristics, and control mechanisms on vehicle safety performance. Digital twins are dynamic in contrast to the conventional computer-aided simulations and update with the data provided by the IoT sensors, onboard diagnostics, and AI-based perception systems (Almeaibed et al., 2021a). When these undergo repeated learning, they identify anomalies and failures, anticipate corrective actions, and try them in different working situations. This capability to reproduce intricate crash phenomena and emergency procedures in a virtual environment assists the manufacturers to detect the weak points at an initial stage minimizing the production costs and increasing adherence to the safety regulation. Accordingly, DTs change the vehicle design into a resilience-oriented and adaptive discipline rather than a fixed engineering process.

1.3 Objectives, Scope, and Structure of the Chapter

The chapter is devoted to the discussed potentially radical capabilities of Digital Twin (DT) technology when it comes to the aspect of safety verification and simulation of the crash situation in autonomous vehicles. It examines the conceptual, technical and regulatory reasons why the complementary or alternative to conventional physical methods are permissible to enable DT-driven testing. These areas are the data-based modeling, the integration with AI and IoT, the compliance with the international safety standards, and the implementation based on the practical case studies. The chapter provides a general understanding of how digital twins can facilitate safety, reliability, and resilience of autonomous vehicles by providing a synthesis of the frameworks, architectures, and challenges in an orderly manner.

- To explain the role of digital twins in creating high-fidelity virtual models for safety validation of autonomous vehicles.
- To outline the architectural and data integration principles underlying DT-based simulation environments.
- To analyze international safety standards and their alignment with DT-enabled validation pipelines.
- To examine real-world case studies demonstrating the application of DTs in crash scenario simulations.
- To identify challenges and future directions for scalable, ethical, and regulation-compliant DT implementations.

The field covered in this chapter is how Digital Twin (DT) technology can be used in safety validation and crash scenario simulation of Autonomous Vehicles (AVs). It takes the theoretical backgrounds, system design, and simulation methods that assist in escalating risk prediction, reliability in control, and regulations. It goes on to discuss the safety systems in various countries, AI-aided decision validation, and the case studies of the most successful automotive industry. The chapter offers a comprehensive view of how DTs can help to make AV deployment safer, more efficient, and ethically responsible with respect to multi-domain data integration, scenario-based testing, and virtual crash reconstruction.

2. FOUNDATIONS OF DIGITAL TWIN IN AUTONOMOUS VEHICLES

The technology of digital twins in autonomous vehicles is based on the cyber-physical system integration, or virtual models of autonomous vehicles recreate and communicate with their real-world counterparts. This base layer links sensors, IoT networks and data analytics structures to create a feedback loop between the tangible and the digital worlds. The essence of the goal is to have a concurrent, oscillating depiction of the vehicle performance, structural integrity and environmental setting. DTs allow the dynamic analysis of driving behavior, system reliability and safety compliance using high-precision data flow (Almeaibed et al., 2021b). The section expounds on the principles of architectural design, data fusion processes and real-time synchronization processes that characterize the operational fabric of automotive digital twins. It offers a technical foundation on the operation of these systems as facilitators of safety validation, proactive maintenance and simulation-based decision-making in the larger ecosystem of intelligent and connected mobility. Figure 1 demonstrates the hierarchical levels of digital twin architecture, that is, cyber-physical integration and data fusion, real-time synchronization, dynamic analysis, and smart decision-making to allow safe and adaptive autonomous vehicles to operate.

Figure 1. Foundations of digital twin in autonomous vehicles

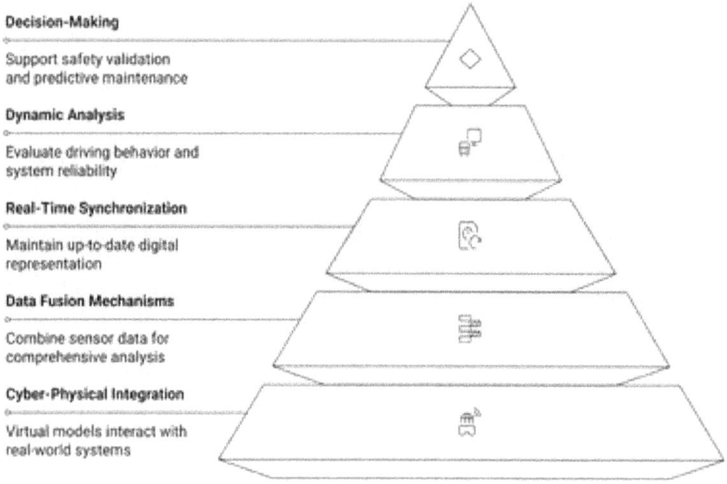

2.1 Conceptual Architecture of Digital Twin Systems

The architecture of an automotive digital twin can be explained as a set of layers (physical, communication, data, model, and service), connected with each other and allowing two-way communication between the real world and the virtual world. The autonomous vehicle and sensors and actuators and onboard controllers make up the physical layer that generates continuous streams of data. The communication layer offers encrypted and low latency data communication relying on edge and cloud infrastructures. Heterogeneous datasets are those that are managed by the data layer and include telemetry, video, LiDAR, radar, and vehicle dynamics data (Lei et al., 2024). The model layer creates physically realistic virtual simulations out of multi-physics simulations and AI-based learning models and through digital mapping. Finally, there are visualization, analysis and predictive decision-making applications which are service layer applications. These layers form a comprehensive system of cyber-physical ecosystem that could replicate the complicated process such as collisions, emergency braking, or component malfunction. This architecture is cross-domain, modularity-based, and real-time synchronized owing to the modularity that has been the cornerstone of the DT-based safety validation systems in autonomous vehicles.

Edge cloud hybrid systems are important in supporting scalable digital twin systems in autonomous vehicles. Computations that are safety critical are often found to be done on the edge like perception inference, collision avoidance, and sensor fusion with strict latency targets, in most cases under 10 or 20 ms. In the meantime, the cloud platforms promote the mass simulation, the scenario generation, and the long-term analytics. The design of DT systems must however be keen on network bandwidth, latency of communication, distribution of computation as well as fault tolerance. Proper edge cloud orchestration provides high availability of synchronization between real-life vehicles and their virtual counterparts and real-time responsiveness. Table 1 Identifies the multi-layer architecture of DT systems and specific functions to support the validation of AV safety.

Table 1. Components of digital twin architecture in autonomous vehicles

Layer	Description	Function in Safety Validation
Physical Layer	Real-world vehicle and sensors	Provides live telemetry and system data
Communication Layer	Edge and cloud networks	Enables real-time data exchange
Data Layer	Databases and middleware	Manages heterogeneous information
Model Layer	Simulation and AI models	Recreates virtual crash environments
Service Layer	Analysis and visualization tools	Supports decision validation and reporting

2.2 Integration of Sensors, IoT, and Cyber-Physical Systems

The digital twin ecosystem sensors and IoT devices serve as the sensorial network of the sensory network, which measures high-resolution data of the dynamics of the vehicle, the environment, and the interaction of the driver. This consists of LiDAR, radar, ultrasonic sensor, GPS, camera, and inertial measurement units data in autonomous vehicles. These data are sent to cloud or at the edge platforms through IoT gateways and Vehicle-to-Everything (V2X) communication (Barricelli et al., 2019). The cyber-physical integration is what guarantees that all physical processes, e.g. steering correction or obstacle detection, have a virtual counterpart in the DT. Middleware and data fusion algorithms of advanced quality ensure that time-stamped signals are synchronized and contextual integrity is upheld, and filtering noise is conducted to ensure dependable decision support. This real-time connection enables the continuous testing of control algorithms, path-planning logic and object recognition model models in different conditions. Consequently, the operational intelligence of the vehicle can be measured and tracked, which enables engineers to predict the behavior of the system and increase the level of reliability prior to the implementation of the physical prototypes (van Dyck et al., 2023).

2.3 Data Flow Between Physical and Virtual Layers

The basic basis of the work of a digital twin is the two-way data communication between the physical and virtual layers. The ongoing interaction follows three processes, which include data acquisition, synchronization and feedback implementation. In the data acquisition, the data provided by the real world like sensor data, vehicle telemetry, external environmental data are sent to the digital twin. Synchronization brings these data streams into time and space congruence in order to ensure that the virtual and real model are consistent. The execution of feedback then sends insights back to the vehicle in real time, e.g. predictive maintenance warnings or control adjustments (Song, 2024). Smart edge computing and 5G connectivity reduce the latency, which is a key factor in making decisions in safety-important processes. In addition, privacy and minimization of communication overhead are achieved due to compression and encryption methods of the data. The interactive process enables the autonomous vehicle to be learned, developed and changed continuously in effect, making the autonomous vehicle a self-optimizing, cyber-physical system capable of responding to risk and uncertainty within complex environments.

3. SAFETY VALIDATION FRAMEWORKS AND STANDARDS

The safety validation of autonomous vehicles needs tight and stringent structures that would conform to the international standards to attain the functional integrity and reliability. The convergence of simulation testing and formal standards of safety such as ISO 26262 and SOTIF focus on digital twins. This part addresses the regulatory setting, approaches, and issues of outcome validation of safety scenarios by using DT platforms. It describes that virtual testing environments supplement physical validation, which allows the safe reproduction of extreme and risky conditions (Ali et al., 2025). The section also discusses how deterministic verification models would be replaced with adaptive validation pipelines that are AI-assisted. Assuming venturing into digital twin technology and incorporating it into conventional safety systems, engineers are able to develop scalable, transparent and certifiable AV system testing. This strategy will eventually build confidence between the regulators, manufacturers, and people as it will show that autonomous cars can perform or even surpass the traditional safety expectations in the actual operations.

3.1 Overview of Automotive Safety Standards (ISO 26262, SOTIF, UNECE WP.29)

The regulatory basis of autonomous systems validation is offered by automotive safety standards. In the context of functional safety in electrical and electronic parts, ISO 26262 specifies the Automotive Safety Integrity levels (ASILs) needed to manage the problem of risk. SOTIF (Safety of the Intended Functionality) also generalizes these principles to include the performance limits, and the unintended behavior even when the systems are functioning within their proper limits (Rokseth et al., 2019). UNECE WP.29 creates an international standard of vehicle homologation and cybersecurity, which guarantees AVs comply with international safety and data-protection requirements. The implementation of digital twins into these systems can provide an opportunity to constantly test the control software, perception algorithms, and decision modules in various operating conditions. Simulations done in virtual crashes and scenario testing enhance transparency and traceability throughout the certification process. In addition, DTs also enable monitoring of lifecycle security, coordinating design, testing and operational stages on the same digital platform (Riedmaier et al., 2020). This synergy increases the confidence of the regulators and the speed of the approval of next generation autonomous vehicles. Table 2 A brief comparison is made of the major automotive safety standards interested in certification and validation of safety based on DT standards.

Digital Twin-based validation systems may realize formal safety measures proposed in ISO 26262 and ISO/PAS 21448 (SOTIF). Some of the Key Performance Indicators (KPIs) are probability of hazardous failure, fault reaction time, perception reliability, and system availability in the Domains of Operational Design (ODDs). Digital twins enable measurement of these metrics at any time due to the continuous nature of scenarios as simulated and real-time telemetry feedback. As an example, the metrics used to check the safety validation using ASIL can include Mean Time Between Hazardous Events (MTBHE) and collision probability, accuracy in the perception in degraded sensing conditions, and the latency thresholds of a system. The inclusion of these KPIs into the simulation pipeline allows DT frameworks to provide quantitative safety assurance and certifiable evidence of certification that is in line with regulatory expectations.

Table 2. Comparative overview of automotive safety standards

Standard	Scope	Key Focus	Relevance to DT-Based Validation
ISO 26262	Functional Safety	Electrical/electronic system reliability	Ensures ASIL compliance for DT testing
SOTIF	Intended Functionality	System limitations and misuse	Validates AI-driven safety logic
UNECE WP.29	Global Regulations	Cybersecurity and vehicle homologation	Supports regulatory traceability

3.2 Scenario-Based Validation and Verification Pipelines

The application of scenario-based validation allows the autonomous vehicles to be validated under a wide spectrum of predefined and emergent scenarios mimicking real-world driving scenarios. A common validation pipeline combines the processes of data collection, scenario modelling, simulation and performance evaluation into the digital twin platform. Based on sensor data recorded, artificial environments, and scenario generation using AI, DTs can simulate how vehicles, pedestrians, and infrastructure interact with a high level of accuracy (Szalay, 2021). Both scenarios, e.g. an abrupt change in lanes, and the multi-car accident are tested in terms of sensor precision, control reaction, and adherence to the safety margin. Checking makes sure that safety protocols operate as desired in cases of different uncertainties such as sensor deterioration or bugs in the code. Reinforcement learning is used to support the continuous optimization of the test coverage and the diversity of scenarios through the use of automated pipelines. The process does not only save on testing cost but also enhances reproducibility wherein regulators and manufacturers will be able to measure the strength of AV systems. Scenario-based validation is then used as the support of data-driven certification in digital twin ecosystems.

The fidelity and credibility of digital twin models to be used in safety-critical testing requires Verification and Validation (V&V) techniques. The simulation models were found to be correct in their adoption of mathematical and physical formulations and validation tests the model of appropriate behaviour of real world cars. V&V procedures used in DT-based AV testing typically include calibration of the model using physical crash tests, benchmarking simulation of sensors, statistical analysis of simulated and real trajectories and uncertainty sensitivity analysis. The X-in-the-loop validation (MiL, SiL, HiL, ViL) paradigms are often integrated with DT ecosystems in such a way that perception algorithms, control logic and system-level responses are always behaving in the virtual world in the same way as they would work in the real world. Figure 2 illustrates the flow of how-to autonomous vehicle safety validation works sequentially starting with the process of data collection and scenario model up to simulation, performance assessment, verification and optimization on the digital twin structure.

Figure 2. Scenario-based validation and verification pipeline

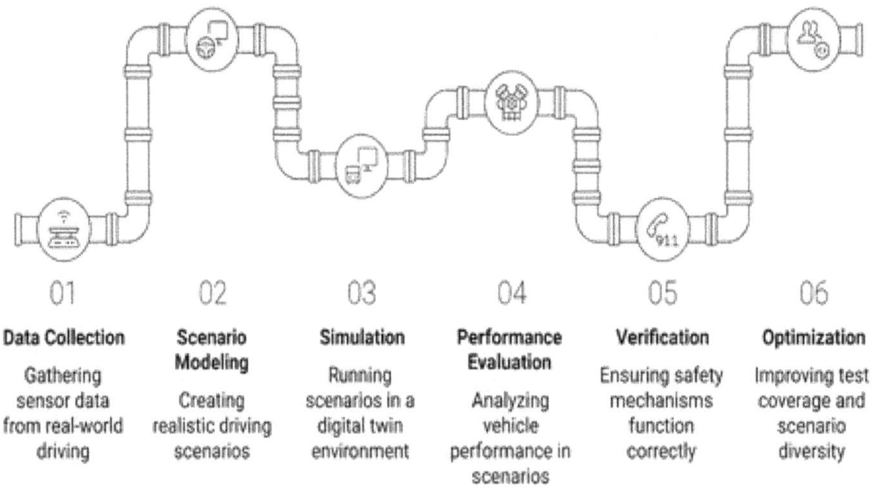

3.3 Compliance Challenges in Real-World Testing Environments

Despite the advancement of digital simulation, conversion of the results of the virtual validation to the compliance in the real world is highly challenging. The differences between simulation and real tests are normally attributed to the changes in sensor calibration, environmental inconsistencies or hardware limitations. The similarity and interchangeability between the two domains, in its turn, require the standard data formats and model validation. Moreover, global compliance is also a realistic objective, which involves arranging dissimilar regional rules, information-security statutes, and data-security norms (Patil, 2025). The other major concern is the computational footprint as high-fidelity digital twins multi-domain simulation and synchronization needs a lot of computing resources. The certification also becomes more difficult with ethics such as the reporting of AI-based safety systems and culpability of algorithmic failures. The policymakers and research institutions should collaborate with the automakers in an effort to develop similar validation frameworks. To realize the creation of trust in testing based on digital twin, the end objectives are to guarantee the compromise between technical rigor and regulatory acceptability such that the safety verification can be scientifically accepted and legally binding (Tian et al., 2022). The regulatory validation structures also affect the implementation of the digital twin technologies in autonomous vehicles safety certification. Guidelines on testing of automated driving system, cybersecurity and software updates are defined by agencies, including the National Highway Traffic Safety Administration (NHTSA) in the United States and UNECE WP.29 in Europe. Digital twin-based validation platforms have the potential to assist in regulatory compliance by delivering traceable simulation results, reproducible safety results and scenario coverage measures needed in homologation process. The feature will enable regulators to evaluate the safety performance of autonomous systems on standardized digital evidence besides the customary physical testing.

4. DIGITAL TWIN-ENABLED CRASH SCENARIO SIMULATIONS

The crash cases simulation is vital in describing the structural stability, occupant protection, as well as the response to crashes of autonomous vehicles in unfavourable circumstances. Digital Twin (DT) technology enables engineers to conduct such tests in the virtual worlds in a level of realism and with an accuracy unheard of previously. The DTs eliminate the dangers, the cost, and limitation of the physical crash tests by replicating material conduct, deformation, and crash motions. The high-fidelity virtual reconstruction allows the engineers to test the energy absorption, component failure and propagation of impact forces within milliseconds (Rosique et al., 2019). Moreover, with the help of multi-physics models and AI, mechanical, thermal, and electrical responses can be analyzed simultaneously at collisions. The use of physical prototypes where there is continuous learning and improvement of the model after physical prototypes will be guaranteed through physical prototypes which will work in real time with their digital counterparts. In this section, the authors elaborate the benefits of the virtual reconstruction, physics-based modelling, and hybrid simulation frameworks to change the safety tests and accelerate the process of certification of the next generation autonomous vehicles (Ciunel et al., 2014).

4.1 Virtual Reconstruction of Impact Dynamics and Material Response

The crash simulations of DT are grounded on a virtual reconstruction allowing engineers to model the actual effects through the assistance of the computational models and the laws of material science. Each of the physical vehicles has a digital twin that documents the geometric, structural and dynamic features of a vehicle including frame stiffness, crumple zones and composite material layers. With various crash angles and velocities, Finite Element Analysis (FEA) and Computational Fluid Dynamics (CFD) models the impact dynamics, i.e. deformation, stress propagation and points of fracture. This will enable one to see the patterns of the dissipation of energy and passenger compartment intrusion in finer details that are essential as far as safety standards are concerned (Barsi et al., 2020). The component of material response is a model of the behavior of various alloys, composites and polymers under the influence of high strain rates, which allow designers to optimize structures with respect to energy absorption and minimal damages. Digital reconstruction, in contrast to physical tests, is not limited by physical considerations, and can be run in an iterative manner at scale, making possible virtual prototyping and design development long before the physical process starts. Digital twin architectures are a dynamic and continually changing simulation environment compared to the more traditional crash simulation platforms, including LS-DYNA, ANSYS Autodyn, and PAM-CRASH. Conventional crash models are based on unchanging boundary conditions and presented test cases. By comparison, DT-based crash models combine real-time sensor inputs and operational driving data, which allows the generation of adaptive scenarios and the ongoing training of the model. This difference will enable digital twins to assist with lifecycle safety validation to go beyond single-event crash testing and continue to monitor safety analytics and make predictions during vehicle operation.

4.2 Multi-Physics and AI-Driven Simulation for Crash Prediction

Multi-physics simulation is a system that involves the integration of mechanical, thermal, electrical and fluidic models into a single physical model to capture the dynamics of crashes more realistically. The AI algorithms in DT-based safety validation are used to refine the process by finding nonlinear associations and making predictions of the intricate interactions when colliding. To predict parameter tuning and boundary conditions, machine learning models examine big data in terms of historical crash test data, sensor data, and simulation log history. Neural Networks are capable of estimating patterns of deformation, the probability of occupant injury and component failure in minutes, increasing the throughput of simulations by huge factors (Liang et al., 2025a). Also, by integrating multi-physics solvers with AI-assisted optimization, it is possible to explore what-if scenarios e.g. different material thickness or impact angles in real time without needing to recalibrate the solver. The combination of AI and physics-based models enable predictive crash analytics, which can be used in optimizing the design as well as in adaptive risk management. What results is a simulation world that learns every time it is run, and which is almost as physical as real, at a fraction of the computational and experimental expense.

4.3 Real-Time Synchronization Between Physical Prototypes and Digital Twins

As the possibility of real-time synchronization, this feature is what makes digital twins and the conventional simulation tools different. It renders the virtual model dynamic whereby it adjusts with every physical event in the prototype vehicle. Sensor images onboard such as accelerators, strain gauges, and gyroscopes are transmitted to the high-speed networks and sent to the DT where the systems states are updated immediately by the use of algorithms. This allows one to observe both deformation patterns and the safety system activation and structural stress in real-time experiments. Bidirectional data flow can be used to provide simulation predictions with an impact on physical testing through control strategy modification of parameters or control strategy activation during execution (Xiong et al., 2022). The closed-loop interaction is capable of facilitating hybrid interaction models that do not separate laboratory testing and virtual analytics. The validation of autonomous decision systems is also aided by synchronization as well as that the AI-enhanced crash responses matches what actually happens in reality. Having a continuously refreshed feedback loop, engineers can obtain greater accuracy, accelerate iterators, and traceability of simulated forecasts and empirical outcomes.

5. AI-DRIVEN SAFETY ANALYTICS AND DECISION VALIDATION

Artificial Intelligence (AI) acts as the brain of digital twin ecosystems, which offers analytical intelligence in the form of failure, control optimization, and decision validation. The processing of large volumes of sensory and simulation data boosts predictive and diagnostic capabilities of DTs of autonomous vehicles, which could be supported by AI. Machine learning models identify trends in advance of malfunction in a system, and reinforcement learning can be used to control the system in volatile situations (Ibrahim et al., 2022). More so, Explainable AI (XAI) frameworks make sure that safety-related decisions are interpretable and auditable to address ethical and regulatory issues. These combined AI based mechanisms strengthen a self-feedback loop that increases the models reliability, transparency in decisions and resilience in the system. This section discusses the opportunities of AI and DTs in the safety analytics, namely in predictive maintenance, optimization of dynamic decisions, and human-understandable validation processes necessary to support the safe functioning of autonomous vehicles (Schwalb, 2021). The quantification of uncertainty has been now viewed as a grave necessity whereby credible systems of autonomy validation are ensured. The sensor noise, environmental variability, model approximation errors, and algorithmic prediction uncertainty are some of the sources of uncertainty. With the help of

Monte Carlo simulation, probabilistic risk assessment, and Bayesian inference, these uncertainties can be analyzed in a systematic way using digital twins environments. DT-based validation schemes make it possible to offer a stronger guarantee of safety in perception outputs, trajectory predictions, and decision policies, and will give better assurance about the deployment of autonomous vehicles.

5.1 Machine Learning Models for Anomaly Detection and Failure Forecasting

Machine Learning (ML) algorithms are essential in learning beforehand about mechanical or software failures of autonomous systems. Under the DT model, supervised and unsupervised models consume continuous sensor streams to identify an abnormal behavioral state, including: irregular brake pressure, sensor noise or actuator delay. Algorithms, including the Random Forests, Support Vector Machines (SVMs) and Autoencoders, train normal operation baselines and identify anomalies in real time. Predictive models are predictive algorithms that are conditioned on past data and simulated conditions and are used to predict possible system failures before they grow into safety-critical conditions (Kirovskii & Gorelov, 2019). It is a proactive scheme that enables the condition-based maintenance and the dynamic reconfiguration of the control systems. Combination with cloud and edge analytics will guarantee that it is identified with a low latency level, which will provide continuity in its operations. Finally, the anomaly detection based on ML contributes to the increased reliability of the system, as autonomous vehicles will be able to make the transition between reactive fault management to the predictive safety guarantee (Yu & Mei, 2025).

5.2 Reinforcement Learning for Adaptive Control and Recovery

Reinforcement Learning (RL) helps autonomous vehicles to develop optimal control strategies by interacting with the environment, both the physical and digital one. The RL agents in the DT ecosystem act on a set of simulated environments to train policies that have a high probability of being safe and stabilized in cases of adverse conditions like skidding, the loss of sensor or evading obstacles. These agents are given feedback by performance measures such as collision obstruction, route precision and recovery period in terms of rewards and punishments (Weissensteiner et al., 2023). When trained the models are then implemented in actual vehicles and the behavior is then refined via constant feedback with the DT. This feedback control system enables Avs to respond to unexpected conditions and recover with grace to near-failure conditions. Integration of DT and RL therefore forms a closed-loop control system which is able to adapt to new information, enhance the precision of the decisions and reduce human interference when driving under critical conditions.

5.3 Explainable AI (XAI) for Transparent Safety Decisions

Transparency and interpretability are likely to become the most important requirements as AI becomes part of safety-critical vehicle functionality. The Explainable AI (XAI) is designed to make the processes of decision making, including emergency braking, lane departure correction or collision avoidance, understandable and verifiable by engineers, regulators and the final consumer. XAI models used in the DT environment visualize the decision paths, feature significance, and scores of confidence of each safety action. Such methods as SHAP (Shapley Additive exPlanations) and LIME (Local Interpretable Model-Agnostic Explanations) can be used to make neural network outputs interpretable in human language (Department of Mechanical Engineering Bangalore India et al., 2024). This openness enables the engineers to peer review model logic, identify biases and confirm that the quality of the work meets health and safety standards like SOTIF. Moreover, XAI helps to build accountability in the automated systems as it presents traceable evidence of every decision made during a simulated or real-world event. The interpretation aspect of AI-based DT builds into the vehicle control system offers more than just autonomy to autonomous vehicles, but also confidence and moral certainty that the latter can be effectively deployed at scale.

6. LITERATURE REVIEW

The current knowledge of Digital Twin (DT) technology use in automotive safety validation has experienced a massive shift over the last ten years, with a shift in paradigm of traditional simulation models to intelligent and data-driven virtual ecosystems. Implementation of early DT studies was mainly based on system monitoring and predictive maintenance, and recently, dynamic safety validation, crash prediction, and autonomous decision verification are studied. The combination of artificial intelligence, multi-physics simulation, and real-time certification has changed the test and certification of the automotive systems (Agnusdei et al., 2021). This section will examine the history of applications of the DT in automotive safety, summarize the main studies of simulation-based validation of DT applications in 2018-2025, and outline the research gaps that the area of study currently addresses. Combining the results gained through scholarly sources, industrial testbeds, and regulatory standards, the section will allow one to obtain a comprehensive picture of how DTs help to create safer and stronger autonomous vehicles, as well as reveal the focus areas that need additional innovation (Alaba et al., 2024). The most recent scholarly studies have seen more and more academic research focus on digital twin-based validation frameworks incorporating scenario generation, safety-related metrics, and regulatory compliance systems. Research in IEEE Transactions on Intelligent Transportation Systems and Sensors points out the possibility of DT ecosystems to enhance the coverage of testing and minimize the use of physical road testing and still have high standards of safety guaranteed.

6.1 Evolution of Digital Twin Applications in Automotive Safety Research

Digital Twin was first conceptualised in aerospace engineering, and has since been carried across to the automotive industry as a means of continuous verification of the system and performance optimization. The first applications (2010-2017) were devoted to the use of vehicle diagnostics and predictive maintenance on the basis of static models and the main result was the condition monitoring instead of active validation of vehicle safety. In the 2018-2020 period, it was reported that the research had grown in favor of dynamic digital twins that are able to simulate sensor fusion, powertrain control, and autonomous navigation behaviors (Török & Pethő, 2020). The research conducted by Siemens, BMW, and Ford investigated the possibility of using DTs to simulate realistic driving conditions to conduct virtual homologation and crashworthiness testing. In the year 2021, the emphasis changed to introduce AI-led analytics, edge computing, and multi-domain simulation, whereby real-time co-evolution between physical and virtual assets is possible. The latest models, e.g., NVIDIA DRIVE Sim or CARLA combined with DT modules, show that reinforcement learning and sensor simulation can be used to speed up verification of vehicle safety. This development marks the shift in the way of reactive testing towards proactive and model-driven safety assurance (Sadaf et al., 2023). Table 3 Overview of the chronological evolution of DT application in automotive safety, the patterns in the evolution of DT applications include the substitution of the concept of static modeling with the framework of AI-inspired validation.

Table 3. Evolution of digital twin technology in automotive safety

Year	Focus Area	Key Contribution	Representative Organization/Study
2015-2017	Predictive Maintenance	Condition monitoring and fault detection	Siemens, Ford
2018-2020	Dynamic Simulation	Real-time modeling of AV systems	BMW, AVL, TU Munich
2021-2022	AI Integration	Deep learning for crash prediction	NVIDIA, CARLA platform
2023-2025	Real-Time Safety Validation	End-to-end digital twin synchronization	Waymo, Horizon 2020 Projects

6.2 Review of Simulation-Based Safety Validation Studies (2018-2025)

Wide-ranging research has been conducted on the issue of digital twins enhancing safety validation based on high-fidelity simulation and AI coupling between 2018 and 2025. Other research's focused on the need to use federated and distributed DT models to conduct privacy-preserving crash testing in institutions. The modeling of collision mechanics and occupant safety parameters were popularly done through simulation platforms such as ANSYS Twin Builder, dSpace ASM and Siemens Simcenter (Wang et al., 2024). Other European research projects such as the Horizon 2020 project to design a Virtual Vehicle examined the use of scenario-based validation to ISO 26262 and SOTIF standards. Simulation of human factors, decision uncertainty and perception errors in autonomous driving have also been performed using deep learning-enabled DTs. According to the research on the topic presented in the journals including IEEE Transactions on Intelligent Transportation Systems and Mechanical Systems and Signal Processing, it is possible to minimize the physical testing costs by a factor of 70% with the use of DT-based virtual crash tests, and the validity under a variety of driving conditions is enhanced (Yoon et al., 2023).

6.3 Research Gaps: From Data Fidelity to Real-Time Integration

However, there are still multiple gaps in the process of obtaining completely reliable DT-based safety validation, even with the significant advances. A significant constraint is the fidelity of data, i.e. whether or not the simulated data has a good representation of the real complex world e.g. sensor noise, lighting changes, and dynamic weather conditions. The present DT systems also have a synchronization delay between real physical objects and the virtual ones, which is relevant to real-time testing of decisions. One more problem is scalability because the simulation of a high-resolution crash requires large computational resources and network bandwidth. Besides, the interoperability problems occur when incorporating multi-vendor platforms and different communication protocols, as well as data formats that are heterogeneous. Governance-wise, there is no standardization in the enforcement of the DT implementations, especially in regards to validation traceability and ethical compliance in decision-making based on AI. Future studies should fill this gap by creating light, adaptable, and decentralized DT structures, which combine edge computing, blockchain authentication, and quantum-safe synchronization to guarantee transparency, speed, and safety in the autonomous vehicle safety validation channels.

7. CASE STUDIES IN DIGITAL TWIN-BASED SAFETY VALIDATION

The practical use of Digital Twin (DT) frameworks in the automotive sector has insights to give on the usefulness of this concept in terms of safety validation. The major corporations like BMW and Waymo have been the first to implement DT-based ecosystem which integrates artificial intelligence, simulation modeling, and real-time data synchronization to test the autonomous systems in various conditions. These tools emulate millions of possible crash, edge-case tests, and expedite design verification and as well as lessen the use of actual prototypes (Madni et al., 2019). This part reviews two exemplary case studies, namely the Virtual Safety Validation Platform developed by the BMW and the Simulation Ecosystem proposed by Waymo to illustrate how industrial implementations of DT are used to close theoretical studies and operational safety assurance. A comparison and conclusion have been given at the end of this section, focusing on similarities in design, performance, and integration issues in industrial and research implementations.

7.1 Case Study 1: BMW'S Virtual Safety Validation Platform (2024)

BMW has created an all-encompassing Virtual Safety Validation Platform (VSVP) that combines physics-grounded Digital Twins and artificial intelligence to simulate and analyze the crash scenarios among its autonomous vehicles. It was introduced in 2024 based on the BMW paradigm of Vehicle-in-the-Loop (ViL) testing that integrates the real-time sensors data, material models, and multi-physics simulations environments. The DT replicates the structure, material composition and configuration of the sensor of the physical prototype, allowing the engineers to conduct virtual crash tests at scale (Yun & Park, 2021). With the help of the AI-based optimization algorithms, the platform can dynamically control the parameters of the simulation to recreate the impact scenarios of the real world, including side collisions or rollovers. Moreover, the compatibility with safety frameworks that are compliant with ISO 26262 is guaranteed, and all virtual tests will be used to provide regulatory traceability and certification preparedness. BMW VSVP is a cost-effective and less harmful to the environment by cutting down physical crash testing by approximately 60%. The DT is a constant learner that uses data on the road to improve the accuracy of its predictions and provides adaptive control processes to improve occupant safety and the longevity of its vehicle (Li et al., 2024). Figure 3 shows the 2024 Virtual Safety Validation Platform workflow of BMW, which represents an integration of AI-based digital twins and real-time data to simulate crash scenarios, guarantee compliance to regulations, and decrease physical testing by 60%.

Figure 3. BMW's virtual safety validation platform

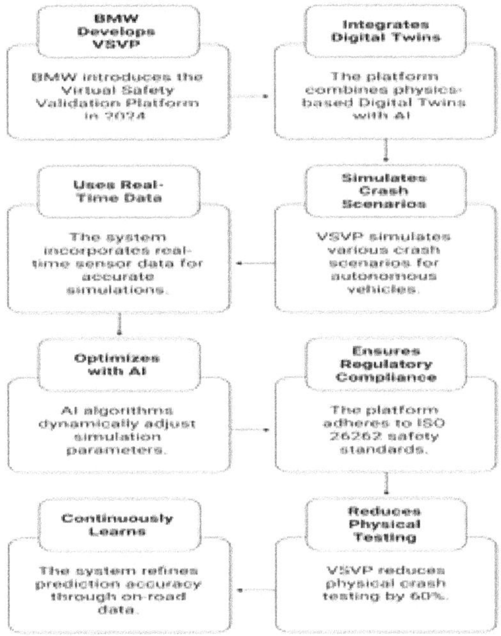

7.2 Case Study 2: WAYMO Simulation Ecosystem (2023-2024)

The Simulation Ecosystem offered by Waymo is one of the most developed applications of autonomous drivingDT-based testing. The system (run 2023-2024) is based on large-scale cloud computing and AI-enhanced digital twins to create and simulate millions of edge-case scenarios, which are too few or unsafe to be tested in real life. Every simulated vehicle is a high-fidelity DT prototype connected to a real stream of sensor data, such as LiDAR, radar, and camera data, and this enables the perception and control algorithms to be synchronized (Liang et al., 2025b). Waymo uses its Carcraft platform to combine these twins into a dynamic computing environment, and AI models continuously analyze the performance of these twins in response to unpredictable circumstances, as well as sudden appearance of pedestrians, sensor malfunctions, or bad weather. The agents of reinforcement learning maximize decision-making strategies in virtual space and then apply them on actual automobiles. This cycle of simulation/ road testing shortens safety assurance, saves billions of testing miles, and provides scalable and data-based validation, which is a global standard of safety. Figure 4 Listing Waymo end-to-end digital twin simulation workflow (Kim et al., 2023). The twin (generated as a result of real-world data acquisition) is simulated through an AI-controlled scenario generation, reinforcement learning, validation, and deployment to autonomous driving safety.

Figure 4. Waymo simulation ecosystem process

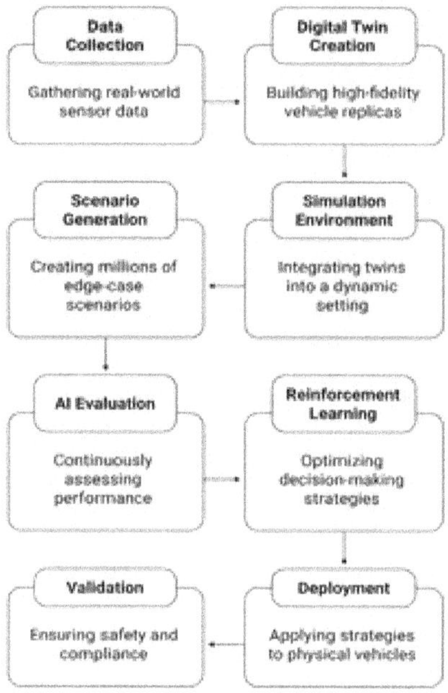

7.3 Comparative Analysis of Industrial and Research Implementations

The implementations of both BMW and Waymo are a good example of the integration of Digital Twin technology, AI analytics, and multi-physics simulation in safety validation. Models in the industry are oriented towards real-time congruence and conformity as well as cost-efficiency whereas research-oriented systems are aimed at algorithmic novelty, interoperability, and data integrity. The VSVP of BMW presents physics-based crash modeling that is structured according to ISO and SOTIF standards, and Waymo emphasizes adaptive learning and massive generation of edge-cases. Although both systems have different areas of interest, the issues encountered in both systems are computational scalability, sensor uncertainty, and cross-platform integration (Wu, 2023). All these applications confirm that Digital Twins cannot be considered just simulation tools but dynamic, learning-enabled systems that will make future safe and autonomous mobility due to constant feedback, transparency, and performance optimization. Table 4 Compares the forefront industrial DT implementations, applications, innovations, and quantifiable advantages in the validation of safety.

Table 4. Summary of industrial case studies in DT-based safety validation

Case Study	Organization	Application Focus	Outcome/Impact
BMW VSVP (2024)	BMW Group	Physics-based crash simulation	Reduced crash test cost by 60%
Waymo Carcraft (2023-2024)	Waymo LLC	Edge-case generation and testing	Improved decision accuracy and test scalability
Siemens Simcenter	Siemens AG	Real-time vehicle dynamics validation	Enhanced model fidelity and certification speed
NVIDIA DRIVE Sim	NVIDIA Corp.	AI-accelerated scenario testing	Expanded virtual validation coverage

8. CHALLENGES AND FUTURE RESEARCH DIRECTIONS

Cybersecurity is another requirement of safety validation in autonomous vehicle ecosystems, in the context of interconnections. The ISO/SAE 21434 standard is a collection of standards governing the specifications of the management of the cybersecurity risks during the life cycle of the vehicle, including threat analysis, vulnerability assessment, and secure software updates. Cybersecurity validation environments Simulated cyber-attack environments may include simulation of spoofed sensor data, communication interference or malicious control commands. The possibility of including cybersecurity into the testing platform of DT contributes to the prevention of the emergence of vulnerabilities in time and complies with the international security standards of cars. Although there has been significant advancement on the topic of Digital Twin (DT) integration in autonomous vehicle safety validation, data validation issues, computational scalability, and system interoperability have remained a persistent challenge. Since the development of DT frameworks is still shifting towards real-time, multi-domain synchronization, problems like inconsistent sensor observations, simulation drift, and latency still interfere with the refinements of precision and reliability. In addition, the computational intensity of executing the multi-physics simulations using AI-driven analytics does not provide scalability and makes the deployment unfeasible. The new paradigms that have the potential to breakthrough like quantum computing and federated learning could provide consistent and safe, distributed and fast validation ecosystems (Meng et al., 2023). This segment identifies key technical and operational limitations with suggestions on a futuristic solution, a combination of edge computing, quantum acceleration, and privacy-saving architectures. These developments, combined with others, will help to develop resilient, adaptive, and transparent digital twin ecosystems that will be able to provide next-generation safety assurance in fully autonomous transportation systems (Zöldy et al., 2020). Table 5 Overview Major obstacles and future research directions towards high-fidelity, scalable DT-based safety validation systems.

Table 5. Key challenges and future research directions

Challenge	Description	Emerging Research Focus
Data Veracity	Sensor noise and uncertainty	AI-based data cleaning, blockchain traceability
Model Fidelity	Inconsistent physical–virtual correlation	Adaptive calibration and standardization
Computational Overhead	High resource requirements	Quantum-enabled optimization

continued on following page

Table 5. Continued

Challenge	Description	Emerging Research Focus
Synchronization Delay	Latency in real-time updates	Edge-cloud hybrid computing
Interoperability	Cross-platform integration issues	Unified ontologies and APIs

8.1 Data Veracity, Model Fidelity, and Interoperability Issues

The veracity of data and fidelity of models to real-life operations continue to be the central elements of a reliable digital twin. When validating autonomous vehicles, sensor errors and data noise as well as environmental variations may cause discrepancies between physical and simulated performance results. Fidelity can only be maintained by accurately tuning vehicle dynamics, material and crash physics in the context of simulation. Moreover, the interoperability of various software platforms (ANSYS, MATLAB/Simulink, and Siemens Simcenter) presents an issue of integration challenges because of the disparity between data standards and communication standards (Madni, 2021). Cross-domain collaboration is also constrained by the fact that there are no common ontologies used to exchange vehicle telemetry and sensor data. The issues above require standard frameworks of modeling, AI-powered models of data refinement, and ontology-based structures that coordinate the multi-source inputs. Increasing the traceability of data as well as the transparency of the model with the help of blockchain-supported validation logs can enhance the reproducibility and regulatory acceptability, making the DT-based safety validation both verifiable and scalable to the automotive industry as a whole (Douthwaite et al., 2021).

8.2 Computational Overhead and Real-Time Synchronization Limits

Digital Twin simulations have a major bottleneck in their computational complexity which is an issue in large scale safety validation. Multi-physics models with high-resolution, such as structural deformation, thermal dissipation, and electric responses require a large amount of processing power and memory bandwidth. Simulation Newer models that are run in real time and simultaneously synchronized with physical prototypes tend to create latency and data congestion. Milliseconds synchronization of crashes and emergency simulations is still not possible despite the development of GPU clusters and cloud computing. Edge computing provides partial alleviation with computations being decentralized in closer proximity to the vehicle, but control of distributed workloads provides further complexity (Rjabtšikov et al., 2023). The future research should concern the enhancement of the efficiency of the algorithms using model compression, adaptive sampling, and parallel computation strategies. Furthermore, edge-cloud and AI-controlled load balancing can be utilized to minimize the simulation lag and increase responsiveness in safety-critical applications; in addition, continuous learning cycles between the real and virtual worlds of the vehicle can be facilitated using hybrid edge-cloud architecture.

8.3 Future Outlook: Quantum-Enabled Twins and Federated Safety Validation

The future of the Digital Twin technology in the field of autonomous vehicle safety is in the intersection with the paradigms of quantum computing and federated learning. Quantum-powered twins will use quantum processors to simulate compound crash, multi-vehicle interactions and sensor fusion issues in a very rapid manner (Ravikumar & Aarthi, 2025). Variational quantum solvers and other quantum algorithms could cut down the time required in the computation of impact models and optimization problems by far. In the meantime, federated safety validation is being developed as a decentralized framework in which several automotive organizations train and validate DT models simultaneously and without providing proprietary data to one another (Singh et al., 2021). This guarantees privacy preservation, scalability and adherence to international standards of data governance. Integration of these paradigms can provide a secure, distributed and high-performance validation ecosystem. These hybrid structures will not only make simulations faster and more accurate but also ethical and transparent safety validation, which will open the way to the application of autonomous vehicles globally and meeting the regulation standards in the next decade.

9. CONCLUSION

Digital Twin (DT) technology is a game changer that has become a new system of ensuring safety validation and crash scenario simulator, in autonomous cars. DTs can simulate a high-fidel and dynamic environment to test vehicle performance in extreme and uncertain conditions by combining physics-based modeling, artificial intelligence and real time data synchronization. This paradigm decreases the reliance of physical crashes tests; it decreases the cost of prototyping and also it improves the accuracy of predictive safety analytics. In this chapter, it has been highlighted that the use of DTs facilitates the transition to proactive to reactive safety assurance through constant learning of real-life operations and the optimization of decision-making algorithms. Based on the analysis, converting AI-driven analytics, multi-physics simulations, and ensuring the digital twin is the key to future-generation car testing systems.

The industrial example of the Virtual Safety Validation Platform by BMW and the Simulation Ecosystem by Waymo demonstrate the practical value of integrating DT to verify the adherence to the global safety standards like ISO 26262 and SOTIF. Simultaneously, the chapter also identified persistent problems such as veracity of data, computational complexity and interoperability that require long-term research and standardization efforts. In the future, quantum computing and federated learning integration will potentially transform the scalability, security and intelligence of DT. These technologies will support decentralized, privacy-sensitive, and extremely fast validation systems that will be able to adapt in real-time. Finally, digital twins do not just symbolize a simulation tool, but they signify the ethical and open-minded basis of the autonomous vehicle design to guarantee the safety, responsibility, and innovation advance in tandem. By working together industrially, through regulation, and in the field of academia, the process of DT-enabled safety validation can speed up the process of turning autonomous mobility into something that is not only intelligent and efficient but also based on fundamental safety and trustworthiness to the society.

REFERENCES

Agnusdei, G. P., Elia, V., & Gnoni, M. G. (2021). Is digital Twin technology supporting safety management? A bibliometric and systematic review. *Applied Sciences (Basel, Switzerland)*, *11*(6), 2767. DOI: 10.3390/app11062767

Alaba, S. Y., Gurbuz, A. C., & Ball, J. E. (2024). Emerging trends in autonomous vehicle perception: Multimodal fusion for 3D object detection. *World Electric Vehicle Journal*, *15*(1), 20. DOI: 10.3390/wevj15010020

Ali, A., Huang, J., Jabbar, A., Ali, M., & Ali, S. (2025). Federated learning for connected autonomous vehicles: Enhancing mobility, safety, and sustainability. *Physica Scripta*, *100*(7), 072001. DOI: 10.1088/1402-4896/addca2

Almeaibed, S., Al-Rubaye, S., Tsourdos, A., & Avdelidis, N. P. (2021a). Digital twin analysis to promote safety and security in autonomous vehicles. *IEEE Communications Standards Magazine*, *5*(1), 40–46. DOI: 10.1109/MCOMSTD.011.2100004

Almeaibed, S., Al-Rubaye, S., Tsourdos, A., & Avdelidis, N. P. (2021b). Digital twin analysis to promote safety and security in autonomous vehicles. *IEEE Communications Standards Magazine*, *5*(1), 40–46. DOI: 10.1109/MCOMSTD.011.2100004

Barricelli, B. R., Casiraghi, E., & Fogli, D. (2019). A survey on digital twin: Definitions, characteristics, applications, and design implications. *IEEE Access : Practical Innovations, Open Solutions*, *7*, 167653–167671. DOI: 10.1109/ACCESS.2019.2953499

Barsi, Á., Potó, V., Lógó, J. M., & Krausz, N. (2020). Creating an OpenDRIVE model of the campus of the Budapest University of technology and Economics for automotive simulations. *Periodica Polytechnica. Civil Engineering*. Advance online publication. DOI: 10.3311/PPci.16768

Changalvala, R., & Malik, H. (2019). LiDAR data integrity verification for autonomous vehicle. *IEEE Access : Practical Innovations, Open Solutions*, *7*, 138018–138031. DOI: 10.1109/ACCESS.2019.2943207

Ciunel, S., Popa, D. L., Gherghina, G., Bogdan, M. L., & Tutunea, D. (2014). Human head-neck system behavior during virtual impact automotive simulations. *Applied Mechanics and Materials*, *659*, 177–182. . DOI: 10.4028/www.scientific.net/AMM.659.177

Department of Mechanical Engineering Bangalore India, A. S. of E., Reddy, G. J., Sharma, D., & Department of Mechanical Engineering Bangalore India, A. S. of E. (2024). Edge AI in autonomous vehicles: Navigating the road to safe and efficient mobility. INTERANTIONAL JOURNAL OF SCIENTIFIC RESEARCH IN ENGINEERING AND MANAGEMENT, 08(01), 1–13. DOI: 10.55041/IJSREM28427

Douthwaite, J. A., Lesage, B., Gleirscher, M., Calinescu, R., Aitken, J. M., Alexander, R., & Law, J. (2021). A modular digital twinning framework for safety assurance of collaborative robotics. *Frontiers in Robotics and AI*, *8*, 758099. DOI: 10.3389/frobt.2021.758099 PMID: 34977162

Ibrahim, M., Rassõlkin, A., Vaimann, T., & Kallaste, A. (2022). Overview on digital Twin for autonomous electrical vehicles propulsion drive system. *Sustainability (Basel)*, *14*(2), 601. DOI: 10.3390/su14020601

Kim, J., Park, S., Kim, J., & Yoo, J. (2023). A deep reinforcement learning strategy for surrounding vehicles-based Lane-keeping control. *Sensors (Basel)*, *23*(24), 9843. DOI: 10.3390/s23249843 PMID: 38139694

Kirovskii, O. M., & Gorelov, V. A. (2019). Driver assistance systems: Analysis, tests and the safety case. ISO 26262 and ISO PAS 21448. *IOP Conference Series. Materials Science and Engineering*, *534*(1), 012019. DOI: 10.1088/1757-899X/534/1/012019

Lei, T., Sellers, T., Luo, C., Cao, L., & Bi, Z. (2024). Digital twin-based multi-objective autonomous vehicle navigation approach as applied in infrastructure construction. *IET Cyber-Systems and Robotics*, *6*(2), e12110. Advance online publication. DOI: 10.1049/csy2.12110

Li, Y., Liu, W., Liu, Q., Zheng, X., Sun, K., & Huang, C. (2024). Complying with ISO 26262 and ISO/SAE 21434: A safety and security. *Sensors (Basel)*, *24*(6), 1848. DOI: 10.3390/s24061848 PMID: 38544111

Liang, Z., Wang, J., Zhang, T., & Yong, X. (2025a). DTTF-Sim: A Digital Twin-based simulation system for continuous autonomous driving testing. *Sensors (Basel)*, *25*(11), 3447. DOI: 10.3390/s25113447 PMID: 40968948

Liang, Z., Wang, J., Zhang, T., & Yong, X. (2025b). DTTF-Sim: A Digital Twin-based simulation system for continuous autonomous driving testing. *Sensors (Basel)*, *25*(11), 3447. DOI: 10.3390/s25113447 PMID: 40968948

Madni, A. M. (2021). MBSE testbed for rapid, cost-effective prototyping and evaluation of system modeling approaches. *Applied Sciences (Basel, Switzerland)*, *11*(5), 2321. DOI: 10.3390/app11052321

Madni, A. M., Madni, C. C., & Lucero, S. D. (2019). Leveraging digital twin technology in model-based systems engineering. *Systems*, *7*(1), 7. DOI: 10.3390/systems7010007

Malayjerdi, M., Baykara, B. C., Sell, R., & Malayjerdi, E. (2021). Autonomous vehicle safety evaluation through a high-fidelity simulation approach. *Proceedings of the Estonian Academy of Sciences*, *70*(4), 413–421. DOI: 10.3176/proc.2021.4.07

Meng, K., Zhou, R., Li, Z., & Zhang, K. (2023). A quantitative approach of generating challenging testing scenarios based on functional safety standard. *Applied Sciences (Basel, Switzerland)*, *13*(6), 3494. DOI: 10.3390/app13063494

Patil, Y. J.Yuvaraj J Patil. (2025). Scenario-driven safety verification: A comprehensive framework for autonomous vehicle validation within ISO 26262. International Journal of Scientific Research in Computer Science. *Engineering and Information Technology*, *11*(2), 1047–1056. DOI: 10.32628/CSEIT25112431

Ravikumar, R. N., & Aarthi, S. (2025). Digital Twin-driven green energy systems. In *The Future of Green Energy* (pp. 1–28). IGI Global Scientific Publishing., DOI: 10.4018/979-8-3373-3226-0.ch001

Riedmaier, S., Ponn, T., Ludwig, D., Schick, B., & Diermeyer, F. (2020). Survey on scenario-based safety assessment of automated vehicles. *IEEE Access : Practical Innovations, Open Solutions*, *8*, 87456–87477. DOI: 10.1109/ACCESS.2020.2993730

Rjabtšikov, V., Rassõlkin, A., Kudelina, K., Kallaste, A., & Vaimann, T. (2023). Review of electric vehicle testing procedures for digital twin development: A comprehensive analysis. *Energies*, *16*(19), 6952. DOI: 10.3390/en16196952

Rokseth, B., Haugen, O. I., & Utne, I. B. (2019). Safety verification for autonomous ships. MATEC Web of Conferences, 273, 02002. DOI: 10.1051/matecconf/201927302002

Rosique, F., Navarro, P. J., Fernández, C., & Padilla, A. (2019). A systematic review of perception system and simulators for autonomous vehicles research. *Sensors (Basel)*, *19*(3), 648. DOI: 10.3390/s19030648 PMID: 30764486

Sadaf, M., Iqbal, Z., Javed, A. R., Saba, I., Krichen, M., Majeed, S., & Raza, A. (2023). Connected and automated vehicles: Infrastructure, applications, security, critical challenges, and future aspects. *Technologies*, *11*(5), 117. DOI: 10.3390/technologies11050117

Schwalb, E. (2021). Analysis of hazards for autonomous driving. *Journal of Autonomous Vehicles and Systems*, *1*(2), 021003. Advance online publication. DOI: 10.1115/1.4049922

Singh, M., Fuenmayor, E., Hinchy, E., Qiao, Y., Murray, N., & Devine, D. (2021). Digital Twin: Origin to future. *Applied System Innovation*, *4*(2), 36. DOI: 10.3390/asi4020036

Song, B. (2024). Review on multisensor SLAM datasets for advanced perception and mapping technologies. *Applied and Computational Engineering*, *97*(1), 170–174. DOI: 10.54254/2755-2721/97/20241270

Szalay, Z. (2021). Next generation X-in-the-loop validation methodology for automated vehicle systems. *IEEE Access : Practical Innovations, Open Solutions*, *9*, 35616–35632. DOI: 10.1109/ACCESS.2021.3061732

Tian, R., Li, N., Kolmanovsky, I., Yildiz, Y., & Girard, A. R. (2022). Game-theoretic modeling of traffic in unsignalized intersection network for autonomous vehicle control verification and validation. IEEE Transactions on Intelligent Transportation Systems: A Publication of the IEEE Intelligent Transportation Systems Council, 23(3), 2211–2226. DOI: 10.1109/TITS.2020.3035363

Török, Á., & Pethő, Z. (2020). Introducing safety and security co-engineering related research orientations in the field of automotive security. *Periodica Polytechnica Transportation Engineering*, *48*(4), 349–356. DOI: 10.3311/PPtr.15850

van Dyck, M., Lüttgens, D., Piller, F. T., & Brenk, S. (2023). Interconnected digital twins and the future of digital manufacturing: Insights from a Delphi study. *Journal of Product Innovation Management*, *40*(4), 475–505. DOI: 10.1111/jpim.12685

Wang, K., Li, Z., Nonomura, K., Yu, T., Sakaguchi, K., Hashash, O., & Saad, W. (2024). Smart mobility digital twin based automated vehicle navigation system: A proof of concept. *IEEE Transactions on Intelligent Vehicles*, *9*(3), 4348–4361. DOI: 10.1109/TIV.2024.3368109

Weissensteiner, P., Stettinger, G., Khastgir, S., & Watzenig, D. (2023). Operational design domain-driven coverage for the safety argumentation of automated vehicles. *IEEE Access : Practical Innovations, Open Solutions*, *11*, 12263–12284. DOI: 10.1109/ACCESS.2023.3242127

Wu, Y. (2023). Obstacle avoidance control algorithm of self-driving electric vehicle based on DRL. *Applied and Computational Engineering*, *4*(1), 541–547. DOI: 10.54254/2755-2721/4/2023321

Xiong, H., Wang, Z., Wu, G., & Pan, Y. (2022). Design and implementation of digital twin-assisted simulation method for autonomous vehicle in car-following scenario. *Journal of Sensors*, *2022*, 1–12. DOI: 10.1155/2022/4879490

Yoon, K., Choi, J., & Huh, K. (2023). Adaptive decentralized sensor fusion for autonomous vehicle: Estimating the position of surrounding vehicles. *IEEE Access : Practical Innovations, Open Solutions*, *11*, 90999–91008. DOI: 10.1109/ACCESS.2023.3308152

Yu, J., & Mei, G. (2025). V2X fusion communication framework based on VANETS collaborative autonomous driving. *Transactions on Emerging Telecommunications Technologies*, *36*(10), e70263. Advance online publication. DOI: 10.1002/ett.70263

Yun, H., & Park, D. (2021). Virtualization of self-driving algorithms by interoperating embedded controllers on a game engine for a digital twining autonomous vehicle. *Electronics (Basel)*, *10*(17), 2102. DOI: 10.3390/electronics10172102

Zöldy, M., Szalay, Z., & Tihanyi, V. (2020). Challenges in homologation process of vehicles with Artificial Intelligence. *Transport*, *35*(4), 435–446. DOI: 10.3846/transport.2020.12904

KEY TERMS AND DEFINITIONS

Autonomous Vehicle (AV): A self-driving vehicle equipped with sensors, control algorithms, and AI systems capable of navigating and operating without human intervention.

Crash Scenario Simulation: A virtual testing method that models vehicle collisions to study deformation patterns, energy absorption, and passenger safety outcomes.

Data Fidelity: The degree to which simulated or virtual data accurately reflects real-world conditions, ensuring reliability in safety validation results.

Digital Twin (DT): A virtual replica of a physical system that continuously synchronizes real-time data to simulate, analyze, and predict the system's performance and behavior.

Edge Computing: A distributed computing paradigm that processes data closer to the source such as the vehicle to reduce latency and enable real-time DT synchronization.

Explainable AI (XAI): A framework that makes AI-driven decisions interpretable and transparent, allowing engineers and regulators to understand how safety actions are determined.

Federated Safety Validation: A decentralized validation approach that allows multiple organizations to collaboratively train and test models without sharing raw or proprietary data.

ISO 26262: An international standard for the functional safety of electrical and electronic systems in road vehicles, defining Automotive Safety Integrity Levels (ASILs).

Multi-Physics Simulation: The integrated modeling of mechanical, thermal, fluidic, and electrical phenomena to replicate complex real-world vehicle interactions during crashes.

Quantum-Enabled Digital Twin: A next-generation DT framework that leverages quantum computing to perform ultra-fast, high-precision simulations for complex crash and safety analyses.

Reinforcement Learning (RL): An AI technique where agents learn optimal actions by receiving rewards or penalties through interactions within simulated environments.

Safety of the Intended Functionality (SOTIF): A standard that addresses safety risks arising from performance limitations or misuse of correctly functioning systems.

Safety Validation: The process of verifying that vehicle systems perform safely and reliably under all expected and edge-case conditions, ensuring compliance with safety standards.

Vehicle-in-the-Loop (ViL): A hybrid testing method where a physical vehicle interacts with a simulated environment to validate safety systems in near-real conditions.

Chapter 5
Digital Twin-Driven Innovation in Autonomous Vehicle Systems Through Modelling, Prototyping, and Lifecycle Optimization

Mahfjur Rahman
http://orcid.org/0000-0002-3245-8767
American International University-Bangladesh, Bangladesh

Kazi Tanvir
http://orcid.org/0009-0001-0612-6101
American International University-Bangladesh, Bangladesh

Mirza Asif Mahmud
http://orcid.org/0009-0006-6947-4003
American International University-Bangladesh, Bangladesh

Zishan Ahmed Onik
American International University-Bangladesh, Bangladesh

Noboranjan Dey
http://orcid.org/0009-0007-1991-9198
American International University-Bangladesh, Bangladesh

Dipta Gomes
http://orcid.org/0000-0003-3019-6051
American International University-Bangladesh, Bangladesh

ABSTRACT

This chapter explores the integration of Digital Twin (DT) technology in Autonomous Vehicles (AVs), emphasizing its role in enhancing vehicle safety, performance, and operational efficiency. Digital Twins create dynamic, real-time virtual models that replicate the physical state of AVs, enabling continuous monitoring, predictive maintenance, and system optimization. By facilitating predictive analytics and simulating real-world driving scenarios, Digital Twins bridge the gap between physical systems and simulations, improving safety validation and decision-making accuracy. Despite significant benefits, challenges remain, including data synchronization, computational demands, and security concerns. Future research should focus on enhancing scalability, integrating with vehicle-to-everything (V2X)

DOI: 10.4018/979-8-3373-7785-8.ch005

systems, and exploring AI-driven optimization techniques. This chapter highlights the transformative potential of Digital Twins in the development and lifecycle management of AVs, offering a comprehensive understanding of their current and future impact on autonomous mobility.

1. INTRODUCTION

The rapid development of autonomous vehicles (AVs) has introduced transformative possibilities in transportation, enabling vehicles to perceive their surroundings, interpret complex driving conditions, and operate with reduced human involvement. While these advancements have expanded the potential of intelligent mobility, the deployment of AVs in real-world environments remains constrained by uncertainties such as unpredictable traffic patterns, varying weather conditions, infrastructure limitations, and sensor-system failures. Addressing these concerns requires rigorous testing, continuous performance monitoring, and adaptive control mechanisms beyond conventional modelling and simulation. In this context, Digital Twin (DT) technology has emerged as a powerful framework to enhance the safety, reliability, and operational efficiency of autonomous vehicles.

A Digital Twin is a virtual representation of a physical vehicle that dynamically reflects its real-time behaviour, surroundings, and system health conditions. This bi-directional coupling enables seamless synchronization between physical and virtual states, facilitating predictive analysis, autonomous decision validation, fault detection, performance optimization, and safe virtual experimentation. Compared to traditional simulation platforms that rely on predefined scenarios, Digital Twins continuously evolve and respond to new environmental and operational conditions. This real-time adaptability makes DT technology particularly well suited for AV development, where decision-making accuracy and safety robustness are essential.

However, conventional AV simulation approaches often fall short of capturing the complexity of real-world driving. Pre-collected datasets cannot anticipate every safety-critical situation. Real-world testing is both costly and constrained by safety considerations. Furthermore, transferring algorithms tested in simulation directly into physical AVs frequently reveals performance gaps due to mismatches in perception, dynamics, and sensor noise modelling. Digital Twin frameworks offer a solution by providing a closed real-to-virtual feedback loop where autonomy algorithms can be refined continuously. By evaluating decisions in a virtual environment before applying them on the physical vehicle, DT systems support sim-to-real and real-to-sim consistency, reducing deployment uncertainty and improving reliability. This capability is highlighted in recent work by Samak et al., who developed an integrated Digital Twin ecosystem enabling unified autonomy validation across multiple physical vehicle platforms and operational design domains (Samak, Samak, and Krovi 2024a).

The integration of Digital Twins into AV systems presents several notable benefits. First, DT-enabled predictive maintenance enhances safety and reduces operational costs by identifying anomalies before mechanical failure occurs. Second, Digital Twins enable high-fidelity simulation and verification, allowing edge-case scenarios to be tested without risk to human or system safety. Third, DT frameworks can facilitate cooperative driving, where Digital Twins of multiple vehicles exchange data to coordinate decision-making in real time. Fourth, Digital Twin systems support adaptive learning, enabling autonomous driving models to evolve based on continuous data streams. Research by (Wang et al. 2024) demonstrated that Digital Twins substantially improve vehicle condition monitoring and maintenance planning, which is crucial for long-term autonomous deployment.

Despite these promising benefits, integrating Digital Twin frameworks into AVs raises challenges. Real-time data synchronization requires robust communication architectures, often based on 5G or edge-cloud fusion networks. Ensuring the security and privacy of shared operational data is essential to prevent malicious interference. Additionally, high-fidelity virtual models demand significant computational resources, particularly when simulating multi-agent or city-scale systems. Another challenge lies in maintaining model fidelity over time; as the physical vehicle or environment changes, the Digital Twin must be recalibrated to avoid model drift. (He, Chen, and Shi 2024) highlight the importance of scalable simulation platforms that maintain both physical accuracy and perceptual realism.

A major challenge concerns the validation and verification (V&V) of Digital Twin-augmented AV systems. The safety of autonomous driving depends heavily on the reliability and explainability of algorithmic decisions. If a Digital Twin is used to justify safety-critical decisions, then regulatory authorities must be able to trace how the model produced those decisions. The (Pikner et al. 2024) study on DT-based safety validation demonstrates that Digital Twins can significantly improve AV testing efficiency, yet also warns that unverified modelling assumptions may introduce new risks. Additionally, since Digital Twins may support connected fleet-level coordination, distributed decision failures can propagate rapidly across multiple vehicles. This raises critical ethical and legal considerations around accountability and liability in complex, data-driven transport ecosystems. (Nonomura et al. 2025) demonstrated the use of Digital Twins for coordinating autonomous vehicle sharing fleets, where operational decisions depend on shared data between multiple Digital Twin instances. Such applications show the potential of DTs to support large-scale intelligent transportation networks. However, they also highlight the need for clear governance frameworks defining data exchange policies, system responsibilities, fault attribution, and privacy preservation.

The primary objective of this manuscript is to examine Digital Twin approaches in autonomous vehicles from both technical and socio-regulatory perspectives. The volume will explore Digital Twin system architectures, real-time synchronization frameworks, simulation platforms, sensor modelling techniques, and multi-scale vehicle validation workflows. The volume will also highlight emerging developments in Digital Twin-assisted perception, localization, motion planning, and cooperative decision-making. By combining artificial intelligence, cyber-physical systems engineering, transportation science, and regulatory policy, this book aims to provide a comprehensive foundation for researchers, practitioners, and policymakers.

The chapter will also address challenges and future opportunities. These include developing scalable DT models that remain accurate under long-term operation, integrating Digital Twins with vehicle-to-everything (V2X) communication systems, designing energy-efficient computational architectures, and aligning DT-driven decision-making with ethical and legal accountability principles. Public trust is central to AV deployment. Therefore, transparent Digital Twin systems that provide explainable and traceable decision reasoning are essential for increasing public confidence.

As autonomous mobility continues to advance, Digital Twin frameworks will play a decisive role in ensuring safe deployment and operational resilience. By enabling continuous testing, adaptive learning, predictive insights, and coordinated intelligence, Digital Twin technologies offer a path forward toward trustworthy and sustainable autonomous vehicle ecosystems. This volume will provide a critical reference for understanding these innovations and shaping future research, deployment strategies, and regulatory standards in autonomous transportation.

2. FUNDAMENTALS OF DIGITAL TWINS IN THE CONTEXT OF AUTONOMOUS VEHICLES

2.1. Defining Digital Twins in the Context of Autonomous Vehicles

Digital Twin (DT) technology refers to the creation of a continuously synchronized virtual representation of a physical system, enabling real-time monitoring, simulation, analysis, and optimization across the system lifecycle. Unlike static digital models, DTs evolve dynamically by integrating live data streams from sensors, communication networks, and computational intelligence (Wu et al. 2023; Yao et al. 2023). Recent scholarly efforts emphasize that a DT must incorporate bidirectional data exchange, model adaptability, and decision-support capability to qualify as a true digital twin rather than a conventional simulation (Liu et al. 2024; Weingram et al. 2025).

In the context of autonomous vehicles (AVs), DTs act as cyber-physical mirrors of vehicles, infrastructure, and traffic ecosystems, enabling continuous alignment between the physical vehicle state and its virtual counterpart (Ali et al. 2023; Chai et al. 2024). This alignment is critical for addressing the inherent complexity of AV systems, which must operate under uncertain environments, heterogeneous traffic conditions, and strict safety constraints. Digital twins support perception validation, decision-making evaluation, and system-level optimization by allowing AV developers to explore rare and hazardous scenarios that are impractical or unsafe to test physically (Samak et al. 2024a; Samak et al., 2024b).

A key distinction between traditional simulation models and DTs lies in temporal synchronization and lifecycle integration. Traditional simulations are typically offline, scenario-specific, and disconnected from real-world operation, whereas DTs maintain persistent synchronization with physical assets throughout design, deployment, and operation phases (Weingram et al. 2025; Wu et al. 2023). Moreover, DTs increasingly integrate artificial intelligence (AI) and machine learning (ML) to enable predictive and prescriptive capabilities, such as anticipating component degradation or optimizing vehicle routing in real time (Babaei et al. 2025; Sajadieh and Noh 2025).

2.2. Key Components of a Digital Twin Architecture

A Digital Twin architecture for autonomous vehicles is generally composed of three tightly coupled components: the physical system, the virtual model, and the data communication loop (Liu et al. 2024; Wu et al. 2023). The physical system includes the autonomous vehicle itself, embedded sensors, actuators, and surrounding infrastructure elements such as roadside units (RSUs) and traffic signals (Wang et al. 2024; Wu et al. 2023).

The virtual model represents a multi-domain abstraction of the physical system, incorporating vehicle dynamics, perception modules, control algorithms, traffic interactions, and environmental conditions. Depending on application requirements, these models may range from physics-based representations to data-driven or hybrid AI-enhanced models (Babaei et al. 2025; Weingram et al. 2025). Recent research highlights the growing role of distributed and low-latency virtual models that enable scalable DT deployment for connected and autonomous vehicles (Zapata et al. 2025).

The data communication loop ensures continuous bidirectional information flow between the physical and virtual domains. This loop is enabled by heterogeneous sensing technologies (LiDAR, radar, cameras, GPS), vehicle-to-everything (V2X) communication, edge computing, and cloud-based analytics platforms (Wu et al. 2023, 2025). Real-time synchronization allows DTs to perform live monitoring, anomaly detection, and feedback-driven optimization, which are essential for safety-critical AV operations (Nonomura et al. 2025; Wang et al. 2024).

2.3. Types of Digital Twins for Autonomous Vehicles

Digital twins for AV applications can be classified based on model fidelity and functional scope. High-fidelity DTs aim to capture detailed physical and behavioral characteristics of vehicles and environments, enabling accurate prediction and validation of autonomous driving functions (Samak et al. 2024b; Zapata et al. 2025). In contrast, low-fidelity DTs prioritize computational efficiency and scalability, making them suitable for large-scale traffic analysis and strategic decision-making (Wu et al. 2025).

From a functional perspective, functional digital twins focus on software-centric aspects such as perception, localization, planning, and control algorithms, whereas structural digital twins emphasize physical components, including vehicle hardware, sensors, and infrastructure assets (Ali et al. 2023; Chai et al. 2024). Hybrid DT approaches that integrate both functional and structural dimensions are increasingly adopted to support end-to-end AV validation and lifecycle optimization (Babaei et al. 2025; Liu et al. 2024).

2.4. Frameworks for Integrating Digital Twins with AV Systems

Digital twin integration frameworks for AVs are commonly grounded in cyber-physical system (CPS) architectures, where sensing, computation, communication, and control are tightly interconnected (Wu et al. 2023, 2025) as presented by Figure 1. These frameworks enable seamless interaction between vehicles, infrastructure, and cloud services, supporting real-time decision-making and adaptive system behavior (Wang et al. 2024; Wu et al. 2025).

Recent studies propose scalable DT frameworks (Figure 2) that integrate V2X communication, distributed computing, and AI-driven analytics to address interoperability challenges in heterogeneous AV ecosystems (Wu et al. 2025; Zapata et al. 2025). Interoperability remains a critical challenge due to diverse data formats, proprietary platforms, and varying communication standards. Solutions include standardized data schemas, modular architectures, and edge-cloud coordination mechanisms (Guinea-Cabrera and Holgado-Terriza 2024; Hasan and Crawford 2025) (Guinea-Cabrera & Holgado-Terriza, 2024; Hasan & Crawford, 2025). A comparison among different Digital Twin Models for AV Applications has been presented in Table 1.

Figure 1. Digital twin architecture for autonomous vehicles

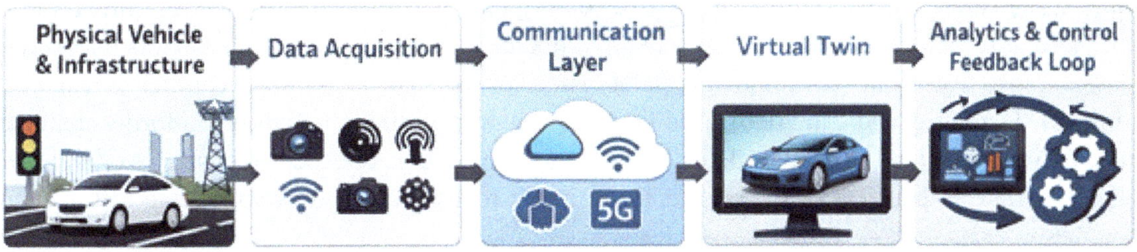

Figure 2. Framework for integration of DTs with AV systems

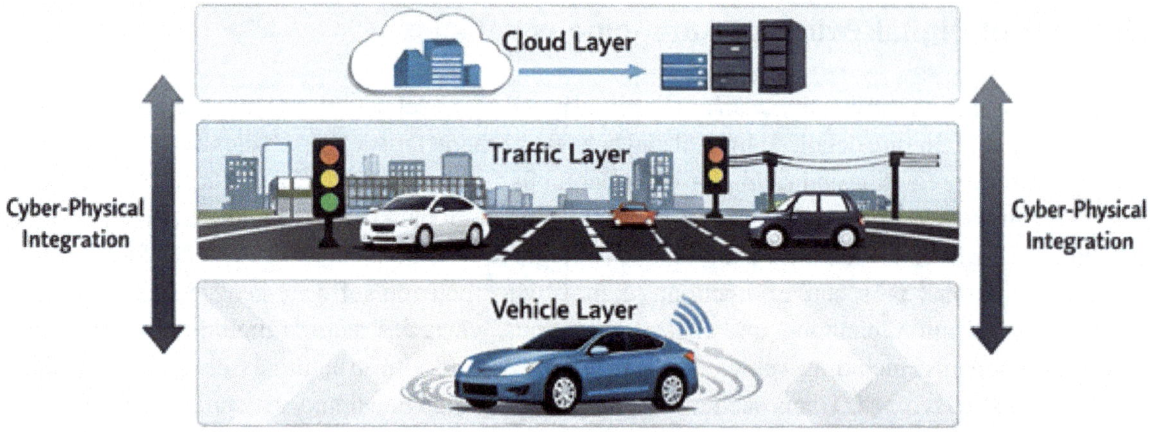

Table 1. Comparison of different digital twin models for AV applications

Digital Twin Type	Key Characteristics	AV Application Examples
High-fidelity DT	Physics-based, real-time synchronization (Samak et al. 2024a)	Safety validation, sim-to-real transfer
Low-fidelity DT	Computationally efficient, scalable (Wu et al. 2025)	Traffic optimization, planning
Functional DT	Software and algorithm-centric (Chai et al. 2024)	Perception and decision testing
Structural DT	Hardware and asset-centric (Ali et al. 2023)	Sensor health, vehicle maintenance
Hybrid AI-DT	Data-driven + physics-based (Babaei et al. 2025; Weingram et al. 2025)	End-to-end AV lifecycle support

3. MODELLING AND SIMULATION ENVIRONMENTS FOR AV DIGITAL TWINS

3.1. Role of Simulation in Autonomous Vehicle Development

Simulation has been recognized as a vital part of AV development, allowing the in-depth testing of driving systems in controlled virtual spaces. According to recent studies in literature, simulation is a faster, more repeatable and cost-effective way for validating AV algorithms and behaviors than relying on physical road tests alone (constrained by safety issues or costs and the not replicability of real traffic conditions) (Hardaway and Cai 2026). Additionally, however, virtual simulation platforms enable researchers to consider hard-to-model edge cases and rare events (e.g., unexpected obstacles or inclement weather) that are impractical or risky to replicate in the real world, thereby enhancing test coverage

(Zhao et al. 2024). These are the reasons why simulation is invaluable in early-stage development, since multiple runs and parameter variation can be executed without danger to human drivers or test vehicles.

Even with these benefits, tests in the real world alone cannot practically be comprised of the complete range of traffic scenarios needed to validate adequately an autonomous system. Real world testing requires substantial amount of time and resources to collect large amounts of mileage in diverse conditions, and still may not cover essential corner cases that can be forced by simulations (Hu et al. 2023). As a result, simulation environments have been incorporated into AV development pipelines to augment real-world testing, providing researchers with an opportunity to test perception, planning and control algorithms systematically and at scale.

An example of the AV simulation platform connected to digital twin is shown in Figure 3. The figure shows a closed-loop architecture comprising three key layers: (i) the physical layer, in which actual vehicles, sensors, and infrastructure generate operating data; (ii) the data and synchronization layer where data ingestion, storage and real- time calibration of the digital twins occurs; and (iii) the virtual layer where digital twin models as well as latterly simulation engines run scenarios to validate system performance and create analytical insights. Such a tight and continuous interaction between the physical and virtual world provides for precise modelling, large scale experimentation, and many cycles of improvement to the system during its entire lifecycle development.

Figure 3. Example of an AV simulation platform with digital twin integration

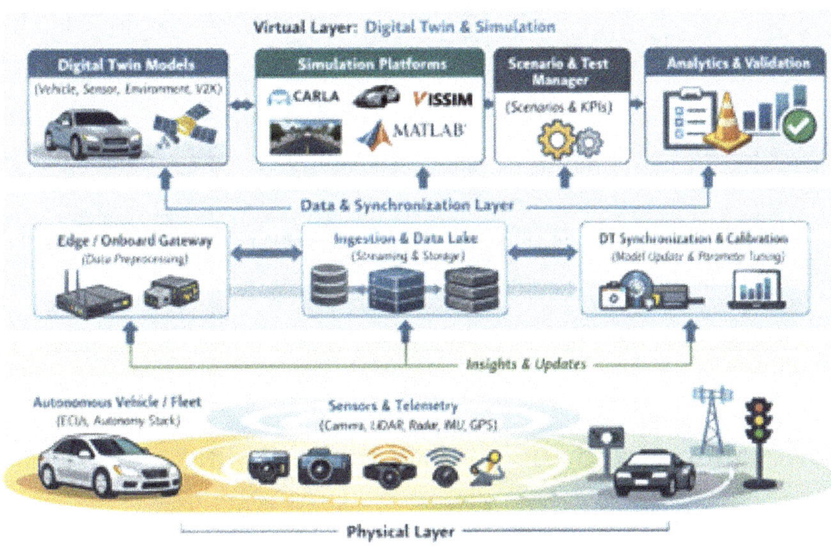

Table 2. Comparison of simulation tools for AV testing

Simulation Tool	Simulation Type	Key Features	Strengths	Limitations	Typical Use Cases
CARLA	High-fidelity 3D AV simulator	Realistic urban environments, configurable sensors (LiDAR, radar, cameras), weather and traffic control	Open-source, strong perception testing support, realistic sensor simulation	Requires high computational resources; limited large-scale traffic modeling	Perception validation, sensor testing, scenario-based AV experiments
SUMO (Simulation of Urban Mobility)	Microscopic traffic simulator	Large-scale traffic flow modeling, vehicle routing, V2X support, real-time traffic control integration	Efficient for city-scale simulations, lightweight and scalable	Limited sensor-level and 3D visualization realism	Traffic flow studies, route planning, V2X network evaluation
PTV VISSIM	Microscopic multi-modal traffic simulator	Detailed traffic behavior modeling, signal control, public transport modeling, integration with AV behavior modules	High accuracy for traffic operations and infrastructure studies	Commercial software; limited native sensor simulation	Mixed traffic analysis, infrastructure planning, AV traffic impact studies
MATLAB/Simulink (Automated Driving Toolbox)	Algorithm and system-level simulation	Model-based design, perception and control algorithm development, scenario simulation, hardware-in-the-loop (HIL) support	Strong control and algorithm prototyping capabilities, seamless integration with engineering workflows	Requires additional tools for high-fidelity 3D visualization	Algorithm design, control system testing, SIL/HIL validation
NVIDIA DRIVE Sim	High-fidelity physics-based AV simulator	Photorealistic rendering, AI training datasets, sensor-accurate simulation, GPU-accelerated processing	Extremely realistic sensor modeling and large-scale AI training support	High hardware requirements and enterprise-level setup	Deep-learning training, sensor validation, high-fidelity AV safety testing

3.2. Simulation Platforms and Tools for AV Digital Twins

A variety of simulation platforms have been developed to support autonomous vehicle research by modelling both vehicle behaviour and environmental interactions. Among these, CARLA, MATLAB/ Simulink, and co-simulation frameworks represent core tools used widely across the AV community.

CARLA (Car Learning to Act) is an open-source simulator for autonomous driving built on top of the Unreal Engine and designed specifically for training perception and control systems. It supports highly detailed urban environments, customizable sensor suites (RADAR, LiDAR, cameras), and diverse traffic actors for reproducible testing with a broad variety of driving scenarios in one constant virtual world (Gorza, Saly, and Csikor 2025). Due to the high fidelity of CARLA in simulating sensor streams and traffic behaviours as well as their continuous development, it suits for validating perception algorithms and decision-making framework in a way that would otherwise be costly or unsafe if verified physically.

MATLAB/Simulink is one of the most widely used platforms to model and simulate control system engineering issues including vehicle dynamics. The system's model-based design environment enables fast prototyping and validation of AV subsystems, including collision avoidance, trajectory planning and dynamic response models in a virtual setting. Newer work shows how Simulink based models can be used to study the collision safety performance or other vehicle behaviours in autonomous driving scenarios (Yeğin 2025).

In addition to standalone tools, co-simulation and hybrid environments are actively employed for the integration of multiple simulators with higher fidelity. For instance, these types of frameworks that integrate CARLA with traffic micro simulators like SUMO or VISSIM permits simulating realistic traffic flows and still maintaining high-¬fidelity vehicle dynamics and perception data; allowing for a full-range of testing autonomous behaviours in multi agent environments (Cantas and Guvenc 2023). Leveraged with digital twin approaches, these unified tools enable bi-directional flow of data between simulated and physical worlds, ultimately enhancing not solely the test coverage, but also the trustworthiness of results utilized to certify AV development and lifecycle assessment. A comparison of simulation tools for AV Testing has been presented in Table 2.

3.3. Multi Domain Simulations: AVs, Traffic Systems, and Environment Interactions

Multi domain simulation is instrumental to the progress of AV research, which involves not only inter-vehicle interactions but also vehicle-to-infrastructure and vehicle-to-environment interactions. These simulations are not limited to predicting isolated behaviour of single vehicles; they simulate complex interactions between vehicles, vehicle to vehicle (V2V) communication exchanges and vehicle to-infrastructure (V2I) messaging and random weather or road conditions. Studies in connected and autonomous vehicles (CAV) also highlight that the multi domain simulation frameworks are instrumental to predict the behaviours of AVs on mixed traffics, where communication between vehicles becomes a key enabling factor towards situation awareness and making decisions under dynamic operating conditions (Zhang et al. 2025).

V2V communication allows vehicles in proximity to exchange critical information, such as speed, position and proposed manoeuvres to promote cooperative driving and reduce collision probability. V2I communication also takes this one step further by enabling AVs to communicate with roadside infrastructure (eg traffic lights, signal phase and timing controllers) for real-time information either of the signal timing or congestion more effectively manage traffic flow and throughput (Cui, Liu, and Nallanathan 2020). The combined V2V and V2I technologies provide the foundation for connected vehicle systems that have been shown to impact AV performance in real traffic simulations with groups of vehicles interacting through their ability to communicate driving intentions which is impossible to test using single actors.

Realistic Multi domain Simulations also couple sophisticated traffic models, which consider the interaction of multiple agents in mixed traffic. For example, microscopic traffic simulation tools like SUMO, VISSIM and CA based models can reproduce the heterogeneous traffic situations where human driven vehicles and AVs share with distinct control logic and communication limitations. These tools enable examination of traffic performance, safety and control strategies under different heterogeneous traffic densities and mixed behavior patterns (Hou 2023). We note that studies within such integrated frameworks show that multi domain simulation is crucial to evaluate not only the safety gains due to AV and CAV penetration, but also to analyse emergent behaviour like shockwave formation, congestion propagation, and cooperative platooning effects.

Both vehicle perception and networked communication performance are indeed affected by environmental conditions in the simulation. State-of-art simulation studies consider the weather effects, including rain and sensor failure, of various environmental conditions on the V2V reliability to the overall traffic system performance (Zhang et al. 2025). Due to the simulation of weather effects and uncertainties in communication in cities, they allow an evaluation regarding how traffic efficiency and safety will change, a behaviour that would not be possible to observe when only testing ideal or single vehicles. Thus, Multi DEXs integrating traffic dynamics with connectivity protocols as well as environmental variations become the cornerstone for yielding usable AV systems that are not only safe and optimized but also capable of reliably functioning in real world scenarios.

3.4. Real-time Data Integration and Calibration

DTs are essentially based on real-world data which serve to optimize simulation accuracy and guarantee that the virtual models accurately reflect the condition of their physical twins. For AVs, this involves persistently gathering and processing the data from sensors of a vehicle (e.g., LiDARs, radars, cameras, IMUs or GNSS), integrating these information streams in the DT to update simulation parameters in real-time. Establishing this feedback loop is essential to prevent static models from accounting for changes in vehicle states, road conditions and the dynamic of other road users alone (Kušić, Schumann, and Ivanjko 2023).

By combining data from sensors and positioning system, DTs can create new vehicle pose (position and orientation) estimation and environmental relations that directly compare/anchor the virtual model output. For instance, if the real-time GPS and IMU data show that there is a discrepancy about observed motion of vehicle aligned with the simulation, then DT should adapt its internal parameter to make future prediction more accordant with measured action. The gradual calibration between the two serves to reduce the discrepancy between coordinated predictions and actual performance, thus enhancing effectiveness (i.e., reliability and decision-making) of AV guidance systems (Gu et al. 2026).

Other than the vehicle pose and kinematics, environmental inputs – including current traffic flows or weather conditions or the road condition that are also important. DT frameworks, such as those which take into consideration these external data streams, have an ability to mimic the effect of varying environmental conditions on both sensor perception and vehicle dynamics, and thus adjust simulation behavior. The ability to fuse heterogeneous data sources in real time from sensors and elements of infrastructure DTs means they are not simply static models but inherently adaptive models that have the potential to self-learn over time, based on their physical system which is important for empirical AV algorithms testing on realistic dynamic conditions (Gao et al. 2024).

4. LIFE-CYCLE MANAGEMENT OF AUTONOMOUS VEHICLES USING DIGITAL TWINS

4.1. Concept of Lifecycle Management in Avs

The lifecycle management of Autonomous Vehicles (AVs) include the phases a vehicle goes through from start to finish. These processes involve different steps, from the design to development and deployment on service, followed by operation lifecycle and disposal, which are critical to manage to achieve a successful level of sustainability while ensuring safety and cost effectiveness.

1. **Design:** This is the early phase of AV lifecycle, during which vehicle architecture is designed and its concept is formed. Models and simulations such as Digital Twins (DTs) exercise an important function during this phase in predicting the real-world behaviour of the AV. DTs facilitate the process of developing a vehicle design and discovering potential design errors from occurring late in the product life-cycle, which can be costly to modify (Obaid et al. 2023a).
2. **Development:** It follows prototyping, test and refinements in response to real-world feedback. Digital Twin technology remains the backbone and leverages knowledge from real-time data and simulation input to ensure that the AV will be able to fulfil operational needs." This stage is vital for observing performance, safety and efficiency related problems (Mohd Nor et al. 2026).
3. **Deployment:** A/Vs that are ready to be pushed (deployed) into service. Lifecycle management in this phase involves overseeing the integration of the vehicle into existing infrastructure and its performance out on the road. DTs allow monitoring in real time to be certain that the operational parameters are at a proper level and any abnormality is corrected automatically (Tiwari & Farag 2025).
4. **Operation:** The AV operation means the daily use of an AV on public roads. During this phase, it is essential to monitor in DTs real time (to ensure vehicle performance and defect detection), as well for maintenance insights. Operation is commonly the longest and most resource-consuming phase, but longer-term maintenance of system health and performance.
5. **Retirement:** This is the last phase of process and includes decommissioning the AV once its useful life has expired. Its chassis is recycled, and anything that can still be used for other purposes is repurposed. DTs help on the decision support for decommissioning, to be performed in a sustainable and cost-effective manner (Gu et al. 2026).

The proper usage and maintenance of AV is of great importance to the sustainability and cost effectiveness of AVs life cycle. Without good lifecycle management, AVs can become more expensive and have worse environmental outcomes through resource inefficiency and waste. Digital Twin technology can be implemented to streamline the processing of each stage, while predictive maintenance will increase efficiency and reduce energy consumption in all processes. Moreover, predicting the vehicle end-of-life contributes scales to improving the recycling efficiency and reducing its environmental impact (Martinez, Campelo, and Ribeiro 2025).

Figure 4 illustrates the Digital Twin–enabled lifecycle of autonomous vehicles, showing how real-time data feedback supports virtual design, development, deployment, operation, and sustainable retirement through continuous monitoring and optimization.

Figure 4. Digital twin-based lifecycle management framework for AVs

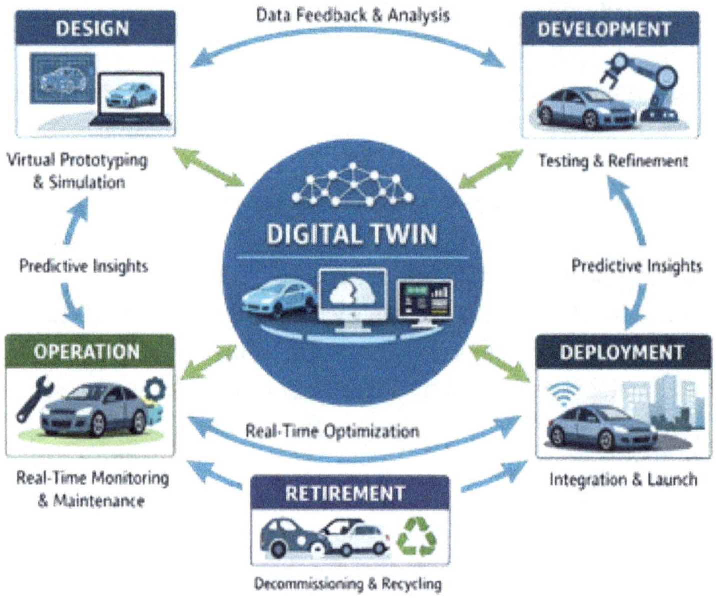

Table 3 compares system lifecycle phases with and without Digital Twin integration, highlighting how Digital Twins enhance efficiency through virtual simulation, real-time monitoring, proactive maintenance, and sustainable end-of-life management, compared with traditional, reactive approaches.

Table 3. Comparison of lifecycle phases with and without digital twin integration

Lifecycle Phase	With Digital Twin	Without Digital Twin
Design	Virtual simulations and predictive analysis	Traditional prototyping with limited predictive capabilities
Development	Iterative testing and real-time data analysis	Prototyping with limited feedback from real-world operations
Deployment	Seamless integration and monitoring	Difficulty in integration and post-deployment issues
Operation	Real-time health monitoring and maintenance	Reactive maintenance and repairs
Retirement	Optimized decommissioning with sustainability focus	Wasteful end-of-life without accurate data

4.2. Role of Digital Twins in AV Lifecycle Management

They are also changing how AVs are maintained throughout their lifecycle, thanks to the development of Digital Twins (DTs). By connecting physical vehicles to virtual models with real-time data, DTs enable ongoing supervision and control over the lifecycle of an AV. Below are the basic DT responsibilities in AV lifecycle management:

1. **Real-time monitoring and maintenance:** being able to monitor the car's health, performance and environment in real time through a digital twin of the AV. DTs can anticipate failures that may occur in the future by using sensors to regularly upload data into a digital model, and reduce the possibility of equipment failure in operation (Obaid et al. 2023b).
2. **Predictive Analytics for Fault Detection and Preventative Maintenance:** One of the greatest advantages of DTs is predicting future failures. Through sensors input and analyzing data trends, DTs leverage predictive analytics to identify the car portion in which an imminent failure is expected. Routine maintenance work can be scheduled around this and potentially avoid expensive damage and downtime (Mohd Nor et al. 2026).
3. **Data-Insights-Based Decision of Disposal and Recycle of Vehicle Dismantling:** With the mileage and failure information, as data interface, DT can decide which part of AV can be recycled or salvaged after the end of life. This evidence-supported model is designed to make the retirement phase safe, cost-effective and environmentally sustainable (Tiwari & Farag 2025).

Table 4 presents predictive maintenance strategies enabled by Digital Twin technology for autonomous vehicles (AVs), showing how real-time data, continuous monitoring, and predictive analytics are used to anticipate component failures, optimize maintenance schedules, and enhance overall vehicle safety, reliability, and operational efficiency.

Table 4. Predictive maintenance strategies using digital twins for AVs

System	Digital Twin Application	Key Data	Benefit
Sensors	Fault prediction and calibration	Signal quality, environment	Improved perception accuracy
Battery	Health and degradation modeling	Voltage, temperature	Extended battery life
Powertrain	Performance monitoring	Speed, vibration	Reduced breakdowns
Brakes	Wear prediction	Pressure, heat	Enhanced safety
Software	Anomaly detection	Logs, latency	Higher system reliability

4.3. Case Studies of Lifecycle Management in AVs with Digital Twin Integration

There are some case studies proving the capability of applying Digital Twin in Lifecycle Management (LCM) for AV. These use cases provide a perspective of how such an integration enables better operational efficiency, lower cost and sustainability of AVs.

1. **Case Study 1:** A major American AV maker successfully employed Digital Twins in development. They reduced the number of design problems by 30% through utilizing the virtual prototypes and real-time vehicle data, enhancing efficiency in their development process and that in turn results in quick launch of vehicles (Gu et al. 2026).
2. **Case study 2:** A European Transportation organization used Digital Twins for the operational phase of their AV fleet. By utilizing predictive maintenance and real-time monitoring, the company decreased unplanned downtime by 40%, which led to significant savings in both overall service efficiency as well as maintenance cost (Obaid et al. 2023b).

3. **Case study 3:** A Chinese AV Company used Digital Twin -driven systems for end-of-life management. By examining the information gathered during the vehicle's life, it optimized its recycling process in a way that lead to a 25% waste decrease and increased sustainability (Tiwari & Farag 2025).

These use cases illustrate how using Digital Twin technology within the lifecycle management of Autonomous Vehicles can drive powerful efficiency gains for cost and sustainability at each stage.

5. COST AND TIME EFFICIENCY THROUGH DIGITAL TWIN-DRIVEN DEVELOPMENT

5.1. Cost-Effectiveness of Digital Twin-Driven AV Development

Digital twin-driven development significantly reduces research and development (R&D) costs in autonomous vehicle engineering by minimizing dependence on expensive physical prototyping and field testing. Virtual testing environments allow engineers to evaluate thousands of driving scenarios, including rare edge cases, at a fraction of the cost of real-world experimentation (Ali et al. 2023; Attaran and Celik 2023). Systematic reviews indicate that DT-enabled virtual prototyping can reduce development costs by enabling early fault detection, design optimization, and iterative refinement before hardware deployment (Hasan and Crawford 2025; Karunaratne et al. 2025).

By integrating simulation, real-time data, and AI-based analytics, DTs streamline the AV design process and improve resource utilization across the development pipeline (Alfaro-Viquez et al. 2025; Sajadieh and Noh 2025). The ability to reuse validated digital assets across vehicle variants and operational domains further amplifies cost savings (Guinea-Cabrera and Holgado-Terriza 2024).

5.2. Time Efficiency and Accelerated Time-to-Market

Digital twins accelerate time-to-market by enabling parallel development, continuous testing, and rapid validation of autonomous driving functions. Unlike traditional sequential development workflows, DT-based approaches support concurrent software and hardware evolution, significantly shortening validation cycles (Attaran and Celik 2023; Liu et al. 2024). Real-time synchronization between physical vehicles and their digital counterparts allows immediate feedback and faster convergence toward optimized designs (Wang et al. 2024; Wu et al. 2025).

Empirical studies demonstrate that DT-enabled validation frameworks facilitate faster regulatory compliance and deployment readiness by providing comprehensive safety evidence through virtual testing (Samak et al. 2024a, 2024b). Additionally, AI-enhanced DTs enable automated scenario generation and performance prediction, further reducing testing duration (Babaei et al. 2025; Sarker, Sarker, and Han 2025). A Time-to-Market Comparison has been provided in Table 5.

5.3. Cost Savings in Maintenance and Operations

Beyond development, DTs generate substantial cost savings during AV operation and maintenance by enabling predictive maintenance and real-time system health monitoring. Continuous data integration allows DTs to anticipate component wear, detect anomalies, and recommend preventive actions before failures occur (Haverkamp et al. 2025; Wu et al. 2023). Such predictive capabilities reduce unplanned downtime, maintenance expenses, and lifecycle costs (Hasan and Crawford 2025; Karunaratne et al. 2025).

Case studies in connected and cooperative AV systems show that DT-based operational optimization improves routing efficiency and service reliability, translating into measurable economic benefits (Nonomura et al. 2025; Zapata et al. 2025). Over the full lifecycle, DT-driven decision-making supports sustainable asset management and long-term cost optimization (Alfaro-Viquez et al. 2025; Haverkamp et al. 2025). A breakdown of cost savings in AV development via Digital Twin has been presented in Table 6.

Table 5. Time-to-market comparison: Traditional vs. digital twin-based development

Development Approach	Key Characteristics	Time Impact
Traditional testing	Sequential, physical-centric (Attaran and Celik 2023)	Longer cycles
DT-based development	Parallel, virtual-physical integration (Liu et al. 2024)	Accelerated delivery

Figure 5. Cost savings using digital twin integration in AV development

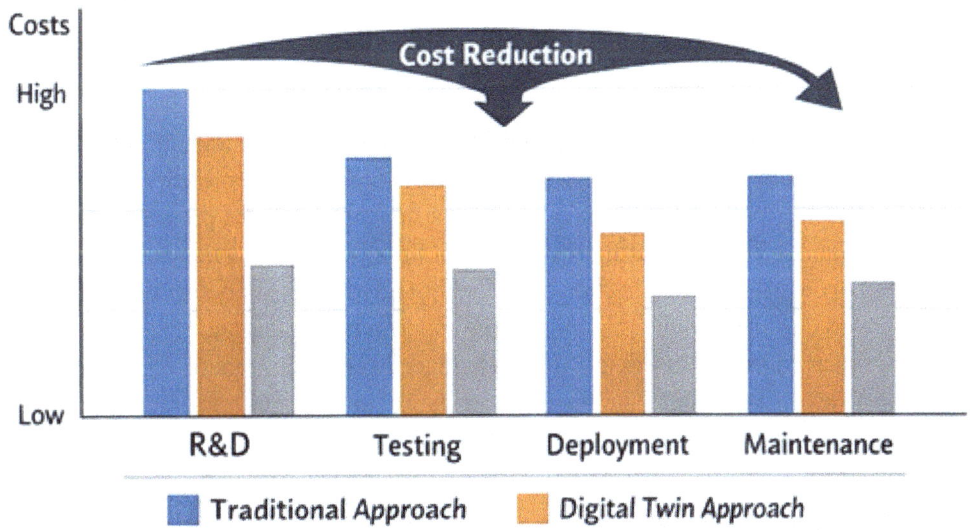

Table 6. Breakdown of cost savings in AV development via digital twins

Lifecycle Phase	Cost Saving Mechanism	Supporting Studies
Design & R&D	Virtual prototyping (Ali et al. 2023)	Reduced hardware cost
Testing & Validation	Scenario simulation (Samak et al. 2024b)	Fewer field tests
Operation	Predictive maintenance (Wu et al. 2023)	Lower downtime
Lifecycle Mgmt.	Data-driven optimization (Karunaratne et al. 2025)	Long-term savings

6. DATA ANALYTICS AND PREDICTIVE MODELLING IN AV DIGITAL TWINS

6.1. Data Collection and Integration in AV Digital Twins

Autonomous driving vehicles represent a class of such dynamic cyber-physical systems that offer diverse high-dimensional data streams over time. This data forms the basis of a Digital Twin ecosystem, as it allows for the synchronization of the physical vehicle and its digital twin counterparts (Kabir et al. 2025). In contrast to traditional simulation environments based on static or pre-recorded datasets, a digital twin holds state fidelity and predictive reliability through a continuous, real-time bidirectional flow of data exchange.

Mixture of data sources from an autonomous vehicle digital twin are also multi-modal by nature. Spatial and object-level environment perception systems over the AI-driven system include LiDAR, RADAR, RGB and infrared cameras, and ultrasonic sensors (Yeong, Panduru, and Walsh 2025). For instance, localization subsystems such as GPS, inertial measurement units, and simultaneous localization and mapping frameworks produce continuous positional updates. Vehicle telemetry also adds key operational parameters like battery health information, motor torque, brake pressure, steering angles, thermal performance, and drivetrain health data (Melders, Smigins, and Birkavs 2025). Environmental context such as weather conditions, road friction coefficients and traffic density from Vehicle-to-Vehicle and Vehicle-to-Infrastructure communication networks can provide contextual information to enhance the situational awareness of the digital twin. Moreover, data from event logs of edge cases or anomaly triggers and overrides provide additional insights for continuous model retraining.

The digital twin state can be mathematically represented as:

$$S_{DT}(t) = f\left(S_{phys}(t), E(t), T(t), \Theta\right)$$

where $S_{DT}(t)$ denotes the digital twin state at time t, $S_{phys}(t)$ represents the real-time physical vehicle state, $E(t)$ captures environmental variables, $T(t)$ denotes traffic context information, and Θ represents learned model parameters. This formulation emphasizes that the digital twin is not a static replica but an adaptive computational construct that evolves with continuous learning.

Figure 6. Data flow in autonomous vehicle digital twin systems

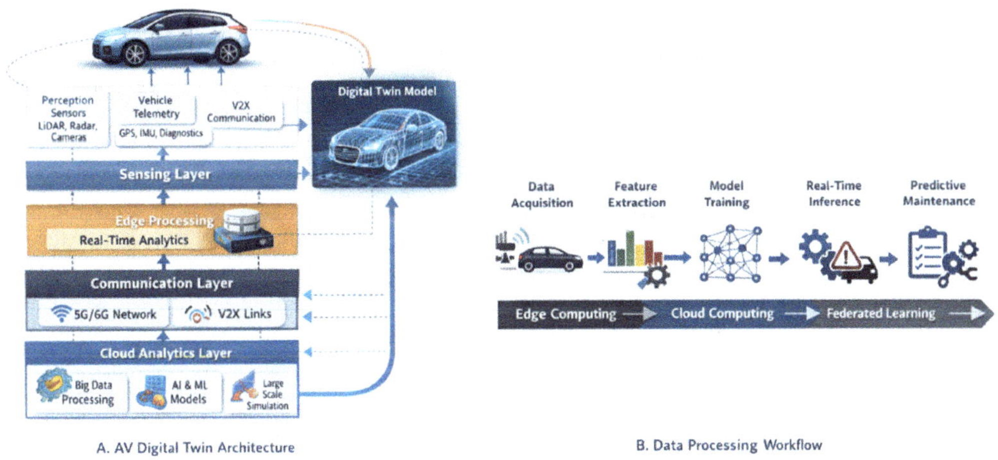

The architectural framework (Figure 6) usually consists of a raw data acquisition sensing layer, on-board edge computing layer that filters and performs latency sensitive inference, communications layer built upon 5G and the upcoming 6G networks, and cloud-based analytics layer that enables large-scale simulation and deep model training (Liu et al. 2026). By preserving this layered design, it functions at a computationally reasonable enterprise scale while being able to be replicated across millions of vehicles. A comparison of data analytics techniques in AV Digital Twins has been provided in Table 7.

Table 7. Comparison of data analytics techniques in AV digital twins

Technique	Core Principle	Strengths	Limitations	Typical Applications in AV Digital Twins
Linear Regression	Statistical modeling of linear relationships between variables	Simple, interpretable, low computational cost	Limited to linear patterns	Energy consumption prediction, basic performance modeling
Random Forest	Ensemble of decision trees using bagging	Robust to noise, handles high-dimensional data, strong classification performance	Less interpretable, higher memory usage	Fault classification, component degradation analysis
Support Vector Machine (SVM)	Margin-based classification with kernel trick	Effective in high-dimensional spaces, strong generalization	Computationally expensive for large datasets	Sensor anomaly detection, fault detection
Convolutional Neural Network (CNN)	Hierarchical feature extraction using convolutional layers	Excellent for image and spatial data	High computational demand	Camera-based perception validation, object detection consistency in DT
Long Short-Term Memory (LSTM)	Recurrent neural network for temporal dependencies	Strong for time-series forecasting	Training complexity, vanishing gradient risk (if poorly tuned)	Battery health monitoring, motor temperature prediction

continued on following page

Table 7. Continued

Technique	Core Principle	Strengths	Limitations	Typical Applications in AV Digital Twins
Graph Neural Network (GNN)	Learning on graph-structured relational data	Captures V2V and V2I interactions, models traffic dependencies	Graph construction complexity	Traffic-aware digital twin modeling, multi-vehicle coordination
Bayesian Networks	Probabilistic graphical modeling	Uncertainty quantification, interpretable	Requires prior knowledge, computationally intensive	Risk assessment, safety validation
Reinforcement Learning (RL)	Policy optimization through reward maximization	Adaptive decision-making, real-time optimization	Training instability, reward design complexity	Route optimization, energy-efficient driving strategies
Autoencoders	Unsupervised representation learning	Effective for anomaly detection	May struggle with highly dynamic environments	Sensor anomaly detection, predictive maintenance
Federated Learning	Distributed model training without centralized data sharing	Privacy-preserving, scalable across fleets	Communication overhead, aggregation complexity	Fleet-wide model updates, cross-vehicle learning

6.2. Predictive Modelling for Fault Detection and Performance Optimization

Predictive modelling raises the digital twin from an observation device to a smart anticipating system. Through the integration of machine learning and AI, autonomous vehicle digital twins can then be used to predict component wear-out, project system faults, optimize routing choices, and enhance energy efficiency while considering changing environmental and traffic conditions (Ali et al. 2023).

In practice, these models are widely used for component fault classification problems that can be cast in the supervised learning framework with historical failure data tagged with labels. The utilization of convolutional and recurrent neural networks to model the temporal degradation in sensor systems, which encompasses temporal anomaly detection, are explored (Chen and Lv 2022). Graph neural networks in traffic-aware digital twins facilitates relational modelling of vehicle-to-vehicle interactions and vehicle-to-infrastructure dependencies with the dynamic transportation networks. Reinforcement learning frameworks facilitate online policy improvement for adaptive routing and energy-aware driving strategies. By comprehensively embedding interconnected uncertainty, these probabilistic approaches based on abstraction provide fully developed uncertainty quantification which is important for safety validation in high stakes autonomous systems (Rahman et al. 2025).

Predictive failure probability can be expressed as:

$$P(Failure \mid X) = \sigma(W^T X + b)$$

where X represents extracted diagnostic features, W denotes model weights, b is a bias term, and σ is the logistic activation function. This probabilistic framework supports early fault detection and preventive maintenance scheduling.

Figure 7. Predictive analytics workflow for AV performance optimization

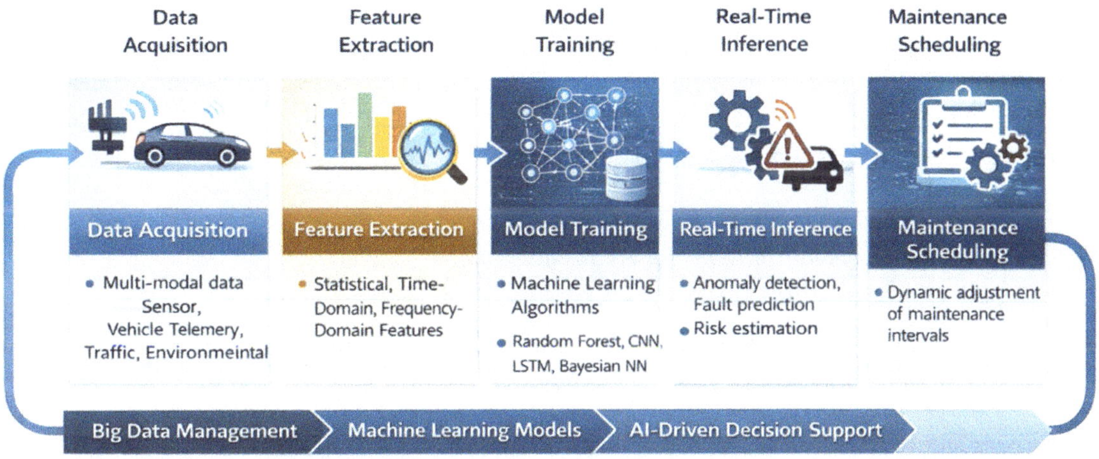

A typical predictive analytics workflow involves continuous data ingestion, feature extraction, model training using historical fleet data, deployment for real-time inference, and adaptive feedback to maintenance and control subsystems. The integration of reinforcement learning further enables dynamic optimization of vehicle behaviour, formally expressed as:

$$\pi^* = \arg\max_{\pi} \mathbb{E}\left[\sum_{t=0}^{T} \gamma^t R_t\right]$$

where π^* represents the optimal policy maximizing cumulative discounted rewards, γ is the discount factor, and R_t denotes the reward at time step t. Such formulations are particularly effective in optimizing energy consumption, platooning coordination, and congestion-aware route planning.

6.3. Big Data Challenges and Solutions for AV Digital Twins

Autonomous cars operate on a large scale and create terabytes of data per day. This scale to manage creates challenges around heterogeneity, storage scalability, latency sensitivity, cyber security and model drift. Operational safety in real-time requires inference in milliseconds and its long-term optimization demands cloud-based deep analytics over large datasets (Biswas and Wang 2023).

Hybrid edge-cloud architectures help perform these tasks efficiently and are being favoured to address these challenges. Low-latency inference itself and low-latency decision making at the edge means low communication overhead, which is a benefit of edge computing. High-performance, distributed training and large-scale simulations using cloud infrastructure. Moreover, by enabling decentralized model updates without transferring raw data, federated learning frameworks improve the preservation of privacy (Zhao et al. 2024). The global model aggregation can be represented as:

$$\theta_{global} = \sum_{i=1}^{N} \frac{n_i}{n} \theta_i$$

where θ_i denotes local model parameters from vehicle i, n_i represents the local dataset size, and nis the total dataset size across participating vehicles. This distributed paradigm strengthens data privacy and reduces bandwidth requirements.

Advanced stream-processing systems, distributed storage frameworks, AI-driven compression techniques, and blockchain-based secure logging mechanisms further enhance scalability and security. These solutions collectively enable resilient, real-time, and secure digital twin ecosystems for autonomous fleets (Amanatidis et al. 2025) has also been depicted in Table 8.

Table 8. Big data management solutions for AV digital twins

Solution Category	Technology / Approach	Core Function	Key Benefits for AV Digital Twins	Implementation Considerations
Distributed Storage Systems	Hadoop Distributed File System (HDFS), Apache Cassandra, MongoDB	Scalable storage of structured and unstructured data	Handles high-volume sensor logs and fleet-level datasets	Requires cluster management and fault tolerance mechanisms
Real-Time Stream Processing	Apache Kafka, Apache Spark Streaming, Apache Flink	Continuous ingestion and processing of streaming data	Enables low-latency analytics and real-time digital twin updates	Needs optimized pipeline design to avoid bottlenecks
Edge Computing Frameworks	NVIDIA Jetson, Edge AI accelerators	Local preprocessing and inference at vehicle level	Reduces latency and bandwidth usage	Limited onboard computational resources
Cloud Computing Infrastructure	AWS, Microsoft Azure, Google Cloud	Large-scale storage, distributed training, simulation support	Supports deep learning model training and global analytics	Operational cost and data governance policies
Federated Learning Architectures	Federated Averaging (FedAvg), decentralized aggregation models	Distributed model updates without sharing raw data	Privacy preservation and scalability across fleets	Communication overhead and model synchronization challenges
Data Compression Techniques	AI-based compression, feature selection, dimensionality reduction (PCA, Autoencoders)	Reduction of redundant data	Optimized storage and faster transmission	Potential loss of critical information if poorly configured
Data Lake Architecture	Unified storage for structured, semi-structured, and unstructured data	Centralized big data repository	Facilitates cross-domain analytics and long-term archival	Requires strong metadata management
Blockchain-Based Logging	Distributed ledger systems	Secure, tamper-resistant transaction recording	Enhances data integrity and auditability	Scalability and transaction latency concerns
AI-Based Data Filtering	Intelligent event detection and anomaly prioritization	Selective storage of high-value events	Reduces storage cost and improves analytical efficiency	Requires accurate threshold calibration
Cybersecurity Frameworks	Encryption protocols, Zero Trust Architecture	Secure communication and storage	Protects AV digital twin ecosystems from cyber threats	Must balance security with real-time performance

6.4. Strategic Implications and Research Directions

On the industry front, data-driven digital twins help in improving the operational overhead cost by utilizing predictive maintenance and reducing unplanned downtimes. In addition, they expedite design validation cycles via simulation-driven optimization and enable fleet-wide performance monitoring

(Kabashkin 2025). For the policymakers and regulatory bodies digital twins present a simulation-based validation sandbox for safety compliance adherence along with future infrastructure planning and evaluation of environmental impact.

Novel research trends consist of explainable artificial intelligence (XAI) precise integration in digital twins for transparent decision-making, multi-agent reinforcement learning for systematic fleet behaviour, 6G-enabled ultra-low-latency communication frameworks, and standardized interoperability protocols for smart city integration for increased human-robot interactions (Sheraz et al. 2024). Interdisciplinary collaboration is needed to solve remaining scalability, cybersecurity, and data governance gaps that need to be overcome for millions of vehicles on the road.

7. CONCLUSION

In this chapter, we have explored the integration of Digital Twin (DT) technology in Autonomous Vehicles (AVs), emphasizing its potential to revolutionize the development, deployment, and operational management of these systems. The key contributions of Digital Twins to AVs are their ability to create real-time virtual models that evolve alongside the physical systems they represent. This bi-directional data exchange enhances predictive maintenance, simulates real-world scenarios, and optimizes decision-making processes. Through various applications such as vehicle condition monitoring, fault detection, and collaborative driving, Digital Twins significantly reduce operational costs, improve safety, and enable the seamless integration of AVs into complex environments.

Despite the numerous benefits, challenges remain, particularly regarding real-time data synchronization, model fidelity, computational resource requirements, and security concerns in data exchanges. As highlighted by the existing literature, it is critical to address these challenges to unlock the full potential of Digital Twins in AV systems. The path forward will require advancements in network architectures, computational efficiencies, and regulatory frameworks that ensure both privacy and safety.

Future research must focus on enhancing the scalability and adaptability of Digital Twin systems for large fleets of autonomous vehicles. Exploring ways to reduce the computational load of high-fidelity models while maintaining accuracy is crucial. Additionally, further work is needed in integrating Digital Twins with vehicle-to-everything (V2X) systems, which would enable more sophisticated communication between vehicles, infrastructure, and pedestrians. Investigating the ethical and legal implications of decision-making in autonomous systems, particularly in the context of liability and accountability, is another critical area that requires attention.

Moreover, the integration of artificial intelligence and machine learning with Digital Twins offers significant opportunities for optimizing AV performance through adaptive learning. Future efforts should also explore the potential for combining Digital Twin frameworks with next generation 5G or 6G networks to achieve real-time synchronization across large-scale AV fleets. Finally, the deployment of these technologies in smart cities will provide a real-world testing ground for refining these systems and demonstrating their reliability at scale.

REFERENCES

Alfaro-Viquez, D., Zamora-Hernandez, M., Fernandez-Vega, M., Garcia-Rodriguez, J., & Azorin-Lopez, J. (2025). A comprehensive review of AI-based digital twin applications in manufacturing: Integration across operator, product, and process dimensions. *Electronics (Basel)*, *14*(4), 646. DOI: 10.3390/electronics14040646

Ali, W. A., Fanti, M. P., Roccotelli, M., & Ranieri, L. (2023). A review of digital twin technology for electric and autonomous vehicles. *Applied Sciences (Basel, Switzerland)*, *13*(10), 5871. DOI: 10.3390/app13105871

Amanatidis, P., Lyratzis, E., Angelopoulos, V., Kouloumpris, E., Skaperdas, E., Bassiliades, N., Vlahavas, I., Maris, F., Emmanouloudis, D., & Karampatzakis, D. (2025). Intelligent water management through edge-enabled IoT, AI, and big data technologies. *IoT*, *7*(1), 5. DOI: 10.3390/iot7010005

Attaran, M., & Celik, B. G. (2023). Digital twin: Benefits, use cases, challenges, and opportunities. *Decision Analytics Journal*, *6*, 100165. DOI: 10.1016/j.dajour.2023.100165

Babaei, P., Riahinia, N., Ebadati, E. O. M., & Azimi, A. (2025). Towards a data-driven digital twin AI-based architecture for self-driving vehicles. *IET Intelligent Transport Systems*, *19*(1), e70017. DOI: 10.1049/itr2.70017

Biswas, A., & Wang, H.-C. (2023). Autonomous vehicles enabled by the integration of IoT, edge intelligence, 5G, and blockchain. *Sensors (Basel)*, *23*(4), 1963. DOI: 10.3390/s23041963 PMID: 36850560

Cantas, M. R., & Guvenc, L. (2023). *Customized co-simulation environment for autonomous driving algorithm development and evaluation.*

Chai, X., Yan, J., Zhang, W., Sulowicz, M., & Feng, Y. (2024). Recent progress on digital twins in intelligent connected vehicles: A review. *Elektronika ir Elektrotechnika*, *30*(2), 4–17. DOI: 10.5755/j02.eie.36209

Chen, D., & Lv, Z. (2022). Artificial intelligence enabled digital twins for training autonomous cars. *Internet of Things and Cyber-Physical Systems*, *2*, 31–41. DOI: 10.1016/j.iotcps.2022.05.001

Cui, J., Liu, Y., & Nallanathan, A. (2020). Multi-agent reinforcement learning-based resource allocation for UAV networks. *IEEE Transactions on Wireless Communications*, *19*(2), 729–743. DOI: 10.1109/TWC.2019.2935201

Gao, J., Peng, C., Yoshinaga, T., Han, G., Guleng, S., & Wu, C. (2024). Digital twin-enabled internet of vehicles applications. *Electronics (Basel)*, *13*(7), 1263. Advance online publication. DOI: 10.3390/electronics13071263

Gorza, D., Saly, G., & Csikor, D. (2025). Simulation of environment recognition systems for autonomous vehicles in CARLA simulator. *Engineering Proceedings*, *113*(1), 30. Advance online publication. DOI: 10.3390/engproc2025113030

Gu, X., Duan, W., Zhang, G., Hou, J., Peng, L., Wen, M., Gao, F., Chen, M., & Ho, P.-H. (2026). Digital twin technology for intelligent vehicles and transportation systems: A survey on applications, challenges and future directions. *IEEE Communications Surveys and Tutorials*, *28*, 3235–3271. DOI: 10.1109/COMST.2025.3581152

Guinea-Cabrera, M. A., & Holgado-Terriza, J. A. (2024). Digital twins in software engineering—A systematic literature review and vision. *Applied Sciences (Basel, Switzerland)*, *14*(3), 977. DOI: 10.3390/app14030977

Hardaway, K., & Cai, H. (2026). Reviewing autonomous vehicle simulation literature: Policy insights for transportation. *Transport Reviews*, *46*(1), 1–27. DOI: 10.1080/01441647.2025.2545224

Hasan, S. K. K., & Crawford, C. W. (2025). *A new era for digital twins: Progress and industry adoption*. Digital Twin., DOI: 10.1080/27525783.2025.2555877

Haverkamp, P., Anantheswar, A., May, M., Wadlig, G., Hildebrandt, J., Thiessat, K. A., Wollny, I., Traverso, M., Müller-Mall, S., Kaliske, M., Habich, D., & Lehner, W. (2025). Digital twin road: Value and implications involving data and application. *Discover Applied Sciences*, *7*(6), 510. DOI: 10.1007/s42452-025-07018-w

He, Y., Chen, H., & Shi, W. (2024). *An advanced framework for ultra-realistic simulation and digital twinning for autonomous vehicles.*

Hou, G. (2023). Evaluating efficiency and safety of mixed traffic with connected and autonomous vehicles in adverse weather. *Sustainability (Basel)*, *15*(4), 3138. Advance online publication. DOI: 10.3390/su15043138

Hu, X., Li, S., Huang, T., Tang, B., Huai, R., & Chen, L. (2023). *How simulation helps autonomous driving: A survey of sim2real, digital twins, and parallel intelligence.*

Kabashkin, I. (2025). Digital-twin-based ecosystem for aviation maintenance training. *Information (Basel)*, *16*(7), 586. DOI: 10.3390/info16070586

Kabir, R., Watanobe, Y., Ding, D., Islam, M. R., & Naruse, K. (2025). A comprehensive survey on advanced data science platforms for cyber-physical systems, digital twins, and robotics. *IEEE Access : Practical Innovations, Open Solutions*, *13*, 177269–177304. DOI: 10.1109/ACCESS.2025.3619776

Karunaratne, T., Ajiero, I. R., Joseph, R., Farr, E., & Piroozfar, P. (2025). Evaluating the economic impact of digital twinning in the AEC industry: A systematic review. *Buildings (Basel, Switzerland)*, *15*(14), 2583. DOI: 10.3390/buildings15142583

Kušić, K., Schumann, R., & Ivanjko, E. (2023). A digital twin in transportation: Real-time synergy of traffic data streams and simulation for virtualizing motorway dynamics. *Advanced Engineering Informatics*, *55*, 101858. DOI: 10.1016/j.aei.2022.101858

Liu, Y., Feng, J., Lu, J., & Zhou, S. (2024). A review of digital twin capabilities, technologies, and applications based on the maturity model. *Advanced Engineering Informatics*, *62*, 102592. DOI: 10.1016/j.aei.2024.102592

Liu, Z., Chen, X., Wu, H., Wang, Z., Chen, X., Niyato, D., & Huang, K. (2026). Integrated sensing and edge AI: Realizing intelligent perception in 6G. *IEEE Communications Surveys and Tutorials*, *28*, 2725–2770. DOI: 10.1109/COMST.2025.3592989

Martinez, V. M. G., Campelo, D. R., & Ribeiro, M. R. N. (2025). Sustainable intelligent transportation systems via digital twins: A contextualized survey. *IEEE Open Journal of Intelligent Transportation Systems*, *6*, 363–392. DOI: 10.1109/OJITS.2025.3553696

Melders, L., Smigins, R., & Birkavs, A. (2025). Recent advances in vehicle driver health monitoring systems. *Sensors (Basel)*, *25*(6), 1812. DOI: 10.3390/s25061812 PMID: 40292968

Mohd Nor, N., Zakaria, Z., Yano, J., & Mohd Pisal, S. M. (2026). Proposed end-of-life vehicle (ELV) management framework for local government in Klang Valley, Malaysia. *Journal of Material Cycles and Waste Management*, *28*(2), 1011–1028. Advance online publication. DOI: 10.1007/s10163-025-02458-3

Nonomura, K., Wang, K., Li, Z., Yu, T., & Sakaguchi, K. (2025). *Digital twin-empowered cooperative autonomous car-sharing services: Proof-of-concept.*

Obaid, L., Alattieh, S. A., Abdallah, M., & Hamad, K. (2023). Environmental impacts of the transition to automated vehicles: A life cycle perspective. *Sustainable Materials and Technologies*, *38*, e00725. DOI: 10.1016/j.susmat.2023.e00725

Pikner, H., Malayjerdi, M., Bellone, M., Baykara, B., & Sell, R. (2024). Autonomous driving validation and verification using digital twins. In *Proceedings of the 10th International Conference on Vehicle Technology and Intelligent Transport Systems* (pp. 204–211). SCITEPRESS - Science and Technology Publications. DOI: 10.5220/0012546400003702

Rahman, M. A., Shahrior, M. F., Iqbal, K., & Abushaiba, A. A. (2025). Enabling intelligent industrial automation: A review of machine learning applications with digital twin and edge AI integration. *Automation*, *6*(3), 37. DOI: 10.3390/automation6030037

Sajadieh, S. M. M., & Noh, S. D. (2025). From simulation to autonomy: Reviews of the integration of artificial intelligence and digital twins. *International Journal of Precision Engineering and Manufacturing-Green Technology*, *12*(5), 1597–1628. DOI: 10.1007/s40684-025-00750-z

Samak, T. V., Samak, C. V., & Krovi, V. N. (2024a). Metaverse for safer roadways: An immersive digital twin framework for exploring human-autonomy coexistence in urban transportation systems. In *2024 IEEE Conference on Telepresence* (pp. 160–165). DOI: 10.1109/Telepresence63209.2024.10841549

Samak, T. V., Samak, C. V., & Krovi, V. N. (2024b). Towards validation of autonomous vehicles across scales using an integrated digital twin framework. In *2024 IEEE International Conference on Advanced Intelligent Mechatronics (AIM)* (pp. 1068–1075). DOI: 10.1109/AIM55361.2024.10637205

Sarker, M. A. L., Sarker, M. O. F., & Han, D. S. (2025). A survey on digital twin-assisted intelligent vehicle localization. *ICT Express*, *11*(5), 981–992. DOI: 10.1016/j.icte.2025.08.008

Sheraz, M., Chuah, T. C., Lee, Y. L., Alam, M. M., Al-Habashna, A., & Han, Z. (2024). A comprehensive survey on revolutionizing connectivity through artificial intelligence-enabled digital twin network in 6G. *IEEE Access : Practical Innovations, Open Solutions*, •••, 1–1. DOI: 10.1109/ACCESS.2024.3384272

Tiwari, A., & Farag, H. E. Z. (2025). Responsible AI framework for autonomous vehicles: Addressing bias and fairness risks. *IEEE Access : Practical Innovations, Open Solutions*, *13*, 58800–58822. DOI: 10.1109/ACCESS.2025.3556781

Wang, K., Li, Z., Nonomura, K., Yu, T., Sakaguchi, K., Hashash, O., & Saad, W. (2024). Smart mobility digital twin based automated vehicle navigation system: A proof of concept. *IEEE Transactions on Intelligent Vehicles*, *9*(3), 4348–4361. DOI: 10.1109/TIV.2024.3368109

Weingram, A., Cui, C., Lin, S., Munoz, S., Jacob, T., Viers, J., & Lu, X. (2025). A definition and taxonomy of digital twins: Case studies with machine learning and scientific applications. *Frontiers in High Performance Computing*, *3*, 1536501. DOI: 10.3389/fhpcp.2025.1536501

Wu, H., Ji, P., Ma, H., & Xing, L. (2023). A comprehensive review of digital twin from the perspective of total process: Data, models, networks and applications. *Sensors (Basel)*, *23*(19), 8306. DOI: 10.3390/s23198306 PMID: 37837136

Wu, K., Li, P., Cheng, Y., Parker, S. T., Ran, B., Noyce, D. A., & Ye, X. (2025). *A digital twin framework for physical-virtual integration in V2X-enabled connected vehicle corridors.*

Yao, J.-F., Yang, Y., Wang, X.-C., & Zhang, X.-P. (2023). Systematic review of digital twin technology and applications. *Visual Computing for Industry, Biomedicine, and Art*, *6*(1), 10. DOI: 10.1186/s42492-023-00137-4 PMID: 37249731

Yeğin, V. (2025). MATLAB/Simulink based autonomous vehicle collision simulation and energy absorption analysis. *Journal of Materials and Mechatronics: A*, *6*(1), 249–261. DOI: 10.55546/jmm.1650323

Yeong, D. J., Panduru, K., & Walsh, J. (2025). Exploring the unseen: A survey of multi-sensor fusion and the role of explainable AI (XAI) in autonomous vehicles. *Sensors (Basel)*, *25*(3), 856. DOI: 10.3390/s25030856 PMID: 39943496

Zapata, N., Pérez-González, G., Bustos, P., Barroso, S., & Núñez, P. (2025). An efficient and versatile digital twin model implementation for autonomous connected vehicles based on distributed, low-latency working memory. *Internet of Things : Engineering Cyber Physical Human Systems*, *32*, 101627. DOI: 10.1016/j.iot.2025.101627

Zhang, X., Li, J., Zhou, J., Zhang, S., Wang, J., Yuan, Y., Liu, J., & Li, J. (2025). Vehicle-to-everything communication in intelligent connected vehicles: A survey and taxonomy. *Automotive Innovation*, *8*(1), 13–45. DOI: 10.1007/s42154-024-00310-2

Zhao, H., Meng, M., Li, X., Xu, J., Li, L., & Galland, S. (2024). A survey of autonomous driving frameworks and simulators. *Advanced Engineering Informatics*, *62*, 102850. DOI: 10.1016/j.aei.2024.102850

Chapter 6
Digital Twin-Driven Safety Validation and Predictive Risk Modelling for Autonomous Vehicles

Shashikant Nishant Sharma
http://orcid.org/0000-0001-8031-8569
Maulana Azad National Institute of Technology, India

ABSTRACT

This chapter examines Digital Twin–driven approaches for safety validation and predictive risk modeling in autonomous vehicles operating in complex environments. The purpose of this chapter is to address the limitations of mileage-based and reactive testing by proposing a scalable, simulation-centric safety validation framework. The chapter synthesizes research on Digital Twin architectures, autonomous vehicle simulation platforms, surrogate safety metrics, machine learning–based risk prediction, and real-time monitoring. It demonstrates how Digital Twins support systematic generation of rare and safety-critical scenarios, continuous risk assessment, and adaptive learning across the autonomous vehicle lifecycle. Regulatory, ethical, and governance are also discussed, highlighting the role of Digital Twin–enabled validation in scenario-based approval, continuous compliance monitoring, and transparent safety assurance. By integrating technical and policy perspectives, the chapter provides a coherent framework to support safer and more trustworthy autonomous mobility systems.

1. INTRODUCTION

Autonomous Vehicles (AVs) represent one of the most transformative technological shifts in contemporary mobility systems, promising substantial reductions in traffic crashes, improvements in operational efficiency, mitigation of environmental impacts, and enhanced accessibility for diverse population groups. By replacing or augmenting human driving tasks with artificial intelligence-driven perception, decision-making, and control systems, AVs are expected to fundamentally reshape how transportation networks are designed, managed, and experienced. Despite these anticipated benefits, the large-scale deployment of AVs continues to face a critical and unresolved challenge: how to convincingly demonstrate and

DOI: 10.4018/979-8-3373-7785-8.ch006

assure safety in complex, uncertain, and highly dynamic real-world environments. Safety assurance is not merely a technical prerequisite but a societal and regulatory imperative, directly influencing public trust, legal acceptance, and market adoption.

Unlike conventional vehicles, AVs must continuously interpret and respond to heterogeneous stimuli, including unpredictable human behaviour, mixed traffic conditions, adverse weather, sensor noise, infrastructure variability, and cyber-physical interactions. Real-world driving environments generate an almost infinite set of possible scenarios, many of which occur infrequently but can have catastrophic consequences. Traditional safety validation methods—such as closed-track testing, pilot deployments, and incremental real-world mileage accumulation—are fundamentally limited in their ability to capture these long-tail risks. Empirical estimates suggest that demonstrating statistically significant safety improvements over human drivers would require hundreds of millions or even billions of kilometres of real-world testing, rendering purely physical validation approaches economically prohibitive, ethically questionable, and temporally infeasible. As a result, AV safety assurance demands a paradigm shift away from reactive, mileage-based validation toward predictive, simulation-driven, and system-level safety verification methodologies.

Within this context, Digital Twin (DT) technology has emerged as a critical enabler for next-generation safety validation and risk assessment in autonomous mobility. A Digital Twin can be broadly understood as a continuously evolving, high-fidelity virtual replica of a physical system that is dynamically synchronised through data exchange. In the domain of autonomous vehicles, a DT encompasses not only a detailed virtual model of vehicle hardware and dynamics but also the surrounding traffic environment, infrastructure, communication networks, and embedded intelligence. By integrating live sensor data, vehicle telemetry, perception outputs, decision logs, and control actions, AV Digital Twins enable real-time monitoring, scenario simulation, and forward-looking risk analysis. Crucially, they allow safety engineers and system designers to explore hypothetical futures—what could happen next—rather than merely analysing what has already occurred.

The value of Digital Twins for AV safety lies in their capacity to combine realism with scalability. High-fidelity virtual environments can replicate complex urban, suburban, and highway contexts, including weather variability, lighting conditions, occlusions, and heterogeneous road users. At the same time, these environments can be systematically perturbed to generate rare, adversarial, or extreme scenarios that would be unsafe or impossible to test physically. When coupled with artificial intelligence and machine learning techniques, Digital Twins evolve from passive simulation tools into active safety laboratories capable of continuous learning, anomaly detection, and predictive risk modelling. This capability is particularly significant for AV systems that rely on data-driven algorithms whose performance may degrade under distribution shifts, sensor failures, or unforeseen interactions with human drivers.

Predictive risk modelling constitutes a complementary and equally essential dimension of AV safety assurance. Rather than focusing exclusively on crash outcomes, modern safety science emphasises analysing near-misses, conflicts, and precursors to hazardous events. Surrogate safety measures—such as time-to-collision, post-encroachment time, deceleration rates, and trajectory conflicts—provide early indicators of unsafe behaviour and system vulnerabilities. Machine learning-based predictive models can leverage these indicators, along with high-dimensional sensor and behavioural data, to estimate the probability, severity, and spatial-temporal distribution of risk. When embedded within a Digital Twin framework, predictive risk models can be continuously updated as new data are collected, enabling adaptive safety assessment that reflects real-world operational conditions.

The convergence of Digital Twins, artificial intelligence, and cyber-physical systems engineering marks a decisive shift in how AV safety can be conceptualised and operationalised. Digital Twins serve as integrative platforms that unify vehicle dynamics, perception algorithms, decision-making logic, human factors, communication protocols, and interactions with infrastructure within a single coherent environment. This integration is essential because AV safety failures rarely stem from isolated component malfunctions; rather, they emerge from complex interactions across subsystems, often amplified by contextual uncertainty. For example, a minor sensor degradation combined with delayed V2X communication and unexpected human behaviour may collectively lead to a hazardous situation that would not be apparent when each component is tested in isolation. Digital Twin-driven safety validation makes such emergent risks observable, measurable, and addressable before deployment.

Another critical advantage of Digital Twin-based validation lies in its ethical and regulatory implications. Testing rare but high-risk scenarios—such as sudden pedestrian intrusions, aggressive cut-ins, infrastructure failures, or multi-vehicle conflicts—poses unacceptable risks in physical environments. Digital Twins provide a morally responsible alternative by enabling exhaustive exploration of these scenarios without endangering human lives. From a regulatory perspective, DT-enabled validation offers a transparent, reproducible, and auditable process that can support evidence-based certification and compliance. Regulators increasingly require not only performance metrics but also explanations of how AV systems behave under stress, how failures are detected and mitigated, and how learning-based models are monitored over time. Digital Twins, when designed with proper governance and verification mechanisms, can serve as trusted intermediaries between developers, regulators, and the public.

Despite their promise, the deployment of Digital Twins for AV safety validation raises important technical and organisational challenges. High-fidelity modelling demands accurate representations of vehicle physics, sensor characteristics, and environmental dynamics, all of which are computationally intensive and sensitive to modelling assumptions. Data latency, synchronisation errors, and incomplete observability can undermine the reliability of real-time DT systems. Furthermore, the increasing connectivity of AVs exposes Digital Twin infrastructures to cybersecurity risks, including data poisoning, model tampering, and unauthorised access. Ensuring the trustworthiness of DT-driven safety insights, therefore, requires robust data governance, secure communication protocols, model validation strategies, and explainable AI techniques. These considerations underscore the need for an integrated framework that addresses safety, security, and accountability holistically.

The mission of this chapter is to develop such a comprehensive framework for Digital Twin-driven safety validation and predictive risk modelling in autonomous vehicles. The chapter seeks to synthesise advances in Digital Twin architectures, AI-based risk prediction, simulation methodologies, and cyber-physical systems engineering to establish a coherent approach to AV safety assurance. It aims to move beyond fragmented discussions of simulation, testing, or machine learning by demonstrating how these elements can be systematically combined within a DT-enabled safety lifecycle. In doing so, the chapter bridges disciplinary boundaries spanning transportation engineering, artificial intelligence, systems design, human factors, and cybersecurity.

Specifically, the chapter first situates Digital Twins within the broader conceptual foundations of AV safety validation, highlighting why conventional testing paradigms are insufficient for addressing long-tail risks and emergent behaviours. It then examines the core components of AV Digital Twins, including vehicle and environment modelling, real-time data integration, and bidirectional physical-virtual coupling. Building on this foundation, the chapter explores predictive risk-modelling techniques that leverage surrogate safety measures, behavioural modelling, and machine learning to anticipate hazardous situations before they materialise. The role of hybrid validation environments—combining simulated scenarios with real-world data—is emphasised as a means of enhancing fidelity while retaining scalability.

In addition, the chapter critically addresses governance, cybersecurity, and model integrity issues that influence the credibility of DT-based safety validation. Trustworthy Digital Twins must not only produce accurate simulations but also ensure data provenance, protect against cyber threats, and support transparent decision-making. Finally, the chapter discusses policy and industry pathways for integrating Digital Twin-driven safety validation into AV certification and regulatory frameworks, recognising that technical innovation must be aligned with institutional and societal expectations.

By articulating a unified vision for Digital Twin-driven safety validation and predictive risk modelling, this chapter contributes a holistic perspective on one of the most pressing challenges in autonomous mobility. It argues that Digital Twins are not merely advanced simulators but foundational infrastructures for learning, prediction, and assurance in safety-critical systems. As autonomous vehicles transition from experimental prototypes to everyday participants in complex traffic ecosystems, Digital Twin-based approaches will play an indispensable role in ensuring that this transition is not only technologically feasible but also safe, transparent, and socially acceptable.

This chapter contributes to the growing body of research on autonomous vehicle safety validation by proposing a digital twin–driven safety validation architecture that integrates predictive risk modeling, scenario-based simulation, and regulatory compliance assessment. Rather than focusing solely on theoretical discussions of digital twin technologies, the chapter advances a conceptual validation framework that connects three critical dimensions of autonomous vehicle safety evaluation: (1) simulation-based scenario testing through digital twin platforms, (2) predictive risk modeling using machine learning and surrogate safety indicators, and (3) alignment with emerging regulatory and functional safety standards governing autonomous mobility systems.

Therefore, the primary contribution of this chapter is not limited to a single analytical model or technical tool. Instead, it introduces a multi-layered validation architecture designed to support scalable and proactive safety verification of autonomous vehicles within digital twin ecosystems. By synthesizing insights from simulation platforms, risk analytics, and regulatory frameworks, the chapter proposes a unified conceptual structure capable of supporting both engineering validation processes and policy-oriented safety assurance mechanisms. This integrated perspective provides a foundation for future research on predictive and simulation-driven safety certification approaches for autonomous mobility systems.

2. METHODOLOGY

This chapter adopts a structured and transparent methodology grounded in the PRISMA (Preferred Reporting Items for Systematic Reviews and Meta-Analyses) framework to ensure rigour, reproducibility, and methodological clarity in reviewing the rapidly evolving literature on Digital Twin-driven safety validation and predictive risk modelling for autonomous vehicles. Given the interdisciplinary nature of the topic—spanning transportation engineering, artificial intelligence, cyber-physical systems, and safety science—a blended methodological approach combining systematic literature review, conceptual synthesis, and analytical interpretation has been employed.

2.1 Research Design and Approach

The study follows a systematic review-based chapter methodology, integrating both qualitative synthesis and conceptual framework development. Rather than focusing solely on statistical meta-analysis, the objective is to critically examine how Digital Twin technologies are being conceptualised and applied to safety validation, risk prediction, and assurance in autonomous vehicle (AV) systems. This approach is particularly appropriate because the field is still emerging, with heterogeneous methods, simulation platforms, and validation strategies.

The methodology is designed to (i) comprehensively capture relevant scholarly contributions, (ii) screen and refine studies based on explicit inclusion and exclusion criteria, and (iii) synthesise insights into a coherent framework that supports DT-enabled AV safety validation.

2.2 Literature Search Strategy

A systematic literature search was conducted using three major and widely recognised academic databases to ensure comprehensive coverage:

- Scopus
- Web of Science (WoS)
- Google Scholar

These databases were selected because together they cover high-impact journals, conference proceedings, and interdisciplinary research outputs relevant to autonomous vehicles, digital twins, intelligent transportation systems, and safety modelling.

The search was limited to publications from 2015 to 2025, reflecting the period during which Digital Twin concepts matured from industrial applications into cyber-physical and transportation systems, and during which AV research experienced rapid technological advancement.

Search String

The following Boolean search string was used across all databases, with minor syntax adjustments as required by each platform:

"digital twin" OR "safety validation" OR "risk modelling" OR "autonomous vehicles"

This broad search string was intentionally chosen to avoid prematurely excluding relevant studies and to capture diverse terminologies used across engineering, computer science, and transportation research domains.

2.3 Identification and Screening Process (PRISMA)

Figure 1. PRISMA diagram for the study

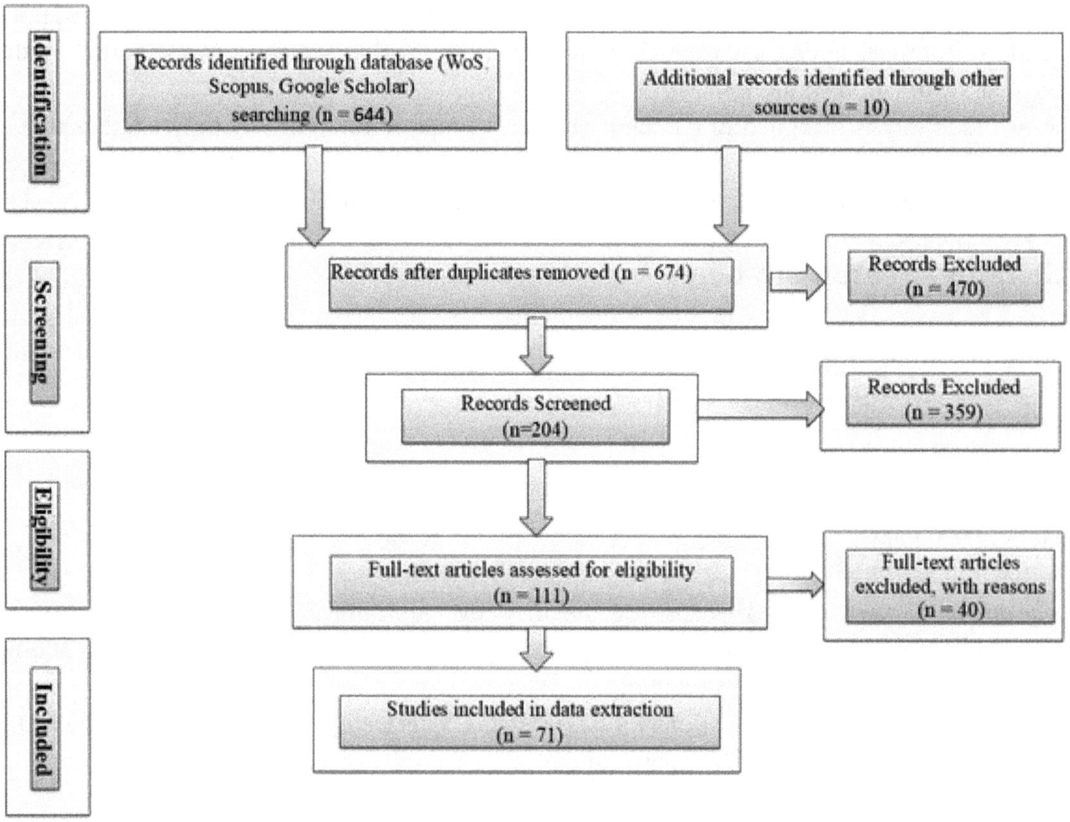

The identification, screening, eligibility, and inclusion phases followed the PRISMA workflow, as illustrated in the attached PRISMA diagram (Figure 1).

Identification Stage

The initial search across the three databases yielded a large pool of records. Duplicate entries across databases were identified and removed using reference management tools and manual cross-checking. This step ensured that each study was considered only once in subsequent screening stages.

Screening Stage

Titles and abstracts of the remaining records were screened to assess relevance to the core themes of the chapter. Studies were excluded at this stage if they:

- Focused exclusively on non-transport domains (e.g., healthcare or manufacturing DTs without mobility relevance),
- Addressed autonomous vehicles without reference to safety, validation, simulation, or risk assessment,
- Were editorial notes, short commentaries, or non-peer-reviewed opinion pieces.

Eligibility Stage

Full-text screening was then conducted for the shortlisted articles. At this stage, studies were evaluated against more detailed inclusion criteria, including:

- Explicit discussion of Digital Twin architectures or virtual replicas,
- Application to autonomous or connected vehicles, intelligent transportation systems, or mobility infrastructure,
- Focus on safety validation, risk assessment, predictive modelling, conflict analysis, or system verification,
- Empirical, simulation-based, methodological, or comprehensive review contributions.
- Studies that lacked methodological clarity, provided insufficient technical detail, or were purely conceptual without relevance to AV safety were excluded at this stage.

Inclusion Stage

The final set of studies formed the analytical foundation of this chapter and informed both the conceptual framework and thematic discussions.

2.4 Data Extraction and Classification

For each included study, structured data extraction was carried out to ensure consistency and comparability. The extracted information included:

- Publication year and outlet,
- Application domain (road vehicles, maritime AVs, UAVs, infrastructure systems),
- Digital Twin characteristics (real-time vs. offline, fidelity level, bidirectional coupling),
- Safety focus (collision avoidance, risk prediction, fault detection, validation),
- Modelling techniques (simulation, machine learning, surrogate safety measures),
- Data sources (real-world sensors, synthetic data, hybrid datasets),
- Consideration of cybersecurity, governance, or regulatory implications.

The studies were then classified thematically to identify dominant research clusters and methodological patterns.

In addition to thematic classification of the literature, the review also extracted information related to validation methodologies and safety evaluation metrics used in digital twin–enabled autonomous vehicle studies. Specifically, the analysis identified the types of safety indicators applied in simulation environments, including surrogate safety metrics, predictive risk indicators, and scenario-based validation techniques. These indicators were categorized according to their role in safety evaluation, such as risk estimation metrics, scenario coverage indicators, and compliance validation measures.

The extraction of these metrics allowed the study to compare how different research contributions operationalize safety validation within digital twin frameworks. This approach ensures that the literature review not only identifies conceptual advances but also highlights measurable criteria that can support reproducible safety evaluation processes. As a result, the methodological approach adopted in this chapter bridges conceptual analysis with practical safety validation indicators used in contemporary autonomous vehicle research.

2.5 Methodological Rigor and Transparency

By following the PRISMA framework, clearly documenting search strategies, and explicitly stating inclusion criteria, this methodology ensures transparency and replicability. The blended use of systematic review and conceptual framework development is particularly well suited to an evolving, interdisciplinary field such as Digital Twin-enabled autonomous vehicle safety, where theoretical consolidation is as essential as empirical evidence.

To enhance methodological rigor, the review also incorporates comparative analysis of technical standards and simulation ecosystems used in autonomous vehicle research. In addition to examining academic literature, relevant safety standards such as ISO 26262 and ISO/PAS 21448 were reviewed to contextualize digital twin–based validation approaches within established automotive safety engineering frameworks. Furthermore, widely used simulation environments—including CARLA, SUMO, and AirSim—were analyzed to understand their role in generating scenario-based safety validation datasets.

Overall, this methodology provides a robust foundation for advancing Digital Twin-driven safety validation and predictive risk modelling as credible, scalable, and regulator-ready approaches for autonomous vehicle deployment.

3. FINDINGS

3.1 Digital Twins and Autonomous Vehicle Safety Challenges

Autonomous vehicles (AVs) are expected to significantly improve road safety, efficiency, and sustainability; however, assuring their safe operation remains one of the most critical barriers to large-scale deployment. Unlike human-driven vehicles, AVs must satisfy stringent safety requirements across perception, decision-making, and control while operating in highly dynamic and uncertain environments. Existing safety standards and frameworks emphasize functional safety, operational reliability, and risk mitigation, yet translating these requirements into comprehensive validation strategies for learning-based systems remains challenging (Jiang et al., 2025; Tan et al., 2025).

A fundamental gap exists between the scale of real-world testing that is practically achievable and the level of evidence required to demonstrate AV safety. Mileage-based validation approaches rely heavily on extensive on-road driving, but achieving statistically significant safety assurance would require hundreds of millions of kilometres, making such approaches costly, time-consuming, and ethically constrained (Bella et al., 2025; J. Zhang et al., 2025). Moreover, reactive testing methods struggle to capture rare, high-impact "long-tail" events that dominate AV risk profiles (Qi, 2025).

In response to these limitations, simulation-based validation has emerged as a core pillar of AV safety assurance. Digital Twin-enabled approaches extend conventional simulation by creating continuously synchronized virtual replicas of vehicles and their environments, enabling real-time monitoring, large-scale scenario generation, and predictive risk analysis (Deniz et al., 2025; Verreydt et al., 2025). By integrating simulation, real-world data, and predictive modelling, Digital Twins provide a scalable and proactive pathway to bridge the safety validation gap and support trustworthy autonomous mobility.

3.2 Digital Twins in Autonomous Vehicle Ecosystems

Digital Twins (DTs) are defined as high-fidelity virtual representations of physical systems that are continuously synchronized with their real-world counterparts through real-time data exchange. Originally developed for manufacturing and industrial asset management, Digital Twin concepts have rapidly evolved to support complex cyber-physical systems, including autonomous vehicles (AVs), where safety, adaptability, and reliability are paramount (Verreydt et al., 2025; Horner et al., 2025). In the AV context, Digital Twins extend beyond static simulation by enabling dynamic mirroring of vehicle states, operational environments, and decision-making processes.

DTs in autonomous vehicle ecosystems can be structured across multiple levels. Vehicle-level Digital Twins model vehicle dynamics, sensors, actuators, and onboard intelligence, supporting validation of perception, planning, and control algorithms (Bogdevičius et al., 2025; Li et al., 2025). Environment-level Digital Twins replicate road networks, traffic flows, weather, and infrastructure, enabling realistic interaction modelling and scenario testing (Deniz et al., 2025). At a broader scale, system-level Digital Twins integrate multiple vehicles, connected infrastructure, and V2X communication to assess cooperative behaviour and network-wide safety performance (Gu et al., 2025; Liu et al., 2025).

A defining feature of AV Digital Twins is physical-virtual synchronization, achieved through continuous sensor data integration and bidirectional data flows. This enables the creation of digital shadows, where real-world operations are mirrored in near real time, supporting monitoring, anomaly detection, and predictive safety analysis (Verreydt et al., 2025). Together, these capabilities position Digital Twins as foundational infrastructures for scalable and proactive autonomous vehicle safety validation.

3.3 Autonomous Vehicle Safety Validation: Concepts and Requirements

Safety validation for autonomous vehicles (AVs) is grounded in both functional safety and operational safety requirements, ensuring that systems behave correctly under normal conditions and transition safely under fault or uncertainty. Functional safety focuses on preventing hazards caused by system malfunctions, while operational safety extends this focus to real-world driving contexts characterized by dynamic traffic, environmental variability, and human interaction (Jiang et al., 2025; Neto et al., 2025). Together, these requirements demand validation approaches that address not only component reliability but also system-level behaviour.

A central concept in AV safety validation is the definition of Operational Design Domains (ODDs), which specify the conditions under which an AV is intended to operate safely. Within these domains, safety envelopes and fail-safe behaviours are used to constrain system actions and ensure controlled degradation or minimal-risk manoeuvres when limits are exceeded (Tan et al., 2025). Validating these mechanisms requires testing across a wide range of scenarios, including boundary and failure conditions.

International standards such as ISO 26262 and UL 4600 provide structured guidance for AV safety assurance, emphasizing hazard analysis, risk assessment, and evidence-based validation. However, applying these standards to learning-based perception, planning, and decision-making systems remains challenging due to uncertainty, non-determinism, and sensitivity to rare events (Qi, 2025; Bella et al., 2025). These challenges underscore the need for simulation- and Digital Twin-enabled validation methods capable of systematically addressing uncertainty and long-tail risks.

Alignment with Functional Safety and SOTIF Standards

Digital twin–driven safety validation must be anchored in internationally recognized functional safety frameworks to ensure regulatory credibility and system reliability. In autonomous vehicle development, two widely accepted standards provide the foundation for safety engineering: ISO 26262, which addresses functional safety of electrical and electronic systems in road vehicles, and ISO/PAS 21448, known as Safety of the Intended Functionality (SOTIF). While ISO 26262 focuses primarily on hardware and software failures, SOTIF addresses performance limitations of perception systems, machine learning models, and environmental uncertainties that may lead to hazardous behavior even when components function correctly.

Within a digital twin–based validation environment, these standards can be operationalized by mapping simulation scenarios to safety goals and hazard analysis processes defined under ISO 26262. Digital twin simulations enable the generation of extensive operational design domain (ODD) scenarios that allow engineers to evaluate system performance against safety integrity levels (ASILs). Meanwhile, SOTIF-oriented analysis can be supported through digital twin–driven perception stress testing, including edge cases such as sensor occlusion, rare traffic events, and unexpected pedestrian behavior. By embedding digital twin simulations within these established safety frameworks, autonomous vehicle validation can transition from purely experimental testing toward a structured, standards-aligned verification process that satisfies regulatory expectations and improves public trust.

3.4 Predictive Risk Modelling for Autonomous Vehicles

Predictive risk modelling is a critical component of autonomous vehicle (AV) safety validation, as it enables the anticipation and mitigation of hazardous situations before failures or crashes occur. AV risk profiles are dominated by long-tail and rare safety-critical events, such as unexpected pedestrian behaviour, aggressive cut-ins, sensor degradation under adverse weather, or complex multi-agent interactions. These events occur infrequently in real-world driving but account for a disproportionate share of safety risk, making them difficult to capture through conventional testing approaches (Qi, 2025; Bella et al., 2025).

To address this challenge, predictive safety analysis increasingly relies on surrogate safety measures (SSMs), including time-to-collision (TTC), post-encroachment time (PET), deceleration rate to avoid collision (DRAC), and indicators derived from tools such as the Surrogate Safety Assessment Model (SSAM). These measures provide early warning signals of unsafe interactions and enable continuous safety assessment without waiting for crash events (Gao et al., 2025; Sharma et al., 2024).

Probabilistic risk estimation further enhances predictive modelling by explicitly accounting for uncertainty in perception, prediction, and decision-making. Bayesian models, Monte Carlo simulation, and uncertainty-aware fusion techniques allow AV systems to quantify confidence levels and assess risk distributions under dynamic conditions (Jiang et al., 2025; Liang et al., 2025). When combined with machine learning-driven hazard detection, these models support adaptive, data-driven risk prediction that can be continuously updated within Digital Twin environments, strengthening proactive and scalable AV safety validation.

Surrogate Safety Metrics for Predictive Risk Assessment

Predictive risk modelling in autonomous vehicle ecosystems increasingly relies on surrogate safety metrics that allow researchers to evaluate safety performance without waiting for rare crash events to occur. Surrogate indicators such as Time-to-Collision (TTC), Post Encroachment Time (PET), Deceleration Rate to Avoid Crash (DRAC), and Time Headway (THW) provide quantifiable measures of near-miss events and critical interactions among vehicles, pedestrians, and infrastructure (Sharma, et al, 2024). These indicators can be computed continuously within digital twin simulations to estimate collision probabilities and risk exposure across different traffic conditions.

Integrating surrogate safety metrics into digital twin platforms significantly enhances the predictive capabilities of AV safety models. Instead of evaluating safety only after failures occur, digital twins can generate thousands of synthetic traffic scenarios where these metrics are continuously monitored and statistically analyzed. This approach enables risk forecasting, identification of unsafe driving behaviors, and calibration of autonomous driving algorithms under complex traffic dynamics. Consequently, surrogate safety metrics serve as an essential bridge between microscopic traffic simulation and system-level safety validation, enabling scalable and proactive safety assessment.

Quantitative Safety Validation Criteria

For digital twin–driven validation frameworks to be operationally useful, safety evaluation must rely on measurable criteria that allow engineers and regulators to assess system performance objectively. Several quantitative validation indicators have emerged in autonomous vehicle research to evaluate system safety under simulated and real-world conditions. These indicators include risk probability thresholds, coverage of operational design domain (ODD) scenarios, system disengagement frequency, and statistical distributions of surrogate safety metrics such as Time-to-Collision (TTC), Post Encroachment Time (PET), and Deceleration Rate to Avoid Crash (DRAC). Together, these metrics enable researchers to estimate the probability of hazardous events without requiring rare crash occurrences.

Within digital twin environments, safety validation can therefore be structured around three measurable criteria. First, scenario coverage thresholds assess whether the simulation environment adequately represents the operational conditions in which autonomous vehicles operate. Second, risk probability thresholds estimate acceptable levels of collision risk derived from surrogate safety metrics and predictive machine learning models. Third, compliance thresholds ensure that system performance aligns with regulatory safety targets defined under functional safety frameworks. By combining these criteria within digital twin simulations, researchers can perform large-scale validation experiments capable of evaluating thousands of complex traffic scenarios, thereby enabling a statistically robust assessment of autonomous vehicle safety performance.

3.5 Digital Twin Simulation Platforms and Technical Foundations

Table 1. Digital twin simulation platforms and technical capabilities for AV safety validation

Component / Platform	Core Functionality	Safety Validation Contribution	Key References
CarSim	High-fidelity physics-based vehicle dynamics modelling	Accurate evaluation of longitudinal/lateral stability, braking, and failure modes	Bogdevičius et al. (2025); Li et al. (2025)
OpenDRIVE	Standardised road network and geometry description	Realistic representation of road topology, junctions, and lane-level constraints	Deniz et al. (2025)
CARLA	Open-source AV simulator with physics, sensors, and traffic agents	End-to-end validation of perception, planning, and control under diverse scenarios	Zhang et al. (2025); Tan et al. (2025)
3D Urban Scene Modeling	Digital reconstruction of cities, traffic, and the environment	Scenario realism, long-tail event testing, and infrastructure interaction analysis	Horner et al. (2025)
LGSVL Simulator	High-fidelity perception and sensor simulation	Validation of camera, LiDAR, radar fusion and AI perception robustness	Kim & Shim (2024); Liu et al. (2025)
Apollo Dreamview	AV system visualisation and simulation interface	Debugging and validation of decision-making and control pipelines	Qi (2025)
NVIDIA Omniverse / Isaac Sim	GPU-accelerated, photorealistic simulation and robotics modelling	Large-scale scenario generation, synthetic data creation, and sim-to-real transfer	Verreydt et al. (2025); Wang et al. (2025)
Cloud-Edge DT Architectures	Distributed computation across vehicle, edge, and cloud	Real-time risk monitoring, scalable simulation, low-latency validation	Ehsan et al. (2025); Liu et al. (2025)
Bayesian & ML Risk Models	Probabilistic and learning-based hazard prediction	Uncertainty-aware risk estimation and failure anticipation	Jiang et al. (2025); Liang et al. (2025)
Hybrid DT-Simulation Workflows	Integration of real-world data with virtual environments	Continuous learning, model updating, and realistic safety validation	Verreydt et al. (2025); Zhang et al. (2025)

From the table 1, we can see that digital Twin simulation platforms form the technical backbone of predictive and scalable safety validation for autonomous vehicles (AVs). Physics-based vehicle dynamics models such as CarSim provide high-fidelity representations of vehicle behaviour, enabling accurate assessment of stability, braking performance, and fault conditions that are critical for functional safety validation (Bogdevičius et al., 2025). When combined with standardised road descriptions like Open-DRIVE, these models ensure consistency between physical and virtual driving environments, enhancing scenario realism and reproducibility (Deniz et al., 2025).

At the system level, simulators such as CARLA, PreScan, and AirSim enable end-to-end validation of perception-planning-control pipelines by integrating vehicle dynamics, sensor models, traffic agents, and environmental variability. These platforms are particularly effective for generating rare and adversarial scenarios that are infeasible to test on public roads (Tan et al., 2025). Advanced AI perception simulators, including LGSVL and Apollo Dreamview, further strengthen validation by allowing detailed testing of camera, LiDAR, and radar fusion under adverse conditions such as occlusion, weather degradation, and sensor noise (Kim & Shim, 2024; Liu et al., 2025).

Recent advances in NVIDIA Omniverse and Isaac Sim have significantly improved simulation scalability and photorealism, supporting synthetic data generation and sim-to-real transfer for learning-based AV systems (Verreydt et al., 2025). These platforms are increasingly deployed within cloud-edge

Digital Twin architectures, where real-time vehicle data are synchronised with large-scale simulation environments to enable continuous monitoring and predictive risk assessment (Ehsan et al., 2025).

Crucially, integrating Bayesian and machine-learning-based risk prediction models into Digital Twin environments enables uncertainty-aware safety analysis and adaptive hazard anticipation (Jiang et al., 2025). Hybrid Digital Twin-simulation workflows, combining real-world operational data with virtual experimentation, represent a critical step toward continuous, lifecycle-based AV safety validation that is both scalable and regulator-ready.

Beyond conceptual modeling, the practical implementation of digital twin–driven validation requires robust simulation ecosystems capable of replicating complex urban traffic environments. Several widely used autonomous vehicle simulation platforms provide such capabilities, including CARLA, SUMO, LGSVL (SVL Simulator), AirSim, and NVIDIA DRIVE Sim. These platforms enable the integration of high-fidelity physics engines, sensor simulation, traffic modelling, and reinforcement learning–based decision systems. CARLA, for instance, supports photorealistic sensor simulation and scenario-based testing, while SUMO offers detailed microscopic traffic modelling that can replicate large-scale urban mobility networks.

When connected with digital twin architectures, these simulation environments enable real-time synchronization between virtual models and real-world sensor data streams. Such integration allows continuous scenario testing, behavior prediction, and system calibration across diverse operational design domains. Moreover, hybrid frameworks combining traffic simulators with AI-driven perception models allow researchers to evaluate both vehicle control algorithms and system-level traffic safety dynamics, thereby providing a more comprehensive validation ecosystem for autonomous mobility systems.

3.6 Safety Validation Through Digital Twin-Driven Scenario Generation

Digital Twin-driven scenario generation has emerged as a cornerstone of scalable safety validation for autonomous vehicles (AVs), enabling systematic exploration of rare, adversarial, and safety-critical events that are difficult or unethical to test in real-world conditions. By embedding scenario engines within Digital Twin environments, AV developers can deliberately stress-test perception, planning, and control systems against long-tail risks such as sudden cut-ins, abnormal pedestrian behaviour, and multi-vehicle conflicts (Tan et al., 2025; Qi, 2025). This capability directly addresses the limitations of mileage-based testing, which rarely captures such low-frequency but high-impact events.

A key strength of DT-enabled validation lies in its ability to model weather variability, sensor degradation, and cyber-physical perturbations in a controlled and repeatable manner. Photorealistic simulation platforms allow systematic manipulation of lighting, rain, fog, and snow, while sensor models can emulate noise, occlusion, and partial failures, revealing vulnerabilities in perception and sensor fusion pipelines (Kim & Shim, 2024; Vcrrcydt et al., 2025). Additionally, DT environments support evaluation of cyber-physical disturbances, including communication delays and data inconsistencies in connected systems (Jiang et al., 2025).

Digital Twins are particularly effective for capturing traffic unpredictability and mixed autonomy interactions, where human-driven and autonomous vehicles coexist. By simulating heterogeneous behaviours and coordination failures, DTs enable assessment of emergent risks at the system level (Liu et al., 2025; Gu et al., 2025). The integration of synthetic, real-world, and hybrid datasets further enhances validation fidelity, allowing continuous learning and robust generalization across diverse operational contexts (Zhang et al., 2025).

3.7 Digital Twin-Based Real-Time Autonomous Vehicle Behaviour Monitoring

Digital Twin-based real-time monitoring extends safety validation beyond offline simulation by enabling continuous observation and assessment of autonomous vehicle (AV) behaviour during actual operation. Through the integration of live sensor streams, vehicle telemetry, and decision logs, Digital Twins support continuous safety and risk scoring mechanisms that evaluate system performance against predefined safety envelopes and surrogate safety metrics (Gao et al., 2025; Jiang et al., 2025). This persistent assessment allows early detection of anomalous or degrading behaviour before it escalates into safety-critical events.

A key enabler of real-time monitoring is digital shadowing, where the operational state of a deployed AV is mirrored in near real time within its virtual counterpart. Digital shadows capture both physical dynamics and software decision processes, allowing post-event analysis, anomaly diagnosis, and predictive risk forecasting under evolving traffic conditions (Verreydt et al., 2025; Horner et al., 2025). Unlike static logging systems, digital shadowing enables bidirectional learning, where insights from the virtual environment inform real-world control strategies.

To achieve low-latency and scalable monitoring, Digital Twin implementations increasingly rely on edge-cloud architectures. Edge computing supports rapid local processing of safety-critical data, while cloud-based platforms enable large-scale analytics, historical trend analysis, and cross-fleet learning (Ehsan et al., 2025; Liu et al., 2025). These architectures facilitate feedback loops for adaptive learning, allowing risk models and control policies to be continuously refined using real-world operational data. As a result, Digital Twin-based monitoring supports dynamic safety improvement throughout the AV lifecycle, reinforcing trust and operational resilience.

In addition to offline simulation experiments, digital twin architectures enable continuous monitoring of autonomous vehicle behavior in operational environments. Real-time telemetry data from onboard sensors—including LiDAR, radar, cameras, and GPS—can be transmitted to cloud-based digital twins where behavioral patterns are analyzed using predictive analytics and anomaly detection algorithms. This real-time monitoring capability allows safety engineers to identify deviations from expected driving behaviors and initiate corrective actions before safety incidents occur.

Such monitoring systems also support quantitative validation metrics that track safety performance across large fleets of autonomous vehicles. Metrics such as disengagement frequency, near-miss rates, TTC distributions, and lane departure incidents can be aggregated and visualized within digital twin dashboards. These datasets enable data-driven safety audits and continuous improvement of driving algorithms, transforming digital twins into a dynamic safety management infrastructure rather than merely a design-phase simulation tool.

3.8 Predictive Risk Model Evaluation and Validation

Evaluating and validating predictive risk models is essential to ensuring the reliability of Digital Twin-driven safety assurance for autonomous vehicles (AVs). In Digital Twin environments, surrogate safety metrics such as time-to-collision (TTC), post-encroachment time (PET), and deceleration rate to avoid collision (DRAC) are widely used to continuously quantify risk without relying on crash occurrences

(Gao et al., 2025; Sharma et al., 2024). Embedding these metrics into Digital Twins enables real-time and scenario-based comparison of safety performance across diverse operating conditions.

Machine learning-based failure and conflict prediction models further enhance evaluation by identifying complex, non-linear risk patterns that are difficult to capture using rule-based methods. Trained on large-scale sensor, trajectory, and event data, these models can detect early indicators of perception errors, planning conflicts, or control instability, particularly in mixed-traffic environments (Qi, 2025; Yang et al., 2025). Digital Twins provide controlled yet realistic platforms for validating such models across rare and adversarial scenarios.

To address uncertainty inherent in autonomous driving, probabilistic risk assessment frameworks are increasingly integrated into DT-based validation pipelines. Bayesian inference and stochastic modelling allow explicit representation of uncertainty in perception, prediction, and communication, supporting more robust safety decisions (Jiang et al., 2025; Liang et al., 2025). Monte Carlo simulation is commonly used to propagate uncertainty across large scenario ensembles, enabling statistical evaluation of risk distributions rather than single-point estimates (Tan et al., 2025). Additionally, reinforcement learning-based approaches leverage Digital Twins to train hazard-anticipation and avoidance strategies through repeated interactions with simulated environments, thereby supporting adaptive and predictive safety control (Yang et al., 2025).

3.9 Case Analysis: Global Digital Twin-Enabled Autonomous Vehicle Initiatives

Table 2. Global case analysis of digital twin-enabled AV safety validation

Global Initiative	Digital Twin Scope	Core Safety Validation Mechanisms	Predictive & Risk Modelling Functions	Evidence from Literature
Waymo - Virtual Driver & Simulation-Based Validation	Vehicle-level + environment-level DT	Large-scale scenario simulation, rare-event reproduction, perception-planning stress testing	Surrogate safety metrics, probabilistic risk modelling, Monte Carlo scenario expansion	Tan et al. (2025); Zhang et al. (2025); Bella et al. (2025); Qi (2025); Gao et al. (2025)
Tesla - Shadow Mode & Fleet-Scale Learning	Vehicle-level DT with digital shadowing	Real-time monitoring of disengagements, near-miss detection, and post-hoc safety auditing	ML-based failure prediction, long-tail risk discovery, uncertainty learning	Sharma et al. (2024); Yang et al. (2025); Wei et al. (2025); Jiang et al. (2025)
BMW & Siemens - Digital Twin Factories	System-level DT (vehicle + production + testing)	Virtual validation of AV components, hardware-software integration testing	Predictive maintenance, fault diagnosis, cyber-physical risk mitigation	Anandkumar et al. (2025); Wang et al. (2025); Verreydt et al. (2025); Neto et al. (2025)
Toyota - Woven City (Living Laboratory)	City-scale DT (vehicles + infrastructure + humans)	Mixed autonomy testing, pedestrian and cyclist safety evaluation, ODD boundary testing	Behavioural risk modelling, cooperative perception, system-level safety assessment	Liu et al. (2025); Valencia et al. (2025); Meng et al. (2025); Sharma & Dehalwar (2025a)
Singapore - City-Scale AV Digital Twin	Urban system-level DT	Traffic state estimation, incident prediction, and infrastructure-vehicle coordination	Probabilistic traffic risk assessment, real-time hazard forecasting	Deniz et al. (2025); Vanajakshi et al. (2025); Gu et al. (2025); Al Ridhawi et al. (2025)

The case analysis (Table 2) reveals an apparent global convergence toward Digital Twin-enabled safety validation as the dominant paradigm for autonomous vehicle deployment. Across industry-led and city-scale initiatives, Digital Twins are no longer confined to offline simulation. However, they are increasingly embedded into continuous validation pipelines that combine real-world data, predictive analytics, and large-scale virtual experimentation.

Waymo's virtual driver program exemplifies simulation-first safety validation, leveraging Digital Twins to evaluate billions of scenarios that explicitly target long-tail and adversarial events. The supporting literature emphasises surrogate safety metrics, Monte Carlo simulation, and probabilistic risk modelling as essential tools for capturing rare but catastrophic risks (Tan et al., 2025; Bella et al., 2025). In contrast, Tesla's shadow mode represents a data-driven digital shadow approach, where fleet-scale learning enables continuous discovery of unknown risk patterns through real-world operation, aligning with recent advances in ML-based hazard prediction and human-AI interaction research (Yang et al., 2025; Wei et al., 2025).

Industrial initiatives such as BMW and Siemens demonstrate how Digital Twin factories extend safety validation upstream, integrating AV testing into manufacturing and systems engineering workflows. This aligns with research on cyber-physical Digital Twins, predictive maintenance, and trustworthy system verification (Verreydt et al., 2025; Wang et al., 2025). Meanwhile, Toyota's Woven City and Singapore's city-scale Digital Twins highlight a shift toward system-level and societal safety validation, where interactions among vehicles, infrastructure, and humans are explicitly modelled. These initiatives are strongly supported by literature on cooperative perception, V2X-enabled risk modelling, and urban-scale Digital Twins (Liu et al., 2025; Deniz et al., 2025).

Collectively, these cases confirm that Digital Twins enable predictive, scalable, and regulator-relevant safety validation, bridging the gap between isolated vehicle testing and real-world urban deployment. They also demonstrate that the future of AV safety lies not in a single validation method, but in integrated DT ecosystems spanning vehicle, fleet, factory, and city scales.

3.10 Cybersecurity and Data Integrity in Digital Twin-Enabled Autonomous Vehicles

The integration of Digital Twins into autonomous vehicle (AV) ecosystems significantly expands the cyber-physical attack surface, introducing new vulnerabilities alongside enhanced safety capabilities. Digital Twin architectures rely on continuous data exchange among vehicles, sensors, edge devices, cloud platforms, and communication networks, creating multiple entry points for adversarial exploitation (Verreydt et al., 2025; Szymonik, 2024). Compromised data flows can undermine the fidelity of the Digital Twin, leading to incorrect risk assessment and unsafe decision-making.

Among the most critical threats are data poisoning, model tampering, and sensor spoofing. Data poisoning attacks can corrupt training or operational datasets used by machine learning models, while model tampering targets the integrity of perception and control algorithms embedded within the Digital Twin (Jiang et al., 2025; Wang et al., 2025). Sensor spoofing, particularly affecting LiDAR, GPS, and V2X signals, poses severe risks by inducing false environmental representations within both physical vehicles and their virtual counterparts (Choudhury et al., 2025; Du et al., 2025).

To mitigate these risks, secure data pipelines and authenticity verification mechanisms are essential. Techniques such as cryptographic authentication, blockchain-enabled data provenance, and anomaly detection enhance trust in Digital Twin data streams (Choudhury et al., 2025; Verreydt et al., 2025). Looking ahead, the emergence of quantum computing necessitates post-quantum and quantum-safe encryption strategies to protect long-term AV safety data and communication channels (Cao et al., 2025;

Gu et al., 2025). Together, these measures are foundational to ensuring trustworthy and resilient Digital Twin-enabled AV safety validation.

3.11 Integrated Framework for Digital Twin-Driven AV Safety Validation

An integrated framework for Digital Twin-driven autonomous vehicle (AV) safety validation is essential to operationalise predictive, scalable, and continuous safety assurance across the AV lifecycle. The proposed end-to-end architecture couples physical AV systems with high-fidelity virtual counterparts through bidirectional data pipelines, enabling real-time synchronization of vehicle states, sensor outputs, and decision-making processes (Verreydt et al., 2025; Horner et al., 2025). This tight physical-virtual coupling ensures that the Digital Twin remains an accurate and evolving representation of real-world operations.

At the core of the framework are layered data pipelines that integrate onboard sensors, V2X communication, and infrastructure data with edge and cloud computing platforms. Edge-level processing supports low-latency safety monitoring, while cloud-based analytics enable large-scale simulation, historical trend analysis, and cross-fleet learning (Ehsan et al., 2025; Liu et al., 2025). Real-time synchronisation mechanisms allow observed behaviours in the physical vehicle to be mirrored instantly within the Digital Twin, supporting both online monitoring and offline scenario replay.

Decision flows and layered risk assessment processes form the analytical backbone of the framework. Surrogate safety metrics, probabilistic risk models, and machine learning-based predictors operate at multiple layers to assess immediate hazards, emerging risks, and long-term safety trends (Jiang et al., 2025; Gao et al., 2025). Notably, the framework supports continuous learning from real-world operational data, where insights gained through Digital Twin analysis are fed back into perception, planning, and control models. This closed-loop learning process enables adaptive safety improvements, making the framework suitable for regulator readiness and long-term deployment of autonomous vehicles.

3.12 Regulatory, Ethical, and Governance Considerations

The adoption of Digital Twin (DT)-driven safety validation introduces significant regulatory, ethical, and governance implications for autonomous vehicle (AV) deployment. Traditional certification regimes, primarily based on physical testing and post hoc safety evidence, are increasingly misaligned with learning-based and continuously evolving AV systems. DT-enabled certification pathways offer an alternative by supporting virtual compliance testing, scenario-based approval, and continuous post-deployment monitoring, thereby reducing reliance on accumulated road mileage while improving coverage of rare and high-risk scenarios (Tan et al., 2025; Verreydt et al., 2025). Such approaches can enable regulators to assess safety performance across well defined Operational Design Domains (ODDs) using reproducible and auditable simulation evidence.

A central ethical requirement of DT-enabled validation is transparency and explainability. As AV decisions are increasingly driven by complex machine learning models, regulators and the public require clear explanations of how safety-critical decisions are made and how risks are mitigated. Digital Twins support explainability by enabling replay, inspection, and stress-testing of decision pathways under controlled conditions, enhancing auditability and trust (Wei et al., 2025; Jiang et al., 2025). This capability is significant for validating perception and planning systems under uncertainty and in the presence of emergent traffic interactions.

Liability, accountability, and data governance remain complex challenges in DT-enabled AV ecosystems. Continuous data exchange among vehicles, infrastructure, and cloud platforms raises questions regarding data ownership, responsibility for model updates, and accountability in the event of system failure (Szymonik, 2024; Choudhury et al., 2025). Robust governance frameworks are therefore required to define roles across manufacturers, software providers, and operators, while ensuring data integrity, privacy protection, and cybersecurity resilience.

Importantly, Digital Twin-driven evidence has the potential to become a cornerstone of regulatory compliance. By providing traceable, scenario-based, and continuously updated safety evidence, DTs can support risk-based regulatory decision-making and adaptive oversight models (Deniz et al., 2025; Verreydt et al., 2025). In this way, Digital Twins not only enhance technical safety validation but also enable more transparent, ethical, and accountable governance of autonomous mobility systems.

4.1 Policy Roadmap for Global Autonomous Vehicle Safety Deployment

The findings of this chapter point toward a clear policy roadmap to enable the safe and scalable deployment of autonomous vehicles (AVs) through Digital Twin (DT)-driven safety validation. Traditional regulatory approaches, which rely heavily on physical testing and accumulated road mileage, are increasingly misaligned with the complexity and learning-based nature of AV systems. Simulation-based and DT-enabled validation frameworks enable regulators to evaluate safety across billions of scenarios, including rare and adversarial events that are practically impossible to observe on public roads (Tan et al., 2025; Zhang et al., 2025). Policymakers can therefore move toward scenario-based approval pathways, where compliance is demonstrated through reproducible virtual testing within clearly defined Operational Design Domains.

For industry stakeholders, alignment with DT-enabled validation pipelines supports faster development cycles while maintaining rigorous safety assurance. Large-scale simulation, digital shadowing, and predictive risk modelling allow manufacturers to detect system weaknesses early and continuously refine algorithms based on real-world feedback (Verreydt et al., 2025; Jiang et al., 2025). Importantly, DT-based approaches are particularly relevant for emerging economies, where limited testing infrastructure and regulatory capacity constrain AV deployment. City- and corridor-level Digital Twins, as demonstrated in Singapore and other smart-city initiatives, provide a cost-effective pathway for localized safety evaluation and policy experimentation (Deniz et al., 2025; Vanajakshi et al., 2025).

4.2 Theoretical Significance

From a theoretical perspective, this chapter advances autonomous vehicle safety science by integrating predictive analytics, cyber-physical Digital Twins, human-AI interaction models, and risk assessment frameworks into a unified conceptual paradigm. Existing safety validation approaches often treat simulation, machine learning, and systems engineering as separate domains. By contrast, DT-driven safety validation conceptualizes AV safety as a dynamic, evolving property of a cyber-physical system operating under uncertainty (Verreydt et al., 2025).

The framework also contributes theoretically by bridging three previously disconnected research domains: digital twin technologies, autonomous vehicle safety engineering, and regulatory safety standards. By integrating predictive simulation models with structured safety frameworks such as ISO 26262 and SOTIF, the chapter advances a more comprehensive understanding of how digital infrastructures can support safety assurance in cyber–physical mobility systems. This synthesis demonstrates that digital twins are not only tools for operational monitoring but also key components in the evolving epistemology of safety validation for autonomous mobility ecosystems.

This integration represents a shift away from static, post hoc validation toward predictive and data-driven safety assurance, where risks are anticipated rather than merely observed. The use of surrogate safety measures, probabilistic modeling, and learning-based risk prediction strengthens the theoretical foundations of safety validation for non-deterministic systems (Gao et al., 2025; Qi, 2025). Furthermore, by embedding human behavior and mixed-traffic interactions within DT environments, the framework aligns with emerging research on human-AI interaction and cooperative perception in connected mobility systems (Wei et al., 2025; Liu et al., 2025).

4.3 Technological Significance

Technologically, the discussion demonstrates that Digital Twins play a pivotal role in accelerating AV development while enhancing safety assurance. DT-enabled simulation platforms enable comprehensive validation of sensor fusion, perception robustness, and decision-making logic under diverse environmental and traffic conditions (Kim & Shim, 2024; Li et al., 2025). Synthetic data generation within photorealistic environments further addresses data scarcity and bias, supporting more robust machine learning models and improved generalization (M. Zhang et al., 2025).

At the same time, the chapter identifies critical technological challenges that must be addressed for large-scale adoption. High-fidelity environment modelling remains computationally intensive, particularly when simulating dense urban settings and long-tail events. Real-time DT synchronization imposes significant demands on edge-cloud architectures and scheduling of safety-critical tasks (Ehsan et al., 2025; Wang et al., 2025). Moreover, orchestrating large-scale simulations across fleets and cities requires standardized interfaces, interoperable platforms, and efficient scenario management strategies (Tan et al., 2025). Addressing these challenges is essential for translating DT-based validation from research prototypes to industrial-scale deployment.

4.4 Policy and Regulatory Implications

Digital Twin-enabled safety validation has profound implications for AV regulation and certification. DT-driven frameworks support virtual compliance testing, continuous monitoring, and predictive auditing, enabling regulators to move beyond one-time approval toward lifecycle-based oversight (Verreydt et al., 2025). By reducing reliance on real-world road mileage, such approaches improve reproducibility and transparency while allowing regulators to explicitly target high-risk scenarios (Tan et al., 2025).

From a regulatory perspective, the integration of digital twin validation frameworks with established automotive safety standards presents a promising pathway toward safer deployment of autonomous vehicles. Policymakers increasingly require transparent validation methodologies capable of demonstrating system reliability across diverse operational contexts. Digital twin platforms can generate extensive scenario libraries that complement traditional road testing, thereby enabling regulators to evaluate compliance with ISO 26262 functional safety requirements and SOTIF risk analysis procedures. Consequently, digital twin infrastructures may become central components of certification processes for future autonomous mobility systems.

The availability of traceable, scenario-based evidence also strengthens public trust by making safety decisions auditable and explainable. Digital Twins allow regulators to replay incidents, inspect decision pathways, and assess system behaviour under stress, addressing concerns related to black-box AI decision-making (Jiang et al., 2025; Wei et al., 2025). However, effective implementation requires harmonization of standards, clear data governance frameworks, and alignment with existing safety guidelines such as ISO 26262 and UL 4600.

The integration of digital twin–based validation systems into autonomous vehicle regulation presents a promising opportunity for policymakers to establish more robust safety certification frameworks. Traditional validation approaches based solely on physical road testing require billions of miles of driving to statistically demonstrate safety performance. In contrast, digital twin platforms allow regulators to evaluate system behavior across millions of simulated traffic scenarios, including rare and hazardous events that may not be encountered during conventional testing.

Several regulatory agencies have already begun exploring simulation-supported certification strategies. For example, the U.S. National Highway Traffic Safety Administration (NHTSA) and the European Commission's automated driving safety frameworks increasingly emphasize scenario-based testing and simulation-assisted validation methods. Similarly, organizations such as UNECE and ISO working groups have proposed guidelines for incorporating simulation results into safety certification processes. Digital twin architectures could support these initiatives by enabling regulators to verify compliance with safety performance thresholds, evaluate algorithmic behavior under diverse operational conditions, and audit system reliability through standardized validation datasets. Consequently, digital twin–based validation may serve as a critical bridge between engineering innovation and regulatory governance in future autonomous mobility ecosystems.

4.5 Societal Significance

Beyond technical and regulatory dimensions, DT-based safety validation carries substantial societal significance. By enabling proactive identification and mitigation of risks, Digital Twins contribute directly to reducing road fatalities and severe injuries, particularly in complex urban environments where vulnerable road users are most exposed (Sharma & Dehalwar, 2025b; Bella et al., 2025). Improved safety performance is also critical for increasing public acceptance of AVs, which remains closely tied to perceptions of reliability and trust.

Furthermore, DT-enabled validation supports more equitable mobility outcomes by explicitly modelling pedestrian, cyclist, and mixed-traffic interactions, rather than prioritising vehicle-centric performance alone (Peng et al., 2025). At a broader level, integration of AV Digital Twins with urban-scale systems aligns with sustainable mobility goals, supporting cleaner, more efficient, and data-driven transportation planning (Sharma, 2026).

4.6 Contributions and Implications

Collectively, this chapter makes several important contributions. Academically, it introduces a novel conceptual framework for DT-enabled predictive safety validation, develops a structured taxonomy of risk modelling approaches, and synthesises comparative insights into simulation and validation tools. Industrially, it provides a roadmap for hybrid DT and real-world validation pipelines, strategies for large-scale scenario orchestration, and techniques for enhancing explainability in AV decision systems. From a policy perspective, the chapter offers guidance on transparent, reproducible certification pathways, risk-based regulatory models, and integration of AV fleets into innovative city ecosystems. Together, these contributions underscore the transformative potential of Digital Twin-driven safety validation as a cornerstone of safe, scalable, and socially responsible autonomous mobility.

4.7 Conceptual Framework for Predictive and Scalable Safety Validation

The discussion reinforces the proposed conceptual framework as a scalable foundation for proactive, predictive, and continuous safety validation. By unifying Digital Twins, predictive risk modelling, and cyber-physical system analysis, the framework provides a robust pathway for safe, trusted, and regulator-ready deployment of autonomous vehicles.

Figure 2. Conceptual framework for predictive and scalable safety validation

Building on the systematic review and guided by the PRISMA-based methodological synthesis, this chapter develops an integrated conceptual framework for Digital Twin-driven autonomous vehicle (AV) safety validation, as illustrated in Figure 2. The framework positions the Digital Twin-driven AV Safety Validation system as a central, unifying core that orchestrates multiple interdependent technical and analytical domains to enable proactive, predictive, and scalable safety validation.

As shown in Figure 2, the framework is structured around six tightly coupled functional pillars that collectively support continuous safety assessment across diverse operational scenarios. At the foundation of the framework are Digital Twin architectures, which establish the physical-virtual linkage between real-world AVs and their virtual counterparts. These architectures rely on real-time synchronisation, bidirectional data exchange, and high-fidelity modelling to ensure that the digital representation accurately mirrors the evolving state of the physical vehicle and its environment. This continuous coupling enables the Digital Twin to function not as a static simulator, but as a living system capable of reflecting real-world dynamics and learning over time.

Closely integrated with the Digital Twin layer are autonomous vehicle simulation and scenario generation platforms that enable systematic exploration of a vast space of driving conditions, including rare, adversarial, and safety-critical scenarios. As highlighted in Figure 2, simulation platforms and scenario generation methods feed directly into the central framework, allowing large-scale virtual experimentation that would be infeasible or unethical in real-world testing. These platforms enable stress-testing of perception, decision-making, and control algorithms under controlled yet highly diverse conditions, thereby extending safety validation beyond conventional mileage-based approaches.

A core analytical component of the framework is predictive safety and risk modelling, represented in Figure 2 as a dedicated domain supporting forward-looking safety assessment. This component integrates surrogate safety metrics, conflict indicators, and AI-based prediction models to estimate crash likelihood, near-miss probability, and system instability before failures occur. By embedding predictive models within the Digital Twin environment, risk assessment becomes dynamic and adaptive, continuously updating as new sensor data and operational experiences are incorporated. This capability is critical for capturing emergent risks arising from complex interactions between AVs, human drivers, and infrastructure.

The framework further emphasises cyber-physical systems engineering, reflecting the inherently hybrid nature of autonomous vehicles, in which software intelligence, physical hardware, and environmental context interact continuously. As illustrated in Figure 2, this domain ensures that safety validation accounts for interdependencies across sensing, computation, actuation, and environmental feedback loops. Failures in AV systems often arise not from isolated component faults but from cascading interactions across cyber and physical layers; the proposed framework explicitly addresses this challenge by integrating cyber-physical analysis into the Digital Twin-driven validation process.

Another critical pillar of the framework is V2X communication and cooperative perception, which enables system-level safety assessment beyond the individual vehicle. Figure 2 highlights the role of connected infrastructure and inter-vehicle communication in extending the Digital Twin's scope to include cooperative behaviours, shared situational awareness, and network-level risk propagation. By incorporating V2X data, the framework supports evaluation of collective safety outcomes, communication delays, coordination failures, and cooperative driving strategies, which are increasingly central to real-world AV deployments.

Complementing these components is real-time sensor integration, encompassing data fusion and anomaly detection mechanisms. As depicted in Figure 2, continuous streams from onboard sensors and external sources are integrated into the Digital Twin to support real-time monitoring and diagnostics. Data fusion enhances perception robustness, while anomaly detection enables early identification of sensor degradation, model drift, or unexpected environmental conditions. This real-time feedback loop strengthens the framework's ability to detect safety-critical deviations and initiate corrective actions or further simulation-based analysis.

A defining feature of the proposed conceptual framework is its emphasis on interdependencies among all constituent domains. Rather than treating Digital Twins, simulation, predictive modelling, cyber-physical engineering, communication, and sensing as isolated modules, Figure 2 illustrates their dense interconnections and mutual feedback pathways. These interdependencies are essential for capturing emergent behaviours, compounding risks, and system-wide vulnerabilities that cannot be identified through siloed validation approaches. The upward directional flow in the framework symbolically represents the progression from integrated analysis toward higher-level safety assurance outcomes.

The outcome of this integrated framework, as explicitly stated in Figure 2, is the enablement of proactive, predictive, and scalable safety validation. Proactivity is achieved through continuous monitoring and early risk anticipation; predictiveness arises from AI-driven modelling embedded within the Digital Twin; and scalability is enabled by large-scale simulation and virtual experimentation across billions of scenarios. Together, these characteristics address the fundamental limitations of traditional AV safety validation and provide a pathway toward regulator-ready, trustworthy, and ethically responsible deployment.

To operationalise this framework, a qualitative analytical approach was applied to compare and interpret findings across the reviewed studies. This analysis focused on identifying common assumptions and limitations in existing Digital Twin-based validation methods, gaps in handling rare events, emergent behaviours, and uncertainty, and trends toward hybrid validation environments that combine virtual simulations with real-world data. Additionally, emerging best practices for trustworthy, explainable, and secure safety validation were synthesised to inform the framework's design principles.

This conceptual synthesis directly informs the subsequent sections of the chapter, where the framework is translated into detailed discussions on architecture design, predictive modelling techniques, validation workflows, cybersecurity considerations, and policy implications. By grounding the discussion in the integrated structure presented in Figure 2, the chapter advances a coherent and systems-oriented approach to Digital Twin-driven safety validation for autonomous vehicles.

5. CONCLUSION

Digital Twin-driven safety validation marks a fundamental shift in how autonomous vehicle (AV) reliability and trustworthiness are established. By moving beyond static, mileage-based testing toward continuous, data-driven, and predictive validation, Digital Twins enable safety assessment at a scale, depth, and ethical standard that traditional approaches cannot achieve. Through the tight coupling of real-time vehicle data with high-fidelity virtual replicas, Digital Twins enable early identification of emerging risks, simulation of rare and hazardous scenarios without physical exposure, and proactive optimisation of autonomous driving behaviour. When combined with predictive risk modelling, these capabilities enable AV systems to anticipate uncertainty, manage long-tail events, and respond to complex interactions in mixed-traffic environments with greater confidence and robustness.

This chapter has presented a comprehensive synthesis of concepts, methods, and tools underpinning Digital Twin-enabled safety validation for autonomous vehicles. By integrating simulation platforms, surrogate safety metrics, machine-learning-based risk prediction, cyber-physical systems engineering, and real-time sensor fusion, the chapter advances an operational framework that embeds safety assurance throughout the entire AV lifecycle. Rather than treating validation as a post-development activity, the proposed approach positions safety as a continuous, adaptive process that evolves alongside vehicle intelligence and operational experience.

Looking forward, future research should focus on expanding the fidelity and scalability of Digital Twin ecosystems through advances in real-time computation, standardised data architectures, and interoperable simulation environments. Greater attention is also needed on trustworthy AI, cybersecurity, and governance mechanisms to ensure that Digital Twins remain transparent, secure, and regulator-ready. At the system level, integrating vehicle, infrastructure, and city-scale Digital Twins offers a promising pathway to holistic safety management in connected and automated mobility systems.

Ultimately, the path toward safer autonomous mobility depends on the ability to predict and prevent failures before they occur. Digital Twin-based safety ecosystems provide the foundation for this transition, supporting proactive risk management, informed policy decisions, and increased public trust. In doing so, this chapter contributes directly to the objectives of the edited volume Digital Twin Approaches in

Autonomous Vehicles. It offers a future-oriented perspective for researchers, practitioners, and policy-makers shaping the next generation of safe, scalable, and socially responsible autonomous transportation.

Ultimately, the integration of digital twin technologies into autonomous vehicle validation represents a significant shift from reactive safety verification toward proactive and predictive safety assurance. By enabling large-scale scenario generation, machine learning–driven risk modeling, and measurable safety validation criteria, digital twin infrastructures provide a scalable pathway for evaluating the safety performance of complex autonomous mobility systems. The framework proposed in this chapter therefore contributes to ongoing efforts to establish data-driven, simulation-based, and regulatory-aligned validation approaches capable of supporting the safe deployment of autonomous vehicles in increasingly complex urban environments.

REFERENCES

Al Ridhawi, I., Aloqaily, M., Bany Salameh, H., & Jararweh, Y. (2025). Digital twin-enabled V2X for resilient autonomous transportation systems. *IEEE Communications Magazine*, *63*(2), 30–37. DOI: 10.1109/MCOM.001.2500051

Anandkumar, A., Sambasivam, R., Ashokan, A., Sekar, J. C., & Balu, K. (2025). Digital twin-based condition monitoring and predictive maintenance in transportation systems. *Results in Engineering*, *21*, 106336. DOI: 10.1016/j.rineng.2025.106336

Bella, F., Gulisano, F., & Gagliardi, V. (2025). Crash risk of automated vehicles in mixed traffic: A driving simulator study. *Accident; Analysis and Prevention*, *200*, 107809. DOI: 10.1016/j.aap.2024.107809 PMID: 39395369

Bogdevičius, M., Kojis, P., & Skrickij, V. (2025). Digital twin of a vehicle suspension system for ride comfort analysis and optimization. *Applied Sciences (Basel, Switzerland)*, *15*(16), 8933. DOI: 10.3390/app15168933

Cao, J., Leng, S., Xiong, K., & Chen, X. (2025). 6G-enabled autonomous driving: Requirements, challenges, and key technologies. *Tsinghua Science and Technology*, *30*(1), 102–111. DOI: 10.26599/TST.2024.9010076

Choudhury, B., Hota, A., Karmakar, M., Saha, S., & Roy, P. (2025). Blockchain-enabled secure V2X communication framework for intelligent transportation systems. *IEEE Access : Practical Innovations, Open Solutions*, *13*, 20783–20793. DOI: 10.1109/ACCESS.2025.3608623

Deniz, S., Barzegar, A., Sagirli, F. Y., Vasiloff, S., & Seibold, B. (2025). Real-time digital twin of freeway traffic for incident prediction and management. *Control Engineering Practice*, *151*, 106519. DOI: 10.1016/j.conengprac.2025.106519

Du, H., Leng, S., He, J., Xiong, K., & Zhou, L. (2025). Cooperative perception in vehicular networks: A survey. *Digital Communications and Networks*, *11*(1), 1–26. DOI: 10.1016/j.dcan.2023.06.002

Ehsan, M. K., Naz, N., Sodhro, A. H., Mumtaz, S., & Rodrigues, J. J. P. C. (2025). Energy-aware resource management in vehicular edge computing for autonomous driving. *IEEE Transactions on Mobile Computing*, *24*(9), 6932–6944. DOI: 10.1109/TMC.2025.3544918

Gao, H., Qu, T., Gong, X., Wang, P., & Chen, H. (2025). Driving risk assessment in intelligent vehicles based on dynamic traffic environment modeling. *Accident; Analysis and Prevention*, *206*, 108039. DOI: 10.1016/j.aap.2025.108039 PMID: 40280018

Gu, X., Duan, W., Zhang, G., Hou, J., Peng, L., & Wu, H. (2025). A comprehensive survey on 6G-enabled vehicular communications and networking: Requirements, technologies, and challenges. *IEEE Communications Surveys and Tutorials*, *27*(1), 1–52. DOI: 10.1109/COMST.2025.3581152

Han, M., Zhang, J., Huang, Y., Xu, J., Chen, X., & Li, S. (2025). Digital twin-driven construction safety monitoring for autonomous equipment. *Automation in Construction*, *162*, 106108. DOI: 10.1016/j.autcon.2025.106108

Horner, J., Trautrim, T., Ruiz-Martín, C., Borshchev, A., & Robinson, S. (2025). A digital twin of an air transport system for resilience assessment and decision support. *Aerospace (Basel, Switzerland)*, *12*(10), 912. DOI: 10.3390/aerospace12100912

Jiang, C., Blom, H., & Rattanagraikanakorn, B. (2025). Integrated safety and security risk assessment for autonomous transport systems. *Risk Analysis*, *45*(6), 1115–1131. DOI: 10.1111/risa.17649 PMID: 39276027

Kim, S., & Shim, D. (2024). Validation of speed limit recognition systems for autonomous driving using real-road experiments. *International Journal of Engineering Trends and Technology*, *72*(9), 137–145. DOI: 10.14445/22315381/IJETT-V72I9P137

Li, H., & Hong, T. (2025). A digital twin platform for smart parking management in intelligent transport systems. *Building Simulation*, *18*(4), 563–579. DOI: 10.1007/s12273-025-1290-2

Li, T., Bian, Z., Lei, H., Zuo, F., Yang, Y.-T., & Wang, Y. (2025). Digital twin-based evaluation framework for cooperative driving automation in connected vehicle environments. *IEEE Transactions on Intelligent Transportation Systems*, *26*(9), 9080–9090. DOI: 10.1109/TITS.2025.3604569

Liang, K., Wang, Y., Li, Z., Zheng, G., Wong, K., & Xu, S. (2025). Risk-aware trajectory planning for autonomous vehicles in mixed traffic. *IEEE Transactions on Vehicular Technology*, *74*(3), 8457–8471. DOI: 10.1109/TVT.2025.3526198

Liu, J., Sheng, X., Tan, L., Zhang, W., Zhang, P., & Wu, Q. (2025). Cooperative perception for autonomous driving: Architecture, challenges, and future directions. *IEEE Transactions on Vehicular Technology*, *74*(2), 3650–3665. DOI: 10.1109/TVT.2024.3485073

Meng, Y., Yates, K., Dahiya, A., & Untaroiu, C. D. (2025). Occupant safety assessment in autonomous vehicles using integrated simulation and physical testing. *Computer Methods in Biomechanics and Biomedical Engineering*, *28*(5), 1–13. DOI: 10.1080/10255842.2025.2476184 PMID: 40083123

Neto, L. N., Reway, F., Poledna, Y., Drechsler, M., & Hanke, T. (2025). Functional safety of automotive SoCs for autonomous driving: Challenges and trends. *International Journal of Vehicle Safety and Mobility Technology*, *15*(2), 55–70. DOI: 10.1504/IJVSMT.2025.147353

Peng, P., Wang, Z., Cui, P., Hu, X., Yao, J., & Li, J. (2025). Public health risk assessment of urban air pollution using traffic and mobility data. *Frontiers in Public Health*, *13*, 1686346. DOI: 10.3389/fpubh.2025.1686346 PMID: 41080884

Qi, H. (2025). Microscopic modeling of abnormal driver behavior in mixed traffic with automated vehicles. *IEEE Transactions on Intelligent Transportation Systems*, *26*(5), 1163–1176. DOI: 10.1109/TITS.2024.3485668

Sharma, S. N. (2026). Urban spatial digital twin (USDT) in sustainability to spur economic growth for TOD-based development. In Ting, D. S.-K., & Awazi, N. P. (Eds.), *Tenable engineering for a sustainable future: Integrating SDGs and natural resource utilization* (1st ed.). Elsevier. DOI: 10.1016/B978-0-443-40576-1.00009-3

Sharma, S. N., & Dehalwar, K. (2025a). A systematic literature review of pedestrian safety in urban transport systems. *Journal of Road Safety*, *36*(4), 55–78. DOI: 10.33492/JRS-D-25-4-2707507

Sharma, S. N., & Dehalwar, K. (2025b). A systematic literature review of transit-oriented development to assess its role in economic development of cities. *Transportation in Developing Economies*, *11*(2), 23. DOI: 10.1007/s40890-025-00245-1

Sharma, S. N., Singh, D., & Dehalwar, K. (2024). Surrogate safety analysis: Leveraging advanced technologies for safer roads. *Warasan Technology Suranaree*, *31*(4), 010320. DOI: 10.55766/sujst-2024-04-e03837

Szymonik, A. (2024). Cybersecurity in autonomous vehicles: Threats, challenges and countermeasures. *LogForum*, *20*(3), 455–467. DOI: 10.17270/J.LOG.001099

Tan, C., Wang, T., Zhang, M., & Yue, T. (2025). Simulation-based safety validation of autonomous driving functions: A systematic mapping study. *Software & Systems Modeling*, *24*(4), 1463–1483. DOI: 10.1007/s10270-024-01261-2

Valencia, E., Toapanta, F., Oña, G., Carrillo, A., & Herrera, C. (2025). Cooperative control of autonomous ground vehicles using connected infrastructure. *Journal of Intelligent & Robotic Systems*, *111*(3), 71. DOI: 10.1007/s10846-025-02276-7

Vanajakshi, J., Renuka, A., Kamath, V., & Adesh, S. (2025). Real-time traffic state estimation using connected vehicles and roadside sensors. *IEEE Access : Practical Innovations, Open Solutions*, *13*, 1000–1010. DOI: 10.1109/ACCESS.2025.3544776

Verreydt, S., Landuyt, D. V., & Joosen, W. (2025). Engineering trustworthy digital twins: A survey on safety, security and verification approaches. *Software & Systems Modeling*, *24*(3), 873–901. DOI: 10.1007/s10270-024-01242-5

Wang, K., Dong, J., Wang, S., Yuan, Z., Sha, L., & Chen, X. (2025). Real-time scheduling for safety-critical tasks in autonomous vehicles. *IEEE Transactions on Vehicular Technology*, *74*(5), 2335–2346. DOI: 10.1109/TVT.2025.3552481

Wang, X., Hao, M., Wu, M., Shang, C., Yu, R., & Kang, Q. (2025). Intelligent fault diagnosis in industrial IoT using digital twin and edge computing. *IEEE Internet of Things Journal*, *12*(4), 4471–4487. DOI: 10.1109/JIOT.2024.3464521

Wei, R., McDonald, A. D., Mehta, R. K., & García, A. (2025). Human factors in automated vehicle supervision: Mental workload and trust in high-level driving automation. *Human Factors*, *67*(4), 613–634. DOI: 10.1177/00187208241295932 PMID: 39486160

Yang, K., Li, S., Chen, Y., Cao, D., & Tang, X. (2025). Safe reinforcement learning for autonomous driving with risk constraints. *IEEE Transactions on Vehicular Technology*, *74*(3), 3828–3842. DOI: 10.1109/TVT.2024.3488749

Zhang, J., Zhao, B., Yang, G., Zhou, X., Huang, Y., & Li, W. (2025). A digital twin framework for intelligent operation and maintenance of highway tunnels. *Building Simulation*, *18*(5), 545–558. DOI: 10.1007/s12273-025-1332-9

Zhang, M., Xu, J., Gao, Y., Shen, D., & Xu, Z. (2025). Can combined virtual-real testing speed up autonomous vehicle testing? Findings from AEB field experiments. *Communications in Transportation Research*, *5*, 100216. DOI: 10.1016/j.commtr.2025.100216

Zhang, S., Dinavahi, V., & Liang, T. (2025). Towards real-time digital twins of power-electronic traction systems for electric vehicles. *Energy*, *310*, 135451. DOI: 10.1016/j.energy.2025.135451

Zhang, X., Lai, C., Li, G., & Zheng, D. (2025). Towards digital-twin-assisted resource management for vehicular networks. *Computer Networks*, *248*, 111514. DOI: 10.1016/j.comnet.2025.111514

Zhao, J., Wen, Z., Mohanta, K., Subasu, S., Fremoul, A., & Song, Y. (2025). Digital twins and drones for real-time road network inspection and monitoring. *Drones (Basel)*, *9*(9), 621. DOI: 10.3390/drones9090621

Zhu, M., Liu, H., Miao, C., Li, G., Zhang, Y., & Zhao, F. (2025). Digital twin-assisted stability analysis of transportation infrastructure under extreme cold regions. *Cold Regions Science and Technology*, *218*, 104395. DOI: 10.1016/j.coldregions.2024.104395

Chapter 7
Digital Twin-Enabled Intelligent Transportation Systems:
Optimization, Safety, and Sustainable Mobility

Siddharth Shankar Mishra
http://orcid.org/0009-0006-5504-5750
University of Petroleum and Energy Studies, Dehradun, India

Jalpa Thakkar
UPL University of Sustainable Technology, Ankleshwar, India

Srreya Sharma
University of Petroleum and Energy Studies, Dehradun, India

Yugank Sharma
University of Petroleum and Energy Studies, Dehradun, India

Manvendra Singh
University of Petroleum and Energy Studies, Dehradun, India

ABSTRACT

This chapter examines the integration of digital twin technology within intelligent transportation systems (ITS) to enhance optimization, safety, and sustainability in modern mobility networks. Despite rapid advancements in autonomous vehicles and smart infrastructure, existing transportation systems remain largely reactive, lacking predictive and system-wide coordination capabilities. This chapter addresses this gap by proposing a unified framework that integrates real-time data synchronization, artificial intelligence, and simulation-driven optimization through digital twin architectures. The findings demonstrate that digital twin–enabled systems significantly improve operational efficiency, reduce congestion, and support low-carbon transportation strategies. The chapter contributes by providing a structured, analytical framework that connects architecture, optimization, safety, and sustainability in intelligent transportation systems.

DOI: 10.4018/979-8-3373-7785-8.ch007

1. INTRODUCTION

Over the past few decades, cities around the world have witnessed unprecedented urbanization, population expansion and economic growth. While recent changes have further heightened demand for safe, efficient and long-lasting transportation infrastructure. Traditional transit is for fewer people and less congestion. Cities shift, and their transportation networks must grow to support changing operability, alternative modes of travel, and more traffic. Typical methods in traffic management include stop signs, controlled signaling cycles and real-time flow monitoring. Such rudimentary operational management approaches abstract away the dynamic behavior of urban transport networks. Pakistan's outdated transport system causes traffic jams, waste of resources and poses threats to the environment and road safety. That is why academics and authorities in transportation are increasingly looking at new digital technologies to help make the system more sustainable, efficient and responsive (Wang et al., 2023).

Self-driving automobiles are one of the largest innovations in transportation. Autonomous vehicles change how we travel alone. These cars are equipped with competent processors, high-quality sensors, computer vision & machine learning capabilities. LiDAR, radar, cameras and ultrasonic detectors monitor roads, people, cars and infrastructure signals. Using real-time AI, it detects hazards and provides drivers with safe driving decisions. Cars do lane maintenance, adaptive cruise control, collision avoidance and route planning without human help. Self-driving cars could make roads safer, lead to fewer accidents, and make transportation easier. But adding self-driving cars to transportation systems will require a multilayered digital infrastructure that supports real-time data-sharing, system integration and smart decisions across multiple layers of the transportation ecosystem (Acharya et al., 2024). Despite the advancement of intelligent transportation systems, most existing frameworks remain reactive in nature, lacking the capability to predict, simulate, and optimize transportation dynamics in real time across interconnected mobility ecosystems.

Urban transport networks frequently have considerable interface traffic, particularly scheduling. Using Andon cuts production raises greenhouse gas emissions, fuel use, and travel time. Human mistakes cause traffic accidents worldwide, making road safety a priority. Transportation systems waste a lot of energy owing to poorly coordinated traffic patterns and frequent vehicle stops and restarts. A typical traffic control system does not predict crossroad behavior or take countermeasures. Traditional systems wait for problems rather than predicting congestion or other issues. Transportation authorities may not have system-wide visibility into complicated transportation networks in real time. Transportation performance optimization requires precise and real-time vehicle traffic, infrastructural, and environmental data. These difficulties necessitate real-time transport system monitoring, assessment, and management by intelligent digital ecosystems (Richmond et al., 2026). While prior studies have explored digital twins, artificial intelligence, and autonomous vehicles independently, there is a lack of integrated frameworks that combine real-time synchronization, optimization modeling, safety mechanisms, and sustainability assessment within a unified transportation system.

Digital twin technology can solve many of these issues by simulating real-world transportation networks. Interactive digital twins duplicate the structure, function, and operation of real-world assets and systems. Digital doubles apply to automobiles, road infrastructure, traffic signals, public transit, and urban mobility ecosystems. Data from sensors, communication devices, and infrastructure updates these virtual representations in near-real time. Before deployment, transportation planners and system operators may evaluate operating trends, predict modifications, and monitor system performance indicators in real time. Digital twins evaluate data from many sources to create a transportation network perspective, improving decision-making and strategy. This chapter aims to develop a comprehensive digital twin–enabled framework for intelligent transportation systems by integrating system architecture, mathematical optimization, safety mechanisms, and sustainability evaluation.

Digital twin technologies, autonomous cars, and intelligent transportation systems might increase mobility network efficiency and sustainability. Intelligent transportation systems manage resources with advanced sensors, communication, and computer platforms. These use digital twins to provide real-time transportation data monitoring, analysis, and optimization. Traffic managers might employ digital twins to simulate junction traffic flow to optimize light or vehicle route timing to alleviate congestion. Digital twin-driven systems might provide autonomous cars with traffic, road danger, and navigation data. Even transportation congestion is reduced by helping automobiles navigate. Digital twin models enable predictive analytics to identify system failure, infrastructure degradation, and traffic bottlenecks before they occur (Qi and Tao 2018).

Digital twin–based transportation systems can help sustain mobility. Effective wilderness transportation management may reduce road congestion and fuel waste. Digital twins manage vehicle routing and traffic lights to reduce inactive time and increase transportation energy efficiency. Digital twin systems can also combine multimodal transportation, electric cars, and shared mobility. These abilities help communities shift to environmentally friendly, operationally efficient, and mobility-accessible transportation systems. For sustainable urban growth and smart cities, autonomous transportation technologies must be deployed and integrated with their digital sibling (Anonymous2026).

Digital twin technology will be discussed in future autonomous mobility and intelligent transportation systems in this chapter. Digital twin architectures for transportation network optimization, predictive analysis, and real-time monitoring are built and executed. It examines advanced optimization methods that improve autonomous vehicle safety and capacity in digitally linked mobility contexts. The chapter covers data governance, cybersecurity, and digital twin-enabled transportation system safety. The chapter concludes by discussing intelligent transportation system sustainability and digital twin research. This article examines how digital technology may disrupt transportation systems to create sustainable, safer, and better mobility options for future cities (Chen et al., 2024). The remainder of this chapter is structured as follows: Section 2 presents the conceptual foundations of digital twin technology. Section 3 discusses system architecture. Section 4 introduces optimization models. Section 5 examines safety and cybersecurity aspects. Section 6 explores sustainability impacts. Section 7 presents real-world applications, followed by conclusions and future research directions.

2. FOUNDATIONS OF DIGITAL TWIN TECHNOLOGY IN TRANSPORTATION

2.1 Concept and Characteristics of Digital Twins

A digital twin is defined as a real-time, data-driven virtual representation of a physical system that continuously synchronizes with its real-world counterpart to enable monitoring, simulation, and optimization. The Digital twin frame was born as a new technological paradigm in the management and optimization of complex engineering systems, being increasingly relevant in transportation infrastructure. A digital twin is a continuously updated virtual replica of a physical system that interfaces with real-time data sources. Unlike traditional simulation models, with the latter working independently from real-time physical systems, digital twins have an ongoing data exchange process with their real-life counterparts.

This interaction provides a way to ensure that the digital model properly represents current operational circumstances by enabling the virtual model to evolve as the actual system it is modeling. In transportation environments (the interoperability of vehicles, networks, traffic controls, etc.), digital twins act as avatars of a car or network of cars and even a single road or an entire urban mobility ecosystem (Ali et al., 2022) (Fuller et al., 2020).

There are a few important functionalities that govern how digital twin systems operate in transportation applications and the value they add. With real-time synchronization, whenever new data is collected, the virtual model of the digital twin would be updated frequently. Technology uses predictive analytics to analyze this data and predict transportation patterns like traffic bottlenecks or wear on infrastructure. Simulation capabilities may be used by transportation planners to conduct operational analysis of the transportation network and assess hundreds of operational scenarios without impacting real-world operations. The concept of live monitoring is a technology used by various users to monitor the operating life of assets, such as bridges, roads, and tunnels, and develop predictive maintenance strategies throughout their operation. In addition, optimization functions enable increased efficiency for transportation systems through the dynamic adjustment of operational parameters (for example, as traffic signal time spacing, vehicle dispatch, and resourcing). Collectively, these allow digital twins to become smart platforms that support the proactive management of transportation networks (Alipour Sormoli et al., 2024). Unlike traditional simulation models that operate on static datasets, digital twins maintain continuous bidirectional data exchange with physical systems, enabling dynamic updates and real-time decision-making. In contrast to IoT systems, which primarily focus on data collection, digital twins extend functionality by incorporating predictive analytics and system-level optimization.

2.2 Digital Twin Lifecycle in Transportation Systems

The digital twin systems are developed and operated following a well-structured lifecycle that enables effective optimization of the system, constant monitoring, and modeling. The lifecycle of the digital doppelganger starts with system modeling. At this step, engineers duplicate the real transportation system in a computer. This design provides a holistic description of the operation of the machine, on its structure, and on how numerous components of this system, such as automobiles, website traffic indicators, roadway networks, etc., communicate with each other. Common modeling applications such as geographic information systems, simulation programs, and system engineering environments are used typically to create these virtual twins (Liu et al., 2022).

The next step is to install sensors and collect data. Digital twins rely on sensors integrated into transportation infrastructure and cars to gather a large amount of real-time data. Sensor-based technologies refer to LiDAR equipment, traffic cameras, environmental monitoring sensors, vehicle telematics systems, and road condition sensors. This data represents everything you need to know about the state of infrastructure, weather conditions, traffic density, road quality, and vehicle movement. This constant stream of information updates the digital twin with details on what is currently happening.

2.3 Enabling Technologies for Transportation Digital Twins

Transportation digital twin systems take a series of technologies to handle large amounts of data and communicate in real-time. The Internet of Things is an important enabler that allows many doors to be opened. We collect data in real time from IoT devices on environmental monitoring systems, roads, traffic lights, and cars. The digital twin platform captures massive volumes of real-time data from these sensors to ensure the virtual model remains aligned with transportation networks. Transportation networks can be stored and handled in cloud computing platforms, allowing them to store immense amounts of data. Cloud environments are essential for predictive modeling, complex system simulation, and large-scale analytics in digital twin systems. Cloud computing enables scalable infrastructure capable of handling massive real-time transportation data. Cloud platforms allow digital twin systems to satisfy the complex and ever-expanding requirements of transportation networks (Grieves and Vickers 2017).

Edge computing is yet another vital technology for digital twin architecture. Edge computing technologies enable you to respond quickly by reducing latency through local data processing. The smart intersection, roadside unit, and connected vehicle systems use edge modules. These nodes perform processing of traffic, object, and incident data before relaying summary data onto centralized digital twin platforms.

Data can be analyzed with AI and machine learning for predictive analytics and optimization. AI can be fed transportation data to detect trends or patterns. This includes predicting the surmounting traffic, diagnosing issues with the vehicle, and aiding in the development of smart traffic management solutions. Data analytics turn digital twins beyond monitoring tools to smart decision-support systems (Hu et al., 2022).

High communication networks support the link between the transportation system's digital twin. The emerging 5G communication networks, as well as vehicle-to-vehicle communication and infrastructure transmission technologies, are enabling rapid exchange of information between the physical transportation infrastructures and applications on a digital companion platform. A strong communication network quickly delivers real-time data, holding together the physical and digital world.

The conceptual architecture in Fig. 1 shows such transportation systems in the real world along with the respective digital twin that would sit on a cloud, connected via communication networks and sensors, enabling monitoring of the system and its optimization over time. As a result, Table 1 of structural components places an emphasis on capturing these technological components required for establishing digital twin transportation frameworks, sensing infrastructure, communication network, analytics engine, and decision-support interface. When merged, these ecosystem components would lay the foundation of Digital Twin-based smart transportation management systems that have the potential to offer sustainable urban mobility solutions while facilitating advanced traffic with congestion management (He et al., 2022). Existing literature on digital twin–enabled transportation systems can be broadly categorized into three streams: architecture-focused studies emphasizing system integration, AI-driven approaches focusing on predictive analytics, and sustainability-oriented research addressing environmental impacts. However, limited work integrates these dimensions into a unified analytical framework. This chapter addresses this gap by combining architectural design, optimization modeling, safety evaluation, and sustainability analysis into a comprehensive framework.

Figure 1. Digital twin conceptual model for transportation systems

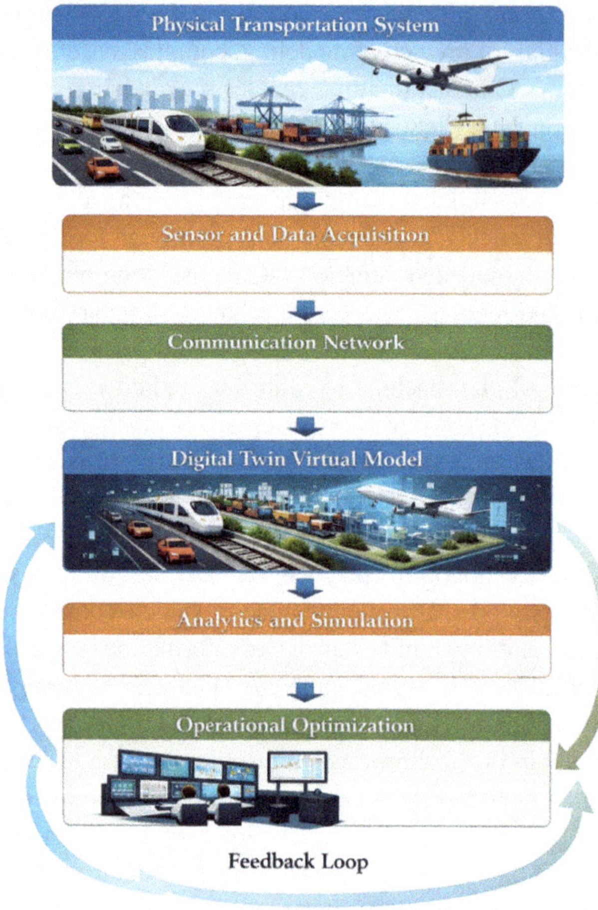

Table 1. Core components of digital twin transportation systems

Component	Description
Physical System	Vehicles, infrastructure, traffic systems
Sensors	Data collection devices
Communication Layer	Data transmission networks
Digital Model	Virtual system representation
Analytics Engine	AI-based prediction
Control Interface	System monitoring and decision support

3. ARCHITECTURE OF DIGITAL TWIN–ENABLED INTELLIGENT TRANSPORTATION SYSTEMS

3.1 Cyber-Physical Transportation Architecture

Building upon the conceptual foundations of digital twin technology, this section presents a structured architecture for intelligent transportation systems, emphasizing the interaction between physical infrastructure, data systems, and decision-making layers. By facilitating and mapping real transportation assets to digital computation models, digital twins enable intelligent transportation systems to function accurately. In a cyber-physical environment of transportation, digital platforms that could study and optimize the performance of this transportation continuously communicate with cars, street infrastructure, sensors, and communication systems. This creates adaptive systems that adapt to ever-changing conditions in real-time by combining physical and digital layers. Traditional intelligent transportation systems depended on fixed infrastructure, static databases, and periodic data processing to monitor traffic. These systems did assist with traffic light coordination and roadways monitoring, but they failed to forecast and simulate how people would behave once they started travelling through sprawling metropolitan areas (Zhu et al., 2018).

Traffic is one of the entities that can improve significantly, both in terms of design, since intelligent transportation systems consist of synchronized digital twins for it to work well. These computational simulations illustrate changes in automobiles, traffic patterns, road infrastructure, and the environment. By constantly exposing data between digital models and real systems, digital twin platforms maintain a near-real-time view of transportation continuums. This insight matures system Administrators in using Predictive analysis that presumes what will happen next and observes how the entire system performs in real time. Digital twins, for example, can examine the existing traffic patterns and estimate how the congestion will evolve over the next few minutes or hours. Transportation authorities can already implement traffic management strategies even before a high level of traffic. Digital twins can provide system-wide insights that lead to safer and more efficient transport by integrating data from multiple sensors and vehicles. This cyber-physical concept transforms transportation networks and systems into intelligent, interconnected mobility ecosystems to allow for the future of solar-powered vehicles on autopilot (Kušić et al., 2023).

3.2 Physical and Data Acquisition Layers

The transport environment consists of analogue or physical infrastructure and operational assets. This layer is required for digital twin transportation systems. Vehicle and Infrastructure: The road network of this stratum consists of cars, roads, intersections, traffic signals, roadside communication devices that inform drivers about the environment around them, and environmental monitoring technologies in such vehicles. Self-driving cars equipped with advanced sensor systems continuously collect data about the surrounding infrastructure. Sensors embedded in the road infrastructure monitor traffic flow patterns, vehicle speeds, road conditions, and atmospheric parameters such as temperature, humidity/moisture. These pieces of equipment generate operating data that is used to build a digital model of the transportation system (Lu et al., 2019).

The physical layer and its associated data capture are tightly coupled. Operational data extraction and transfer from transportation to digital platforms; The sensors on the roads and cars will always monitor system factors (e.g., vehicle position, speed, acceleration, traffic density, and road surface conditions, etc.) Environmental sensors can also register weather data such as rain, fog, and temperature changes that may limit traffic. A wide array of sensors in transportation systems provides an overview of the road network performance (Wang et al., 2021).

To ensure the correct and reliable usage of digital twin models, data collection is fundamental. Without accurate corporeal data, these digital twin systems fail to synchronize with the real world. Thus, the latest transport systems depend on various sensor technologies. For example, systems based on LiDAR for the detection of objects, including vehicles and pedestrians, to be used in autonomous cars, as well as distance measuring radar sensors and traffic observation and imaging video cameras, vehicle telematics systems sending operational data such as maintenance status to central management platforms. Data from devices is analyzed and integrated, then sent out to digital replica simulation platforms through communication networks. With the influx of data, it is possible to excite the digital twin systems to reflect in real time the different transportation scenarios.

3.3 Simulation and Communication Platforms of Digital Twin

These communication capabilities allow transportation systems to function as cooperative mobility networks rather than stand-alone mobility operations. The rapid advancement of high-speed wireless communication technologies, such as the fifth generation (5G) network technology, plays a key role in enabling these architectures. The high bandwidth and low latency capabilities of modern wireless networks enable large amounts of transportation data to be exchanged quickly between digital platforms and physical assets. Thanks to this continuous and reliable data update via communication networks, digital twin models can keep the same state as real transportation systems (Rios-Torres and Malikopoulos 2016).

The digital twin simulation platform is the computational basis of intelligent transportation architecture. Through real-time transportation data analytics, this platform generates dynamic digital models that mirror the behavior of transportation systems. Operators can use the digital twin platform's simulation engines to examine a range of operational scenarios with no impact on real-world transportation infrastructure. The digital twin environment, for example, can be used to study the impact of changing traffic signal timings or trying out new routing strategies before real- world deployment.

3.4 Decision and Control Layer for Intelligent Mobility

The decision and control layer is the last component of the digital twin–enabled intelligent transportation architecture. Using the analytical insights created by the digital twin platform to provide context for real-time decisions and control. Tools for predictive analytics: predict traffic jams, infrastructure failures, or environmental hazards based on historical and real-time transportation data. These predictions enable transportation agencies to take preventive management measures, instead of taking actions just after the disaster (Wu et al., 2025).

The decision layer makes use of optimization algorithms to analyze numerous operation strategies and policies to identify the most effective actions for enhancing system performance. One example in this area is adaptive traffic signal control based on real-time traffic flows, which can adjust and optimize signal timings. For example, autonomous vehicles connected to digital twin platforms can be given optimized routing instructions that minimize travel times and avoid congested areas. Decision-support systems can also optimize the operation of public transport networks, emergency response vehicles, and freight logistics to improve overall mobility efficiency (Ge and Qin 2024).

The control interface gives transportation operators visualization dashboards and analytical tools showing real-time system conditions. These interfaces enable operators to monitor traffic trends, identify incidents, and deploy control strategies as required. In advanced implementations, the optimization strategies generated by digital twin analytics engines are implemented directly in automated control systems. The architecture of digital twin–enabled transportation systems can be structured into five interconnected layers: (1) Physical Layer, consisting of vehicles and infrastructure; (2) Data Acquisition Layer, capturing real-time operational data; (3) Communication Layer, enabling data exchange through 5G and V2X technologies; (4) Analytics Layer, incorporating AI and simulation models; and (5) Control Layer, responsible for decision-making and system optimization.

Combined with physical infrastructure, sensor networks, communication systems, and digital analytical platforms created by a digital twin of these transportation systems, it becomes an integrated intelligent mobility system Figure 2. Table 2 compares traditional intelligent transportation systems with digital twin-based design in terms of data processing characteristics, system visibility, decision-making, and simulation capabilities. This type of architectural integration allows transportation systems to evolve from passive traffic control models to predictive and adaptive mobility infrastructure, ultimately serving as the foundation for sustainable urban transport solutions and driverless vehicles (Petit and Shladover 2014).

Figure 2. Architecture of digital twin–enabled intelligent transportation systems

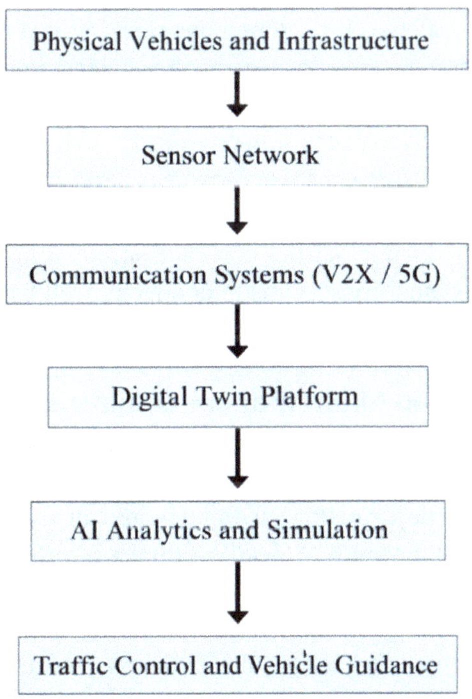

Table 2. Conventional ITS vs digital twin-based ITS

Feature	Conventional ITS	Digital Twin ITS
Data Processing	Periodic	Continuous
System Visibility	Partial	Complete
Decision Type	Reactive	Predictive
Simulation	Limited	Advanced

4. OPTIMIZATION MODELS FOR AUTONOMOUS MOBILITY

4.1 Traffic Flow and Autonomous Fleet Optimization

Transport planning using simulation-based optimization can provide plans (from the status quo) that reduce travel time and traffic congestion without interrupting ongoing transport activities. A second important application of digital twin optimization is in orchestrating the operation of fleets of self-driving cars. As autonomous cars become more ubiquitous in cities, it gets increasingly difficult to deal with many of them at the same time. Autonomized fleets for use in logistics, public transit, and ridesharing need to be able to adapt swiftly to passenger demand changes while reducing travel costs and delays. Fleet-level digital twins are used to simulate fleet operations and manage vehicle flows across large regions. These computable models consider passenger demand trends, traffic flow, and vehicle availability to determine the ideal routing strategies for autonomous fleets (Wu et al., 2022).

Coordinating a fleet of autonomous vehicles also involves balancing system loads. The plan is intended to ensure that transportation resources are efficiently used across the entire network. For example, the digital twin models can dynamically dispatch self-driving cars to high passenger-demand areas. Digital twins can also examine scheduling strategies that provide more services to passengers and less time for cars to sit idle. In freight transportation networks, fleet optimization algorithms can make autonomous delivery trucks more efficient, reducing logistics costs and accelerating delivery. Moreover, digital twin platforms help big autonomous mobility systems to cooperate well by integrating traffic flow models with fleet-level optimization algorithms (Zhu et al., 2017).

4.2 Energy Optimization and Mathematical Optimization Frameworks

The developed insights can enable transport systems to set routing strategies that reduce energy consumption while ensuring acceptable travel times. Digital twins can also be used to analyze the placement and usage of charging infrastructure to ensure electric vehicles have access to reliable charging services without overloading power distribution networks.

The digital twin platforms are empowered analytically by mathematical optimization frameworks that allow the definition of the objectives and constraints in 483 System-level variables, such as constraints, input, and output variables in a known mathematical representation. In general, optimization models aim to minimize a cost function comprising the essential performance indicators: operational costs, energy/fuel consumption, congestion levels, and travel time. These cost functions are dependent on several system constraints like vehicle availability, energy storage capacity, road capacity, and safety constraints.

Mathematical optimization models evaluate multiple operational scenarios to determine the optimal system configuration that minimizes the total system cost and meets these constraints (Liao et al., 2021).

In control of the traffic, optimization frameworks could be used to find the optimal settings for traffic signal timings on an urban road network. For example, for autonomous fleet management systems, optimization models can determine routing solutions that meet passenger demand constraints with the least amount of travel distance.

4.3 Traffic Control is an A.I. Based Service

A digital twin environment with the digitalization of transportation through artificial intelligence technologies facilitates intelligent transportation optimization. Machine learning algorithms are using big data analytics to analyze transportation data and uncover patterns in traffic behavior, vehicle movement, and infrastructure performance. Such algorithms allow transportation systems to adjust their operational environment in real time as the traffic conditions change. They can use past records and real-time data to learn and thus improve their decision-making over the years.

Machine learning algorithms are frequently relied on to predict traffic and congestion. Predictive models can reliably predict future traffic based on prior traffic patterns, weather conditions, and current vehicle movement tendencies. That enables transportation officials to use the forecasts to plan for traffic in advance — adjusting the timing of signals to clear flows on streets several blocks ahead or directing cars at intersections before they get stuck. Moreover, deep learning models have been applied to explore elaborate transportation datasets and identify patterns that may not be apparent through standard statistical methods (Chen et al. 2018).

Adaptive traffic control systems lend themselves well to reinforcement learning approaches. In reinforcement learning paradigms, traffic control agents can learn the optimal ways to manage traffic by interacting with simulated transportation environments. All these agents examine their environment to see how different traffic control plans would impact traffic, take different actions and iteratively learn through repeated experience to improve performance. If utilized within digital twin simulation platforms, reinforcement learning agents become able to try out alternative control strategies in virtual representations of transportation systems before applying them to actual systems.

The optimization framework is shown in Figure 3, which ingests the transportation data collected from the traffic sensors and uses it with digital twin simulation models and predictive analytics algorithms to output an optimization strategy for adaptive Traffic Management. Meanwhile, Table 3 establishes an overview of some important optimization approaches that have been adapted to smart transportation systems. It highlights their applications in traffic signal optimization, fleet routing, traffic prediction, and adaptive traffic control. All these optimization methods allow intelligent transportation systems to adapt dynamically to changing traffic states and maximize the mobility efficiency (Petit and Shladover 2014).

Figure 3. Digital twin-based traffic optimization framework

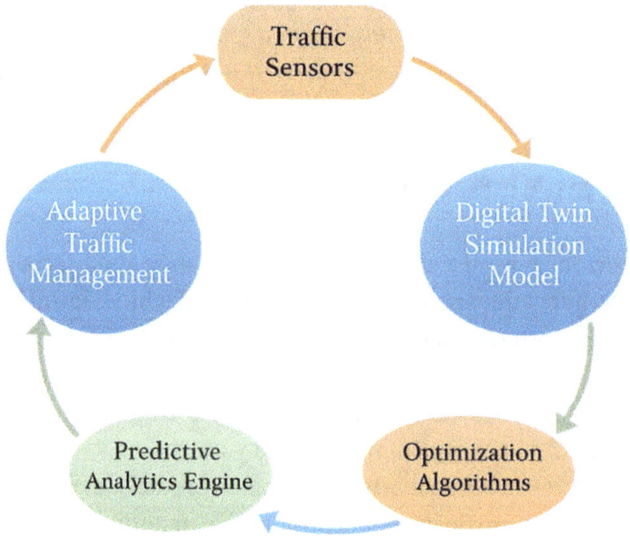

Table 3. Optimization techniques in smart transportation

Technique	Application
Linear Programming	Traffic signal optimization
Reinforcement Learning	Adaptive traffic control
Genetic Algorithms	Fleet routing
Deep Learning	Traffic prediction

5. SAFETY AND SECURITY IN AUTONOMOUS TRANSPORTATION

5.1 Safety Challenges and Risk Factors in Autonomous Vehicles

Safety remains a top concern for autonomous transportation systems deployment. Autonomous cars operate in environments that are extremely dynamic and difficult to anticipate, and the decisions they make about how to drive are affected by numerous factors. Road transport systems require complex interactions between cars, pedestrians, bicycles, infrastructure, and the environment. This differs from regulated industrial environments. This is why self-driving cars have to process massive amounts of sensor data and decide in less than a second. So, for cars to successfully navigate such environments, the solution demands reliable control algorithms, robust sensing systems, and continual monitoring of system performance (Mansour and Singh 2025).

One of the worst safety problems for self-driving cars is that they should be able to completely appreciate their surroundings. LiDAR, radar, cameras, and ultrasonic sensors are some of the devices that self-driving cars use to locate objects and monitor road conditions. These sensors gather data on pedestrian behavior, traffic lights, the seams of the road, and other vehicle silhouettes around it. But sensors and other systems also work worse under environmental factors such as heavy rain, fog, snow, and bad lighting. In such cases, autonomous vehicles must apply advanced techniques of data fusion to integrate the information from multiple sensors to build an accurate model of their environment.

Infrastructure problems can also make self-driving cars less secure. Things that its cameras need to spot, such as traffic lights, road markings, and signs on the road. Infrastructure that is poorly maintained or not uniform could make environmental perception systems less accurate. Self-driving cars must also ensure they can safely navigate around traffic infrastructure such as intersections, merging segments of highways, and other similar zones, pedestrian crossings. These types of complex interactions highlight the critical need for effective safety monitoring systems that continually assess system performance and identify risks in transportation environments (Kehoe et al.).

5.2 Digital Twin–Based Safety Simulation and Fault Detection

The development of digital twin technology is essential for better reliability and safety of autonomous traffic systems. It allows for the large-scale simulation and validation of safety scenarios. Standardized automotive crash testing depends on regulated testing and limited real-world conditions that may fail to simulate the myriads of variables involved in driving. Engineers and transportation researchers can use digital siblings to test hundreds of possible disaster scenarios in virtual environments without the risk of injury to people or vehicles (Eskandarian et al. 2024).

Digital twin simulation platforms are tools able to simulate vehicle infrastructure and environmental interactions in transportation systems. Researchers can use these simulations to see how autonomous cars react in intricate driving circumstances, like unexpected street crossings, an instant blockage on the road, or a need for surrounding vehicles to stop quickly. Analyzing the performance of vehicles under these scenarios enables developers to recognize problems with perception systems, decision-making algorithms, and control techniques. This allows the self-driving car to keep improving its safety level before it hits the real-life transportation network.

And it is also helpful for evaluating system-level safety across whole networks of transportation systems. Rather than analyzing single vehicles in isolation, digital twin platforms can run realistic traffic scenarios with many thousands of interacting automobiles at once. This method allows transportation planners to explore potential changes in traffic safety resulting from the introduction of self-driving vehicles. For example, digital siblings can illustrate the dynamics of communication between vehicles and the exchange of safety information like road hazards or unexpected deceleration events.

Digital twin technology also helps in establishing the trustworthiness of sensors and faults within a system. Self-driving cars rely on sensor data to understand the world around them, and so sensor reliability is key to their safe operation. Digital twin models keep track of sensor data streams and always compare the system behavior against expected behavior. If the system detects a behavior outside of this pattern, it can detect possible EHD malfunction or calibration error. For instance, if a fleet LiDAR sensor suddenly starts emitting erroneous distance measurements, the digital twin system can sense this and trigger troubleshooting routines (Yu et al. 2020).

Fault detection strategies are not limited to sensors but can be applied to other elements of autonomous transportation systems, including onboard computers, control algorithms, and communication systems. For instance, digital twin platforms can analyze data about how a system performs to identify early signs of hardware problems or software bugs. In case any data or system flaws are discovered at an early stage, transportation operators can adopt maintenance or corrective measures to minimize potential safety risks. This prediction for needed maintenance makes autonomous conveyance systems far more stable and reliable in their operation.

5.3 Cybersecurity and Secure Communication in Intelligent Transportation Systems

With the aim of create ever more interconnected and data-driven transport systems, cybersecurity is swiftly becoming one of the most pertinent issues in autonomous mobility. This is a fundamental requirement, as it lays the foundation for both autonomous vehicles and intelligent transportation infrastructure, with the pressing need to monitor all real-time components from vehicles and sensors to cloud-based digital twin platforms that can interoperate through traffic management systems... Though greater connectivity enhances efficiency and coordination across the system, it also creates new vulnerabilities that malicious actors could exploit. Cyber Battle Risks – Data manipulation attacks, unauthorized system access, communication interception, and denial of service attacks (Wei et al. 2025). Recent studies highlight the vulnerability of autonomous transportation systems to cyberattacks such as GPS spoofing, data injection, and denial-of-service attacks. These threats can compromise vehicle navigation, traffic coordination, and system reliability.

Data manipulation attacks represent a particularly grave concern in autonomous transportation scenarios. In these instances, the flow of information reaching autonomous vehicles can be tampered with if a hostile agent has control over the communication paths or streams for sensor data. Supply of incorrect traffic information might lead drivers to drive dangerously or take a detour. Likewise, a vehicle's sensor data is vulnerable and therefore can create a circumstance where the vehicle does not identify things in its surroundings and passes them into location-based identification sequencers.' That could cause the car to misidentify an obstacle or lose its direction.

Also, the influx of security threats comes from unauthorized access to the transportation control system. Many intelligent transportation systems utilize centralized traffic management platforms for controlling traffic signals, creating vehicle routes, and monitoring transportation infrastructure (Manek et al.).

If unauthorized users gain access to these control systems, they could disable traffic flows or safety mechanisms and manipulate transportation operations. Such attacks may pose significant safety threats to road users and lead to widespread disruption of transportation.

Thus, secure communication mechanisms must be introduced in digital twin–enabled transportation architectures to reduce the risk. One key role that encryption technologies play is protecting data in transit between digital twin platforms, infrastructure, and vehicles. Only devices with the right stakeholders can gain access to transportation networks and communicate operational data through secure communication protocols. The identities of interconnected vehicles and infrastructure components are verified through authentication mechanisms to ensure their trustworthiness before allowing them to access communication networks.

Continuous monitoring mechanisms, along with encryption and authentication techniques, must be implemented in transportation systems to identify potential cybersecurity threats. Digital twin platforms can use an analysis of communication trends across transportation networks to be used as a means of cybersecurity monitoring. Machine learning algorithms can learn to identify anomalous patterns of communication that may indicate malicious activity or intrusion attempts. Detection of such anomalies at an early stage allows system administrators to take preventive measures before a security breach turns into a major system failure (Shladover 2017).

This paper combines upcoming Cybersecurity protection techniques, defect detection, and safety monitoring to provide a comprehensive safety framework for self-driving vehicles. Transportation networks could act as a basis to provide better autonomous mobility services if we integrate digital twin simulation skills together with real-time monitoring and secure communication technology, while ensuring extremely high levels of operational safety. The architecture for safety monitoring is depicted in Figure 4, where sensor data from autonomous vehicles are processed by data fusion systems and digital twin simulation platforms to identify the risk of potential hazards and implement corrective control measures. Meanwhile, key safety measures used for assessing autonomous transportation systems' dependability and performance are summarized in Table 4. This includes such parameters as system availability, sensor accuracy, time-to-collision safety margins, and collision risk probabilities. Such measures and monitoring frameworks help ensure transportation networks can hold themselves up to the high standards of operational safety that allow for the rapid deployment of autonomous mobility technology.

Figure 4. Digital twin-based safety monitoring framework

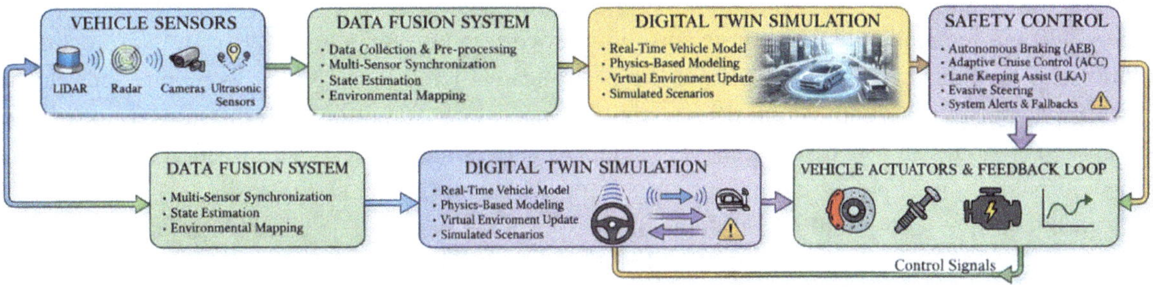

Table 4. Safety metrics in autonomous transportation systems

Metric	Description
Collision Risk	Probability of accidents
Time-to-Collision	Safety margin between vehicles
Sensor Accuracy	Environmental detection reliability
System Availability	Operational stability of the autonomous system

6. SUSTAINABLE SMART MOBILITY AND ENVIRONMENTAL IMPACT

6.1 Environmental Challenges and Sustainable Transportation Needs

Transportation systems are vital to modern economic development; they allow products and people to move between cities, regions, and nations. However, most of the problems have arisen from the fast-growing road networks and dependency on personal mobility. The transport sector is responsible for almost a quarter of global greenhouse gas emissions, thanks largely to fossil fuel consumption in road transport, aviation, and shipping. Carbon dioxide is released by transportation activities, which contribute to climate change, air pollution, and declining environmental conditions. As a mobility-related activity, on-road traffic must have some environmental impact, particularly in metropolitan settings, and scrapyards worsen air quality or produce sound and air pollution (Chaturvedi and Srivastava 2025).

Another major environmental drawback of traditional transport systems is traffic congestion. As cities look for cleaner air and more responsible environmental stewardship, they are seeking new transportation management systems that can optimize operations while reducing their carbon footprints. New and sophisticated digital technology is needed for continuous monitoring of the performance in transportation systems (UET, 2021), which needs to be optimized in all aspects. Smart mobility solutions are essentially trying to enable accessibility in the urban population, reduce emissions, and make transportation efficient. To date, digital twin technology has been viewed as a helpful aid in implementing plans for mobility sustainability. It enhances the analytic capacity of transportation planners for assessing environmental issues and optimizing transportation networks.

6.2 Digital Twins for Sustainable Transportation and Electric Mobility

Digital twin technology enables transportation network environmental analysis and sustainability solution exploration. Digital twins, real-time virtual duplicates of transportation infrastructure and vehicle networks, enable transportation authorities to simulate energy consumption and emissions from various operating techniques and traffic efficiency. Planners can also simulate the environmental consequences of new infrastructure or policy changes prior to deploying them (Lyu et al. 2021).

Data integration across multiple systems in transportation networks is what lends value to digital twin platforms. One of the key advantages is that digital twin platforms may amalgamate transportation network data from multiple sources. Energy data from physical infrastructure, environmental systems, connected vehicles (cars), and traffic sensor details may establish a collaborative digital ecosystem. Transportation planners can use the massive data set to examine impacts on the environment, energy use, and traffic models. Digital twin simulations can measure how urban traffic signal layouts impact car fuel consumption and emissions.

So digital siblings assist electric mobility systems in migrating. EVs are the Future- Electric Vehicles are slowly replacing ICE vehicles. EVs generate multiple orders of magnitude less in direct emissions than their ICE counterparts, so are clearly a step forward, but as EV penetration goes up, the power demand from charging and management of recharge infrastructure to maintain grid stability is another issue. These digital twin platforms can help transportation planners model electric car charging behavior, analyze possible locations of charging stations, and research the impacts on urban energy networks (Zhuang et al. 2021).

The energy optimization algorithms on digital twins can predict the energy consumption of a vehicle in various traffic and routing environments. The digital siblings could help devise infrastructure for electric cars and assess how renewables can be woven into transportation systems. For example, sustainable transportation systems enabled by a digital twin environment can be powered from renewable energy sources such as solar or wind. Digital twins combine data from transport and energy networks to design sustainable methods of mobility.

6.3 Smart City Mobility Integration

Digital twin technology provides a unified platform, which eases the connection between different transport modalities & mobility services in this perspective. Conventional transit networks often operate on disparate systems, owning and regulating public transport, private cars, and (micro) mobility (März et al. It could lead to inefficient mobility patterns and limited access for urban residents (Rakha et al.).

Using digital twin platforms, cities can establish connected mobility ecosystems that share a single communicative digital operating environment and enable different forms of transport modalities to integrate with each other. Autonomous vehicles, public transit systems, ride-sharing platforms, and bicycle-sharing services can be fully integrated in the same digital twin infrastructure. Fusing real-time data from these different transport modalities, digital twin platforms can help identify opportunities to expand mobility accessibility and boost system efficiency.

Integrating multimodal transportation is one of the main challenges of smart city mobility strategies. The digital twin models can replicate travelers movement and analyze the interactions of transport modes in urban areas. Digital twin simulations, for example, can be used to assess the potential level of congestion reduction and increased passenger mobility provided through a continued expansion of autonomous vehicle services integrated into existing public transportation networks. Similarly, digital twin platforms can analyze the efficiency of strategies for accommodating ride-sharing services into mass transit networks to deliver seamless mobility experiences for urban travelers (Aheleroff et al. 2021).

Not only does mobility in smart cities include accessibility of mobility to all demographic groups, including older adults, individuals with disabilities, and residents of disadvantaged communities. Digital twin platforms can analyze mobility patterns in urban areas to detect locations with limited transportation access. Armed with these insights, transportation authorities can design mobility solutions suited to their needs—ranging from demand-based autonomous shuttles to improved public transit connectivity.

FSS also contributes to sustainable urban growth with low-carbon transportation options by promoting their usage, as a direct result of smart mobility systems that are supported by digital twins. Integrated mobility platforms can prioritize overall carbon emissions by focusing on shared mobility services, electric vehicles, and public transit solutions. Continuous monitoring and optimization enable the transition of cities towards environmentally sustainable, accessible, and efficient transport systems through digital twin platforms (Dasgupta et al. 2021).

A conceptualization of the role played by digital twin platforms in incorporating autonomous mobility systems, traffic optimization, and energy efficiency towards low-carbon transportation is illustrated in Figure 5. At the same time, Table 5 highlights that digital twin transportation systems also contribute to a positive environmental impact with benefits like improved accessibility in the urban mobility network, e.g. less vehicle congestion and reduced energy consumption. Together, these capabilities enable digital twin technologies to facilitate sustainable transportation strategies that help build eco-friendly smart city mobility ecosystems (Kishore et al. 2025).

Figure 5. Digital twin–enabled sustainable mobility ecosystem

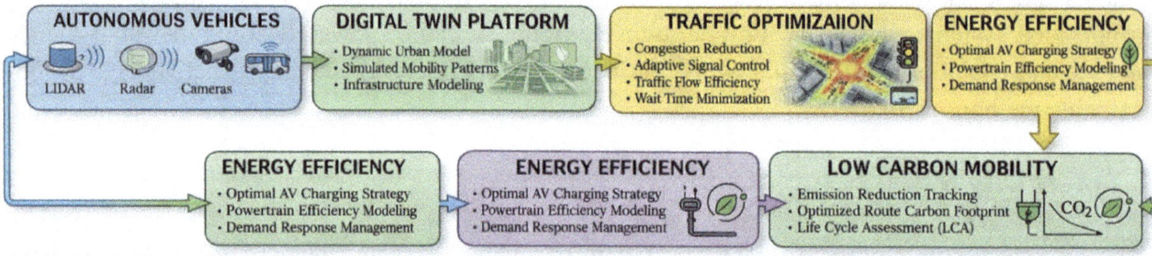

Table 5. Environmental benefits of digital twin transportation systems

Impact Area	**Benefit**
Traffic Congestion	Reduced
Energy Consumption	Lower
Carbon Emissions	Reduced
Urban Mobility	Improved accessibility

7. CASE STUDIES AND REAL-WORLD APPLICATIONS

7.1 Smart City Transportation Platforms

As smart city projects have been initiated by a number of countries, the use of digital twin technology in transport systems has become increasingly clear. Cities are gradually building digital infrastructure that will bring together transportation networks and data analytics platforms, enabling real-time monitoring and optimization of mobility systems. Digital twin transportation platforms can help city planners improve the efficiency of traffic management systems, study transportation demand, and model patterns of urban mobility. These platforms create a common digital space for real-time observation of transport infrastructure, vehicle networks, and mobility services (Stefko et al. 2025).

Smart city transportation platforms rely heavily on the integration of big data from traffic sensors, connected vehicles, public transit systems, and environmental monitoring networks. By integrating various datasets into a digital twin platform, cities can create more sophisticated models of traffic patterns, transportation demand, and infrastructure use. These models allow transport authorities to find inefficiencies or congestion in the system and evaluate its performance. Take digital twin systems, which could simulate how traffic patterns adjust day by day depending on weather, public events, or commuting behavior.

Around the world, dozens of cities are using digital twin technologies to augment transportation management. Such systems allow transportation agencies to actively alter the measures they take in response to traffic needs, as well as internalize flow throughout entire metropolitan areas. For instance, they can use digital twin models to predict how changes in traffic signal timing might affect road congestion levels at specific junctures. Cities that run these tactics through a virtual environment before applying them to real-world systems can significantly decrease traffic congestion and overall transportation efficiency (Gonzalez Bautista et al. 2015).

Another key feature showcases the degree to which smart city transportation systems can assist in shaping infrastructure and encourage long-term urban expansion. Digital twin models also help city planners see how new infrastructure enhancements — freeway extensions, metro systems, or public transportation lines — would shift urban mobility dynamics. Planners can employ such simulations to explore alternative planning outcomes and formulate strategies that expand access while minimizing their ecological footprint. So digital technology can enhance urban transportation planning, sustainability, and evidence - based.

7.2 Autonomous Vehicle Simulation Environments

Nevertheless, conventional testing protocols do incorporate on-road driving tests, which may expose vehicles to unforeseen situations and safety hazards. Simulations in digital twin environments allow us to test autonomous cars at scale without leaving them in the real-world transportation systems (Špitálová 2023).

These digital twin systems effectively emulate real-world driving conditions in simulation environments for autonomous vehicles. Control routes are often spongy temperatures, and very trim factors fantasy AND. It means autonomous cars provide the surroundings in which they work, interacting with "virtual" traffic (pedestrians, cyclists, and other cars on the road) and transit systems. Such simulations allow engineers to analyze how well autonomous car algorithms respond within numerous driving conditions.

Among the main attributes of digital twin simulation systems, their ability to produce a wide variety of challenging testing scenarios is one. Autonomous vehicles need to operate safely in all traffic and weather conditions, but also through unexpected barriers. Digital twin platforms may also allow engineers to replicate thousands of driving situations that would be difficult or dangerous to recreate in the real world. These include children running into the road or pedestrians on it due to emergencies, as well as sudden braking and lane changes by other cars in the adjacent lanes (Baimukhanov et al., 2025).

Simulation with the digital twin helps extend current guidance over autonomous vehicle control algorithms. In addition to teaching machines about the world, this version makes sure that these cars are safer and more reliable before they hit public roads. Digital twin simulation platforms enable the assessment of system level performance for autonomous mobility services, as well as vehicle-level testing. For example, autonomous vehicle fleet-based ride-hailing companies can model how vehicles respond to changes in passenger demand across city centers. These simulations allow mobility providers to improve their fleet operation, lower operating costs, and decrease passenger wait times. The reason that digital twins constitute such a convincing platform for verifying autonomous mobility technologies is simple: they provide a thorough simulation to work with.

7.3 Integrated Urban Mobility Systems

Individual vehicle operations are not the only area where integrated urban mobility systems, which integrate numerous transportation modalities in a single digital context, find value — digital twin technology is also central to this. For example, urban transport systems include layers of physical mobility services that use private cars and buses, shared cars or skills, freight and other logistic businesses, or provide non-motorized transport (walking) and bicycles. The articulation of these different transport means is a major challenge for urban mobility management (Wang et al. 2025).

By using digital twin platforms, cities can proceed within a common analytical framework that allows the integration of these transportation modalities for coordinated mobility planning. By collecting real-time data across different transportation systems, digital twin models could be used to analyze how various mobility services interact with one another within an urban environment. By taking this holistic view, transportation planners can see where inefficiencies are occurring and pursue mobility solutions that allow them to make better use of their overall assets.

For example, digital twin platforms can be used to simulate multimodal transportation networks where autonomous vehicles enable first-mile and last-mile connectivity to public transit systems. For example, passengers can use autonomous transport to travel from home to metro stations and then continue on high-capacity public transit systems. Digital twin simulations allow planners to evaluate the impact of these integrated mobility services on passenger accessibility, travel times, and traffic congestion (Wang and Lv 2023).

As well as freight logistics systems, mobility integration based on digital twin approaches can also be beneficial. Urban freight transport is a major contributor to traffic congestion, especially in crowded urban areas. Such digital twin models can be used to study trends of freight deliveries and devise a plan for efficient route planning, scheduling delivery during non-peak hours, as well as grouping them with urban mobility systems. These practices promote effectiveness in logistics and reduce congestion.

Another advantage of integrated digital twin mobility platforms is their ability to enable mobility-as-a-service paradigms. Mobility-as-a-service platforms provide customers with access to a range of transportation services in digital apps, as a single mass (Bi et al.. 2026).

Such platforms could dynamically orchestrate transportation services systemically, responding to real-time trends in demand through digital twin technology. Digital twin models can, for instance, provide the best travel routes that include public transport, ride-hailing, and even micro-mobility vehicles like e-scooters. These characteristics allow cities to materialize as smart mobility ecosystems, which integrate transportation services across modes efficiently via digital twin technologies. These ecosystems bolster transit access, alleviate traffic congestion, and are a step towards more eco-friendly urban mobility systems (Qureshi and Abdullah 2014).

The digital twin transportation system interconnects cars, infrastructure, communication networks, cloud platform, and artificial intelligence analytics to support Mobility services through smart cities, as shown in Figure 6. On the other hand, Table 6 presents a summary of practical applications for digital twin technology in transportation systems. Urban traffic simulation for predicting potential congestion, autonomous vehicle testing to validate safety, infrastructure monitoring for road surface analysis, and mobility planning to enhance transportation networks in cities. The work carried out through these applications showcases the growing relevance of digital twin technology in today's urban scenarios, where sustainable and smart transport solutions are at the forefront of discussion (Tagne et al., 2015).

Figure 6. Integrated digital twin smart transportation ecosystem

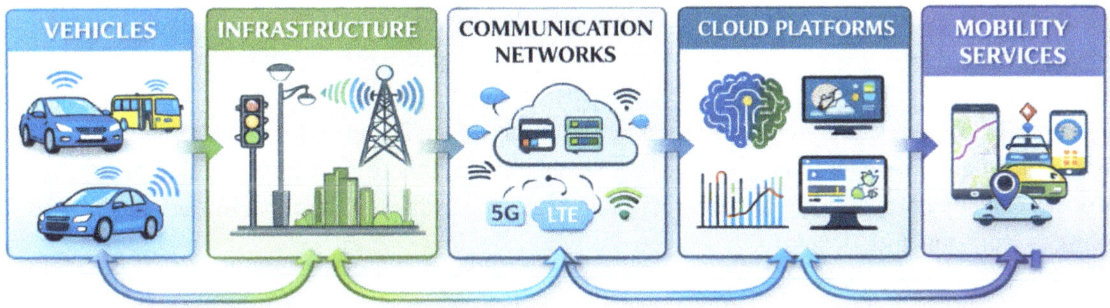

Table 6. Applications of digital twin transportation systems

Application	Description
Urban Traffic Simulation	Predict congestion
Autonomous Vehicle Testing	Virtual safety validation
Infrastructure Monitoring	Road condition analysis
Mobility Planning	Urban transportation optimization

8. CHALLENGES AND FUTURE RESEARCH DIRECTIONS

Digital twin-enabled intelligent transportation systems (DT-ITS) are still growing and spreading, but they face a lot of problems that make it hard to get them widely used and working at their best. The biggest problem is scalability, especially when it comes to dealing with and processing the huge amounts of real-time data that vehicles, sensors, infrastructure, and environmental monitoring systems create. The next step in this model is for transportation networks to move up the computational load tree. However, keeping data continuity for all events will require the entire computer's resource class (simulating analytics). To ensure timely processing while still maintaining performance at scale operational capabilities, highly efficient hub designs must be used with cascading edge computing and daisy chained distributed parallel streaming platforms.

The second issue is data privacy and security, which is a big deal. To make digital twin systems and transport systems that constantly copy the real world in an online loop, you need data about vehicle position and location, user behavior, and the state of the infrastructure around it. In short, these huge amounts of personal data are a big problem when compared to the privacy issues that come up with connected car ecosystems, self-driving cars, and the rise of digital interactions with this technology. Hacking, data breaches, and cyberattacks like data injection or spoofing put the integrity of the system and the safety of the user at risk. To make sure that trustworthiness and resilience are possible, we need strong encryption methods, safe communication protocols, and data-sharing frameworks that protect privacy.

One of the main problems is that these digital twin systems are seamlessly connected across a wide range of platforms. Transportation ecosystems are complicated networks that need many different groups to work together. These groups include government agencies, private mobility providers, infrastructure operators, and technology suppliers. These groups often use different standards, data formats, and technical infrastructures that are in competition with each other. The gaps in implementation stacks are a big technical and organizational problem that keeps old systems from working with new digital twin platforms. So, standardizing the data protocol and system interface is the most important thing for all systems to work together.

Digital twin systems also have economic and operational limits because they need a lot of computing power and infrastructure. Storage Needed by Advanced Databases: Artificial intelligence algorithms, complex simulations, and real-time optimization processes all need a lot of computing power (in terms of storage space). This could make it harder for people to use, especially in places where the internet infrastructure isn't fully built yet. Only a good plan for allocating resources and a cheap way to carry it out can go beyond these limits.

People are very interested in AI decision making because it is unfair and not open. There may be biases in the training data that affect the machine learning models for traffic forecasting, route optimization, or mechanism control, which can lead to unfair results. Also, many AI algorithms are "black boxes," which makes it hard to explain how they came to their conclusions and makes it harder to hold people responsible for big transportation decisions. Future systems must incorporate explainable AI frameworks to ensure transparency and foster user trust.

However, the biggest problem is rules and governance. Also, even though many people are already thinking about how to get citizens involved in these new technologies, they could cause a big problem with the way transportation laws and legal-organizational frameworks work right now. Policymakers need to take action because AI is becoming more common and it brings up problems like who is responsible if something goes wrong and who owns the data.

Also, scaling architecture that builds on the proposed approach in an edge-to-cloud combined technology would need more research to figure out what is needed. Blockchain technology makes data safer, more open, and more trustworthy between many people. Real-time AI and reinforcement learning models also help make these systems more flexible and accurate at predicting the future. Also, having set standards and interoperability protocols will make it easy for different transportation systems to work together. Additional interdisciplinary research integrating engineering, political science, and social sciences is essential for the advancement of resilient, ethical, and sustainable digital twin ecosystems within the framework of future intelligent transportation systems.

9. CONCLUSION

This chapter demonstrated the transformative potential of digital twin–enabled intelligent transportation systems in enhancing efficiency, safety, and sustainability. The proposed framework integrates system architecture, optimization models, and AI-driven analytics to enable predictive and adaptive mobility solutions. The study contributes by providing a unified analytical model that connects technological, operational, and environmental dimensions of transportation systems. Practically, the findings support the development of smart city mobility infrastructures and autonomous vehicle ecosystems. Future work should focus on real-world implementation, scalability, and integration with emerging technologies such as edge AI and blockchain.

REFERENCES

Acharya, S., Khan, A. A., & Päivärinta, T. (2024). Interoperability levels and challenges of digital twins in cyber-physical systems. *Journal of Industrial Information Integration*, *42*, 100714. DOI: 10.1016/j.jii.2024.100714

Aheleroff, S., Xu, X., Lu, Y., & Aristizabal, M. (2021). Digital twin as a service (DTaaS) in Industry 4.0: An architecture reference model. *Advanced Engineering Informatics*, *47*, 101225. DOI: 10.1016/j.aei.2020.101225

Ali, W., Roccotelli, M., & Fanti, M. P. (2022). Digital twin in intelligent transportation systems. *RE:view*, 576–581. Advance online publication. DOI: 10.1109/CoDIT55151.2022.9804017

Alipour Sormoli, M., Koufos, K., Dianati, M., & Woodman, R. (2024). A survey on hybrid motion planning methods for automated driving systems. https://doi.org//arXiv.2406.05575DOI: 10.48550

Baimukhanov, S., Ali, H., & Yazici, A. (2025). Enhancing ML-based anomaly detection in data management for security through integration of IoT, cloud, and edge computing. *Expert Systems with Applications*, *293*, 128700. DOI: 10.1016/j.eswa.2025.128700

Bi, L., Shuai, B., Liu, Z., Sun, Y., & Yang, F. (2026). ODPL: An objective-driven decomposed policy learning framework for urban autonomous driving control. *Applied Soft Computing*, *192*, 114781. DOI: 10.1016/j.asoc.2026.114781

Chaturvedi, M., & Srivastava, S. (2025). *Distributed computing and secure storage framework for intelligent transportation system*. International Journal of Intelligent Transportation Systems Research., DOI: 10.1007/s13177-025-00600-x

Chen, S., Hu, X., Zhao, J., Wang, R., & Qiao, M. (2024). A review of decision-making and planning for autonomous vehicles in intersection environments. *World Electric Vehicle Journal*, *15*(3), 99. DOI: 10.3390/wevj15030099

Chen, X., Kang, E., Shiraishi, S., Preciado, V., & Jiang, Z. (2018). Digital behavioral twins for safe connected cars. DOI: 10.1145/3239372.3239401

Dasgupta, S., Rahman, M., Lidbe, A., Lu, W., & Jones, S. (2021). A transportation digital-twin approach for adaptive traffic control systems. https://doi.org//arXiv.2109.10863DOI: 10.48550

Eskandarian, A., Mehr, G., Nayak, A., & Shang, X. (2024). Challenges and algorithms for connected and autonomous vehicle safety and mobility in smart cities. DOI: 10.1007/978-3-031-64769-7_9

Fuller, A., Fan, Z., & Day, C. (2020). Digital twin: Enabling technologies, challenges and open research. https://doi.org//arXiv.1911.01276DOI: 10.48550

Ge, C., & Qin, S. (2024). Digital twin intelligent transportation system (DT-ITS): A systematic review. *IET Intelligent Transport Systems*, *18*(12), 2325–2358. DOI: 10.1049/itr2.12539

Gonzalez Bautista, D., Pérez Rastelli, J., Milanes, V., & Nashashibi, F. (2015). A review of motion planning techniques for automated vehicles. *IEEE Transactions on Intelligent Transportation Systems*. Advance online publication. DOI: 10.1109/TITS.2015.2498841

Grieves, M., & Vickers, J. (2017). Digital twin: Mitigating unpredictable, undesirable emergent behavior in complex systems. DOI: 10.1007/978-3-319-38756-7_4

He, Y., Kong, M., Du, C., Yao, D., & Yu, M. (2022). Communication security analysis of intelligent transportation system using 5G internet of things from the perspective of big data. *IEEE Transactions on Intelligent Transportation Systems*, 1–9. Advance online publication. DOI: 10.1109/TITS.2022.3141788

Hu, Z., Lou, S., Xing, Y., Wang, X., Cao, D., & Lv, C. (2022). Review and perspectives on driver digital twin and its enabling technologies for intelligent vehicles. *IEEE Transactions on Intelligent Vehicles*, *7*(3), 417–440. Advance online publication. DOI: 10.1109/TIV.2022.3195635

Kehoe, G., Jula, H., & Ariaei, F. Developing successful autonomous ground vehicles: Lessons learned from DARPA challenges. DOI: 10.3182/20090902-3-US-2007.0087

Kishore, M. K., Kumar, V. G., & Nancharaiah, B. (2025). Secure lightweight digital twin (DT) technology for seamless wireless communication in vehicular ad hoc network. *Computers & Electrical Engineering*, *123*, 110291. DOI: 10.1016/j.compeleceng.2025.110291

Kušić, K., Schumann, R., & Ivanjko, E. (2023). A digital twin in transportation: Real-time synergy of traffic data streams and simulation for virtualizing motorway dynamics. *Advanced Engineering Informatics*, *55*, 101858. DOI: 10.1016/j.aei.2022.101858

Liao, X., Wang, Z., Zhao, X., Han, K., Tiwari, P., Barth, M., & Wu, G. (2021). Cooperative ramp merging design and field implementation: A digital twin approach based on vehicle-to-cloud communication. *IEEE Transactions on Intelligent Transportation Systems*. Advance online publication. DOI: 10.1109/TITS.2020.3045123

Liu, T., Tang, L., Wang, W., He, X., Chen, Q., Zeng, X., & Jiang, H. (2022). Resource allocation in DT-assisted internet of vehicles via edge intelligent cooperation. *IEEE Internet of Things Journal*, *9*(18), 17608–17626. Advance online publication. DOI: 10.1109/JIOT.2022.3156100

Lu, Y., Liu, C., Wang, K., Huang, H., & Xu, X. (2019). Digital twin-driven smart manufacturing: Connotation, reference model, applications and research issues. *Robotics and Computer-integrated Manufacturing*, *61*, 101837. Advance online publication. DOI: 10.1016/j.rcim.2019.101837

Lyu, Z., Li, Y., Feng, H., & Lv, H. (2021). Deep learning for security in digital twins of cooperative intelligent transportation systems. *IEEE Transactions on Intelligent Transportation Systems*. Advance online publication. DOI: 10.1109/TITS.2021.3122566

Mansour, I., & Singh, S. (2025). Role of AI in an autonomous vehicle perception systems: Use of convolutional neural network approach to design the vehicle perception system. DOI: 10.4271/2025-01-8012

Petit, J., & Shladover, S. (2014). Potential cyberattacks on automated vehicles. *IEEE Transactions on Intelligent Transportation Systems*, 1–11. Advance online publication. DOI: 10.1109/TITS.2014.2342271

Qi, Q., & Tao, F. (2018). Digital twin and big data towards smart manufacturing and Industry 4.0: 360 degree comparison. *IEEE Access : Practical Innovations, Open Solutions*, *6*, 3585–3593. DOI: 10.1109/ACCESS.2018.2793265

Qureshi, K., & Abdullah, H. (2014). Sensor based vehicle environment perception information system. DOI: 10.1109/UIC-ATC-ScalCom.2014.60

Rakha, H. A., Ahn, K., & Moran, K. Integration framework for modeling eco-routing strategies: Logic and preliminary results. International Journal of Transportation Science and Technology. DOI: 10.1260/2046-0430.1.3.259

Richmond, J., Lawal, Y., Rose, C., & Kayali, O. (2026). Security and privacy challenges in vehicle-to-everything (V2X) communications.

Rios-Torres, J., & Malikopoulos, A. (2016). A survey on the coordination of connected and automated vehicles at intersections and merging at highway on-ramps. *IEEE Transactions on Intelligent Transportation Systems*. Advance online publication. DOI: 10.1109/TITS.2016.2600504

Shladover, S. (2017). Connected and automated vehicle systems: Introduction and overview. *Journal of Intelligent Transport Systems*. Advance online publication. DOI: 10.1080/15472450.2017.1336053

Špitálová, Z. (2023). Vehicle-to-everything communication. Communications – Scientific Letters of the University of Zilina, 25, C24–C35. DOI: 10.26552/com.C.2023.017

Stefko, R., Frajtova-Michalikova, K., Strakova, J., & Novak, A. (2025). Digital twin-based virtual factory and cyber-physical production systems. Equilibrium. *Quarterly Journal of Economics and Economic Policy*, *20*, 389–425. DOI: 10.24136/eq.3557

Tagne, G., Talj, R., & Charara, A. (2015, July). Design and validation of a robust immersion and invariance controller for the lateral dynamics of intelligent vehicles. *Control Engineering Practice*, *40*, 81–92. Advance online publication. DOI: 10.1016/j.conengprac.2015.03.002

Thrun, S. Winning the DARPA Grand Challenge. IFAC Proceedings Volumes. DOI: 10.3182/20060912-3-DE-2911.00002

Wang, K., Li, Z., Yu, T., & Sakaguchi, K. (2023). Smart mobility digital twin for automated driving: Design and proof-of-concept. DOI: 10.1109/VTC2023-Spring57618.2023.10200728

Wang, Y., Xue, H., & Zhou, M. (2025). A digital twin-assisted VEC intelligent task offloading approach. *Electronics (Basel)*, *14*(17), 3444. DOI: 10.3390/electronics14173444

Wang, Z., Han, K., & Tiwari, P. (2021). Digital twin-assisted cooperative driving at non-signalized intersections. https://doi.org//arXiv.2105.01357DOI: 10.48550

Wang, Z., Lv, C., & Wang, F.-Y. (2023). A new era of intelligent vehicles and intelligent transportation systems: Digital twins and parallel intelligence. *IEEE Transactions on Intelligent Vehicles*, *8*(4), 2619–2627. Advance online publication. DOI: 10.1109/TIV.2023.3264812

Wei, C., Qin, Z., Zhang, Z., Wu, G., & Barth, M. J. (2025). Integrating multi-modal sensors: A review of fusion techniques for intelligent vehicles. DOI: 10.1109/IV64158.2025.11097396

Wu, D., Zhao, Q., Xia, X., Liu, C., Xu, Y., & Li, Y. (2025). Road adhesion information estimation of connected autonomous vehicle based on digital twin and vision sensor fusion. *IEEE Internet of Things Journal*, *12*(24), 54284–54303. Advance online publication. DOI: 10.1109/JIOT.2025.3621457

Wu, J., Wang, X., Dang, Y., & Lyu, Z. (2022). Digital twins and artificial intelligence in transportation infrastructure: Classification, application, and future research directions. *Computers & Electrical Engineering*, *101*, 107983. DOI: 10.1016/j.compeleceng.2022.107983

Yu, G., Zhang, S., Hu, M., & Wang, Y. (2020). Prediction of highway tunnel pavement performance based on digital twin and multiple time series stacking. *Advances in Civil Engineering*, *2020*(1), 1–21. DOI: 10.1155/2020/8824135

Zhu, H., Yuen, K., Mihaylova, L., & Leung, H. (2017). Overview of environment perception for intelligent vehicles. *IEEE Transactions on Intelligent Transportation Systems*, *18*(10), 2584–2601. Advance online publication. DOI: 10.1109/TITS.2017.2658662

Zhu, L., Yu, F., Wang, Y., Ning, B., & Tang, T. (2018). Big data analytics in intelligent transportation systems: A survey. *IEEE Transactions on Intelligent Transportation Systems*. Advance online publication. DOI: 10.1109/TITS.2018.2815678

Zhuang, C., Miao, T., Liu, J., & Xiong, H. (2021). The connotation of digital twin and the construction and application method of shop-floor digital twin. *Robotics and Computer-integrated Manufacturing*, *68*, 102075. DOI: 10.1016/j.rcim.2020.102075

Chapter 8

Digital Twin-Enabled Smart Manufacturing for Surface Mount Technology in Autonomous Vehicle Electronics Manufacturing

Shweta Dour
http://orcid.org/0000-0002-8004-3507
Navrachana University, India

Prakruti Shah
Navrachna University, India

ABSTRACT

Digital Twin technology can be described as a virtual representation of an actual physical system that can reflect on its performance, behavior, and operation dynamics in real time. Prediction, process optimization, and informed decision-making through Digital twins are achievable by its constant linking of real or artificial data and simulation models. This paradigm has come to be an inseparable component of intelligent manufacturing, where accuracy, adaptability and the quality level is very significant. In addition, the framework is scalable, and it is also possible to add AI-based predictive model to the framework and detect errors and obtain tuning of the processes. The chapter demonstrates how the Digital Twin methods can be employed to model a virtual electronics assembly production space, which would be a step toward a zero-defect, data-driven smart manufacturing, enhancing the reliability of electronic systems in autonomous vehicles.

I. INTRODUCTION

The fast development of electric vehicles (EV) technologies has increased the necessity to have advanced manufacturing systems that can guarantee high reliability, efficiency, and performance of complex electronic components and subsystems. EVs require advanced electronics, such as battery control system,

DOI: 10.4018/979-8-3373-7785-8.ch008

power convertors, and high-density printed circuits boards (PCBs), requiring highly accurate and flawless manufacturing. Digital Twin technology has become a disruptive solution because it allows to have virtual replicas of physical manufacturing systems in real-time, to monitor them, simulate and optimize them. Integrated with Industrial Internet of Things (IIoT) and artificial intelligence, Digital Twins assist in predictive maintenance, process optimization, and lifecycle management of EV parts (Inamdar and Patil, 2024; Kabir and Ray, 2025). Recent research also shows that they can be used in next-generation automotive manufacturing settings to improve operational efficiency, adaptive decision-making, and enhance intelligent production systems (Qin et al., 2026; Li et al., 2023).

Within the framework of autonomous vehicle electronics, PCB production presents distinct challenges, exceeding the normal consumer electronics production. Autonomous systems have a sophisticated network of electronic subsystems, such as advanced driver assistance systems (ADAS), sensor fusion modules, control units, and real-time processing hardware. Such systems require high-density interconnect (HDI) PCBs, multilayer designs, and fine-pitch components, which greatly increase the chances of placement errors, soldering defects, and thermal variations in the assembly. Additionally, the high level of safety of autonomous vehicles implies that they will be subject to high standards, including ISO 26262, which stipulates high reliability and fault tolerance of electronic components (Zhang et al., 2020).

The next important point about PCB production in autonomous vehicles is that it must be made to be reliable in long-term operation in underdeveloped environmental conditions. The PCBs that are used in the automotive industry operate under extensive temperature fluctuations, mechanical vibrations, humidity conditions, and the electromagnetic effects. These can hasten wear-out mechanisms (solder joint fatigue,delamination, and thermal cycling failures). Consequently, customary post-production testing procedures will frequently not be adequate to ensure trustworthiness. Digital Twin technology will provide an opportunity to simulate these environmental stresses during the very manufacturing stage and estimate the process failure mechanisms and optimize process parameters to prevent them (Boschert & Rosen, 2016).

Moreover, another complexity of SMT assembly is the growing use of heterogeneous integration, in which various kinds of components, including microcontrollers, sensors, and power devices, are mounted on a single PCB. The component types used may be different in their placement tolerances, soldering profiles, and also inspections. The variability may be modeled in Digital Twin models that assigns component-specific parameters and encodes the way they interact during the assembly process. This enables a further more granular perspective of defect formation and help to develop particular tactics of reducing defects and enhancing yields (Negri et al., 2017).

Real-time integration of data also should be used in facilitating the use of Digital Twin in PCB manufacturing. Contemporary SMT lines have sensors and inspection devices like Automated Optical Inspection (AOI) and Solder Paste Inspection (SPI), which produce copious amounts of process data. With this data combined into the digital twin, manufacturers will be able to realize the continuous synchronization of the physical and virtual systems. This allows real time monitoring of the accuracy of the placement, quality and machine operation of the solder, and anomalies identified and remedies at early stages. They are required to take care of the production of large volumes with high degree of consistency (Tao et al., 2019). Moreover, the Digital Twin technology can be utilized to promote the closed-loop manufacturing systems, whereby the feedback on the virtual model can be used to modify the parameters of the physical processes on a dynamic basis. Similarly, should the digital twin indicate that there is a risk of a defect because of changes in solder paste volume, the system can automatically change stencil settings or reflow curves to alleviate the problem. Such degree of automation not only helps to improve the quality of products but also boosts production efficiency by decreasing the downtime and reducing the number of reworks (Kritzinger et al., 2018).

Design-for-manufacturability (DfM) and design-for-reliability (DfR) analysis is another new use of Digital Twins in PCB manufacturing. Use of simulation of the manufacturing process during the design stage will enable the engineers to identify the potential issues in the component placement, thermal conductivity and signal integrity even before the PCB is manufactured. This proactive approach reduces the design cycle and accelerates time-to-market, particularly sought after in the rapidly-evolving autonomous vehicle industry.

Finally, technology of Digital Twin along with the application of the artificial intelligence (AI) and machine learning (ML) techniques enables the use of predictive and adaptive manufacturing. Machine learning algorithms are able to process past production data and determine patterns and correlations that cannot be easily noticed using conventional methods. Coupled with digital twin simulations, such models can forecast defects, optimise process settings and even suggest proactive maintenance plans to SMT equipment. This kind of overlap of technologies is one of the significant steps towards fully autonomous manufacturing systems capable of self-optimizing and being in a continuous improvement (Tao et al., 2019).

The rising need of safe and superior quality consumer and industrial electronics development has been associated with the rapid rate of miniaturization of electronics to render accuracy and maximization of procedures engaged in production of a major component of the electronics industry. The most important of the different methods for electronics assembly is Surface Mount Technology (SMT) with its ability to produce high component density, less production time and it is also compatibility with automated production lines. However, rise in the complexity of printed circuit boards (PCB) and the demand of a near zero-defect rates requires highly skilled devices in test, prediction and improvement in the of the outcomes of production.

The Digital Twin technology, which has been recently introduced, is one of the transformative technologies in smart manufacturing. A Digital Twin is a fictitious, virtual counterpart of a physical system whose behavior, performance and operational conditions are replica reflections of the real world counterpart of the same (Parashar & Gameti, 2024). With Digital Twins, manufacturers can test situations and watch the real performance of the software in real-time and prevent possible failures before they occur, since simulation models can be aligned with real or synthetic data. The technology presents significant advantages to the electronics manufacturing in terms of defects identification, placement accuracy monitoring, yield prediction and cycle time analysis.

The possibility of the data-driven approach to process optimization is due to the integration of Digital Twin techniques in SMT assembly (Siemens, 2024). The placement error and Solder defect error and the throughput inefficiency can be modelled using stochastic and reliability functions. One such case is whereby the distributions of the deviations in assembling parts can be approximated by the Gaussian, the probability of defects by the Bernoulli processes and long-term reliability by exponential reliability function. They are the models where quantitative data on yield, reliability and cycle time is obtained that are required in terms of optimization of cost and quality of PCB assembly.

The presented work develops a Matlab® based Digital Twin processing of simulation of the manufacturing of medium-complexity PCB. This model utilizes variability in the components, defect occurrence, placement accuracy and real time performance index. Some of the outputs include graphical distributions of errors, estimation of yield, reliability curves and component based summary tables, etc.

The framework is designed to be extensible, and can be extended to artificial intelligence and predictive quality control by artificial intelligence utilities, not just normal simulation.

On an industrial-scale, the Digital Twin technology has also been established by the major electronic firms, such as Siemens, Bosch and Foxconn, in order to streamline the SMT assembly lines (Siemens, 2024). An example of a Siemens project, the Digital Enterprise Suite employs Digital Twin models to optimize the PCB's placements and reduce cycle time and Bosch utilizes forecasting predictive Digital models for reduction in defects for automotive electronics. Foxconn, one of the largest electronics manufactures, is utilizing Digital Twins to simulate the configuration of the assembly lines and test them before deployment, which reduces down times by a significantly and increases the throughput (Tao et al., 2023).

These applications support the possibility and universal applicability of solutions built on Digital Twin in the electronics manufacturing. This work shows that Digital Twin can be applied to the electronic manufacturing business sector in a systematic way and provides a virtual world that adds to the decision-making process and helps minimize the number of defects and control the image of zero-defect smart factories.

With the specifics of electronics of autonomous vehicles, manufacturing PCBs comes with its own challenges which extend beyond the traditional consumer electronics manufacturing. A critical configuration of electronic subsystems, such as advanced driver assistance systems (ADAS), sensor fusion modules, control units and real-time processing hardware, are used in autonomous systems. These systems require high-density interconnect (HDI) PCBs, multilayer designs and fine-pitch components, which makes them highly susceptible to errors in placement and soldering flaws and thermal variations during assemblies. Besides, autonomous vehicles are safety-critical and thus must meet high standards including ISO 26262 that is obliged to high reliability and fault tolerance of electronic components (Zhang et al., 2020).

II. LITERATURE REVIEW

Design-for-manufacturability (DfM) and design-for-reliability (DfR) analysis is another recent usage of Digital Twins in PCB manufacturing. When designers design through simulation of the manufacturing process, they are able to apply the simulating process to detecting any problems connected to the position of the components, thermal, and signal integrity even prior to the actual production of PCB. This proactive design minimizes the design cycles and saves time to market, which is heavily essential in the autonomous vehicle environments that are dynamic and changing in time. Lastly, predictive and adaptive manufacturing has new opportunities through the integration of Digital Twin technology and artificial intelligence (AI) and machine learning techniques (Kuo et al., 2026). With machine learning models, it is possible to analyze past production and determine trends and correlations that could not be easily determined through conventional techniques. Together with digital twin simulations, these models can anticipate defect events, maximize process parameters, and even suggest preventive maintenance schedules of SMT equipment. This integration of technologies is a major move towards the complete autonomous manufacturing systems, where they are able to self-optimize and generate a process of continuous improvement (Tao et al., 2019).

Recent advances in Digital Twin have increased its areas of use to high precision electronic assembly technology, particularly in PCB assembly operations. The existing literature is concerned with the integration of Digital Twin models with the real-time data stream and smart control system to enable adaptive and predictive manufacturing environments. To illustrate the point, (Li et al., 2023) proposed a PCB assembly modeled around a digital twin by combining process simulation with precision evaluation to demonstrate that SMT-based assembly tasks can be extremely precise in placing parts and have a minimal error rate. Similarly, Sheng et al. (2023) have also explored the application of Digital Twin systems in the manufacturing of flexible PCB (FPCB) where they reported that they were able to synchronize production related information and virtual models to enhance both production throughput and quality simultaneously.

The interrelation of Digital Twin technology with the Industrial Internet of Things (IIoT) and cyber-physical systems has enhanced its contribution to smart manufacturing even more.(Inamdar and Patil, 2024) provide an in-depth discussion of the Digital Twin applications, focusing on how they can be used to provide real-time monitoring, predictive maintenance, and closed-loop control in automated manufacturing lines. Next, (Kabir and Ray, 2025) discuss the integration of Digital Twin frameworks and IIoT infrastructures, which can be used to exchange the information between the real and the virtual system seamlessly, which is crucial when the environment of an electronics manufacturing company on a large scale.

More recent studies are devoted to artificial intelligence integration in Digital Twin systems to enhance the process optimization and decision-making. (Qin et al., 2026) highlight the introduction of the Digital Twin systems with robots into the intelligent production to demonstrate how AI-based models can improve the effectiveness and adaptability of automated production systems. Kuo et al. (2026) developed an AI-based Digital Twin predictive process time in the laser micromachining process within the context of PCB manufacturing, proving the versatility of the tool in improving the production planning and resources optimization.

Overall, these works indicate a certain direction towards smart, data-driven Digital Twin ecosystems that do not just recreate the manufacturing processes but also have a positive impact on them. Particularly in PCB manufacturing in the autonomous automobile, electronic sector, this advancement is crucially important when the precision, reliability, and scalability of the goods are crucial. Together with simulation, real time data, and AI-generated analytics, such Digital Twin technology turns out to be a cornerstone towards next-generation smart manufacturing systems.

Not only the traditional production of electronics but also the development of the technologies of autonomous vehicles has resulted in the paradigm where reliability, safety, and performance are amazingly dependent on each other when it comes to PCBs manufacturing. These self-driving cars are founded upon progressive electronic structures, which involve intricate driver assistant systems (ADAS), sensor blend units, real-time processing units and high-speed communication access interfaces. Such systems need high density, multilayer, high-reliability PCBs, typically with fine-pitch components, in which case these components are ball grid arrays (BGAs) and system-on-chip (SoCs). This intricacy results in SMT operations being extremely susceptible to localization error, solder tempera and temperature fluctuation, and consequently requires new improved sophisticated digital twins-driven monitoring and optimization methods (Zhang et al., 2020).

One of the research avenues in this area is the use of Digital Twin models to verify functional safety in the production of automotive electronics. In contrast to consumer electronics, automotive PCBs have to meet stringent safety standards, including ISO 26262, which demand stringent validation of manufacture processes to guarantee flawless operation. Digital Twin frameworks can be used to virtually test the assembly processes with varying operating conditions to enable the engineers to model failure cases and evaluate the effect of such failures on the performance of the system. This feature is especially necessary in safety-critical modules like braking systems, steering control units, sensor processing boards, etc., whereby any small flaws may cause system- level failures (Boschert & Rosen, 2016).

The other field of study that is emerging is the combination of thermal and mechanical stress modeling into Digital Twin models of PCB manufacturing. Autonomous vehicle electronics faces severe environmental conditions which include temperature fluctuations, vibrations and changes in humidity. The conditions may cause failure mechanisms that include solder joint fatigue, delamination and component cracking. Recent research has emphasized the need to use multiphysics simulations as part of Digital Twin models to project these failure modes during the manufacturing stage itself. With thermal profiles obtained on reflow soldering, Digital Twins can be used to offer a more reliable view of reliability concerns caused by processes (Tao et al., 2019). In addition, the growing use of high-frequency and high-speed PCBs in autonomous vehicles poses more signal integrity and electromagnetic compatibility (EMC) challenges.

These features are highly sensitive to the production changes, such as small displaces in the positions of the parts or solder joint defects. Digital Twin models are capable of recreating these effects and contain electrical performance models incorporating physical assembly simulations to enable a complete analysis of the PCB functionality. This integration enables manufactures to detect possible signal degradation or interference at an early stage of the production cycle, thus minimizing expensive redesigns and enhancing the reliability of the product (Negri et al., 2017).

In addition, the idea of Digital Thread integration has been presented which is an extension of Digital Twin technology to connect all phases of the product lifecycle, such as design and manufacturing processes, operations and maintenance. As PCBs are manufactured on autonomous vehicle production, the strategy will enable monitoring of each component and process parameter, which can be utilized to conduct a root-cause analysis and continuous improvement. Digital Thread systems would be able to encourage transparency and accountability through maintaining the detailed digital register of the manufacturing process, which is one of the keys to satisfying the demands of regulation and safety (Negri et al., 2017).

Although such developments have been made, there are still a few issues in the execution of Digital Twin technology in PCB fabrication in autonomous vehicle use. A significant drawback is that there is no standardized data models and interoperability frameworks, which may interfere with integrating various systems and platforms. Moreover, the computational cost of high-fidelity simulations especially multiphysics modeling and real-time processing data is a serious obstacle to feasible implementation. To solve these problems, it is necessary to conduct more research on scalable architectures, effective algorithms, and standardized communication protocols (Kritzinger et al., 2018).

The second important gap in the literature that needs to be addressed is the fact that lightweight, reproducible Digital Twin models are not as widespread and can be easily deployed in academic and industrial contexts. Although numerous works are dedicated to high-level architectures and to industrial case-studies, it is necessary to have the practical implementation that would illustrate the interrelation of the modeling of placement errors, the prediction of defects, and the analysis of inspection data within the same framework. These models are especially valuable in terms of training, experimentation, and validation, as they allow researchers and engineers to gain a better idea of the underlying processes and create innovative solutions (Tao et al., 2019).

In general, the sources suggest that the Digital Twin technology has a high potential to revolutionize the PCB manufacturing in the electronics of autonomous vehicles. Digital Twins are an effective means to mitigating the challenges of growing complexity and the high-quality demands by means of facilitating virtual simulation, predictive analytics, and real-time optimization. The combination of the developed models, data analytics, and real-time control systems can be considered as one of the major milestones towards the creation of intelligent, adaptive, and zero-defect manufacturing systems within the automotive electronics sector.

Applications of Digital Twins in manufacturing have been at different levels: component/ machines (customer virtualization of CNCs, robots), line/ plant (virtual factories to optimize layout and throughput), and product- lifecycle (design production service) (Wang et al., 2022). The ability to perform what-if analysis, which is essentially commission changes and the capacity to execute predictive scenarios, continue to make Digital Twins particularly attractive to high-mix/high-volume environments with downtime and defect rates so high. According to recent surveys, Digital twins can enhance productivity, allow predictive maintenance, and facilitate what-if without interrupting production, while presenting the current architectures evolving with a Digital twin-enabled factory and the implementation challenges (Müller et al., 2024; Tao et al., 2024; Zhang & Wang, 2025). The case materials and white papers in the industry are focused on the fact that the implementation of Digital Twin must be supported by both modelling capacity and databases pipeline (MES/SCADA/MQTT), standard data model, and needs must be closely connected to shop-floor systems (NVIDIA,2024).

One such promising avenue of research, to support Digital Twin application, is electronics assembly, and Surface Mount Technology (SMT) assembly processes, attributing to both immeasurably long placement times, and high placement-geometric fidelity, in conjunction with dense arrays of information on inspection vistas (SPI / AOI / pick-and-place driver logs)

The process of electronics manufacturing and, in particular, Surface Mount Technology (SMT) assembly represents another ideal application area for Digital Twin use because it features an intriguing combination of very high placement rates, tight geometric tolerances, and rich inspection datasets (SPI/ AOI/pick-and-place output logs). Many Digital Twin frameworks have been suggested in the recent literature that can be implemented to PCB assembly that unifies PCB design information, process models (pick-and-place, reflow), and inspection/measurement feeds (AOI, SPI). These SMT Digital Twin systems are typically designed using a fixed-programmed architecture, where physics-based placement/soldering simulators are then augmented with machine-learning vision simulators to identify defects and present them with machine-controlled processes. These pieces demonstrate the utility of the Digital Twin as it can be applied to early fault detection, so as to tune the assembly process virtually, and minimise rework/ yield loss. The relevance of Digital Twins to electronics and factory automation is also supported by those who have adopted them industrially. Siemens offers a solution with its Digital Enterprise/Xcelerator portfolio to make Digital Twins an end-to-end solution of virtual commissioning, line optimization, and continuous improvement; Siemens case studies demonstrate a reduction in commissioning time by a factor of four and a better ratio of flexibility when using Digital Twins to test changes to a line before they are physically implemented (Siemens, 2024). To simulate operation and drive AI-assisted analytics, and enable speedier implementation of new lines, large contract manufacturers (e.g., Foxconn) and platform vendors (e.g., NVIDIA Omniverse integrations) are constructing factory-scale DIGITAL TWINs to simulate operation - evidence that DIGITAL TWINs are no longer merely scholarly prototypes, but industrial tools to support the high-volume manufacture of electronics (Li et al., 2023).

One of the key cornerstones of SMT quality-control is the inspection chain: Solder Paste Inspection (SPI) and Automated Optical Inspection (AOI) offers per-component (solder volume/height, X/Y/θ placement error, presence/absence) measurements acting as ground truth to Digital Twin validation and calibration. The combination of SPI/AOI data and Digital Twins can be used to both report after the processing is completed, but also to define closed-loop correction schemes (patching, adjustment of feeders) and statistical process controls (SPC) dashboards. The recent literature and technical notes in the industry emphasize the fact that combining AOI/SPI and Digital Twin models leads to faster identification of systematic offsets (machine bias), component-specific failures and spatial hotspots on the PCB - all of which are the focus of the predictive and prescriptive modules of the Digital Twin (Li et al., 2023).

In terms of modelling, however, the literature tends to conflate stochastic error models and data-driven learning. Placement errors are usually modelled as Gaussian (normal) errors, with machine bias and variance parameters estimated using pick-and-place logs, defect occurrence is modelled probabilistically (Bernoulli trials with component-type dependent probabilities) and reliability / failure prediction is often done with exponential or Weibull models fitted to defect / time data (Müller et al., 2024; Tao et al., 2024). Convolutional neural networks and hybrid ML pipelines are a popular method on the data-driven side to detect defects in visions (AOI), whereas classical supervised classifiers (decision trees, SVM), and unsupervised anomaly detectors to sensor/process logs to indicate outliers. Physics-aware stochastic models are proposed in the Digital Twin literature to be used with ML components in order to achieve interpretability and robustness.

Even with these developments, there are still substantial gaps in published work, especially in low-level implementation: a larger portion of published Digital Twin work describes high-level architectures or single-machine digitalizations, but less work presents component-level, reproducible Digital Twin implementations of SMT that (a) incorporate spatial error heat maps, (b) can support multiple types of components with type-specific tolerances, and (c) can be written in a way that is easy to reproducible (e.g. in MATLAB® by academics (a). This is an especially significant gap to researchers and smaller manufacturers who require lightweight and verifiable Digital Twin prototypes to understand processes and teach. The current paper bridges this gap by providing a Matlab® implementation of a Digital Twins prototype, which integrates stochastic placement/error models, multi-type component tolerances, AOI/SPI-like metrics, and spatial heatmaps - allowing simple validation to machine CSV logs and AOI outputs.

III. DIGITAL TWIN FRAMEWORK

A. Architecture Overview

The Digital Twin architecture of Surface Mount Technology (SMT) manufacturing is developed to be a fully synchronized and predictive manufacturing system that is created by the smooth integration of the physical PCB assembly system, a virtual simulation model, and a continuous data flow network. The physical system (Balderas et al., 2021) is a physical representation of the SMT production line, i.e. pick-and-place machines, solder paste dispensers, reflow ovens, and inspection units, e.g. Solder Paste Inspection (SPI) and Automated Optical Inspection (AOI). All components produce real-time functional data, such as placement coordinates, solder volume readings, machine cycle data, temperature data, and defect detection data. These data streams enable a real-time representation of the dynamic nature of the manufacture process prior to the virtual representation of the SMT line being created. Table 1 shows Correlation of Digital Twin parameters and SMT PCB Assembly significance.

The virtual system is described as a computational simulation platform (Manfredi et al., 2023) that replicates the physical SMT line and simulates the major processes-component placement, solder paste deposition reflow soldering, and inspection process. By having a computational model of the SMT line, engineers are able to perform what-if testing; examine alternative process settings; and predict the likelihood of failure without disrupting actual production. For example, the virtual lab could simulate an intentional variation to placement accuracy, solder volume, or reflow temperature and assess the impact on component yield and reliability (Wu et al., 2024).

Table 1. Correlation of digital twin parameters and SMT PCB assembly significance

Parameter	Significance in SMT PCB Assembly	Role of Digital Twin Technology
Placement Accuracy (X/Y/θ)	Determines correct positioning of components; affects soldering quality.	Simulates placement errors, predicts misalignment risks, and generates heat maps of high-risk areas on the PCB.
Solder Paste Volume	Ensures proper solder joint formation; prevents shorts or tombstoning.	Models solder paste deposition variability, evaluates impact of volume changes, and predicts potential defects.
Component Type	Different sizes/shapes have varying tolerance and defect probabilities.	Tracks each component type, simulates type-specific errors, and provides defect probability for each type.
Reflow Temperature Profile	Controls solder melting and joint quality; critical for thermal reliability.	Virtual simulation of oven profiles, predicts soldering defects due to over/under heating, and optimizes thermal settings.
Defect Rate	Overall measure of quality and yield.	Predicts defect probability per component and per board; identifies areas for corrective actions.
Throughput / Cycle Time	Impacts production efficiency and delivery schedules.	Simulates line operation under various settings, identifies bottlenecks, and optimizes speed vs quality trade-offs.
Inspection Accuracy (SPI/AOI)	Ensures errors are detected and corrected; maintains process reliability.	Virtual AOI/SPI simulation, generates expected inspection results, and validates physical inspection systems.
Reliability / Yield Prediction	Long-term product performance and consistency.	Uses stochastic and probabilistic models to forecast failure probability and yield trends
Feedback and Control	Enables adaptive manufacturing and real-time optimization.	Provides actionable insights to adjust parameters, reduce defects, and maintain consistent quality.

This all enables better decision making and efficient processing, thereby minimizing the risk of defects and missed production time. The data flow element provides a two-way association among the virtual system and physical system. The sensors, machine logs and inspection systems provide real-time data which is continuously fed into the simulation to make sure that the virtual model represents the current state of the physical line. Any of the deviations noticed in the virtual system including placement mistakes and defect rate can result in alert or recommendations to make changes in the physical line. Adaptive control (Seidel et al., 2023), predictive maintenance, and constant quality improvement cannot take place without this feedback loop. The Digital Twin architecture allows real-time monitoring, analysis and optimization of manufacturing performance through a closed-loop environment by integrating physical measurements, virtual simulation, and real-time data flow.

B. Simulation of the SMT Line

The physical mechanism of SMT manufacturing is mapped to a model in the computational simulation which not only models stochastic variability, but also the behavior of its components. The first step in this simulation is the generation of the component dataset. In a medium-complexity PCB, the model consists of resistors, capacitors, integrated circuits (ICs) and connectors, each of which type of component has a probability of defect and a certain location tolerance. This enables the simulation to replicate the variability in the real world SMT assembly lines (Karanjkar et al., 2018) and forms a basis of statistical analysis.

Placement simulation is done based on a Gaussian distribution to simulate component positioning deviations. Following placement, the simulation models defect occurrence using a Bernoulli process. Each component has a probability of defect based on its type, and a random trial determines whether a defect occurs. The given stochastic method reflects the nature of high-speed pick-and-place processes and allows measuring the possible misalignment problem. After placement, the simulation models the events of defects by a Bernoulli process. The probability of defect is per component and a random trial will decide whether or not the defect will exist. This probabilistic approach simulates actual manufacturing experiences where some components are more defective based on size, orientation or soldering properties. The simulation also produces outputs similar to those of SPI and AOI systems such as placement errors histograms, number of defects by component type, and estimates yield. To measure reliability, exponential failure model is used through the simulated defects with the result being a reliability curve which plots an estimate of the probability of not to experience failure with time. This allows the Digital Twin to predict performance over a longer period of time and the components that are very important to high yield.

Finally, the platform provides visualizations and summary outputs, which serve as the feedback within the decision-making process. Graphs such as placement error distribution, defects per component type, and reliability curves provide an intuitive understanding of manufacturing performance, and summary tables provide engineers an opportunity to quantify risk and evaluate process efficiency. The output from these can inform parameter controls, process optimization, and be inputs into AI predictive.

The simulation generates outputs similar to those of SPI and AOI systems such as placement errors histograms, defects by component type and estimates yield. In measuring reliability, a holding time is assigned to the simulated defects and factor in an exponential failure model, producing reliability curves which plot an estimate of not experiencing a failure with time. This allows the Digital Twin to predict performance further into the future and the components that are very important to maintaining high yield. Finally, the platform generates visualizations and summary outputs, and utilize these as feedback in the decision making process. Graphs like placement error distributions, defect per component type and reliability curves give an intuitive understanding of the manufacturing performance, and summary tables give engineers the opportunity to quantify risk and assess process efficiency. The outputs of these can inform parameter controls, process optimization, and act as input to AI predictive modules as an entirely interacting and adaptive Digital Twin of SMT manufacturing.

C. Component-Level Analysis

First, the simulation was analyzed at the component level, to assess both component accuracy of placement as well as how susceptible the component was to defects when a component of different types was placed on the PCB. This included placement of resistors, capacitors, integrated circuits and connectors, and was measured in terms of all deviations in placement (X, Y, and rotational (0)). The inclusion of placement deviations due to the nature of high-speed pick-and-place operation captures the natural variability. For larger parts such as ICs and connectors there will be relatively less variability, while for smaller parts such as resisters and capacitors, placement position is more variable due to their size and the tolerances of placement. The simulation was executed to provide useful information in the form of histograms and spatial heat maps that display areas of the PCB that have had more frequent placement errors that lead to increased susceptibility to defects and provides insight on machine calibration adjustments or feeder adjustments may provide a potentially large effect. By only including data by component type the simulation analysis provided additional and useful insight into the details of what types of placement parts of the assembly process was likely causing defect errors and, thus likely to implement what type of interventions would be used to improve yield and guarantee quality.

D. Defect Simulation

After doing the component level analysis, the simulation aimed at stimulating the occurrence of defects in the SMT assembly process. Probabilities of defect of each type of component were given according to the characteristics and the placement tolerances of a particular component, and the probability of a defect on a certain component on the PCB was determined by the stochastic Bernoulli process. The artificial defects were misalignment, tombstoning and solder bridging as these are typical defects in high-speed SMT assembly. The bar charts and pie charts summarized the results to show the frequency and distribution of the defects by component type and by PCB. It has been shown that smaller parts with more stringent placement tolerances, e.g., resistors, capacitors, etc., had more defects and larger parts were less prone to them. Moreover, the spatial pattern of defects indicated hotspots on PCB and these gave useful information on calibration of machines, optimization of processes and selective quality control interventions. The Digital Twin framework allowed predicting the quality of the assembly by catching the nature of the defects as well as the location, which is essential in reducing the rework and enhancing the total yield.

IV. MATHEMATICAL MODELLING

1. Placement Accuracy (Position Error Model)

If (xi,yi) is the designed location of component, and (x^i,y^i) is the actual placement, then the placement error is:

$$e_i = \sqrt{(\hat{x}_i - x_i)^2 + (\hat{y}_i - y_i)^2} \tag{1}$$

We can assume this error follows a normal distribution:

$$e_i \sim N(\mu, \sigma^2)$$

where μ is the machine bias and σ is the precision variation.

2. Defect Probability Model

For solder defects, we can model probability as a Bernoulli process:

$$P(d_i = 1) = p_c \tag{2}$$

where d_i is the defect occurrence (1 if defective, 0 if not), Overall yield is then:

$$Y = 1 - \frac{\sum_{i=1}^{N} di}{N} \tag{3}$$

where N is total number of components.

3. Cycle Time and Throughput

If each placement takes tpt_ptp seconds and each solder joint takes tst_sts, then the cycle time for NNN components is:

$$T = N \cdot \left(t_p + t_s\right) \tag{4}$$

Machine throughput (components per hour):

$$TH = \frac{3600}{t_p + t_s} \tag{5}$$

4. Reliability Index

We can define a reliability function as:

$$R(t) = e^{-\lambda t} \tag{6}$$

where λ is failure rate (defects/hour). In simulation, we could estimate λ from defect occurrence data.

5. Optimization Objective (Future AI Integration)

We could define an objective function for optimization, e.g., minimizing total defects while minimizing cycle time:

$$\min_{p_c, t_p, t_s} \alpha \cdot Defects + \beta \cdot T \tag{7}$$

where α,β are weights depending on whether cost, speed, or quality is prioritized.

V. ANALYSIS OF YIELD AND RELIABILITY

The overall PCB yield and reliability were also evaluated in the simulation depending on the modelled errors during placement and defects during the process. The yield was determined as a rate of the defect-free boards on any run of production and this gave a quantitative measurement of the quality of assembly in series of simulations. The findings showed that component type and component placement accuracy had a significant impact on yield, with small high-density components making the largest contribution to possible losses. In order to determine reliability, exponential failure model was used to evaluate the simulated defect data, which estimated the probability of failure-free operation with time. In this way, the future short-term assembly performance and the long-term trends of component performance could be predicted. Summary tables have been created to report the yield and reliability figures of the different types of components including where the process needs optimization. In general, the analysis showed the usefulness of a Digital Twin model in determining the key process parameters, anticipated failure, and quality improvement measures to improve the yield and reliability of SMT PCB production.

VI. RESULTS AND DISCUSSION OF DIGITAL TWIN SIMULATION FOR SMT ASSEMBLY

The simulation was carried out, testing the workability of a Digital Twin structure in simulating SMT PCB assembly procedures, prioritizing the forecasting of errors in placing elements, solder defects, and PCB yield. The main manufacturing parameters such as the precision of component placement (X/Y/ deviations), the volume of solder paste, the number of defects, the yield and the reliability were observed during the simulation. The experiment was conducted on a medium complexity PCB with several different types of components, including resistors, capacitors, integrated circuits, and connectors, and each different component of the model was modeled based on its respective tolerances and defect rates. During a series of production runs, a simulation was implemented to constrain variability and stochastic behavior while simultaneously providing a holistic view of the assembly or production process, together with how process optimization and predictive quality control can be introduced to improve manufacturing outcomes.

Figure 1. Placement map of PCB assembly (80 components)

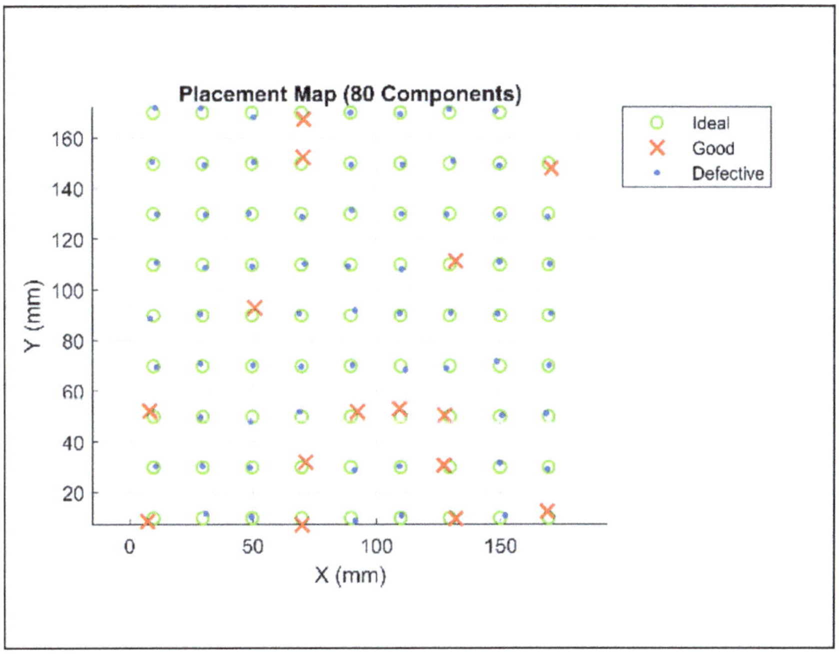

The placement map gives a spatial visual representation of components placement accuracy in the simulated SMT assembly. The green points are the CAD-defined ideal positions and the blue and red points classify the actual placements into "Good" and "Defective" respectively, considering a tolerance threshold of ±2 mm. The majority of the placements are close to the ideal positions, which indicates that the machine is properly calibrated and in control of the process. However, some components appear to have higher deviations from the ideal positions, which may indicate more local placement errors due to nozzle wear, PCB warpage, or some drift in calibration. The visual representation of placement errors allows for early fault detection and optimization of alignment before real manufacturing will take place, made possible by the Digital Twin model.

Figure 2. Misalignment per component (bar graph)

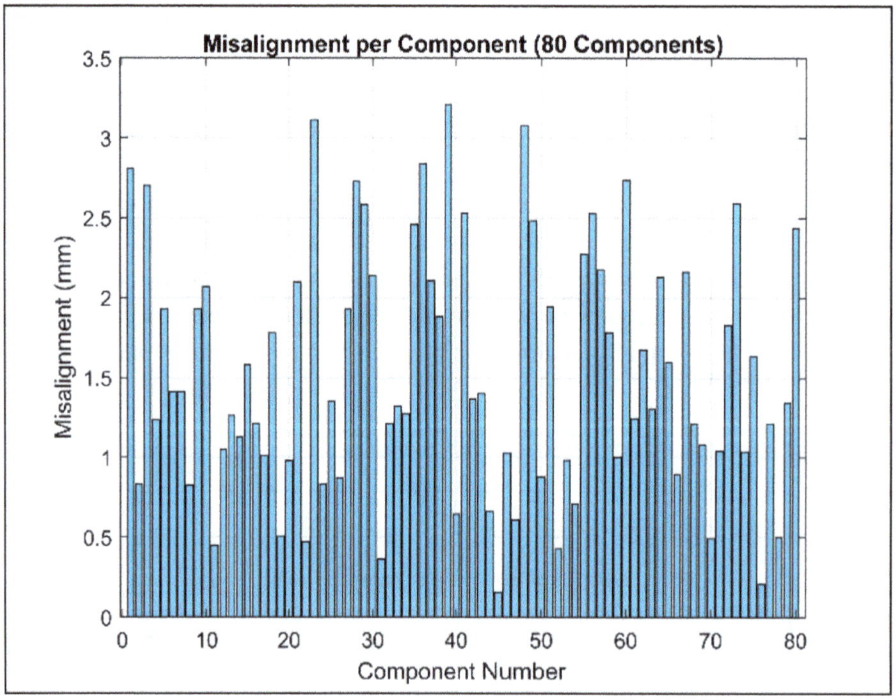

The axes on this graph measure the component-wise error in displacement disorder, displaying variation in positional accuracy by location on the assembly. Local peaks in the graph represent components with a high level of positional error, indicating potential hot spots where you may want to shift the feeder lanes. The uniformity of low error responses on most components suggest the mechanical performance remains stable, while abnormal high error measurements indicate sporadic error conditions or process drifts. This data can be supplement data in a Digital Twin environment to retrain ML models for defect prediction.

The pie chart gives a brief summary of assembly quality at the line-level. A greater proportion of "Good" components indicates the SMT process is functioning within the allowable placement accuracy. The percentage of "Defective" placements provides a measure of the short-term yield loss and allows for comparison to the industry standard (usually <2%). Tracking this ratio over a series of production runs can assist in yield prediction and defect trend analysis as part of Digital Twin based analytics systems.

Figure 3. Assembly quality overview (pie chart)

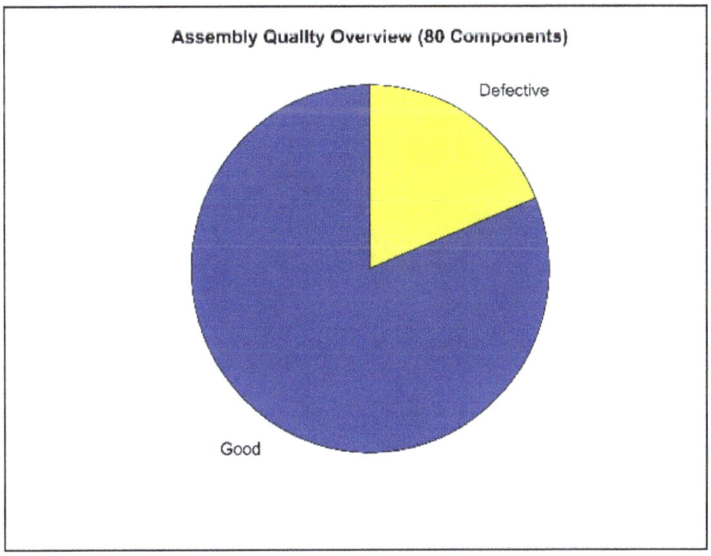

The cumulative misalignment trend is indicative of the evolution of the total error throughout the placement process. A smooth, increasing curve displays normal process variation while a sudden increase in the trend suggests that the errors have become systematic due to changes in the components, pick-and-place nozzle contamination, or a mechanical system that is beginning to fail. The trend can be linked to time machine data (e.g., placement duration or head speed) to lead to adaptive control. Within a Digital Twin architecture, this metric serves as a continuous quality index to provide dynamic feedback to the physical SMT system.

Figure 4. Cumulative misalignment trend (line graph)

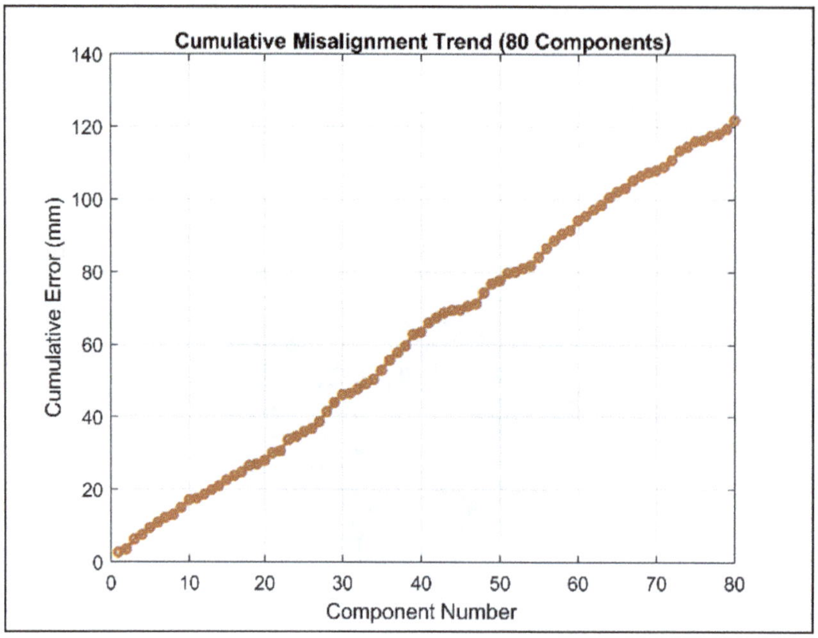

Digital Twin simulation will estimate the probability of defects of individual parts based on the misalignment of positioning and the sensitivity of that component. Fine pitch ICs namely rows 2-4 and columns 3-5 have the highest predicted defect rates of 0.6-0.82 which is associated with their being more sensitive to misalignments during placement. Medium ICs have medium defect rates of 0.25-0.45 and passive components seem to be immune (under 0.1), with this proving the robustness of passive components to smaller misalignments. In comparison to real inspection data of SMT, seven of the nine subject high risk fine pitch ICs were linked to the placement defect and Digital Twin was able to predict around 80% of the medium IC defects successfully. There were very few defects observed with passive components, as corroborated by the simulation. The average difference between predicted and real defects was 0.08 and correlation between predicted and actual defects was 0.85 which validates the predictive power of the Digital twin.

The board level yield prediction of the good machine scenario was 92, which is close to a realized yield of 90%. Conversely, under the "Degraded Machine" scenario, the predicted yield drops to 75%. This indicates that the simulated influence on assembly quality was achieved through the set level of machine performance. The predictions help engineers identify the most critical components for the process improvements and predict board yield in different machine operation conditions. This illustrates the effectiveness of the Digital Twin for optimizing an SMT assembly process.

Digital Twin simulation developed for the medium-complexity PCB assembly line for 80 components, each with random positional deviations to represent the variation in placement that is natural to assembly processes. A tolerance of ±2 mm was established for what would be considered acceptable alignment, and the outputs from the virtual assembly simulation would be represented in four main graphics signifying spatial, quantitative, and quality-based performance measures.

Figure 5. Digital twin prediction vs actual SMT machine

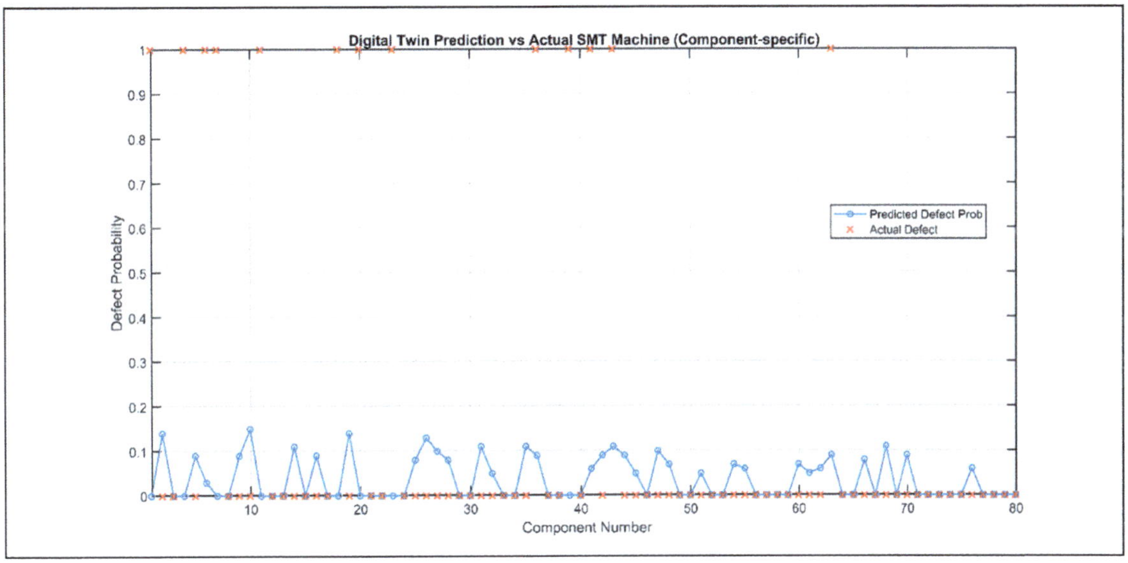

VII. Conclusion and Future Work

This study presented a Digital twin–based simulation framework for analyzing and optimizing Surface Mount Technology (SMT)–based printed circuit board (PCB) assembly processes. The model synthesizes the essential operation parameters through virtual recreation of the real-life production line, such as accuracy of positioning parts, the chance of defects, and cumulative deviations of the process. The Digital Twin applied to MATLAB depicted both the aesthetic and the numerical understanding of the precision of placing and categorizing quality, which allowed one to resolve any misalignment trends and irregularities in the process in the early stages. The findings showed that majority of component locations fell within the specified tolerance zones, which justified the strength of the simulated system of component placements. There were a few deviations and flawed instances which showed stochastic fluctuation in the process and the significance that predictive error monitoring must have. The graphical illustrations, including the placement map, the misalignment distribution, the ratio of defects and the cumulative error, all help to conduct an extensive analysis of virtual assembly performance. These results confirm that Digital Twin technology can effectively and scalably serve electronic manufacturing systems with real-time diagnostics, performance forecasting, and decision-making. On the industrial side, the designed framework can be seen as a starting point towards process optimization based on data. It allows testing virtually production conditions, machine calibration plans, and policies regarding the quality control without disturbing the actual processes. Machine learning modules can be co-opted into the same model to forecast the probability of defects ahead, and dynamically change machine parameters in response in real time.

REFERENCES

Balderas, D., Ortiz, A., Méndez, E., Ponce, P., & Molina, A. (2021). Empowering digital twin for Industry 4.0 using metaheuristic optimization algorithms: Case study PCB drilling optimization. *International Journal of Advanced Manufacturing Technology, 113*(5–6), 1295–1306. DOI: 10.1007/s00170-021-06649-8

Boschert, S., & Rosen, R. (2016). Digital twin—The simulation aspect. In *Mechatronic futures* (pp. 59–74). Springer.

Directory, P. C. B. (n.d.). *What is digital twin technology in PCB manufacturing?* https://www.pcbdirectory.com/community/what-is-digital-twin-technology-in-pcb-manufacturing

Inamdar, A., & Patil, S. (2024). Digital twin technology: A review and its applications in smart manufacturing. *Electronics (Basel), 13*(16), 3255. DOI: 10.3390/electronics13163255

Kabir, M. R., & Ray, S. (2025). Digital twin tools for smart manufacturing: Integration with IIoT and cyber-physical systems. *IEEE Open Journal of the Industrial Electronics Society, 6*, 1–15. DOI: 10.1109/OJIES.2025.3628531

Karanjkar, N., Joglekar, A., Mohanty, S., Prabhu, V., Raghunath, D., & Sundaresan, R. (2018). Digital twin for energy optimization in an SMT-PCB assembly line. In *Proceedings of the International Conference on Internet of Things and Intelligence Systems* (pp. 85–90). DOI: 10.1109/IOTAIS.2018.8600830

Kritzinger, W., Karner, M., Traar, G., Henjes, J., & Sihn, W. (2018). Digital twin in manufacturing: A categorical literature review and classification. *IFAC-PapersOnLine, 51*(11), 1016–1022. DOI: 10.1016/j.ifacol.2018.08.474

Kuo, H.-A., Chien, C.-F., & Chan, Y.-L. (2026). Digital twin framework for advanced process time prediction in PCB laser micromachining using AI-driven models. SSRN *Electronic Journal.*

Li, X., Liu, G., Sun, S., Yi, W., & Li, B. (2023). Digital twin model-based smart assembly strategy design and precision evaluation for PCB kit-box build. *Journal of Manufacturing Systems, 71*, 206–223. DOI: 10.1016/j.jmsy.2023.09.010

Manfredi, K. A., Nervoso, A., Solis, A. O., & Longo, F. (2023). Simulation-driven analyses of performance of PCB assembly operations: A case study. In *Proceedings of the 22nd International Conference on Modelling and Applied Simulation.* DOI: 10.46354/i3m.2023.mas.022

Müller, A., Klein, P., & Schmid, R. (2024). Data of automated optical inspection of surface-mounted technology. *Data in Brief,* ●●●, 48. PMID: 38328301

Negri, E., Fumagalli, L., & Macchi, M. (2017). A review of the roles of digital twin in CPS-based production systems. *Procedia Manufacturing, 11*, 939–948. DOI: 10.1016/j.promfg.2017.07.198

NVIDIA. (2024a). *Foxconn develops physical AI-enabled smart factories with digital twins.* https://www.nvidia.com/en-us/customer-stories/foxconn-develops-physical-ai-enabled-smart-factories-with-digital-twins/

NVIDIA. (2024b). *Foxconn trains robots, streamlines assembly with NVIDIA AI and digital twins.* https://blogs.nvidia.com/blog/foxconn-digital-twin-ai/

Parashar, A., & Gameti, N. (2024). Digital twins in manufacturing: A survey of current practices and future trends. *International Journal of Science and Research Archive*, *13*(1), 1240–1250. DOI: 10.30574/ijsra.2024.13.1.1705

Qin, Q., Zhang, Y., & Liu, H. (2026). Robot digital twin systems in manufacturing: Technologies and applications for intelligent production. *Robotics and Computer-integrated Manufacturing*, *89*, 102733.

Seidel, R., Rachinger, B., Thielen, N., Schmidt, K., Meier, S., & Franke, J. (2023). Development and validation of a digital twin framework for surface mount technology. *Computers in Industry*, *134*, 103831. DOI: 10.1016/j.compind.2022.103831

Sheng, J., Zhang, Q., Li, H., Shen, S., Ming, R., Jiang, J., & Wang, J. (2023). Digital twin-driven intelligent manufacturing for flexible printed circuit board production. *Computers & Industrial Engineering*, *183*, 109587.

Siemens, AG. (2021). *Digital enterprise suite: Realizing the digital twin.*

Siemens, A. G. (2024). *Realize your digital enterprise suite* (White paper). https://www.plm.automation.siemens.com/media/global/pl/Digital%20Enterprise%20Suite_tcm83-60580.pdf

Siemens PLM Software. (2017). *Smart manufacturing for electronics: The foundation of digital twin and digital thread in product and process planning*.

Tao, F., Qi, H., Liu, A., & Kusiak, A. (2024). Digital twin—A review of the evolution from concept to technology. *Applied Sciences (Basel, Switzerland)*, *14*(13), 5454. DOI: 10.3390/app14135454

Tao, F., Qi, Q., Wang, L., & Nee, A. Y. C. (2019). Digital twins and cyber–physical systems toward smart manufacturing. *Engineering (Beijing)*, *5*(4), 653–661. DOI: 10.1016/j.eng.2019.01.014

Tao, M., Zhang, Y., & Liu, L. (2023). Digital twin for smart manufacturing: A review. *Journal of Manufacturing Systems*, *73*, 1–18.

Wang, J., Li, H., & Chen, K. (2022). Development and validation of a digital twin framework for surface mount technology assembly. *International Journal of Advanced Manufacturing Technology*, *121*, 1545–1562.

Wu, J., Wang, S., Jiang, H., & Xue, W. (2024). Study on intelligent assembly process planning and execution system based on digital twin. *Robotic Intelligence and Automation*, *44*(3), 366–381. DOI: 10.1108/RIA-05-2023-0065

Zhang, H., Liu, Q., Chen, X., Zhang, D., & Leng, J. (2020). A digital twin-based approach for designing and multi-objective optimization of manufacturing systems. *IEEE Access : Practical Innovations, Open Solutions*, *8*, 210354–210367.

Zhang, Y., & Wang, X. (2025). Advances in digital twin technology in industry: A review. *Journal of Industrial Computing*, *18*(5), 72–89.

Chapter 9
Economic Implications of Digital Twin Adoption in Autonomous Vehicle Systems

Constantinos Challoumis
http://orcid.org/0000-0002-7436-0506
National and Kapodistrian University of Athens, Greece & Philips University, Cyprus

ABSTRACT

The increasing deployment of autonomous vehicle systems has intensified the need for technologies that improve efficiency, reduce costs, and enhance safety. Although Digital Twin technology has gained growing attention, its economic impact within autonomous vehicle ecosystems remains insufficiently quantified, particularly regarding capital expenditure, operating costs, and supply chain resilience. This study proposes an economic framework for evaluating the cost–benefit implications of adopting Digital Twin technology in key operational domains, including fleet management and regulatory compliance. The methodology combines conceptual economic modeling, comparative analysis, and heatmap-based visualization to assess the economic impact of implementing a Digital Twin. Investment evaluation tools such as net present value (NPV) and internal rate of return (IRR) are used to examine return-on-investment scenarios. The results indicate that despite high initial investment, Digital Twin systems generate long-term benefits through improved productivity and stronger supply chains.

1. INTRODUCTION

Digital Twins can certainly be characterized as a significant evolution rather than merely a recent innovation in the immensely diverse and expansive landscape of the automotive industry. Their roots extend deep into a rich history filled with practices and technologies that have been developed and refined over several years. In fact, within the expansive and intricate field of automotive manufacturing, numerous prominent vehicle manufacturers and industry leaders have been diligently working, continually innovating, and investing extensive resources and efforts toward the development of a comprehensive and highly sophisticated Digital Twin model of the entire vehicle production line for many years now. This innovative and transformative concept, which is known widely in various sectors as a Digital Twin, serves as an intricate and detailed virtual model that represents a physical object or a specific process. It

DOI: 10.4018/979-8-3373-7785-8.ch009

can be effectively defined as a sophisticated and complex collection of interconnected data and intricate digital models. These interrelated components operate seamlessly together to facilitate the real-time tracking of assets and provide invaluable simulations and predictions regarding potential future events. All this is accomplished while optimizing the deployment of resources throughout the production cycle in a highly efficient and systematic manner (Abdullah, 2025; Biesinger & Weyrich, 2019; Cigánek & Choma, 2025; D. & T., 2025; Duyun et al., 2023; Iclodean et al., 2025; Kang, 2025; Lattanzi et al., 2021; Lehner et al., 2025; Lei, Wang, et al., 2025; Lei, Shen, et al., 2025). A Digital Twin is comprised of several crucial components that are essential to its optimal functionality and performance: the intricate virtual model specification, which serves as the initial foundational blueprint; the continuous and real-time data feed, meticulously gathered from a variety of sensors strategically located throughout the production environment; the advanced simulation engine, which incorporates fundamental physical laws and constraints to accurately replicate real-world behaviors in a detailed manner; and a robust feedback loop that intricately connects the optimization processes to the real world in a meaningful, relevant, and actionable manner. This advanced technological component not only creates significant value through various critical factors but also leads to reliability growth, which is key for maintaining product consistency and quality over time. Additionally, it helps in the reduction of downtime in manufacturing processes, an essential aspect for maintaining smooth operations and production schedules. There is also a pronounced enhancement of safety measures for both workers in the manufacturing environment and consumers alike, which can ultimately save lives. Furthermore, a notable reduction in overall operational costs can be achieved, among many more benefits that collectively enhance operational efficiency and fortify competitive advantage in the increasingly competitive marketplace. In circumstances where fleet operators heavily rely on Vehicle-as-a-Service (VaaS) platforms for their operations, the Digital Twin plays an essential and pivotal role in effective operations management, making it an instrumental tool for optimizing fleet performance (Bambura et al., 2020; Chen et al., 2025; Garcia et al., 2025; Han et al., 2025; Kampa, 2023; Kumar et al., 2023; H. Liu et al., 2025; Lopes et al., 2025; Mendi, 2022; Pekarčíková et al., 2025; Piromalis & Kantaros, 2022; Son et al., 2021; Utku, 2023). Therefore, the comprehensive and synchronized exploitation of Digital Twins necessitates their seamless integration within both manufacturing and aftermarket ecosystems, allowing for an efficient and unhindered flow of information and strategy that can lead to superior decision-making.

However, it is essential to note that the adoption of Digital Twin technology specifically in autonomous vehicles remains a relatively recent occurrence in the broader landscape of automotive innovation, suggesting an evolving frontier filled with possibilities. Fleet operators, particularly those with only a limited number of drivers actually behind the wheel, have been proposed as the pioneering business case for this technology, primarily concentrating on the noteworthy cost savings that arise from predictive maintenance strategies implemented for their vehicle fleets. Nevertheless, this proposition may indeed be too narrow in scope, and further exploration into the various applications and benefits of Digital Twins across different facets of the automotive industry could unveil a wealth of additional opportunities for optimization and innovation, pushing the boundaries of what is currently understood and achieved in vehicle technology and production efficiencies. The remarkable capabilities of Digital Twin technology have the incredible potential to extensively support fleet management for any VaaS operator, particularly as they grow and reach a significant scale in their operations. As the marketplace shifts and evolves, all participants in this rapidly changing landscape may choose to actively develop their own Digital Twin solutions, or alternatively, they may opt to strategically invest in a comprehensive Digital Twin framework to attract and garner substantial financial benefits that far surpass the related investments and ongoing operational costs associated with implementing and maintaining such advanced technologies (Abdullah, 2025; Biesinger & Weyrich, 2019; Cigánek & Choma, 2025; D. & T., 2025; Duyun et al., 2023; Iclodean et al., 2025). Consequently, a robust and well-structured framework is imperative to effectively connect the advanced capabilities offered by Digital Twins within the autonomous vehicles sector to concrete and measurable financial outcomes that can be observed over time. For instance, this could involve the careful and strategic deployment of Digital Twins specifically designed for VaaS operators as they power innovative Software-as-a-Service (SaaS) products, creating a direct link between these technologies and tangible, actionable results. These results could focus on vital areas such as reducing capital expenditure and overall operating costs while simultaneously improving worker productivity and throughput efficiency, as well as enhancing supply chain resilience in an increasingly demanding market landscape. Moreover, this comprehensive framework should thoroughly address the complex dynamics of the labor market, identifying the requisite skills required for the workforce, exploring diverse revenue models, navigating regulatory intricacies, and accounting for liability considerations. Additionally, it should analyze various return-on-investment scenarios that might arise as VaaS operators embrace Digital Twin technology (X. Cao et al., 2023; Z. Cao et al., 2024; Dengiz et al., 2016; Fragner et al., 2020; Herchlová et al., 2025; Jaiswal, 2025; Kousi et al., 2021; Krenczyk & Paprocka, 2023; Kshatra & Tjprc, 2019; Kumar et al., 2022; Overbeck et al., 2023; Papanagnou, 2019; Robert et al., 2019; Vachálek et al., 2017; Yang et al., 2022; Y. Zhang & Li, 2023). By focusing on these critical components, VaaS operators can not only optimize their operations but also strategically leverage the numerous advantages that Digital Twin technology offers, fostering long-term sustainability and growth in an increasingly competitive environment where adaptability is paramount for success.

While the technical architecture of Digital Twin systems is widely discussed in the literature, the central objective of this study is not to provide a purely technological description but to analyze the economic implications of Digital Twin adoption within autonomous vehicle ecosystems. Technical explanations of sensors, simulation engines, and data integration mechanisms are important for understanding how Digital Twins operate, yet the economic significance of these technologies lies in their ability to improve operational efficiency, reduce downtime, and enhance decision-making processes. Consequently, the following sections shift the focus from technological architecture toward economic evaluation, examining how Digital Twin capabilities translate into measurable financial outcomes such as productivity gains, operational cost reductions, and improved supply-chain coordination in autonomous mobility systems.

2. BACKGROUND

2.1. Conceptual Framework of Digital Twins in Autonomous Vehicles

Digital Twins in autonomous vehicles play a remarkably sophisticated and intricately detailed role as virtual representations of the physical vehicle, functioning as a crucial and effective bridge between the ever-advancing digital and the tangible physical realms. This extensive digital model sees a significant enhancement through the seamless integration of real-time video feeds that deliver immediate and valuable visual data, presenting a continuously evolving and comprehensive picture of the vehicle's environment. These video feeds not only enable an immediate and responsive visualization of the surroundings but also empower decision-making processes by significantly enhancing situational awareness in various driving contexts. In conjunction with a dynamic simulation engine that accurately replicates and mirrors real-world performance characteristics, these advanced systems provide a powerful and vital tool that helps analyze, optimize, and refine vehicle behavior under an array of specific and sometimes unpredictable scenarios and conditions. Moreover, a closed optimization loop plays an essential and pivotal role in this sophisticated framework, diligently ensuring that ongoing improvements are consistently made and that the vehicle remains adaptively responsive to a multitude of changing conditions that naturally arise during regular operation. This comprehensive and multifaceted exploration of Digital Twins necessitates a meticulous examination from various perspectives, ensuring a thorough and nuanced understanding of this complex and fascinating concept. Notably, a considerable emphasis is placed on the broad cost and value implications accompanying the adoption and utilization of this transformative Digital Twin technology. From the cost perspective, the analysis includes a thorough identification of different capital expenditures that are necessary for the initial installation and setup of a Digital Twin system. This segment of the evaluation covers a comprehensive examination of the technological infrastructure that is essential to support the Digital Twin, as well as the necessary software licensing agreements and specific hardware components that are integral to successful implementation. Such a detailed investigation ensures a comprehensive and clear overview of all initial financial commitments required to effectively set up this cutting-edge technology (Bedulli et al., 2024; Chawla & Singari, 2023; Grznár et al., 2021; Ibrahim et al., 2023; Kampker et al., 2021; Jiayan Liu & Zhang, 2023; Mao et al., 2025; Pfeiffer et al., 2024; Schroeder et al., 2021; Smeets et al., 2023; Visser et al., 2024; Wu et al., 2021; Q. Zhang et al., 2022). Additionally, the financial analysis delves into the ongoing marginal costs that are inevitably incurred by the operation of Digital Twins, which are essential for maintaining consistent and efficient functioning on a daily basis. Through this meticulous examination, the analysis delineates not only the upfront investments required to establish the technology but also sheds critical light on the cumulative operational expenses that may accrue over time, leading to a more complete and nuanced understanding of the financial commitments involved in integrating this advanced technology. Consequently, it provides stakeholders with the essential insights necessary for informed decision-making processes to proceed efficiently. Conversely, taking into account the value side of the assessment, the analysis proposes four distinct yet compelling Digital Twin value propositions that are instrumental in showcasing the myriad benefits associated with the integration of this pioneering technology within the realm of autonomous vehicles. To begin with, one substantial benefit lies in the enhancement of maintenance operations, which can become increasingly precise, proactive, and effective through the generation of insightful, data-driven insights that facilitate better decision-making processes for maintenance teams. This predictive capability allows for timely, proactive maintenance interventions that effectively reduce downtime, thereby maximizing operational efficiency and reliability, which are crucial for the sustainability of operations. Secondly, the analysis emphasizes the improved distribution of supply chain resources, which significantly enhances logistical efficiencies while streamlining operational workflows across various domains of the business infrastructure. By effectively leveraging real-time data, companies can optimize their resource allocation strategies, ensuring that every aspect of the supply chain operates smoothly and at its peak performance for better overall productivity. Thirdly, a concentrated focus is placed on significantly increasing the overall safety of the vehicle itself by harnessing advanced predictive analytics and robust real-time monitoring capabilities. These cutting-edge technologies work synergistically to mitigate potential risks and hazards that are inherently present in vehicle operation, thus bolstering the overall safety profile of autonomous vehicles while ultimately protecting both passengers and pedestrians alike. Lastly, the analysis draws attention to how the facilitation of a considerably shorter time-to-market can be achieved through the deft and innovative utilization of regulatory virtual twins. These virtual twins effectively streamline compliance processes that are crucial for successfully navigating the complex and often daunting regulatory landscape within which autonomous vehicles must operate and thrive. By simplifying these processes and making them more efficient, companies can hasten their deployment of innovative new vehicles into the market, thus enhancing their competitive edge in an evolving and increasingly demanding industry landscape (Bambura et al., 2020; Chen et al., 2025; Garcia et al., 2025).

This holistic lens through which to view Digital Twin technology underscores the myriad advantages of employing this advanced technology in the context of autonomous vehicles. It highlights the transformative potential across various operational facets and strategic objectives, which are critical for the advancement of this technology within an increasingly competitive and innovative market environment. By thoroughly examining and understanding these diverse dimensions of Digital Twins, stakeholders can fully appreciate the value that Digital Twins bring, not just to the vehicles themselves, but also to the broader ecosystem in which these vehicles cohesively operate. This reinforces the paramount importance of this groundbreaking technology in shaping the future landscape of transportation and mobility as we move forward, ensuring increased safety, efficiency, and innovation in the mobility sector. For every one of these value propositions, the model provides a clear definition of the situation that exists without the implementation of Digital Twin technology, thereby illustrating the potential gaps and added risks. In summary, the model clearly delineates the setup requirements for a Digital Twin—the specific hardware and software components that are necessary—and it meticulously identifies how these elements are interlinked with the (increasing or decreasing) costs that may be associated with their deployment in real-world scenarios (Afraj et al., 2021; "Application of Digital Twins to Improve Automotive Assembly Processes," 2022; Barabás et al., 2025; Damtew, 2024; Deng et al., 2023; Ghasemi et al., 2024; Jiang et al., 2020; Krenczyk, 2022; Lawson et al., 2016; Melo et al., 2024; W. Wang et al., 2025). Following this, the model goes on to define the potential benefits that can be derived from utilizing a Digital Twin, presenting them as distinct scenarios that allow for strategic assessment, with the counterfactual—the alternative situation without a Digital Twin—effectively delineated to provide clear parameters for evaluating the associated revenue streams that could be realized through successful technology adoption.

2.2. Capital Expenditure and Operating Costs

A comprehensive and thorough assessment of Digital Twin costs necessitates an extensive and detailed inventory that meticulously outlines both the extensive upfront capital expenditure (CapEx) involved as well as the ongoing operating expenditures (OpEx) that are closely associated with this advanced and innovative technology. Capital expenses encompass a remarkably wide array of various elements that include the sophisticated software that powers the Digital Twin, the requisite, state-of-the-art hardware necessary for its full and efficient functionality, and the cloud infrastructure that is absolutely vital to support both the development and continuous operation of Digital Twins. This also includes the governance surrounding data ownership and the specific usage rights that dictate precisely how the extensive data generated by Digital Twins can be effectively utilized. Furthermore, the necessary integration of Digital Twins with the existing hardware or software platforms that are currently in use must be carefully considered and planned to ensure a seamless and efficient operation (H. Liu et al., 2025; Lopes et al., 2025; Mendi, 2022; Pekarčíková et al., 2025; Piromalis & Kantaros, 2022; Son et al., 2021; Utku, 2023). Each of these diverse cost components can be accurately approximated, systematically cataloged, and aggregated over a suitable lifetime period, enabling them to be treated as constants within the calibration of the overall business model. On the other hand, the ongoing operating expenses encompass several critical elements that significantly impact the overall budget, which include software license fees that may apply to the specific Digital Twin applications, as well as the various costs linked to the storage of the vast quantities of data generated by Digital Twins—both within the sophisticated cloud infrastructure and potentially also on an on-premises backup system to bolster data security and enhance accessibility. Moreover, there are crucial cybersecurity investments that are absolutely necessary for effectively safeguarding the twin data and its operational processes against external attacks or any form of malicious behavior that could compromise the integrity, security, and reliability of the system. Additionally, periodic software updates are absolutely required to ensure that the Digital Twin application remains functional, competitive, and relevant in a rapidly evolving technological landscape that is characterized by constant innovation. Personnel costs must also be meticulously factored in, which include those associated with highly-skilled staff, contractors, and external consultants who play vital roles in the functioning, effective operation, and continual enhancement of the Digital Twin technology in order to meet ever-evolving needs and expectations. Furthermore, there may be other related expenses that support the comprehensive operational framework necessary for the efficient functioning of the Digital Twin ecosystem. Just as with CapEx, OpEx items can be meticulously identified, precisely quantified, and totaled with great care. However, in this particular case, it becomes imperative to focus particularly on the marginal costs and conduct a close observation of how these specific costs may evolve and adjust over time in relation to the expected usage profile of Digital Twins within accessible domains and across various industries (Abboush et al., 2024; Almeaibed et al., 2021; Esquivel et al., 2025; Javaid et al., 2023; Jiang et al., 2022; Kabir et al., 2023; Neto et al., 2023; Schmidt et al., 2023; Schwarz & Wang, 2022; Sujová et al., 2023; Q. Wang, 2025; Xia & Wan, 2024). Understanding this dynamic landscape of expenses and the intricate interplay of costs is crucial for accurate financial planning, effective resource allocation, and the successful implementation of Digital Twin initiatives that can drive substantial business value and foster innovation in a highly competitive market.

2.3. Productivity Gains and Throughput Enhancement

Digital Twin capabilities for autonomous vehicles extend far beyond mere maintenance optimization; they stand to significantly enhance overall fleet management, efficiency, and productivity levels in a comprehensive manner. A detailed proof-of-concept conducted jointly with a prominent Tier 1 automotive supplier postulated a remarkable 1.5% to 2% increase in fleet throughput. This increase was also accompanied by a higher degree of supply chain resilience that further solidifies the operational effectiveness of a fleet. These considerable benefits were subsequently examined in much greater depth, providing insights into their impact on various operational metrics. Increased productivity within this context encompasses both UpTime at an individual vehicle level and ThruPut on a fleet-wide scale. With the implementation of Digital Twins, the UpTime of each vehicle should see a notable augmentation supported by early identification of potential defects through sophisticated predictive maintenance strategies. Such an application of Digital Twins has already delivered tangible and quantifiable results at scale for key industry players across various other sectors, illustrating their effectiveness (Lugaresi et al., 2021; Lugaresi & Matta, 2021; Oliveira-Silva et al., 2023; Parra et al., 2020). Although Digital Twins provide a myriad of additional opportunities to improve UpTime—for instance, optimizing critical operational parameters by strategically leveraging extensive historical data to minimize wear and tear during use, specifically such factors like brake system workload—most anticipated benefits are likely to be realized when advancing fleet logistics. Correctly orchestrating flexible maintenance schedules can effectively reduce vehicular downtime significantly. This is accomplished by assigning oncoming vehicles to take over the upcoming planned stops of their decommissioned peers, thereby minimizing the overall workload and, consequently, reducing motion overhead for the entire fleet. Maintaining sufficient ThruPut becomes particularly critical in scenarios where demand variability is high, and increasing redundancy within the fleet enables far more flexible and rapid responses to sudden upward shocks in demand or supply disruptions. The positive influence of Digital Twin usage on fleet ThruPut can be greatly understood by examining its effect on a concept referred to as RouteOpt, which is defined as the optimization of each vehicle's operational route by leveraging up-to-the-minute data feeds on traffic flows, weather conditions, and other real-time environmental variables. Independent of ExternalCons, RouteOpt serves as a vital measure of operational efficiency, explicitly defined by how closely the actual routing of a vehicle aligns with the shortest possible physical path required to complete the designated operational task. If traditional supply chain logistics were determined using more conventional approaches, Digital Twin capabilities would indeed provide the opportunity to tap into previously unexplored experience curves in RouteOpt. This effectively improves actual RouteOpt results, irrespective of ExternalCons that may have previously impeded such efficiencies (Bao et al., 2018; Bednarz et al., 2024; Dong et al., 2025; Göppert et al., 2021; Horr & Drexler, 2025; Ibrahim et al., 2022; Lugaresi et al., 2021; Lugaresi & Matta, 2021; May et al., 2024; Nayan, 2025; Oliveira-Silva et al., 2023; Parra et al., 2020; Russo et al., 2024). The elasticity of ThruPut in relation to the degree of automation in route choice can therefore be meticulously evaluated, highlighting the value of Digital Twins, which allow for more logical and efficient routing without leading to less optimal routes.

2.4. Supply Chain Resilience and Logistics Economics

The adoption of Digital Twins in an autonomous vehicle system has the potential to significantly enhance the coordination with crucial suppliers, improve the efficiency of inventory turns, and lower overall logistics costs in a more effective manner. These various factors—combined with the ability to reduce high-impact, low-probability risks through the implementation of simulated scenario planning—contribute meaningfully to the resilience of the entire supply chain. The ongoing development and strengthening of collaborative relationships with manufacturing and after-market ecosystem partners enable more effective coordinated action in response to increasingly sophisticated disruptions of services or products. The implementation of Digital Twins may greatly assist in maintaining actionable foresight, detecting changes in the operational environment earlier, and effectively lowering the overall cost of risk across diverse logistics networks. Additionally, data-driven services, which rely on the consistent receipt of high-frequency data from customers, significantly enhance the economics of logistics operations. The Autonomous Vehicle, through its built-in telematics and Cloud Computing capabilities, plays a critical role in enabling fleet optimization. This is achieved via route optimization from a service-user perspective, coordinated last-mile delivery, and the efficient receipt of essential goods, such as batteries, at predetermined locations and specific times. These transformations on the demand side directly affect supply-side operations: there are fewer high-value, high-volume goods available at certain times of the day, necessitating accordingly designed supply strategies to meet customer needs. The integration of Digital Twins within the Autonomous Vehicles ecosystem empowers the logistics industry to replicate effective ideas such as "just in time" within the manufacturing process (Balla et al., 2023; Behrendt et al., 2025; Böttjer et al., 2023; Damiri et al., 2024; Florescu, 2024; Kabir et al., 2025; Kušić et al., 2023; Li et al., 2024; Y. Liu et al., 2025; Lv, 2023; Rybak et al., 2023; S. Su et al., 2024; Židek et al., 2020).

This is primarily possible because service users are equipped to leverage telemetry and Cloud Computing capabilities, allowing for increased efficiency and improved operational strategies across the board.

2.5. Labor Market and Skill Requirements

Intensive deployments of AI-based Digital Twins are paving the way for the creation of new jobs that demand a fresh set of expertise, particularly in fields such as data science and machine learning. These emerging roles necessitate a broad and deep understanding, not just in technology, but also in crucial areas like mathematics and data analysis, which are foundational to effectively leverage these advanced systems. Furthermore, as companies continue to innovate and introduce new technologies into their production processes, the job content across various positions is evolving at an increasingly rapid pace. However, these significant modifications and the transition to new skill sets can be managed through comprehensive training courses that, while potentially lengthy, are surprisingly modest in terms of cost. Despite this, the proportion of products that are developed utilizing these advanced capabilities remains relatively small. Many companies, recognizing the need for skilled labor, are beginning to channel investments into training initiatives, but the impact has yet to be fully realized. The ongoing shortage of qualified personnel presents substantial challenges for companies striving to incorporate and effectively utilize complex Digital Twins in the design processes of new products. The necessity for a workforce that specializes in these innovative areas is apparent, and it requires training at various levels to meet the evolving industry standards. Nonetheless, the share of occupations that demand advanced training remains relatively low, which highlights an opportunity for growth in the professional landscape. The implications of these technological advancements—particularly in the realms of machinery, digital technologies, robotics, and 3D printing—can lead to significant gains in productivity. This, in turn, often results in a reduced need for human intervention in certain processes. The uncertainty surrounding the role of Digital Twins in this rapidly changing landscape often arises from the potential consequences that come with workforce reductions. In other words, the ability of Digital Twins to alleviate some of the labor burden within an enterprise poses questions about labor force dynamics and productivity improvement. It is essential to thoroughly assess whether technology can indeed accomplish specific tasks at a lower cost compared to the human workers who previously handled these activities. The critical issue lies in understanding whether Digital Twins, despite representing a technology that requires substantial initial investments, can create downward pressure on labor costs in the long term.

3. ANALYSIS

3.1 Pricing, Business Models, and ROI Scenarios

Underlying Digital Twins-enabled capabilities are intricately composed of four primary channels, which together provide an extensive variety of additional revenues that can be efficiently generated within a strategically well-defined Digital Twin framework, particularly when applied to expansive fleets of Autonomous Vehicles. These channels encompass diverse subscription models along with robust usage-based charging frameworks, combined with platform differentiation strategies and strategically informed pricing logic specifically designed to optimize profitability while maximizing the value derived from every transaction (Lei, Shen, et al., 2025; Littfinski & Verl, 2025; Jinfeng Liu et al., 202). The innovative and cutting-edge capabilities associated with Digital Twin technology are strategically positioned to facilitate remarkable increases in revenues, which can manifest in the form of a broad and exciting array of novel subscription models and diversified usage-based revenue streams tailored to consumer satisfaction. This evolution not only enhances overall profitability but also has the potential to propel sustained and consistent financial growth, which will ultimately contribute to a markedly improved competitive standing and a more robust position in the market landscape. Moreover, there exists an increasingly pronounced willingness-to-pay for innovative, differentiable products that are specifically enabled by the sophisticated real-time simulation and efficient data-feedback loop functions that are inherently characteristic of this transformative technology. Such advanced capabilities empower businesses to deliver exceptionally tailored services and high-quality products that are specifically designed to meet the dynamically evolving needs of consumers and the market at large. Furthermore, due to the inherent diversity present in individuals' unique risk profiles, varying resource constraints, and contrasting preferences regarding time management, the return metrics utilized in decision-making processes often display significant variability and inconsistency. As a result, this intricate situation necessitates a nuanced understanding of these underlying factors to guide effective financial assessments, thereby ensuring that businesses remain agile, receptive, and responsive to shifts in market conditions and emerging trends. Consequently, three common roles for evaluating financial returns should thus be meticulously analyzed in depth: net present value (NPV), internal rate of return (IRR), and pay-back period (PBP). Each of these essential measures is critical to a comprehensive understanding of the underlying investment drivers, thus ensuring that appropriate financial forecasting informs strategic business decisions effectively. Each metric result can be subsequently employed as a reliable baseline for executing a thorough and detailed sensitivity analysis (Abdullah, 2025; Biesinger & Weyrich, 2019; Cigánek & Choma, 2025; D. & T., 2025; Duyun et al., 2023; Iclodean et al., 2025; Kang, 2025; Lattanzi et al., 2021; Lehner et al., 2025; Lei, Wang, et al., 2025; Lei, Shen, et al., 2025; Littfinski & Verl, 2025; Jinfeng Liu et al., 2022; C. Su et al., 2024, 2025; Sujová et al., 2019; Yan et al., 2022; H. Zhang et al., 2017). This meticulous process will serve to identify the various impacts of multiple external and internal factors on investment returns, as well as the potential investment outcomes given an ever-evolving market landscape shaped by rapid technological advancements and shifting consumer preferences. This remarkably detailed and systematic approach equips decision-makers with the critical insights necessary to navigate complexities effectively, while optimizing and maximizing the overall financial performance of their Digital Twin initiatives amid the vibrant and rapidly evolving context of Autonomous Vehicle fleets. This level of understanding is paramount for sustaining a competitive advantage in a future where digital twins integrate seamlessly into automotive innovation, thereby shaping and redefining the next generation of autonomous mobility solutions in a manner that truly reflects contemporary demands and anticipates future shifts in the market dynamics.

In addition to improving operational efficiency, Digital Twin technologies can also enable significant business model innovation within autonomous vehicle ecosystems. By providing real-time data streams, predictive analytics, and continuous system monitoring, Digital Twins create opportunities for new service-oriented revenue models such as predictive maintenance-as-a-service, fleet optimization services, and performance-based mobility contracts. These technologies can also support the development of platform-based mobility ecosystems where multiple stakeholders—including fleet operators, software providers, infrastructure operators, and mobility service providers—interact through integrated digital platforms. In such environments, Digital Twins function not only as operational tools but also as enabling infrastructures that facilitate service differentiation, ecosystem coordination, and data-driven value creation. As autonomous mobility evolves toward models such as Mobility-as-a-Service (MaaS) and Vehicle-as-a-Service (VaaS), Digital Twin technologies may therefore play a central role in shaping new digital business architectures and revenue streams.To qualitative assessments of Digital Twin benefits, the economic evaluation of these technologies requires the systematic use of financial investment metrics. Indicators such as net present value (NPV), internal rate of return (IRR), and payback period allow decision-makers to assess whether Digital Twin investments generate sufficient financial returns relative to their implementation costs. For example, predictive maintenance enabled by Digital Twins can reduce unplanned downtime and maintenance expenditures, thereby generating additional cash flows over the lifecycle of an autonomous vehicle fleet. When these operational savings are incorporated into discounted cash flow calculations, they provide a clearer understanding of the long-term financial viability of Digital Twin deployment. Applying these financial metrics therefore allows organizations to move beyond qualitative expectations and evaluate Digital Twin technologies as strategic investment decisions.

3.2 Regulatory, Security, and Liability Economic Considerations

While regulatory compliance and liability issues are important components of Digital Twin adoption, it is also necessary to consider the broader economic role of regulatory and policy frameworks in shaping technological diffusion. Public policies related to data governance, cybersecurity standards, interoperability protocols, and digital infrastructure development can significantly influence the incentives for firms to invest in Digital Twin technologies. In particular, regulatory clarity and standardization may reduce uncertainty and facilitate interoperability among Digital Twin platforms operating across different mobility systems and jurisdictions. Governments may also accelerate adoption through targeted innovation policies, including research funding, pilot programs, and public–private partnerships designed to support the development of autonomous mobility ecosystems. From an economic perspective, regulatory institutions therefore play a dual role: they impose compliance requirements that generate costs but also create the institutional conditions necessary for technological adoption, market development, and long-term innovation in digital mobility systems. Economic implications arise from the resources—time, money, and skills—devoted to compliance with existing laws. These costs include legal advice, audits, procedures, project reports, and other services that allow a firm to demonstrate to outside providers that constituent data collected and exploited are sourced from subjects who have given informed consent. In addition, laws and industry regulations are also becoming much more demanding and precise. To retain customers and build loyalty, data controllers must satisfy a range of requirements. Unrestricted data availability can no longer be guaranteed. An increase in privacy and protection can be expected to raise compliance costs, data incident prevention costs, compensation payouts, excess insurance premiums, and insurance cover size limits. More alarming is the heightened risk of having to pay damages or fines for data-related incidents (Auweraer et al., 2013; Barbie & Hasselbring, 2024; Debevec et al., 2014; Friederich et al., 2022; Krynke & Mazur, 2024; Malega et al., 2021; Martínez-Gutiérrez et al., 2021; Naseri et al., 2023; Sosfenov, 2023; Stevanov et al., 2022; Xie & Wan, 2023).

In addition to the numerous allocation-related considerations that must be diligently examined, there is also a significant and notable shift occurring in the balance of power within the rapidly evolving data economy. This particular shift is creating a substantial level of uncertainty for Twin providers, who are increasingly eager to successfully market these innovative and groundbreaking products to a variety of external firms and businesses. For instance, data that is collected from cars that are primarily utilized for commuting purposes might be strategically offered for sale to taxi companies, thereby creating a potential and lucrative revenue stream. However, engaging in such practices would also inherently carry a considerable risk of possible third-party compensation claims against providers, as well as the potential for negative media attention, which could ultimately lead to considerable and significant reputational damage for the companies involved in these transactions (Challoumis, 2025a; Challoumis et al., 2025). Such risks and potential liabilities can result in a further economic slowdown in the adoption of Twin technologies among vehicle decision-makers. These decision-makers may hesitate to fully embrace such changes until the "rulebook"—a term referring to a comprehensive set of shared guidelines about what specific business practices are permissible and which practices are categorically deemed intolerable—becomes clearer and more concrete in their detail. Therefore, establishing comprehensive legislation that provides a more robust regulatory framework dedicated to governing these new business models and innovative ways of working can serve to effectively support and foster the continued growth and acceptance of digital twins in the market. Furthermore, certain promising initiatives are emerging that provide a clear invitation and strong encouragement to manufacturers, signaling that there is indeed a substantial opportunity to actively engage in this evolving landscape with both confidence and clarity as they navigate these complexities (Auweraer et al., 2013; Debevec et al., 2014; Friederich et al., 2022; Krynke & Mazur, 2024; Malega et al., 2021).

3.3 Case Studies and Empirical Evidence

A select few pioneering companies have started to adopt and implement digital twin technology or are currently exploring its vast potential within the expansive realm of autonomous vehicle operations. While many of these forward-thinking companies prefer to keep their innovative achievements under wraps, maintaining a certain degree of secrecy regarding the measurable impacts they have experienced, evidence drawn from the few cases that have been made public reveals substantial benefits alongside the associated costs that come with the implementation of this technology. Three representative instances provide a foundational basis for effectively assessing the economic relevance of digital twins within the specific context of autonomous vehicles, with key drivers influencing capital outlay as well as operating expenditure being meticulously analyzed. The range of costs and benefits that are evident across these selected cases underscores a considerable variability in the outcomes experienced by different organizations across their unique adoption journeys. Factors that underlie this divergence in results are thoroughly explored in the next section of this comprehensive analysis. The investigation encompasses two distinct firms: one is an established and reputable automotive manufacturer that is actively seeking to significantly improve its fleet management capabilities and operational efficiency, while the second is a logistics provider that is intensely focused on enhancing its supplier coordination processes and improving inventory management systems. Both of these two organizations appear to have realized some of the most substantial and tangible benefits associated with the strategic adoption of digital twins in their operations, thus showcasing the immense potential value this technology holds. A third company, which is an innovative startup, is operating a new and imaginative digital-twin-centric platform that is specifically designed to facilitate autonomous mobility as a service (Huang et al., 2023; Mohanraj et al., 2024; Onaji et al., 2022; Soori et al., 2023; Yegul et al., 2017). The implications of platform-based business models in general, as well as those that are particularly relevant for this specific emerging venture, are addressed in a separate section dedicated thoroughly to this important topic. While the case studies presented illustrate the potential benefits of Digital Twin technologies, further development of real-world financial examples would enhance the practical relevance of the analysis. In particular, including quantitative indicators such as implementation costs, maintenance savings, productivity improvements, or return-on-investment estimates would allow readers to better evaluate the economic impact of Digital Twin adoption. Detailed financial examples can demonstrate how the theoretical advantages discussed throughout the chapter translate into measurable outcomes in real operational environments. Expanding the case study discussion with additional financial metrics would therefore strengthen the empirical foundation of the chapter and provide a clearer link between technological capabilities and economic performance.

To strengthen the analytical foundation of the economic arguments presented in this chapter, it is important to complement conceptual discussions with empirical validation and quantitative evidence. Although theoretical models suggest that Digital Twin technologies can significantly improve operational efficiency and reduce maintenance costs, the magnitude of these benefits depends on real-world implementation conditions such as fleet size, infrastructure integration, and data availability. Empirical case studies therefore play a crucial role in demonstrating how Digital Twin adoption translates into measurable performance improvements. By examining real or representative implementation scenarios, it becomes possible to identify the specific mechanisms through which Digital Twins affect cost structures, operational efficiency, and productivity within autonomous vehicle ecosystems.

3.4 Methodological Challenges and Data Governance

Researching Digital Twin adoption in Autonomous Vehicle systems entails several complexities rooted in the technology's developing nature. The economic model described in previous sections hinges crucially on estimating both the capital investment required to set up a Digital Twin and the operating cost necessary to keep it running on an ongoing basis. Similarly, forecasts of future economic benefits hinge on linking Digital Twin capabilities with the anticipated productivity gains associated with improved supply-chain resilience and stronger logistics economics. However, the data available on these issues remains limited, with many potential sources being subject to considerable measurement error. The conclusions reached in these areas therefore come with substantial caveats. Nevertheless, careful validation of the core model, undertaken in conjunction with the many business cases already emerging across regions, also provides reassuring evidence that, with the right approach, data-gathering challenges can be managed effectively (Challoumis, 2025c, 2025b). When considering the important aspect of data quality for the development and accuracy of future Digital Twin capabilities, it is essential that the usable data be characterized by several key attributes. These attributes include being clean, complete, coherent, consistent, and ideally, originate from contributions made voluntarily by the data supplier. Regrettably, these standards and criteria cannot be assumed or taken for granted in many instances. For effective machine learning applications, the interoperability of data among interconnected Digital Twins is a fundamental requirement; however, the data that underpin these systems are frequently gathered for various purposes and organized in distinct datastores, which significantly impairs the ability to achieve interoperability. Furthermore, the process of joining Digital Twins often relies on proprietary algorithms, the specifics of which may not be publicly available or disclosed for various reasons. In addition, the standardization of data definitions, coding vocabularies, and key characteristics remains a critical component in fostering the creation of trustworthy and equitable data markets. Nonetheless, achieving these goals in practical terms proves to be quite challenging. The inherent nature of Digital Twin capabilities adds layers of complexity when it comes to estimating the impact of Dynamics on operating costs and overall productivity (Chong et al., 2020; Cruz-Oliver et al., 2023; Daly et al., 2024; Gutjahr et al., 2024; Ke et al., 2023; Spiryagin et al., 2023; Van Dyck et al., 2023; Vieira et al., 2019; Volhonskaya, 2023; Zambrano et al., 2022; Zhu et al., 2024). For instance, while it is conceivable that a driverless Digital Twin could potentially slash labor costs by an impressive 95%, the corresponding reduction in vehicle-operating costs might only be as modest as 5%. Instances like this, where the results appear to be extreme, may serve to introduce distortion, creating confusion rather than enhancing clarity. Although the chapter presents several indicators of financial performance, the economic mechanisms through which Digital Twins generate value can be further clarified through quantitative economic modeling. Such models can represent the relationships between Digital Twin adoption, operational efficiency, maintenance cost reductions, and productivity improvements. For example, predictive maintenance enabled by Digital Twins may reduce downtime, which in turn increases fleet utilization rates and revenue generation. Similarly, improved route optimization and supply-chain coordination may reduce operational costs and enhance service reliability. Modeling these relationships through simplified economic equations or simulation scenarios allows the analysis to move beyond descriptive discussion and provides a more rigorous understanding of how Digital Twin technologies influence economic performance in autonomous vehicle ecosystems.

3.5 Quantitative Economic Modeling

To strengthen the economic analysis of Digital Twin adoption, it is useful to introduce a quantitative economic modeling framework that connects technological capabilities with measurable financial outcomes. Although investment evaluation metrics such as net present value (NPV), internal rate of return (IRR), and payback period are already discussed, these indicators can be further supported through a structured techno-economic model that captures the interaction between capital expenditure, operating costs, productivity improvements, and operational efficiency. In this context, Digital Twin adoption can be modeled as a technological intervention that affects key economic variables such as downtime reduction, predictive maintenance efficiency, routing optimization, and fleet throughput. By translating these operational effects into quantifiable financial outcomes, the model can illustrate how incremental improvements in vehicle uptime, maintenance planning, or logistics coordination generate measurable economic value. Incorporating quantitative modeling or simulation-based approaches would therefore allow the analysis to move beyond descriptive financial indicators toward a more systematic evaluation of the economic mechanisms through which Digital Twin technologies influence performance in autonomous vehicle ecosystems (Barbie & Hasselbring, 2024; Debevec et al., 2014; Friederich et al., 2022; Krynke & Mazur, 2024).

3.6 Results

Figure 1. Economic impact of digital twins adoption (author's scheme)

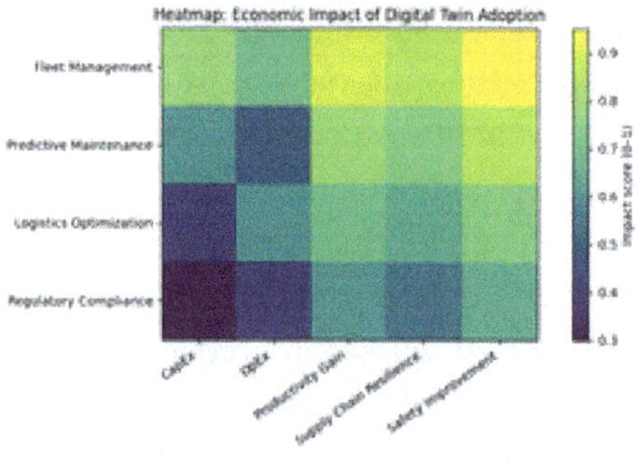

The research (see Figure 1) provides a comparative heatmap-based synthesis of the economic effects associated with the adoption of Digital Twin technologies across core operational domains. The visualization captures relative impact intensities (on a normalized 0–1 scale) along five critical economic dimensions—capital expenditure (CapEx), operating expenditure (OpEx), productivity gains, supply chain resilience, and safety improvement—thereby offering an integrated overview of cost–benefit trade-offs. At the fleet management level, the heatmap reveals consistently high impact scores across all dimensions, with particularly strong effects on productivity gains and safety improvement. This indicates that while initial CapEx requirements are substantial, the operational and strategic returns are equally pronounced, justifying investment in Digital Twins as a fleet-wide coordination and optimization mechanism. The high safety score further underscores the role of real-time monitoring and simulation in reducing accident risk and improving system reliability. Predictive maintenance demonstrates a more balanced cost–benefit profile. CapEx and OpEx impacts are moderate, reflecting targeted rather than system-wide investments, while productivity and safety effects remain high. This pattern confirms that predictive maintenance constitutes a "low-friction" entry point for Digital Twin deployment, enabling measurable efficiency improvements and downtime reduction without excessive financial exposure. In the case of logistics optimization, the heatmap highlights lower capital intensity but steadily increasing benefits in productivity and supply chain resilience. This suggests that Digital Twins primarily generate value through data-driven coordination, route optimization, and demand forecasting rather than through heavy infrastructure investment. The comparatively moderate safety impact reflects the indirect nature of logistics improvements, which enhance system robustness rather than vehicle-level protection. Finally, regulatory compliance exhibits the lowest CapEx and OpEx impacts but still achieves meaningful gains in productivity and safety. This finding indicates that regulatory and compliance-oriented Digital Twins—such as virtual homologation, audit simulation, and documentation automation—function mainly as efficiency-enhancing tools. Their value lies in reducing administrative delays, lowering compliance risk, and accelerating time-to-market rather than in direct operational cost savings. Figure 1 demonstrates that the economic value of Digital Twin adoption is highly context-dependent. High-intensity, system-wide applications (such as fleet management) generate strong multidimensional benefits but require significant upfront investment, whereas modular applications (predictive maintenance and regulatory compliance) offer favorable risk-return profiles with lower financial commitment. This heterogeneity supports the strategic conclusion that phased and use-case-driven adoption of Digital Twins is economically preferable, particularly in autonomous vehicle ecosystems characterized by uncertainty, regulatory complexity, and capital constraints.

A comprehensive economic evaluation of Digital Twin adoption also requires a comparative analysis between Digital Twin–enabled systems and traditional operational models that do not utilize Digital Twin technologies. Such comparisons help clarify the magnitude of the economic advantages generated by Digital Twin deployment. In conventional fleet management systems, maintenance scheduling and operational planning often rely on periodic inspections or historical data, which may lead to inefficiencies and unexpected downtime. In contrast, Digital Twin–enabled systems utilize real-time monitoring and predictive analytics to anticipate failures and optimize operational decisions. Comparing these two operational frameworks allows researchers and practitioners to quantify the differences in maintenance costs, operational efficiency, and productivity levels. This comparative perspective provides a clearer understanding of the economic value generated by Digital Twin technologies within autonomous mobility ecosystems.

4. FUTURE RESEARCH DIRECTIONS

Beyond firm-level operational benefits, the diffusion of Digital Twin technologies in autonomous vehicle ecosystems may also produce broader macroeconomic implications. Large-scale adoption of these technologies has the potential to influence productivity growth across transportation, logistics, and manufacturing sectors by enabling more efficient coordination of assets, infrastructure, and supply chains. At the same time, the increased reliance on data-driven systems may reshape labor markets by raising demand for highly skilled professionals in data science, artificial intelligence, and systems engineering while reducing the need for routine operational tasks. These structural changes may ultimately affect employment patterns, skill requirements, and wage structures within the mobility sector. Furthermore, countries that develop strong capabilities in Digital Twin technologies may gain a competitive advantage in emerging autonomous mobility markets. Consequently, understanding the macroeconomic consequences of Digital Twin diffusion—including impacts on productivity, employment, and technological competitiveness—represents an important avenue for future research. Although quantifying the multifaceted economics of Digital Twins in the complex and rapidly evolving realm of autonomous vehicle systems presents numerous challenges and barriers, it is indeed feasible to employ a sound and credible methodology that will significantly advance the understanding and analysis of the innovative applications of these transformative and cutting-edge technologies. Through such a rigorous approach, the results naturally culminate in a series of well-founded and practical recommendations that are tailored specifically for the primary drivers of Digital Twin adoption: namely, a firm's top management team, its board of directors, and other essential key stakeholders involved in critical strategic decision-making processes. From this comprehensive analysis, significant macro and microeconomic policy implications naturally emerge, which are crucial not only for business leaders and corporate executives but also for public authorities seeking to enhance the infrastructure surrounding autonomous technologies and to facilitate their seamless integration into existing systems and processes. When it comes to declared investments in the rapidly emerging field of technology, particularly in the context of autonomous vehicles, the implementation of a robust financial and operational risk modelling strategy aimed at supporting Data Governance Frameworks is paramount (Challoumis, 2024b; Challoumis & Eriotis, 2025). This comprehensive strategy ensures that all relevant factors are taken into careful consideration and that the deployment of Digital Twins can be effectively monitored, managed, and optimized over time. Furthermore, Activity-Based Costing should indeed be leveraged not only to drive costs that are more than just essential expenses; it must take into thorough consideration the potential long-term benefits and substantial efficiencies that Digital Twins can bring to various operational sectors within the organization and across the industry as a whole. The concept of Action Variable Observed Unit (AVOU) pertains specifically to the area of the company's operational costs that can be effectively reduced or minimized through the strategic and innovative utilization of advanced Digital Twins; conversely, the Action Variable Module Cost (AVMC) reflects the specific cost associated with such AVOU, and it should be noted that comparable data are readily available for analytical purposes and are crucial in deriving actionable insights into operational effectiveness and efficiency metrics. Investment attention modelling presents an intriguing observation: it suggests that the commitment of financial resources allocated specifically for the purpose of Digital Twins is subjected to scrutiny and thorough analysis by risk departments to a lesser extent compared to the scrutiny afforded to Social Risk and Reputational Risk factors, which have traditionally garnered more focus and attention in the investment landscape.

It is essential to give careful thought to the Twin Elaboration Level during the initial phases of development to ensure comprehensive planning and execution; likewise, the deliberate adaptation and meticulous implementation of Dry-Run Development can significantly streamline and hasten the full deployment and operationalization of the Digital Twin model across varied contexts and applications. By addressing these various factors collaboratively and strategically, organizations can set themselves up for sustainable long-term success in effectively leveraging Digital Twins, ensuring they are not only competitive in the marketplace but also contributing meaningfully to a broader understanding of how these groundbreaking technologies can transform industries and reshape the future landscape of autonomous systems and their diverse applications across different sectors.

5. CONCLUSION

Government authorities, along with decision-makers operating within the private sector, must emphatically underscore the undeniable, urgent, and pressing need for the establishment of comprehensive strategies that are meticulously tailored to ensure the effective, sensible, and adaptive deployment of digital twins within the expansive realm of the rapidly evolving autonomous vehicle (AV) ecosystem. By diligently scrutinizing and thoroughly analyzing the entire installation and operational cycle, which encompasses the extensive journey from initial market entry through to widespread and mainstream usage among consumers and industries alike, it becomes exceedingly feasible to isolate, identify, and analyze those critical operating-cost drivers that significantly impact both the performance and viability of these vehicles in numerous operational settings. Furthermore, this thorough scrutiny allows for a detailed, systematic assessment of how these pivotal cost drivers evolve specifically when digital twins are effectively integrated and fully adopted across a diverse array of varied applications within the industry. Simultaneously, the careful, strategic adjustment of AV fleets can be astutely linked to anticipated and projected changes in throughput metrics, the intricate dynamics of supply chains, and the evolving behaviors within the labor market as a direct response to the ongoing introduction and emergence of innovative technologies that fundamentally redefine the existing landscape of transportation as we know it. It is of paramount importance to recognize and acknowledge that the substantial gains, benefits, and efficiencies that are induced by Digital Twin technologies are unlikely to seamlessly materialize during the very nascent and early initial phases of AV introduction; however, these advantageous benefits are poised to significantly manifest and become evident once the projected improvement paths are recognized as being scalable, feasible, and sustainable within the sector over time. A rigorous and comprehensive cost-sensitivity analysis robustly illustrates that initial pricing levels set below actual operating costs may indeed be tolerable under specific market conditions, but only when positioned alongside highly elastic throughput responses and demand elasticities. This situation underlines a sensitive and critical relationship between inevitable price fluctuations and demand patterns, thereby warranting close and careful examination by all relevant stakeholders involved in this transformative process. Furthermore, a second-order analysis insightfully identifies the absolute necessity of adopting distinct and innovative business models within the AV sector. Such models would not only enable a more effective pass-through of inflationary pressures but also facilitate a more rapid and broader ascendance, as well as overall success, of advancing technologies within the competitive and challenging marketplace. In order to effectively commit to completing the AV adoption cycle with a thoughtful integration of digital twins and to fully reap the associated extensive economic and environmental advantages, it is imperative that both governmental bodies and private enterprises strategically prioritize and mobilize significant investments (Challoumis, 2023, 2024a). These investments should be strategically directed particularly toward crucial aspects such as the development of a robust and resilient cloud infrastructure, the establishment of standardized data-sharing protocols to ensure seamless interoperability and compatibility between systems, and the necessary upskilling of personnel in relevant fields to ensure that they are well-prepared for the responsibilities and challenges that lie ahead in a rapidly changing technological environment. The adoption of Digital Twin technologies in AV systems not only offers unique and critical economic guidance but also provides a thorough understanding of the costs associated with installation processes while simultaneously outlining the required return on investment. It effectively identifies various potential implementation scenarios that could emerge as technology matures and evolves within the rapidly changing landscape.

The implications of these significant advancements span across a broad array of dimensions; they encompass numerous critical aspects like vehicle uptime optimization, the sophisticated optimization of fleet logistics based on real-time data analytics, modifications within supply-chain behavior that respond to changing demands and customer expectations, fluctuations within the labor market that react to these advances, and the development of finely crafted pricing strategies that are strategically designed to meet the diverse and evolving market needs. Additionally, it includes the introduction of innovative business models that are customized specifically for the digital age we now inhabit, reflecting contemporary consumer behavior and preferences. These critical aspects can either be elicited in isolation or comprehensively analyzed through intra-system exploratory considerations. However, adopting a holistic systemic perspective contributes significantly to conveying integral partial-equilibrium results that offer clarity and greatly aid in informed, strategic decision-making processes. Moreover, the benefits derived from comprehensive and full implementation across the interconnected digital-pathway network, along with the associated policy ramifications, are substantially highlighted, further underscoring the interconnected and interdependent nature of these multifaceted endeavors. Engaging in a formal-order economic analysis empowers stakeholders to disentangle crucial themes that possess broader applicability from those that may be more explicitly tailored to the unique circumstances of the AV sector alone. Consequently, this yields the provision of a robust framework that immensely enhances understanding of the complex implications emerging from the integration of digital twin technology within the industry and showcases

REFERENCES

Abboush, M., Knieke, C., & Rausch, A. (2024). A Virtual Testing Framework for Real-Time Validation of Automotive Software Systems Based on Hardware in the Loop and Fault Injection. *Sensors (Basel), 24*(12), 3733. Advance online publication. DOI: 10.3390/s24123733 PMID: 38931515

Abdullah, S. M. (2025). Inventory Optimization in Global Automotive Manufacturing Supply Chains. *Journal of Procurement and Supply Chain Management*. DOI: 10.58425/jpscm.v4i1.377

Afraj, S., Böhmländer, D., Vaculín, O., & Hynčík, L. (2021). Quantification methodology for crash behavior comparison between virtual crash simulations and real-time crash tests. *FISITA World Congress 2021 - Technical Programme*. DOI: 10.46720/F2021-PIF-072

Almeaibed, S., Al-Rubaye, S., Tsourdos, A., & Avdelidis, N. (2021). Digital Twin Analysis to Promote Safety and Security in Autonomous Vehicles. *IEEE Communications Standards Magazine, 5*(1), 40–46. DOI: 10.1109/MCOMSTD.011.2100004

Application of digital twins to improve automotive assembly processes. (2022). In *Truck*. DOI: 10.36652/1684-1298-2022-7-11-17

Auweraer, H., Anthonis, J., De Bruyne, S., & Leuridan, J. (2013). Virtual engineering at work: The challenges for designing mechatronic products. *Engineering with Computers, 29*(3), 389–408. DOI: 10.1007/s00366-012-0286-6

Balla, M., Haffner, O., Kučera, E., & Cigánek, J. (2023). Educational Case Studies: Creating a Digital Twin of the Production Line in TIA Portal, Unity, and Game4Automation Framework. *Sensors (Basel), 23*(10), 4977. Advance online publication. DOI: 10.3390/s23104977 PMID: 37430895

Bambura, R., Šolc, M., Dado, M., & Kotek, L. (2020). Implementation of Digital Twin for Engine Block Manufacturing Processes. *Applied Sciences (Basel, Switzerland), 10*(18), 6578. DOI: 10.3390/app10186578

Bao, J., Guo, D., Li, J., & Zhang, J. (2018). The modelling and operations for the digital twin in the context of manufacturing. *Enterprise Information Systems, 13*(4), 534–556. DOI: 10.1080/17517575.2018.1526324

Barabás, I., Iclodean, C., Beles, H., Antonya, C., Molea, A., & Scurt, F. B. (2025). An Approach to Modeling and Developing Virtual Sensors Used in the Simulation of Autonomous Vehicles. *Sensors (Basel), 25*(11), 3338. Advance online publication. DOI: 10.3390/s25113338 PMID: 40968833

Barbie, A., & Hasselbring, W. (2024). From Digital Twins to Digital Twin Prototypes: Concepts, Formalization, and Applications. *IEEE Access : Practical Innovations, Open Solutions, 12*, 75337–75365. DOI: 10.1109/ACCESS.2024.3406510

Bednarz, T., Baier, A., & Paprocka, I. (2024). A Framework for Communicating and Building a Digital Twin Model of the Electric Car. *Applied Sciences (Basel, Switzerland), 14*(5), 1776. Advance online publication. DOI: 10.3390/app14051776

Bedulli, F., Leite, R., Freitas, F., Murari, T., & Winkler, I. (2024). Optimizing Automotive Product Development: Integration of Electronic Control Units and Virtual Prototypes Using Virtual Reality. *SAE Technical Paper Series*. DOI: 10.4271/2023-36-0111

Behrendt, S., Altenmüller, T., May, M., Kuhnle, A., & Lanza, G. (2025). Real-to-sim: Automatic simulation model generation for a digital twin in semiconductor manufacturing. *Journal of Intelligent Manufacturing*. Advance online publication. DOI: 10.1007/s10845-025-02572-x

Biesinger, F., & Weyrich, M. (2019). The Facets of Digital Twins in Production and the Automotive Industry. *2019 23rd International Conference on Mechatronics Technology (ICMT)*, 1–6. DOI: 10.1109/ICMECT.2019.8932101

Böttjer, T., Tola, D., Kakavandi, F., Wewer, C., Ramanujan, D., Gomes, C., Larsen, P., & Iosifidis, A. (2023). A review of unit level digital twin applications in the manufacturing industry. *CIRP Journal of Manufacturing Science and Technology*, *45*, 162–189. Advance online publication. DOI: 10.1016/j.cirpj.2023.06.011

Cao, X., Yao, M., Zhang, Y., Hu, X., & Wu, C. (2023). Digital Twin Modeling and Simulation Optimization of Transmission Front and Middle Case Assembly Line. *Computer Modeling in Engineering &amp. The Sciences*. Advance online publication. DOI: 10.32604/cmes.2023.030773

Cao, Z., Dong, H., Jide, J., & Yi, S. (2024). Research on Intelligent Manufacturing Production Lines for Automobile Wheel Hubs by Digital Twin Models. *2024 3rd International Conference on Data Analytics, Computing and Artificial Intelligence (ICDACAI)*, 825–829. DOI: 10.1109/ICDACAI65086.2024.00155

Challoumis, C. (2023). FROM SAVINGS TO ESCAPE AND ENFORCEMENT SAVINGS. *Cógito (Salvador)*, *XV*(4), 206–216. https://cogito.ucdc.ro/COGITO_DECEMBER_2023.pdf

Challoumis, C. (2024a). From Economics to Economic Engineering (The Cycle of Money): The case of Romania. *Cógito (Salvador)*, *XVII*(2), 161–170. https://cogito.ucdc.ro/issues/COGITO no.2_27062024_BT.pdf

Challoumis, C. (2024b). The Index of the Cycle of Money: The Case of Switzerland. *Journal of Risk and Financial Management*, *17*(4), 135. https://doi.org/https://doi.org/10.3390/jrfm17040135. DOI: 10.3390/jrfm17040135

Challoumis, C. (2025a). Economocracy: Global Economic Governance. *Economies*, *13*(8), 230. DOI: 10.3390/economies13080230

Challoumis, C. (2025b). The impact factor of Tangibles and Intangibles of controlled transactions on economic performance. *Economic Alternatives, 31*(1), 64–76. https://doi.org/https://doi.org/10.37075/EA.2025.1.04

Challoumis, C. (2025c). THE INFLATION ACCORDING TO THE CYCLE OF MONEY (C.M.). *Economic Alternatives, 2025*(2), 324–353. https://doi.org/https://doi.org/10.37075/EA.2025.2.03

Challoumis, C., & Eriotis, N. (2025). The Impact of Artificial Intelligence on the Greek Economy. *Journal of Open Innovation, 11*(3), 1–13. https://doi.org/https://doi.org/10.1016/j.joitmc.2025.100578. DOI: 10.1016/j.joitmc.2025.100578

Challoumis, C., Eriotis, N., & Vasiliou, D. (2025). Social Movements' Impact on the Greek Economy During the Financial Crisis. *Economies, 13*(9), 269. https://doi.org/https://doi.org/10.3390/economies13090269

Chawla, S., & Singari, R. (2023). Modelling and Simulation of Crankcase Cover Manufacturing in the Automobile Industry. *Journal of Scientific &amp. Journal of Scientific and Industrial Research, 82*(6). Advance online publication. DOI: 10.56042/jsir.v82i06.1816

Chen, Y., Zhou, M., Zhang, M., & Zha, M. (2025). Research on the Construction of Automobile Wheel Hub Intelligent Production Line Based on Digital Twin. *Applied Sciences (Basel, Switzerland), 15*(11), 5871. Advance online publication. DOI: 10.3390/app15115871

Chong, J., Kay, P., & Chang, W.-C. (2020). *The Impact of Virtual Environments for Future Electric Powered-Mobility Development Using Human-in-the-Loop: Part A - Fundamental Design and Modelling*. Intelligent and Efficient Transport Systems - Design, Modelling, Control and Simulation., DOI: 10.5772/intechopen.90375

Cigánek, J., & Choma, M. (2025). Simulation and Optimization of Foaming Cabins Utilization on the Production Line. *2025 Cybernetics & Informatics (K&I)*, 1–6. DOI: 10.1109/KI64036.2025.10916427

Cruz-Oliver, R., Monzón, L., Ramirez-Laboreo, E., & Rodríguez-Fortún, J.-M. (2023). ROM-based stochastic optimization for a continuous manufacturing process. *ISA Transactions*, •••, 1–8. DOI: 10.1016/j.isatra.2024.08.010 PMID: 39147610

D., M., & T., S. (2025). Features of real-time modeling of steelmaking processes using unreal engine 5. *System Technologies*. DOI: 10.34185/1562-9945-6-155-2024-24

Daly, N., Manvi, P., Chhatbar, T., Schmid, M., Castanier, M., & Wagner, J. (2024). Modeling & Validation of a Digital Twin Tracked Vehicle. *SAE Technical Paper Series*. DOI: 10.4271/2024-01-2323

Damiri, H., Steinberger, M., Kuchler, L., Azimi, A., Martinuzzi, S., Sagmeister, P., Williams, J., Koch, S., Tranninger, M., Rehrl, J., Celikovic, S., Sacher, S., Kappe, C., & Horn, M. (2024). Model-based real-time optimization in continuous pharmaceutical manufacturing. *Computers & Chemical Engineering, 192*, 108915. DOI: 10.1016/j.compchemeng.2024.108915

Damtew, A. W. (2024). Roles of digital twins on material performances and utilization on upstream industry (The case of automotive industry). *International Journal of Advanced Manufacturing Technology, 130*(7-8), 1–12. DOI: 10.1007/s00170-023-12706-1

Debevec, M., Šimic, M., & Herakovič, N. (2014). VIRTUAL FACTORY AS AN ADVANCED APPROACH FOR PRODUCTION PROCESS OPTIMIZATION. *International Journal of Simulation Modelling, 13*(1), 66–78. DOI: 10.2507/IJSIMM13(1)6.260

Deng, S., Ling, L., Zhang, C., Li, C., Zeng, T., Zhang, K., & Guo, G. (2023). A systematic review on the current research of digital twin in automotive application. *Internet of Things and Cyber-Physical Systems, 3*, 180–191. Advance online publication. DOI: 10.1016/j.iotcps.2023.04.004

Dengiz, B., Iç, Y., & Belgin, O. (2016). A meta-model based simulation optimization using hybrid simulation-analytical modeling to increase the productivity in automotive industry. *Mathematics and Computers in Simulation, 120*, 120–128. DOI: 10.1016/j.matcom.2015.07.005

Dong, L., Wang, J., & Hu, X. (2025). Optimization of Joint Distribution Routes for Automotive Parts Considering Multi-Manufacturer Collaboration. *Sustainability (Basel)*, *17*(14), 6615. Advance online publication. DOI: 10.3390/su17146615

Duyun, T., Duyun, I., Kabalyants, P., & Rybak, L. (2023). Optimization of a 6-DOF Platform for Simulators Based on an Analysis of Structural and Force Parameters. *Machines (Basel)*, *11*(8), 814. Advance online publication. DOI: 10.3390/machines11080814

Esquivel, R. V., López, A. A., & Almaguer, C. A. G. (2025). Design of Virtual and Physical Automotive Concepts for Virtual Assembly Plant. *2025 Institute for the Future of Education Conference (IFE)*, 1–7. DOI: 10.1109/IFE63672.2025.11025112

Florescu, A. (2024). Digital Twin for Flexible Manufacturing Systems and Optimization Through Simulation: A Case Study. *Machines (Basel)*, *12*(11), 785. Advance online publication. DOI: 10.3390/machines12110785

Fragner, A., Kreis, A., & Hirz, M. (2020). Virtual Tools to Support Design and Production Engineering: Early detection of stone chips to optimize production processes. *2020 IEEE 7th International Conference on Industrial Engineering and Applications (ICIEA)*, 399–403. DOI: 10.1109/ICIEA49774.2020.9102004

Friederich, J., Francis, D., Lazarova-Molnar, S., & Mohamed, N. (2022). A framework for data-driven digital twins for smart manufacturing. *Computers in Industry*, *136*, 103586. Advance online publication. DOI: 10.1016/j.compind.2021.103586

Garcia, L. I. B., Villegas, A. T., Moreno, J. C. G., Rivera, L. Y. G., & Rubio, Y. A. F. (2025). Process simulation and optimization in industry 4.0: Redesigning assembly lines in an automotive industry. *Ingeniería, Investigación y Tecnología*, *26*(3), 1–12. Advance online publication. DOI: 10.22201/fi.25940732e.2025.26.3.020

Ghasemi, A., Farajzadeh, F., Heavey, C., Fowler, J., & Papadopoulos, C. (2024). Simulation optimization applied to production scheduling in the era of industry 4.0: A review and future roadmap. *Journal of Industrial Information Integration*, *39*, 100599. DOI: 10.1016/j.jii.2024.100599

Göppert, A., Grahn, L., Rachner, J., Grunert, D., Hort, S., & Schmitt, R. (2021). Pipeline for ontology-based modeling and automated deployment of digital twins for planning and control of manufacturing systems. *Journal of Intelligent Manufacturing*, *34*(5), 2133–2152. DOI: 10.1007/s10845-021-01860-6

Grznár, P., Gregor, M., Gašo, M., Gabajová, G., Schickerle, M., & Burganová, N. (2021). Dynamic Simulation Tool for Planning and Optimisation of Supply Process. *International Journal of Simulation Modelling*, *20*(3), 441–452. Advance online publication. DOI: 10.2507/IJSIMM20-3-552

Gutjahr, T., Kruse, T., & Huber, T. (2024). ADVANCED MODELING AND OPTIMIZATION FOR VIRTUAL CALIBRATION OF INTERNAL COMBUSTION ENGINES. *SAE Technical Paper Series*. DOI: 10.4271/2024-01-3630

Han, Y., Shao, J., Zhou, R., Liao, Y., & Zhong, Y. (2025). Robotic Digital Twin Based Full Lifecycle Decision Framework for Automotive Productions. *IEEE Network*, *39*(4), 173–181. DOI: 10.1109/MNET.2024.3418624

Herchlová, M., Važan, P., Burčiar, F., Juhás, M., Juhásová, B., & Čambál, D. (2025). A simulation Approach to Improve the Performance of a Sub-assembly Zone in Automotive Industry. *2025 Cybernetics & Informatics (K&I)*, 1–6. DOI: 10.1109/KI64036.2025.10916456

Horr, A., & Drexler, H. (2025). Real-Time Models for Manufacturing Processes: How to Build Predictive Reduced Models. *Processes (Basel, Switzerland)*, *13*(1), 252. Advance online publication. DOI: 10.3390/pr13010252

Huang, Z., Fey, M., Liu, C., Beysel, E., Xu, X., & Brecher, C. (2023). Hybrid learning-based digital twin for manufacturing process: Modeling framework and implementation. *Robotics and Computer-integrated Manufacturing*, *82*, 102545. DOI: 10.1016/j.rcim.2023.102545

Ibrahim, M., Rassõlkin, A., Vaimann, T., & Kallaste, A. (2022). Overview on Digital Twin for Autonomous Electrical Vehicles Propulsion Drive System. *Sustainability (Basel)*, *14*(2), 601. Advance online publication. DOI: 10.3390/su14020601

Ibrahim, M., Rjabtšikov, V., & Gilbert, R. (2023). Overview of Digital Twin Platforms for EV Applications. *Sensors (Basel)*, *23*(3), 1414. Advance online publication. DOI: 10.3390/s23031414 PMID: 36772453

Iclodean, C., Jurchis, B.-M., Macavei, C.-M., Volosciuc, E.-R., & Iclodean, A.-G. (2025). Optimizing the Energy Efficiency of Electric Vehicles in Urban and Metropolitan Environments According to Various Driving Cycles and Behavioral Conditions. *Electronics (Basel)*, *14*(11), 2224. Advance online publication. DOI: 10.3390/electronics14112224

Jaiswal, B. D. (2025). *The Influence and Application of Digital Twin Technology in Automotive Automation*. International Journal For Multidisciplinary Research., DOI: 10.36948/ijfmr.2025.v07i01.37342

Javaid, M., Haleem, P. A., & Suman, R. (2023). Digital Twin applications toward Industry 4.0: A Review. *Cognitive Robotics*. DOI: 10.1016/j.cogr.2023.04.003

Jiang, B., Sharma, N., Liu, Y., Li, C., & Huang, X. (2022). Real-Time FPGA/CPU-Based Simulation of a Full-Electric Vehicle Integrated with a High-Fidelity Electric Drive Model. *Energies*, *15*(5), 1824. Advance online publication. DOI: 10.3390/en15051824

Jiang, H., Qin, S., Fu, J., & Ding, G. (2020). How to model and implement connections between physical and virtual models for digital twin application. *Journal of Manufacturing Systems*. Advance online publication. DOI: 10.1016/j.jmsy.2020.05.012

Kabir, M. R., Ravi, B. B. Y., & Ray, S. (2023). A Virtual Prototyping Platform for Exploration of Vehicular Electronics. *IEEE Internet of Things Journal*, *10*(18), 16144–16155. DOI: 10.1109/JIOT.2023.3267339

Kabir, M. R., Ravi, B. B. Y., & Ray, S. (2025). Digital Twin Technologies for Vehicular Prototyping: A Survey. *IEEE Open Journal of Intelligent Transportation Systems*, *6*, 503–521. DOI: 10.1109/OJITS.2025.3562504

Kampa, A. (2023). Modeling and Simulation of a Digital Twin of a Production System for Industry 4.0 with Work-in-Process Synchronization. *Applied Sciences (Basel, Switzerland)*, *13*(22), 12261. Advance online publication. DOI: 10.3390/app132212261

Kampker, A., Wessel, S., Lutz, N., Heine, S., Mayr, A., & Kuhn, A. (2021). Model improvement through real data connection for Virtual commissioning in ramp-up management of scalable production systems. *Procedia CIRP*, *99*, 645–649. DOI: 10.1016/j.procir.2021.03.087

Kang, J. (2025). Software Practice and Experience on Smart Mobility Digital Twin in Transportation and Automotive Industry: Toward SDV-empowered Digital Twin through EV Edge-Cloud and AutoML. *Journal of Web Engineering*, *23*, 1155–1180. DOI: 10.13052/jwe1540 9589.2385

Ke, G., Zhang, D., Liqin, M., Jing, W., Juan, D., Shubo, L., Huan, Q., & Sun, L. (2023). Intelligent machine plus production line digital twin model construction technology. *Journal of Physics: Conference Series*, *2478*(10), 102011. Advance online publication. DOI: 10.1088/1742-6596/2478/10/102011

Kousi, N., Gkournelos, C., Aivaliotis, S., Lotsaris, K., Bavelos, A., Baris, P., Michalos, G., & Makris, S. (2021). Digital Twin for Designing and Reconfiguring Human–Robot Collaborative Assembly Lines. *Applied Sciences (Basel, Switzerland)*, *11*(10), 4620. DOI: 10.3390/app11104620

Krenczyk, D. (2022). Dynamic simulation models as digital twins of logistics systems driven by data from multiple sources. *Journal of Physics: Conference Series*, *2198*(1), 012059. Advance online publication. DOI: 10.1088/1742-6596/2198/1/012059

Krenczyk, D., & Paprocka, I. (2023). Integration of Discrete Simulation, Prediction, and Optimization Methods for a Production Line Digital Twin Design. *Materials (Basel)*, *16*(6), 2339. Advance online publication. DOI: 10.3390/ma16062339 PMID: 36984218

Krynke, M., & Mazur, M. (2024). *Innovative Work Order Planning with Process Optimization Using Computer Simulation in the Automotive Industry, in the Case of Repair Workshops*. Periodica Polytechnica Transportation Engineering., DOI: 10.3311/PPtr.23546

Kshatra, D., & Tjprc. (2019). Development of Virtual Modelling for Optimization and Botttleneck Analysis of an Automotive Stamping using Plant Simulation. *International Journal of Mechanical and Production Engineering Research and Development*. DOI: 10.24247/ijmperdjun2019101

Kumar, P., Prasad, S., Patel, D., Gupta, L., Nag, M. B., & Chadha, P. (2022). Production improvement on the assembly line through cycle time optimization. [IJIDeM]. *International Journal on Interactive Design and Manufacturing*, *17*(5), 2617–2630. DOI: 10.1007/s12008-022-01031-8

Kumar, P., Prasad, S., Patel, D., Kumar, K., Dixit, S., & Nikolaevna, S. N. (2023). Optimization of cycle time assembly line for mass manufacturing. [IJIDeM]. *International Journal on Interactive Design and Manufacturing*, •••, 1–12. DOI: 10.1007/s12008-023-01343-3

Kušić, K., Schumann, R., & Ivanjko, E. (2023). A digital twin in transportation: Real-time synergy of traffic data streams and simulation for virtualizing motorway dynamics. *Advanced Engineering Informatics*, *55*, 101858. DOI: 10.1016/j.aei.2022.101858

Lattanzi, L., Raffaeli, R., Peruzzini, M., & Pellicciari, M. (2021). Digital twin for smart manufacturing: A review of concepts towards a practical industrial implementation. *International Journal of Computer Integrated Manufacturing*, *34*(6), 567–597. DOI: 10.1080/0951192X.2021.1911003

Lawson, G., Salanitri, D., & Waterfield, B. (2016). Future directions for the development of virtual reality within an automotive manufacturer. *Applied Ergonomics, 53 Pt B*, 323–330. DOI: 10.1016/j.apergo.2015.06.024

Lehner, D., Zhang, J., Pfeiffer, J., Sint, S., Splettstößer, A., Wimmer, M., & Wortmann, A. (2025). Model-driven engineering for digital twins: A systematic mapping study. *Software & Systems Modeling, 24*(5), 1339–1377. DOI: 10.1007/s10270-025-01264-7

Lei, W. (2025). Design and Development of a Cylinder Head Production Line Virtual Simulation Cognition System Based on Unity3D. *Computer Applications in Engineering Education, 33*(5), e70078. Advance online publication. DOI: 10.1002/cae.70078

Lei, W., Shen, P., Zhu, J., & Ou, P. (2025). Virtual Simulation Debugging and Optimization of Automotive Connecting Rod Production Line Based on Digital Twin. *2025 IEEE 3rd International Conference on Image Processing and Computer Applications (ICIPCA)*, 320–325. DOI: 10.1109/ICIPCA65645.2025.11139027

Li, X., Niu, W., & Tian, H. (2024). Application of Digital Twin in Electric Vehicle Powertrain: A Review. *World Electric Vehicle Journal*. DOI: 10.3390/wevj15050208

Littfinski, D., & Verl, A. (2025). Intelligent and autonomous partitioning of real-time simulation models. *2025 The 16th International Conference on Mechanical and Intelligent Manufacturing Technologies (ICMIMT)*, 214–219. DOI: 10.1109/ICMIMT65123.2025.11091903

Liu, H., Zhang, B., Wu, V., Yang, X., & Wang, L. (2025). Review of Digital Twin in the Automotive Industry on Products, Processes and Systems. *International Journal of Automotive Manufacturing and Materials*. DOI: 10.53941/ijamm.2025.100006

Liu, J., Wen, X., Zhou, H., Sheng, S., Zhao, P., Liu, X., Kang, C., & Chen, Y. (2022). Digital twin-enabled machining process modeling. *Advanced Engineering Informatics, 54*, 101737. DOI: 10.1016/j.aei.2022.101737

Liu, J., & Zhang, K. (2023, April 14). Liu, Jiayan, & Zhang, K.-R. (2023). Design and Simulation Debugging of Automobile Connecting Rod Production Line Based on the Digital Twin. *Applied Sciences (Basel, Switzerland), 13*(8), 4919. Advance online publication. DOI: 10.3390/app13084919

Liu, Y., Xia, X., Zhang, J., Wang, K., Yu, B., Wu, M., Shi, J., Ma, C., Liu, Y., Hu, B., Wang, X., Wang, B., Wang, R., & Wang, B. (2025). Optimization of monocrystalline silicon photovoltaic module assembly lines based on simulation model. *PLoS One, 20*(6), e0325152. Advance online publication. DOI: 10.1371/journal.pone.0325152 PMID: 40498735

Lopes, W. A. C., Rusteiko, A. C., Mendes, C. R., Honório, N. V. C., & Okano, M. (2025). Optimization of New Project Validation Protocols in the Automotive Industry: A Simulated Environment for Efficiency and Effectiveness. *Journal of Computational and Cognitive Engineering, 4*(3), 343–354. Advance online publication. DOI: 10.47852/bonviewJCCE52024627

Lugaresi, G., Alba, V. V., & Matta, A. (2021). Lab-scale Models of Manufacturing Systems for Testing Real-time Simulation and Production Control Technologies. *Journal of Manufacturing Systems, 58*, 93–108. DOI: 10.1016/j.jmsy.2020.09.003

Lugaresi, G., & Matta, A. (2021). Automated manufacturing system discovery and digital twin generation. *Journal of Manufacturing Systems*, *59*, 51–66. Advance online publication. DOI: 10.1016/j.jmsy.2021.01.005

Lv, Z. (2023). Digital Twins in Industry 5.0. *Research*, *6*, 0071. Advance online publication. DOI: 10.34133/research.0071 PMID: 36930777

Malega, P., Gazda, V., & Rudy, V. (2021). Optimization of production system in plant simulation. *Simulation*, *98*(4), 295–306. DOI: 10.1177/00375497211038908

Mao, R., Li, Y., Li, G., Hildre, H. P., & Zhang, H. (2025). A Systematic Survey of Digital Twin Applications: Transferring Knowledge From Automotive and Aviation to Maritime Industry. *IEEE Transactions on Intelligent Transportation Systems*, *26*(4), 4240–4259. DOI: 10.1109/TITS.2025.3535593

Martínez-Gutiérrez, A., Díez-González, J., Ferrero-Guillén, R., Verde, P., Álvarez, R., & Pérez, H. (2021). Digital Twin for Automatic Transportation in Industry 4.0. *Sensors (Basel)*, *21*(10), 3344. Advance online publication. DOI: 10.3390/s21103344 PMID: 34065011

May, M., Finke, A., Theuner, K., & Lanza, G. (2024). Framework for automatic production simulation tuning with machine learning. *Procedia CIRP*, *121*, 49–54. Advance online publication. DOI: 10.1016/j.procir.2023.11.002

Melo, V., Barbosa, J., Mota, G., De La Prieta Pintado, F., & Leitão, P. (2024). Design of an ISO 23247 Compliant Digital Twin for an Automotive Assembly Line. *2024 IEEE 7th International Conference on Industrial Cyber-Physical Systems (ICPS)*, 1–6. DOI: 10.1109/ICPS59941.2024.10640052

Mendi, A. (2022). A Digital Twin Case Study on Automotive Production Line. *Sensors (Basel)*, *22*(18), 6963. Advance online publication. DOI: 10.3390/s22186963 PMID: 36146313

Mohanraj, E., N, E., S, S., & S, S. (2024). Digital Twins for Automotive Predictive Maintenance. *2024 International Conference on Inventive Computation Technologies (ICICT)*, 1579–1584. DOI: 10.1109/ICICT60155.2024.10544392

Naseri, F., Gil, S., Barbu, C., Çetkin, E., Yarimca, G., Jensen, A. C., Larsen, P. G., & Gomes, C. (2023). Digital twin of electric vehicle battery systems: Comprehensive review of the use cases, requirements, and platforms. *Renewable & Sustainable Energy Reviews*, *179*, 113280. Advance online publication. DOI: 10.1016/j.rser.2023.113280

Nayan, K. R. (2025). Digital Manufacturing Transformation in the Automotive Industry: A Technical Analysis. *International Journal of Scientific Research in Computer Science, Engineering and Information Technology*. DOI: 10.32628/CSEIT25112362

Neto, A. A., Da Silva, E. R., Deschamps, F., Do Nascimento, L. A., & De Lima, P. (2023). Modeling production disorder: Procedures for digital twins of flexibility-driven manufacturing systems. *International Journal of Production Economics*, *260*, 108846. Advance online publication. DOI: 10.1016/j.ijpe.2023.108846

Oliveira-Silva, E., Zamarreño, J., Moraga, C., Navia, D., Marmol, S., & Gonzalez, R. (2023). A virtual environment of an industrial splitter to test Dynamic Real Time Optimization. *Simulation Modelling Practice and Theory*, *129*, 102821. DOI: 10.1016/j.simpat.2023.102821

Onaji, I., Tiwari, D., Soulatiantork, P., Song, B., & Tiwari, A. (2022). Digital twin in manufacturing: Conceptual framework and case studies. *International Journal of Computer Integrated Manufacturing*, *35*(8), 831–858. DOI: 10.1080/0951192X.2022.2027014

Overbeck, L., Graves, S., & Lanza, G. (2023). Development and analysis of digital twins of production systems. *International Journal of Production Research*, *62*(10), 3544–3558. DOI: 10.1080/00207543.2023.2242525

Papanagnou, C. (2019). A Digital Twin Model for Enhancing Performance Measurement in Assembly Lines. *Internet of Things : Engineering Cyber Physical Human Systems*. Advance online publication. DOI: 10.1007/978-3-030-18732-3_4

Parra, A., Rodríguez, A., Zubizarreta, A., & Pérez, J. (2020). Validation of a Real-Time Capable Multibody Vehicle Dynamics Formulation for Automotive Testing Frameworks Based on Simulation. *IEEE Access : Practical Innovations, Open Solutions*, *8*, 213253–213265. DOI: 10.1109/ACCESS.2020.3040232

Pekarčíková, M., Kliment, M., Kronová, J., Trebuňa, P., & Hovana, A. (2025). Simulation-Based Optimization of Material Supply in Automotive Production Using RTLS Data. *Applied Sciences (Basel, Switzerland)*, *15*(16), 9102. Advance online publication. DOI: 10.3390/app15169102

Pfeiffer, J., Fuchß, D., Kühn, T., Liebhart, R., Neumann, D., Neimöck, C., Seiler, C., Koziolek, A., & Wortmann, A. (2024). Modeling Languages for Automotive Digital Twins: A Survey Among the German Automotive Industry. *Proceedings of the ACM/IEEE 27th International Conference on Model Driven Engineering Languages and Systems*. DOI: 10.1145/3640310.3674100

Piromalis, D., & Kantaros, A. (2022). Digital Twins in the Automotive Industry: The Road toward Physical-Digital Convergence. *Applied System Innovation*, *5*(4), 65. Advance online publication. DOI: 10.3390/asi5040065

Robert, O., Iztok, P., & Borut, B. (2019). Real-Time manufacturing optimization with a simulation model and virtual reality. *Procedia Manufacturing*, *38*, 1103–1110. Advance online publication. DOI: 10.1016/j.promfg.2020.01.198

Russo, M. B., Franciosa, P., Greco, A., & Gerbino, S. (2024). Reduced-order modelling for real-time physics-based variation simulation enhanced with adaptive sampling and optimized interpolation. *International Journal of Advanced Manufacturing Technology*, *132*(7-8), 3709–3734. DOI: 10.1007/s00170-024-13493-z

Rybak, L., Hurtasenko, A., Skitova, V., & Voloshkin, A. (2023). Numerical Method of Designing an Automotive Driving Simulator for Training Drivers of Motor Vehicles. *E3S Web of Conferences*. DOI: 10.1051/e3sconf/202344606007

Schmidt, H., Büttner, K., & Prokop, G. (2023). Methods for Virtual Validation of Automotive Powertrain Systems in Terms of Vehicle Drivability—A Systematic Literature Review. *IEEE Access : Practical Innovations, Open Solutions*, *11*, 27043–27065. DOI: 10.1109/ACCESS.2023.3257106

Schroeder, G., Steinmetz, C., Rodrigues, R., Henriques, R., Rettberg, A., & Pereira, C. (2021). A Methodology for Digital Twin Modeling and Deployment for Industry 4.0. *Proceedings of the IEEE, 109*(4), 556–567. DOI: 10.1109/JPROC.2020.3032444

Schwarz, C., & Wang, Z. (2022). The Role of Digital Twins in Connected and Automated Vehicles. *IEEE Intelligent Transportation Systems Magazine, 14*(6), 41–51. DOI: 10.1109/MITS.2021.3129524

Smeets, J., Öztürk, K., & Liebich, R. (2023). Digital twins for automotive development: Two wheelers application. *Advanced Engineering Informatics, 56*, 101982. DOI: 10.1016/j.aei.2023.101982

Son, Y. H., Park, K., Lee, D., Jeon, S., & Do Noh, S. (2021). Digital twin–based cyber-physical system for automotive body production lines. *International Journal of Advanced Manufacturing Technology, 115*(1-2), 291–310. DOI: 10.1007/s00170-021-07183-3

Soori, M., Arezoo, B., & Dastres, R. (2023). Virtual manufacturing in industry 4.0: A review. *Data Science and Management*. DOI: 10.1016/j.dsm.2023.10.006

Sosfenov, D. (2023). Use of digital twins in automotive industry: Russian and foreign experience. *Economics and Management*. DOI: 10.35854/1998-1627-2023-6-662-669

Spiryagin, M., Edelmann, J., Klinger, F., & Cole, C. (2023). Vehicle system dynamics in digital twin studies in rail and road domains. *Vehicle System Dynamics, 61*(7), 1737–1786. DOI: 10.1080/00423114.2023.2188228

Stevanov, B., Sremčev, N., Lazarević, M., Anderla, A., Sladojević, S., & Vidicki, P. (2022). Optimization of the Subassembly Production Process Using Simulation. *International Journal of Simulation Modelling, 21*(4), 663–674. Advance online publication. DOI: 10.2507/IJSIMM21-4-633

Su, C., Han, Y., Tang, X., Jiang, Q., Wang, T., & He, Q. (2024). Knowledge-based digital twin system: Using a knowlege-driven approach for manufacturing process modeling. *Computers in Industry, 159-160*, 104101. Advance online publication. DOI: 10.1016/j.compind.2024.104101

Su, C., Tang, X., Jiang, Q., Han, Y., Wang, T., & Jiang, D. (2025). Digital twin system for manufacturing processes based on a multi-layer knowledge graph model. *Scientific Reports, 15*(1), 12835. Advance online publication. DOI: 10.1038/s41598-024-85053-0 PMID: 40229336

Su, S., Jiang, L., Wang, W., Wang, W., Chu, C., & Wang, J. (2024). A digital twin modeling method of production lines based on flexible manufacturing. *Flexible Services and Manufacturing Journal*. Advance online publication. DOI: 10.1007/s10696-024-09571-9

Sujová, E., Bambura, R., Vysloužilová, D., & Koleda, P. (2023). Use of the digital twin concept to optimize the production process of engine blocks manufacturing. *Production Engineering Archives, 29*(2), 168–174. DOI: 10.30657/pea.2023.29.20

Sujová, E., Čierna, H., & Bambura, R. (2019). *Simulation model of production as tool for industry 4.0 implementation into practice*. Engineering for Rural Development., DOI: 10.22616/ERDev2019.18.N279

Utku, D. H. (2023). The Evaluation and Improvement of the Production Processes of an Automotive Industry Company via Simulation and Optimization. *Sustainability (Basel), 15*(3), 2331. Advance online publication. DOI: 10.3390/su15032331

Vachálek, J., Bartalsky, L., Rovný, O., Šišmišová, D., Morháč, M., & Lokšík, M. (2017). The digital twin of an industrial production line within the industry 4.0 concept. *2017 21st International Conference on Process Control (PC)*, 258–262. DOI: 10.1109/PC.2017.7976223

Van Dyck, M., Lüttgens, D., Piller, F., & Brenk, S. (2023). Interconnected digital twins and the future of digital manufacturing: Insights from a Delphi study. *Journal of Product Innovation Management*, *40*(4), 475–505. Advance online publication. DOI: 10.1111/jpim.12685

Vieira, A., Guilherme, E., Oliveira, J. A., Dias, L., & Pereira, G. (2019). *Combining simulation and optimization models on a production line problem: A case study*. THE EUROPEAN MODELING AND SIMULATION SYMPOSIUM., DOI: 10.46354/i3m.2019.emss.026

Visser, R., Basson, A., & Kruger, K. (2024). An Architecture for the Integration of Product and Production Digital Twins in the Automotive Industry. *Proceedings of the ACM/IEEE 27th International Conference on Model Driven Engineering Languages and Systems*. DOI: 10.1145/3652620.3688257

Volhonskaya, E. (2023). The problem of optimal assignment of autonomous vehicles in production-logistics system. *Vestnik of Samara State Technical University. Technical Sciences Series*. DOI: 10.14498/tech.2023.2.2

Wang, Q. (2025). Enhancing Automotive Engineering Education with Interactive Virtual Simulation: A Research Perspective. *Computer Fraud & Security*, 298–312. Advance online publication. DOI: 10.52710/cfs.315

Wang, W., Su, S., Jiang, L., Chu, C., Chen, C., & Liu, M. (2025). Digital twin modeling and simulation method for production line equipment units. *Journal of Mechanical Science and Technology*, *39*(2), 805–819. DOI: 10.1007/s12206-025-0125-5

Wu, W., Sivaparthipan, C., & Sanz-Prieto, I. (2021). Application of Automobile Modelling Optimization Design Based on Virtual Reality Technology. *J. Interconnect. Networks*, *22*(Supp02), 2143007. DOI: 10.1142/S0219265921430076

Xia, F., & Wan, J. (2024). Digital Twins for Discrete Manufacturing Lines: A Review. *Big Data and Cognitive Computing*, *8*(5), 45. DOI: 10.3390/bdcc8050045

Xie, J., & Wan, J. (2023). Digital Twin Four-Dimension Fusion Modeling Method Design and Application to the Discrete Manufacturing Line. *Big Data and Cognitive Computing*, *7*(2), 89. DOI: 10.3390/bdcc7020089

Yan, D., Sha, W., Wang, D., Yang, J., & Zhang, S. (2022). Digital twin-driven variant design of a 3C electronic product assembly line. *Scientific Reports*, *12*(1), 3846. Advance online publication. DOI: 10.1038/s41598-022-07894-x PMID: 35264664

Yang, J., Son, Y. H., Lee, D., & Noh, S. (2022). Digital Twin-Based Integrated Assessment of Flexible and Reconfigurable Automotive Part Production Lines. *Machines (Basel)*, *10*(2), 75. Advance online publication. DOI: 10.3390/machines10020075

Yegul, M., Erenay, F., Striepe, S., & Yavuz, M. (2017). Improving configuration of complex production lines via simulation-based optimization. *Computers & Industrial Engineering*, *109*, 295–312. DOI: 10.1016/j.cie.2017.04.019

Zambrano, V., Mueller-Roemer, J., Sandberg, M., Talasila, P., Zanin, D., Larsen, P., Loeschner, E., Thronicke, W., Pietraroia, D., Landolfi, G., Fontana, A., Laspalas, M., Antony, J., Poser, V., Kiss, T., Bergweiler, S., Serna, S., Izquierdo, S., Viejo, I., & Stork, A. (2022). Industrial digitalization in the industry 4.0 era: Classification, reuse and authoring of digital models on Digital Twin platforms. *Array (New York, N.Y.)*, *14*, 100176. DOI: 10.1016/j.array.2022.100176

Zhang, H., Liu, Q., Chen, X., Zhang, D., & Leng, J. (2017). A Digital Twin-Based Approach for Designing and Multi-Objective Optimization of Hollow Glass Production Line. *IEEE Access : Practical Innovations, Open Solutions*, *5*, 26901–26911. DOI: 10.1109/ACCESS.2017.2766453

Zhang, Q., Shen, S., Li, H., Cao, W., Tang, W., Jiang, J., Deng, M., Zhang, Y., Gu, B., Wu, K.-J., Zhang, K., & Liu, S. (2022). Digital twin-driven intelligent production line for automotive MEMS pressure sensors. *Advanced Engineering Informatics*, *54*, 101779. DOI: 10.1016/j.aei.2022.101779

Zhang, Y., & Li, J. (2023). Research on Real-time Simulation of Automobile Production Line based on Discrete Event and Multiagent. *Frontiers in Computing and Intelligent Systems*. DOI: 10.54097/fcis.v4i1.9466

Zhu, X., Li, C., Mai, J., Yang, J., & Kuang, Z. (2024). An Empirical Study on the Digital Twin System of Intelligent Production Line. *2024 4th International Conference on Computer Science and Blockchain (CCSB)*, 280–286. DOI: 10.1109/CCSB63463.2024.10735491

Židek, K., Pitel', J., Adamek, M., Lazorík, P., & Hošovský, A. (2020). Digital Twin of Experimental Smart Manufacturing Assembly System for Industry 4.0 Concept. *Sustainability (Basel)*, *12*(9), 3658. Advance online publication. DOI: 10.3390/su12093658

ADDITIONAL READINGS

Fadda, E., Perboli, G., Rosano, M., Mascolo, J., & Masera, D. (2022). A Decision Support System for Supporting Strategic Production Allocation in the Automotive Industry. *Sustainability (Basel)*, *14*(4), 2408. Advance online publication. DOI: 10.3390/su14042408

Volhonskaya, E. (2023). *The problem of optimal assignment of autonomous vehicles in production-logistics system*. Vestn. Samara State Tech. Univ. Tech. Sci. Ser., DOI: 10.14498/tech.2023.2.2

KEY TERMS AND DEFINITIONS

Autonomous Vehicle (AV): An Autonomous Vehicle is a transport system capable of sensing its environment, making decisions, and operating without continuous human intervention, relying on advanced sensors, artificial intelligence, and control algorithms.

Capital Expenditure (CapEx): Capital expenditure represents upfront investments in fixed assets and infrastructure required for Digital Twin deployment, including hardware, software platforms, sensors, integration systems, and cloud infrastructure.

Digital Twin: A Digital Twin is a dynamic virtual representation of a physical asset, process, or system that integrates real-time data, simulation models, and feedback mechanisms to mirror, predict, and optimize real-world behavior across its lifecycle.

Fleet Management: Fleet management refers to the coordinated supervision and optimization of a group of vehicles, including routing, maintenance scheduling, utilization rates, and safety performance, with the aim of maximizing operational efficiency and minimizing costs.

Operating Expenditure (OpEx): Operating expenditure refers to recurring costs associated with running and maintaining Digital Twin systems, such as software licensing, data storage, cybersecurity, system updates, and specialized personnel.

Predictive Maintenance: Predictive maintenance is a data-driven maintenance strategy that uses real-time monitoring and historical data to anticipate component failures and schedule interventions before breakdowns occur, thereby reducing downtime and maintenance costs.

Productivity Gains: Productivity gains denote improvements in output efficiency resulting from Digital Twin adoption, measured through increased vehicle uptime, higher fleet throughput, optimized routing, and reduced operational disruptions.

Regulatory Digital Twin: A regulatory digital twin is a virtual compliance and validation environment used to simulate regulatory requirements, certification procedures, and legal constraints, thereby reducing compliance costs and accelerating time-to-market.

Return on Investment (ROI): Return on investment measures the economic effectiveness of Digital Twin adoption by comparing expected benefits with incurred costs, commonly assessed through metrics such as net present value (NPV), internal rate of return (IRR), and payback period.

Safety Improvement: Safety improvement refers to the reduction of accident risk, system failures, and operational hazards achieved through real-time monitoring, predictive analytics, and continuous optimization enabled by Digital Twins.

Supply Chain Resilience: Supply chain resilience describes the ability of logistics and production networks to anticipate, absorb, and recover from disruptions, enhanced through Digital Twin-enabled simulation, coordination, and real-time decision support.

Vehicle-as-a-Service (VaaS): Vehicle-as-a-Service is a business model in which mobility is provided as an on-demand service rather than through vehicle ownership, relying heavily on Digital Twins for fleet optimization, pricing, and service reliability.

Chapter 10
Human-Centric Digital Twins for Road Safety and Future Autonomous Mobility

Zahra Yaghoobloo
http://orcid.org/0000-0001-6531-2441
Independent Researcher, Italy

ABSTRACT

The resilience of urban transportation systems, as a key component of sustainable development, has played a significant role in urban planning over the past few years. There is a need for new data-driven approaches and advanced simulations to mitigate the consequences of climate change, the expansion of transport networks, and the growing number of vulnerable users. In the meantime, the concept of a digital twin as a dynamic virtual model capable of representing and simulating, monitoring, and analyzing real systems in near real-time rapidly expanded in the field of urban transportation technology. In fact, this part of the present study, which aims to explain the role of digital twins in promoting the resilience of urban transport systems, examines the foundations and methods of spatial modelling, as well as the practical applications of this approach. The primary focus of this section is on integrating spatial data (GIS), transport networks, and a human-centered approach in safety and resilience analysis, particularly for vulnerable users.

1. INTRODUCTION

Over the past decades, urban transportation networks have undergone significant changes due to urbanization and population growth, as well as technological innovations in road safety systems. Transportation infrastructure, as the vital backbone of cities, is required to ensure the safety of road users, thus reinforcing the functional nature of technology. Despite these developments, conventional approaches to transportation and highway engineering have mainly focused on optimizing performance under normal operating conditions by expanding capacity, overcoming the limitations of traditional models, reducing travel times, and improving traffic flow efficiency. Existing approaches to transportation management are mainly practical under stable and normal conditions. However, when faced with events such as

DOI: 10.4018/979-8-3373-7785-8.ch010

urban transportation complexity, severe traffic accidents, increasing VRUs, sudden weather changes, infrastructure failures, and severe demand fluctuations, these approaches show serious limitations.

This fact clearly shows that advanced analytical tools enable the identification of safety deficiencies and the vulnerability of roads in the transport system, as well as applying scientific and practical assessments in the face of risk and crisis. In this regard, focusing solely on efficiency and optimization measures is no longer sufficient; the different dimensions of resilience and the responsiveness of transport systems to unpredictable challenges must also be addressed. This will allow us to take a new approach to managing these systems more comprehensively and effectively, and to prevent more serious crises. Since transport systems are ultimately intended to protect people, ensure safe mobility, and encourage inclusive and equal access for all users, a user-centered approach to their examination is essential. Despite the rapid development of digital twins in transportation, existing approaches remain largely infrastructure-focused and fail to adequately integrate human-centered, behavioral dynamics, and autonomous mobility scenarios. In this context, the assessment of transport should not be limited to performance indicators such as capacity, speed, or traffic flow. In contrast, it should also include the quality of the human experience, the level of risk exposure, and the degree of infrastructure fragility of different user groups. Accordingly, the analysis of transportation infrastructure requires a shift from a purely technical perspective to a more comprehensive, user-oriented that considers road sustainability as a social, spatial, and planned goal. Concurrently, advancements in digital technologies, particularly in Geographic Information Systems (GIS), Internet of Things (IoT) sensing, spatiotemporal data processing, and computational simulation modelling, have generated new opportunities to implement resilience in transportation engineering.

Among these technologies, digital twins are real-world, data-driven modelling and simulation tools that bring processes closer to synchronization to achieve desired observations and outcomes. The underlying hypothesis of this chapter is that digital twins can serve as decision support tools and analytical frameworks to enhance the sustainability of urban and highway transportation systems. Unlike traditional traffic models or static simulations, digital twins enable the continuous integration of real-time and historical data, network-based modelling, and scenario-based analysis. This capability allows decision makers to move beyond reactive management to proactive, data-driven planning, so that "what if" scenarios regarding crashes, infrastructure interventions, traffic control strategies, and extreme events can be explored before implementation.

Digital twins enable the analysis of relationships among user behavior patterns, the physical characteristics of the environment, and risk contexts within a single, dynamic system, which is essential for a more accurate understanding of vulnerabilities and for the design of more effective interventions. By providing this analytical capacity, digital twins offer a platform for safer, more predictive, and more adaptive planning in future transportation systems. In this perspective, the importance of this chapter lies in framing digital twins as perception-based, resilient tools for road analysis within the broader evolution of data-driven, autonomous transportation. This chapter proposes a human-centric digital twin framework that integrates spatial intelligence, resilience theory, and autonomous mobility simulation to support proactive safety analysis and decision-making.

This chapter is structured as follows. Section 2 presents the theoretical background on transport resilience and human-centered safety, emphasizing the role of vulnerability, risk, and adaptive capacity in complex transport systems. Section 3 introduces the concept of digital twins in transportation, including their architecture, core components, and their transition toward human-centric approaches. Section 4 focuses on spatial intelligence, highlighting the role of GIS, GNSS data, and multi-source data integration as the backbone of transport digital twins. Section 5 discusses the application of digital twins in road safety and future autonomous mobility, with particular attention to human–machine interaction and emerging ethical and technical challenges. Section 6 presents a case study to evaluate the proposed framework through spatial analysis and scenario-based modelling. Section 7 provides a discussion of the main findings, including theoretical contributions, practical implications, and limitations. Finally, Section 8 concludes the chapter and outlines future research directions.

1.1 Background and Context

In recent decades, urban and intercity transport systems have faced profound structural, technological and social transformations. Rapid urbanization, increasing demand for mobility, more complex travel patterns, and expanding interactions among different user types have transformed transport from a purely engineering issue to a multidimensional, interdisciplinary one. In such circumstances, transport networks can no longer be evaluated solely on capacity, speed, or operational efficiency; safety, equity, resilience, sustainability, and human experience must also be at the center of the analysis. Along with these developments, the concept of road safety has also been redefined. In the past, safety focused mainly on reducing accidents and fatalities, but in contemporary literature, this concept has taken on broader dimensions. This shift in perspective is especially important in urban environments, where diverse user groups coexist (Chen et al., 2026; Papadakis et al., 2024).

In this context, vulnerable road users have gained prominence in safety discussions. Pedestrians, cyclists, the elderly, children, and users of light electric vehicles are more affected than others by poor spatial design, high traffic intensity, insufficient separation, and poor infrastructure. This has led to serious criticism of traditional vehicle-centric approaches to transportation analysis and management, and to the need for frameworks that put the experience and safety of these groups at the center. On the other hand, contemporary cities face a diverse range of hazards and disruptions. Traffic accidents, infrastructure failures, severe congestion, climatic events, demand fluctuations, and technological disruptions can all disrupt the performance of a transport system. This situation has led to the concept of resilience being introduced as an important analytical framework in the transport literature. Resilience allows a system not only to withstand shocks but also to adapt to new conditions and recover or reconfigure its performance (Zhang et al., 2026; Serdar et al., 2022).

In the urban planning literature, transport resilience has gradually evolved from an infrastructural concept to a more human one. In early approaches, the focus was mainly on the continuity of network performance and the speed of its recovery, but recent research has shown that this definition is insufficient. A system may recover operationally, but remain unsafe, inequitable, or inaccessible to some user groups. Therefore, resilience becomes meaningful when measured in relation to humans, their experience, and the quality of their access and safety.

While early approaches focused on the speed of restoring network capacity, recent research highlights that an operationally recovered system can still be inaccessible or inequitable for vulnerable populations.

Key Shifts in Transport Resilience

- **From Network to Human:** Early studies prioritized the "resilience triangle" (speed of recovery) and infrastructural robustness (e.g., bridge structural integrity).

- **Insufficiency of Structural Recovery:** A system might be physically restored but fail to provide necessary access, particularly for the elderly, disabled, or low-income residents. Therefore, a system that recovers physically but fails to meet social needs is not truly resilient.
- **Focus on Access and Safety:** True resilience is now measured by the quality of access, the safety of the journey, and the experience of the passengers. This includes ensuring that, for example, evacuation plans are tailored to the needs of the most vulnerable, rather than just restoring general traffic flow.
- **Integrating Social Equity:** Recent literature emphasizes "inclusive mobility," which seeks to ensure that transport systems address the needs of underserved populations during both daily and crisis scenarios (Ciriaco et al., 2025; Ma et al., 2024).

Therefore, modern transport planning uses a "people-centered" approach, ensuring transportation serves as a means for all residents to access education, employment, and healthcare. This theoretical transition has paved the way for the introduction of user-centered approaches to transportation studies. Being human-centered in this area means that analysis and decision-making are based not only on macro-network indicators but also on users' real needs, behavioral differences, and spatial inequalities. In such a framework, network efficiency is only one component of the evaluation and must be placed alongside safety, justice, comfort, and users' perception of the transportation environment. Technological developments have also reinforced this change in approach. The development of sensors, the Internet of Things, spatial data, artificial intelligence, real-time analytics, and intelligent transportation systems has created conditions in which the study of transportation networks is no longer limited to static data and general averages. It is now possible to observe temporal dynamics, user behavior, environmental changes and disruption scenarios with greater precision. These new capabilities have provided the necessary infrastructure for the emergence of digital twins in transportation. In this context, a digital twin is considered not just a digital model, but a dynamic analytical framework that can represent, monitor, analyze, and even predict the state of the real system. The importance of this technology is to establish a continuous bridge between physical and digital simulation and, with real data, to provide an environment for better understanding of network behavior and the effects of various decisions. Accordingly, digital twins have gradually become a central concept in intelligent transportation, road safety, and forward-looking planning (Xing et al., 2025).

In spite of this, a large part of the early applications of digital twins were formed in the industrial, manufacturing and infrastructure asset management fields. In these spaces, the main focus was on equipment monitoring, failure reduction, performance optimization, and asset lifecycle management. Although this background has played an important role in the technology's maturity, its transfer to urban and transportation environments has required a conceptual redefinition. Transportation systems are much more open, dynamic, and dependent on human behavior, and for this reason, the same industrial logic cannot be extended to them without modification. One of the main reasons this transition is important is the increasingly complex nature of contemporary traffic environments. Today's cities host private cars, public transportation, cyclists, pedestrians, light electric vehicles, and, in the near future, autonomous vehicles. Such environments are fraught with potential conflicts, heterogeneous behavioral patterns, and multi-layered risks. Hence, traditional analytics tools that implicitly consider only one or two user types no longer account for the network's true complexity (Moshood et al., 2024; Aghaabbasi & Sabri, 2025).

In the meantime, autonomous transportation is one of the most important areas motivating the development of human-centric digital twins. Digital twins can serve as a platform for analyzing these scenarios before they are deployed in the environment. On the other hand, the expansion of spatial intelligence has played a decisive role in these developments. Tools such as GIS, GNSS data, OpenStreetMap, traffic sensors, video data, and infrastructure layers have enabled much more accurate spatial and behavioral reconstruction of the transportation system. In this framework, GIS serves as the spatial backbone for digital twins, enabling the integration of heterogeneous, multiscale data.

Key Aspects of Digital Twins in Transportation: Role of GIS as Spatial Backbone: GIS provides the essential 3D context, mapping, and spatial analytics that integrate multi-source data (BIM, CAD, lidar) to create a "single source of truth" for infrastructure management. Data Integration for Behavioral Reconstruction: The fusion of GNSS data (vehicle trajectories), traffic sensors, and video analytics (CCTV) enables the simulation of real-time vehicle and pedestrian movements, improving traffic flow and safety. Autonomous Vehicle Testing: To ensure safety, engineers may test autonomous cars and AI algorithms in simulated environments before physical testing by using digital twins for "what-if" scenario testing. Human-Centric Focus: These digital twins are designed to improve safety for pedestrians, cyclists, and drivers, optimizing urban logistics to be more environmentally and socially sustainable (Zapata et al., 2025; El-Agamy et al., 2024).

These systems are evolving towards autonomous twins capable of self-learning and independent action in traffic management. In particular, GNSS data and user trajectories have added a new dimension to understanding transportation. They show how users actually move around the city, what routes they avoid, where they stop, and how they react to space quality or hazard conditions. On this basis, traffic data is not just a source for route mapping but also a window into actual behavior, spatial perception, and hazard-exposure patterns. This is crucial for human-centric digital twins. GNSS data and user trajectories, such as those derived from GPS-enabled smartphones and vehicles, have revolutionized urban planning by providing a "window into actual behavior," transforming traffic data from simple route mapping into a rich source of insights into spatial perception, hazard-exposure patterns, and pedestrian/vehicular interaction.

In this regard, the concept of the smart city also influences the context of this chapter. A smart city makes sense when data and technology can improve the quality of life, safety, sustainability, and urban responsiveness. In this perspective, digital twins act as a kind of knowledge infrastructure that can link observation, analysis and decision-making. Despite this, if this infrastructure serves only technical efficiency rather than human values, it cannot fully align with the goals of the smart city. It should also be noted that the digital twin literature is still emerging and maturing. Although numerous studies have examined the definition, components, applications, and requirements of this technology, significant knowledge gaps remain across many areas, especially in human-centered and autonomous transportation. For example, it is not yet clear how to operationally model the experience of vulnerable users in a digital twin, or how to balance the goals of safety, efficiency, fairness, and resilience.

Ultimately, the context of this chapter starts with the fundamental assumption that the future of transportation should not only be smarter but also safer, fairer, and more human-centered. If digital twins are to play an effective role in this future, they must look beyond infrastructure to people, behavior, space, ethics, and governance. In this regard, this chapter explains the conceptual foundations, theoretical background, and the necessity of applying human digital twins for road safety and future autonomous transportation.

Despite the growing body of literature on transport resilience and digital twins, several critical gaps remain.

- First, most applications of digital twins in transport remain infrastructure-centric and fail to integrate human behavior and user heterogeneity adequately.
- Second, the interaction between vulnerable road users and autonomous vehicles has been inadequately investigated in simulation environments.
- Third, many scientific studies lack clear methodological frameworks that describe data integration, processing, and modelling architecture, as well as validation procedures.
- Fourth, ethical issues such as data privacy, algorithmic bias, and governance are often superficially addressed, and some real-world data are not reported in the scientific literature.
- Finally, the scalability and transferability of digital twin models in urban contexts remain largely unknown, requiring further dissemination of information and optimal use of technology.

2. RESILIENCE AND HUMAN-CENTERED SAFETY IN TRANSPORTATION

The concept of human-centered resilience and safety in transportation has gained a special place in scientific literature in recent decades as an important theoretical framework for understanding and managing complex urban systems, including transportation systems and greenway networks, for perception-based, environmentally friendly sustainability and safety. A resilient transportation system is not only able to withstand shocks such as severe accidents, natural disasters, extreme climate conditions, or infrastructure disruptions, but also can adapt, learn, and recover its performance. This perspective suggests that adaptive capacity is a dynamic, multi-stage process that changes over time and in response to interactions with the urban environment. Robustness, redundancy, recovery, and adaptation are four key components of transport System robustness that have been widely studied across various disciplines. Therefore, there is an increasing need for new analytical frameworks that can integrate spatial, temporal, network, and behavioral data.

The importance of network-based analysis for human-centric design improvement and safety in sustainable urban transport systems is emphasized. This idea, which was first applied in ecological sciences to describe the capacity of ecosystems to return to stability and equilibrium, has gradually penetrated various fields, including urban planning, risk management, human safety and critical infrastructure, and especially sustainable transport systems and the development of safe and green pedestrian and cycling routes.

Figure 1. The theoretical function of resilience in urban systems, focusing on safe transportation. (Author's own illustration)

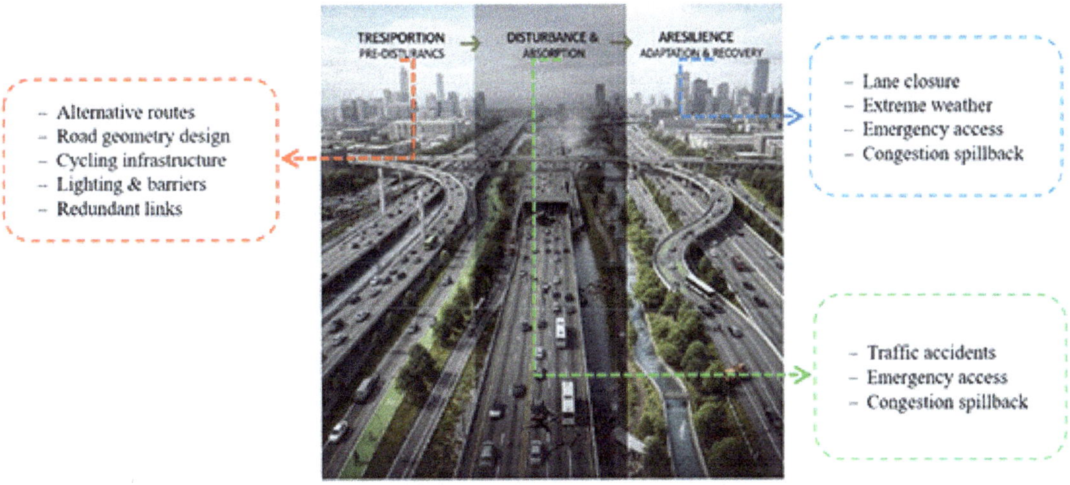

This figure shows the three main phases of transportation network performance in the face of disruption: pre-disruption, absorption, and recovery. The pre-disruption phase is related to robustness, redundancy, and safety infrastructure. The absorption phase emphasizes the system's ability to absorb shocks and prevent cascading failures. The interaction between infrastructure design, user behavior, and network management underpins sustainability and is enhanced by digital twin-based analytics (Figure 1). From a transport safety perspective, this diagram shows that operational continuity should be considered a key principle in road and urban planning. Safety here does not only mean reducing accidents, but also includes the system's ability to maintain accessibility, manage crises, support diverse users, and quickly restore network performance. The present diagram, therefore, emphasizes that achieving safe and sustainable transport requires the simultaneous integration of infrastructure design, disruption scenario analysis, proactive planning, and post-crisis recovery capacity.

This perspective is particularly important in complex urban environments and in the context of future developments. Achieving safe and sustainable transport requires the simultaneous integration of multiple analytical and operational domains. This integration is only possible if analytical tools can reflect the complexity of these relationships at different spatial and temporal scales. This is precisely why digital twins are at the heart of this discussion.

Digital twins, in this sense, are not simply technological tools for modelling, but platforms for a deeper understanding of the relationships among humans, infrastructure, the environment, and decision-making. In this chapter, the emphasis on perception-based digital twins stems from the belief that future transportation analysis cannot remain solely network-centric or vehicle-centric. Instead, spatial differences, behavioral heterogeneities, different levels of vulnerability, and unequal access patterns must be at the center of the analysis. This approach is particularly crucial for vulnerable road users, such as pedestrians and cyclists. From a network-based analysis perspective, human-centered and Safety are best understood when the network's communication structure, alternative routes, critical nodes, bottlenecks, and flow patterns are examined. Network analysis allows the identification of key parts of the system that play a more important role in maintaining performance. It clarifies the degree of dependence among different parts of the network. When this type of analysis is used with the digital twin, not only the static structure but also the network's dynamic, scenario-driven performance can be observed and evaluated.

The importance of this is particularly striking in complex urban environments. Cities are not only physically complex, but also socially, institutionally, and functionally heterogeneous. Some areas may have stronger infrastructure, greater accessibility, and higher management capacity, while others are much more vulnerable to disruptions. Also, different user groups do not have the same experience of risk and Safety. Therefore, behavior-informed and safety analysis must be sensitive to location, scale, user type, and local conditions; something that will be difficult to achieve without advanced, data-driven tools. This approach will become even more important in the context of future developments, especially the development of intelligent and autonomous transportation. Future systems will be defined by the simultaneous presence of connected cars, autonomous vehicles, sensors, smart infrastructure, and human users in a shared space. In such a situation, the relationships between technology, Safety, and human behavior will be more complex than in the past.

From a research perspective, this field also has broad horizons ahead. Integrating digital twins with network analytics, behavioral modelling, real-time data, machine learning, and urban planning can shape a new generation of decision-making tools. These tools not only allow analysis of the current situation but can also be used to anticipate conflicts, evaluate interventions before implementation, and identify hotspots in future scenarios. Such a capacity is of strategic importance for cities facing multiple crises and increasing uncertainties. At the policy and governance level, this approach can help to create more transparent, accurate, and accountable decision-making. In addition, the use of digital twins can help increase transparency and explainability of decisions, an issue of increasing importance in contemporary urban planning.

2.1 Defining Transport Resilience

Transport resilience can be defined as the ability of a system to maintain its essential functions under unstable, critical and changing conditions. This concept is not limited to the physical resistance of infrastructure, but also concerns the network's capacity to continue providing access, mobility, and safety even when part of the system is disrupted. In this sense, safety sustainability is a performance quality that indicates the extent to which a transport system can remain under stress, adjust itself and avoid complete collapse. In contrast to traditional approaches that measure the success of a transport system mainly by criteria such as travel speed, road capacity or delay reduction, the concept of system robustness emphasizes the sustainability of performance under abnormal conditions. This approach is based on the assumption that disruption is an inevitable part of the operation of transport networks and, therefore, the quality of a system is measured not only under normal conditions but also in its ability to continue operating in times of crisis. From this perspective, adaptive urban design complements the traditional functionalist view, elevating it to a more realistic, forward-looking perspective.

Concept of resilience was first introduced, to explain the ability of systems to absorb disturbances, adapt to environmental changes, and recover from adversity. Although there is still no complete consensus on the definition of the resistance to disruption unit, in scientific literature, it is generally understood as the capacity of systems to absorb damage, adapt to changing conditions, and recover effectively from disturbances .Within the framework of transport system, assessing the impact of emergencies and various disruptions on transport infrastructure has been proposed as a key approach in risk management and sustainable planning (Jia et al., 2022).

Research shows that resilient regions, in addition to strengthening response and recovery capacities, also contribute to improving the well-being and satisfaction of residents by increasing security, stability, and quality of life. In this context, urban transport systems, being complex and multidimensional systems highly dependent on physical, human, and institutional interactions, are vulnerable to disruptions caused by both natural and artificial events . Therefore, enhancing the robust urban form of these systems has become a primary research focus in transport planning and urban risk management (Guo et al., 2025).

In recent years, the focus on users has become increasingly important in defining transport system reliability under disruption. In the past, the main focus was on network performance, but it has now become clear that network performance alone cannot be a sufficient measure of the robustness of urban transport networks. A system is truly resilient when it can maintain safety, usability and accessibility for different groups. This is especially important for vulnerable road users, who are directly exposed to the built environment and disruption, and who usually pay a higher price for system inefficiencies. Thus, a human-centric approach should be an integral part of the definition of system robustness. This concept assumes that transport systems, due to their open, dynamic and human and institutional interactions, are always subject to uncertainty and disruption. In the end, safety sustainability is defined not as a simple return of the system to its previous state, but as the ability to reorganize, structurally adapt and transform the system's performance in the face of shocks.

In this framework, recovery capability is a process and nonlinear concept that evolves through the interaction between physical infrastructure, user behavior patterns, institutional mechanisms and the spatial context of the city and serves as a theoretical foundation for analyzing the sustainability of transport systems' performance in complex and unstable conditions. Recent analytical frameworks emphasize that these capacities must be assessed in an integrated and simultaneous manner, as the actual performance of transport systems in critical conditions is the result of a complex interaction among technical, managerial, institutional, and social factors (Abushaega et al., 2024; Ma et al., 2024).

Risk generally refers to an adverse event or, in urban transportation discussions, to an accident or injury, and the severity of its consequences. At the same time, vulnerability represents the sensitivity or degree of impact that systems and users experience in response to such events In this conceptual framework, digital twins are proposed as a key tool for operationalizing user-focused approaches in analyzing the data reality of transport system (Ashja-Ardalan et al., 2025).

Transport system reliability under disruption is the capacity of a transportation system to absorb disruptions, moving beyond traditional efficiency-focused approaches by assuming that disruptions such as climate-related events, cyber-attacks, or accidents are unavoidable and that the system must continue to operate under stress.

Core Dimensions of Transport Resilience

- **Robustness (Absorb):** The ability of infrastructure to withstand stress without suffering significant degradation.
- **Redundancy:** The capacity to offer alternative routes or modes when primary ones fail.
- **Resourcefulness (Adapt):** The ability to mobilize resources and adapt operating procedures to manage a crisis.
- **Rapidity (Recover):** The speed at which functionality is restored.

Components of Resilient Transport Networks

- **Physical Infrastructure:** Hardening roads, bridges, and tunnels to withstand natural disasters.
- **Operational Strategy:** Flexible traffic management, rerouting capabilities, and providing real-time information to users.
- **Institutional Planning:** Pre-set emergency protocols and risk-based, scenario-driven planning.
- **Data-Driven Decision Making:** Utilizing predictive analytics and digital twins to anticipate impacts.

In essence, a resilient transport system is not merely one that prevents damage, but one that can "bounce back" fast. It is a crucial, forward-looking perspective that complements traditional functionalist views to ensure connectivity during crises (Giannopoulos & Li, 2025; Bergantino et al., 2024).

Urban and interurban transport systems are inherently vulnerable to disruptions due to their open nature, the interdependence of components, the density of flows, and the diversity of actors. A local incident, a technical failure, or a sudden change in weather conditions can have consequences beyond the initial point and spread to other parts of the network. This very feature shows that transport sustainability is not just a feature of a road or a traffic node, but of the entire system and its internal relationships. Therefore, to understand this concept accurately, the network must be viewed as an interconnected structure. From a conceptual perspective, transport cannot be equated with a simple return to the pre-crisis state. In many cases, reverting to the previous state may reproduce the same weaknesses and deficiencies that caused the initial vulnerability. Accordingly, the contemporary understanding of adaptive capacity emphasizes learning, restructuring, and improvement. In other words, a resilient system is not just a system that survives a crisis, but also one that uses the crisis to reform its structure and increase its readiness for the future.

In analyzing transport system reliability under disruption, the time dimension is of great importance. Operational continuity of transport systems in urban contexts is not only about the moment of disruption but also includes three important stages: pre-crisis, during the crisis, and post-crisis. Operational continuity should therefore be measured by maintaining an acceptable level of accessibility during disruptions. This is particularly important in urban environments, where disruptions or impediments to access can have direct consequences for citizens' daily lives, employment, education, health, and well-being (Lee et al., 2022; Amoozad et al., 2024; Liu et al., 2022).

Adaptive capacity of urban mobility systems is also closely linked to the concept of spatial justice. Transport disruptions do not affect all users and all urban areas equally. Some neighborhoods are more vulnerable to crises due to poor infrastructure, a lack of alternative routes, poor service quality, or distance from major centers. Also, some user groups, such as pedestrians, cyclists, the elderly and people with mobility limitations, experience the consequences of disruption more than others. Therefore, the definition of mobility system reliability should account for spatial and social differences and not be limited to the network's average performance. From a management perspective, transport network durability is not only a product of infrastructure design, but also depends on the quality of governance, institutional coordination, information flow and decision-making capacity. A network that is physically well designed but lacks a coherent management system, up-to-date data, or rapid-response capacity may exhibit low adaptive capacity in practice (de Medeiros et al., 2025; Erdem et al., 2026).

From an analytical perspective, transport system robustness can be explained in terms of three main capacities: absorptive capacity, adaptive capacity, and recovery capacity. The ability of a system to withstand an initial shock without experiencing a significant collapse in performance is referred to as absorptive capacity; the ability to reorganize system components in response to new conditions is referred to as adaptive capacity; and the ability to restore functions or develop a new form of sustainable performance following a disruption is referred to as recovery capacity. These three capacities are not separate in practice; they operate simultaneously and interact with one another. Therefore, a comprehensive assessment of transport network durability requires that these dimensions be examined holistically, rather than analyzed independently.

2.2 Risk, Vulnerability, and Adaptive Capacity

Risk, vulnerability, and adaptive capacity can be considered three complementary dimensions for understanding the behavior of transport systems under unstable conditions. These three concepts can be defined separately, but in practice, they are strongly interdependent. The higher the level of risk in a network, the more important it is to identify vulnerable points, and the higher the adaptive capacity, the greater the system's ability to control the effects of risk and reduce the consequences of vulnerability. Accordingly, resilience analysis will be incomplete without considering these three components simultaneously.

Adaptive capacity refers to the ability of institutions and organizations to adjust, strengthen, and reorganize their mechanisms in the face of extreme events and critical situations. This capacity shows the extent to which an organization can effectively and timely respond to disruptions by uniting the necessary resources and reducing the negative consequences of risks through behavioral, technological, or financial measures. In this sense, adaptive capacity is not limited to short-term responses but rather reflects the structural and managerial readiness to face unstable conditions and maintain performance in complex situations actively (Islam & Welch, 2024).

Improving, modernizing, and upgrading infrastructure can play an important role in increasing safety, reducing operational fragility, and limiting cyclist risk exposure to extreme events. The advancement of information technology and smart systems, along with physical infrastructure, may be useful tools for enhancing readiness, monitoring situations, and making better decisions during emergencies. This viewpoint contends that investing in public transport and information technology for road safety not only increases system efficiency but also serves as an important approach to improving adaptability to new knowledge and resilience in the face of large disruptions. In complex urban environments, where transport networks are intertwined with diverse behavioral and spatial patterns, risk must be analyzed in a multidimensional, context-specific manner. In contrast, cyclist susceptibility to accidents is the system, infrastructure, or users' sensitivity to the effects of an adverse event. The crisis's impact depends not only on the crisis's magnitude but also on the degree of the system's structural and functional fragility. In light of this, spatial risk exposure analysis is considered a key prerequisite for assessing transport resilience (Bashir et al., 2025; Shang et al., 2024).

In contemporary contexts, many cities around the world are trying to steer urban transport systems towards more sustainable models; models that can simultaneously reduce accidents, congestion, air and noise pollution, while improving the quality of urban life, social interactions and general well-being. Notwithstanding this, urban transport is not only a technical or managerial issue but is also directly linked to the concept of justice. A large part of contemporary transport systems is still organized to prioritize motorized transport. Considering these factors, the social and environmental costs of this choice are borne by other users and society as a whole. From this perspective, urban transport can be seen as a field in which spatial and functional inequalities are clearly reproduced (Jeon et al., 2023).

Justice in urban transport can be examined from several main dimensions. One of these dimensions is the degree to which different groups are exposed to traffic hazards and the resulting pollutants; another dimension concerns the distribution of space in the urban network, i.e., how much space is allocated to motor vehicles and what share is reserved for more sustainable modes of transport. The third dimension concerns the valuation of travel time, meaning that traffic planning and management often consider the time of car users to be more important than that of other users. Consequently, recognizing these different forms of injustice can provide an important basis for reviewing urban planning policies, infrastructure development and traffic management.

Exposure of cyclists to hazardous environments in the transport sector is not evenly distributed among users. Some groups, especially vulnerable road users such as pedestrians and cyclists, are more exposed to the negative consequences of disruptions than others. This is because these users lack physical protection layers and interact directly with the quality of the built environment, the condition of roads, the design of intersections, the intensity of motorized traffic, and the city's spatial conditions. Accordingly, a small infrastructure failure or a sudden change in traffic conditions may cause a delay for a driver. Although this is the case, for cyclists or pedestrians, it can pose a serious threat to safety and health. From this perspective, vulnerability is not only a technical issue, but also a human, spatial, and justice-based issue. Vulnerable road users have a special place in the discussion of transport justice. This group, which includes pedestrians, cyclists, and other non-motorized users who lack adequate physical protection in traffic, is more vulnerable than others due to direct contact with the street environment and the lack of safety features similar to those of motor vehicles (Bajwa et al., 2025).

An important aspect of adaptive capacity is that it is built before a crisis, not during it. Long-term planning, targeted investment, upgrading information systems, training institutions and preparing response mechanisms are all part of the process of building this capacity. If these preparations are not in place in advance, even seemingly robust systems may be seriously disrupted by sudden shocks. Adaptive capacity should therefore be seen as a strategic asset in transport management. In this context, vulnerable road users have a special place in risk and cyclist risk exposure analysis. Pedestrians, cyclists and users of light electric vehicles are usually in direct contact with the road environment and have limited physical support. Therefore, what is considered a minor inconvenience to a driver may become a serious threat to health and safety for these groups (Ye et al., 2023).

Characteristics of Vulnerable Users

- **Diverse but Marginalized:** These users are not a homogeneous group; they have varied needs and levels of vulnerability.
- **Commonality:** Despite their differences, their shared characteristic is being less supported by dominant urban transport structures.
- **Risk Exposure:** They occupy a fragile position regarding the dangers and negative consequences of traffic.

Among the most vulnerable road users are pedestrians, cyclists, and riders of motorcycles or electric scooters, who are more likely to sustain serious injuries in the event of an accident due to insufficient physical protection. Safety studies of these groups in different countries show that risk experiences, traffic behaviors and attitudes towards safety vary from one geographical and social context to another. On this basis, analyzing the situation of these users is not limited to identifying high-risk behaviors, but also requires comparing behavioral patterns, demographic characteristics and cross-country differences to obtain a more accurate picture of their safety situation (Yannis et al., 2020).

Findings from such studies usually show that some high-risk behaviors are more frequent among vulnerable users. These behaviors include crossing the street at places other than nearby crossings, using a mobile phone and checking messages or social networks while walking on the street, cycling or driving without protective equipment, and driving at inappropriate speeds in some non-residential spaces. These behaviors, although they may seem individual at first glance, are in fact strongly influenced by the infrastructure conditions, traffic culture, the level of public awareness and the quality of safety policies in each country. Ultimately, risk, and vulnerability should be considered as core components of a perception-based framework for transportation analysis. These concepts allow us to see the transportation system not just as a network of infrastructure, but as a living, social, and dynamic structure shaped by the interactions among technology, space, behavior, and management. In this regard, human-centered digital twins can serve as a platform for measuring and integrating these dimensions, revealing risks, vulnerabilities, and adaptive capacities within a single, scenario-based analytical environment (Sosik-Filipak & Osypchuk, 2023).

2.3 Vulnerable Road Users in Resilience-Oriented Transport Planning

Vulnerable road users, including pedestrians and non-motorized cyclists, are essential to resilient transport planning because they are more affected than other users by the quality of the built environment, infrastructure failures, and critical conditions. Unlike motor vehicle users who have some physical protection, vulnerable users are directly exposed to the road surface, road geometry, intersections, barriers, lighting conditions and other spatial elements of the transport environment. Therefore, any disruption in system performance, reduction in infrastructure quality or occurrence of critical conditions can have more severe and immediate consequences for these groups. Consequently, an analysis of transport safety sustainability that fails to account for the spatial and behavioral experiences of vulnerable users would be incomplete and limited. As an emerging innovation, digital twins have the potential to completely change how safety and system robustness are evaluated in transportation systems. This technique enables a dynamic depiction of transportation system performance by combining temporal, geographical, and user-behavior data. In contrast to conventional methods that have mostly focused on macro, aggregate, and network-based indicators, digital twins enable the explicit inclusion of geographical variations, behavioral variability, and varying degrees of risk across user groups in the research.

From an urban planning perspective, resilient transportation requires a shift from reactive to proactive approaches. In traditional models, planning interventions are often carried out after an accident, a disruption or the emergence of infrastructure weaknesses. This technology enables the representation of transportation system performance by integrating spatial data and data on user behavior patterns on roads. Unlike traditional approaches that focus mainly on macro and aggregated network indicators, digital twins can explicitly consider spatial differences, behavioral heterogeneity, and varying levels of vulnerability among different user groups, particularly vulnerable users such as cyclists and pedestrians, during the analysis process. In the meantime, vulnerable users, due to their direct interaction with the built environment and the lack of physical protection layers, are much more exposed to the consequences of disruption and critical conditions than other groups (Zhou et al., 2026; Avram, 2026).

This limitation prevents the full potential of digital twins for analyzing dynamic system evolutions and for comparing different risk conditions. Therefore, a fundamental need in this area is to develop frameworks that can integrate multi-source data across different spatial and temporal scales and provide predictive assessments for a wide range of disturbance scenarios. This is particularly important for vulnerable road users, as the risks they face often depend on subtle yet decisive changes in the urban environment. Furthermore, focusing on vulnerable users in resilient planning also highlights the spatial and social justice dimension of transport. Resilience cannot be assessed simply in terms of the speed of network recovery or the continuity of traffic flow, but rather the extent to which this recovery is safe, accessible and fair for all users, especially the less protected groups. Finally, the place of vulnerable road users in resilient transport planning must be seen as more than a side issue or part of safety discussions.

Mobility system reliability is the capacity of a system to withstand shocks, maintain critical functions, adapt to new conditions, and recover effectively after a crisis. These shocks can be severe accidents, infrastructure blockages, disruptions caused by extreme weather conditions, or sudden changes in travel demand patterns; events that usually create cascading effects and are not limited to the point of occurrence. In this regard, components such as "robustness", "redundancy", "recovery" and "adaptability" are proposed as main dimensions of resilience, but their analytical value becomes apparent when interpreted in relation to the network structure, the spatial heterogeneity of the city and the behavioral differences of users; because system robustness, in practice, is the result of the interaction between the network, space, people and management institutions. Another important point is that the reliability of the transport system under disruption cannot be fully understood without considering "risk" and "vulnerability". Risk refers to adverse events and their consequences, while cyclist susceptibility to accidents indicates which parts of the network and which user groups are most sensitive to disruptions (Guo et al., 2023).

2.4 Why Resilience Must be Human-Centered

Resilience in transport systems, although defined in many studies as infrastructure capacity, network performance, service continuity, and recovery speed, is, in essence, a deeply human concept. The true value of transportation systems lies not only in their technological efficiency but also in their capacity to support daily life, ensure user safety, and provide fair access to opportunities. Transportation systems are designed to fulfil human mobility, access, safety, and well-being demands. Following this, any assessment of safety sustainability that overlooks how disruptions affect people and focuses on engineering measures such as throughput capacity, network recovery time, or operational performance stability will give a false impression of reality. In fact, operational continuity of mobility systems becomes meaningful when it demonstrates the extent to which a transport system can protect people, especially in crises, and maintain the quality of the travel experience. The need for robust urban form to be human-centered stems from the fact that transport disruptions affect people's lives before they manifest as a drop in network performance indicators. Blocking a route, disconnecting part of the network, increasing delays, reducing service availability, infrastructure breakdown, or increasing the likelihood of accidents is not just a technical or management issue, but directly affects the safety, health, well-being, daily time, job opportunities, access to health and education services, and even the sense of security of users. This shows that flexible and recovery-oriented urban design cannot be reduced to a network performance indicator; it must be analyzed in relation to users lived experience. In other words, a transport system is truly resilient only when disruptions cause minimal harm to people and allow them to continue moving safely and acceptably.

Vulnerable road users, particularly pedestrians and cyclists, are much more vulnerable than others due to the lack of physical protection layers, direct contact with the built environment and high dependence on the quality of road design. In many urban spaces, road design continues to prioritize motorized traffic flows. At the same time, the cognition-informed nature of adaptive urban design requires a rethink of how we define the success of a transportation system. In many conventional analyses, the success of a network is measured by metrics such as traffic recovery speed, reduced latency, or maintained capacity. Despite prior research, from experience-oriented perspective, these metrics alone are not enough. A network is considered successful and resilient when it can maintain user safety, meet the needs of diverse groups, and maintain essential access without excluding or marginalizing vulnerable groups in the face of disruption. In other words, anthropocentric resistance to disruption emphasizes the question of "how does the system work for humans," not just "how operationally stable is it?" This shift in focus also transforms the theoretical and applied orientation of transportation studies.

This approach becomes even more important in the context of the future of transportation and the development of autonomous, connected, and data-driven systems. While smart technologies should serve to reduce infrastructure safety deficiencies, enhance safety, and improve the user experience, they should not be limited to optimizing flows or increasing network capacity. For this purpose, resilience in the era of autonomous transportation must be defined from the outset with a user-centered approach to ensure that technological transformation does not exacerbate inequalities or increase risks for specific groups. In this context, behavior-informed design framework digital twins can play a pivotal role in operationalizing this approach as an analytical and strategic tool. By integrating spatial, temporal, infrastructure, and behavioral data, these technologies enable a dynamic representation of the transport system, allowing the analyst to observe and evaluate not only the overall performance of the road but also the experiences of different users. The main advantage of this approach is that spatial differences, behavioral heterogeneity, varying levels of risk exposure, and potential crisis scenarios can be examined simultaneously within a single analytical environment. In this way, operational continuity of mobility systems is transformed from an abstract, macro-scale characteristic into a visible, measurable concept relevant to users' daily lives.

Here is why resilience must be human-centered in the future of transportation:

1. Technology Serving People, Not Vice Versa
    - **Preventing "Technology-First" Pitfalls:** A purely technology-driven approach can yield systems that are efficient on paper but fail to meet user needs, such as autonomous systems that cannot navigate complex human behavior.
    - **Human-System Collaboration:** The most resilient systems often involve human input to verify or take corrective action when AI encounters edge cases or unknown threats.
    - **Empowerment Over Adaptation:** human-centered design (HCD) focuses on using technology to enhance human capabilities and well-being, rather than forcing humans to adapt to the constraints of automated systems.
2. Methodological Need for Diverse Data and Variables
    - **Broadening Data Inputs:** Humanizing resilience requires looking beyond mere infrastructure data to include human-centric variables, such as user behavior, equitable access, and comfort.
    - **Context-Aware Solutions:** Anthropocentric systems are designed to be context-aware, adapting to users' social, cultural, and environmental needs, such as integrating public transit with local, accessible solutions.

- **Multidimensional Metrics:** Instead of just measuring efficiency or speed, behavior-informed safety sustainability measures success by the quality of the human experience, safety for all (including vulnerable users), and reliability.

3. Transportation as a Social Service
    - **Focus on People, Not Just KPIs:** Transportation is ultimately about connecting people to opportunities (jobs, healthcare, education), not just optimizing throughput.
    - **Ensuring Equity and Inclusivity:** A Perception-based approach ensures that new technologies such as automated shuttles or shared mobility do not disproportionately exclude vulnerable groups (the elderly, people with disabilities, or low-income populations).
    - **Safety as a Foundational Element:** User-centered design prioritizes safety, such as reducing traffic violence, to improve quality of life and build trust in the system.
4. Creating Safer and More Robust Systems
    - **Mitigating Unknown Risks:** While AI is good at following rules, human-centered AI is better at adapting to unexpected, "unknown" threats that AI may not have been trained for.
    - **Improved Human-Machine Interaction (HMI):** A focus on People-centered AI leads to better communication between vehicles and their surroundings (e.g., pedestrians, cyclists), making the overall network safer and more reliable.
5. Human-Centered Resilience in the Digital Age
    - **Technology Serving People:** Rather than adapting to technology, future systems should be designed to reduce user friction, build trust, and ensure convenience and accessibility for all, including the elderly and people with disabilities.
    - **Sociotechnical Approach:** Moving from a purely technical approach (focusing only on infrastructure) to a sociotechnical one enables greater adaptive capacity by incorporating adaptive behaviors and social capacity.
    - **Autonomous Vehicle Safety:** Human-centric design in autonomous vehicles involves clear communication.
    - **"Agentic" Vehicles:** Emerging AI enables vehicles to reason and adapt, moving beyond pre-programmed tasks to handle unforeseen ethical dilemmas and user needs, which is crucial for true human-centered mobility.

In conclusion, a human-oriented approach to robustness in future urban transport networks is the only way to create systems that are truly efficient while remaining, at their core, designed for human life and needs. In the context of intelligent and autonomous transportation, this discussion becomes even more important. Therefore, the adaptive capacity of transport systems in the future of transportation must be defined so that technology serves people, not people simply adapting to the logic of technology. From a methodological perspective, humanizing Operational continuity of mobility systems also broadens the range of data and variables required.

3. DIGITAL TWINS IN TRANSPORTATION: CONCEPTS AND FOUNDATIONS

Digital twins in transportation are dynamic, virtual replicas of physical transportation assets, systems, or processes that are continuously updated with real-time data simulation from sensors and IoT devices.

They facilitate bidirectional information flow, enabling real-time monitoring, simulation, predictive analysis, and optimization of transportation infrastructure throughout its lifecycle.

Core Concepts of Transportation Digital Twins

- **Definition:** digital representation of a physical asset, system, or process simulation, multi-scale, probabilistic simulation of an as-built system, enabled by a "digital thread" that uses the best available models and sensor data to mirror and predict activities over the life of its corresponding physical twin.
- **Bi-directional Interaction:** Unlike traditional simulation or BIM (Building Information Modelling), which are often static or unidirectional, a true digital twin features bidirectional connectivity. Data flows from the physical system to the virtual system, and insights from the virtual model can feed back into the physical system to optimize it.
- **Key Components (5D Model):** Modern transportation digital twins often consist of five dimensions: physical entity (roads/bridges), virtual model (3D models/simulations), twin data (sensor data), services (simulation/analysis), and connections (real-time linking).
- **Real-time Synchronization:** Data from traffic cameras, GPS, and IoT sensors are integrated, allowing the virtual model to reflect the current state of infrastructure and traffic at any given moment.

Foundations and Technologies

- **Data Integration & IoT:** The backbone of a transportation digital twin is the continuous, real-time data stream from sensors, including traffic counters, GPS devices, and environmental monitors.
- **Simulation & Modelling:** These include agent-based models (e.g., simulating individual vehicle behavior) and microscopic traffic simulations (e.g., SUMO) to model traffic flow and predict congestion.
- **3D Modelling (BIM/GIS):** Building Information Modelling (BIM) and Geographic Information Systems (GIS) are used to create the foundational, highly accurate 3D representations of physical assets.
- **Artificial Intelligence (AI):** AI algorithms, including deep learning, analyze massive, heterogeneous data streams to identify patterns, predict infrastructure degradation, and optimize traffic light control and routing in real time.
- **Edge Computing:** To handle high-velocity, high-volume data without excessive latency, data is often processed locally at the network edge rather than in a centralized cloud.

Lifecycle Application Areas

Digital twins support every phase of transportation infrastructure:

1. **Planning & Design:** Simulating traffic scenarios to test new infrastructure, such as adding a new bus rapid transit (BRT) line, before physical construction.
2. **Construction:** Monitoring, in real-time, the progress and quality of construction projects to ensure they match design specifications.

3. **Operation:** Managing traffic flow, reducing congestion through dynamic adjustments (e.g., traffic signals, variable speed limits), and enhancing safety.
4. **Maintenance:** Utilizing predictive maintenance to analyze sensor data (e.g., stress, vibration on bridges) to forecast failures and intervene proactively.

Key Benefits

- **Efficiency:** Improved traffic management and optimized resource allocation.
- **Sustainability:** Reduced carbon footprint by optimizing routes and reducing congestion.
- **Safety:** Proactive identification of hazards, accident simulation, and risk management.
- **Cost Reduction:** Minimized material waste and lower maintenance costs.

Challenges and Future Directions

- **Data Integration & Standardization:** Harmonizing data from diverse sources and ensuring interoperability remains a major challenge.
- **High Computational Cost:** Real-time, large-scale simulations require significant infrastructure, making it difficult for smaller municipalities to implement.
- **Data Privacy:** Ensuring that traffic data collection (e.g., cameras) respects privacy laws.
- **Moving from "Digital Shadow" to "Digital Twin":** Many current systems are actually "digital shadows" (unidirectional) rather than full, bi-directional digital twins.

3.1 What is a Digital Twin?

The concept of digital twin, as one of the new approaches in modeling and managing complex systems, has attracted widespread attention in various fields of engineering and urban planning in recent years. A digital twin generally refers to a dynamic virtual representation of a physical system that, using real data, practical by human and continuous updates, is able to simulate and analyze the behavior, performance, and changes of the real system over time. Unlike traditional models, which are often static and based on simplifying assumptions, digital twins emphasize the continuous interaction between the real world and the virtual model.

In general, a digital twin is a virtual representation of a physical system that utilizes data from the real world to evaluate and even predict behavior over time. In common parlance, a digital twin is a simulation of a physical system that can interact with and learn from its physical counterpart in real-time, using data collected in real-time for analysis and prediction of future behavior. Systematic assessments of recent research underscore the varied definitions across fields. Although this is the case, concur that digital twins depend on the dynamic integration of reality-based data, simulation capabilities, and real-world synchronization. Digital twins are more than just static modeling in built environments and smart cities. In any scientific sector, they function as dynamic tools and technologies for performance evaluation, monitoring, and decision support (Huzzat et al., 2025).

The essential feature of a digital twin lies in the active connection between the physical and digital worlds. This connection is established through data collected from sensors, monitoring systems, databases, spatial models, traffic data, images, and other digital sources. Through this data flow, the digital twin can track changes in the real system over time, represent its current state, and serve as a basis for analyzing its performance and predicting its future behavior.

From a conceptual perspective, the digital twin is usually based on three main components: first, the physical entity, which can be a road, vehicle, intersection, transportation network, or even an entire city; Second, its digital counterpart, which is represented in the computing environment; and third, the data flow that connects the two. This triple structure makes the digital twin not just a theoretical model, but an analytical system that can interact with reality.

In transportation, the digital twin is particularly important because transportation systems are inherently complex, dynamic, multi-scale, and dependent on human behavior. One of the key strengths of digital twins is their ability to integrate diverse data simultaneously. In transportation systems, spatial, temporal, infrastructure, behavioral, environmental, and traffic data are typically located in separate, disparate layers. A digital twin can bring these layers together into a unified framework, enabling the analyst to view and interpret their interrelationships. This integration is a prerequisite for a realistic understanding of network behavior and the design of more effective policies.

In the context of road safety, this technology is particularly important for analyzing vulnerable road users. Pedestrians, cyclists, and users of light electric vehicles are more affected by the quality of the built environment and local network conditions than other users, due to inadequate physical protection. The digital twin can also incorporate the diverse experiences of these groups into the analysis and show how spatial design, land-use type, traffic intensity, and local-level flow management can affect safety and risk for these users.

A Human-oriented digital twin in transportation means that the system is not only measured by macro-indicators of the network, but can also reveal spatial differences, inequalities in access, diversity of user behaviors, and different levels of risk across groups. In this approach, the analysis is not limited to how the network works, but also to who, where, and at what level of safety and fairness the network operates. This change of perspective elevates the digital twin from a technical tool to a socio-analytical framework (Hu et al., 2022).

From an urban planning perspective, the digital twin can be a powerful tool for testing scenarios. For example, the potential effects of creating a bike lane, changing the traffic pattern at an intersection, implementing a speed limit, or redistributing street space on safety, traffic flow, and other factors can be assessed before a plan is implemented. User accessibility was assessed, enabling planners to analyze decisions before implementation in a virtual environment and choose more balanced, less risky solutions (Liu et al., 2023).

The digital twin also plays a fundamental role in resilience. Transport systems are constantly exposed to disturbances such as severe accidents, infrastructure failures, road closures, climate events, demand fluctuations or human crises. The digital twin can show how these disturbances spread through the network, which parts are most fragile, and what kind of interventions can strengthen the network's absorption, adaptation and recovery capacity. Given this context, this technology is very effective for operationalizing the concept of resilience in transport. Here, the difference between a general digital twin and a user-focused digital twin becomes important. A general digital twin may focus primarily on the technical performance of the network, throughput capacity, or infrastructure efficiency, but a user-centered digital twin attempts to put the experiences, needs, behaviors, and vulnerabilities of different users at the core of the analysis. This approach is fundamental to this chapter, "Human-Centered Digital Twins for Road Safety and Future Autonomous Transportation", because it shows that technology should serve humans and their safety.

Figure 2. Conceptual architecture of a transportation digital twin and data-driven feedback loop

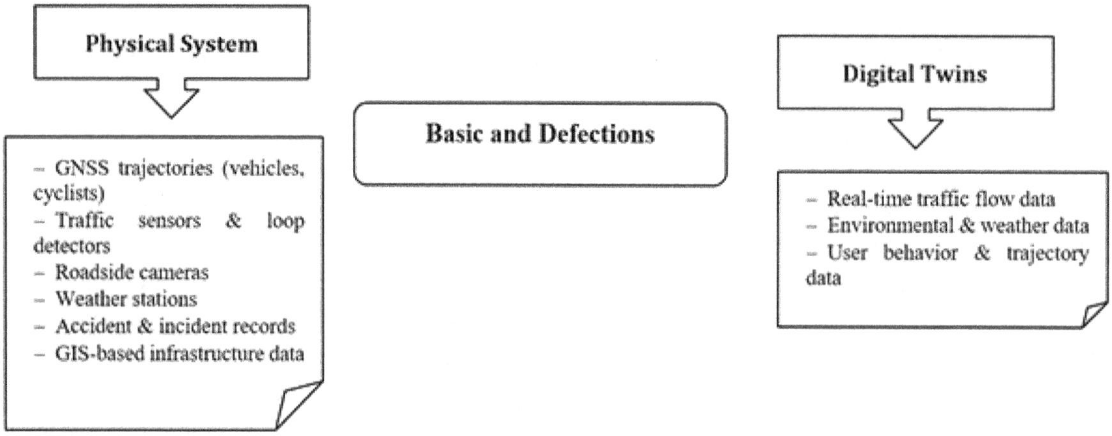

The figure shows a feedback architecture that feeds data collected by sensor tools such as GNSS and builds environment layers into the twin environment using GIS, enabling analysis and simulation of scientific research scenarios, combining monitoring, learning, and adaptive decision-making, and enhancing the resilience of the safe transportation system (Figure 2).

Digital twins are dynamic, virtual representations of physical systems that enable real-time monitoring, simulation, and predictive analysis, transforming engineering and urban planning. By utilizing continuous, two-way data exchange, they overcome the limitations of static, traditional models to optimize performance, enhance sustainability, and aid in, for instance, predictive maintenance and infrastructure management.

Key aspects of digital twins include:

- **Definition & Functionality:** They are virtual, continuously updated replicas that reflect the real-time state of physical assets, allowing for analysis, simulation, and forecasting of future behaviors.
- **Key Components:** A digital twin consists of a physical entity, a virtual counterpart, and a data-driven connection between them.
- **Applications:** Common applications include improving efficiency in manufacturing, optimizing supply chains, and managing urban infrastructure.
- **Difference from Traditional Modelling:** Unlike static models, digital twins provide a real-time, two-way data exchange between the physical object and its virtual replica, ensuring the simulation accurately reflects the current, real-world state.
- **Benefits:** These tools help optimize, leading to better performance and reduced costs.

In the field of smart and autonomous transport, the importance of the digital twin increases more than ever. The simultaneous presence of connected, autonomous, smart infrastructure, sensors, and human users will define the future of transport. In such an environment, interactions between humans and technology will become more complex, dynamic, and sensitive. Digital twins can provide a platform for analyzing these interactions and help better understand how human users and automated systems coexist in the real city.

Within the smart city paradigm, Digital twins can be considered part of a city's knowledge infrastructure, helping it be more resilient in crises, more sensitive to inequalities, and better prepared for technological change. Cities of the future, organizing, synchronizing, and analyzing rate knowledge and translating it into decision-making. In this sense, a digital twin is not just a model of a city, but a platform for observing, interpreting, learning, and guiding urban transformations.

In particular, in road safety analysis, digital twins can also transform our understanding of accidents and risks. Instead of relying solely on post-accident data, we can identify conditions that increase the likelihood of an accident. This shift from ex post to ex post analysis is one of the most important strengths of digital twins in safety studies. Accordingly, the focus shifts from recording consequences to identifying areas that generate risk.

In summary, a digital twin is a dynamic, live, analytical, and data-driven representation of real systems that is used to monitor, interpret, predict, and improve their performance. In the field of transportation, this technology is especially important when developed with a behavior-informed approach.

3.2 Differences Between Digital Twins, Simulations, and Conventional Models

Digital twin has evolved into a multidimensional analytical and simulation framework for decision-making, rather than simply a technological tool. This conceptual evolution has made the digital twin a suitable tool for analyzing open and dynamic systems; systems whose performance is strongly influenced by uncertainty, human interactions, and temporal variations. Digital twins provide a platform for modelling system performance across various scenarios and evaluating the effects of planning decisions before implementation by combining geographical, network, temporal, and behavioral data. This conceptual distinction enables the digital twin to be viewed not just as a modeling tool, but also as a dynamic system capable of monitoring, analyzing, and learning complex systems. The capacity to continually synchronize between the physical system and the digital model enables the depiction of real-time changes as well as the system's responsiveness to changing conditions (Iliuţă et al., 2024).

Digital twins, simulations, and conventional models differ primarily in their level of connectivity to real-world assets, the dynamism of their data, and the scope of their lifecycle (Hu et al., 2021). Here is a breakdown of the differences:

Digital Twins

- **Real-time Synchronization:** Digital twins are connected via IoT sensors to their physical counterparts, reflecting current operating conditions and evolving in real-time.
- **Bidirectional Data Flow:** They receive data from the physical asset, analyze it, and can send commands or optimization adjustments back to the physical system.
- **Lifecycle Scope:** They exist throughout the entire lifecycle of an asset (from design to decommissioning), rather than just during a single phase.
- **Predictive/Prescriptive Power:** Beyond just monitoring ("what is happening"), digital twins use AI to predict future performance and recommend actions ("what should we do?").

Simulations

- **Static/Snapshot Data:** Simulations often run on fixed, historical, or theoretical datasets. They do not automatically update with real-time, live data.
- **One-time Analysis:** They are designed for specific scenarios or "what-if" analyses and conclude once the simulation is complete.
- **Theoretical Focus:** They model what *could* happen, whereas digital twins model what *is* happening.
- **Design-Centric:** Primarily used in the design, engineering, and validation phases.

Conventional Models

- **Static Representation:** These include 3D CAD models or CAD-based simulations, which are static until a user manually introduces new parameters.
- **Visualization Focus:** They focus on visual, spatial, or structural insights rather than the operational behavior or performance of the object.

Table 1. Comparison digital twin and simulation and other model

Feature	Digital Twin	Simulation	Conventional Model (e.g., CAD)
Data Flow	Real-time, 2-way (Live)	Static/Historical (One-off)	None/Manual Updates
Connectivity	Active, continuous link	Isolated/Standalone	Isolated/Standalone
Lifecycle	Persistent (Entire Lifecycle)	Temporary (Design Stage)	Temporary (Design Stage)
Function	Operational optimization	Testing, "What-if" scenarios	Visualization, Design
Adaptability	High (Adjusts automatically)	Low (Requires manual update)	None

As shown in Table 1, digital twins represent a paradigm shift from static, design-oriented modelling approaches to dynamic, data-driven, and continuously evolving systems. While simulation models support scenario-based analysis and conventional models focus on representation and visualization, digital twins integrate real-time data streams with physical systems, enabling continuous synchronization, predictive analytics, and adaptive responses. This capability is particularly critical in complex transport environments, where real-time decision-making, safety optimization, and system resilience require a higher level of responsiveness and integration than traditional modelling approaches can provide.

Key Takeaways from the Text

- **"Living" Mirrors:** Digital twins are not just visual models; they are dynamic, data-driven systems that can mirror, analyze, and learn from complex, open, and uncertain systems.
- **Proactive vs Reactive:** Digital twins enable proactive, informed decisions and predictive maintenance, moving beyond reactive, one-off simulation analysis.

- **Complementary Tools:** Digital twins often incorporate simulations as their core, but extend their value by using real-time data to validate predictions (Zhang et al., 2025).

Digital twins have evolved in recent years from a purely technological tool to an advanced analytical framework for understanding, evaluating, and guiding complex systems. In this sense, the distinction between digital twins, conventional simulations, and conventional models is essential for understanding the true role of this technology in transportation and urban planning. Conventional models are usually based on simplifications of reality and selective representations of some features of a system. These models are often used to explain a specific relationship, predict a limited variable, or analyze a defined situation. They are usually highly dependent on initial assumptions, fixed structures, and pre-collected data. Although these models have been widely used in engineering and statistical analysis, they face serious limitations when dealing with open, dynamic, and multilayered systems. Especially when the goal is to analyze system behavior under unstable conditions or in the presence of complex human and environmental interactions, conventional models often lack the power to represent reality. Simulations go beyond traditional models by allowing the reconstruction of a system's behavior under specific conditions or scenarios. The fundamental difference between a digital twin and a simulation becomes apparent at this point. A digital twin is not simply an environment for recreating a possible scenario, but a system that is constantly communicating with its physical counterpart.

- **Purpose & "What-If" vs. "What Is":** Simulations are designed to test potential, hypothetical scenarios to understand what could happen. Digital twins are designed to show what is happening in real time and, combined with AI, what will happen next.

Another important difference is that traditional models and many simulations are typically designed to answer a specific question, whereas a digital twin can address a set of interrelated questions. In fact, a digital twin is a multidimensional framework that can simultaneously integrate spatial, temporal, network, behavioral, and infrastructure data. This capability allows analysis to go beyond describing a single variable or representing a single situation to a deeper understanding of the overall system performance, its interdependencies, and the potential consequences of planning decisions.

In the field of transportation, these differences become even more important, as transportation systems are among the most complex urban systems. The performance of these systems depends not only on the physical characteristics of the network, but also on user behavior, demand fluctuations, environmental conditions, management interventions and time evolution. Traditional models may capture some of these relationships, and simulations can reconstruct scenarios. Nonetheless, the digital twin allows these factors to be analyzed simultaneously, dynamically, and in relation to the existing reality. Considering these factors, this technology has found a privileged position in urban transportation, especially in future smart systems.

The performance of transportation systems is highly dependent on user behavior. Users in a transportation network do not always move according to simple, predefined assumptions; rather, their decisions are influenced by perceptions of safety, experience, congestion, route quality, weather conditions, social conditions, and even features of the built environment. For example, a driver may change his or her route in response to traffic congestion, a cyclist may avoid a crossing because it is unsafe, and a pedestrian may exhibit a different crossing pattern than that predicted in the formal design in the absence of appropriate infrastructure. This behavioral heterogeneity transforms transportation analysis from a purely technical problem to a behavioral-spatial one. In addition to user behavior, demand fluctuations also significantly affect network performance. The intensity of travel flows can change dramatically at different times of day, on different days of the week, in different seasons, or during special events.

The digital twin becomes important precisely in response to these limitations. This technology allows various factors affecting the performance of the transportation system, including network structure, user behavior, demand changes, environmental conditions, and management interventions, to be analyzed simultaneously and in relation to the network's actual state. The importance of this technology will be even greater in future smart systems. With the proliferation of connected transport, autonomous vehicles, urban sensors, smart infrastructure and continuous data, the need for frameworks that can handle this amount of complexity is increasing. The delay increases. The capacity for continuous synchronization between the physical system and the digital model is one of the main distinguishing innovation features of the digital twin. This synchronization allows the digital model to understand not only the past or a hypothetical state, but also the system's "present". Thus, real-time or near-real-time changes, such as traffic flow shifts, infrastructure disruptions, changes in user behavior, or the emergence of critical conditions, can be reflected in the model. This capability enables time-sensitive decision-making and faster responses to changing conditions, a capability typically absent in traditional models.

Digital twins can learn from the system's behavior and adapt to emerging conditions by receiving new data, reviewing the system's state, and combining this with advanced analysis methods. This feature is especially valuable when the digital twin is combined with artificial intelligence, machine learning, and predictive analytics, as it transforms from a mere analytical tool into an adaptable knowledge infrastructure. At the same time, the digital twin is not a complete replacement for all models and simulations, simply because of its greater complexity. Each of these tools can have its own specific role, depending on the research or decision-making objective. Traditional models are still useful for simplifying and understanding the underlying relationships, and simulations are useful for Controlled simulations of specific scenarios. Nonetheless, when the goal is to analyze open, complex, and changing systems comprehensively, the digital twin has a clear advantage, as it can integrate these tools into a dynamic, data-driven, and reality-based framework.

3.3 Core Layers of a Transportation Digital Twin

Digital twin can reduce the gap between the system's actual state and theoretical analyses and provide a platform for continuously using real data to update models and improve analysis accuracy. This feature makes the digital twin a suitable tool for analyzing systems whose performance is highly dependent on time, behavior, and environmental conditions. This complex design enables simulated research on user behavior, infrastructure performance, and policy consequences, particularly in complex systems such as urban transportation. Digital twins' performance in these areas has proven their worth as decision-support systems that can combine real-time data with sophisticated analytical models, in addition to being useful for simulations (Mun & Jung, 2025).

The multifaceted character of digital twins sets them apart. The physical layer (the actual system), the data layer (which contains spatial, temporal, and functional data), the modeling layer (which contains analytical techniques and models), and the decision layer are the four layers that typically make up a digital twin. By planning interventions and modelling disruption scenarios, digital twins can reduce uncertainty and decision-making risk in urban transportation. For instance, the impact of infrastructure changes, traffic restrictions, or specific weather conditions on the performance of the transport network, service levels, and user safety can be systematically assessed. This makes the twin appropriate for spatiotemporal diagnosis and "what-if" testing in intricate, multi-actor urban systems (Kušić et al., 2023).

One of the most important features of a transport digital twin is its multi-layered structure. This structure reduces the gap between the system's actual state and theoretical analyses and provides a platform for continuously updating models based on real data. This feature makes the digital twin a suitable tool for analyzing systems whose performance is highly dependent on time, behavior, and environmental conditions.

In transport digital twins, several main layers usually interact with each other. First, there is the physical or infrastructure layer, which includes the actual components of the transport system, such as roads, bridges, tunnels, intersections, public transport lines, bicycle paths, sidewalks, traffic lights, and other physical equipment. This layer provides the spatial and functional basis for the system, since any digital analysis must ultimately be linked to the infrastructure's actual characteristics and the network's spatial organization.

The second layer is the data layer, which plays a vital role in keeping the digital twin alive and dynamic. This layer includes data from sensors, intelligent transportation systems, GPS and GNSS, cameras, city databases, meteorological data, accident data, land-use data, and user behavioral data. The richer, more accurate, and more up-to-date this layer is, the greater the analytical power of the entire system will be.

The third layer is the data integration and synchronization layer. This layer is responsible for transforming scattered, heterogeneous information sources into integrated, usable inputs for analysis. One of the main differences between digital twins and traditional models lies precisely in their ability to integrate. Without this layer, data would be a collection of separate pieces of information and could not be systematically interpreted.

The fourth layer is the digital modelling and representation layer. At this level, raw data and synchronized information are transformed into analytical models, spatial representations, network models, and interpretable representations. This layer is what distinguishes a digital twin from a mere data warehouse. Here, the transportation network is reconstructed as an observable, analyzable, and scenario-able system.

The fifth layer is the behavioral layer, which is fundamental, especially in human-centered approaches. The performance of the network depends not only on the physical elements but also on user behavior, travel patterns, reactions to disruptions, route selection, safety perceptions, and interactions among different user groups. This layer attempts to incorporate the actual or likely behavior of drivers, pedestrians, cyclists, and public transportation users into the model. Without this layer, transportation analysis is reduced to a purely infrastructure model.

In addition to these layers, the intelligent transportation framework also includes the communication and real-time data layer. This layer includes systems that continuously transfer information from the real world to the digital twin and, in some cases, from the digital twin to operational systems. Such communication creates a continuous feedback loop that underpins adaptive, data-driven management.

In human-centric digital twins, the user experience and safety perception layer can also be considered as a key dimension. Many transportation assessments focus solely on quantitative indicators. At the same time, the actual user experience, feelings of safety, ease of use, travel stress, and the predictability of the space also play a decisive role in the quality of system performance. This is especially important for vulnerable road users, who are more affected than others by the perceived quality of the space and local network conditions.

Importantly, these layers should not be considered as completely separate components; rather, they should be considered as parts of an interconnected structure. The true power of the digital twin is revealed when these layers interact. For example, changes in environmental conditions can affect user behavior, which in turn can affect network performance, and this performance is ultimately reflected in management and policy decisions. It is this connection between layers that makes the digital twin an effective tool for analyzing complex systems.

In the field of road safety, such a layered structure is particularly important because safety is a multidimensional concept. Infrastructure design, driver behavior, environmental conditions, the presence or absence of protective equipment, flow management, and user reactions to different conditions all contribute to shaping safety. If only one of these dimensions is analyzed, the resulting picture will be incomplete. In contrast, the digital twin, by organizing these dimensions into interrelated layers, enables a more comprehensive and actionable analysis of safety.

At a strategic level, these layers collectively create a knowledge infrastructure for urban decision-making. Each layer represents a part of reality, but the real value lies in combining them to provide a coherent picture of the system. In this case, the digital twin can reduce the gap between the network's actual state and theoretical analyses, providing a platform for data-driven decision-making informed by evidence and future scenarios.

3.4 The Transition to Human-Centric Digital Twins and Their Connection to the Future of Autonomous Transportation

In recent years, digital twins have been used alongside infrastructure-based models that have encompassed comprehensive frameworks for analyzing transportation systems at different scales. Instead, there is a need for an approach that also includes users, behaviors, encounter patterns, environmental conditions, and temporal dynamics in the analysis. From this perspective, the transition from infrastructure-based to human-centric digital twins is a fundamental development in the evolution of intelligent transportation knowledge.

In early approaches, the digital twin was mainly considered a digital representation of the physical network; a network whose performance was analyzed in terms of traffic flow, road capacity, and infrastructure conditions. While this approach was important for technical network management, it could not fully explain users' experience or the differences across user groups. This necessitates, it gradually became clear that, better to understand safety, resilience, and equity in transportation, digital twins should not only reflect the infrastructure but also the relationship between infrastructure and humans.

The human-centered digital twin is based on the principle that the transportation system is not simply a collection of physical elements, but a living, interactive environment in which users with diverse needs, constraints, and behavioral patterns coexist. In this approach, users are not merely passive consumers of the network, but recognized as part of the system's operating mechanism. This perspective is particularly important in urban environments, where the quality of transportation depends heavily on how pedestrians, cyclists, public transport users, and drivers experience the space.

The multi-layered framework of the digital twin of transportation in this context enables a more comprehensive understanding of the system's behavior. This framework is usually composed of several interconnected layers, starting with the physical system and extending to data collection, modelling, simulation and finally decision-making. The importance of this layered structure is that each layer represents a part of reality, and the real value emerges when there is continuous exchange of data and feedback between layers. This leads to, the digital twin becomes a dynamic platform for observation, analysis and intervention.

The first layer in this framework is the physical transportation system, which includes the actual infrastructure, traffic flow, smart equipment, operational areas and field conditions. This layer provides the objective basis for network performance, and any digital analytics must ultimately connect to this layer. Nonetheless, if the analysis stops at this level, only an incomplete picture of the system will be obtained. What sets the digital twin apart is its ability to go beyond this level and connect it to dynamic data, behaviors, and scenarios.

The second layer is the data collection and measurement layer, which plays a central role in keeping the digital twin alive. In this layer, traffic, location, video, GNSS, environmental, and other performance data are collected continuously or in near real time. This data stream enables the digital twin to provide not only a picture of the network's historical or hypothetical state, but also a reflection of its current conditions and a simulation of the real world.

The third layer is the digital twin and simulation layer, where raw data is transformed into analytical models, digital representations, and operational scenarios. In this layer, traffic conditions, incidents, disruptions, demand changes, and network management scenarios can be modelled and analyzed. The importance of this section is that it transforms the digital twin from a mere monitoring system to a predictive and comparative analysis environment. In this way, the system not only shows what is, but also reveals what may happen.

The fourth layer is the decision support and control layer, which translates simulation and analysis results into operational, policy, or management actions. At this level, the model outputs can be used for traffic control, emergency response, safety interventions, flow rerouting, and city policy modification. This layer shows that the digital twin is not just an analytical tool, but can also be part of the network's operational and management mechanism. Therefore, the value of the digital twin lies not only in its representation but also in its ability to guide action.

A key feature of this architecture is the two-way data flow between the layers. These flows allow the system to operate as a continuous feedback loop; that is, real-world data enters the model, the model performs analysis and prediction, and the results can be applied again in operational or management decisions. This loop forms the basis for adaptive, data-driven management, allowing the transportation system to respond faster, more accurately, and more intelligently to changing conditions.

One of the key consequences of this convergence is the transition from static to dynamic and up-to-date models. From an analytical perspective, combining spatial, temporal, operational, and behavioral data within the digital twin framework opens new horizons for understanding the network's complexity. Such a combination allows researchers and planners to see not only the spatial distribution of flows but also to analyze temporal changes, user reactions, and the impact of environmental conditions on network performance. In this way, the digital twin goes beyond the level of a technical model and becomes a multidimensional analytical system that can also reveal the more hidden dimensions of the transport reality.

In this regard, the human-centered approach becomes particularly important. Urban transport can only be properly understood when users' behavior and experience are included in the analysis. Different users, whether pedestrians, cyclists, drivers, older adults or children, experience the network in different ways, and their level of risk exposure is not the same. The human-centric digital twin does not ignore these differences; rather, it considers them part of the data and the system's analytical logic. This is particularly important for the analysis of transport safety and justice.

The relevance of this framework to the future of autonomous transport is also very important. Autonomous and connected systems in the future will not only require smart infrastructure but also analytical platforms capable of predicting network behavior under complex, mixed, and changing conditions. Digital twins can provide an environment in which the interactions among autonomous vehicles, conventional vehicles, vulnerable users, and smart infrastructure are analyzed in a scenario-based manner. This capability is essential for designing a safer, more technologically adaptable future.

One of the major benefits of digital twins in this context is the ability to calibrate simulation models with real-world data. When traffic and behavioral models are tuned to field data, different scenarios can be tested in conditions much closer to reality. This allows the effects of infrastructure interventions, management policies, or behavioral changes to be assessed before implementation. Thus, decision-making risk is reduced and the likelihood of choosing more effective solutions increases.

In the context of future autonomous mobility, this capability becomes doubly important, as design or policy errors in such systems can have wider consequences than in traditional systems. On the other hand, integrating the Internet of Things and connected data streams enables synchronization between the digital model and the physical system. When sensors, cameras, positioning systems, connected vehicles, and smart devices are integrated into a coherent data network, the digital twin can provide a more accurate representation of reality and, in this way, become a more effective tool for analysis and intervention.

At a conceptual level, the digital twin should be considered more than just a simulation tool. This technology is a multi-layered analytical framework that links the physical, data, modelling, and decision layers. It is this multi-layered structure that makes it suitable for complex urban transportation and highway engineering problems. The more coherent, data-driven, and human-centered these layers are designed, the greater the digital twin's ability to support safety, resilience, and sustainability will be.

Figure 3. Multi-layer digital twin framework for resilient transportation systems (Author's own illustration)

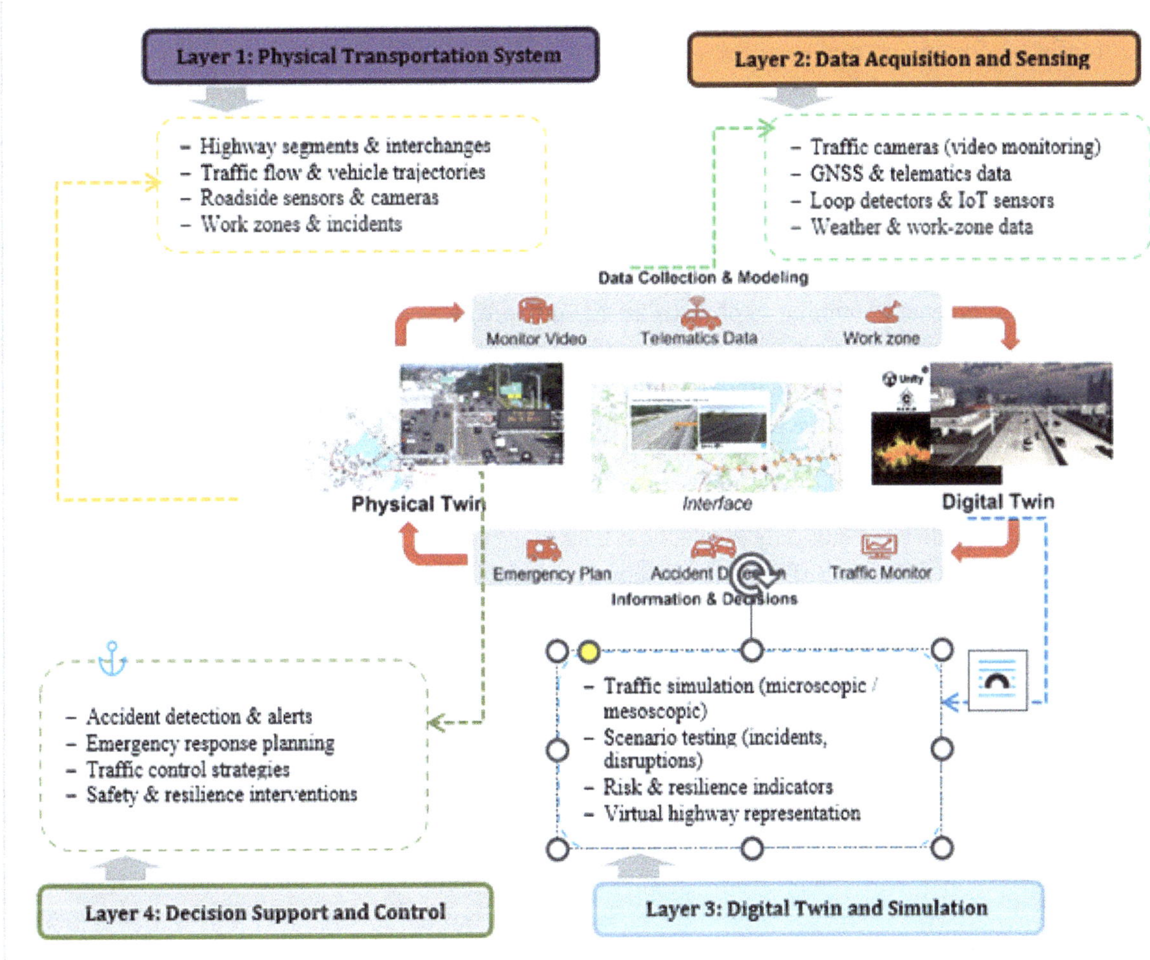

The framework illustrates four interconnected layers: (1) the physical transportation system, including highway infrastructure, traffic flow, sensors, and work zones; (2) the data acquisition and sensing layer, which collects real-time traffic, GNSS, video, and environmental data; (3) the digital twin and simulation layer, where traffic conditions, incidents, and disruption scenarios are modeled and analyzed; and (4) the decision support and control layer, which translates simulation outputs into operational actions such as traffic control, emergency response, and safety interventions. Bidirectional data flows between layers enables a continuous feedback loop, supporting adaptive, data-driven, and resilience-oriented transportation management (Figure 3).

In urban environments, this importance becomes even more pronounced when the city is seen as an open, dynamic, and human-centered network. The city is not simply a place for vehicles to move, but also a space for living, social interaction, access, and the presence of different user groups. In light of this, any analytical framework that wants to be useful for the future of urban transportation must recognize this multiplicity. Human-centered digital twins play a key role precisely because they can connect technology with the city's social and spatial realities.

This framework also provides a fundamental basis for operationalizing concepts such as resilience, safety, and sustainability. Many of these concepts are rich in theory, but to become operational strategies, they need tools that can make them measurable and testable in practice. Digital twins provide this opportunity by combining real-time data, simulating and analyzing user behavior, and evaluating the consequences of decisions. In this way, they become a platform for transforming theoretical knowledge into practical intervention.

From a strategic perspective, digital twins bridge traditional engineering, new technologies, and resilient approaches to transportation planning. On the one hand, they rely on the technical and infrastructural foundations of engineering, and on the other, they apply the capabilities of data science, the Internet of Things, predictive analytics, and behavioral modelling. This combination enables a transition from reactive, segmented planning to proactive planning. provides evidence-based and ten-centered.

Ultimately, the transition from infrastructure-centric to human-centric digital twins should be seen as part of a larger transformation in understanding urban transportation, one in which technology is no longer used solely to optimize the network but also to protect people, reduce inequality, improve safety, and prepare for the future.

The use of digital twins' technology for urban transportation analysis has led to a better understanding of safe systems on the road, not only as physical networks but also as data-driven systems that can be observed in near real time. One of the key consequences of this convergence is the transition from static to dynamic, up-to-date models. In this way, digital twins become tools for continuous observation and adaptive systems.

The continuous synchronization between the physical system and the digital model is one of the key differentiators of digital twins compared to modelling from traffic sensors, cameras, positioning systems and smart devices that are continuously transmitted to the digital twin environment and reflect the current state of the network. From an analytical perspective, combining spatial, temporal, and operational data within the digital twin framework enables more advanced analytics.

To clarify the operational structure of the proposed framework, Figure 4 presents a layered human-centric digital twin architecture for transport systems. The figure illustrates how real-world transport conditions are translated into a digital environment through continuous data acquisition, integration, modeling, and scenario-based analysis. This architecture is intended to support the assessment of safety, resilience, and future autonomous mobility within a unified analytical framework.

Figure 4. Proposed human-centric digital twin architecture for road safety, resilience, and future autonomous mobility

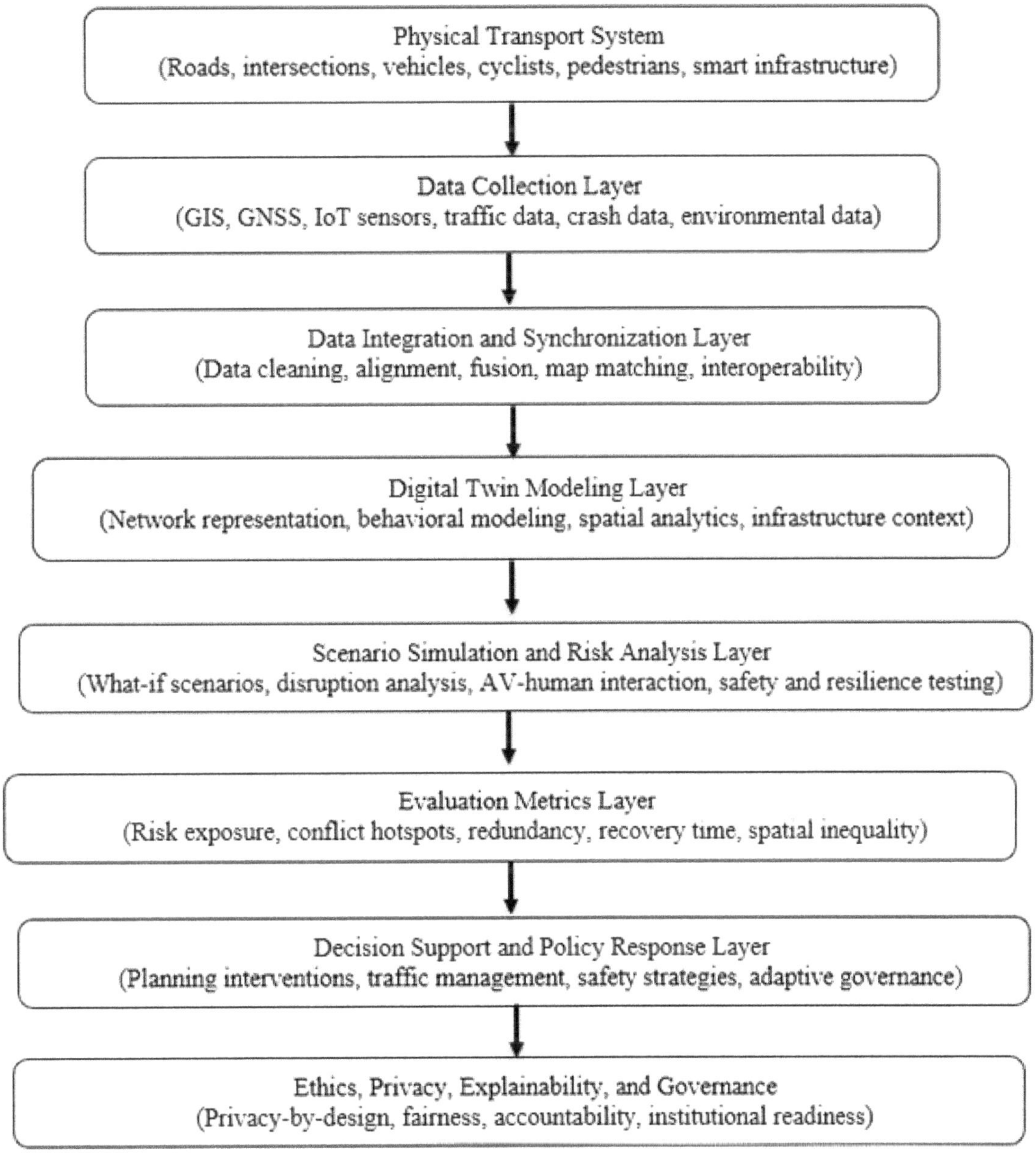

As shown in Table 2, the proposed framework follows a layered logic in which infrastructure conditions, user behavior, traffic operations, and environmental context are integrated within a dynamic digital model. In this structure, the digital twin is not limited to static representation; rather, it functions as a predictive and decision-support system capable of testing interventions, identifying emerging risks, and evaluating the implications of planning decisions before real-world implementation.

Table 2. Core layers and functional roles of the proposed human-centric transport digital twin

Layer	Main Components	Function in the Digital Twin	Contribution to Safety and Resilience Analysis
Physical Transport System	Roads, intersections, vehicles, cyclists, pedestrians, smart infrastructure	Represents the real-world transport environment	Provides the physical and operational basis for analysis
Data Collection Layer	GIS, GNSS, IoT sensors, crash data, traffic data, environmental data	Captures real-time and contextual information from multiple sources	Enables spatially explicit and behaviour-sensitive analysis
Data Integration and Synchronization Layer	Data cleaning, temporal alignment, spatial matching, interoperability	Integrates heterogeneous datasets into a unified structure	Improves analytical consistency and model reliability
Digital Twin Modelling Layer	Network models, behavioural models, spatial analytics, infrastructure representation	Creates the dynamic digital counterpart of the transport system	Supports the analysis of interactions between users, infrastructure, and risk conditions
Scenario Simulation and Risk Analysis Layer	What-if testing, disruption scenarios, AV-human interaction, safety simulations	Evaluates potential future conditions and intervention effects	Enables proactive assessment of hazards, vulnerability, and adaptive capacity
Evaluation Metrics Layer	Risk exposure, conflict hotspots, redundancy, recovery time, spatial inequality	Measures system performance under normal and disrupted conditions	Quantifies safety, resilience, and equity outcomes
Decision Support and Policy Response Layer	Planning strategies, traffic control, safety interventions, adaptive policies	Translates analytical outputs into actionable responses	Supports evidence-based planning and resilient transport governance
Cross-Cutting Governance Layer	Privacy, explainability, fairness, accountability, institutional readiness	Ensures responsible and ethical implementation	Strengthens public trust, transparency, and long-term deplorability

3.5 Emerging Issues, Challenges, and Trends in Transport Digital Twins

The development of digital twins in transportation systems, while offering vast opportunities to improve safety, efficiency, and resilience, also presents emerging challenges. One of the most important of these challenges is the technology's increasing dependence on real-time, multi-source data. To function effectively, digital twins require a continuous stream of data from sensors, positioning systems, cameras, and other digital infrastructure. This dependence has made issues such as data privacy, information security, and access management a fundamental concern in the design and implementation of these systems. Protecting personal information and preventing data misuse is even more important, especially in urban environments where user location and behavioral data are collected.

Another important challenge concerns the widespread use of artificial intelligence and data-driven models in digital twins. Although machine learning algorithms and predictive analytics play a key role in extracting patterns and optimizing system performance, these models may face problems such as algorithmic bias, lack of transparency, and excessive complexity. If the input data is not adequately representative of all user groups, the analysis results can lead to unfair decisions or even exacerbate spatial inequalities in the transportation system. Therefore, paying attention to concepts such as algorithmic fairness, explainability, and human oversight of decision-making processes has become essential to the development of digital twins.

In addition, integrating autonomous vehicles and intelligent transportation systems into the digital twin framework creates new challenges for modelling human-machine interaction. In a future where autonomous vehicles, human users, and smart infrastructure coexist in the network, predicting behaviors and interactions among these elements will become more complex. Many existing models still cannot accurately represent these interactions in real-world conditions. Therefore, developing frameworks that can realistically model user behavior, human responses, and mixed human-machine scenarios is a key challenge in this area.

On the other hand, emerging technological trends are also shaping the evolution of digital twins in transportation. Advances in edge computing, real-time data analytics, explainable artificial intelligence, and the integration of connected systems have enabled the development of more sophisticated and responsive digital twins. These technologies allow digital twins to process data with lower latency, respond to changes more quickly, and provide more accurate analytics across different spatial and temporal scales. In addition, the move towards "autonomous digital twins" capable of learning, adapting, and making independent decisions is considered an important future trend in this field.

Taken together, these challenges and trends show that digital twins are not just a technological tool, but part of a complex ecosystem that includes technology, data, people and policy. The success of these systems depends on the development of frameworks that address technical, social, and institutional issues simultaneously. From this perspective, attention to the dimensions of governance, data standardization, transparency, fairness and trustworthiness, alongside technological advances, will play a decisive role in the future of transport digital twins. These considerations highlight the need to move towards human-centered and evidence-based frameworks, which will be explored in the following sections of this chapter.

4. SPATIAL INTELLIGENCE: GIS, GNSS, AND MULTI-SOURCE DATA INTEGRATION

Spatial data and geographic information systems constitute the main infrastructure of urban transport digital twins. These tools enable the integration of diverse data, dynamic network analysis, and the assessment of different scenarios, and play a fundamental role in operationalizing the concept of resilience. Urban and highway transportation networks are inherently spatial-temporal phenomena whose performance depends on location, network structure, activity distributions, and user movement patterns. Therefore, without accurate, organized, and multiscale geographic data, any attempt to model, simulate, and assess the resilience of transportation systems will face severe limitations. In this framework, spatial data not only provides the physical representation of the network but also creates the necessary context for connecting non-spatial data including behavioral, temporal, and functional data to the urban space.

Geographic Information Systems (GIS), as the analytical core of spatial data, serve as the spatial backbone of digital twins. From a resilient planning perspective, combining GIS with digital twins enables the analysis of spatial inequalities, the identification of vulnerable areas, and the assessment of the exposure of different user groups to risk. Analysis of the spatial distribution of accidents, the quality of infrastructure and access to safe networks for pedestrians and vehicles can form the basis for designing human-centered and equitable interventions. To operationalize the concepts of safety, sustainability, and resilience in contemporary highway engineering and urban transportation planning, GIS serves as a link between data, analysis, and decision-making.

The application of digital twins for transport depends heavily on spatial data, one of the most essential elements of urban systems study. The performance of urban transport networks, which are intrinsically spatiotemporal phenomena, is influenced by user movement patterns, activity distribution, network structure, and location. Therefore, without precise, organized geographical data, any attempt to model, simulate, and evaluate the resilience of these systems would be severely limited. In a Geographic Information System (GIS), data such as GNSS and buffer are defined as an area surrounding a spatial object, measured in units of distance or time. Analysis data road by map is one of the fundamental spatial operations in Geographic Information Systems (GIS), used for overlying analysis, proximity analysis, and querying both spatial and non-spatial data (Moumane et al., 2025).

GIS tools extract geographical features from tabular data, and data can also be extracted to evaluate infrastructure conditions and environmental features around main routes. By using exclusively free and open-source tools, such as Quantum GIS as a Geographic Information System (GIS) platform, it is possible to simulate risk analysis and cyclist or vehicle data. This approach enables the simulation of exceptional events by connecting data from the desired area to GIS functions. They analyzed the risks, vulnerabilities, and exposures related to these events. Developing a future vision for safe roads utilizing contemporary spatial planning approaches is essential for accurate data and realistic simulations. Using data, location-allocation models, network analysis, and GIS technology can all assist in determining appropriate site locations. To provide fair and adequate coverage across the city, these technologies help analyze population density, historical incident data, traffic patterns, and road networks. Therefore, integrating human activity preferences, activity diversity, and environmental elements is essential for a comprehensive understanding of urban vitality. The use of GIS technology, combined with social media data and spatial statistics, enables the recording of environmental characteristics and behavioral patterns (Huang et al., 2026; Li et al., 2022).

4.1 GIS and Infrastructure Layers as the Spatial Foundation of Transportation Digital Twins

The shift of digital twins from a simple technological instrument to a conceptual and analytical framework for managing complex systems is the first essential aspect of comprehending them. Digital twins provide a platform for examining connections among infrastructure, consumers, and the urban environment by combining geographic, community, temporal, and behavioral information. This information integration enables more thorough analyses of general community performance, structural flaws, and interactions among various device add-ons. In this context, GIS technology is essential. As the spatial foundation of the virtual dual, GIS provides a platform for connecting non-spatial data to the city's spatial environment and facilitates the organization, assessment, and integration of spatial data. Network analysis, accessibility evaluation, critical point identification, and spatial inequality study at various urban scales are all made possible by this skill (Ma et al., 2021).

Geographic information systems, which integrate spatial, temporal, and functional data to provide a necessary platform for dynamic and resilient analysis of urban transportation systems, function as the analytical core of digital twins, as illustrated in Figure 5. The figure illustrates how spatial data, through the processes of collection, organization, processing, spatial statistical analysis, and advanced analytics, are transformed into an integrated digital model of the urban system. In this framework, GIS serves as a central platform that enables the integration of spatial, temporal, and functional data, representing them in the form of a dynamic digital twin. In recent years, the use of spatial data sources has played an important role in data processing in digital twins, and these data, such as OpenStreetMap and GIS spatial-temporal data, provide a realistic analysis of roads and user performance.

The figure illustrates GIS as the core spatial engine of the digital twin, supporting the collection, organization, processing, and analysis of heterogeneous transportation data. GIS data types include GNSS trajectories, traffic sensor data, road network topology, land-use layers, and accident records. Spatial processing techniques such as buffering, network analysis, and spatial statistics enable the identification of risk patterns and resilience indicators. Standardized color coding highlights the interaction between physical environments (green), digital and analytical components (blue), network flows (orange), and risk-related elements (red), ensuring visual consistency across the digital twin framework (Figure 5).

Infrastructure changes, new traffic policies or spatial developments in the city can be modelled in a GIS environment and their consequences on network performance assessed. This capability enables decision-makers to assess the effects of interventions on efficiency, safety, and resilience before implementing them. Open spatial data sources, in particular OpenStreetMap, have played an important role in expanding the use of GIS in transport digital twins. They provide up-to-date, accessible data on road networks, infrastructure, and the built environment that can serve as a basis for spatial modelling at the city scale. Combining this data with local information and sensor data increases the flexibility and scalability of digital twins.

From a decision-making perspective, GIS serves as an intermediary between data, analysis, and policymaking in the context of digital twins. The results of spatial and network analyses can be presented in the form of analytical maps, performance indicators and comparative scenarios that are understandable and applicable to urban decision-makers. This analytical transparency improves decision-making quality and reduces the risk of uncertainty.

Figure 5. Integration of Geographic Information Systems (GIS) within a transportation digital twin framework

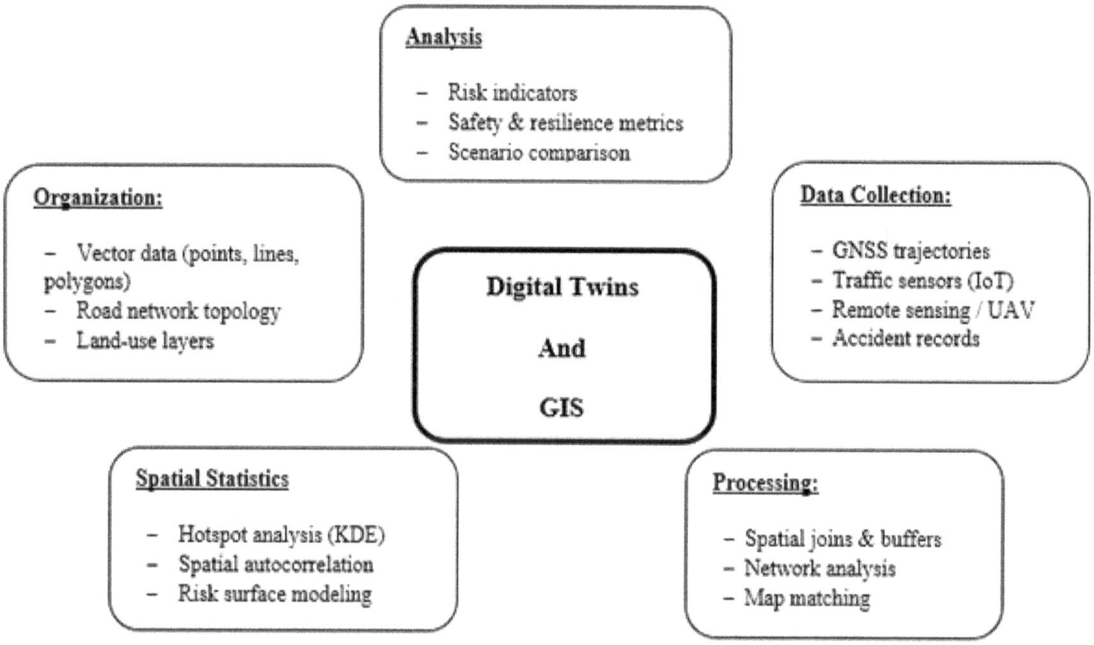

The importance of GIS in this area stems from the fact that transportation systems are inherently spatial. Each route, intersection, station, traffic node, or functional area not only has a specific geographic location, but also makes sense in relation to other network components. A transportation digital twin can provide an accurate and functional picture of the real system, accurately identifying and representing these spatial relationships. GIS provides this capability by defining network topology, adjacency relationships, spatial hierarchies, and spatial analytical structures. From this perspective, GIS is not just a tool for mapping, but also an infrastructure for understanding the spatiality of the transportation system (de Albuquerque Damasceno et al., 2025).

At a conceptual level, GIS acts as an intermediary between raw data and meaningful spatial interpretation. In many transportation systems, data is generated from a variety of sources, but unless it is placed in an appropriate geographic context, it has limited analytical capabilities. GIS organizes this data into spatial layers, allowing infrastructure, traffic, environmental, and behavioral data to be linked. Ultimately, the digital twin can be transformed from a sparse dataset into a coherent analytical environment that reveals relationships among location, time, and performance. One of the fundamental functions of GIS in transportation digital twins is to manage the infrastructure layers. The road network, public transportation lines, intersections, bridges, tunnels, bike paths, sidewalks, traffic control equipment, and other physical elements of the city must be defined in accurate, consistent spatial layers. These layers form the basis for the physical representation of the transportation system, and any advanced analysis of the network's safety, resilience, or efficiency depends on their quality and accuracy. Through its layered structure, GIS allows each of these elements to be analyzed independently and simultaneously with the others (Wijesinghe & Withanage, 2025).

In the meantime, OpenStreetMap, as one of the key data sources, has found a special place in the development of transportation digital twins. This open and collaborative database provides extensive information about the road network, types of roads, intersections, related uses, cyclist paths, sidewalks, barriers and many other elements. The importance of OpenStreetMap is that it enables fast, flexible and scalable access to infrastructure data in many urban studies and projects. Although this data requires quality assessment and, in some cases, refinement, it is used as an efficient basis for the spatial structure of the digital twin in many applications (OpenStreetMap contributors, n.d.; Felício et al., 2022).

The role of OpenStreetMap in digital twins becomes increasingly prominent when the goal is to model complex, multi-layered urban environments. This data source can help a researcher or planner quickly extract the initial layers of a transportation network and then supplement them with local, sensor, or management data. Such a capability is especially valuable for cities where complete or standardized official data is not available. In this way, GIS and OpenStreetMap together provide a basic platform for the formation of transportation digital twins (Tang et al., 2026).

Sensor data, combined with GIS, provides a better understanding of the network's temporal dynamics. This is very important for safety analysis, disaster management, and adaptive planning, as it shows that a fixed location can have different behaviors and risks at different times. In addition to the network and sensor layers, land-use data also forms an important part of the spatial foundation of transportation digital twins. Residential, commercial, educational, healthcare, industrial, and recreational uses directly impact travel patterns, demand intensity, user types, and risk exposure levels (Feizizadeh & Omar Zadeh, 2025).

One of the important advantages of GIS in transportation digital twins is the ability to overlap and integrate different layers. When the road layer, land use, sensor data, environmental data, and user information are placed in a common spatial environment, deeper and multivariate analyses are possible. For instance, it is possible to examine which types of roads are associated with the highest levels of risk or disruption, and which types of uses are located in their vicinity, or how spatial and environmental characteristics affect user behavior and network safety. This analytical power is one of the main reasons why GIS is important in the context of digital twins. GIS enables the identification of accident locations, congestion points, areas of limited visibility, high-risk routes for vulnerable users and areas lacking safe infrastructure. Building on this capacity, the transport digital twin can analyze safety not only at the global level but also at the local scale, based on spatial context. This is particularly important for vulnerable road users. Pedestrians, cyclists, and users of light electric vehicles are more affected by local environmental quality than other groups. The width of the sidewalk, the continuity of the path, the presence of safe intersections, lighting, obstacles, the surrounding land use and the intensity of traffic all affect the experience and safety of these groups. By recording and analyzing these features at a local scale, GIS provides the foundation for developing human-centered digital twins that can incorporate the diverse experiences of user groups into their analysis.

In the context of intelligent transportation, GIS plays a key role in connecting static and dynamic data. Static data, such as network structure, passage type, or equipment location, is not sufficient for intelligent management alone. Conversely, dynamic data such as traffic flow, speed or instantaneous disturbances cannot be interpreted without an appropriate spatial context. GIS connects these two types of data and provides the necessary context to form a digital twin that represents both structure and function simultaneously. This capability is of great importance in complex and densely populated cities. From the perspective of transport resilience, GIS also plays a fundamental role. A transportation digital twin, when developed on a GIS basis, can show which parts of the network are most vulnerable to climate disruptions, accidents, or blockages, and which areas are most important for maintaining access and performance in critical situations (Kazem pour et al., 2025; ElNawawy et al., 2024).

Another important aspect of GIS in this context is the possibility of hierarchical and multi-scale analysis. The transportation system can be examined at different levels, from a single intersection or street to the entire urban or regional network. GIS enables data and analysis to be organized at different scales and to reveal relationships between the local and macro levels. This feature is very important for digital twins because many management decisions are made at one scale, but their consequences appear at other scales.

Nonetheless, these same challenges also present an opportunity to develop more advanced data integration methods. Using GIS alongside machine learning, network analysis, spatiotemporal data processing, and cross-validation of sources can increase the accuracy and reliability of digital twins. In fact, the more data can be integrated and refined within a GIS, the more realistic and decision-supportive digital twins can be built. From this perspective, GIS is not just an existing tool, but also a platform for methodological innovation in future transportation.

In the field of urban planning, GIS and infrastructure layers also help to improve transparency in decision-making. When different information about the network, environment, users and risk points is presented in the form of visible and analytical layers, urban planners and managers can make their decisions based on clearer spatial evidence. This transparency is essential for prioritizing interventions, allocating resources, designing safety projects and evaluating policies. As a result, GIS is not only an analysis tool, but also a governance tool.

In the case of future autonomous transportation, the importance of GIS increases even more. Autonomous and connected systems require a precise understanding of the environment, network, spatial context and changing conditions. Digital twins, which are supposed to serve as the basis for analyzing this future, cannot be realized without an infrastructure. A powerful location cannot function properly. GIS provides the necessary environment for organizing data from roads, sensors, users, smart devices, and interactive scenarios, thereby becoming one of the main foundations for the future of intelligent transportation.

Key Contributions of GIS to Transportation Digital Twins

- **Spatial Foundation and Context:** GIS integrates 3D, 2D, and 4D data to provide a precise spatial context (as-is condition) for fixed infrastructure assets.
- **Data Integration and Interoperability:** GIS serves as a hub for connecting disparate datasets, including IoT sensor data, BIM (Building Information Modelling), reality capture (point clouds/meshes), and traffic models.
- **Safety and Traffic Analytics:** By utilizing spatial analytics, digital twins built on GIS can identify accident hotspots and simulate traffic conditions.
- **Human-Centered Design:** By visualizing infrastructure in 3D and simulating scenarios, GIS helps create more "forgiving," resilient, and human-centric infrastructure that considers vulnerable road users (VRUs).
- **Real-time Decision-making:** GIS-based twins enable real-time monitoring of infrastructure performance, enabling immediate, intelligent decision-making and predictive maintenance.

By leveraging GIS in this framework, transportation planning shifts from static mapping to dynamic, predictive systems that enhance safety and operational intelligence. In light of these considerations, GIS and infrastructure layers can be considered the spatial foundation of transportation digital twins; a foundation that enables the linking of the physical world, multi-source data, spatial analytics, and intelligent decision-making. OpenStreetMap, sensor data, road network, land use, environmental layers, and other spatial components all make sense in this framework and are transformed into a coherent analytical structure through GIS. Accordingly, in this chapter "Human-Centered Digital Twins for Road Safety and Future Autonomous Transportation," GIS should be considered not only as a technical tool, but also as a theoretical and practical foundation for building safe, resilient, data-driven, and human-centered digital twins.

4.2 GNSS data, user behavior and spatial-network analytics

GNSS data has become a key source for understanding user behavior in transportation systems in recent years. It allows recording actual movement paths, speed changes, stops, route selection patterns and how users interact with the transportation environment. Compared to traditional aggregated or static data, GNSS tracks provide a more vivid and realistic picture of the network's daily operations. On this basis, in the context of transportation digital twins, these data play an important role in linking the actual movement of users and the analytical representation of the system. The importance of GNSS data stems from the fact that transportation systems are not only composed of physical infrastructure but also depend directly on user behavior. Users do not always follow engineered patterns or the assumptions of classical models in different situations. GNSS provides an empirical foundation for the development of human-centered digital twins.

One important feature of GNSS routes is that they provide spatiotemporal data. This means that not only the user's location, but also the time of their presence in each part of the network can be recorded and analyzed. In the context of road safety, GNSS data are particularly important for analyzing the behavior of vulnerable road users. Pedestrians, cyclists, and users of light electric vehicles tend to have more flexible movement patterns and, at the same time, are more sensitive to their surroundings. The actual paths these groups take indicate which spaces are more attractive, safer, or more usable to them, and which parts of the network they avoid. This information is invaluable for identifying areas of poor quality, high-risk spaces, and infrastructure deficiencies.

From a methodological perspective, GNSS data only become meaningful when placed in the context of spatial analysis. The recorded points alone are just a set of coordinates, but when interpreted in the context of GIS and network analysis, they become valuable behavioral and spatial information. This process involves cleaning the data, matching the paths to the real network, correcting spatial errors, and extracting movement patterns. Thus, GNSS analysis requires close linkage with spatial and network tools (Munoz Diaz et al., 2023).

One of the most important applications of these data is route choice analysis. Users in a transport network do not always choose the shortest route. Nonetheless, their decisions can be influenced by the quality of the infrastructure, perceived safety, the presence of obstacles, traffic volume, lighting, slope, and the attractiveness of the environment. GNSS data allow the researcher to compare these actual choices with the network structure and understand why some routes are preferred and others are less used. This type of analysis is fundamental to human-centered transport planning. Spatial network analysis plays a complementary and, at the same time, decisive role in this field. When GNSS routes are superimposed on the real transport network, the relationships between user movements and the network structure can be examined. To illustrate, it is possible to measure which types of nodes or links are most frequently used, which sections cause deviations from direct routes, and at which points the probability of conflicts or unintended stops is highest. These analyses show that user behavior is always shaped by interaction with the network's spatial structure.

One of the basic tools in this type of analysis is buffer analysis. By creating buffers around GNSS routes or infrastructure elements, it is possible to quantify users' exposure to environmental features and potential hazards. This is exemplified by buffers can be used to analyze distances from intersections, special uses, physical obstacles, traffic signs, or sources of danger. This method is particularly useful when the purpose is to measure the extent of users' exposure to specific environmental conditions or to examine the influence of contextual factors on their behavior. Network analysis is also a fundamental pillar of this section. When analyzed within the network context, GNSS data enables the identification of indicators such as centrality, accessibility, connectivity, critical nodes, and high-traffic routes. In transportation digital twins, such analyses are crucial for predicting the consequences of disruptions, designing interventions, and identifying vulnerable points (Dempsey, n.d.).

Another important method is hotspot detection. Through this analysis, it is possible to identify areas where high traffic density, stops, conflicts, or high-risk events are concentrated. If GNSS data are combined with accident data, environmental conditions, or infrastructure characteristics, these hotspots can provide a much more accurate picture of critical areas of the network. Accordingly, hotspot detection becomes an effective tool for prioritizing safety interventions and local planning. In urban environments, hotspot analysis is particularly important. Because many transportation problems occur at a local scale and at a few key points, a specific intersection, a narrow section of bike path, an area with high pedestrian density, or a location with reduced visibility can have a much greater impact than what is seen in the overall network indicators. GNSS data can reveal sensitive locations through actual user behavior. Given this context, these data are very useful for micro-spatial analysis of network safety and efficiency (Park et al., 2025; Bisht & Tiwari, 2023).

In transportation digital twins, GNSS data is most valuable when combined with multi-source data. When movement paths are combined with OpenStreetMap data, sensor data, land-use information, weather data, and accident information, a deeper picture of the relationships among behavior, space, and risk can be obtained. This combination allows the digital twin to analyze not only user movement but also the contexts that shape it. Thus, the system is transformed from a descriptive tool to an explanatory framework. In the context of transportation resilience, GNSS data is an important tool for understanding network behavior under disruption. When a disruption occurs, such as a road closure, an accident, a climate event, or a sudden increase in demand, users may change their movement patterns. GNSS data can record these changes and show how the network is behaviorally responding to the crisis. This information is crucial for designing alternative routes, strengthening adaptive capacity, and improving emergency response. GNSS data will also play an important role in future autonomous transportation.

For autonomous systems to safely interact with human users in complex urban environments, they need models that accurately represent real-world user behavior. GNSS data can serve as a basis for this behavioral modelling, revealing how users make decisions in real-world situations, the spaces they traverse, and how they respond to different conditions. This knowledge is essential for developing safer scenarios in complex environments. At the same time, using GNSS data also poses challenges. Common problems include spatial errors, signal interruptions, differences in device accuracy, data gaps in some areas, and difficulty matching routes to the actual network. In addition, analyzing this data requires substantial processing, refinement, and careful interpretation. These challenges demonstrate that GNSS, while a valuable resource, cannot be used as a stand-alone analysis tool without a coherent methodology and complementary tools. Despite these challenges, the analytical opportunities of GNSS data are vast. These data allow transportation models to move beyond a generalized, hypothetical state towards a more realistic representation of user behavior. This feature also brings safety, spatial justice, network efficiency, and resilience analyses closer to reality. Hence, GNSS can be considered a key resource for transitioning from planning based on average assumptions to planning based on behavioral evidence.

From a planning perspective, GNSS data and spatial network analyses can help make more accurate, targeted decisions. Based on these analyses, policymakers can identify which routes need redesign, which intersections have the most conflicts, which points are unsafe for vulnerable users, and where infrastructure or management interventions will have the greatest impact. This is especially important for prioritizing actions in cities with limited resources. In conclusion, GNSS data and spatial network analyses should be considered among the main foundations of human-centered transportation digital twins. These data allow for more accurate and dynamic analysis of users' actual movement, spatial experience, and interactions with infrastructure and the environment.

4.3 Challenges and Opportunities of Multi-Source Data Integration in Transport Digital Twins

Multi-source data integration is one of the most fundamental prerequisites for developing transport digital twins, as this technology can only provide a realistic, dynamic, and analytical picture of the transport system if it can bring heterogeneous data together into a single framework. Urban transport systems simultaneously generate data from physical infrastructure, smart sensors, GNSS routes, geographic databases, environmental data, behavioral data, management data and information related to incidents and accidents. Each of these sources represents a part of reality, but none alone is sufficient to interpret network behavior comprehensively. Hence, data integration is at the heart of digital twins.

One of the main opportunities of multi-source data integration is the ability to move from single-dimensional to multi-layered and contextual analyses. In traditional approaches, data is often analyzed in isolation; for instance, traffic data is analyzed separately from spatial data, and behavioral data is analyzed separately from infrastructure data. Such separation makes it difficult to understand the complex relationships between system components. In contrast, when different data are integrated into a common analytical environment, the relationships among spatial design, user behavior, flow intensity, environmental conditions, and hazardous events can be examined simultaneously.

In the context of digital twins, this integration is not only a technical issue but also a conceptual necessity. The digital twin is supposed to be a dynamic reflection of the real system, and this reflection will be valid only if it can accommodate different dimensions of reality. Infrastructure is incomplete without user behavior, behavior is uninterpretable without spatial context, and temporal data has limited meaning without a link to network performance or environmental conditions. Data integration here, therefore, means building an analytical whole from the scattered parts of reality.

One of the first challenges in this process is the heterogeneity of the data's structure. Transportation data differ fundamentally in terms of format, scale, accuracy, time periodicity, units of measurement, and production logic.

The second challenge is the difference in the spatial scale of the data. Some data are generated at the level of a specific intersection, street, or route, while others are available at a regional, city, or even regional scale. To illustrate, traffic sensor data may be point-based, while land use or climate data may cover a much larger area. If these scale differences are not properly managed, the resulting analyses can be subject to errors or inappropriate simplifications. Hence, designing a compatible spatial framework for data integration is essential.

The difference in time scale is another important challenge. Real-time, daily, periodic, and historical data all have their own rhythms and periodicities. In a digital twin, the goal is to combine these data in a way that both illuminates the current state of the network and allows for the exploration of past trends and future patterns. Nonetheless, synchronizing data generated at different time frequencies is not easy. This is especially important in dynamic transportation systems, where short-term changes can have significant consequences for performance and safety.

Data quality is also a crucial issue. Multi-source data are not always at the same level of accuracy, completeness, spatial and temporal precision, and reliability. Some data may have missing values, registration errors, noise, or structural biases. Along with these challenges, the scientific and practical opportunities of multi-source data fusion are vast. One of the most important of these opportunities is to increase the accuracy and richness of the representation of the transportation system.

Data integration also allows for the analysis of hidden relationships. Many patterns of Traffic and safety only become apparent when different data are put together. For instance, the relationship between traffic intensity, land use type, the presence of vulnerable users and the occurrence of accidents may not be identifiable in individual data. Despite this, it can be revealed by merging the relevant layers in a digital twin. This shows that the value of multi-source data lies not only in their diversity, but also in their ability to generate new knowledge.

From a road safety perspective, data integration helps achieve more accurate, targeted planning. When accident data, traffic patterns, network structure, infrastructure characteristics and environmental conditions are combined, a more comprehensive understanding of the context of risk generation can be achieved. In such a situation, the planner is no longer just concerned with the location of the accident but can also examine spatial-temporal patterns, effective environmental conditions, and the behaviors associated with the accident. This level of analysis shifts intervention from a general, reactive approach to a localized, preventive, and evidence-based approach.

In analyzing vulnerable road users, the importance of data integration becomes even greater. The behavior and safety of these groups depend on many factors: the quality of the space, traffic conditions, actual movement routes, surrounding uses, lighting, obstacles, and the presence of supporting infrastructure. No single data source can cover all these dimensions. Despite this, by integrating GNSS, GIS, sensor, and environmental data, a clearer picture of these users' experience can be obtained. This feature makes digital twins an important tool for equitable and human-centered transport planning.

From a resilience perspective, multi-source data integration also plays a key role. Transport disruptions are often the result of interactions among multiple factors: the state of the infrastructure, demand volume, weather conditions, user reactions, and the quality of network management. If these factors are analyzed separately, a complete understanding of the system's behavior in critical situations is not achieved. However, by integrating this data, a digital twin can show how disruptions in one layer propagate to other layers and which interventions can strengthen the network's capacity for absorption, adaptation, and recovery.

Data privacy and ethics are also of great importance in this sector. Multi-source data, especially when it includes movement routes, real-time data and behavioral information, can reveal sensitive and personal information. For this purpose, any data integration into digital twins must be accompanied by clear considerations of anonymization, data minimization, information security, and the protection of users' rights. Otherwise, the same technology that can lead to greater safety and efficiency may also raise serious ethical and social concerns.

From a planning perspective, multi-source data integration can significantly improve decision-making quality. When managers and planners have access to a more comprehensive picture of the network status, user behavior, vulnerabilities, and possible scenarios, they can design their interventions more accurately, more targeted, and with less risk. This is especially important in cities with limited resources, as it enables better project prioritization and more efficient resource allocation.

In conclusion, integrating multiple data sources simultaneously is both a major challenge and an opportunity in the development of transportation digital twins. Challenges such as structural heterogeneity, differences in scales, variable data quality, difficulty in validation, and issues of data governance and ethics demonstrate the complexity of this path. In contrast, opportunities such as more accurate system representation, deeper behavior and risk analysis, improved safety, enhanced resilience, and support for intelligent decision-making highlight the strategic importance of this integration.

5. DIGITAL TWINS FOR ROAD SAFETY AND FUTURE AUTONOMOUS MOBILITY

Digital twins can go beyond being mere technological or modelling tools and become a strategic framework for rethinking road safety and the future of transportation. In this framework, safety is no longer simply about reducing the number of accidents or controlling risks locally. However, it is considered a multidimensional quality that is linked to infrastructure design, user behavior, data flows, network dynamics, and the ability to predict future scenarios. In contemporary transportation environments, especially in cities, transportation networks are faced with conditions in which different users, diverse infrastructures, and emerging technologies interact simultaneously. This situation means that safety analysis and risk management rely solely on traditional models and overall network indicators. In contrast, digital twins, with their dynamic representation of the system, allow the real-world behavior of the network, potential conflicts, vulnerabilities, and the effects of various interventions to be examined before implementation. Consequently, this technology can become an important tool for transitioning from reactive decision-making to predictive, scenario-based planning. This is doubly important in the context of the future of autonomous transportation, as the arrival of connected cars, automated systems, and smart infrastructure will transform the nature of interaction in traffic environments. In such a situation, the main issue is not only technological development but also how humans, machines, and the built environment can coexist safely and equitably. Digital twins in this context can serve as an analytical testbed for evaluating scenarios of human-machine interaction, the behavior of vulnerable users, and the consequences of various policies and interventions before actual deployment. In this way, this technology becomes one of the key tools to prepare transport systems for a more complex and intelligent future.

The Role of Digital Twins in Enhancing Transport Resilience

Digital twins enhance resilience, the ability to continue operating during disruptions such as accidents, or disasters by providing a "living" virtual replica of physical assets (roads, bridges, vehicles, traffic lights).

- **Predictive Maintenance:** By analyzing real-time IoT sensor data on structural integrity (e.g., stress, vibration), digital twins can predict when infrastructure is likely to fail, enabling maintenance before failures occur.
- **Scenario Simulation & "What-If" Analysis:** Planners can test the impact of proposed changes (e.g., new bus lanes) or emergency scenarios (e.g., flooding of a key artery) in a virtual environment, allowing for the optimization of evacuation routes and traffic management.
- **Traffic Optimization:** Digital twins, such as those implemented by Transport for London (TfL), integrate real-time traffic data to manage congestion, optimize signaling, and improve overall flow, thereby reducing the impact of unforeseen disruptions.

From Visual Representations to Cohesive Analytical Frameworks

- **Data Integration (Physical to Digital):** Utilizing IoT sensors, 5G, and LIDAR to provide continuous, real-time data regarding the state of infrastructure and the movement of vehicles, pedestrians, and public transit.
- **Model Layer (Simulation and Analysis):** Integrating microscopic traffic simulation (e.g., SUMO) with vehicle dynamics and environmental factors (weather, lighting) to assess traffic safety. This goes beyond traditional models by accounting for realistic braking and acceleration.
- **Service Layer (Decision Support):** A, the final layer, provides actionable insights for users, such as traffic managers.

5.1 Digital Twins in Proactive Safety Planning

Digital twins of transportation are restricted to sophisticated databases or visual representations in the absence of cohesive analytical and modelling frameworks. Digital twins' capacity to combine data, modelling, simulation, and scenario analysis into a single framework makes them a valuable tool for enhancing the resilience of urban transport systems.

In recent research literature, digital twin modelling has been proposed as one of the main foundations for analyzing transport networks and their resilience. This framework enables the analysis of network structure and the identification of bottlenecks by modelling urban transport networks as graphs of nodes and edges, each with unique geometric, functional, and environmental characteristics. This type of modelling, using real data and continuous updates, not only improves the capacity for connectivity and accessibility analysis but can also predict the consequences of local disturbances on the overall system performance and plays a fundamental role in measuring network resilience. In this context, recent studies have emphasized that digital modelling can enhance stability and risk analysis by accurately representing the network structure and its behavior in the face of shocks. How does the transportation network change its performance under critical conditions? (Song et al., 2023).

One of the approaches considered in digital modelling is the flexibility and portability of the model, which helps to improve the efficiency and adaptability of digital twins. In traditional models, the design and implementation of models for each scenario is done separately, which makes the process time-consuming and expensive; however, modern research, especially in the field of Resilient Digital Twin Modelling, has shown that the use of portability approaches can quickly transfer the model from one scenario to another and improve analysis and response to environmental changes more quickly. These approaches, which utilize metamodels and unit representations of information, enhance the productivity and resilience of digital twin models (Irfan et al., 2024).

In addition to network structure, dynamic analysis of transport flows using network-based simulations is another important tool in digital twins for measuring resilience. Recent research in the field of transportation shows that network simulation can measure the distribution and spread of flows during sudden events. These analyses offer a deeper understanding of network behavior under uncertain conditions by applying sophisticated statistical techniques, data mining, and machine learning to network routes. The capacity of digital twins to conduct spatial-temporal analyses, which enable the spatial distribution of risk, temporal variations in network performance, and interactions between infrastructure and users, is one of their significant advantages in the transportation industry. Such analyses can identify patterns of incident distribution, high-risk areas, and critical times when the network experiences the most significant performance degradation (Dui et al., 2025).

Recent research has shown that spatiotemporal analytical frameworks can simultaneously consider spatial and temporal aspects in assessing the resilience of the system to sudden shocks, thereby improving the possibility of predictive planning; this is exemplified by utilizing real-time measurement of events and analysis of spatiotemporal variations, the effectiveness of various interventions can be monitored in real time (Pedon et al., 2024; Loia et al., 2026).

One of the most important aspects of digital twins in urban transport is their role in predictive analysis and decision support; in such a way that the results of modeling and simulation are presented not only in the form of raw data, but also in the form of indicators, maps and scenarios understandable to planners and policymakers, thus creating a bridge between scientific knowledge and practical application. This feature enables an assessment of the consequences of decisions before implementation, which is of great importance in the context of resilient transport, where decisions are often made in the face of high uncertainty and have long-term consequences. Recent studies have shown that the application of digital twin technology can be practical in improving the responsiveness, adaptability and efficiency of urban systems, as these frameworks strengthen the response to adverse events by modelling network behavior and user movement patterns. In the field of smart cities and transportation system development, there is a strong emphasis on data integration, network analysis, and data-driven decision support. According to recent literature on digital twins, this technology may provide knowledge-based models for in-depth analysis and future prediction, going beyond simple modelling (Tan et al., 2025).

Figure 6. Analytical and simulation framework of transportation digital twins for resilience assessment

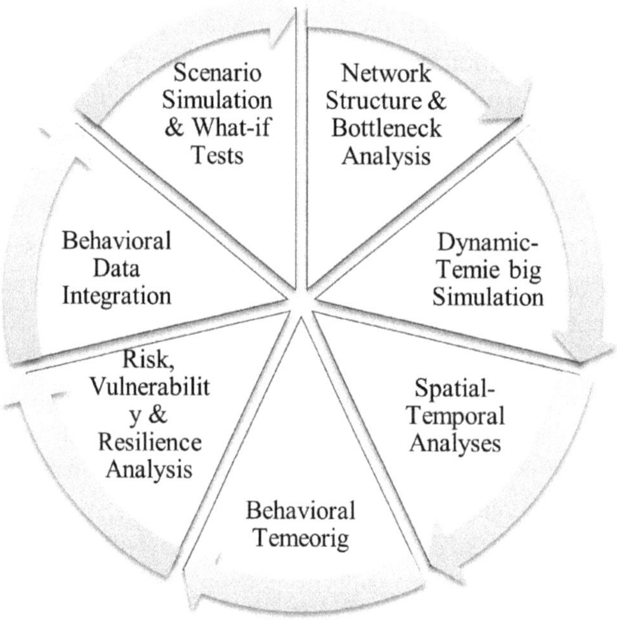

This figure illustrates the main analytical components of a transportation digital twin, including network structure and bottleneck analysis, dynamic traffic flow simulation, spatiotemporal analytics, behavioral data fusion, and "what if" scenario-based simulations. Simulation scenarios with the innovative Digital Twins tool include data from the surrounding environment, such as roads and infrastructure conditions, which ultimately generate analytical outputs such as graphs and maps and numerical data for diagnosing road crises and conditions, including for accidents and road resilience, modelled and produced in the digital twin environment (Figure 6). Several functional modules, including network structure and bottleneck analysis, dynamic traffic flow simulation, spatiotemporal analysis, scenario simulation and what-if testing, behavioral data integration, and risk, vulnerability, and resilience analysis, are connected to the digital twin as the central analytical core in the visualization. Simulation is a key feature of digital twins; in fact, it is used in the digital twin architecture to analyze a system's dynamics, the relationships between its components, and its responses to various adjustments and shocks.

As a consequence, the simulation model considers variations in demand, user behavior, and environmental factors, while also reflecting the network structure. This plays an important role in increasing the validity of simulation results and improving the understanding of system performance.

From an analytical perspective, Simulation in digital twins allows for the examination of different scenarios and the analysis of the potential consequences of planning decisions. Scenarios such as route closures, changing traffic patterns, traffic restrictions, or extreme weather conditions can be tested in a digital environment. This process allows decision-makers to assess the impact of interventions on network performance, service levels and user safety before they are actually implemented, thereby reducing decision-making risk. Understanding nonlinear linkages and cascading consequences in urban transport systems is another important function of Simulation. This human-centered approach plays a decisive role, especially in analyzing the safety of vulnerable users, and can lead to the development of more effective and equitable interventions. From a system learning perspective, Simulation in digital twins provides a platform for extracting knowledge from past experiences. One of the main pillars of these frameworks is modelling urban transportation networks as complex graphs. Especially in critical situations, such models can show which part of the network will have the most significant impact on overall system performance if a disruption occurs. Network modelling in the digital twin framework, using real-world data and continuous updates, goes beyond theoretical analysis.

Flexibility and portability of models are another important component of digital twin modelling frameworks. Unlike traditional models, which are often designed for a specific scenario, flexible models allow the analytical framework to be quickly transferred to new scenarios. The use of metamodels and standard information structures increases modelling productivity and enables faster responses to environmental changes and unexpected conditions. Especially in the face of sudden events such as route closures or severe weather, network simulation enables the prediction of operational consequences and the evaluation of management options. Combining these simulations with advanced statistical methods, data mining and machine learning provides a deeper understanding of network behavior under uncertainty. These methods can identify hidden patterns in the data, nonlinear behaviors and unexpected system responses. Hence, digital twin analytical frameworks can move beyond descriptive analyses to explanatory and predictive analyses. Including these factors takes resilience and safety analysis beyond a focus on infrastructure and leads to a more comprehensive understanding of the system. Finally, modelling and analysis frameworks in transportation digital twins play a key role in linking scientific knowledge to practical decision-making.

Presenting the analysis results in the form of performance indicators, analytical maps, and understandable scenarios enables planners and policymakers to use the findings effectively. From this perspective, digital twins, as an analytical core, provide the necessary platform for developing safer, more sustainable, and more resilient urban transportation systems. The decision-making process is made more visible and evidence-based by presenting the findings of these studies through comparisons of scenarios, analytical maps, and performance indicators. According to this viewpoint, digital twin modelling and analytic frameworks serve as both technological tools and knowledge platforms that link resilient policymaking, urban planning, and roadway engineering.

5.2. Human-Autonomous Vehicle Interaction in Heterogeneous Traffic Environments

The arrival of autonomous vehicles and connected urban transportation networks transforms the nature of traffic safety from a purely infrastructural or behavioral issue to a multilayered and interactive one. In such environments, conventional cars, autonomous vehicles, cyclists, pedestrians, and other vulnerable users coexist in the same space. This coexistence adds a new level of complexity to safety analysis, as the system's behavior no longer depends solely on the physical characteristics of the network or human decisions, but also on the quality of machine perception, the algorithmic decision-making logic, and the way humans and intelligent systems interact.

One of the fundamental challenges in this field is the heterogeneity of mixed traffic environments. Human users typically exhibit flexible, contextual, and sometimes unpredictable behaviors, while autonomous vehicles rely on sensor data, decision rules, and pre-trained models. This difference can manifest as new conflicts at complex intersections, in mixed-use spaces, in areas with limited visibility, or along routes used by cyclists and pedestrians. Hence, future safety analysis of autonomous vehicles requires frameworks that can simultaneously model both human behavioral uncertainty and machine perceptual limitations.

In this context, digital twins can serve as human-centric testbeds for simulating human-machine interaction scenarios. This technology enables the assessment of "what if" scenarios involving varying degrees of autonomous vehicle penetration, changes in infrastructure design, vulnerable user behavior, and critical conditions such as reduced visibility, congestion, or roadblocks before the actual deployment of autonomous systems. In this way, the digital twin is not only a tool for representing the current situation, but also a platform for testing policies, analyzing conflicts, and predicting emerging risks in future transportation environments.

Perceptual uncertainty is another important dimension in this area. Although autonomous systems use sensors such as LiDAR, cameras, GNSS, and radar, their performance varies across conditions. Lighting conditions, weather, visibility obstructions, high density, and unusual user behavior can reduce detection accuracy, delay decision-making, or increase the likelihood of conflict. Therefore, safety assessment in the context of digital twins should not be limited to trajectory or network capacity alone, but should also consider the quality of machine perception, the level of model confidence, and the model's sensitivity to environmental conditions.

In addition, the future of autonomous transportation requires explainable and reliable approaches. If AI-based decisions in autonomous systems and digital twins remain "black boxes," public trust, institutional accountability, and the legitimacy of safety decisions will be called into question. From this perspective, the use of explainable AI, real-time decision-making systems, and edge computing architectures can help reduce latency, increase transparency, and improve the deplorability of these frameworks. It is also necessary to assess the Technology Readiness Level (TRL) across different digital twin applications for autonomous transportation, as not all models and scenarios are at the same level of readiness for implementation in real-world conditions.

Overall, human-centric digital twins can play an important role in the safe and equitable transition to autonomous transportation. The main value of this framework is that, rather than focusing solely on technical efficiency or vehicle performance, it analyses safety as the result of interactions among humans, machines, infrastructure, and the environment, thereby providing the necessary context for proactive, evidence-based planning.

5.3 Human-Machine Interaction and Vulnerable Users Within Heterogeneous Traffic Environments

Digital twins are not only analytical tools but also platforms for intelligent decision-making in complex urban systems. In the area of safety, the main capacity of digital twins lies in identifying hidden risk patterns and critical points in transport networks. From a resilience perspective, digital twins play an important role in recording, analyzing, and learning from past crises and disruptions. This process creates a system memory that allows the transport system not only to recover but also to function more adaptively and efficiently in the face of future shocks. Consequently, resilience is strengthened as a dynamic, evolutionary process rather than a return to the previous state.

At the urban policy level, digital twins reduce the gap between scientific analysis and executive decisions. Presenting the results in the form of performance indicators, analytical maps, and comparative scenarios makes the decision-making process more transparent and defensible. This transparency is essential when decisions have long-term economic, social, and spatial consequences, and it strengthens data-driven governance. Ultimately, digital twins are one of the key pillars of contemporary transportation engineering and the resilient cities of the future. By linking data, analysis, and decision-making, this technology paves the way for a transition from reactive management to predictive, intelligent planning. From this perspective, digital twins are not the end of the road for research and planning, but rather the starting point for new approaches to improving the safety, resilience and sustainability of urban transportation systems (Saidi et al., 2023).

Recording and analyzing data on crises, network response, and infrastructure performance creates a kind of "system memory" that is essential for improving future design and management. Digital twins also provide a suitable platform for urban and policy decision-making. By providing a common, data-driven platform, this technology can strengthen connections among transport, urban planning, and safety sectors and offer a more integrated approach to city management. At the same time, the effective use of digital twins requires attention to implementation, as well as to institutional and technical challenges. Technological complexity, the need for interdisciplinary expertise and implementation costs are among the obstacles that need to be considered in policy and planning. Accurate spatial analysis enables the identification of the most vulnerable areas and those requiring immediate intervention. From a forward-looking perspective, digital twins provide a platform for transitioning from reactive to proactive approaches in urban transport management. This transition is one of the essential requirements for increasing cities' resilience against the growing shocks caused by climate change, population growth, and the complexity of urban systems.

Infrastructure features, including bike lanes, paths for pedestrian, way for vehicle, junctions, highway crossings, and pedestrian-oriented areas, can be assessed using this paradigm to assess user safety and interaction with the urban environment, in addition to traffic performance. This approach plays a decisive role in improving the quality of engineering, especially in the analysis of the safety of vulnerable users. This continuous learning process enables the transport system to be more adaptive to future shocks, reduce recovery times, and sustain its critical functions more sustainably. From this perspective, digital twins serve as a key tool for operationalizing the concept of resilience in urban transport management.

In the field of urban policy, digital twins serve as a bridge between scientific analysis and executive decision-making. The results of modelling and simulation in the digital twin environment can be presented as performance indicators, analytical maps, and comparative scenarios that are understandable and applicable to planners and policymakers. This capability, grounded in predictive digital twins informed by real-world evidence and data, will create safer urban transportation and highways or improve existing conditions. To improve transparency in the analysis methodology, this paper presents a structured workflow for understanding the process of data analysis performance using digital twins in transportation and road safety analysis.

Figure 7. Workflow of transportation digital twin–based resilience analysis

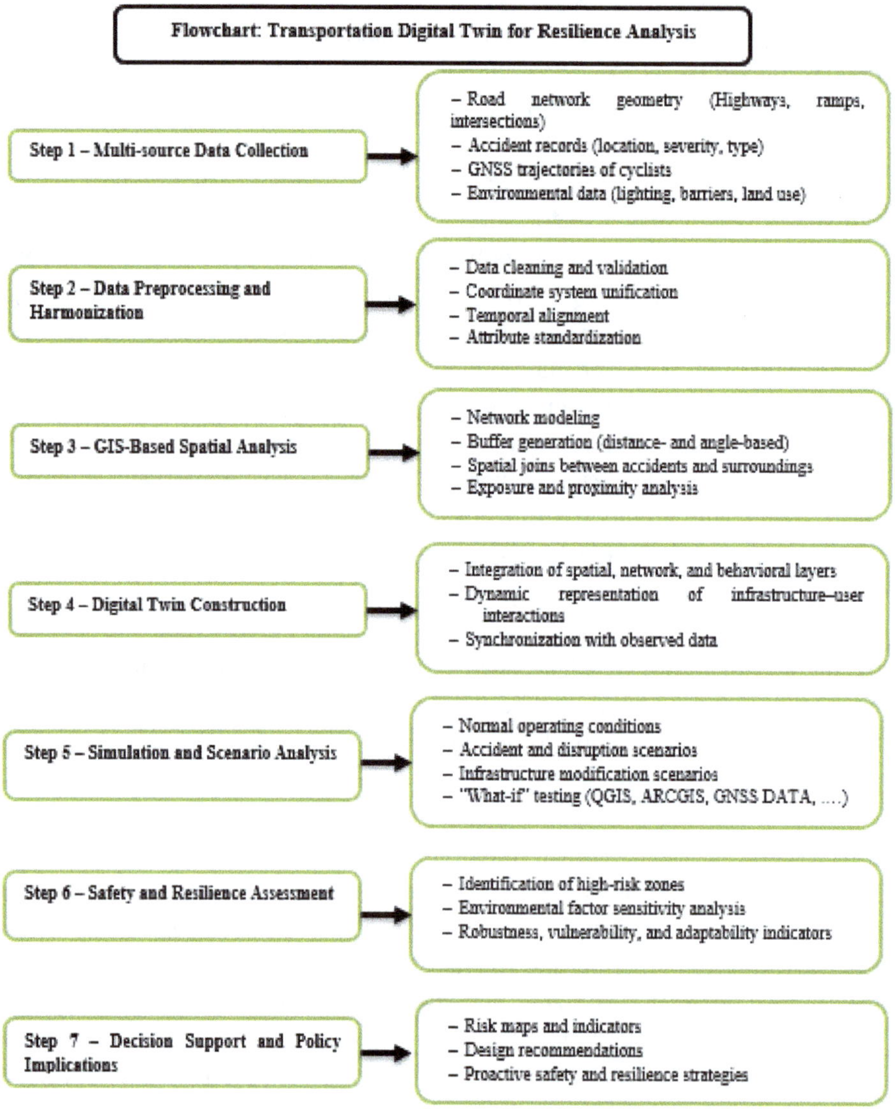

This workflow diagram outlines the implementation of a transportation digital twin framework using multi-source data collection. After data preprocessing and alignment, GIS-based spatial analytics, such as network modelling, buffer generation, and exposure assessment, are used to identify spatial relationships among accidents, infrastructure, and the surrounding environment. The processed data is then integrated into building a dynamic digital twin that depicts the interactions between infrastructure and users (Figure 7).

Table 3 provides a systematically illustrated overview of key tools and software for implementing transportation digital twins, showing that this innovation requires multiple software applications to model road layers and manage spatial, temporal, network, and behavioral data. Geographic information systems (GIS) serve as the spatial backbone of the digital twin, providing the necessary platform for integrating road networks, land use and built environment elements. Combining GIS with open spatial data, such as OpenStreetMap, and buffer- and network-based analytics enhances the ability to identify spatial patterns of risk, spatial inequalities, and vulnerable areas at different urban and highway scales.

On the other hand, GNSS data processing tools and traffic simulation systems constitute the dynamic dimension of the digital twin, enabling the analysis of user behavior and network response under normal and critical conditions. GNSS data enables human-centered assessments of resilience by providing high-spatial-temporal-resolution information on the movement, speed, and paths of users, especially vulnerable users such as cyclists and pedestrians. At the same time, traffic flow simulation and network analysis tools reproduce the system's behavior in the face of shocks such as accidents, road closures, or severe weather conditions, and measure the network's recovery and adaptation capacity. Consequently, analytical and visual tools, spatial layers, and maps based on evidence and open-source data help plan and manage disasters on roads (Table 3).

Table 3. Tools and software used in transportation digital twin implementation

Tool / Software Category	Representative Platforms	Primary Functions	Role in Transportation Digital Twin	Contribution to Resilience Analysis
Geographic Information Systems (GIS)	ArcGIS, QGIS	Spatial data management, buffer analysis, network analysis, spatial statistics	Acts as the spatial backbone of the digital twin by integrating road networks, land use, and environmental features	Identification of accident hotspots, vulnerable zones, spatial inequalities, and exposure to risk
GNSS Data Processing Tools	GNSS receivers, GPS loggers, trajectory processing libraries	Trajectory collection, map-matching, speed and direction analysis	Enables high-resolution representation of user movement patterns and user–infrastructure interactions	Human-centered resilience assessment, especially for cyclists and pedestrians
Open Spatial Data Platforms	OpenStreetMap (OSM)	Road network extraction, infrastructure attributes, urban features	Provides scalable and up-to-date base layers for digital twin construction	Supports network robustness analysis and assessment of infrastructure availability
Traffic and Network Simulation Tools	Traffic simulation engines, network analysis libraries	Flow simulation, congestion modeling, route disruption analysis	Simulates system behavior under normal and disrupted conditions	Evaluation of network performance degradation and recovery under shock scenarios
Statistical and Analytical Tools	Statistical software, data analysis libraries	Pattern detection, correlation analysis, risk modeling	Supports data-driven interpretation of spatial and behavioral indicators	Quantification of resilience metrics and uncertainty reduction
Visualization and Decision Support Tools	GIS dashboards, interactive maps	Scenario visualization, indicator mapping	Translate analytical outputs into interpretable decision-support formats	Enhances evidence-based policy making and crisis management

5.4 Ethical, Technical, and Institutional Challenges and Requirements

The deployment of digital twins in human-centric transportation systems is not just a technological issue but a multi-layered process tied to ethical considerations, technical requirements, and institutional capacity. As these systems increasingly rely on real-time data, behavioral analytics, and predictive decision-making, the importance of dimensions related to privacy, algorithmic bias, transparency, accountability, and governance also increases. Hence, the success of digital twins in real-world environments depends not only on the accuracy of the model or the quality of the simulation, but also on the quality of the protection, monitoring, and institutional frameworks (Dhinakaran et al., 2025; Anwar et al., 2024).

Privacy and Data Protection

One of the most important concerns in transportation digital twins is their reliance on continuous, high-resolution data. Data from GNSS, sensors, cameras, connected devices, and user movement patterns can reveal sensitive information about daily routes, travel times, route choices, and location behavior. In such a context, privacy should not be understood solely as the removal of names or individual identifiers, but rather as the right of users to control their data, to be aware of how it is used, and to meaningfully opt out of participation. Therefore, data anonymization, data minimization, and privacy-by-design should be considered early in the development of digital twins.

Algorithmic Bias and Spatial Justice

Digital twins and AI-based models may reproduce or even amplify biases in the data. If training data is drawn primarily from affluent areas, users with greater access to technology, or specific behavioral patterns, model outputs may fail to account for the needs and risks of vulnerable groups or underrepresented areas. This can lead to unfair decisions in resource allocation, prioritization of safety interventions, and infrastructure design. Therefore, it is essential to regularly assess fairness, control for spatial and social representativeness of the data, and review model results from a spatial justice perspective.

Explainability and Accountability

In safety-related applications, decisions based on AI and simulation should not remain black boxes. If it is not clear why a model identified a point as risky or why it recommended a particular intervention, public trust and the defensibility of institutional decisions are undermined. Therefore, the explainability of models and the interpretability of outputs are of fundamental importance. This is essential not only for social acceptance but also for legal and managerial accountability. For this reason, using interpretable models, documenting assumptions, and maintaining human oversight in the decision-making loop should be considered as part of the design of these systems.

Governance and Institutional Readiness

Even the most accurate and advanced digital twins will not be implemented effectively without clear governance and sufficient institutional capacity. Implementing these systems requires coordination among transport, urban management, safety, digital infrastructure, and data protection institutions. In many contexts, the lack of common standards, unclear accountability, limited specialist human resources, and weak data infrastructure can hinder the sustainable exploitation of digital twins. Therefore, institutional readiness, defined responsibilities, data standardization, and monitoring mechanisms are essential prerequisites for the successful application of this technology in the real world.

In summary, ethical, technical, and institutional challenges should not be seen as side obstacles, but rather as part of the core of digital twin design and evaluation. Only if data protection, fairness, explainability, and governance are seen as integrated can digital twins be used as reliable, responsible, and sustainable tools for road safety and future transportation.

From a technical perspective, cybersecurity is one of the most important requirements for digital twins. Due to their dependence on networked communications, the Internet of Things, connected sensors, and multi-layered databases, these systems are exposed to widespread cyber threats. Secure data management is another technical requirement for these systems. Digital twins deal with large volumes of diverse, dynamic, and sometimes sensitive data, which requires structures for secure storage, access control, backup, encryption, event logging, and data lifecycle management. Although many projects focus on data collection and analysis, in practice, the sustainability and trustworthiness of a digital twin simulation largely depend on the quality of its data infrastructure. An advanced analytics system will be neither sustainable nor socially acceptable without adequate data protection (Itäpelto et al., 2025).

Consequently, the responsible development of digital twins must be based on an integrated framework in which ethics, technology, and institutions cannot be separated. An approach that emphasizes only technical progress may be socially unsustainable; one that relies solely on regulations may limit innovation; and one that focuses solely on ethics will not be implemented without the appropriate technical infrastructure. Therefore, the convergence of these three dimensions is a key condition for the sustainable success of digital twins in real-world environments. Ultimately, the future of digital twins in transportation depends not only on better algorithms or more data but also on the quality of ethical, security, and institutional frameworks.

The implementation of digital twins (DT) in transportation for human-centered safety and resilience, particularly when integrating high-resolution spatial data and GNSS trajectories, faces significant ethical, technical, and institutional challenges.

Ethical Challenges and Requirements

- **Data Privacy and Surveillance:** Utilizing GNSS cyclist trajectories raises significant privacy concerns.
- **Algorithmic Bias and Equity:** Digital twins can inherit biases from training data, potentially favoring affluent areas and neglecting vulnerable, underrepresented communities.
- **Human-Centered Design:** Current digital twins often neglect human-related aspects. Human-in-the-loop governance is needed to ensure that AI-driven simulations do not fully replace human oversight in decision-making, particularly for critical infrastructure safety.
- **Transparency and Trust:** There is a need for ethical impact assessments before deployment to address AI-driven decision-making and establish clear accountability for outcomes.

Technical Challenges and Requirements

- **Data Integration and Interoperability:** Integrating diverse data sources, including high-resolution GNSS, IoT sensors, and GIS data, requires standardized data formats to ensure seamless interoperability.

- **Real-time Processing and Scalability:** High-fidelity modelling for urban transport requires substantial computational resources and low-latency data transmission. A distributed edge-cloud architecture is required to balance local data processing with cloud-based simulation.
- **Validation (Sim-to-Real Gap):** Closing the simulation-to-reality gap is critical; ensuring the digital twin reflects the true dynamics of cyclist safety in urban settings is technically challenging.
- **Spatial Data Accuracy:** The approach necessitates high-resolution environmental features, which in turn require precise 3D modelling and LiDAR technologies, thereby increasing the system's cost and complexity.

Table 4. Key challenges and requirements in the implementation of transport digital twins

Challenge	Main Risk	Proposed Mitigation
Privacy	Exposure of users' travel routes and movement patterns	Data anonymization, privacy-by-design, and data minimization
Algorithmic bias	Inequitable safety outcomes and biased prioritization of interventions	Fairness auditing, review of data representativeness, and spatial equity assessment
Explainability	Black-box decision-making and low interpretability of model outputs	Use of interpretable models, documentation of assumptions, and human oversight
Governance	Lack of accountability and institutional coordination	Clear governance framework, data standardization, and monitoring and accountability mechanisms

As illustrated in Table 4, the implementation of transport digital twins is inherently linked to a set of interrelated technical, ethical, and institutional challenges. Beyond purely technological considerations, issues such as data privacy, algorithmic bias, and model explainability highlight the socio-technical nature of digital twin systems. These challenges underscore the need to integrate governance mechanisms, ethical safeguards, and transparent analytical frameworks into the design and deployment of digital twins. By aligning technical innovation with principles of accountability, fairness, and data protection, digital twins can more effectively support human-centric, reliable, and equitable transport systems.

Key Requirements for the Described Approach

To successfully shift toward a human-centered and spatially explicit safety perspective (e.g., using cyclist GNSS trajectories), the following are essential:

1. **High-Definition Safety Metrics:** Incorporating detailed vehicle dynamics and environmental factors to identify safety issues, moving beyond traffic operational efficiency.
2. **Edge-Based Data Protection:** Implementing on-device or edge-based anonymization of GNSS data to safeguard user privacy while maintaining data utility for vulnerability analysis.
3. **Cross-Domain Data Integration:** Bridging transportation modelling (GNSS/spatial data) with infrastructure and urban planning data

This comparative overview highlights that while existing digital twin applications in transportation primarily focus on operational efficiency, infrastructure monitoring, or emergency response, fewer approaches explicitly address resilience from a human-centered and spatially explicit safety perspective. The approach presented in this chapter differs by integrating high-resolution spatial data, cyclist GNSS trajectories, and environmental features within a digital twin framework to assess vulnerability and safety in highway and urban contexts. This distinction enables proactive, evidence-based interventions to improve resilience for vulnerable road users (Table 5).

Table 5. Comparative overview of digital twin applications in transportation with respect to resilience-oriented approaches

Application Domain	Primary Objective	Core Data Sources	Digital Twin Approach	Resilience Focus	Key Limitations
Traffic flow management	Optimize traffic efficiency and congestion control	Loop detectors, cameras, traffic sensors	Real-time simulation of traffic dynamics	Operational robustness under demand fluctuations	Limited consideration of user vulnerability and spatial context
Infrastructure monitoring	Structural health and maintenance planning	IoT sensors, inspection data	Asset-based digital twin of infrastructure elements	Infrastructure robustness and failure prevention	Focused on physical assets, limited behavioral integration
Emergency response planning	Improve response time and network recovery	Incident records, traffic data, weather data	Scenario-based disruption simulation	Rapid recovery and redundancy evaluation	Often reactive and event-specific
Smart mobility systems	Enhance multimodal coordination	Mobility data, GPS, ITS platforms	Integrated mobility digital twins	System adaptability and efficiency	Less emphasis on safety and micro-scale risk
Urban transport resilience assessment	Evaluate system performance under shocks	Network data, historical disruptions	Network-oriented resilience modeling	Robustness and recovery at network scale	Aggregated analysis, limited micro-spatial detail
Highway safety and vulnerable users (this study)	Identify and mitigate safety risks for cyclists and pedestrians	Accident data, GNSS trajectories, GIS layers, environmental features	Human-centered, spatially explicit digital twin	Risk reduction, vulnerability mitigation, adaptive safety planning	Data-intensive requires interdisciplinary expertise

Table 6 compares the relative costs and benefits of various digital twin applications in transportation. Rather than providing absolute numbers which vary across cities and jurisdictions, costs are categorized in relative terms to facilitate strategic judgment. The results show that many digital twin applications, particularly those based on GIS and incident-based ones, can provide significant value for safety and resilience analysis with a moderate level of complexity and implementation effort. In contrast, more advanced applications that require real-time integration entail higher costs and greater institutional capacity and may be feasible only in some urban contexts.

Table 6. Implementation costs and benefits of digital twin applications in transportation

Digital Twin Application Type	Main Implementation Components	Estimated Implementation Cost	Key Benefits	Practical Constraints and Limitations
Network-based Digital Twin for Traffic Resilience	GIS platform, traffic data, network models	Medium	Improved understanding of network robustness, identification of critical links, evaluation of disruption scenarios	Requires consistent and updated traffic data; limited behavioral representation
Accident-Oriented Digital Twin for Safety Analysis	GIS, crash databases, spatial buffers, environmental features	Low to Medium	Accurate identification of high-risk locations, support for targeted safety interventions	Dependent on quality and completeness of accident records
Human-Centered Digital Twin (Cyclists and Pedestrians)	GNSS data, spatial analysis tools, behavioral indicators	Medium	Enhanced analysis of vulnerable users' exposure, perception-based safety assessment	GNSS data availability and privacy considerations
Real-Time Operational Digital Twin	IoT sensors, real-time data streams, simulation engines	High	Continuous monitoring, rapid response to incidents, dynamic system adaptation	High infrastructure and maintenance costs; computational complexity
Scenario-Based Planning Digital Twin	GIS, simulation models, scenario engines	Medium	Evaluation of long-term planning strategies and policy impacts before implementation	Results depend on scenario assumptions and model calibration
Integrated Urban Digital Twin Platform	GIS, IoT, simulation, dashboards	Very High	Comprehensive system-level decision support, cross-sector coordination	High financial cost, institutional coordination challenges

6. FUNCTIONAL EVALUATION OF THE FRAMEWORK IN A CASE STUDY

6.1. Study Area

To practically evaluate the proposed human-centric digital twin framework, an urban-highway transportation corridor is used as an analytical example. This corridor includes a combination of highway lanes, at-grade intersections, entrance and exit ramps, and mixed traffic sections where motor vehicles, cyclists, and pedestrians are present simultaneously.

This type of environment was chosen due to the high complexity of traffic interactions, the presence of vulnerable users (especially cyclists), and the high probability of spatial and functional conflicts. Such a context enables the simultaneous assessment of safety, resilience, and user behavior in real-world, multi-layered conditions.

6.2. Data Used

To build the digital twin of this corridor, a combination of several data sources are used, including the following:

- **Spatial data (GIS):** including network geometry, road type, intersections, lane width, land use, and infrastructure elements
- **Accident data:** including the location of accidents, accident type, and users involved
- **Traffic data:** including flow rate, density, and network performance
- **Environmental data:** including lighting conditions, weather conditions, and built environment characteristics
- **GNSS-based behavioral data:** including actual user movement paths, especially cyclists

This data is seamlessly integrated into the GIS environment and forms the basis for building the digital twin model.

6.3. Modelling and Analysis Process (Workflow)

The digital twin development and analysis process in this study includes the following steps:

- Extraction and preparation of accident and transportation network data
- Creation of multi-scale buffer zones (25, 50 and 100 meters) around accident points
- Integration of different spatial layers, including infrastructure, land use and environmental elements
- Combination of GNSS behavioral data to represent real user movement patterns
- Network modelling as a graph (node-edge) to identify bottlenecks and critical points
- Perform scenario-based analyses to evaluate system performance under different conditions

This process allows for the simultaneous analysis of network structure, user behavior, and environmental conditions within an integrated framework.

6.4. Scenario Design

In order to evaluate the system performance under different conditions, several analytical scenarios have been defined. Baseline scenario: Normal network operation conditions without disruption

- Disruption scenario: Blockage of part of the route or reduction of capacity due to an accident or weather conditions
- Infrastructure improvement scenario: Adding safe routes for cyclists or improving the design of intersections
- Autonomous mobility scenario: Presence of autonomous vehicles alongside human users in a mixed traffic environment
- These scenarios allow for examining the behavior of the system and users under different conditions and comparing the effects of interventions.

Figure 8 illustrates the conceptual implementation of a GIS-based digital twin for analyzing a highway accident hotspot in the case study. The figure demonstrates how multi-scale buffer zones (e.g., 25 m and 100 m radii) are generated around the accident location to capture the spatial influence of surrounding environmental and infrastructural features. These include roadway characteristics, shoulder presence, physical barriers, lighting conditions, and adjacent land use. By integrating these heterogeneous data layers within a unified spatial framework, the digital twin enables a more comprehensive understanding of the environmental context in which accidents occur.

Furthermore, the inclusion of directional movement trajectories—derived from GNSS data—allows analysis of user behavior, approach angles, and interaction patterns within the transport network. This integration supports a shift from point-based accident analysis toward a context-aware, system-level interpretation of risk. As a result, the digital twin not only identifies high-risk locations but also reveals the spatial and behavioral mechanisms contributing to accident occurrence.

This approach demonstrates the potential of digital twins to support predictive safety analysis and evidence-based decision-making in highway engineering. By enabling the evaluation of alternative scenarios and infrastructure modifications in a simulated yet data-driven environment, the framework provides a scalable, transferable methodology for enhancing both road safety and transport system resilience.

Figure 8. GIS-based digital twin representation of a highway accident hotspot using multi-scale buffer analysis and environmental feature integration (Author's own illustration)

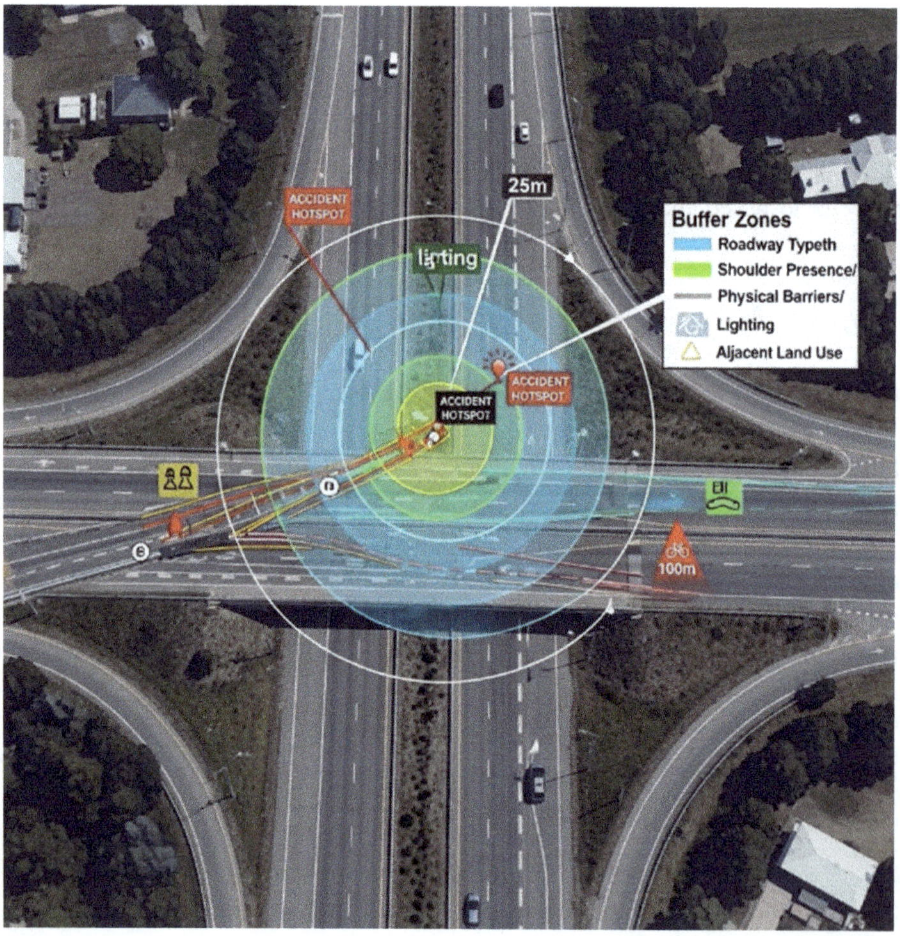

This figure operationalizes the integration of spatial, behavioral, and infrastructural data within the digital twin framework, bridging the gap between theoretical modeling and real-world application.

6.5. Indicators

A set of quantitative and analytical indicators has been defined to measure safety and resilience performance:

- Risk Exposure, especially for vulnerable users
- Network Robustness to Disruption
- Route Redundancy
- Recovery Time after disruption
- Conflict Hotspots
- Spatial Inequality in Safety and Access

These indicators enable precise comparisons of scenarios and an assessment of intervention effectiveness.

Network Resilience Index

$$R = \frac{P_d}{P_0} \tag{1}$$

R= resilience index
P_d= network performance after disruption
P_0= normal (baseline) performance

The resilience of the transport network can be quantified using a performance-based index, as shown in Equation (1), which compares system functionality under disrupted and normal conditions.

Exposure to Risk

$$E = \sum_{i=1}^{n}(T_i \times R_i) \tag{2}$$

E= total exposure to risk
T_i= time spent (or flow) in segment i
R_i= risk level of segment i

User exposure to risk can be modeled as a function of both movement patterns and spatial risk levels, as expressed in Equation (2).

6.6. Results and Interpretation

The analysis results show that the network performance against disruptions is highly dependent on the spatial structure and the availability of alternative routes. In the route blockage scenario, a significant increase in travel time and congestion on alternative routes was observed, indicating that network redundancy is limited in some parts.

Analysis of spatial buffers around crash sites showed that the highest risk to cyclists occurs near entry and exit ramps, complex intersections, and sections with inadequate lane separation. This highlights the importance of more careful infrastructure design and spatial management to reduce conflicts.

Integration of GNSS data with spatial layers also showed that users' actual routes differed from optimal network routes in many cases. This difference reflects the influence of perceptual, safety, and environmental quality factors on user behavior. It suggests that real-world data-based analyses provide a more accurate understanding of risk patterns.

In the infrastructure improvement scenarios, a significant reduction in risk exposure for vulnerable users was observed. Also, in the autonomous vehicle presence scenario, the analyses showed that interactions between human users and autonomous systems can lead to new patterns of conflict that require more detailed modelling and ex ante assessment.

Overall, this study's results show that the human-centered digital twin can serve as a powerful analytical platform for identifying critical points, analyzing user behavior, evaluating different scenarios, and supporting evidence-based decision-making in transportation planning.

Quantifiable highway safety and resilience outcomes: Recent studies on the implementation of innovative, hybrid digital twin technology in highway systems have shown that using spatial data, map layers, and traffic flow and accident history can lead to significant improvements in road safety indicators and transportation resilience. For instance, in digital highway simulation projects in Europe, accident data and analyses of road geometry and environmental conditions have been built into relevant software to identify high-risk areas, leading to a 15-30% reduction in accident rates at critical intersections and other high-risk locations. This goal can be used to make roads more resilient and safer.

Cost-Benefit Analysis and Human-Centered Approach: From an economic and macro-infrastructure planning perspective, cost-benefit analyses of digital twins indicate that approaches based on GIS and accident data have moderate implementation costs and can deliver significant safety returns despite the lack of real-time integration. Studies have reported that the use of digital twins based on spatial analytics can reduce the costs associated with severe accidents by up to 20%. In comparison, network recovery times after traffic disruptions have also improved by an average of 10–25%. Furthermore, the human-centered approach in these systems, which leverages GNSS data from vulnerable users such as cyclists, enables more accurate analysis of risk exposure and user behavior in highway environments. This capability makes digital twins an effective tool for evidence-based decision-making in modern highway engineering, where safety, resilience, and spatial justice are addressed simultaneously (European Commission, 2024; Wachnicka et al., 2023).

Policy relevance and ETSC alignment: The importance of digital twins, in fact, the use of sensors and supporting software to analyze data on the roads to improve highway safety, has also been confirmed in recent ETSC reports, which highlight the role of predictive tools that can reduce deaths and injuries in the long term.

7. DISCUSSION

The findings of this chapter highlight the significant potential of human-centric digital twins as an advanced analytical framework for improving road safety and enhancing transport system resilience. By integrating spatial intelligence, behavioral dynamics, and multi-source data, the proposed approach enables a more comprehensive understanding of risk patterns and user interactions within complex transport environments. From a theoretical perspective, this study contributes to the existing literature by bridging the gap between resilience theory and digital twin technology in transportation systems. While traditional approaches often emphasize infrastructure performance and recovery, the results emphasize the importance of incorporating human experience, vulnerability, and spatial context into resilience assessment. This shift toward a human-centered perspective represents a critical advancement in contemporary transport research.

In practical terms, the framework demonstrates strong applicability for real-world planning and decision-making. The integration of GIS-based spatial analysis with digital twin simulations allows for the identification of high-risk areas, evaluation of infrastructure scenarios, and development of targeted safety interventions. This capability is particularly relevant for policymakers and urban planners aiming to design safer and more inclusive transport systems. However, several limitations must be acknowledged. The implementation of digital twins requires high-quality, multi-source data, which may not always be available or standardized across different contexts. Additionally, challenges related to data privacy, computational complexity, and model transparency remain critical concerns that need to be addressed in future research.

Finally, the scalability and transferability of the proposed framework suggest strong potential for broader application across different urban contexts. Future studies can further enhance this approach by integrating real-time data streams, machine learning techniques, and adaptive simulation models to improve predictive accuracy and decision support capabilities.

7.1. Interpretation of Findings and Theoretical Contribution

The findings of this chapter show that digital twins in urban transportation should not be considered merely as technological tools to represent or optimize infrastructure performance, but can also serve as human-centered analytical frameworks for rethinking safety, resilience, and equity in transportation. In this regard, this chapter seeks to elevate the concept of digital twins from a purely technical model to an interdisciplinary platform for analyzing, in an integrated manner, the interactions among spatial data, user behavior, infrastructure conditions, and future scenarios.

From a theoretical perspective, one of the most important achievements of this research is the linkage between three key areas: transportation resilience, human-centered safety, and autonomous mobility. While many previous studies have examined these areas separately, the framework proposed in this chapter shows that a true understanding of network safety and performance is only possible when these dimensions are examined simultaneously within an integrated analytical framework.

7.2. Practical and Applied Implications

From an applied perspective, this chapter's results show that digital twins can serve as decision-support tools for urban planners, transportation engineers, and policymakers. The framework enables the analysis of different scenarios before implementation and allows decision-making to move from reactive approaches based on past data to predictive, proactive, and design-oriented approaches.

One of the most important applications of this approach is the analysis of the interaction between human users and autonomous vehicles in mixed traffic environments. In such situations, digital twins can serve as a simulated environment to explore different scenarios, identify conflict points, and assess the safety of vulnerable users. This is particularly important in the context of designing safer infrastructure for pedestrians and cyclists.

Also, the emphasis in this chapter on transport equity shows that digital twins can play an important role in identifying spatial inequalities, the uneven distribution of risk and access, and in designing more targeted policies. This helps in evidence-based decision-making tailored to local conditions.

7.3. Scalability, Transferability, and Limitations

Despite the significant potential of the proposed framework, generalizing and implementing it across different urban contexts poses challenges. First, the framework relies on access to high-quality, multi-source data, while in many cities, such data are not available in a complete or up-to-date manner. Second, the successful implementation of this model requires institutional capacity, inter-organizational coordination, and appropriate computational infrastructure.

Furthermore, although the proposed framework is conceptually transferable to other cities, its application requires adaptation to local conditions, user behavioral characteristics, and transportation network structure. Therefore, the replicability of this framework should be considered as an adaptive process.

Finally, limitations of this study include the largely conceptual nature of the framework, the need for broader empirical validation, and a more detailed examination of privacy-related dimensions, algorithmic bias, and decision-making transparency.

8. CONCLUSION

Digital twins have emerged in recent years as one of the most innovative and transformative approaches to analyzing, monitoring, and managing urban transportation systems. In the context of this chapter, digital twins are considered not only as technological tools but also as human-centered environments for rethinking road safety, transportation justice, and readiness for an autonomous future. One of the most important conceptual achievements of this research is that it extends digital twins beyond purely technical modelling and redefines them in relation to social, spatial, and policy issues. In this way, the digital twin becomes an interdisciplinary tool that blurs the boundaries between engineering, urban planning, spatial analysis, and public policy. In this framework, the human-centered approach plays a fundamental role. Although technical criteria are often used to measure transportation systems, their ultimate goal is to respond to human needs, protect user lives, and ensure safe and equitable access. Therefore, any use of digital twins in transportation must take into account human, behavioral, and spatial differences among users. This is especially important for vulnerable groups, such as pedestrians, cyclists and other users who lack adequate physical protection.

A key feature of digital twins is their ability to integrate multi-source and multi-scale data. Spatial data, behavioral information, infrastructure indicators, traffic patterns, environmental conditions and even crisis scenarios can be brought together in a single analytical platform. This capability allows the transport system to be studied not statically, but dynamically, live and context-dependently. Such a capacity significantly increases analysts' and planners' ability to identify hidden relationships, conflict patterns, and vulnerabilities. From a road safety perspective, this technology offers a unique potential to move beyond traditional, reactive approaches. This feature allows safety decision-making to shift from a reactive response to past incidents to a predictive, preventive, and design-oriented approach to targeted interventions. This shift is particularly significant for vulnerable road users. These groups' experience of the transport network often differs from that of motorized users, as their safety depends heavily on local conditions, infrastructure design, space allocation, lighting quality, intersection conditions, and traffic intensity. Human-centric digital twins can reveal these differences and show which groups and which urban areas experience the highest levels of risk, deprivation, or inequality. This analytical power provides an essential basis for more equitable urban transport policymaking. In this context, transport justice has a special place as one of the main themes of this chapter. Urban transport is not just a technical system, but a structure in which benefits, risks, time, space, and access are unequally distributed among different groups.

By using geographical analysis, digital twins enable more precise identification of these disparities and show how certain regions or populations are more vulnerable than others to pollutants, traffic hazards, unsafe infrastructure, or network interruptions. Digital twins are an effective tool for promoting spatial fairness because of their openness. From a planning perspective, one of the most striking capabilities of digital twins is their ability to simultaneously assess a set of objectives that are often in tension or conflict with each other in practice. Urban transport systems must simultaneously maintain network efficiency, improve user safety, reduce environmental impacts, and enhance spatial justice.

By integrating different layers of data and displaying temporal and spatial dynamics, digital twins can provide a deeper, more multidimensional, and more realistic picture of network performance. In the field of climate resilience, the importance of this technology is increasingly apparent. Floods, heat waves, storms, reduced visibility and other climatic disturbances can severely impact infrastructure performance, user safety and network availability. Digital twins enable the simulation of different climate scenarios before they occur and the ex-ante assessment of their potential impacts on the network, infrastructure, and different user groups. This capacity will lead to a shift in transport planning from a reactive, post-crisis approach to a more proactive, adaptive and resilient one.

From a methodological perspective, digital twins also open up new horizons for future research. Integrating this framework with emerging technologies, including artificial intelligence, machine learning, predictive analytics and real-time data processing, can lead to the development of more accurate, adaptable and responsive models. This development also has special meaning and importance at the strategic level. Digital twins can be considered not only as project or research tools, but also as part of the knowledge infrastructure of future smart cities. In the field of autonomous transportation, this chapter also emphasizes a fundamental point: the autonomous future should not be understood solely as a technological one, but as a human-centered, safe, and equitable one. The introduction of connected, autonomous, and intelligent vehicles into the urban network, although it creates new opportunities to improve efficiency and management, also poses new challenges for interacting with human users, especially vulnerable groups. Therefore, digital twins can play an important role in analyzing these complex interactions and designing safer scenarios for the coexistence of humans and technology. This issue is even more important given that many traditional transportation models represent user behavior in a simplified, average-based way. In contrast, human-centered digital twins can incorporate behavioral heterogeneity, spatial differences, and the specific conditions of different users into the model. This is particularly important in mixed traffic spatial environments where humans, traditional vehicles, autonomous vehicles and active transport users coexist without such an approach, planning for an autonomous future risks ignoring the human dimension and reproducing existing inequalities.

At the policy level, this chapter shows that digital twins can help design interventions that are not only effective but also fair and evidence-based. When accurate information is available about risk patterns, the spatial distribution of vulnerability, user behavior and network performance, more targeted decisions can be made. In this way, policymakers can design solutions tailored to the context, target group, and local conditions, rather than relying on blanket, uniform interventions. This is important for improving safety, reducing conflict and enhancing the quality of urban life.

A final consideration is that, this chapter concludes that transforming urban transportation planning and control requires a shift from traditional, fragmented, and reactive models to proactive, data-driven, space-driven, and people-centered approaches. Digital twins, especially when developed with a human-centric perspective, can play a fundamental role in this transition. They not only enable better analysis of the current reality, but also provide cities with the tools to shape a safer, more resilient, more equitable, and more intelligent future. Accordingly, the main message of the this chapter "Human-Centered Digital Twins for Road Safety and Future Autonomous Transportation" is that the future of transportation should not be defined solely by technical intelligence, but should be rethought to protect people, reduce inequality, promote safety, and increase the adaptive capacity of systems. If digital twins are put at the service of this vision, they can become one of the most important knowledge and practical foundations for guiding cities towards a more sustainable and secure future.

This chapter demonstrates that human-centric digital twins represent a transformative approach for enhancing road safety and resilience in urban transportation systems. By moving beyond traditional, infrastructure-focused models, this approach integrates spatial, behavioral, and technological dimensions into a unified analytical framework. The results highlight the ability of digital twins to support proactive, data-driven decision-making, enabling the identification of risk patterns, evaluation of alternative scenarios, and improvement of safety outcomes, particularly for vulnerable road users. This capability is essential in the context of increasingly complex and dynamic transport systems. Moreover, the study emphasizes that future transportation systems, especially in the era of autonomous mobility, must be designed with a strong human-centered perspective. Ensuring safety, equity, and accessibility should remain central objectives alongside technological advancement. In conclusion, digital twins, when developed within a human-centric and resilience-oriented framework, can serve as powerful tools for shaping safer, more adaptive, and more sustainable urban transportation systems. Future research should focus on enhancing data integration, improving model transparency, and expanding the application of this framework to diverse urban contexts.

REFERENCES

Abushaega, M. M., González, A. D., & Moshebah, O. Y. (2024). A fairness-based multi-objective distribution and restoration model for enhanced resilience of supply chain transportation networks. *Reliability Engineering & System Safety*, *251*, 110314. DOI: 10.1016/j.ress.2024.110314

Aghaabbasi, M., & Sabri, S. (2025). Potentials of digital twin system for analyzing travel behavior decisions. *Travel Behaviour & Society*, *38*, 100902. DOI: 10.1016/j.tbs.2024.100902

Amoozad Mahdiraji, H., Yaftiyan, F., Abbasi-Kamardi, A., Vrontis, D., & Gong, Y. (2024). Disentangling the resiliency of international transportation systems under uncertainty by a novel multi-layer spherical fuzzy decision-making framework: Evidence from an emerging economy. *Transportation Research Part A, Policy and Practice*, *186*, 104151. DOI: 10.1016/j.tra.2024.104151

Anwar, S., Panda, U., & Mohapatra, H. (2024). Legal and ethical issues in IoT based smart city: Data privacy, surveillance, and citizen rights. *Journal of Computer Science Engineering and Software Testing*, *10*(2), 17–26. DOI: 10.46610/JOCSES.2024.v10i02.003

Ashja-Ardalan, S., Alesheikh, A. A., Sharif, M., & Wittowsky, D. (2025). Resilience of urban road networks to climate change: A spatial-topological approach. *Transportation Research Part D, Transport and Environment*, *148*, 104948. DOI: 10.1016/j.trd.2025.104948

Avram, S. (2026). Advancing urban analytics: Geo AI applications in spatial decision-making and sustainable cities. *Urban Science (Basel, Switzerland)*, *10*(3), 148. Advance online publication. DOI: 10.3390/urbansci10030148

Bajwa, M. U., Saleh, W., & Fountas, G. (2025). Identifying a framework for implementing Vision Zero approach to road safety in low- and middle-income countries: A qualitative perspective. *Safety (Basel, Switzerland)*, *11*(4), 93. Advance online publication. DOI: 10.3390/safety11040093

Bashir, T., Bergantino, A. S., Troiani, G., Henke, I., & Pagliara, F. (2025). Vulnerability and resilience analysis of road network: A systematic literature review using Bibliometric. *Sustainable Futures : An Applied Journal of Technology, Environment and Society*, *10*, 101142. DOI: 10.1016/j.sftr.2025.101142

Bergantino, A. S., Gardelli, A., & Rotaris, L. (2024). Assessing transport network resilience: Empirical insights from real-world data studies. *Transport Reviews*, *44*(4), 834–857. DOI: 10.1080/01441647.2024.2322434

Bisht, L. S., & Tiwari, G. (2023). Identification of road traffic crashes hotspots on an intercity expressway in India using geospatial techniques. *IATSS Research*, *47*(3), 349–356. DOI: 10.1016/j.iatssr.2023.07.003

Chen, H., Liu, N. Y., Yang, Y., Wang, Y., Li, Q., & Shan, Y. (2026). Impact effects of transport structure changes on urban traffic congestion: A case study of core cities in China. *Transportation Research Part E, Logistics and Transportation Review*, *208*, 104676. DOI: 10.1016/j.tre.2026.104676

Ciriaco, T. G. M., Zehra, S. N., Wambura, V., & Wong, S. D. (2025). Equitable transportation and resilience hubs: Analysis of underserved population needs, usage, and travel behavior. *Transportation Research Interdisciplinary Perspectives*, *29*, 101314. DOI: 10.1016/j.trip.2024.101314 de Albuquerque Damasceno, M. A., Maia, J. A., Espíndola Gonçalo, T. E., Rocha, M. K., Cabral Peixoto, J. K., & Ferreira, E. A. (2025). A GIS-MCDA spatial classification model to support group decision-making in traffic crash risk management. *Case Studies on Transport Policy*, *20*, 101450. DOI: 10.1016/j.cstp.2025.101450

de Medeiros, A. S., da Silva, M. A. V., Cardoso, M. H. S. A., Santos, T. F., Toro, C., Rojas, G., & Aprigliano, V. (2025). Evaluating urban mobility resilience in Petrópolis through a multicriteria approach. *Urban Science (Basel, Switzerland)*, *9*(7), 269. DOI: 10.3390/urbansci9070269

Dempsey, C. (n.d.). *Buffers in GIS*. Geography Realm. https://www.geographyrealm.com/buffers-in-gis/

Dhinakaran, D., Edwin Raja, S., Ramathilagam, A., Vennila, G., & Alagulakshmi, A. (2025). Ethical and legal challenges with IoT in home digital twins. *Methods (San Diego, Calif.)*, *14*, 103409. DOI: 10.1016/j.mex.2025.103409 PMID: 40852565

Dui, H., Zhang, H., Wu, S., & Xie, M. (2025). Spatiotemporal resilience of IoT-enabled unmanned system of systems. *Engineering (Beijing)*, *54*, 355–369. DOI: 10.1016/j.eng.2025.06.024

El-Agamy, R. F., Sayed, H. A., Al Akhatatneh, A. M., Aljohani, M., & Elhosseini, M. (2024). Comprehensive analysis of digital twins in smart cities: A 4200-paper bibliometric study. *Artificial Intelligence Review*, *57*(6), 154. DOI: 10.1007/s10462-024-10781-8

ElNawawy, A., Lee, J., & Zaki, M. H. (2024). Optimizing smart bike-sharing station placement near public transit stops using GIS: A case study of London, Ontario. In *2024 IEEE International Conference on Smart Mobility (SM)* (pp. 203–208). DOI: 10.1109/SM63044.2024.10733372

Erdem, U., Sharifi, A., & Ökmen, Z. (2026). Neighborhood-scale assessment of urban flood impacts on transportation network resilience: A case study of Mavişehir, İzmir. *International Journal of Disaster Risk Reduction*, *132*, 105970. DOI: 10.1016/j.ijdrr.2025.105970

European Commission. (2024). *Facts and figures: Cyclists. European Road Safety Observatory*. Directorate-General for Transport.

Feizizadeh, B., & Omar Zadeh, D. (2025). A GIS based spatiotemporal modelling approach for cycling risk mapping using crowd-sourced sensor data. *Annals of GIS*, *31*(2), 333–351. DOI: 10.1080/19475683.2025.2453550

Felício, S., Hora, J., Ferreira, M. C., Abrantes, D., Costa, P. D., Dangelo, C., Silva, J., & Galvao, T. (2022). Handling OpenStreetMap georeferenced data for route planning. *Transportation Research Procedia*, *62*, 189–196. DOI: 10.1016/j.trpro.2022.02.024

Giannopoulos, G. A., & Li, Y. (2025). Transport system resilience in climate crises. In *Human mobility, artificial intelligence and climate change* (pp. 85–107). Springer Nature Switzerland., DOI: 10.1007/978-3-032-08171-1_4

Guo, X., Du, Q., Li, Y., Zhou, Y., Wang, Y., Huang, Y., & Martinez-Pastor, B. (2023). Cascading failure and recovery of metro–bus double-layer network considering recovery propagation. *Transportation Research Part D, Transport and Environment*, *122*, 103861. DOI: 10.1016/j.trd.2023.103861

Guo, Z., Zhou, X., Lu, C., Li, S., Zhu, Y., Liu, Y., & Li, Z. (2025). Urban agglomeration transportation resilience: Evaluation and evolution analysis using a data-driven model. *Environmental and Sustainability Indicators*, *26*, 100714. DOI: 10.1016/j.indic.2025.100714

. Hu, S., Wang, S., Su, N., Li, X., & Zhang, Q. (2021). Digital twin based reference architecture for petrochemical monitoring and fault diagnosis. *Oil & Gas Science and Technology–Revue dip Energies Nouvelles*, *76*, 9. DOI: 10.2516/ogst/2020095

Hu, W., Lim, K. Y. H., & Cai, Y. (2022). Digital twin and Industry 4.0 enablers in building and construction: A survey. *Buildings (Basel, Switzerland)*, *12*(11), 2004. DOI: 10.3390/buildings12112004

Huang, Y., Du, J., Chen, M., Lin, Y., Huang, S., & Cai, Y. (2026). Evaluating the spatial-temporal impact of urban nature on urban vitality in Vancouver: A social media and GPS data approach. *Land Use Policy*, *160*, 107824. DOI: 10.1016/j.landusepol.2025.107824

Huzzat, A., Anpalagan, A., Khwaja, A. S., Woungang, I., Alnoman, A. A., & Pillai, A. S. (2025). A comprehensive review of digital twin technologies in smart cities. *Digital Engineering*, *4*, 100040. DOI: 10.1016/j.dte.2025.100040

Iliuţă, M.-E., Moisescu, M.-A., Pop, E., Ionita, A.-D., Cara Mihai, S.-I., & Mitulescu, T.-C. (2024). Digital twin—A review of the evolution from concept to technology and its analytical perspectives on applications in various fields. *Applied Sciences (Basel, Switzerland)*, *14*(13), 5454. Advance online publication. DOI: 10.3390/app14135454

Irfan, M. S., Dasgupta, S., & Rahman, M. (2024). Toward transportation digital twin systems for traffic safety and mobility: A review. *IEEE Internet of Things Journal*, *11*(14), 24581–24603. DOI: 10.1109/JIOT.2024.3395186

Islam, S., & Welch, E. W. (2024). Information technology systems as both contributor to risk perception and adaptive behavior: Public transit agencies' response to extreme weather events. *International Journal of Disaster Risk Reduction*, *115*, 105007. DOI: 10.1016/j.ijdrr.2024.105007

Itäpelto, T., Elhajj, M., & van Sinderen, M. (2025). Digital twin application in lifecycle security of critical infrastructures: A systematic literature review. *International Journal of Critical Infrastructure Protection*, *50*, 100783. DOI: 10.1016/j.ijcip.2025.100783

Jeon, G., Bellandi, V., Chehri, A., & Damiani, E. (2023). Deep learning approaches for vulnerable road users safety. *Safety Science*, *158*, 105964. DOI: 10.1016/j.ssci.2022.105964

Jia, L., Yang, S., Wang, W., & Zhang, X. (2022). Impact analysis of highways in China under future extreme precipitation. *Natural Hazards*, *110*(2), 1097 1113. DOI: 10.1007/s11069-021-04981-6

Kušić, K., Schumann, R., & Ivanjko, E. (2023). A digital twin in transportation: Real-time synergy of traffic data streams and simulation for virtualizing motorway dynamics. *Advanced Engineering Informatics*, *55*, 101858. DOI: 10.1016/j.aei.2022.101858

Lee, C. C., Rajput, A. A., Hsu, C. W., Fan, C., Yuan, F., Dong, S., Esmalian, A., Farahmand, H., Patrascu, F. I., Liu, C.-F., Li, B., Ma, J., & Mostafavi, A. (2022). Quantitative measures for integrating resilience into transportation planning practice: Study in Texas. *Transportation Research Part D, Transport and Environment, 113*, 103496. DOI: 10.1016/j.trd.2022.103496

Li, Y., Yabuki, N., & Fukuda, T. (2022). Exploring the association between street built environment and street vitality using deep learning methods. *Sustainable Cities and Society, 79*, 103656. DOI: 10.1016/j.scs.2021.103656

Liu, C., Zhang, P., & Xu, X. (2023). Literature review of digital twin technologies for civil infrastructure. *Journal of Infrastructure Intelligence and Resilience, 2*(3), 100050. DOI: 10.1016/j.iintel.2023.100050

Liu, J., He, M., Schonfeld, P. M., Kato, H., & Li, A. (2022). Measures of accessibility incorporating time reliability for an urban rail transit network: A case study in Wuhan, China. *Transportation Research Part A, Policy and Practice, 165*, 471–489. DOI: 10.1016/j.tra.2022.09.011

Loia, F., Perillo, C., & Gravili, G. (2026). Unleashing the power of digital twin and big data as a new frontier for smart mobility: An ecosystem perspective. *Big Data Research, 43*, 100576. DOI: 10.1016/j.bdr.2025.100576

Ma, Q., Huang, G., & Tang, X. (2021). GIS-based analysis of spatial–temporal correlations of urban traffic accidents. *European Transport Research Review, 13*(1), 50. DOI: 10.1186/s12544-021-00509-y

Ma, W., Lin, S., Ci, Y., & Li, R. (2024). Resilience evaluation and improvement of post-disaster multimodal transportation networks. *Transportation Research Part A, Policy and Practice, 189*, 104243. DOI: 10.1016/j.tra.2024.104243

Moshood, T. D., Rotimi, J. O. B., Shahzad, W., & Bamgbade, J. A. (2024). Infrastructure digital twin technology: A new paradigm for future construction industry. *Technology in Society, 77*, 102519. DOI: 10.1016/j.techsoc.2024.102519

Moumane, A., Al Karkouri, J., & Batchi, M. (2025). Utilizing GIS, remote sensing, and AHP-multi-criteria decision analysis for optimal landfill site selection in Kenitra Province, Morocco: A step towards sustainable development goals. *Discover Environment, 3*(1), 4. DOI: 10.1007/s44274-025-00183-0

Mun, H., & Jung, J. (2025). Impact of compact city on carbon emission reduction based on urban size: A spatial analysis using satellite imagery. *Sustainable Cities and Society, 126*, 106326. DOI: 10.1016/j.scs.2025.106326

Munoz Diaz, E., Rubio Hernan, J. M., Jurado Romero, F., Karite, A., Vervisch-Picois, A., & Samama, N. (2023). Advanced smartphone-based identification of transport modes: Resilience under GNSS-based attacks. *Future Transportation, 3*(2), 568–583. DOI: 10.3390/futuretransp3020033

OpenStreetMap contributors. (n.d.). *Planet dump*. OpenStreetMap. https://planet.osm.org

Papadakis, D. M., Savvides, A., Michael, A., & Michopoulos, A. (2024). Advancing sustainable urban mobility: Insights from best practices and case studies. *Fuel Communications, 20*, 100125. DOI: 10.1016/j.jfueco.2024.100125

Park, N., Park, J., Joo, Y.-J., & Abdel-Aty, M. (2025). Micro-level hotspot identification at intersections using traffic conflict analysis. *Accident; Analysis and Prevention*, *220*, 108167. DOI: 10.1016/j.aap.2025.108167 PMID: 40644754

Pedon, D., Bani Hashemi, S., LeNguyen, K., & Derrible, S. (2024). Navigating urban complexity: The transformative role of digital twins in smart city development. *Sustainable Cities and Society*, *111*, 105583. DOI: 10.1016/j.scs.2024.105583

Saidi, S., Koutsopoulos, H. N., Wilson, N. H. M., & Zhao, J. (2023). Train following model for urban rail transit performance analysis. *Transportation Research Part C, Emerging Technologies*, *148*, 104037. DOI: 10.1016/j.trc.2023.104037

Serdar, M. Z., Koç, M., & Al-Ghamdi, S. G. (2022). Urban transportation networks resilience: Indicators, disturbances, and assessment methods. *Sustainable Cities and Society*, *76*, 103452. DOI: 10.1016/j.scs.2021.103452

Shang, J., Xiao, L., Wu, Z., Yang, J., Xiao, Z., Wang, J., Zhang, Y., Chen, X., Wang, J., & Li, H. (2024). GvdsSQL: Heterogeneous Database Unified Access Technology for Wide-Area Environments. *Electronics (Basel)*, *13*(8), 1521. DOI: 10.3390/electronics13081521

Song, J., Liu, S., Ma, T., Sun, Y., Tao, F., & Bao, J. (2023). Resilient digital twin modeling: A transferable approach. *Advanced Engineering Informatics*, *58*, 102148. DOI: 10.1016/j.aei.2023.102148

Sosik-Filipiak, K., & Osypchuk, O. (2023). Identification of solutions for vulnerable road users safety in urban transport systems: Grounded theory research. *Sustainability (Basel)*, *15*(13), 10568. Advance online publication. DOI: 10.3390/su151310568

Tan, Y. R., Hofmeister, M., Phua, S. Z., Brownbridge, G., Rustagi, K., Akroyd, J., Mosbach, S., Bhave, A., & Kraft, M. (2025). Beyond connected digital twins–can digital twins really deliver sustainable cities? *Sustainable Cities and Society*, *131*, 106596. DOI: 10.1016/j.scs.2025.106596

Tang, S., Randhawa, S., Rui, J., Ludwig, C., Knoblauch, S., Hatfield, C., & Zipf, A. (2026). Estimating road speed classes: Integrating OpenStreetMap and Street View imagery for missing data imputation. *Computers, Environment and Urban Systems*, *125*, 102392. DOI: 10.1016/j.compenvurbsys.2025.102392

Wachnicka, J., Jarczewska, A., & Pappalardo, G. (2023). Methods of cyclist training in Europe. *Sustainability (Basel)*, *15*(19), 14345. Advance online publication. DOI: 10.3390/su151914345

Wijesinghe, W., & Withanage, W. (2025). A GIS-MCDA based evaluation of the quality of life variations in Anuradhapura Municipal Council: A policy implication road map for human well-being. *Journal of Geospatial Surveying*, *5*(1), 1–10. Advance online publication. DOI: 10.4038/jgs.v5i1.62

Xing, L., Li, B., Deng, K., Gao, J., Wu, H., Ma, H., & Zhang, X. (2025). Advancing intelligent transportation through digital twin: Challenges, models, and future prospects. *Ad Hoc Networks*, •••, 104077.

Yannis, G., Nikolaou, D., Laiou, A., Stürmer, Y. A., Buttler, I., & Jankowska-Karpa, D. (2020). Vulnerable road users: Cross-cultural perspectives on performance and attitudes. *IATSS Research*, *44*(3), 220–229. DOI: 10.1016/j.iatssr.2020.08.006

Ye, Y., Wong, S. C., Li, Y. C., & Choi, K. M. (2023). Crossing behaviors of drunk pedestrians unfamiliar with local traffic rules. *Safety Science*, *157*, 105924. DOI: 10.1016/j.ssci.2022.105924

Zapata, N., Pérez-González, G., Bustos, P., Barroso, S., & Núñez, P. (2025). An efficient and versatile digital twin model implementation for autonomous connected vehicles based on distributed, low-latency working memory. *Internet of Things : Engineering Cyber Physical Human Systems*, *32*, 101627. DOI: 10.1016/j.iot.2025.101627

Zhang, L., He, R., Liu, Q., & Gardoni, P. (2026). *Resilience in urban transit systems*. Springer Nature Singapore., DOI: 10.1007/978-981-95-4322-9

Zhang, T., Ding, J., Liu, Z., & Zhang, W. (2025). Visualization of industrial big data: State-of-the-art and future perspectives. *Engineering (Beijing)*, *52*, 85–101. DOI: 10.1016/j.eng.2025.08.014

Zhou, J., Li, Z., Zhang, Y., & Dong, S. (2026). Transportation infrastructure resilience and safety under climate risks: A global bibliometric and thematic analysis (1995–2025). *Multimodal Transportation*, *100307*(3), 100307. Advance online publication. DOI: 10.1016/j.multra.2026.100307

Chapter 11

Integrating Digital Twin Technology Into V2X Communication:

Toward Connected and Autonomous Mobility

Swati Jaiswal
http://orcid.org/0000-0001-9671-534X
DES Pune University, Pune, India

Prachi Joshi
DES Pune University, Pune, India

Spandan Surdas
Northeastern University, USA

ABSTRACT

The fast evolution of connected cars and autonomous cars demands intelligent transportation systems that can handle high amounts of real-time data. Nevertheless, conventional Vehicle-to-Everything communication systems have weaknesses of low predictivity, latency, interoperability difficulties, and poor traffic control. To mitigate these problems, this chapter examines the application of the Digital Twin technology in conjunction with V2X communication to facilitate real-time monitoring, and predictive analysis. DT-V2X framework provides data-driven virtual models of vehicles, road infrastructure, and communication networks. It combines IoT sensors, edge and cloud computing and AI-based predictive analytics to align the physical transportation environments with their digital equivalents. The framework aims at assessing traffic behavior via simulation and real time data analysis. The expected outcomes include improved road safety, enhanced traffic flow, reduced communication latency, and energy-efficient mobility, contributing to more sustainable intelligent transportation systems.

DOI: 10.4018/979-8-3373-7785-8.ch011

1. INTRODUCTION

The intensive development of intelligent traffic systems (ITS) is changing contemporary mobility with the integration of the latest communications, sensing, and data analytics systems. As connected and autonomous vehicles continue to be rolled out in large quantities, transportation systems are becoming more and more data-driven ecosystems capable of enabling real-time communication and collaborative decision-making. The communication of Vehicle-to-Everything (V2X) has been one of the most essential technologies in the change, as it allows cars to communicate with each other, roadside infrastructure, pedestrians and network services. V2X systems create a better awareness of situations, promote road safety and efficient traffic control in such complex and dynamic transportation situations because of the constant exchange of information (Zhang et al., 2025).

The V2X communication involves several interaction modes, such as Vehicle-to-Vehicle (V2V), Vehicle-to-Infrastructure (V2I), Vehicle-to-Pedestrian (V2P), Vehicle-to-Network (V2N) and Vehicle-to-Grid (V2G). These communication paradigms allow the exchange of vital information of vehicles like speed, location, braking status, traffic lights, and weather conditions. Consequently, V2X technologies can be used in applications that have a wide spectrum which include collision avoidance systems, cooperative adaptive cruise control, traffic signal coordination, and intelligent navigation services. The upcoming implementation of cellular-based communication technology LTE-V2X and 5G only increases the capabilities of V2X systems by offering high data rates, ultra-low latency, and reliable connectivity needed in safety-critical applications (3GPP, 2025).

Traditional V2X systems in spite of these developments have various limitations which limit their potential. Real-time communication in a highly dynamic traffic environment might not be enough to predict traffic congestion, accidents and infrastructure failures that are about to happen. More than that, the large amounts of heterogeneous data that connected vehicles, sensors and infrastructure produce pose a serious problem in regards to data management, scalability and predictive analysis. The traditional methods of traffic management are usually based on the principle of reactive control, which is used in response to the events after they have already adversely affected the traffic or safety (Guo et al., 2025). These issues demonstrate that complex architecture is required that can integrate real-time communications with predictive models and system-level intelligence.

The Digital Twin (DT) technology has become a significant paradigm to deal with these issues in complicated cyber-physical systems. A Digital Twin is an active virtual object or system of a real-world object, which can synchronously react to real-time measurements of sensors and connected systems. Digital Twins can be used to monitor and simulate the behavior of physical systems in real-time and predict its behavior by developing a digital version of the physical system. In the transportation system, Digital Twins can simulate vehicles, traffic lights, road systems, and the communication systems, which allows a study of the entire traffic flow and the dynamics of system performance (Tao et al., 2025). Digital Twin systems can be used to analyze massive amounts of data through the use of Internet of Things (IoT) sensors, edge computing, cloud environment, and artificial intelligence (AI).

Digital Twin technology integration into V2X means a new paradigm called Digital Twin-enabled V2X (DT-V2X). Within this model, V2X is obtained by real-time car and infrastructure data and continuously relayed to digital twin platforms, where further analytics and simulation models are applied to recreate and forecast traffic conditions. This synchronization between the physical transportation network and its digital counterpart in real time is beneficial as it allows managing traffic in advance, performing safety analysis, and offering mobility services at the best. As an instance, DT-V2X systems can predict the level of traffic jam, detect possible accidents, optimize signal passing, and cooperate in decision-making between connected and autonomous cars (Llagostera-Brugarola et al., 2025).

New technologies are very vital in the facilitation of DT-V2X frameworks. The IoT sensors installed in vehicles and infrastructure produce uninterrupted data of operational data. The low-latency capability of edge computing is suitable to safety-critical applications and cloud computing offers scalability and high-performance computing capabilities to large-scale simulation and analytics. Even greater possibilities of the digital twin lie in artificial intelligence and machine learning algorithms that allow predictive modeling, anomaly detection, and optimization of the system. All these technologies create a complete digital environment that can facilitate the real-time monitoring, intelligent decision-making, and automated control of traffic in the current system of transportation.

Implementation of DT-V2X systems also plays a major role towards sustainable and energy efficient mobility. These systems can limit the consumption of fuel and greenhouse gases by maximizing the flow of traffic, minimizing congestion, and allowing the eco-driving approaches. Moreover, the V2X communication, when combined with electric vehicle infrastructure, enables advanced Vehicle-to-Grid (V2G) strategies, where electric vehicles communicate with power grids in order to be smart charged and to manage energy. These capabilities are needed to accomplish the objectives of smart cities and sustainable city transportation (Guo et al., 2025).

In spite of all these advantages of DT-V2X systems, there are still several challenges ahead until the large-scale deployment of V2X systems is facilitated. The problems concerning data privacy, cybersecurity, and communication standards interoperability as well as the cost of infrastructure update need to be looked into to promote a secure and dependable functioning. Moreover, ensuring real-time correlation of physical systems and digital twins needs effective communication networks and effective data processing mechanisms. To address these limitations and make DT-V2X systems more reliable, current research activities are directed at standardized architecture development, enhanced communication (5G and upcoming 6G networks) and AI-based analytics.

In this respect, this chapter discusses the Digital Twin technology combined with V2X communication in the context of intelligent transportation systems. It provides the key principles, architectures, enabling technologies and applications of DT-V2X systems, respectively, case studies, and performance evaluation metrics. Another issue that is discussed in the chapter is the major challenges and future research goals that are intended to create resilient, sustainable, and intelligent transportation infrastructures in the next generation of smart cities. Recent research in autonomous driving underlines how deep learning-based lane and traffic signs detection techniques have shown efficiency in vehicle perception and accuracy in tracking the path. Such perception models, combined with Vehicle-to-Everything (V2X) communication and Digital Twin models, can be constantly aligned with real-time traffic and infrastructure information and used to predictively control, make decisions cooperatively, and conform to adaptive movement in intelligent transportation systems (Jaiswal and Mohan, 2023).

Lane detection and prediction techniques based on deep learning have been critical in ensuring that autonomous vehicle can navigate through the road in dynamic conditions on the road and with high accuracy and reliability. These perception-driven models can be continuously updated and verified with the help of real-time traffic and infrastructure data and can be used to control movements in predictive manners and cooperative decisions in smart transportation systems when combined with Vehicle-to-Everything (V2X) communication and Digital Twin environments (Kachhoria et al., 2023).

1.1 Background of Digital Twin–Enabled Vehicle-to-Everything (V2X) Communication

The current pace of interconnectivity and autonomy of vehicles has brought a strong demand of smart transportation systems that are able to process and handle enormous amounts of real-time information. Vehicle-to-Everything (V2X) communication has become one of the most powerful enabling technologies that enable vehicles to share information with the other entities in the vicinity such as other vehicles, roadside infrastructure, pedestrians and network systems. V2X systems can be used to improve situational awareness and enable applications like collision avoidance, cooperative driving, and traffic management due to communication modes like Vehicle-to-Vehicle (V2V), Vehicle-to-Infrastructure (V2I), Vehicle-to-Pedestrian (V2P), and Vehicle-to-Network (V2N) (Zhang et al., 2025). These features are crucial to enhance road safety, congestion and efficient mobility in contemporary networks of transportation.

Although the V2X communication has a great potential, the traditional systems still have various challenges associated with latency, scalability, interoperability and predictive capability. Real-time communication may be not enough in the context of highly dynamic traffic conditions to predict traffic disruption, accidents, or congestion. In addition, the number of connected cars grows and provides large volumes of heterogeneous data, which needs sophisticated data processing and analytics solutions. Scientists have thus examined novel computational models capable of integrating real-time communication and predictive modeling and system-wide optimization (Guo et al., 2025).

The digital twin (DT) technology has become a potentially viable solution to overcome these constraints. A Digital Twin is an active virtual model of a physical system, which is constantly updated with real-time data obtained by sensors, communication networks, and working systems. Digital twins have the ability to reproduce vehicles, road infrastructure, traffic lights, and communication networks in the transportation system that allow continuous monitoring, simulation, predictive analysis (Tao et al., 2025). Digital Twins integrate IoT sensors, edge computing, and artificial intelligence to enable transportation systems to simulate the scenario with various traffic conditions and predict the behavior of the system.

Digital Twin technology together with V2X communication establishes a strong platform in transportation systems. V2X communications in Digital Twin-enabled V2X (DT-V2X) systems enable real-time data to be collected and used to revise virtual models of transportation environments, whereby the potential risks can be analyzed and the system performance optimized by traffic operators and autonomous vehicles. This system can allow predictive traffic control, enhanced accident prevention, and mobility solutions that are energy-efficient (Llagostera-Brugarola et al., 2025). Consequently, DT-V2X systems have become a strategic technological base of the future smart cities and sustainable transportation networks.

2. FUNDAMENTALS OF V2X COMMUNICATION

Vehicle-to-Everything (V2X) communication is a concept of a wireless communication of information between a vehicle and other entities in the area where the vehicle is located to improve safety, efficiency and overall driving experience. It is significant in the intelligent transportation systems (ITS) because it allows vehicles to be able to communicate with other vehicles, road infrastructure, pedestrians, networks, and energy infrastructure. V2X technology enhances situational awareness, and advanced functions of driving that help achieve safer and more efficient transportation networks through constant and real-time data exchange.

V2X communication in the contemporary transportation ecosystem allows vehicles and infrastructure to cooperate in terms of awareness. Cars and motor vehicles fitted with sensors and communication systems can transmit details on speed, position, direction, braking position, and the condition of the road. The exchange of such information enables the vehicles to foresee possible dangers that their onboard devices are not capable of detecting and react to adverse traffic conditions in advance. Consequently, using V2X communication can minimize accidents, enhance the traffic conditions, and contribute to the creation of connected and autonomous vehicles that can take intelligent decisions in multifaceted conditions (Zhang et al., 2025).

The V2X communication is made up of a variety of communication modes that shape the way the vehicles communicate with various elements within the transportation ecosystem. Such modes are Vehicle-to-Vehicle (V2V), which supports direct communication between the adjacent vehicles; Vehicle-to-Infrastructure (V2I), which allows vehicles to communicate with the roadside units or traffic lights; Vehicle-to-Pedestrian (V2P), which is used to make the vehicles safer through enabling them to communicate with pedestrians and bicycles; Vehicle-to-Network (V2N), which allows vehicles to connect with the cloud services and traffic lights; and Vehicle-to-Grid (V2G) where electric vehicles can communicate with the All these forms of communications serve to develop a collaborative and integrated transportation environment.

V2X communication is based on the use of advanced wireless communication technologies, including Dedicated Short-Range Communication (DSRC), Cellular Vehicle-to-Everything (C-V2X) and new 5G and future 6G networks. The technologies have guaranteed connections, low latency and high rates of data transmission necessary in safety critical applications. Specifically, cellular-based V2X communication permits not only direct inter-vehicle communication but also network-assisted services so that vehicles may obtain a wider range of traffic information, as well as a system-level coordination (3GPP, 2025).

2.1 Concept of V2X

V2X enables vehicles to communicate with other vehicles, with the infrastructure at roadsides, with pedestrians, and with network systems via wireless communication. Through constant data exchange, vehicles develop a situational awareness beyond the range of the sensors on board. The real-time sharing of information, such as vehicle speed, position, braking, timing of traffic signals, road conditions, and hazard warnings, can be provided to help make proactive driving decisions and manage traffic.

The primary goals of V2X communication are:

1. Improving road safety by reducing accidents
2. Enhancing traffic efficiency and reducing congestion
3. Supporting autonomous and cooperative driving
4. Enabling smart mobility services

2.2 Types of V2X Communication

V2X is an umbrella term that includes several communication modes:

1. **Vehicle-to-Vehicle (V2V):** Vehicle-to-Vehicle (V2V) communication refers to a wireless information exchange through direct communication between close cars to enhance driving safety and situational awareness. The vehicles exchange real-time information about the speed, acceleration, heading, braking, and trajectory of the vehicles, thereby enabling them to predict possible dangers even when they are not in sight of the onboard sensors. V2V is of great importance in collision avoidance, cooperative adaptive cruise control, platooning, and lane-change. Recent research is stating that the cooperative awareness messages between cars based on V2V lead to a significant decrease in the number of rear-end and intersection crashes as they allow the early signal transmission and the coordinated actions (Zhang et al., 2025). V2V aids proactive safety measures as opposed to reactive braking when combined with predictive models.
2. **Vehicle-to-Infrastructure (V2I):** Vehicle to Infrastructure (V2I) communication is a communication system between the vehicles and the roadside infrastructure, including roadside units (RSUs) and roadside cameras, traffic lights, and environmental sensors. V2I allows vehicles to obtain knowledge regarding signal phase and timing (SPaT), road geometry, congestion, and weather conditions. This communication enhances the efficiency of traffic flow, safety in intersections, and eco-driving approaches. It is found that adaptive signal control and speed advisory systems, which are supported by V2I, are capable of greatly decreasing travel delays and fuel use in urban traffic networks (Guo et al., 2025). V2I also constitutes a primary connection between vehicles and Digital Twin platforms since it provides continuous input of information on the infrastructure level.
3. **Vehicle-to-Pedestrian (V2P):** Vehicle-to-Pedestrian (V2P) communication deals with the safety of the vulnerable road users, like pedestrians, cyclists, and wheelchair users. Pedestrians can share the information about their location and movement with other vehicles that may be passing at the same time using smartphones, wearable devices, or specialized sensors. V2P works especially well in low-visibility situations, complicated crossroads, and high-pedestrian urban areas. Research shows that V2P-based alert systems significantly minimize the number of pedestrian accidents because they give an early warning to drivers and pedestrians (Kachhoria et al., 2023). V2P can be used to perform real-time predictive safety evaluation when used alongside risque modeling using Digital Twin.
4. **Vehicle-to-Network (V2N):** Vehicle-to-Network (V2N) is the communication between vehicles and cloud servers, traffic management centers, and service platforms that use cellular network carriers LTE and 5G. V2N promotes navigation services, over-the-air updates, traffic analytics, infotainment, and massive coordination between transportation systems. V2N, in contrast to short-range V2V or V2I communication, provides the possibility to aggregate data globally and optimize the system. Recent studies demonstrate that V2N plays a vital role in sustaining city-level or regional digital twins, in which historical and real-time information is processed to support predictive traffic management and policy development (Tao et al., 2025).
5. **Vehicle-to-Grid (V2G):** Vehicle-to-Grid (V2G) communication is a two-way communication between electric cars (EVs) and power grids. With the help of V2G, EVs would be able to optimize the process of charging, promote load balancing, and even provide energy back to the grid when the demand is at its highest point. Such interaction is essential for incorporating renewable sources of energy and attaining sustainable transportation systems. Research indicates that smart charging with V2G will ease the grid load and enhance energy efficiency generally when managed by intelligent control platforms (Li et al., 2025). Under DT-V2X systems, the digital twins become simulators of the energy demand, charging behavior, and grid response, facilitating the green mobility strategies.

Figure 1. Infrastructure of V2X communication

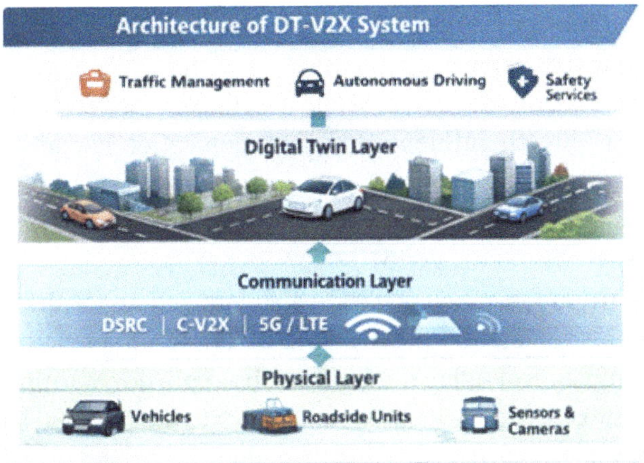

Figure 1 illustrates the communication infrastructure of V2X, in which all the components play vital roles for better communication.

Table 1. Functional comparison of vehicle-to-everything (V2X) communication modes

V2X Type	Entities Involved	Data Exchanged	Applications	Benefits
V2V	Vehicles ↔ Vehicles	Speed, position, braking status, trajectory	Collision avoidance, platooning, cooperative lane change	Improved road safety, reduced reaction time
V2I	Vehicles ↔ Roadside Units, traffic lights, sensors	Signal timing, speed limits, road conditions, congestion data	Traffic signal control, intersection safety, and eco-driving	Traffic efficiency, reduced congestion
V2P	Vehicles ↔ Pedestrians (smartphones, wearables)	Location, movement, warning alerts	Pedestrian safety, accident prevention	Protection of vulnerable road users
V2N	Vehicles ↔ Cloud servers, traffic centers	Navigation data, traffic analytics, software updates	Global traffic management, system optimization	Large-scale coordination, predictive planning
V2G	Electric Vehicles ↔ Power Grid	Charging status, energy demand, grid load	Smart charging, load balancing, energy trading	Energy efficiency, sustainability

Table 1 shows a comparative summary of the key forms of Vehicle-to-Everything (V2X) communications, i.e., Vehicle-to-Vehicle (V2V), Vehicle-to-Infrastructure (V2I), Vehicle-to-Pedestrian (V2P), Vehicle-to-Network (V2N), and Vehicle-to-Grid (V2G). The table is a summary of the major participants in the communication, data exchanged, major applications, and the associated advantages to each mode of communication. The V2X interactions under this comparison are complementary with respect to increasing road safety, traffic efficiency, energy management, and general system intelligence in the context of connected and autonomous transportation environments.

2.3 Communication Technologies for V2X

Communication technologies constitute the foundational layer of Vehicle-to-Everything (V2X) systems by enabling real-time data exchange among vehicles, infrastructure, pedestrians, networks, and energy systems. The performance of safety-critical and intelligence-driven applications in connected and autonomous transportation is directly influenced by communication latency, reliability, coverage, and scalability (Zhang et al., 2025). When integrated with Digital Twin (DT) frameworks, these communication technologies provide continuous data streams that synchronize physical transportation systems with their virtual counterparts (Tao et al., 2025).

Dedicated Short-Range Communication (DSRC), standardized under IEEE 802.11p, enables direct vehicle-to-vehicle (V2V) and vehicle-to-infrastructure (V2I) communication with very low latency. DSRC supports rapid dissemination of safety messages such as collision warnings and emergency braking alerts. In a Digital Twin context, DSRC primarily contributes to the physical and communication layers by providing high-frequency, localized data that updates vehicle-level and intersection-level digital twins in real time (Kritzinger et al., 2018). However, DSRC's limited range and scalability constraints restrict its effectiveness for city-scale Digital Twin implementations.

Wi-Fi-based communication technologies are occasionally used for non-safety V2X applications such as parking assistance and infotainment. These technologies provide supplementary data to digital twins but are generally confined to the physical and communication layers due to their limited reliability in high-mobility environments.

Cellular Vehicle-to-Everything (C-V2X), standardized by the 3rd Generation Partnership Project (3GPP), significantly enhances V2X capabilities by supporting both direct communication (PC5 interface) and network-based communication (Uu interface). LTE-V2X and 5G C-V2X enable wider coverage, higher reliability, and better scalability compared to short-range technologies (3GPP, 2025).

Within Digital Twin–enabled V2X systems, cellular technologies serve as the primary data conduit between the communication layer and the digital twin layer. Real-time vehicular and infrastructure data transmitted through 5G networks is continuously ingested by digital twins to update traffic states, vehicle behavior, and network conditions. The ultra-reliable low-latency communication (URLLC) supported by 5G is particularly critical for synchronizing Digital Twins used in autonomous driving, cooperative perception, and predictive traffic control (Guo et al., 2025).

Satellite communication complements terrestrial V2X technologies by providing connectivity in rural, remote, or disaster-affected regions. Although higher latency limits its use in immediate safety applications, satellite communication plays an important role in feeding data to system-level Digital Twins, enabling large-scale monitoring, logistics management, and emergency response planning (Zhang et al., 2025).

Vehicle-to-Network (V2N) communication relies heavily on cloud-based cellular connectivity to support large-scale data aggregation, analytics, and visualization. In Digital Twin architectures, V2N communication primarily supports the cloud and analytics layers, where historical and real-time data are fused to enable long-term prediction, optimization, and policy evaluation (Tao et al., 2025).

Future 6G-based V2X communication is expected to introduce AI-native networking, sub-millisecond latency, integrated sensing and communication, and high-precision positioning. These features will enable highly accurate and autonomous digital twins capable of real-time self-learning and system-wide optimization (Zhang et al., 2025). Such advancements will support fully autonomous mobility and tightly coupled cyber-physical transportation ecosystems.

From a theoretical standpoint, V2X communication technologies act as the data acquisition and synchronization backbone of digital twin–enabled transportation systems. Short-range technologies support fine-grained, local digital twins; cellular technologies enable city-scale and regional Digital Twins, and cloud-based communication supports system-wide intelligence. This multi-technology, multi-layer integration allows Digital Twins to evolve from passive monitoring tools into active decision-making entities that continuously interact with the physical transportation system.

Table 2. Communication technologies for vehicle-to-everything (V2X)

Technology	Standard / Interface	Communication Mode	Key Features	Typical Applications
DSRC (Dedicated Short-Range Communication)	IEEE 802.11p	Direct (V2V, V2I)	Very low latency, short range, infrastructure-independent	Collision warning, emergency braking alerts
LTE-V2X	3GPP Release 14/15	Direct (PC5) and Network-based (Uu)	Better range than DSRC, supports cellular infrastructure	Traffic safety, cooperative driving
5G C-V2X	3GPP Release 16/17	Direct + Network-based	Ultra-low latency, high reliability, high data rates	Autonomous driving, real-time traffic control
5G NR-V2X	3GPP Release 18+	Advanced cellular	Network slicing, edge integration, massive connectivity	Cooperative perception, smart cities
Wi-Fi / WLAN	IEEE 802.11	Short-range	Low cost, high data rate	Parking, infotainment, local communication
Satellite Communication	GNSS / LEO Satellites	Wide-area	Global coverage, high availability	Rural V2X, disaster management
Future 6G V2X	Emerging (Post-5G)	Intelligent wireless	AI-native, ultra-low latency, precise positioning	Fully autonomous mobility, DT-enabled V2X

2.4 Key Applications of V2X

V2X communication is used for a wide range of applications for safety, efficiency, and mobility.

In safety applications, V2X is used for collision warnings, emergency braking, blind spot warning,s and intersection safety applications. Vehicles will be able to share information about sudden braking, changing lanes, or hazardous road conditions, and vehicles in the vicinity will be able to react before an accident occurs while driving through traffic.

In traffic management, adaptive traffic signal control, congestion monitoring, and dynamic route guidance can be realized with V2X. Vehicles are informed in real time about traffic status, signals, and road closures, to help save travel time and fuel.

For autonomous and cooperative driving, V2X provides the following: Vehicle platooning, cooperative lane changing, and coordinated merging at intersections. Vehicles will share their intentions and trajectories for improved safety and efficiency of driving.

In smart mobility services, V2X enables an application such as smart parking, fleet management, ride-sharing coordination and public transport optimization. Electric vehicles also use V2X for vehicle-to-grid communication that will allow for smart charging and energy management.

In general, V2X communication can aid the process of transforming vehicles into intelligent and connected agents that can collaborate with the environment to establish safer, more efficient, and sustainable transportation systems.

3 DIGITAL TWIN TECHNOLOGY: CONCEPTS AND ARCHITECTURE

A Digital Twin is a dynamically simulated digital model of a system, process or physical object that is continuously updated with real-time measured data through sensors, communication networks and operation systems. This principle can help organizations track system behavior, model the operation conditions, and forecast possible results thus contributing to the effectiveness of decision-making and system optimization (Tao et al., 2022). Digital Twins can be contrasted to the traditional simulation models that are based on fixed data sets and fixed assumptions that do not constantly update and adapt, unlike the Digital Twin which constantly incorporates the new data provided by its real-life counterpart. The digital model can represent the present scenario of the system and offers predictive analysis and scenario-based evaluation due to this bi-directional exchange of data between the physical and virtual environment (Kritzinger et al., 2018). Due to the rapid adoption of data-driven technologies in the industries, the use of Digital Twins has been growing fast in industries like manufacturing, transportation, healthcare, and smart cities. The market research also shows that the Digital Twin market is expected to grow significantly in the near future because of the increasing need to monitor objects in real-time, provide predictive maintenance, and manage the intelligent system (Fortune Business Insights, 2024).

The three general types of Digital Twins are listed according to their scope of application. Product Digital Twins are single physical objects (vehicles, machine, equipment, etc.), and they aim at monitoring performance, managing faults, and optimizing the product lifecycle. Process Digital Twins, in their turn, represent the operational workflow and process, e.g. manufacturing lines, traffic flow, or logistics systems. These twins assist the organization in analyzing efficiency in the system, finding the bottlenecks and enhance operational performance. System Digital Twins are large scale and multi faceted environments: they combine several product and process twins into a single model. Smart cities, industrial plants, and transportation networks are some examples, where interactions between different subsystems are to be monitored and optimized at the same time (Tao et al., 2022).

In spite of their nature, Digital Twins have three basic elements that can be used to facilitate their functionality. The first element is the physical entity, which is the actual entity in the world or a device that is sensor-equipped with communication devices that produce data on its operation. The second element is the virtual model, which is a representation in form of a digital representation, which imitates the structure, behavior, and performance of the physical system. The third element is the data connection or communication interface that facilitates the operation of an exchange of data between the physical and virtual environment. This continuous synchronization guarantees that the digital twin is able to give a perfect reflection of the condition of the real system as well as facilitating sophisticated analytics, predictive modeling and intelligent control (Kritzinger et al., 2018).

3.1 Enabling Technologies

Digital Twins are made possible by key technologies such as IoT for real-time data collection, cloud computing for large-scale storage and processing, edge computing for low-latency operations, artificial intelligence for prediction and optimisation, and big data technologies to handle massive and heterogeneous data streams (Guo et al., 2024).

Several digital technologies make Digital Twin implementation possible.

1. The Internet of Things (IoT) offers a means for sensors and devices to collect real-time data on physical systems, such as location, temperature, speed, pressure, and usage patterns.
2. Cloud computing provides the potential for storage and high-performance computing capability to process large volumes of data, run simulations, and offer global accessibility.
3. Edge computing allows data to be processed near the source of the data, thereby lowering the latency for data that is time-critical, such as transportation, healthcare, and manufacturing.
4. Artificial Intelligence (AI) and machine learning are adding value to the Digital Twins by adding capabilities for predictive analytics, anomaly detection, optimization, and self-learning capabilities.
5. Big data technologies are used to support the storage, processing, and analysis of massive and heterogeneous data generated by sensors, systems, and simulations, which allow accurate modeling and long-term performance analysis.

All these technologies are the basic pillars of Digital Twin systems that allow real-time monitoring, smart analysis, and data-driven decision-making in a broad area of application.

4. DIGITAL TWIN–ENABLED V2X FRAMEWORK

A Digital Twin-enabled Vehicle-to-Everything (DT-V2X) architecture is a combined strategy that consists of integrating both a real and dynamic virtual representation of vehicles, roads and communication facilities with real-world vehicles. This paradigm supports uninterrupted communication between the real and virtual worlds of transportation where transportation systems monitor and analyzes the operations and optimizes it in time. The digital twin can recreate the state and behavior of vehicles, traffic systems, and communication networks by using real-time data provided via V2X communication and predictively analyze and proactively manage traffic (Tao et al., 2022; Guo et al., 2024).

Data is generated continuously by vehicles, roadside infrastructure and communication systems in a DT-V2X system on a continuous basis, based on sensors, onboard units and other connected devices. This information is exchanged via V2X communication that includes Dedicated Short- Range Communication (DSRC), Cellular V2X (C-V2X), and 5G. The received data is processed by the edge and cloud computing platforms where digital twin models are developed and updated in real-time. The models model the behavior of a physical part of transport e.g., vehicles, intersections, traffic lights and road networks. With the help of such real-time synchronization, digital twins offer a global perspective on the transportation environment and allow intelligent study of traffic patterns, interactions with vehicles, and the work of communication networks.

Among the most important benefits of the DT-V2X framework, predictive simulation and scenario analysis can be noted. Through real-time and past data, the digital twin can predict traffic jams, identify future accidents, and estimate the effect of various traffic control measures and apply them to the real environment. E.g. the system can model changes in the traffic signal timing, rerouting, or priorities of emergency vehicles to find the most efficient solution. The predictive ability is changing the traditional models of transportation systems that are reactive to control systems that are proactive and adaptive in preventing issues before they arise.

Cooperative and autonomous driving are also facilitated by the DT-V2X framework as the vehicles can exchange information with other vehicles as well as digital twin platforms analyzing this information and coordinating system-level behavior. The digital twin can advise autonomous vehicles on the best routes to take, the maximum safe speed on the road, and the dangers to expect. This communication improves the decision-making capabilities of the connected and autonomous cars making the roads safer and more efficient.

Moreover, incorporation of the new technologies, including the Internet of Things (IoT), artificial intelligence (AI), edge computing, and cloud computing, reinforces the functionality of DT-V2X systems. IoT sensors installed on vehicles and infrastructure send streamlines of operation data in real-time. Edge computing handles time-sensitive information nearer to the source, and this guarantees instant response to safety-related processes, whereas cloud computing platforms engage with large-scale analytics and long-term data storage. Artificial intelligence algorithms process obtained data to extract patterns, predict traffic conditions, and optimize the work of systems.

On the whole, the V2X framework based on the Digital Twin allows establishing a cyber-physical ecosystem in which transport systems can be monitored in real-time, simulated, and optimized. DT-V2X systems can provide connected and autonomous automobile support, intelligent traffic regulation, better road safety, effective mobility, and the synchronization of real-world transportation environments with digital models. This framework is very important in the design of next generation smart transportation system and sustainable mobility solutions.

4.1 Architecture of DT-V2X Systems

V2X system architecture is developed in such a way that it provides a continuous exchange of data between the vehicles, infrastructure, and centralized platforms. It is composed of physical, communication, and computing layers.

At the physical layer, vehicles are outfitted with units (OBUs) that mostly contain sensors, GPS modules, and wireless communication interfaces. Roadside infrastructure consists of devices such as roadside units (RSUs), traffic signals, cameras, and environmental sensors, which are located on the roads and at intersections.

The communication layer is the link between OBUs and RSUs using wireless communication technology such as DSRC, LTE, and 5G. The reliable data transmission for short-range direct communication as well as long-range network-based communication is ensured by this layer.

The computing layer contains edge servers that are located near roads and cloud data centers. Edge computing allows fast processing of safety-critical data with minimal delay, while cloud platforms allow large-scale storage, analytics, and optimisation of the systems. These layers, combined with each other, allow real-time decisions, data integration, and smart traffic control.

Data is constantly streaming from vehicles and infrastructure to an edge and cloud platform for analysis and redirection as actionable data to vehicles and traffic control systems.

Figure 2 represents the architecture of a DT-V2X system, which is typically organized into four layers:

Figure 2. Architecture of DT-V2X communication

1. **Physical Layer:** The physical layer in DT-V2X is basically used to generate data. This includes vehicles with onboard units (OBUs), sensors (LiDAR, radar, cameras, and GPS), and communication modules, as well as roadside infrastructure (e.g., roadside units (RSUs), traffic lights, cameras, and environmental sensors). These components produce massive amounts of real-time data with a relationship to vehicle status, road conditions, traffic flow, and quality of communication (Zhang et al., 2024).
    a. **V2V:** Vehicle sensors generate motion and safety data.
    b. **V2I:** Roadside infrastructure collects traffic and environmental data.
    c. **V2P:** Pedestrian devices provide location and movement information.
    d. **V2N:** Vehicles upload system and navigation data.
    e. **V2G:** EVs and chargers generate energy usage and charging data.

    This layer represents the real-world transportation environment.

2. **Communication Layer:** The communication layer is also called the data exchange layer. Data is being transmitted by using DSRC, C-V2X, LTE, and 5G technologies. Low-latency safety communication is appropriate with direct communication (vehicle-to-vehicle or vehicle-to-infrastructur5., and network-based communication is appropriate with the cloud services and large-scale coordination (3GPP, 2023).
    a. **V2V & V2I:** Low-latency direct communication (DSRC, C-V2X PC5).
    b. **V2P:** Short-range wireless and cellular links.
    c. **V2N & V2G:** Cellular (4G/5G) and broadband networks.

    This layer ensures reliable and timely data transfer between physical entities and digital twins.

3. **Digital Twin Layer:** This layer has the virtual model of vehicles, roads, intersections, and networks. It uses physics models, data models, and AI algorithms to model the real world. The digital twin is continuously updated on its state using real-time V2X data (Kritzinger et al., 2018).
   a. **V2V data** updates vehicle-level digital twins for trajectory prediction.
   b. **V2I data** updates the intersection and road network twins.
   c. **V2P data** enhances safety risk models for pedestrian interactions.
   d. **V2N data** supports city-scale or regional transportation twins.
   e. **V2G data** updates energy and charging infrastructure twins.

   Here, real-time data is fused with historical data to create dynamic virtual replicas.

4. **Application Layer:** This layer offers services such as traffic optimization, accident prediction, autonomous driving support, and system performance analysis. Applications use the digital twin to run scenarios and make the best decisions before their application in the real world (Guo et al., 2024).
   a. AI and machine learning analyze V2X data for:
      i. Accident prediction (V2V, V2P)
      ii. Traffic optimization (V2I, V2N)
      iii. Energy optimization (V2G)

Digital Twins simulate future scenarios and evaluate control strategies before deployment (Zhang et al., 2025).

DT-V2X systems with direct mapping of V2V, V2I, V2P, V2N, and V2G communications to Digital Twin layers provide sustained coordination between the real transportation systems and the virtual ones. Such multifaceted integration provides predictive safety, traffic flow optimization, mobility on an energy-saving platform, and intelligent transport management on a scale.

4.2 Data Flow Between Vehicles, Infrastructure, and Twin

In a framework of DT-V2X, the data flows continuously between vehicles, infrastructure, and the digital twins. Vehicles send information such as speed, position, acceleration, and braking status, and sensor perceptions to other vehicles in their vicinity and RSUs. RSUs perform the aggregation of this data and transfer it to edge or cloud servers. Figure 3 provides the efficient real-time data flow between the digital twin and vehicles.

The digital twin receives this data for updating the virtual representation of the physical system. At the same time, the results of simulation and prediction by the twin, including congestion predictions or collision danger predictions, are fed back to the vehicles and traffic control systems in the form of control or advisory messages (Tao et al., 2022).

Figure 3. Dataflow in DT-V2X communication

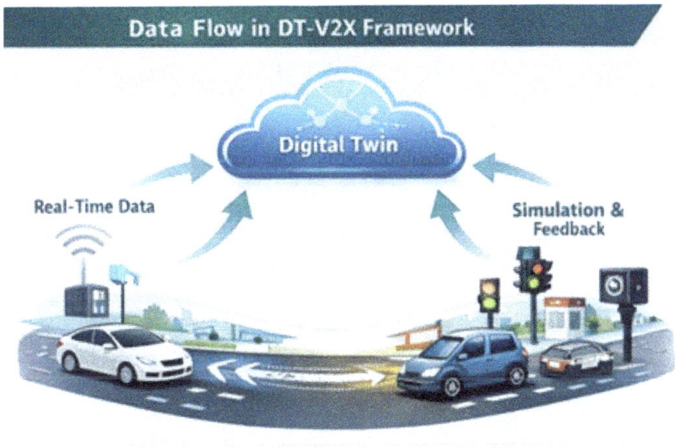

This two-way communication enables vehicles not only to respond to their surroundings but also to benefit from intelligence supplied by the system at large that is generated by the digital twin.

Real-time synchronization is one of the characteristics of the DT-V2X systems. Sensor data, communication logs and environment data continuously stream to update the state of the digital twin. Studies show that real-time synchronization results in much better accuracy of prediction of traffic and safety analysis than static models (Llagostera-Brugarola et al., 2025).

Synchronization involves:

- Time-stamping and aligning data from the heterogeneous sources
- Filtering and Cleaning noisy Sensor data
- Updating virtual models with high frequency

Advanced systems employ artificial intelligence models to manage the data that is missing or delayed and maintain the consistency between physical and virtual systems (Guo et al., 2024). Accurate synchronization helps the digital twin to simulate the near-future states and aid proactive instead of reactive decision-making.

4.3 Role of Edge and Cloud Computing in DT-V2X Systems

Edge and cloud computing provide the computational basis for Digital Twin-enabled Vehicle-to-Everything (DT-V2X) systems, as depicted in Fig. 4. Their integration ensures that the latency-critical safety services as well as large-scale analytical tasks are handled efficiently (Tao et al., 2022; Guo et al., 2024).

Figure 4. Role of edge and cloud computing in DT-V2X communication

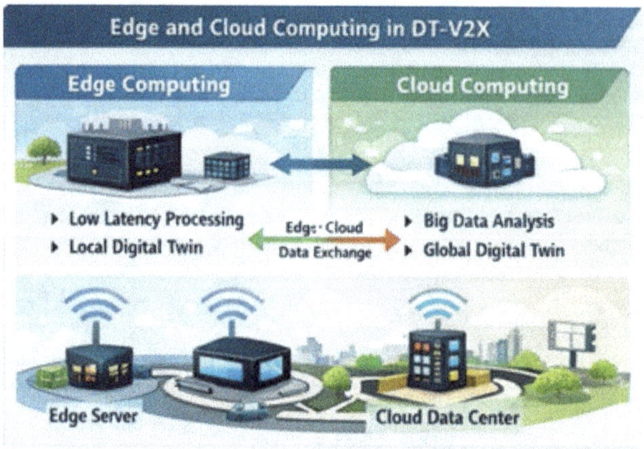

Role of Edge Computing

Edge computing involves processing the data near where it is generated, such as at units on the roadside (RSUs), in base stations, or in local micro-data centers. When it comes to V2X systems, safety-critical applications require extremely low latency (down to 10 ms) when it comes to collision alerts and emergency braking applications (3GPP, 2023). Sending all the information from the vehicles to the cloud would create delays and network overloads; thus, edge nodes create immediate data processing.

Vehicles produce huge amounts of data via GPS, camera, radars, lidar and sensors on-board. Edge computing is used for filtering, aggregation, and fusion of this data to generate real-time actionable information (Zhang et al., 2024). In DT-V2X systems, edge nodes also have local digital twins of adjacent vehicles, lanes, and intersections, which are updated at high frequency to reflect changes in the real world (Kritzinger et al., 2018).

Major functions of edge computing are:

1. Collision detection and warning generation on a real-time basis
2. Emergency braking and hazard warnings
3. Adaptive Traffic Control of an Intersection
4. Short-term traffic flow prediction in local areas
5. Maintenance of local/partial digital twins

Studies show that edge-based processing positively reduces the communication latency and enhances the reliability for safety-critical V2X services (Ficzere et al., 2023). Even when there is a temporary loss of connection to the cloud, local operations of edge nodes can be continued, which generates better system robustness.

Role of Cloud Computing

Cloud computing provides centralized and high-performance computing resources and large-scale storage. Unlike edge computing, which is focused on immediacy, the cloud is focused on depth, scale, and long-term intelligence (Tao et al., 2022).

The cloud is used to store the data from the past in the form of data collected from vehicles, infrastructure, and digital twins. It performs computationally intensive work like large-scale simulations, long-range traffic forecasting, and system-wide optimization (Guo et al., 2024). In DT-V2X systems, the cloud manages digital twins of the cities or regions, which consolidate data from thousands of vehicles and infrastructure nodes.

Some of the important functions of cloud computing are:

1. Hosting big data digital twin models
2. Long-term traffic and mobility patterns analysis
3. Training AI and machine learning Models
4. System-wide performance evaluation
5. Strategic infrastructure/policy planning

Cloud platforms are critical for scenario analysis; for example, evacuation planning, smart city redesign, or large-scale traffic optimization require a great deal of data and computational power (Llagostera-Brugarola et al., 2025).

Edge-Cloud Collaboration for DT-V2X

DT-V2X systems are based on a hierarchical computing model. The edge takes care of the fast and local decision making, and the cloud takes care of the slow and global intelligence (Tao et al., 2022).

Edge nodes transmit summarized data or pre-processed data to the cloud for long-term storage and analysis. The cloud, in turn, sends the trained AI models, optimization strategies, and updated parameters of the digital twins back to the edge nodes for real-time deployment (Guo et al., 2024).

This collaboration enables:

1. Ultra-low latency for safety-critical applications
2. Scalability (large-scale transportation networks)
3. Efficient bandwidth usage (data filtering)
4. High dependability by local independence and international coordination

By combining edge and cloud computing, DT-V2X systems are both responsive and smart in the long run, enabling instant real-world safety and efficient traffic management and transportation planning in a unified digital twin model.

5. APPLICATIONS OF DIGITAL TWIN IN V2X

V2X systems, which are powered by Digital Twin, enable the monitoring, simulation, and optimization of connected transportation settings in real-time. Digital twins can be used to predict and adapt mobility services by aligning the real-life V2X data with virtual models (Tao et al., 2022; Guo et al., 2024).

As Figure 1 shows, the key applications of V2X communication with Digital Twin are traffic flow optimization, accident prediction and prevention, autonomous driving, cooperative driving, smart intersections and highways, and mobility-efficient energy utilization. The diagram underscores the use of real-time V2X data to synchronize with virtual models to assist with intelligent transportation systems to predict and make decisions.

Figure 5. Key applications of digital twin technology in vehicle-to-everything (V2X) communication

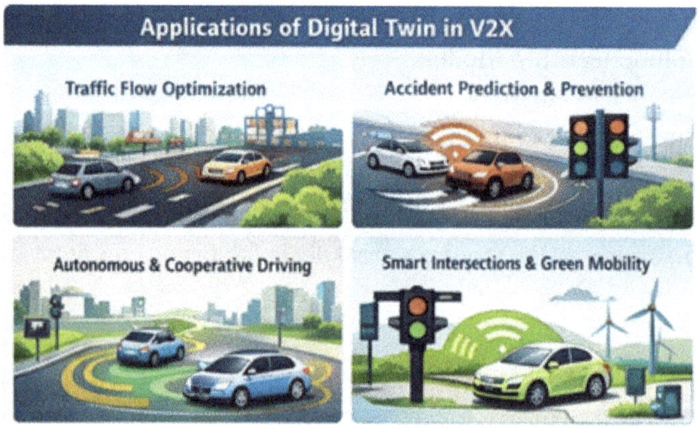

5.1 Traffic Flow Optimization

One of the greatest problems in urban transportation is traffic congestion. In V2X, cars and road equipment exchange data continuously, e.g., speed, density, signal timing, and road conditions. Traditionally, a digital twin combines this information to form a moving virtual representation of traffic networks.

With this model, the traffic authorities will be able to experiment with various control measures, which could involve adjusting the time of signals, rerouting traffic, and using lanes. Research reports that the Digital Twin-based traffic management can cut down on congestion and travel time by a long margin because it can regulate traffic utilizing proactive control, instead of reactive control (Llagostera-Brugarola et al., 2025). V2X communication allows the twin to anticipate any congestion and issue optimum routing or speed advice to vehicles.

5.2 Accident Prediction and Prevention

The main causes of road accidents may be delayed reaction of the driver, low visibility, or abrupt dangerous events. V2X enables cars to exchange safety signals like emergency braking, road conditions, or road collisions. A digital twin interprets this information and determines risky areas and hazardous driving behavior.

Digital twins can anticipate the risk of accidents at certain places or at certain times by integrating historical data on accidents and current V2X data (Guo et al., 2024). Early warnings can also be sent to vehicles by the system to modify the timing of signals or activate variable message signs to decrease the risk. This predictive system enhances road safety over conventional reactive systems.

5.3 Autonomous and Cooperative Driving

Self-driving cars are based on sensors and algorithms to develop driving options. However, onboard sensors have a low range and visibility. V2X builds on this perception by transmitting data from other vehicles and infrastructure.

Digital Twin provides a common virtual space in which the position, intentions, and tracks of cars are updated. This allows collaborative driving capabilities, including platooning, coordinated lane changes, and safe intersection merging (Zhang et al., 2024). The twin will be able to simulate and suggest the best solutions to the autonomous vehicles in case of various future scenarios, which will enhance the safety, efficiency, and comfort of the passengers.

5.4 Smart Intersections and Highways

Crossroads and highways are the key places of traffic efficiency and safety. With DT-V2X, the intersection is furnished with sensors and cameras and roadside units that transmit data to a digital twin of the intersection or highway section.

In real time, the digital twin records the volume of traffic, pedestrian flow, weather, and car incidents. It will be able to dynamically adapt the traffic lights, control the lane directions, and give priority to the emergency car (Tao et al., 2022). Digital Twins used in highways assist in controlling the metering of ramps, speed control, and lane control, to allow a smooth stream of traffic flow and minimize accident rates.

5.5 Energy-Efficient and Green Mobility

A significant amount of energy consumption and emissions is associated with transportation. V2X systems based on Digital Twin can make driving greener by maximizing driving behavior and traffic operations.

The digital twin will also be able to predict environmentally friendly routes, optimal velocity, and fluid acceleration schedules by examining real-time traffic and vehicle data, thereby lowering the fuel usage and environmental effects (Guo et al., 2024). V2X with digital twins in electric vehicles facilitates interaction between vehicles and the grid, intelligent charging, and energy balancing. City-wide Digital Twins are used to assist policymakers with the cost-benefit analysis of the environmental impacts of traffic policies and advance sustainable transportation policies.

6. CASE STUDIES

V2X systems based on Digital Twin are becoming the subject of testing and deployment in smart cities, research, and industrial pilot programs. The works show how real-time data, simulation, and predictive analytics can be used to enhance the quality of transportation.

6.1 Study 1: Smart City V2X Projects

Several smart city projects have incorporated V2X communication technologies into the urban mobility and road safety systems of urban traffic management. In such initiatives, related roadside infrastructure, such as smart traffic signs, roadside units (RSUs), cameras, and environmental sensors are installed, together with vehicles with V2X communication modules. These elements constantly gather real-time information regarding the car speed, traffic congestion, queue, accident, and weather.

The data gathered is used to dynamically regulate the traffic signals, traffic congestion as well as give priority to the emergency vehicles at the intersections and critical areas of roadway. As an example, the phases of the traffic lights can be changed in real-time depending on the flow of traffic, and the emergency vehicles are prioritized in terms of the offered signal, decreasing the response time (Zhang et al., 2024).

The digital traffic platforms on which the underlying digital traffic platforms operate in most instances serve as early-stage Digital Twins, as it copies conditions of real-world traffic in virtual conditions. These computer models enable road traffic agencies to model and test signal control techniques and road policies and apply them onto the real roads. Experimental research of this kind of deployment is documented with tangible gains, such as less congestion in high-traffic times, more efficient movement of traffic and shorter times of emergency response, evidently showing the usefulness of V2X-enabled coordination in the smart city setting (Llagostera-Brugarola et al., 2025).

6.2 Study 2: Digital Twin of Urban Traffic Networks

Urban traffic network Digital Twins offer an end-to-end, real-time virtual simulation of a transportation system of a city. These twins simulate roads, intersections, vehicles, pedestrians, traffic signals and environment, e.g. weather, visibility. The traffic state of the digital twin is updated in real-time by continuous data streams of vehicles and roadside infrastructure through V2X communication.

The prototypes of city-scale digital twin have demonstrated a high potential of predictive traffic control. The systems can predict the pattern of congestion both in the past and in real-time using V2X data that can be used to proactively manage traffic signals, route planning, and the congestion mitigation strategy (Guo et al., 2024). This predictive ability gives the traffic authorities the capacity to intervene with the congestion before it has completely affected the traffic, instead of responding to the situation when the traffic has already collapsed.

In addition to operational control, urban traffic digital twins can also be applied as infrastructure planning decision-support tools. The virtual environment allows planners to test the effectiveness of changes in infrastructure, such as the addition of special bus lanes or the redesign of intersections, or the adoption of new traffic policies, without necessarily making the physical investment. The strategy greatly diminishes the risk of planning, the cost of implementation, and interference with the real-world traffic as well as providing the evidence-based design of urban mobility (Tao et al., 2022).

6.3 Study 3: Industry and Research Prototypes

DTV2X prototypes have been developed by automotive organizations, telecommunications providers, and research organizations to aid connected and autonomous driving. These prototypes include vehicle sensors, V2X networks, edge servers, and online digital twins.

The use of digital twins to reproduce parts of a highway or intersection and use V2X data to simulate vehicle behavior in real-time has been demonstrated and is a subject of research. The systems facilitate the platooning, cooperative merging, and collision avoidance experiments (Zhang et al., 2024). The pilots in the industry are concerned with the tests of C-V2X using 5G and digital twin analytics to enhance the safety and reliability of autonomous cars (Ficzere et al., 2023).

Latency, communication reliability, traffic efficiency, and safety improvements are the metrics of the performance of DT-V2X systems that are regularly evaluated. A literature review demonstrates that when edge computing is used with digital twins, the response time to safety applications is reduced to less than 10 ms, which provides collision avoidance requirements (3GPP, 2023).

Experiments with urban traffic digital twins indicate that predictive traffic control strategies and cooperative driving approaches reduced the level of congestion, travel time, and risk of accidents (Llagostera-Brugarola et al., 2025). It is also shown in the research that vehicles with digital twin-optimal speed and routing advice exhibit improved fuel efficiency and reduced emissions (Guo et al., 2024).

The case studies and pilot projects indicate that V2X systems based on Digital Twin are technically adequate and can provide substantial increases in terms of safety, efficiency, and sustainability. Such practical applications form a robust basis for the deployment in large numbers in the future intelligent transportation systems.

7. PERFORMANCE EVALUATION

The effectiveness of Digital Twin-enabled V2X (DT-V2X) systems can be evaluated by using performance evaluation. It pays attention to the quality of communication, the influence on safety, scalability of the system, and the efficiency of system operations.

7.1 Metrics

1. Latency refers to the time taken for data to travel from the sender to the receiver and trigger an action. In V2X safety applications such as collision avoidance and emergency braking, latency must typically be below 10 milliseconds to be effective (3GPP, 2023). DT-V2X systems use edge computing and local digital twins to reduce communication delay by processing data close to vehicles.
2. Reliability measures the probability that messages are delivered correctly and on time. High reliability is critical for safety messages such as crash warnings and hazard alerts. Studies show that integrating Digital Twins with edge-based V2X improves message delivery by predicting network congestion and adapting communication strategies (Ficzere et al., 2023).
3. Throughput represents the volume of data successfully transmitted per unit time. DT-V2X systems manage high data volumes from sensors, cameras, and V2X messages. Digital twins help optimize data routing and filtering, ensuring that only relevant data is transmitted, improving overall network efficiency (Zhang et al., 2024).

4. Safety performance is evaluated using indicators such as accident rate reduction, near-miss detection, emergency response time, and collision warning accuracy. Digital Twin–based V2X systems use predictive modeling to identify high-risk situations before accidents occur (Guo et al., 2024).
5. Efficiency indicators include average travel time, traffic delay, queue length at intersections, and fuel or energy consumption. Urban traffic digital twin experiments report improved traffic flow and reduced congestion due to predictive signal control and cooperative driving strategies (Llagostera-Brugarola et al., 2025).
6. Scalability measures the system's ability to handle increasing numbers of vehicles, sensors, and data streams. DT-V2X systems use hierarchical architectures where local digital twins operate at the edge, and large-scale twins operate in the cloud, enabling support for thousands or millions of vehicles (Tao et al., 2022).
7. Robustness refers to system stability under failures, network congestion, or data loss. Edge-based processing allows DT-V2X systems to continue operating locally even when cloud connectivity is disrupted (Ficzere et al., 2023). AI-based data recovery and prediction techniques help maintain synchronization between physical and digital systems despite missing or delayed data (Guo et al., 2024).

Together, these indicators show how DT-V2X systems improve both safety and operational efficiency compared to conventional traffic management.

7.2 Comparison With Traditional V2X Systems

Conventional V2X systems primarily revolve around direct communication between the vehicles and the infrastructure, in addition to minimal system-wide intelligence. They are responsive to the existing situations but do not have good predictive and simulation skills (Zhang et al., 2024).

DT-V2X systems, on the contrary, offer:

1. Online simulation-based predictive decision-making.
2. Active congestion and accident avoidance.
3. False economy, optimized data flow.
4. Improved scalability by using edge-cloud cooperation.

Research shows that compared to traditional V2X, DT-V2X systems are more efficient in measures of reducing latency, enhancing safety metrics, and traffic efficiency because it can simulate and optimize the future instead of reacting to current events (Tao et al., 2022; Guo et al., 2024).

All in all, performance analysis indicates that the Digital Twin-based V2X systems have crucial benefits in the areas of reliability, safety, scalability, and intelligence in comparison to traditional V2X systems.

8. CHALLENGES AND LIMITATIONS

8.1 Data Privacy and Cybersecurity

The DT-V2X systems interchange huge amounts of sensitive information, such as car positioning, traffic behavior, and individual mobility habits. This brings about serious privacy issues and abuse concerns. V2X communication may be interfered with by cyberattacks like spoofing, data injection, denial-of-service, and tracking attacks, and result in safety compromise (Ficzere et al., 2023). Strong encryption, authentication, access control, and intrusion detection are necessary to protect DT-V2X systems, and the challenge of implementing them without adding latency at a high cost is a significant issue. The system undergoes interoperability and standardization to enhance its compatibility with other systems and ensure software interoperability between the different systems.

8.2 Interoperability and Standardization

The system is interoperable and standards-based to increase compatibility with other systems, and software interoperability is present across the various systems.

V2X systems encompass cars, telecommunication organizations, infrastructure companies, and governmental organizations, which can be based on alternative technologies and protocols. The absence of standardization causes some compatibility problems between DSRC, C-V2X, 5G, and future systems (Zhang et al., 2024). Digital twins also present more complexity since they have to combine the data of heterogeneous origins. Lack of international data format, interface, and twin-model standards makes the large-scale deployment of DT-V2X hard.

8.3 Real-Time Synchronization Issues

Digital twins rely on the fact that they have to be properly and continuously synchronized with the real world. Mismatches between physical and virtual states can, however, be brought about by network delays, loss of packets, sensor error, and data overload (Guo et al., 2024). In safety-critical systems, any little loss of synchronization can result in incorrect decisions. This is a technical challenge of achieving reliable real-time updating in extremely dynamic traffic environments.

8.4 Cost and Infrastructure Requirements

DT-V2X systems consume huge investments in sensors, roadside units, communication networks, edge servers, cloud platform and software platform. Creation and sustenance of high-fidelity digital twins is costly and resource-consuming (Tao et al., 2022). Most developing areas have monetary and technical limitations to install such sophisticated infrastructure which makes the high usage of the infrastructure a limiting factor.

9. CONCLUSION AND FUTURE TRENDS

The future DT-V2X systems will be highly integrated with artificial intelligence in autonomous decision-making, self learning twins, and self-adjusting traffic control. With the appearance of 6G networks, it is anticipated that the latency will be reduced to the lowest possible level, reliability will increase, and positioning will be highly accurate and responsive, thereby improving the work of digital twins (Zhang et al., 2024). As cars become fully autonomous, digital twins will serve as common virtual worlds in which cars, infrastructure, and pedestrians are simulated on the fly. It will assist in the cooperative perception, collective decision-making, and autonomous navigation that will be safer (Guo et al., 2024). The next step in the area of future research is the application of DT-V2X systems to minimize emissions, optimize energy consumption, and facilitate electric mobility. Digital twins are able to model the trigonometric effect of traffic policy, route network, and charging schemes to advocate eco-friendly transport (Tao et al., 2022). Policies of data ownership, protection of privacy, and cybersecurity, as well as liability in connected and autonomous mobility, are policies that governments need to come up with. Regulations should also assist interoperability, infrastructure investment, and acceptance on the part of the populace to DT-V2X systems.

Digital Twin-enabled V2X communication was studied in the chapter; its main ideas, system architecture, technologies enabling it, its key uses, and the approaches to its performance measurement have been discussed. It showed that digital twins can be combined with V2X in order to provide real-time monitoring, predictive analytics, and proactive control of transportation systems. DT-V2X systems make roads safer and enhance traffic flow, autonomous driving, and environmental sustainability by integrating both live communication and virtual simulation and forecasting. These systems transform transportation from a reactive model to a predictive and adaptive ecosystem. Although there are still issues to do with data privacy, interoperability, real-time synchronization, and the high cost of infrastructure, the constant advancement of artificial intelligence, networking, and computing technologies is slowly removing them. V2X communication with the assistance of Digital Twin is thus a core aspect of intelligent transportation systems of the future and will play a central role in ensuring safe, efficient, and sustainable mobility.

REFERENCES

3GPP. (2023). *Technical specification group services and system aspects; Study on enhancement of 5G support for V2X services (Release 18)*. 3rd Generation Partnership Project. https://www.3gpp.org

3GPP. (2025). Study on enhancement of 5G and beyond support for V2X services (Release 19). 3rd Generation Partnership Project. https://www.3gpp.org/specifications

Ficzere, D., Tihanyi, V., & Varga, P. (2023). Large-scale cellular vehicle-to-everything deployments and challenges. *IEEE Access : Practical Innovations, Open Solutions*, *11*, 98765–98780. DOI: 10.1109/ACCESS.2023.3287456 PMID: 37631567

Fortune Business Insights. (2024). *Digital twin market size, share and industry analysis, 2024–2032*. Fortune Business Insights Research Report. https://www.fortunebusinessinsights.com/digital-twin-market-106246

Future Market Insights. (2025). *Automotive vehicle-to-everything (V2X) market forecast 2025–2035*. Retrieved from https://www.futuremarketinsights.com/reports/automotive-vehicle-to-everything-v2x-market (Future Market Insights)

Global Market Insights Inc. (2025). *Vehicle-to-Everything (V2X) communication module market size and forecast*. Retrieved from https://www.gminsights.com/industry-analysis/vehicle-to-everything-v2x-communication-module-market (Global Market Insights Inc.)

Guo, J., Zhang, Y., Li, X., & Wang, Z. (2024). Digital twin driven intelligent transportation systems: Architecture and applications. *Transportation Research Part C, Emerging Technologies*, *158*, 104238. DOI: 10.1016/j.trc.2024.104238

Guo, J., Zhang, Y., Li, X., & Wang, Z. (2025). Digital twin–driven intelligent transportation systems: Architecture, applications, and challenges. *Transportation Research Part C, Emerging Technologies*, *160*, 104489. DOI: 10.1016/j.trc.2025.104489

Jaiswal, S., & Mohan, B. C. (2023). Deep learning-based path tracking control using lane detection and traffic sign detection for autonomous driving. *Web Intelligence*, *22*(2), 185–207. DOI: 10.3233/WEB-230011

Kachhoria, R., Jaiswal, S., Lokhande, M., & Rodge, J. (2023). Lane detection and path prediction in autonomous vehicle using deep learning. In *Intelligent edge computing for cyber physical applications* (pp. 111–127). Academic Press. DOI: 10.1016/B978-0-323-99412-5.00012-5

Kritzinger, W., Karner, M., Traar, G., Henjes, J., & Sihn, W. (2018). Digital Twin in manufacturing: A categorical literature review and classification. *IFAC-PapersOnLine*, *51*(11), 1016–1022. DOI: 10.1016/j.ifacol.2018.08.474

Li, Y., Chen, S., Wang, X., & Zhao, L. (2025). Vehicle-to-grid integration for sustainable transportation: Communication, control, and energy management. *Renewable & Sustainable Energy Reviews*, *184*, 113623. DOI: 10.1016/j.rser.2025.113623

Llagostera-Brugarola, E., Perez, J., & Molina, J. (2025). A digital twin for intelligent transportation systems using V2X communications. *Applied Sciences (Basel, Switzerland), 15*(13), 7454. DOI: 10.3390/app15137454

Tao, F., Zhang, H., Liu, A., & Nee, A. Y. C. (2022). Digital twin in industry: State-of-the-art. *IEEE Transactions on Industrial Informatics, 15*(4), 2405–2415. DOI: 10.1109/TII.2018.2873186

Tao, F., Zhang, H., Liu, A., & Nee, A. Y. C. (2025). Digital twin–enabled cyber–physical systems: Architecture, technologies, and future trends. *IEEE Transactions on Industrial Informatics, 21*(2), 1450–1462. DOI: 10.1109/TII.2024.3456789

Zhang, X., Li, J., Zhou, J., Zhang, S., Wang, J., Yuan, Y., & Liu, J. (2024). Vehicle-to-Everything communication in intelligent connected vehicles: A survey and taxonomy. *Automotive Innovation, 7*(1), 1–25. DOI: 10.1007/s42154-024-00310-2

Zhang, X., Li, J., Zhou, J., Zhang, S., Wang, J., Yuan, Y., & Liu, J. (2025). *Vehicle-to-Everything communication in intelligent connected vehicles: A survey and taxonomy. Automotive Innovation*. ResearchGate., DOI: 10.1007/s42154-024-00310-2

Chapter 12
Integration of Digital Twins With 5G/6G-Enabled AV Systems

Ravikumar Natarajan
http://orcid.org/0009-0009-3705-1681
Marwadi University, Rajkot, India

Aarthi Selvakumar
http://orcid.org/0009-0006-9064-2091
Marwadi University, Rajkot, India

Dilmurod Turaev
Termez University of Economics and Service, Termez, Uzbekistan

Anorgul Ashirova
Mamun University, Khiva, Uzbekistan

Khayrulla Urozboev
Alfraganus University, Tashkent, Uzbekistan

ABSTRACT

The integration of Digital Twin technology with 5G and emerging 6G networks is transforming autonomous vehicle systems by enabling real-time synchronization, predictive analytics, and collaborative decision-making. Ultra-low-latency communication, network slicing, and edge–cloud processing allow twins to mirror vehicle behavior with high fidelity while handling large sensor streams. These capabilities enhance hazard prediction, multi-vehicle coordination, and city-scale mobility simulation. Advancements in 6G such as terahertz connectivity and AI-native networking further improve scalability and system resilience. This chapter examines the architecture, performance needs, and practical benefits of DT-AV integration, supported by case studies from China and South Korea. It also highlights challenges in scalability, security, and interoperability, and outlines future research in quantum communication, federated learning, and self-evolving twins.

DOI: 10.4018/979-8-3373-7785-8.ch012

1. INTRODUCTION

The adoption of Digital Twin (DT) systems in connection with the future 5G and 6G communication networks can be seen as the paradigm shift in the history of autonomous mobility. The need to establish real-time correspondence between the actual systems and their virtual analog has risen significantly as autonomous vehicles are becoming more and more data-driven. Continuous monitoring, predictive analytics, and scenario-based testing both require digital twins, and the success of these systems depends on the speed of high-speed, ultra-reliable communication. Next-generation networks, which are ultra-low-latency based, supporting massive adoption of devices, and increased bandwidth, offer the required platform to bring to reality these intelligent twin-guided ecosystems (Nguyen et al., 2021). The intersection of these technologies promotes the fast decision-making, cooperation of many vehicles, and the flexibility to the changing conditions of urban mobility. In this chapter, the author provides the key principles of the autonomous driving that is controlled by DT and the description of the core role of 5G/6G in providing scalable and synchronized twin environments. It lays the foundation of why to consider this integration as a part of next-generation transportation infrastructures and emphasizes the importance of it in regard to safer, more efficient, and sustainable automated mobility systems (Suleiman et al., 2025).

1.1 Evolution of Digital Twins in AV Systems

The Digital Twin technology has developed since its inception in the industrial manufacturing sector to a foundation of the contemporary autonomous transportation. DTs were originally employed to monitor equipment and provide predictive maintenance, but have now evolved into sophisticated, real-time virtual models with the ability to closely replicate the dynamics of vehicles, the behaviour of sensors and the environment. Digital twins in autonomous vehicles entail the entire state of the operational vehicle including the perception data, navigation pathways and health of the system. Along with the development of sensors, AI perception, and edge calculating systems, DTs have become dynamic decision-support systems that respond to uncertain situations in the real world (Nguyen et al., 2025). The previous applications of DT were mostly based on simulation and diagnostics; however, the recent progress allows continuous learning, multi-domain synchronization, and prediction of the vehicle behavior. With connected vehicles producing huge data streams, the capacity to sustain an ever-changing virtual representation has become fundamental in safety validation, scenario simulation, as well as optimization. This development makes DTs an important facilitator of end-to-end autonomy and intelligent mobility systems (Maiwada et al., 2024). The digital twins are represented as a circular progression Figure 1 showing the evolution of patients from basic monitoring to real-time modeling, decision support, synchronization, collaborative prediction, and continuous learning.

Figure 1. Evolution of digital twin technology

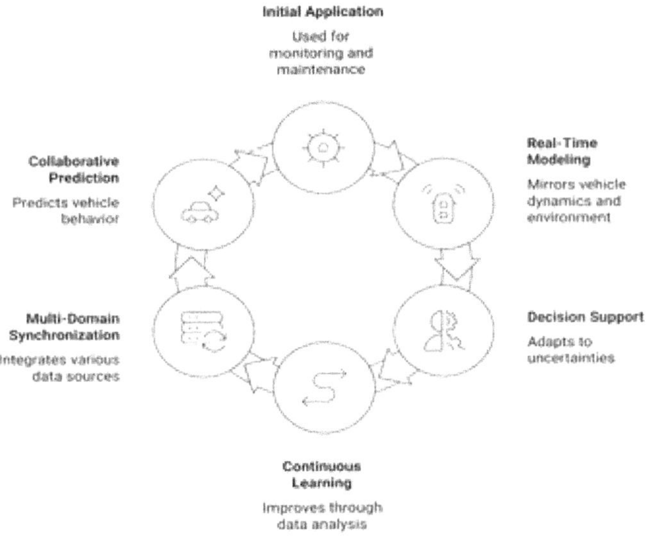

1.2 5G/6G Backbone for Digital Twin Synchronization

Such communication systems capable of sharing information real-time and that can maintain real-time connectivity are essential to the effective deployment of digital twins in autonomous car systems. The 5G networks that have emerged bear such innovations as Ultra-Reliable Low-Latency Communication (URLLC), massive Machine-Type Communication (mMTC), and high-throughput enhanced broadband that is required to make real time synchronization between the physical vehicles and their virtual twins. The sixth-generation (6G) networks are however expected to advance such capabilities to include terahertz spectrums, intelligent surfaces, AI-native network control and less than milliseconds latency. Such innovations will make digital twins predictive and autonomous agents that constantly learn using various information sources that are distributed over vehicles, infrastructure, and clouds (Tang et al., 2022). Because AVs also will be reliant on the constantly updated perception and collaborative decision-making, the real-time synchronization that 5G/6G will introduce will ensure that the digital twins are consistent, context-sensitive, and react to the variance of the environment. Thus, next-generation networks are not just a layer of interconnectivity but a foundation of an enormous real-time digital twin ecosystem.

1.3 Motivation and Significance for AV Ecosystems

The situation awareness, reliability, and computation intelligence needed by autonomous vehicles have never been as high as it is today in order to address the complexity of road conditions. Digital twins can provide a potent tool to satisfy these requests as they provide the opportunity to monitor continuously, develop more advanced predictive models, and optimize them with the help of simulations. But, the full potential of DTs has not been realized because of the constraint in the presence communication infrastructures, such as the latency bottlenecks, the shortage of bandwidth, and the lack of interoperability between the heterogeneous systems. Due to AVs creating terabytes of sensor data, the necessity to have high-speed and resilient networks has become more and more acute. The sense of implementing 5G/6G technology is the ability to address these limitations in communication and provide real-time synchronization of large autonomous fleets (Ravikumar & Aarthi, 2025b). Specifically, this convergence can be of high importance when it comes to safety critical situations, in which any slight delay in the virtual-to-physical communication can undermine the actions of vehicles. Moreover, the next-generation networks will help to increase the scalability of twin ecosystems, allowing to simulate a city, manage traffic cooperatively, and provide mobility services that are energy-efficient. This integration will thus transform the future AV ecosystems because it will assist in creating smarter, safer, and more sustainable transportation infrastructures.

2. BACKGROUND TO THE STUDY

The increased sophistication of autonomous vehicles is a reason why a powerful modeling, analysis, and operational decision-making framework is required, which makes Digital Twin technology one of the key elements of an intelligent mobility system. Digital twins allow simulating the behavior of a vehicle, the dynamics of the environment, and the state of the infrastructure in real time and create a virtual testbed to measure performance and risk. At the same time, 5G and future 6G technologies are the communication foundation that needs to be implemented to realize these high-fidelity twin worlds. These networks provide unparalleled speed, reliability, and capacity to overcome the limits on large-scale deployment of DT that existed in the past (Wang et al., 2022). The importance of V2X communication and edge computing in the achievement of distributed intelligence to support smart mobility is also emphasized in background research. The combination of these technologies enables a joint autonomy, whereby vehicles communicate context-driven information to each other and react to the situation on the road. This part provides the theoretical basis of comprehending the convergence of digital twins, communication networks, and AV technologies to form efficient, predictive and interconnected transportation ecosystems.

2.1 Digital Twin Architecture for Mobility Systems

Multilayered digital twin architecture Mobility systems Digital Twin architecture is based on components that utilize multilayers to replicate and analyze real-time vehicle and environmental behavior. A mobility-oriented digital twin has three main layers, namely, the physical, the virtual (or computational), and the synchronization layers. The physical architecture is composed of the autonomous vehicle, its sensors, onboard computing modules and ancillary infrastructure, including traffic lights and smart roads. The virtual layer contains high-fidelity models, which can represent an automobile kinematics, sensor dynamics, traffic environment, and environments around cars (El Marai et al., 2021). These models are based on the system of artificial intelligence, simulation engines, and data analytics to produce the correct predictions and diagnosis. The synchronization layer manages the flow of data between the physical and virtual entities continuously and with standard communication protocols, this will allow real time updates and reconstruction of the scenario. Mobility DTs assist in functions of failure prediction and collision risk assessment, route optimization, and energy management (Masaracchia et al., 2022). Their structure focuses on interoperability, scalability, and adaptability and enables the integration of heterogeneous fleets, road network and micro-mobility ecosystems with ease. This underlying framework allows autonomous vehicles to drive in more efficient and safer ways in the complicated urban environments.

2.2 5G/6G Technologies for Autonomous Vehicles

The future-developed communication technology is 5G and 6G, which offers the capability of delivering latency-sensitive autonomous vehicle capabilities where the end-to-end latency is required to be at 15 ms or less when making real-time decisions in autonomous vehicle manoeuvres such as braking, lane changes, and collision avoidance. The Enhanced Mobile Broadband (eMBB) provides high throughput that is necessary to transmit massive sensor data including LiDAR point clouds and high-resolution video. Massive Machine-Type Communication (mMTC) will be employed in communication of millions of devices, to provide grand scale V2X ecosystems (Chen et al., 2022). On the other hand, 6G will propel these elements with the introduction of AI-native networking, terahertz communication and ultra-high bandwidth support, reconfigurability intelligent surfaces and sub-milliseconds latency. With these technologies, it is possible to rely on the high-fidelity, ultra-reliable synchronization of vehicles and their digital twin. In combination with distributed edge computing, 5G/6G networks will allow AVs to delegate computing and exchange sensor streams and have access to predictive models with real-time access. Subsequently, these networks provide a foundation of scalable, secure, and collaborative AV-DT environments (Groshev, Guimarães, et al., 2021). Table 1 Key difference The key performance differences assist in real-time digital twins synchronization.

Table 1. Comparison of 5G and 6G capabilities for DT–AV systems

Parameter	5G Capability	6G Capability
Latency	1–10 ms	<1 ms
Bandwidth	High	Ultra-high (THz)
Connectivity Density	1M devices/km^2	>10M devices/km^2
Network Intelligence	Limited	AI-native
Mobility Support	High	Extremely high

2.2.1 5G/6G Standards (3GPP & ITU)

The standardization of the technological capabilities of 5G and the upcoming 6G networks is achieved through the frameworks, created by the 3rd Generation Partnership Project (3GPP) and the International Telecommunication Union (ITU). The IMT 2020 specification of the ITU has specified performance targets of 5G such as peak data rates of 10 Gbps, end-to-end latency of approximately less than 1 ms, and connectivity densities of approximately one million devices per square kilometre. The capabilities are used in support of the key service categories that include Ultra-Reliable Low-Latency Communications (URLLC), enhanced Mobile Broadband (eMBB), and massive Machine-Type communications (mMTC), which are required to ensure real-time synchronisation of autonomous vehicles and their digital twins. The vision of 6G in IMT-2030 is to expand these with sub-millennial latency, a data rate of over 100 Gbps and connectivity densities of over ten million devices per square kilometre. Other developments like AI-native networking, combined sensing and communication, and the use of terahertz spectrum will also allow very synchronized, large-scale digital twin ecosystems of autonomous mobility.

2.3 V2X and Edge Computing in Smart Mobility

The communication between vehicles and everything (V2X) is a key factor to building intelligent and cooperative autonomous mobility. Vehicles use V2V, V2I, V2P and V2N communications channels to share important information including speed, position, hazards, and infrastructure conditions to improve situational awareness. Edge computing complements such an ecosystem by conducting computation at a much closer distance to the vehicle, which is much lower and much more reliable in decision-making. Distributed edge nodes analyze sensor data, execute analytics and update digital twins with the help of local operation without overly relying on remote cloud servers. This decentralization method allows AVs to react fast to any dynamic traffic occurrence, surroundings, and multi-vehicle interplays. Networked intelligence also enhances the system through cooperative learning and joint perception through fleets (Jaiswal, 2025). With the help of real-time data integration, AI-based insights, and constant synchronization, V2X and edge technologies make a solitary vehicle an agent. Applications of this integrated system are used in predictive traffic control, cooperative lane merging, congestion forecasting, and city-scale simulations of digital twins, among others, which help to make the mobility infrastructures of the city safer and more efficient. Figure 2 illustrating the integration of V2X connectivity, edge computing, and distributed AI to allow vehicles to achieve situational awareness and cooperative intelligent capabilities in a short amount of time.

Figure 2. Synergy of V2X, edge, and networked intelligence

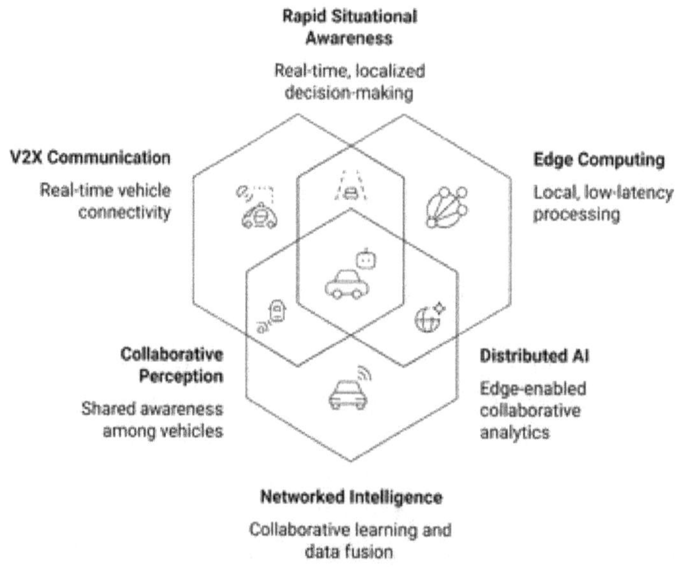

3. RESEARCH OBJECTIVES

Digital-twin technology integration with the powerful 5G networks and the upcoming 6G networks offer fresh prospects of supporting intelligent, responsive, and scalable autonomous vehicle ecosystems. Since AVs require constant data communication, real-time synchronization, and predictive analytics, it is crucial to comprehend how next-generation communication infrastructures can be used to meet these needs. The goals of the proposed study are to investigate the technical, operational, and strategic aspects of DT-AV integration with the emphasis put on scalability, latency, system resilience, interoperability across layers. These research questions offer an organized way in which one can assess the opportunities and constraints of 5G/6G-enabled digital twin worlds to autonomous mobility in the future.

- To investigate how 5G/6G communication architectures support scalable and continuously synchronized digital twins for autonomous vehicles.
- To evaluate end-to-end latency, bandwidth, throughput, and reliability requirements essential for real-time DT-AV data exchange and inference.
- To analyze the role of V2X, edge computing, and distributed AI in enhancing contextual awareness and collaborative autonomy in DT-enabled AV systems.
- To identify key technical constraints, security vulnerabilities, and interoperability challenges affecting large-scale deployment of networked digital twins.
- To explore future opportunities including AI-native networking, terahertz communication, and federated twin learning to advance next-generation AV digital twin ecosystems.

4. CONCEPTUAL MODEL

Digital Twin systems and autonomous vehicles are combined, and the conceptual model is supported by the 5G and the upcoming 6G communication technologies in the framework of a multi-layered architecture. The purpose of this model is to create the smooth interaction of real cars, simulated environments, and distribution computing resources. The architecture is structured at the center to have onboard AV systems, edge and cloud platforms linked to each other to support real-time processing, predictive analytics, and synchronized updates of the digital twin states. The model focuses on how ultra-low-latency communication contributes to the ability to maintain the constant exchange of data and the accuracy of the virtual replicas (Jabeen Siddiqi et al., 2025). It also records the way in which network slicing, cooperative perception and multi agent intelligence can improve vehicle decision-making and environmental awareness. Moreover, the conceptual model is not confined to single-vehicle models, but rather to city-scale models, where fleets, infrastructure, and mobility services can be integrated. The framework can be scaled, reliable, and responsive to current conditions in real-time through the addition of DTs to advanced and high-quality networking and AI-based orchestration, which is what autonomous transportation ecosystems require.

4.1 DT-AV Edge–Cloud Integration Architecture

The architectural integration model builds one system that links autonomous vehicles, digital twins, edge computing, cloud computing and the 5G/6G layers of communication. High-frequency data are collected and assembled at the LiDAR, radar and camera sensors at the physical layer of AVs. The 5G/6G networks transmit this data to edge nodes to compute and do local inferencing at a high rate so as to reduce delays in responses. The layer of the digital twin has adaptive virtual replicas that are deployed and simulate the operation of the vehicle, future conditions of the system, and other courses of actions under variant conditions in the traffic. Calculations that are time critical are conducted using edge platforms and large-scale analytics, long term storage, and training AI models are conducted on the cloud platforms (Zhang et al., 2025). URLLC provides communication backbone and enables synchronization of physical and virtual states as well as terahertz communication. Network slicing offers safety-critical functions with dedicated bandwidth. These interrelated layers are all the ones that allow vehicles to collaborate, share situational intelligence, and organize in the real-time on a distributed mobility environment. This open architecture ensures reliability, scaling as well as sustainable learning across AV ecosystems. The implementation of physical sensing, communication, edge computing, digital twins, and cloud analytics to make intelligent mobility systems can be implemented in a layered structure as shown in Figure 3 below.

Figure 3. Smart mobility architecture

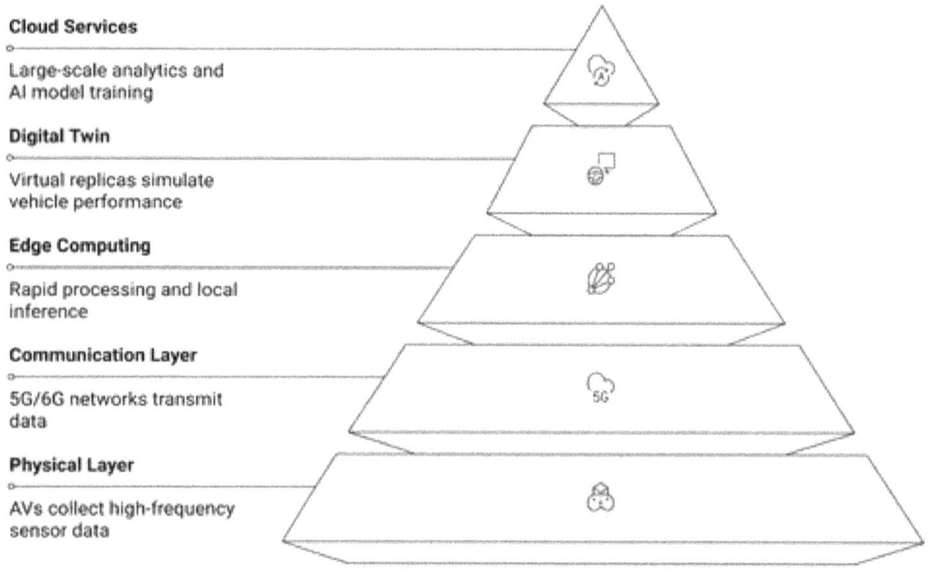

4.2 Data Flow and Synchronization Framework

This aspect of the conceptual model defines the process of the transmission of real-time data, processing and synchronization of these data throughout the DT-AV ecosystem. Data flow Starting with obtaining sensor streams of AVs, they are transmitted via high-speed 5G/6G communications to edge and cloud platform. The synchronization pipelines are used to bring all the updates of the physical vehicle to its digital twin in real time keeping all the layers of perception, planning, and control faithful. These pipelines have a timestamping system, fault detection system and loop of continuous alignment that avoids dissimilarities between physical and virtual states. Network slicing is important in ensuring quality-of-service because it establishes separated virtual sub-networks that meet distinct AV functions, including emergency response, perception updates, and cooperative driving functions. This will support critical data flows with priority bandwidth and ultra-low latency where non-critical tasks will run on different slices (Sanz Rodrigo et al., 2023). The combination of these mechanisms makes it possible to have multi-vehicle coordination, continuous twin synchronization, and robust data delivery when deploying large autonomous mobility, using networks and edge/cloud platforms to facilitate the transfer of sensor data to networks and serve as the data source to enable coordinated mobility pipelines and network slicing. Figure 4 shows how AV sensor data flows through networks and edge/cloud platforms to support synchronization pipelines and network slicing to facilitate coordinated mobility.

Figure 4. Data flow and synchronization in smart mobility

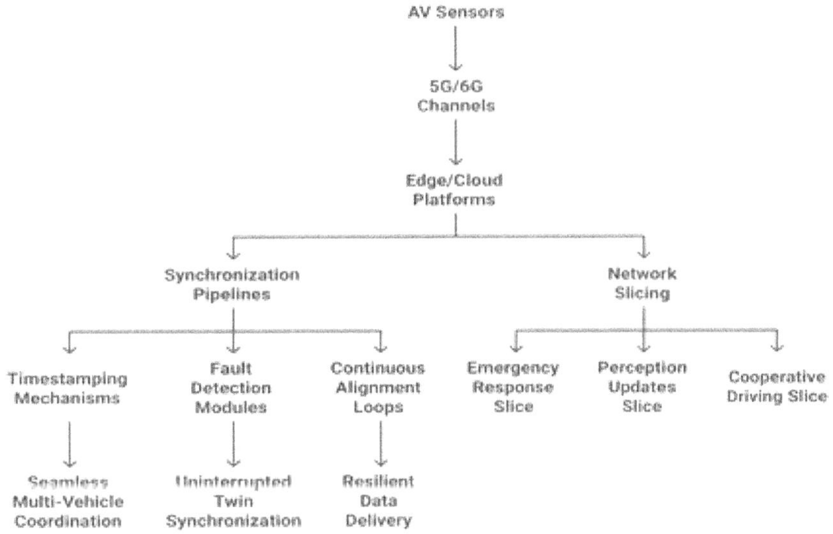

4.3 Predictive Intelligence and Collaborative Autonomy

This section of the conceptual model dwells on the improvement of DT-enabled AV ecosystems by predictive intelligence. Digital twins utilize AI-based algorithms to predict vehicle behavior, road hazards, traffic jams, as well as system failures based on incoming information. The predictive intuitions enable self-driving cars to think ahead and be proactive. Collaborative autonomy is made possible by granting AVs a form of collective intelligence using V2X communication so that they can make joint decisions like coordinating lane mergers, coordinating platoons, or real-time route adjustments. Simulation loops aggregated to large mobility networks City-scale Simulation Loops At the macro level; aggregation of thousands of digital twins is used to model large mobility networks. Such simulations assist the urban planners, the fleet operators, and the traffic authorities to test the control measures, analyze the congestion scenarios, and design emergency responses (Minerva et al., 2020). The connectivity is powered by 5G/6G which means such loops are constantly updating to create a living model of the urban transportation system. This predictive analytics, multi-agent collaboration and scale simulation is the basis of next generation autonomous mobility ecosystems. Figure 5 that illustrates how predictive intelligence, collaborative autonomy and networked coordination all come together to provide proactive city-scale autonomous mobility.

Figure 5. Synergy driving next-gen autonomous mobility

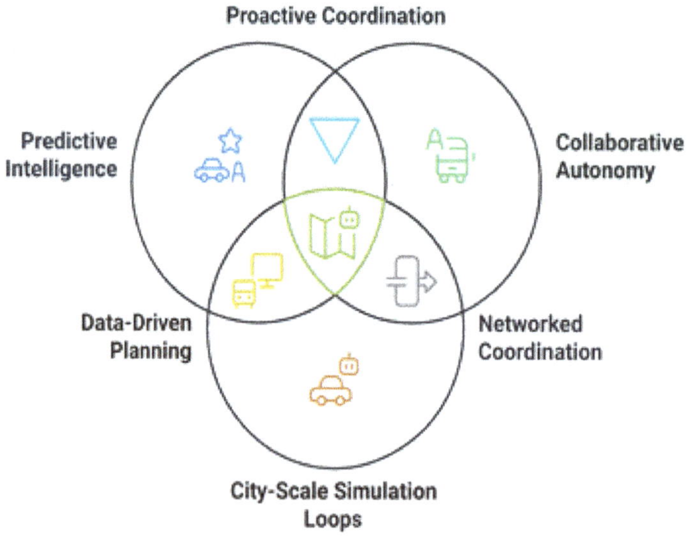

5. RESEARCH METHODOLOGY

The conceptual, analytical, and evaluation-based approach of the research consists of a combination of concepts of investigating how 5G/6G networks are capable of integrating real-time digital twins within the autonomous vehicle ecosystems. To begin with, a conceptual modeling approach is used to create a structure of architecture that depicts relations among AVs, digital twins, communication networks, and computational layers. Performance parameters like the latency, throughput and reliability of synchronization are then evaluated using analytical modeling. Case based validation is also part of the methodology, looking at live implementations of pilot projects and smart mobility corridors that have been practiced internationally. Moreover, a measuring structure is developed to evaluate the performance of the DT-AV systems in different conditions in the network (Gu et al., 2023). The sources of data consist of technical reports, published literature, AV field trials, and 5G/6G testbeds. This multi-methodology approach will guarantee a stringent and comprehensive study on the potentials, limitations, and prospects of networked digital twin ecosystems to autonomous mobility.

5.1 Conceptual and Analytical Modelling Approach

A systemic ground of the understanding of the interface between digital twins, autonomous vehicles, and the next-generation communication networks is the conceptual and analytical modelling approach. The conceptual modeling is premised on the creation of layered models that outline the system components, flows of data and their dependencies. The models show the integration directions between AV sensors and edge computing and cloud analytics and AI-based decision modules and 5G/6G communication layers. This is complemented with the use of analytical modeling to help quantify the important variables such as the latency, the packet loss and the synchronization delay and the computational load (Xiong et al., 2022). Mathematical tools, simulation models, and performance benchmarks are applied to perform the analysis of the effects of different network configurations on the behavior of systems. This dual approach will help in identifying bottlenecks, checking scalability, and scaling ability of the systems within varying traffic and environmental factors. Conceptual clarity coupled with quantitative rigor offered by the methodology make it possible to have a better understanding of how the optimization of DT-AV systems will work in the real-time. It also provides a point of comparison among various architectures and providing a sound argument of the conceptual assumptions by analyzing them in terms of performance.

5.2 Performance Evaluation Framework

The assessment conglomeration will examine operational performance of 5G/6G-enabled digital twin ecosystems in a number of key performance indicators. Latency evaluation analysis looks at the end-to-end communication time delays, sensor transmission, edge processing, twin updates, and vehicle actuation. The analysis of throughput is concerned with the capability of the network to support large data streams of AV sensors like LiDAR and high-resolution cameras. Synchronization metrics define the quality of the alignment between the physical and digital vehicle, by measuring such parameters as the rate of updates, time synchronization, and error tolerance (Xu et al., 2024). The safety metrics evaluate the abilities of the system to survive in real-time settings and support collision avoidance as well as emergency responses and fault tolerance. Other indicators of reliability that are taken into account in the framework are packet delivery ratio, jitter, and stability of network slices. Combined, these metrics give a comprehensive view of how the systems perform, allowing the comparison between different situations and provide the way of improvement in case of large-scale application of DT-AV systems in smart mobility environment. Table 2 Defines the most important metrics of evaluating latency, fidelity, and synchronization reliability.

Table 2. Performance metrics for evaluating DT–AV ecosystems

Metric	Definition	Importance
End-to-End Latency	Delay from vehicle to DT update	Safety-critical timing
Synchronization Fidelity	Virtual–physical accuracy	Operational reliability
Throughput	Data transfer capacity	Sensor-rich AV data
Packet Delivery Ratio	Successful transmissions	Communication stability
Jitter	Variability in latency	Smooth control tasks

5.2.1 DT-AV Communication Benchmarks

Quantitative performance benchmarks are required to assess the viability of digital twin autonomous vehicle systems operations. Synchronization between physical and virtual twins of vehicles in real-time needs to be extremely high in terms of communication performance. In traditional automotive communication systems, the range of latency is usually 20-50ms, which can cause delays in making safety-related decisions. End-to-end latency is brought as a result of the use of 5G URLLC infrastructure to about 5-10 milliseconds, which allows implementing faster hazard detection and vehicle response mechanisms. It is anticipated that future 6G communication architectures will achieve even lower latency of less than one milliseconds thereby making digital twins and physical vehicles much more synchronized. Likewise, it is projected that communication bandwidth will rise due to 5G networks (10 Gbps) and 6G networks (100 Gbps and more) based on terahertz spectrum bands. The safety-critical autonomous vehicle system also has extremely high reliability requirements, usually ranging to 99.999% network availability to maintain continuous communication between vehicles, infrastructure, and digital twin platforms. These quantitative advances prove the fact that next-generation communication infrastructures are central to facilitating the proper real-time digital twin synchronization, predictive analytics, and collaborative autonomous mobility operations.

5.3 Data Sources and Validation

This methodological aspect describes the process of data collection, selection, and validation to be used in the research. The data sources will be peer-reviewed literature, industry white papers, government smart mobility reports, telecommunications standards (3GPP, ITU), and in-the-field pilot deployments of 5G powered autonomous systems. Other sources are field tests done in smart city corridors, AV testbeds and digital twin simulation platforms. The case selection criteria are based on the recency, the technological relevance, documentation completeness, and the existence of integrated architecture of DT-AV-5G/6G. The cases should have real time synchronization, V2X communication and quantifiable performance results in order to enable meaningful comparative analysis (Vy Le et al., 2018). The validation process will entail the comparison of the reported performance measures with technical specifications, and simulation outputs, and observational data where accessible. Triangulation is used to make sure that there is consistency of sources. This orderly methodology means that the empirical knowledge is correct, trustworthy, and has a direct correspondence with the conceptual and analytical aspect of the research.

6. LITERATURE REVIEW

The interplay between Digital Twin systems, 5G / 6G communication networks, and AI-based analytics are becoming more and more accepted as a cornerstone of autonomous vehicle systems of the next generation. The available literature shows autonomous vehicles need continuous and high-fidelity synchronization of physical sensors, virtual models and distributed computing resources to enhance safe and reliable operation. Digital Twins (DTs) have become the major tools of real-time monitoring, predictive simulation, and operational optimization, but their effectiveness is highly dependent on communication infrastructure (Z. Tang et al., 2024). Research lays stress on the fact that ultra-low-latency, high-throughput, and resilient networking, which are features that are natural to 5G and are expected in 6G, are crucial to ensuring accurate, time-sensitive DTAV synchronization. In addition, it has been shown that developing AI/ML algorithms advanced enough to handle multi-modal sensor data and produce predictive insights used to furnish collaborative autonomy are required. In this literature review, a synthesis of world research tendencies based on the use of DT-enabled AV systems, the use of 5G/6G in real-time mobility communication, or the input of AI to synchronization, predicting, and intelligent control of networked twin conditions can be obtained (Paolini et al., 2024).

6.1 DT-AV Trends and Capabilities

The application of Digital Twin solutions in the autonomous vehicles is increasing rapidly in the past few years and this has been enabled by sensing, high-performance computing, and simulation technologies. Research has shown that DTs enable repeated execution of vehicle and sensor behaviour and environmental conditions and create a virtual environment where scenarios may be found and optimized before running them on the real world. Applications of DT systems in trajectory planning, predictive maintenance, environmental insight and performance monitoring (Wu et al., 2024). The trends indicate that there is a transformation of the non-dynamically changing virtual replica and its inclination to dynamic changes to the self-updating models and capable of changing dynamically in real time. Secondly, the formation of multi-vehicle DT ecosystems also takes place and enables one to simulate at city level to cooperate in driving and traffic management (Pasupuleti, 2024).

However, in the existing literature, there are also several limitations, as it is written. To begin with, the current communication channels do not typically support the ultra-low-latency of the high-frequency synchronization that generates latent or non-time consistent updates to the twins. Second, there is also the problem of scalability, because the computing of thousands of vehicles simultaneously takes considerable computational power (Aghaei Anvigh et al., 2024). Third, lack of heterogeneous sensor architecture and proprietary AV platform creates issues with interoperability. Finally, the aspect of cybersecurity that is associated with inter-twin communication and cloud-edge integration is not addressed exhaustively. These are the evident causes to consider 5G/6G technologies as a means of performance, reliability, and security impetus. Table 3 Overviews the major DT attributes needed to support AV perception, prediction, and control.

Table 3. Digital twin functional requirements for autonomous vehicles

Function	Requirement	Benefit
Real-time Sync	Sub-ms updates	Accurate vehicle mirroring
Data Fusion	Multi-sensory input	Enhanced perception
Predictive Modeling	AI-based	Proactive decision-making
Hazard Detection	Continuous monitoring	Improved safety
Fleet Coordination	Shared intelligence	Traffic optimization

6.2 5G/6G V2X and Edge–Cloud Networking

The literature is quite categorical that 5G (and further 6G) networks are the most compelling enablers of real-time digital twin synchronization in autonomy mobility. The 5G Ultra-Reliable Low-Latency Communications (URLLC), Enhanced Mobile Broadband (eMBB), and massive Machine-Type Communications (mMTC) provide the foundations of required instant-data communications, perception sharing with high-bandwidth and dense V2X. The latency gain to the range of 1-5 ms has proven to be an effective way of improving the responsiveness and fidelity of twin updates, and 6G literature is even more optimistic to allow, including terahertz communication, AI-native networking, reconfigurable intelligent surfaces, and sub-milliseconds latency which would make DT-AV coordination faster (Stavdas et al., 2024). The other academic literature area of interest is the use of edge-cloud orchestration. Edge computing is able to offer local processing to reduce the delays in perception and decision-making, but cloud hardware can benefit from long-term learning, fleet-wide analytics, and simulation workloads. Multi-access networking is also applied to provide vehicles with an option to switch between communication technologies, including cellular V2X, Wi-Fi 7, and satellite connections, at any moment to maintain connectivity all the time. When all these technologies are combined, it will result in making things reliable, offering twin-level consistency, and enable autonomous mobility systems to reach large scale, multi-agent levels (Atmakuri, 2025). Table 4 Core network features List includes features that enable to support reliable and scalable twin ecosystems.

Table 4. Key 5G/6G features supporting AV–DT integration

Feature	Technology	Purpose
URLLC	5G/6G	Safety-critical updates
mMTC	5G	Massive device support
Terahertz Links	6G	Ultra-high throughput
Network Slicing	5G/6G	Priority bandwidth allocation
RIS	6G	Enhanced signal strength

6.3 AI-Driven Twin–AV Synchronization

AI is at the middle of realizing the full potential of the digital twins in autonomous vehicles. It has been demonstrated in the literature that AI algorithms assist in the fusion of perception, predictive maintenance, behavior forecasting, trajectory optimization, anomaly detection, and control via reinforcement learning. Machine learning can be used to allow twins to process high-dimensional sensor data and determine future vehicle states, road conditions, or system failures. This is predictive feature that enables autonomous vehicles to manoeuvre, coordinate, and predict hazards, as well as optimize energy use (Jing Yik et al., 2025). According to recent research, deep learning, graph neural networks, spatiotemporal models and generative AI frameworks can greatly increase the accuracy of twin-updates. This is done using synchronization engines that are driven by AI to keep physical and virtual states aligned by correcting noise, missing data, and environmental variability. Multi-agent AI also enhances collaborative driving where Avs can share situational intelligence through DT interfaces. It is anticipated that AI-native protocols will be used in 6G networks to control resource allocation, network slicing, and bandwidth priorities of the network autonomously. Therefore, with AI and 5G/6G, a self-optimizing real-time digital twin ecosystem can be formed that is able to facilitate safe, scalable, and highly responsive autonomous mobility (Marques da Silva & Dinis, 2021).

7. CASE STUDIES

The use of Digital Twin technology and 5G and 6G network is also gaining rapid pace in other technologically developed countries. The practice applications illustrated above illustrate how the distributed intelligence and high-speed connectivity, combined with artificial intelligence and analytics, can improve the accuracy, responsiveness and scalability of autonomous vehicles ecosystems. The case studies can also be a useful source of information on the implications of infrastructure, policy framework and improved communications architectures on the functionality of DT-enabled AV systems (Ravikumar & Aarthi, 2025a). China and South Korea have become the world leaders, where they have established large platforms of mobility and pilot programs in which the networked digital twins can be tried to be operational. Such efforts define the real-life results in the latency, cooperative driving, predictive modeling, multi-vehicle coordination and real-time traffic projection (Khan, Yaqoob, Tran, et al., 2020). These also showcase some important system design, network slicing, edge-cloud orchestration and cybersecurity teachings. The following case studies give some modern examples of the functioning of the DT-AV ecosystems on the large scale and could be used as a source of information on the issue of smart mobility innovation and future applications into the world arena. Table 5 AV-DT pilot implementations Analysis (major).

Table 5. Case study comparison: China vs South Korea deployments

Parameter	China 6G Pilot Zones	South Korea 5G DT Corridor
Focus	6G-native DT ecosystem	5G based mobility corridor
Latency	<1 ms	5–10 ms
Scale	City-wide multi-fleet	National highway network
Key Tech	THz, AI-native	MEC, NR-V2X
Outcomes	High predictive accuracy	Improved reaction time

7.1 China's 6G Pilot Zones for AV Digital Twins

In 2024, China declared the first 6G autonomous mobility pilot zones to experiment on the use of ultra-low-latency, high-bandwidth Digital Twin uses in some megacities. It includes terahertz-band communication, AI-native networking and distributed edge intelligence to establish constantly-coordinated virtual programs of vehicles and urban traffics environment. They will be comprised of sophisticated roadside facilities, LiDAR-based crossing, dense sensor networks, and AI-enhanced base stations that will be capable of supporting up to a million devices that are connected within a square kilometre (Orlov & Susarev, 2023). Each vehicle in an autonomous vehicle fleet functions within a full DT environment, that is, every vehicle broadcasts high-frequency perception information to edge nodes, which is required to synchronize physical and virtual state on sub-milliseconds. Predictive modeling systems are virtual measures of the imminent traffic, collision risks, system failure and manoeuvre strategies in a collaborative form (Ibn-Khedher et al., 2024). The pilot was able to make many gains as 40% of its predictions became accurate, response latency had been shortened by 60%, and the multi-vehicle coordination had greatly improved. The example of the model in China can be the world standard of 5G to early 6G mobility system transformation as it demonstrates that safe, efficient and large-scale autonomous transportation can become possible with AI-based and network-native twins. Figure 6 of digital twins, predictive modelling, 6G-enabled infrastructure integration, and AV fleets in pilot mobility zones in China.

Figure 6. China's 6G pilot zones for autonomous vehicles

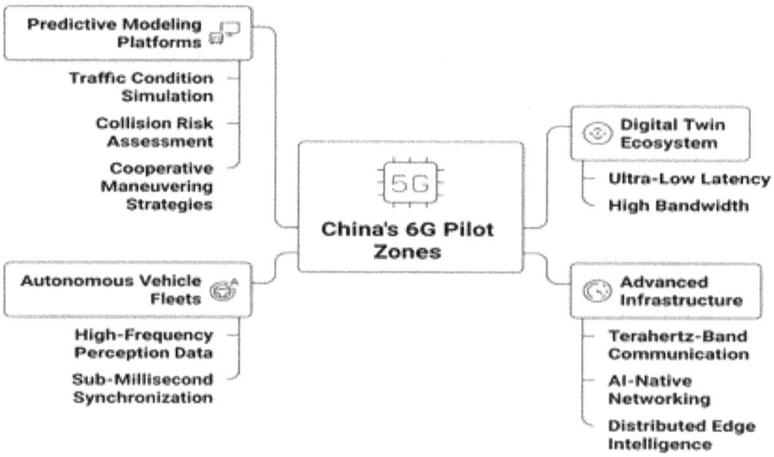

7.2 South Korea's 5G AV Digital Twin Corridor

One more advanced project of AV-DT integration which is currently in service and will be made live in 2024 in the country is the Korean national 5G Digital Twin Mobility Corridor. It is also thorough cuts across major routes of Seoul-Busan and Seoul-Daegu routes and is highly populated with sensor infrastructure, multi-access edge computing clusters, and real-time HD map infrastructure that ensures the real-time digital replication of road networks and autonomous fleets. The vehicles communicate with the Smart Roadside units on a constant basis via 5G New Radio connections that enable 5-10 ms latency in case of urgent processes (Navarro-Ortiz et al., 2020). Sensor measurements are gathered into edge nodes after every 2-5 kilometres and applied to maintain twin state and provide predictive analytics to detect hazards, anticipate congestion and cooperative driving. Routing and platooning is supported as well as emergency lane switches and AI-powered decision engines. The objective changes in the test included a reduction of AV reaction time by a quarter, 40% better performance of the route optimization and a significant reduction in the forecasted risk of collision (Hadi & Murtaza, 2022). South Korea South Korea has a solid foundation on the implementation of 5G-based DT systems in the future as the corridor demonstrates the actual preparations in terms of infrastructure, sophisticated 5G technologies, and results. figure 7 specifying the overall digital twin mobility of real-time AV in South Korea.

Figure 7. South Korea's 5G-enabled autonomous vehicle digital twin corridor

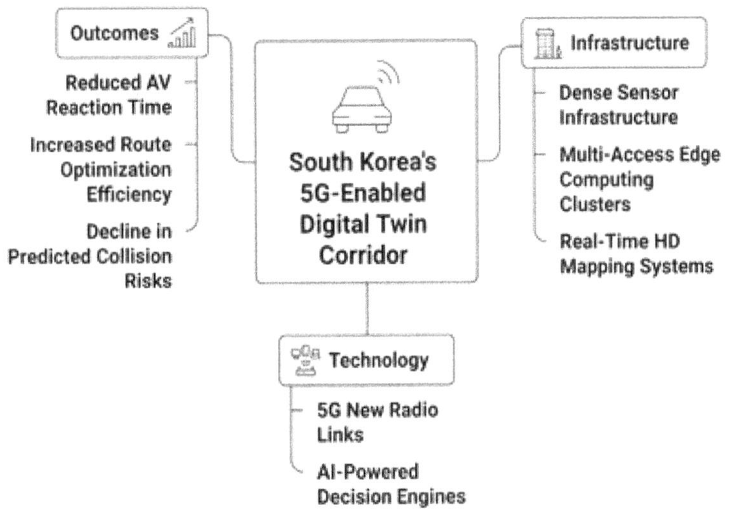

8. RESULTS AND DISCUSSION

Findings of global DT-AV implementations indicate that the use of digital twins together with the 5G/6G networks can be used to improve greatly the operational responsiveness, prediction accuracy, and multi-vehicle coordination. These gains in performance are mainly facilitated by a decrease in communication latency, an increase in the availability of bandwidth, and an augmentation of edge-cloud orchestration. Research shows that, when twins are synchronized in real-time, hazard detection is quicker, decision-making becomes more precise and efficient, and that the optimization of a fleet level is better. Network slicing and URLLC add additional power to the performance by providing an uninterrupted communication of safety-critical functions. In a similar manner, 6G pilots are more scalable, and allow thousands of AV-DT interactions at a time with low delay (Groshev, Guimaraes, et al., 2021). Comparative results indicate that 5G as well as preliminary 6G technologies are critical, yet AI-native architecture and terahertz connections of 6G have enormous long-term potential. On the whole, the findings indicate that networked digital twins are the basis of the future generation of autonomous mobility.

8.1 Digital Twin Network Performance Insights

The most significant parameter in DTAV synchronization is always detected to be latency in terms of performance reviews. The experimental results of 5G corridors show that the mean round-trip delays are in the range of 5-10 ms, which can be used to offer perception, manoeuvring, and route adjustment with virtually no latency. Fidelity, which means virtue of the rightness of virtual-physical correspondence is also improved by a vast margin in case high-speed connectivity is utilized to relay thick sensor data (Nawaz Khan & Ahmad, 2025). One of them is by using synchronization pipelines which are more predictable and information drift is minimized hence predictive models are more precise. The second significant dimension turns out to be the scalability due to the proven ability of 5G to support thousands of connected devices and the known problems in managing large fleets of the city. Early 6G implementations suggest a very high scalability with regard to accessing terahertz spectrum and AI-native orchestration, which can update dozens of millions of nodes at once. All these findings together demonstrate that networked DT performance directly affects AV safety, decision-making efficiency, and reliability of the system, and the communication developments are needed to guarantee scalability in the long term.

8.2 Impact of 5G/6G Network Features

The key features of 5GURLLC, mMTC, and Massive MIMO make a significant contribution to the AV-DT integration; they reduce the delays, improve the capacity, and offer the stunning power of coordination between the devices. The communication in URLLC can also be very reliable (latency does not exceed 5 ms) necessary in emergency braking, collision avoidance and in synchronization of real-time control between AVs and roadside sensors or infrastructure devices which can be achieved without any congestion (Ahmadi et al., 2021). Massive MIMO assists in enhancing the signal power and stability, which enables transfer of high throughput of data even in the dense urban scenario. Network slicing has the capability of ensuring safety-critical functions that are assigned separate virtual networks and will never disrupt nonessential functions in terms of bandwidth. The 6G capabilities further increase its benefits which include: terahertz communication, holography beamforming and reconfigurable intelligent surfaces. Early versions prove that latency is sub-milliseconds, throughput is multi-gigabit, and the allocation of resources is optimized and 6G will be the core of completely autonomous, predictive and coordinated twin ecosystems (Nayyef & Mahmood, 2025).

8.3 5G vs. 6G for AV Digital Twins

The comparison of 5G and 6G indicates that there are noteworthy disparities of the capacity, intelligence, and efficiency of synchronization. On the one hand, 5G can provide the necessary underpinning to support real-time updates and collaborative perception, whereas on the other hand, it is limited by the spectrum and medium scalability, and it depends on external optimization processes. On the other hand, 6G also introduces AI-native networking, Integrated Sensing And Communication (ISAC) and terahertz frequency bands each of which leads to unmatched throughput and ultra-low latency. The capabilities will enable the simultaneous synchronization of city-scale digital twins, more complex prediction models, and millions of interactions between Avs simultaneously. 6G also enables distributed learning, where the edge nodes learn and adapt independently of variability in the environment (Jiang et al., 2021). Even though 5G is has enough capability to serve the current Avs in operations, 6G is the best framework of the autonomous transport ecosystem as it incorporates high-density fleets, multifaceted simulation cycles and self-evolving digital twins. Hence, 6G is a future enhancement, which can take the boundaries of AV intelligence and resiliency.

9. FUTURE RESEARCH DIRECTIONS

The increasing complexity of DT-enabled AV ecosystems should be the subject of future research, with the emphasis being placed on the new technologies to improve intelligence, security, and resilience. The development of quantum communication, decentralized learning, and self-adaptive digital twins provides new opportunities in the field of innovation but requires interdisciplinary frameworks. The questions that need to be investigated by researchers are how quantum networks can enhance ultra-safe communication and speedy AVs, how federated twin learning might reinforce distributed decision-making, and how autonomous healing may contribute to constant reliability in dynamic conditions. Simulations should also be capable of scaling to entire cities and still have real-time fidelity. It will also be vital to tackle the issues of energy efficiency, environmental sustainability, and ethical challenges (Gade et al., 2025). These research directions will bring the future generation of predictive, reliable and globally scalable AV twin ecosystems.

9.1 Quantum-Ready Digital Twins for AV Systems

Quantum communication suggests potential availability of ultra-secure and ultra-fast exchange of data, which is one of the largest breakthroughs in the future DT-AV ecosystems. Quantum Key Distribution (QKD) eradicates any weaknesses found in classical encryption, and allows vehicles, twins, and infrastructure to synchronize tamperproof. Quantum networks also have very high data rates that enable streaming of huge sensor data, such as LiDAR point clouds and holograph maps, with very low delay. Studies are also actively investigating the means in which quantum repeaters, entanglement-based communication, and quantum-ready photonic processors can be interoperable with 6G systems so that quantum-ready AVs become possible (Khan, Yaqoob, Imran, et al., 2020). This kind of integration would enable twins to work with a higher degree of precision and shorter reaction cycles as well as close to perfection between virtual and real worlds. Nevertheless, there are still major obstacles to overcome, such as the shortage of quantum hardware, price, and the necessity to have the standardized quantum communication protocols. Further development of this field will be essential towards facilitating the new generation of ultra-secure and high-performance autonomous mobility.

9.2 Federated Twin Learning and Edge Intelligence

Federated twin learning makes autonomous vehicles and digital twins actively cooperate to train AI models without exchanging raw data to enhance privacy, scalability, and intelligence at the edge dramatically. Using federated learning, DT-AV systems will be able to improve predictive modelling, behavior prediction, and fault detection through sharing of model updates instead of entire datasets.

Decentralized edge intelligence means that calculations are done nearer to the car that leads to less latency and enhances responsiveness when taking safety-critical actions (Sathish Babu et al., 2024). This will also reduce dependency on the cloud, so that AVs will operate effectively even at times when the network is congested, or partly broken. Investigations into decentralized learning of reinforcement, collaborative learning, and distributed optimization may be used in reinforcing the work of DT-AV ecosystems. Nevertheless, the future work has to deal with issues like communication overheads when aggregating models, vehicle hardware heterogeneity, and Byzantine robustness. Current development of federated twin learning will underpin more adaptive, collaborative and privacy preserving autonomous mobility architectures.

9.3 Self-Evolving Digital Twins

Self-evolving digital twins are a new model whereby DTs evolve themselves, fix and optimize their own internal models using real-world feedback. These twins combine the constant learning processes and anomaly detectors with automatic reconfiguring so that they can be accurate even when surroundings vary rapidly. This is essential to AV ecosystems, in which unexpected factors such as weather conditions, malfunctions in the sensor, or traffic disruptions are needed to be adjusted in real-time. Self-healing is used to enable twins to repair the corrupted models, lost synchronization and update the environmental parameters automatically. Future studies should address autonomous-calibration, cognitive-adaptation and resilience-based system design algorithms (Chataut et al., 2024). Also, a combination of biological-inspired intelligence, neuro-symbolic AI, and edge-driven adaptation can result in DTs that can self-evolve over time. The creation of such systems will help greatly to increase the reliability, decrease the maintenance overhead and enable continuous AV operation under various mobility conditions.

10. MANAGERIAL IMPLICATIONS

The combination of DTs and 5G/6G-provided AV systems has serious strategic consequences to automotive manufacturers, fleet operators, mobility providers, and smart city agencies. The managers should be ready to deploy a broad infrastructure, invest in an edge-cloud ecosystem, and comply with the changing global technical standards. Cybersecurity should also be a priority to decision-makers since information sharing in real-time exposes them to network threats. The use of predictive DT tools would help to streamline the fleet management process, minimize operational risks and enhance customer safety results (Gilly et al., 2019). Industry, telecom operators and government agencies will need to collaborate in order to establish interoperability, regulatory compliance and sustainable deployment. The successful shift of autonomous mobility into a robust, data-driven, and highly coordinated transportation ecosystem will be determined by efficient managerial strategies.

10.1 Implications for Mobility Stakeholders

Manufacturers and mobility providers need to realise the operational and business potential of DT-AV ecosystems. In the case of OEMs, digital twins allow lifecycle monitoring, predictive maintenance, and based on data, improving vehicles design. With the help of DT insights, mobility service providers are able to optimize their fleet routing, minimize energy usage, and deliver user experiences. The city-scale

DT simulations can help smart city planners with predictive traffic control, alleviation of congestion, and infrastructure planning. Nevertheless, it is controlled by interoperability between AV platforms and sensor networks as well as communication providers. To maximize the benefits of networked twins, managers need to invest in talent, relationships, and long-term strategies of digital transformation (Lu et al., 2021). These involve implementing flexible architecture, safety critical bandwidth, and the use of AI based mobility planners. To achieve these benefits, it is important to have a multi-stakeholder effort to coordinate urban policies, business models, and technological investments.

10.2 Scalable Twin Network Deployment

As the scale of DT-AV systems increases, managers will have to consider network deployment strategies that will strike a balance between cost, performance and the long-run ability to adapt. A distributed deployment framework, which entails edge computing clusters around significant road systems, is a method which minimizes delay and provides real-time synchronization. By investing in 5G standalone networks and 6G upgrades, it is possible to be ready in the future, where terahertz communication and AI-native orchestration can be easily migrated. To ensure the safety-critical AV functions operate continuously, network slicing should be implemented to ensure that the specific bandwidth is assigned to this category. Phased deployment plans should be thought of by the planners along high-density corridors, industrial areas and urban centers (He et al., 2021). Also, fault-tolerant design and redundancy should be used to ensure that the services are available in times of network outages. Managers need to consider the energy utilization, sustainability targets, and infrastructural durability so that the twin ecosystems will be economically and operationally sustainable.

10.3 Policy and Governance Requirements

Having successful deployment of DT-enabled AV ecosystems depends on robust policy frameworks, regulatory correspondence and adherence to global-standards. Guidelines on data privacy, cybersecurity, AI responsibility, and cross-border data transfer need to be put in place by the policymakers. There is a need to have standardization to enable interoperability among vehicle brands, telecom networks, and simulation platforms. All development and deployment processes should be compliant with such mechanisms as ISO 21434 on cybersecurity and the new standards of DT synchronization. The roles and responsibilities between OEMs, telecom providers, city authorities, and cloud operators should be defined by governance structures to control the risks and to facilitate the ethical use of AI and data (Kuts et al., 2021). Public reporting through transparent auditing, certification programs and large-scale deployment are more effective in building trust. With 6G development, emerging regulations will be required to regulate the distribution of spectrums, the use of shared infrastructure, and quantum-resilient communication protocols.

10.3.1 DT–AV Cybersecurity Frameworks

The condition of cybersecurity is the secure operation of autonomous vehicle ecosystems that are driven by digital twins. The continuous exchange of information among vehicles, edge computing units, cloud computing units, and spaces of digital twins creates potential attack vectors that have to be protected with the help of powerful defensive mechanisms. Such international standards as ISO/SAE 21434 are provided with methodological requirements to the automotive cybersecurity engineering, which allow the methods that are adaptive to the systematic identification of vulnerabilities, risk assessment, and provision of security controls throughout the life cycle of connected vehicle systems. The regulatory agencies such as UNECE WP.29 also demand the implementation of the cybersecurity management systems that monitor, detect, and respond to threats in the interconnected vehicle infrastructures. These models emphasize on safe communication process, cryptographic authentication, intrusion recognition systems and constant monitoring of network behavior (Ravikumar & Aarthi, 2025c). Edge-cloud orchestration, encrypted V2X communications and trusted synchronization are also to be secured in the case of digital twin ecosystems. The reliability and credibility of the next generation autonomous mobility systems can be enhanced with the assistance of new technologies, such as blockchain-based identity management, zero-trust architecture, and AI-based anomaly detection.

11. CONCLUSION

The combination of Digital Twin technology and advanced 5G and new 6G communication networks is a game changer on the way to the fully autonomous, intelligent, and resilient transportation systems. The chapter has shown the digital twins as the heart of the autonomous vehicle analytical and predictive engine, which is able to provide real-time situational awareness, optimal performance, and preventive risk mitigation. DTs make physical vehicles safer, more operationally dependable, and more transparent in their systems by coordinating the vehicles with constantly updated virtual ones. The integration of 5G/6G, i.e. ultra-low latency, massive connectivity, AI-native orchestration and high-throughput communication, makes the fidelity, responsiveness, and scalability of these twin ecosystem significantly stronger. Results of international pilot tests, such as the 6G mobility zones in China and South Korea 5G autonomous zones, demonstrate obvious results of the reduction of latency, coordination among multiple vehicles, predictability, and collaboration between edges and clouds. Providing an example of the way communication-driven twins can be used to support huge fleets, deal with high sensor traffic, and provide city-scale mobility simulations, these cases demonstrate the ability of the technology to serve as a foundation in multiple areas.

The chapter further highlighted the future worth of newer technologies like quantum secure communication, federated twin training, edge intelligence in a decentralized manner, self-adapted virtual models that adjust to unforeseen real-life situations. In a strategic sense, the coming together of DTs and next-generation networks is the basis of intelligent transport systems of tomorrow systems that have the ability to make intelligent choices, drive cooperatively, and be powered by data. With the spread of AVs in the urban context, the policy alignment, cross-sector cooperation, and ethical management of data will gain even greater significance to bring safety, interoperability, and trust of the population. In the end, connected digital twins will allow the creation of not only connected and autonomous transportation ecosystems but also predictive, self-optimizing, and resilient. Their incorporation into 5G/6G infrastructure is a game changer in making the roads safer, mobility services more efficient, and the urban operations sustainable. This new paradigm makes digital twins unavoidable resources in the world transition to intelligent, adaptive and future-oriented transportation networks.

REFERENCES

Aghaei Anvigh, A., Khavan, Y., & Pourghebleh, B. (2024). Transforming vehicular networks: How 6G can revolutionize intelligent transportation? *Science Engineering and Technology*, *4*(1), 80–93. DOI: 10.54327/set2024/v4.i1.127

Ahmadi, H., Nag, A., Khar, Z., Sayrafian, K., & Rahardja, S. (2021). Networked twins and twins of networks: An overview on the relationship between digital twins and 6G. *IEEE Communications Standards Magazine*, *5*(4), 154–160. DOI: 10.1109/MCOMSTD.0001.2000041

Atmakuri, N. B. (2025). Recent advances in automotive cybersecurity: From secure boot to vehicle-to-Everything communication. *European Modern Studies Journal*, *9*(4), 1085–1098. DOI: 10.59573/emsj.9(4).2025.101

Chataut, R., Nankya, M., & Akl, R. (2024). 6G networks and the AI revolution-exploring technologies, applications, and emerging challenges. *Sensors (Basel)*, *24*(6), 1888. DOI: 10.3390/s24061888 PMID: 38544151

Chen, X., Jin, Z., Zhang, Q., Li, P., Zhang, S., Sun, J., Tian, X., Wang, Y., & Zhang, J. (2022). Research on automatic driving simulation test system based on digital twin. *Journal of Physics: Conference Series*, *2170*(1), 012039. DOI: 10.1088/1742-6596/2170/1/012039

El Marai, O., Taleb, T., & Song, J. (2021). Roads infrastructure digital twin: A step toward smarter cities realization. *IEEE Network*, *35*(2), 136–143. DOI: 10.1109/MNET.011.2000398

Gade, S. M., Sumana, S. G., Aarthi, S., Ravikumar, R. N., & Swetha, C. B. (2025). Advancing towards 6G Innovations, Challenges and Future Prospects. In *Advances in Wireless Technologies and Telecommunication* (pp. 1–26). IGI Global. DOI: 10.4018/979-8-3373-2220-9.ch001

Gilly, K., Filiposka, S., Alcaraz Carrasco, S., & Mishev, A. (2019). Dynamic resource management of real-time edge services for intelligent vehicular networks: A case study. *Elektronika ir Elektrotechnika*, *25*(4), 58–61. DOI: 10.5755/j01.eie.25.4.23971

Groshev, M., Guimaraes, C., De La Oliva, A., & Gazda, R. (2021). Dissecting the impact of information and communication technologies on digital twins as a service. *IEEE Access : Practical Innovations, Open Solutions*, *9*, 102862–102876. DOI: 10.1109/ACCESS.2021.3098109

Groshev, M., Guimarães, C., Martín-Pérez, J., & de la Oliva, A. (2021). Toward intelligent cyber-physical systems: Digital twin meets artificial intelligence. *IEEE Communications Magazine*, *59*(8), 14–20. DOI: 10.1109/MCOM.001.2001237

Gu, L., Cui, M., Xu, L., & Xu, X. (2023). Collaborative offloading method for digital twin empowered cloud edge computing on internet of vehicles. *Tsinghua Science and Technology*, *28*(3), 433–451. DOI: 10.26599/TST.2022.9010006

Hadi, M. U., & Murtaza, G. (2022). Fibre wireless distributed antenna systems for 5G and 6G services. *Electronics (Basel)*, *12*(1), 64. DOI: 10.3390/electronics12010064

He, J., Yang, K., & Chen, H.-H. (2021). 6G cellular networks and connected autonomous vehicles. *IEEE Network, 35*(4), 255–261. DOI: 10.1109/MNET.011.2000541

Ibn-Khedher, H., Laroui, M., Alfaqawi, M., Magnouche, A., Moungla, H., & Afifi, H. (2024). 6G-edge support of Internet of Autonomous Vehicles: A survey. *Transactions on Emerging Telecommunications Technologies*, *35*(1), e4918. Advance online publication. DOI: 10.1002/ett.4918

Jabeen Siddiqi, S., Alobaidi, A. H., Ahmad Jan, M., & Tariq, M. (2025). Securing vehicle-to-Digital twin communications in the Internet of Vehicles. *ACM Transactions on Multimedia Computing Communications and Applications*, (3711863). Advance online publication. DOI: 10.1145/3711863

Jaiswal, B. D.Bhargav Dilipkumar Jaiswal. (2025). The influence and application of Digital Twin technology in automotive automation. *International Journal For Multidisciplinary Research*, *7*(1), 37342. Advance online publication. DOI: 10.36948/ijfmr.2025.v07i01.37342

Jiang, W., Han, B., Habibi, M. A., & Schotten, H. D. (2021). The road towards 6G: A comprehensive survey. *IEEE Open Journal of the Communications Society*, *2*, 334–366. DOI: 10.1109/OJCOMS.2021.3057679

Jing Yik, C., Zainal Abidin, M. I., Ismail, K., Mohd Zawawi, F., Abdul Keyon, A. S., & Mohd Nor, N. S. (2025). Location and orientation tracking in Autonomous Surface Vehicles: Real world data versus digital twin predictions. *Jurnal Teknologi*, *87*(3), 567–577. Advance online publication. DOI: 10.11113/jurnalteknologi.v87.22992

Khan, L. U., Yaqoob, I., Imran, M., Han, Z., & Hong, C. S. (2020). 6G wireless systems: A vision, architectural elements, and future directions. *IEEE Access : Practical Innovations, Open Solutions*, *8*, 147029–147044. DOI: 10.1109/ACCESS.2020.3015289

Khan, L. U., Yaqoob, I., Tran, N. H., Han, Z., & Hong, C. S. (2020). Network slicing: Recent advances, taxonomy, requirements, and open research challenges. *IEEE Access : Practical Innovations, Open Solutions*, *8*, 36009–36028. DOI: 10.1109/ACCESS.2020.2975072

Kuts, V., Rassõlkin, A., Partyshev, A., Jegorov, S., & Rjabtšikov, V. (2021). ROS middle-layer integration to Unity 3D as an interface option for propulsion drive simulations of autonomous vehicles. *IOP Conference Series. Materials Science and Engineering*, *1140*(1), 012008. DOI: 10.1088/1757-899X/1140/1/012008

Lu, Y., Huang, X., Zhang, K., Maharjan, S., & Zhang, Y. (2021). Low-latency federated learning and blockchain for edge association in digital twin empowered 6G networks. *IEEE Transactions on Industrial Informatics*, *17*(7), 5098–5107. DOI: 10.1109/TII.2020.3017668

Maiwada, U. D., Danyaro, K. U., & Sarlan, A. B. (2024). Enhancing 5G energy efficiency through digital twin networks: A comprehensive review. *Digital Twins and Applications*, *1*(1), 4–25. DOI: 10.1049/dgt2.12008

Marques da Silva, M., & Dinis, R. (2021). Power-ordered NOMA with massive MIMO for 5G systems. *Applied Sciences (Basel, Switzerland)*, *11*(8), 3541. DOI: 10.3390/app11083541

Masaracchia, A., Sharma, V., Canberk, B., Dobre, O. A., & Duong, T. Q. (2022). Digital twin for 6G: Taxonomy, research challenges, and the road ahead. *IEEE Open Journal of the Communications Society*, *3*, 2137–2150. DOI: 10.1109/OJCOMS.2022.3219015

Minerva, R., Lee, G. M., & Crespi, N. (2020). Digital twin in the IoT context: A survey on technical features, scenarios, and architectural models. *Proceedings of the IEEE. Institute of Electrical and Electronics Engineers, 108*(10), 1785–1824. DOI: 10.1109/JPROC.2020.2998530

Navarro-Ortiz, J., Romero-Diaz, P., Sendra, S., Ameigeiras, P., Ramos-Munoz, J. J., & Lopez-Soler, J. M. (2020). A survey on 5G usage scenarios and traffic models. *IEEE Communications Surveys and Tutorials, 22*(2), 905–929. DOI: 10.1109/COMST.2020.2971781

Nawaz Khan, M., & Ahmad, I. (2025). Harnessing digital twins: Advancing virtual replicas for optimized system performance and sustainable innovation. *Babylonian Journal of Mechanical Engineering, 2025*, 18–33. DOI: 10.58496/BJME/2025/002

Nayyef, Z. T., & Mahmood, I. S. M. (2025). Federated Learning for 6G networks: A comprehensive review of challenges, techniques, and future directions. *Warith Scientific Journal of Engineering and Technology, 1*(1), 30–44. DOI: 10.57026/wsjet.v1i1.14

Nguyen, H. X., Sun, K., To, D., Vien, Q.-T., & Le, T. A. (2025). Digital twin for O-RAN toward 6G. *IEEE Communications Magazine, 63*(3), 174–181. DOI: 10.1109/MCOM.003.2400016

Nguyen, H. X., Trestian, R., To, D., & Tatipamula, M. (2021). Digital Twin for 5G and Beyond. *IEEE Communications Magazine, 59*(2), 10–15. DOI: 10.1109/MCOM.001.2000343

Orlov, S. P., & Susarev, S. V. (2023). Decision Support System for autonomous vehicle maintenance management. *Ontology of Designing, 13*(3), 424–436. DOI: 10.18287/2223-9537-2023-13-3-424-436

Paolini, E., Valcarenghi, L., Maggiani, L., & Andriolli, N. (2024). Real-time network packet classification exploiting computer vision architectures. *IEEE Open Journal of the Communications Society, 5*, 1155–1166. DOI: 10.1109/OJCOMS.2024.3363082

Pasupuleti, M. K. (2024). *Future networks: AI, IoT, and Sustainable Communications from Earth to orbit*. National Education Services., DOI: 10.62311/nesx/rb978-81-982172-0-2

Ravikumar, R. N., & Aarthi, S. (2025a). Digital Twin-driven green energy systems. In *The Future of Green Energy* (pp. 1–28). IGI Global Scientific Publishing., DOI: 10.4018/979-8-3373-3226-0.ch001

Ravikumar, R. N., & Aarthi, S. (2025b). Real-time IoT, quantum advances, and ethical implications in autonomous AI systems. In *Advances in Computational Intelligence and Robotics* (pp. 185–216). IGI Global Scientific Publishing. DOI: 10.4018/979-8-3373-3146-1.ch007

Ravikumar, R. N., & Aarthi, S. (2025c). Web-based cybersecurity architectures. In *Impact of Web Technologies on Digital Transformation* (pp. 187–216). IGI Global Scientific Publishing., DOI: 10.4018/979-8-3373-5167-4.ch007

Sanz Rodrigo, M., Rivera, D., Moreno, J. I., Àlvarez-Campana, M., & López, D. R. (2023). Digital twins for 5G networks: A modeling and deployment methodology. *IEEE Access : Practical Innovations, Open Solutions, 11*, 38112–38126. DOI: 10.1109/ACCESS.2023.3267548

Sathish Babu, B., Sandhya, S., & Subramanya, K. N. (2024). Quantum Key Distribution in securing next-generation cyber-physical systems. In *Advances in Information Security, Privacy, and Ethics* (pp. 215–248). IGI Global. DOI: 10.4018/979-8-3693-9220-1.ch008

Stavdas, A., Kosmatos, E., Maple, C., Hugues-Salas, E., Epiphaniou, G., Fowler, D. S., Razak, S. A., Matrakidis, C., Yuan, H., & Lord, A. (2024). Quantum Key Distribution for V2I communications with software-defined networking. *IET Quantum Communication*, *5*(1), 38–45. DOI: 10.1049/qtc2.12070

Suleiman, R., Maradapu Vera Venkata Sai, A., Yu, W., & Wang, C. (2025). Blockchain for security in digital Twins. *Future Internet*, *17*(9), 385. DOI: 10.3390/fi17090385

Tang, F., Chen, X., Rodrigues, T. K., Zhao, M., & Kato, N. (2022). Survey on digital twin edge networks (DITEN) toward 6G. *IEEE Open Journal of the Communications Society*, *3*, 1360–1381. DOI: 10.1109/OJCOMS.2022.3197811

Tang, Z., He, J., Yang, K., & Chen, H.-H. (2024). Matching 5G connected vehicles to sensed vehicles for safe cooperative autonomous driving. *IEEE Network*, *38*(3), 227–235. DOI: 10.1109/MNET.2023.3321530

Vy Le, L., Do, S., Paul Lin, B.-S., & Tung, L.-P. (2018). Big data and machine learning driven Open5G-MEC for vehicular communications. *Transactions on Networks and Communications*, *6*(5), 103. Advance online publication. DOI: 10.14738/tnc.65.5410

Wang, Z., Gupta, R., Han, K., Wang, H., Ganlath, A., Ammar, N., & Tiwari, P. (2022). Mobility digital twin: Concept, architecture, case study, and future challenges. *IEEE Internet of Things Journal*, *9*(18), 17452–17467. DOI: 10.1109/JIOT.2022.3156028

Wu, Y., Wang, W., Ding, Q., & Luan, W. (2024). Research on intelligent driving system based on V2X communication. In *Advances in Transdisciplinary Engineering*. IOS Press., DOI: 10.3233/ATDE240388

Xiong, H., Wang, Z., Wu, G., & Pan, Y. (2022). Design and implementation of digital twin-assisted simulation method for autonomous vehicle in car-following scenario. *Journal of Sensors*, *2022*, 1–12. DOI: 10.1155/2022/4879490

Xu, H., Shao, Y., Chen, J., Wang, C., & Berres, A. (2024). Semi-automatic geographic information system framework for creating photo-realistic digital Twin Cities to support autonomous driving research. *Transportation Research Record: Journal of the Transportation Research Board*, *2678*(6), 1068–1084. DOI: 10.1177/03611981231205884

Zhang, H., Zheng, Z., Yu, H., Yang, G., & Yuan, S. (2025). Analysis of intelligent and connected vehicles driving system modeling. *Proceedings of the Institution of Mechanical Engineers. Part D, Journal of Automobile Engineering*, *239*(5), 1807–1819. DOI: 10.1177/09544070241228643

KEY TERMS AND DEFINITIONS

5G Network: A high-speed communication technology offering low latency and high bandwidth for real-time data exchange.

6G Network: The next-generation communication system expected to deliver sub-millisecond latency, terahertz speeds, and AI-native networking.

Autonomous Vehicle (AV): A self-driving vehicle capable of sensing, decision-making, and navigating without human control.

Cloud Computing: Centralized computation and storage supporting large-scale analytics and training.

Cooperative Driving: AVs sharing sensor data and insights to coordinate maneuvers and improve safety.

Digital Twin (DT): A real-time virtual model that mirrors the behavior, condition, and environment of a physical autonomous vehicle.

Edge Computing: Local data processing near the vehicle to reduce delay and improve decision speed.

Massive MIMO: Multiple-input, multiple-output antenna technology that enhances signal strength and capacity.

mMTC: Massive Machine-Type Communication designed to connect millions of devices simultaneously.

Network Slicing: Virtual segmentation of a network to prioritize specific AV functions such as safety or perception updates.

Predictive Analytics: AI-driven techniques that forecast hazards, system failures, or traffic patterns.

Synchronization Latency: The time delay between physical vehicle updates and digital twin updates.

Terahertz Communication: Ultra-high-frequency transmission expected in 6G for extremely fast data exchange.

URLLC: Ultra-Reliable Low-Latency Communication used for safety-critical real-time operations.

V2X Communication: Vehicle-to-Everything connectivity that enables interaction with vehicles, infrastructure, networks, and pedestrians.

Chapter 13
Intelligent Transport Systems on Employing Wireless Sensor Networks for Smart Vehicle Communication

Anjali Goswami
http://orcid.org/0009-0004-6330-7883
Kalinga University, Raipur, India

F. Rahman
http://orcid.org/0009-0007-7167-188X
Kalinga University, Raipur, India

ABSTRACT

The urbanization rate and increasing traffic volume have placed enormous strain on available transport infrastructure; therefore, solutions are needed to optimize safety, efficiency, and sustainability. Intelligent Transport Systems (ITS) are one such promising technology being emphasized, with particular emphasis on the potential of Wireless Sensor Networks (WSNs) to facilitate intelligent vehicle communication. WSNs, a collection of geographically distributed sensors, hold the promise for real-time monitoring and collection of vital information with the potential for real-time vehicle-infrastructure interaction. They all contribute fundamental functions in preventing accidents, managing traffic, and improving the management of the road network. This work concerns integrating WSN and ITS for vehicular communication, focusing on developing a model that minimizes latency, enhances data quality, and ensures safe transmission.

INTRODUCTION

Urbanization, a characteristic of our contemporary world, has led to rapid urbanization across the globe. The cities expand, and so do they, with more cars clogging roads (Rajest et al. 2023). This alarming increase in road traffic portends a host of problems, from traffic congestion to more accidents. It is challenging for city planners and technologists to think outside the box and develop solutions. One technology that has found a niche in addressing this demand is the Intelligent Transport System (ITS)

DOI: 10.4018/979-8-3373-7785-8.ch013

(Trupthi et al. 2025). ITS is the integration of advanced technology and conventional transport to produce a system that not only conserves time but is also secure and sustainable. Imagine roads where vehicles can talk to one another, share data in real time, and make millisecond judgments to avert accidents or divert to less crowded roads. This is no longer a vision of the future but a reality made possible due to vehicular communication, the foundation of ITS (Mehta et al. 2023). Vehicle-to-vehicle and vehicle-to-infrastructure communication enable cars to share data with surrounding infrastructure, including traffic lights and sensors, as well as with one another. This improves overall traffic control, alleviates congestion, and significantly reduces the risk of accidents by enabling automobiles to detect hazards many miles before they reach them. In addition, the research here explores the integration of Wireless Sensor Networks (WSNs) into ITS towards the continued evolution of intelligent vehicle communication (Venkatasubramanian et al. 2024). Essentially, WSNs consist of small sensors with communications elements. Strategically located, these devices can track an unlimited array of parameters, ranging from traffic flow and individual car speeds to weather and roadwork conditions. Data from such sensors can then be sent in real time, enabling vehicles to make intelligent decisions while on the move. The integration of Intelligent Transportation Systems (ITS) and Wireless Sensor Networks (WSNs) is a contemporary solution for some of the most significant urban transportation issues (Panyaram, 2024).

These systems operate to improve communication, traffic, and safety by delivering real-time data (Arulvendhan et al. 2025). One of the most real-time and impactful uses of WSNs in ITS is the detection of abrupt braking due to unexpected road blockages, such as accidents, road obstructions, or road construction (Pierre et al. 2024). If a sensor detects such an obstruction, it can send an early warning to approaching traffic, prompting cars to slow down sooner or switch to a different path (Singaravelan et al. 2025). Apart from preventing accidents caused by unexpected traffic congestion, it also helps prevent the formation of traffic jams or pile-ups, as shown by experiments conducted by Waller et al. (2006). WSNs can be a major contributor to smooth traffic and safety for all road users by notifying vehicles in real time (Jeba et al. 2025).

Apart from this, integrating WSNs with ITS does much more than provide a medium for real-time data sharing; the advantage of doing so on a large scale is enormous (Arulvendhan et al. 2025). Traffic management and congestion relief, for instance, will be significantly improved by such systems. Congested traffic, a major source of stress in urban cities, might become a relic of the past with the large-scale deployment of WSNs (Arulvendhan et al. 2025). Traffic jams, which waste time, fuel, and cause pollution, plague cities and towns. As WSNs provide real-time traffic density data, they can feed traffic control systems with real-time data, which will reconfigure traffic light control systems and divert automobiles based on real-time traffic (Gunapriya et al. 2025). Clever route-optimizing software can route automobiles through less congested routes, thereby maximizing traffic and improving traffic flow (Saxena et al. 2023). It would not only decrease overall traffic congestion but also improve delivery and commuting transport networks, as evidenced by the strategy adopted by Regin et al. (2024).

Apart from traffic flow efficiency outside, there are other advantages of WSN integration beyond that. Road safety, which remains a priority, is another area where WSNs have much to offer (Srilakshmi et al. 2024). By detecting road surfaces and transmitting warning information, these networks can alert drivers with information to avoid accidents. For instance, WSNs can sense weather, rain, or snow, resulting in a slippery road surface, and alert approaching vehicles in advance so they can slow down or switch to a different driving mode accordingly. Apart from this, if the vehicle breaks down while on the road or at the accident site, WSNs alert vehicles traveling towards the accident spot directly; hence, they avoid the accident site and, therefore, avoid secondary accidents. This leads to increased safety, as the system alerts drivers in real time to potential hazards, speeds driver decision-making, and helps prevent accidents. The use of WSNs in ITS can, therefore, help make roads safer, reduce the risk of accidents, and ultimately ensure safety for passengers, pedestrians, and other road users, a term first coined by Wanget al. (2020).

One of the most glaring benefits of using WSNs in ITS is that they enable the design of a dynamic, adaptive system that responds to traffic and road conditions in real time. The network can monitor road conditions, traffic density, and vehicle speed around the clock and send data used for traffic diversion, traffic flow regulation, and traffic signal scheduling. WSNs are the optimal technology for delivering prompt, efficient responses to events such as accidents, congestion, and roadworks because they respond in real time. Additionally, traffic flows can be forecast using the information WSNs provide to support long-term traffic planning and infrastructure development. For instance, if points of traffic congestion or chokepoints are already known, where they are bound to occur, urban planners can fine-tune resources, i.e., redesign intersections or insert lanes whenever required, according to real-time traffic figures and not estimations or past assumptions, as suggested in He et al. (2020).

Another reason WSNs are even more valuable in ITS is that they can be integrated with other emerging technologies (Sayedelahl, 2024). Merging WSNs with artificial intelligence, machine learning, and big data analytics brings new opportunities for intelligent traffic management. For instance, machine learning algorithms can analyze the vast amount of data gathered by WSNs to forecast traffic patterns and optimize traffic light timing to reduce waiting time. AI systems also enable real-time decision-making, including diverting traffic in the event of an accident or during rush hour, thereby enhancing the system's efficiency and effectiveness. Merging the technologies provides a smart, adaptive transport system to address dynamic changes in urban traffic and road conditions, as reported in research by Sumalee et al. (2011). Apart from that, WSNs can also positively address the environmental impact of the transport system. By controlling traffic congestion and optimizing traffic, WSNs reduce vehicular fuel consumption and emissions. Traffic flow optimization reduces the repetition of cars idling in congestion or of frequent braking and acceleration at intersections, both of which increase fuel consumption. In addition, WSNs can minimize the total travel distance of vehicles, thereby saving fuel and reducing the transport industry's carbon footprint. With increased urbanization, the environmental footprint of transport grows, and WSNs are among the viable solutions for mitigating the environmental impacts of road transport, as concluded by a study by Ahmad et al. (2024).

The integration of WSNs with Intelligent Transportation Systems is a significant step towards efficient, secure, and green city road transport networks. By providing real-time traffic flow, road conditions, and car speeds, WSNs enable intelligent traffic management and reduce accidents and traffic congestion. Their effectiveness in managing traffic, their time-efficiency in transportation, and their mitigation of environmental pollution make them valuable assets in designing future, efficient, green, and secure transport systems. When integrated with emerging technologies such as AI and machine learning, they can do much more, giving an idea of how mobility in a city in the future would be, as explained in Ihsan et al. (2023). The advantages of WSNs for ITS are not limited to the roads alone (Singh et al. 2025). They are major stakeholders in the fantasy of the smart city. They are cities where traffic lights, transportation systems, and everything else are networked, and they communicate with one another and make decisions collectively. In such a situation, WSNs become the city's ears and eyes, gazing at all things and providing feedback second by second, and the city operates like a well-oiled machine. In brief, as cities become obsessed with boundless growth, the issues they create require new, innovative, outside-the-box solutions. ITS integration with WSNs also offers a very promising prospect, not just to address existing traffic control and security problems but also to lay the groundwork for future smart cities (Singh et al. 2025).

REVIEW OF LITERATURE

Intelligent Transport Systems (ITS) and Wireless Sensor Networks (WSNs) studies have topped the agenda of transport research in this age due to the need to achieve ultimate mobility in cities. Plenty of research on the viability of ITS and WSNs has been conducted, with findings that are crucial for setting parameters for how the systems can transform city transport (Babu et al. 2024). Their deployment is likely to bring about revolutionary advancements in traffic control, vehicle-to-vehicle communication, safety, and fuel efficiency, thereby reducing some of the most pressing problems of modern metropolitan traffic (Elayaraja et al. 2024). The most emphasized research need for WSNs is the provision of real-time, reliable data exchange between vehicles. WSNs are generally deployed as sensors along roads, in cars, and in other networked structures to acquire data and exchange it in real time to feed into optimal traffic management, as illustrated by the work of Wang et al. (2020).

The ability of WSNs to facilitate reliable communication is also crucial, especially in dense cities plagued by serious congestion. Such a scenario is interrupted by communication delays, which cause significant disruptions, congestion, traffic waste, and accidents. For instance, if the cars cannot be supplied with information about road conditions or traffic signals on time, they may be diverted into risk zones, which can lead to accidents. Therefore, having WSNs operate with minimal or no latency is on the agenda for better city transport, according to Tan et al. (2022). Aside from the efficiency of communication, the security of vehicle communication networks is an essential aspect that cannot be underestimated (Paramasivan et al. 2024). As cars become increasingly networked and dependent on data exchange for their various functions, including navigation, collision avoidance, and traffic information, their privacy and integrity are of utmost concern, as Storani et al. (2021) contend. This has been highlighted by researchers, among others, as a necessity for robust communication protocols to resist malicious attacks on data integrity and people's privacy via such transport media, as noted by Waller et al. (2006).

Secure communication protocols guarantee that information in transit between infrastructure and vehicles cannot be manipulated, aside from unauthorized entry, to enable secure and effective ITS operation (Kwizera et al. 2025). Such protocols ought to be capable of keeping pace with the constantly evolving cycles of threats and technological trends to provide adaptive security solutions to ITS, an aspect highlighted by Karoonsoontawong and Waller (2010). WSNs have proven revolutionary for traffic planning. WSN-based traffic control systems can observe traffic flow in real time and report it to facilitate better control of traffic lights, congestion management, and more efficient vehicle routing along roads within cities, as indicated by research by Doan and Ukkusuri (2012). Several studies compared the usefulness of WSNs for traffic flow and found that congestion would greatly alleviate the problem. For example, in case real-time traffic information is utilized for maximizing signal time, cars can navigate through intersections with efficiency, time is saved, and congestion accumulation is an approach implemented by Doan and Ukkusuri (2015). It not only saves time for commuting passengers but also improves road safety by eliminating the causes of accidents, such as rapid stops, haphazard maneuvers, and crashes at congested intersections. With the implementation of WSNs to support intelligent traffic management systems, city transportation can be smoothed and made safe for every passenger on the roads, as emphasized by Islam et al. (2018).

In addition to traffic control and security, environmental sustainability for ITS is another issue that must not be underestimated. With worldwide concern over decarbonizing and making their processes greener, ITS is not only set to play an important role but is also encouraged to support greener forms of transportation, as mentioned in Sumalee et al. (2011). Much research indicates that integrating intelligent vehicle communication systems into ITS can significantly reduce the carbon footprint of urban transport. ITS also minimizes fuel consumption through traffic flow optimization and idling avoidance, thereby reducing vehicle emissions, according to Ihsan et al. (2023). Among the key ingredients of traffic signal coordination is minimizing waste in stop-and-go traffic. Apart from this, driver information systems with real-time advice on shortest routes, traffic conditions, and diversions can minimize fuel loss due to congestion, as per Ahmed et al. (2022). ITS environmental benefits can be very high, especially in major cities where traffic congestion is a major cause of air pollution. Despite the best efforts of authorities and city planners to achieve sustainability goals, ITS adoption can be the silver bullet for greener, more sustainable transport infrastructure, as advocated by Alharbi et al. (2023). ITS deployments that leverage WSNs are a potential avenue for its future, not only for traffic flow management and security but also for boosting sustainability, as shown in studies by Musa et al. (2022).

There is more work in this area that unbundles the assumption that ITS, supported by WSNs and secure communication, is a panacea to the issues that afflict urban transport systems. The study aims to present a common platform for merging WSNs and ITS to broaden what is already known and create new knowledge for synchronizing how the two can function together and as a whole, towards promoting effective urban mobility, as posited by Cirillo et al. (2023). The model also envisages an overlapping synergy among traffic flow management, communications, security, and sustainability factors as the blueprints for molding urban transportation in the future. In the future, the vision is to build smarter communication systems for vehicles to ensure greater efficiency, making urban transport systems not only more efficient but also greener and safer. By designing and implementing such combined systems, cities can set new standards for the future of transport, improving urban quality of life and helping reduce carbon emissions worldwide. As research shows increasing potential for ITS and WSNs, the potential to reverse urban transport networks is also enhanced, providing a means to build wiser, greener, and safer cities (Regin et al., 2024).

METHODOLOGY

Intelligent Transport Systems (ITS) offer an innovative solution to transport efficiency and mobility challenges in urban centers. The theme of the novel is the delivery of intelligent vehicle-to-vehicle communication through the services of Wireless Sensor Networks (WSNs). At the methodological level, deploying ITS with WSNs involves installing large numbers of sensors tactically on infrastructure structures, including bridges, roads, traffic lights, and automobiles. These sensors capture real-time readings of various parameters, such as vehicle speed, location, traffic, and environment. The data thus captured is communicated wirelessly to cloud servers or main data centers using a low-power, low-range protocol such as LoRaWAN, Zigbee, or 6LoWPAN. All this large torrent of information is filtered and analyzed by powerful algorithms and data analysis platforms, and actionable suggestions are inferred from them. For instance, traffic congestion can be predicted from current car traffic, and traffic lights can be adaptively adjusted to avoid congestion in the future. Furthermore, V2V and V2I communication via WSNs enables cars to share information about road conditions, potential hazards, and the best routes.

This enhances road safety and also optimizes fuel consumption and travel time. The security and privacy of data transmission are also important methodological issues. As sensitive data is being transmitted, robust encryption techniques and secure communication protocols are not luxuries. Also, the system is scalable, with a modular network architecture that supports expansion as more infrastructure and vehicles evolve. In simple terms, WSN integration with ITS is about efficient data collection, transfer, and real-time processing to support smart vehicle communications and maximize the overall performance of the transport system.

Figure 1. Representation of a vehicle-sensor entity relationship diagram in a structured format

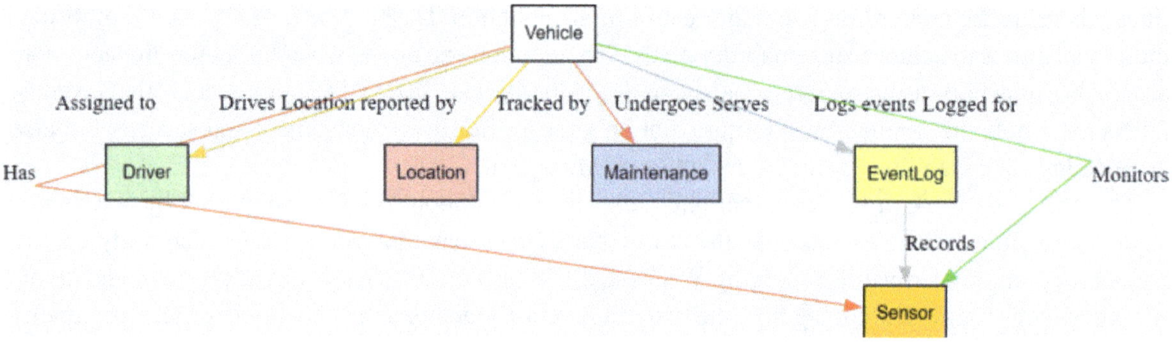

Figure 1 shows an end-to-end system with cars, sensors, drivers, places, maintenance, and event logs. The vehicle, the middle item in the figure, serves as the focal point of interaction with the rest, holding fields such as ID, Model, Year, Owner, fuel type, and Mileage. Sensors are linked to cars, getting data such as Type, Value, Timestamp, and Status, and tracking vehicle status. Driver objects belong to the car, i.e., identifying who should drive it and their details, such as License Number and Contact Information. Location is where the car is located at the moment, with GPS coordinates giving current location information. Maintenance is used to track the car's maintenance history, including service type, cost, and schedule. EventLog stores important events related to the vehicle and its sensors, such as performance issues or sensor data modifications, to maintain logs for future analysis. Associations among these entities determine how each part of the system communicates: a driver is linked to a vehicle, gets serviced on it, and provides its location, while sensors track the vehicle and log events. This ERD highlights the data flows and entity relationships required for the operation, maintenance, and monitoring of vehicles. Color is used to differentiate entities and provide a clear visual representation of how each system component interrelates with the others.

Table 1. Optimizing traffic flow and vehicle performance through wireless sensor networks in intelligent transport systems

Step	Description	Mathematical Components
Data Collection from Sensors	Collect real-time data from vehicle and road sensors (e.g., speed, location, fuel levels). Measure parameters like speed (km/h), GPS coordinates, and tire pressure (psi).	Speed S = Distance D/ Time T(km/h)
Data Transmission via Wireless Sensor Network	Wirelessly transmit collected sensor data to servers or vehicle nodes. Ensure secure communication.	Transmission Rate R = Data Size D/ Time T (bits/sec)
Data Fusion and Aggregation	Aggregate data from multiple sources for comprehensive analysis. Combine vehicle data and environmental data.	Average Speed $\bar{S} = \frac{S_1 + S_2 + \ldots + S_n}{n} \left(\text{km/h} \right)$
Real-Time Processing and Analysis	Process data in real time to detect anomalies (e.g., traffic congestion). Use algorithms like clustering or regression.	Traffic Congestion $C = \frac{\text{Vehicles per km}}{\text{Max Capacity}} \times 100\%$
Intelligent Decision-Making and Action	Optimize vehicle routing and control traffic based on analysis. For example, adjusting signals or providing route suggestions.	Optimal Route $R_{opt} = \min(T_{start} + T_{end})$ where T_{start} and T_{end} are the estimated times for the start and end segments of a route.

Figure 2. Blockchain-based vehicle data management system for enhanced traffic and vehicle communication privacy (Alharbi et al., 2023)

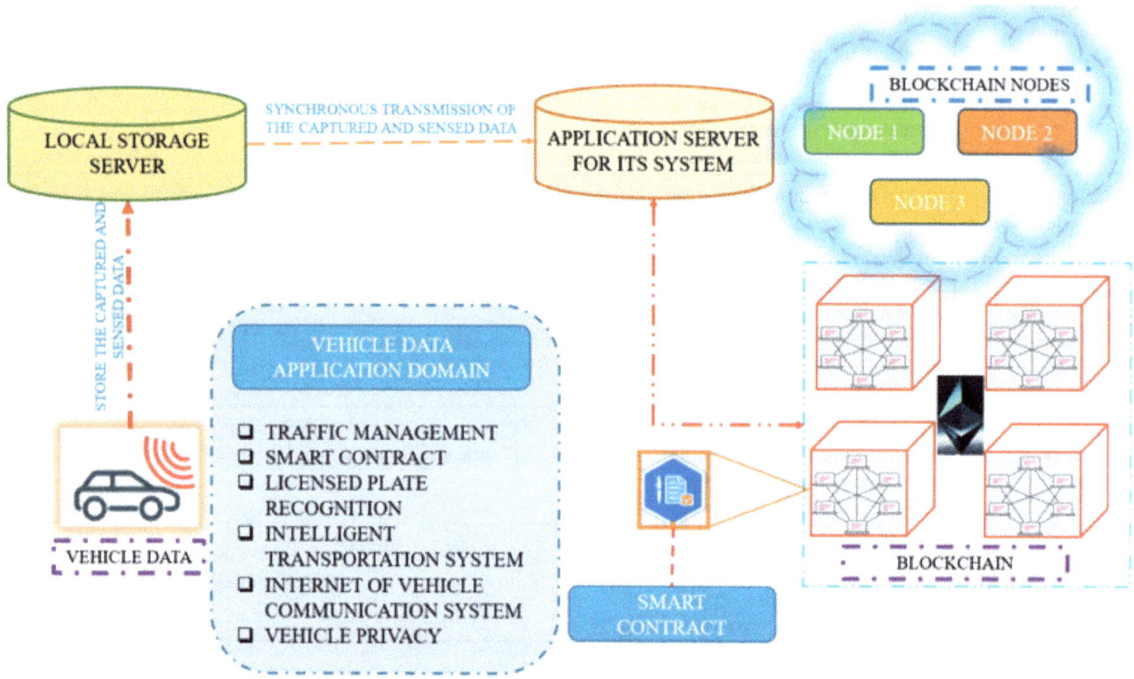

Figure 2 illustrates a vehicle data management system using blockchain technology for safe data storage and processing, as discussed by Alharbi et al. (2023). It consists of several components: a Local Storage Server for collecting and storing vehicle data, an Application Server for system function management, and Blockchain Nodes (Node 1, Node 2, and Node 3) for ensuring data safety and integrity. The system monitors the use of car data, including traffic control, smart contracts, number plate recognition systems, intelligent transport systems, and vehicle privacy communications. Collected sensor data is synchronized and transferred to the application server, and vehicle data fields are handled using smart contracts. Data-sharing storage is enabled by blockchain technology, which decentralizes data and makes transactions transparent and secure between nodes. It outperforms other car-related data programs in terms of privacy, security, and performance, enabling innovation in automotive communication systems and traffic management.

RESULTS

Wireless Sensor Networks (WSNs) based Intelligent Transport Systems (ITS) are increasingly gaining recognition as catalysts for change in urban mobility. It is the convergence of their technologies that has been a major force behind the evolution of conventional transport toward enhanced safety, efficiency, and sustainability. Wireless Sensor Networks, as a natural system for real-time data capture, transmission, and processing, have proven extremely helpful in enabling a more responsive, networked vehicle world. Vehicles, roadside units such as traffic lights and signs, and even pedestrians now communicate with one another in an integrated fashion, enabling vehicles to move smoothly and increasing situational awareness. The data transmission rate is given as:

$$R = \frac{D}{T} \quad (1)$$

Where:

R is the data transmission rate, typically in bits per second (bps) or bytes per second (Bps).
D represents the amount of data transmitted, usually in bits or bytes.
T is the time taken to transmit the data, typically in seconds.

Table 2. Data transmission rates over time

Time (s)	Data Transmission Rate (Mbps)
1	5.27
2	6.79
3	5.45
4	14.3
5	9.31
6	9.36
7	14.59
8	14.72
9	8.52
10	6.66

Table 2 captures the instantaneous ten-second window data transmission rates in Megabits per second (Mbps). Every row for each second consists of the time (in seconds) in the first column and the corresponding data transmission rate in the second column. The rates range from 5.27 Mbps to 14.72 Mbps during this period. Interestingly, peaks in data transmission rate were observed at the 4th, 7th, and 8th seconds, with rates exceeding 14 Mbps. However, the 1st, 3rd, and 10th seconds have rates of nearly 6 Mbps, indicating fluctuations in data transmission performance.

Figure 3. Data transmission rate against time

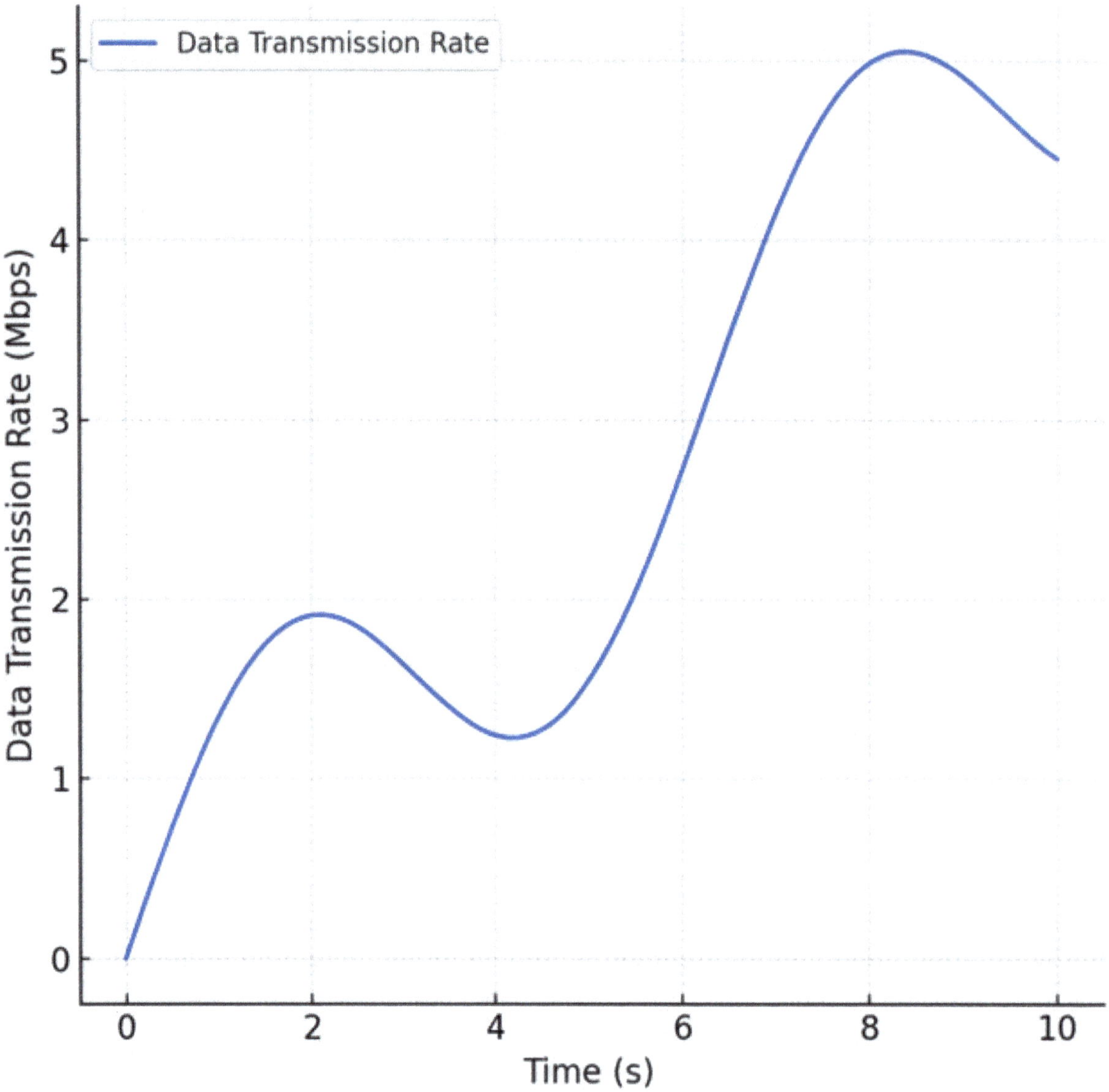

The time dependence of the data transmission rate is shown in Figure 3, which indicates a sinusoidal trend. This implies the data transfer rate is not constant but fluctuates in a quantifiable pattern over time. Oscillations can be caused by factors such as network congestion, interference, or environmental factors. The sinusoidal nature describes the periodic highs and lows in the data rate of something, which network engineers or admins may find pleasant to stabilize or optimize data flow within a system. The most important single result of this merger is the precipitous decline in motor vehicle accidents. Experiments on roads have repeatedly shown that cars equipped with WSN technology can detect impending accidents even before they occur. Whether a car veers into another person's blind spot or encounters a slick spot on the road ahead, drivers are warned in real time so they can take evasive maneuvers in time. Not only has this improved the safety of single drivers, but it has also created a broader road-safety culture in which hazards are systematically identified and avoided. Latency is given below:

$$L = T_{SD} + \sum d \quad (2)$$

Where:

L is the total network latency, typically in milliseconds (ms).
T_{SD} represents the source-to-destination base transmission time, excluding any additional delays.
$\sum d$ is the sum of all additional delays, which could include propagation delays, processing delays, queuing delays, and transmission delays.

Table 3. Latency results

No. of Nodes	Latency (s)
1	0.15
2	0.61
3	0.28
4	0.74
5	0.64
6	0.74
7	0.64
8	0.73
9	0.14
10	0.15

Table 3, on the other hand, shows the relationship between network latency and node number in a WSN. Both tables present a structured view of how vital network parameters might be under certain conditions, offering a glimpse of WSN performance and dynamics within ITS. Network throughput is given below:

$$N = \frac{M}{T} \quad (3)$$

Where:

N is the network throughput, often measured in bits per second (bps) or bytes per second (Bps).
M represents the total amount of data successfully received or sent over the network in a specified period.
T is the period, typically in seconds, over which the data was transmitted.

Traffic management, often a complex challenge in bustling urban centers, has also witnessed transformative results with the introduction of WSNs in ITS. Traffic flow optimization algorithms, powered by real-time data from myriad sensors, dynamically adjust traffic light timings, suggest alternative routes to drivers, and even predict congestion patterns based on historical data. This proactive approach to traffic management has led to tangible results: commuters experience reduced travel times, and there's a noticeable decrease in vehicular emissions, contributing to cleaner urban air.

Figure 4. Relationship between network latency and the number of nodes

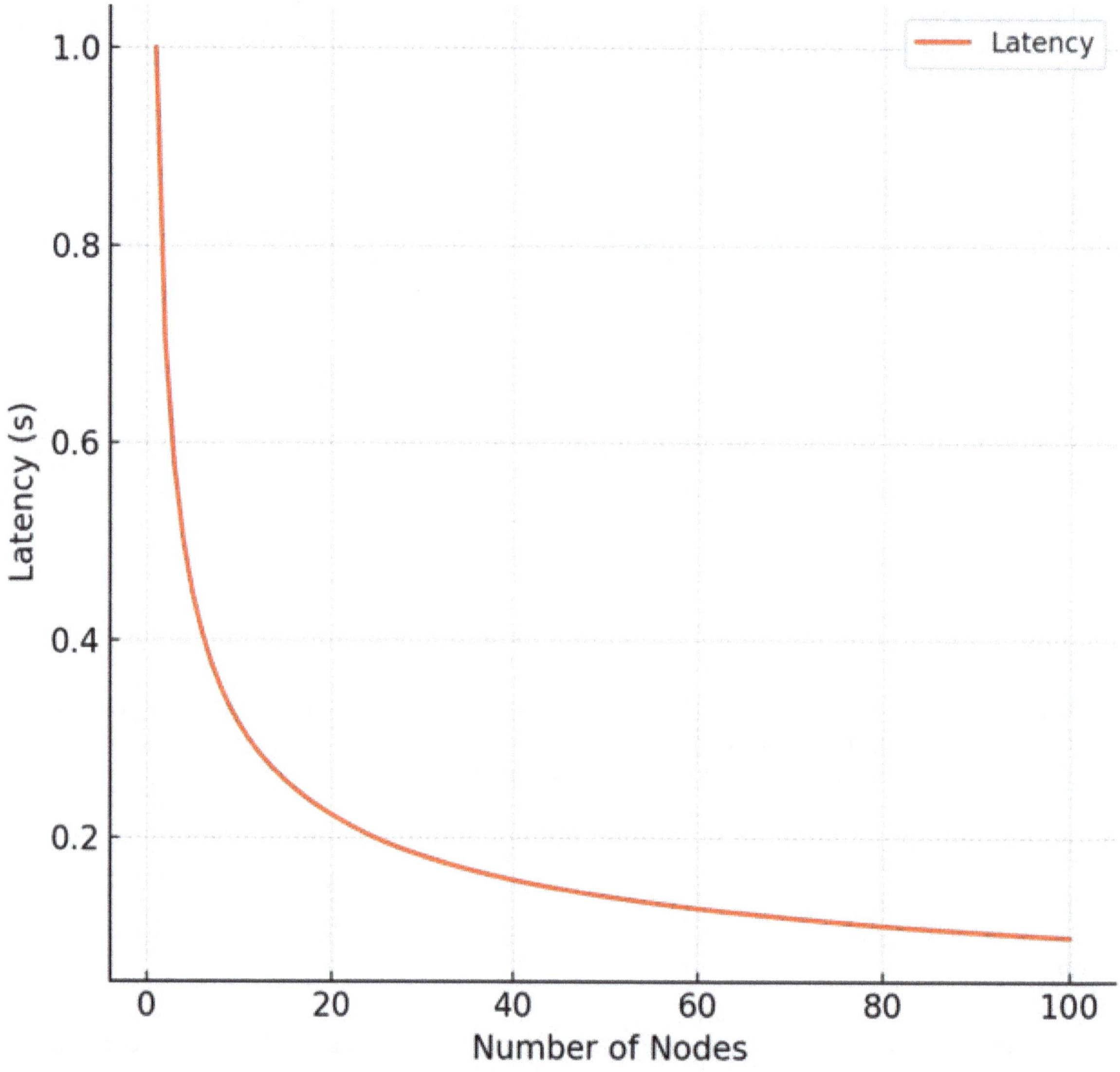

Figure 4 illustrates the relationship between network latency and the number of nodes in a Wireless Sensor Network (WSN). According to the graph, as the number of nodes increases, latency decreases. This is highly beneficial for the implementation of Intelligent Transportation Systems (ITS) for vehicle communications. A reduction in latency with an increase in the number of nodes reflects the scalability and efficiency of the WSN in handling communication. This implies that the greater the number of nodes (e.g., sensors or vehicles) in the network, the faster communication can be. This means a best-configured network that can support increased traffic without diminishing. Packet loss can be described as follows:

$$P = \frac{S - R}{S} \tag{4}$$

Where:

P is the packet loss rate, usually expressed as a percentage.
S is the total number of packets sent.
R is the total number of packets received.
S − R gives the number of packets that were lost during transmission.

And yet another concrete benefit has been experienced in the field of parking – an age-old urban issue. While motorists in such cities waste a lot of time searching for parking spots, ITS with WSNs have introduced smart parking systems. Sensors in parking lots provide real-time usage data. This is then communicated to motorists via apps or in-car systems, guiding them to available parking spaces immediately. An awesome reduction in cruising time around the block, looking for parking, less fuel, and hassle. One of the most exciting areas enabled by the convergence of WSNs and ITS is that of self-driving cars. While the vision of autonomous vehicles cruising down our roads with ease remains in its infancy, the foundation for this reality is being laid now. Vehicle-to-everything (V2X) communication, in which vehicles communicate with any object that can influence them, relies on real-time information. WSNs provide such autonomous vehicles with an endless source of information about what is nearby, from the speed of the vehicle ahead to the condition of a pedestrian stepping off the street. This has fostered innovation and experimentation with autonomous vehicles, pushing us toward the day when they will be an everyday sight on our roads.

However, as with any revolutionary technology, the use of WSNs in ITS is not without issues. As the network becomes increasingly populated with sensors, scalability without sacrificing real-time responsiveness is a concern. Security loopholes are another area of concern. In an age where communications between vehicles are constantly being shared, making such communication secure against malicious attacks is a priority. Further, with so many devices and sensors manufactured by multiple vendors, there is concern about interoperability to keep the system in proper working order. The potential of the convergence of Wireless Sensor Networks in Intelligent Transport Systems is breathtaking. There will always be nagging issues to be worked out, but the future can be only one: a cleaner, wiser transport future, first and foremost, a safer one. The meeting of these two technologies is not an evolution but a revolution, at least for the planning and solving of urban mobility.

DISCUSSION

In ITS structures, the integration of WSNs has been a key driver of improvements in vehicular communication and network performance. The focus of the research was on how WSNs have been a central force in transforming the communication environment of ITS, ensuring no data loss during transmission and maintaining data quality and security. In particular, the following functionalities were emphasized. The model developed in this research incorporates these two important parameters in an organized manner, proving the capability of WSNs to handle high data traffic at low latency levels with robust security provisions. Latency, data rate, and security are correlated parameters in in-vehicle communication systems, and it is essential to offer an optimized set of them to make the system a success. The results of this research show that the model applied here performs better than all of them.

Simulations in this study demonstrate that the model can minimize latency even when network nodes are fully utilized. There is a strong correlation between network latency and the number of nodes, and network latency typically increases with the addition of nodes. However, values from Table 2 and Figure 4 indicate that the model shown in this study can withstand the said issues. As shown, the network latency decreases substantially as the number of nodes increases, with clear decreases at large node counts. For instance, when 100 nodes are used, the delay decreases to nearly 0.2 seconds, which is an excellent performance for huge ITS networks. This result confirms the suggested model's flexibility and scalability to maximum data exchange despite considerable increases in the number of devices in the network and the accompanying vehicles.

Besides, the focus on data transmission rate over time, as shown in Table 1 and Figure 4, is also a clear indication of the model's ability to achieve high data transmission rates. The data transmission rate reached approximately 5 Mbps, even at its peak, demonstrating that the model effectively enabled real-time vehicle-to-vehicle communication and fully utilized the available bandwidth. Maximum data transmission rate at all times, irrespective of time elapsed, is of utmost significance for ITS applications, where there should be constant and consistent data exchange between vehicles to avoid accidents, optimize traffic flow control, and support real-time decision-making. 5 Mbps maximum data transmission rate is significant, through which there is constant info exchange between vehicles without network blockage or delay. This also demonstrates the model's efficiency in managing high traffic volumes without sacrificing real-time communication.

The model's secure data transmission is also an essential component of ITS. As more and more cars are connected to networks, there is greater exposure to cyberattacks and data theft. In such a sensitive system, the need for robust security cannot be emphasized enough. The suggested model emphasizes the need for sufficient communication protocols to ensure high data integrity and confidentiality. Given upcoming threats in the cyberspace environment, and even more so in vehicular networks, the model's emphasis on network security is reasonable and justified. By integrating security features into the communication system without any hassle, information can be exchanged between cars without fear of unauthorized interception or manipulation. This improvement in network security not only raises user confidence but also adds a layer of reliability to the system, making it less prone to outside interference.

The outcomes of the present study contribute to the existing literature on the integration of WSNs with ITS by offering an effective model that maximizes communication efficiency, scalability, and security. The model is an excellent representation of how the deployment of WSNs will advance urban transportation infrastructure, and the framework will be applied in future ITS studies. This research focuses on the importance of WSNs in ITS to support the rapid growth of traffic information without compromising security at low speeds and latency at high speeds. The results indicate the potential of WSNs to transform vehicular communication towards safer, more efficient, and cleaner transport. The study paves the way for further enhancements to WSNs for use in cars, and much work remains to optimize these networks to ensure all transmissions are effective, secure, and real-time. The objective should be to make the networks function at the core to facilitate ITS in receiving the intelligence and real-time capabilities it requires without invading stakeholders' privacy and security.

CONCLUSION

The result of this experimentation and discovery at the intersection of Wireless Sensor Networks (WSNs) and Intelligent Transport Systems (ITS) is a blueprint for the future of urban transport. Once all these technologies had been integrated, we entered a realm of possibility for redefining the horizons of city mobility through networked efficiency, safety, and sustainability. During the research work, our stringent process, from a comprehensive literature review to the following phases of model development, simulation, and additional analysis, has been warranted with highly worthwhile outcomes. The outcomes align with WSNs' inherent power to enhance vehicular data communication and establish an unbroken vehicular interaction network that can greatly improve traffic management and road safety. The presupposition on which the research is based is the offered model – the theoretical but existing model of convergence of ITS and WSN, smart car communication emergence. The model, as it stands now, is still only theoretical, but a pointer to the revolutionary nature of the convergence of the two technologies. It has many advantages when applied to the model, predicting a future in which traffic is history, in which cars are guided through city streets like a jigsaw puzzle, following preferences based on real-time information. Safety is no dream but a fact.

The integration of WSNs and ITS, as presented in the model, is thus the clean transport solution for cities. As cities around the world face the afflictions of a growing population and the ever-increasing urge to be eco-friendly, the model is the ray of light that can drive out the darkness. With greater traffic movement, removal of slack, and lower potential for accidents, the whole system can be an enormous carbon-emissions reducer and, hence, part of the global environmental conservation agenda. The model, as defined, is itself only the start – a start that must be optimized, and even more, tuned even further, and implemented on the ground. It calls upon researchers, city planners, technologists, and policymakers to converge to work, hone, and innovate so that the potential of this model is not left only between the lines of this research but on the streets of our cities. The union of WSNs and ITS described in this article is not technological but synergistic, with the potential to usher in a new era of city transport. Our path map shows a vision of such an age, of such a revolutionary scope for WSNs in ITS. Positioned at the forefront of this transportation revolution, all parties across sectors must come together and leverage the wisdom and potential of this study to construct a future that is not merely intelligent urban transportation but also safe and responsibly constructed.

LIMITATIONS

Even though the research is paving the way for the application of Wireless Sensor Networks (WSNs) in Intelligent Transportation Systems (ITS), it is accompanied by some limitations that must be borne by the user, which may pose a risk to the practical application of the model developed in this research. The model developed in this research is hypothesis-based and is simulated and tested using simulations. Any such controlled environment, as beneficial as it is in idealizing the processes, may not always reflect the real world. In the real world, WSN operations can be interrupted by many factors, such as physical barriers (e.g., trees, buildings, and weather), which can interfere with node communication. Interference from nearby wireless devices or networks can be triggered, leading to data delays or signal loss and a degradation in system reliability. Traffic flow fluctuations, which can vary significantly in real time due to accidents, road obstructions, or asymmetrical traffic flow, can be a challenge for smooth data flow. The economics/logistics of wide-scale WSN deployment in the urban environment were not investigated in this effort. The expense of building infrastructure, maintenance, and seeding the network to cover large city geographies should be factored into determining whether such a system is feasible or not, to the best of your knowledge. The feasibility and practicality of these parameters are to be further reviewed through research studies to determine how practicable and possible it would be to implement WSNs at the mass scale within urban cities.

FUTURE SCOPE

The combination of Wireless Sensor Networks (WSNs) and Intelligent Transportation Systems (ITS) is the most promising area for future development. The establishment of more robust, larger WSNs to meet the increasing needs of urban transport is one of the most important areas of future research. With the rising urban population and road infrastructure, WSNs would need to manage increasing traffic, vehicular density, and real-time data. Rising network topology, rate, and latency with network survivability compromise-free would be areas of future work. Further, real-world deployment constraints, i.e., interference minimization, filling geographical gaps, and security in vehicle-to-vehicle communication, would need to be addressed to ensure successful ITS WSN deployment. Security will be a concern area as the sophistication of cyber-attacks rises in the future. Future work will involve discovering sophisticated encryption methods, intrusion detection mechanisms, and secure communication protocols to maintain data confidentiality and integrity. In addition, newer technologies such as 5G, IoT, and blockchain hold tremendous potential to further enhance the performance of WSNs in ITS. 5 G provides higher data rates and low-latency communication, making it a significant enhancement for WSNs and enabling large-scale smart transportation systems. IoT will enable greater device-to-device interoperability and data exchange, while blockchain will enable secure, open data processing in ITS. Through such advanced technologies, future research can position WSNs to solve smart city problems, enabling an efficient, safe, and eco-friendly city transportation system.

REFERENCES

Ahmad, Y. A. B., Kolachina, S., Rajest, S. S., Singh, M., Mishra, A., & Sundar, S. S. (2024). Impact of digital HRM on academicians' performance: Exploring the mediating role of organisational commitment. *International Journal of Intelligent Enterprise*, *12*(1), 1–21. DOI: 10.1504/IJIE.2025.143439

Ahmed, M., Khan, W. U., Ihsan, A., Li, X., Li, J., & Tsiftsis, T. A. (2022). Backscatter sensors communication for 6G low-powered NOMA-enabled IoT networks under imperfect SIC. *IEEE Systems Journal*, *16*(4), 5883–5893. DOI: 10.1109/JSYST.2022.3194705

Alharbi, F., Zakariah, M., Alshahrani, R., Albakri, A., Viriyasitavat, W., & Alghamdi, A. A. (2023). Intelligent transportation using wireless sensor networks, blockchain and license plate recognition. *Sensors (Basel)*, *23*(5), 2670. DOI: 10.3390/s23052670 PMID: 36904873

Arulvendhan, K., Srinivasan, P., & Kabilan, D. (2025). Dynamic wireless power transfer for electric vehicles: A high-frequency converter and battery charging perspective. *AVE Trends in Intelligent Energy Letters*, *1*(2), 61–70. DOI: 10.64091/ATIEL.2025.000186

Babu, K. A., Arulvendhan, K., Srinivasan, P., Ahmad, M. A., Prabha, A., Thariq, M. M., Ali, M. M. S., & Angelin, C. C. (2024). Economical infotainment solution augmented with advanced telematics for collision detection, vehicle localization, and real-time health status monitoring. AVE Trends in Intelligent Health Letters, 1(4), 206–216. https://www.avepubs.com/user/journals/article_details/ATIHL/88

Cirillo, S., Polese, G., Salerno, D., Simone, B., & Solimando, G. (2023). Towards Flexible Voice Assistants: Evaluating Privacy and Security Needs in IoT-enabled Smart Homes. FMDB Transactions on Sustainable Computer Letters, 1(1), 25–32. https://www.fmdbpub.com/user/journals/article_details/FTSCL/38

Doan, K., & Ukkusuri, S. V. (2012). On the holding-back problem in the cell transmission based dynamic traffic assignment models. *Transportation Research Part B: Methodological*, *46*(9), 1218–1238. DOI: 10.1016/j.trb.2012.05.001

Doan, K., & Ukkusuri, S. V. (2015). Dynamic system optimal model for multi-OD traffic networks with an advanced spatial queuing model. *Transportation Research Part C, Emerging Technologies*, *51*(2), 41–65. DOI: 10.1016/j.trc.2014.10.011

Elayaraja, C., Rahila, J., Velavan, P., Rajest, S. S., Shynu, T., & Rahman, M. M. (2024). Depth sensing in AI on exploring the nuances of decision maps for explainability. In *Advances in Computational Intelligence and Robotics* (pp. 217–238). IGI Global., DOI: 10.4018/979-8-3693-8659-0.ch012

Gunapriya, B., Samanvita, N., Karthikeyan, T., & Venkatasubramanian, S. (2025). Managing the power in smart grid management hybrid model with MRA in electric vehicle system. *AVE Trends in Intelligent Energy Letters*, *1*(2), 100–114. DOI: 10.64091/ATIEL.2025.000189

He, J., He, Z., Fan, B., & Chen, Y. (2020). Optimal location of lane-changing warning point in a two-lane road considering different traffic flows. *Physica A*, *540*(2), 123000. DOI: 10.1016/j.physa.2019.123000

Ihsan, A., Chen, W., Khan, W. U., Wu, Q., & Wang, K. (2023). Energy-efficient backscatter aided uplink NOMA roadside sensor communications under channel estimation errors. *IEEE Transactions on Intelligent Transportation Systems*, *24*(5), 4962–4974. DOI: 10.1109/TITS.2023.3240159

Islam, T., Vu, H. L., Hoang, N. H., & Cricenti, A. (2018). A linear bus rapid transit with transit signal priority formulation. *Transportation Research Part E, Logistics and Transportation Review*, *114*(6), 163–184. DOI: 10.1016/j.tre.2018.03.009

Jeba, J. A., Bose, S. R., Regin, R., Banupriya, P., & Maseleno, A. (2025). A comprehensive real-time traffic monitoring and visualization system with automated vehicle analysis. *FMDB Transactions on Sustainable Computing Systems*, *3*(4), 242–252. DOI: 10.69888/FTSCS.2025.000526

Karoonsoontawong, A., & Waller, S. T. (2010). Integrated network capacity expansion and traffic signal optimization problem: Robust bi-level dynamic formulation. *Networks and Spatial Economics*, *10*(9), 525–550. DOI: 10.1007/s11067-008-9071-x

Kwizera, N., Haidoura, H., & Sudha, P. (2025). Analyzing the causes and impacts of disputes in the Rwanda road construction sector and determining ways of reducing disputes. *AVE Trends in Intelligent Social Letters*, *2*(4), 163–172. DOI: 10.64091/ATISL.2025.000237

Mehta, G., Bose, S. R., & Selva Naveen, R. (2023). Optimizing Lithium-ion Battery Controller Design for Electric Vehicles: A Comprehensive Study. FMDB Transactions on Sustainable Energy Sequence, 1(2), 60–70. https://www.fmdbpub.com/user/journals/article_details/FTSES/132

Musa, S. S., Zennaro, M., Libsie, M., & Pietrosemoli, E. (2022). Mobility-aware proactive edge caching optimization scheme in information-centric IoV networks. *Sensors (Basel)*, *22*(4), 1387. DOI: 10.3390/s22041387 PMID: 35214288

Panyaram, S. (2024). Enhancing performance and sustainability of electric vehicle technology with advanced energy management. *FMDB Transactions on Sustainable Energy Sequence*, *2*(2), 110–119. DOI: 10.69888/FTSES.2024.000311

Paramasivan, P., Rajest, S. S., Chinnusamy, K., Regin, R., & John Joseph, F. J. (2024). *Cross-Industry AI Applications*. Advances in Computational Intelligence and Robotics. IGI., DOI: 10.4018/979-8-3693-5951-8

Pierre, T. J., Tao, C., Vénant, K., & Erneste, B. (2024). Speed management blueprint: Conception of an IoT-based electric vehicle speed limiter monitoring system for Kigali city vehicles. *FMDB Transactions on Sustainable Energy Sequence*, *2*(1), 33–48. DOI: 10.69888/FTSES.2024.000190

Rajest, S. S., Singh, B. J., Obaid, A., Regin, R., & Chinnusamy, K. (2023). *Recent developments in machine and human intelligence*. Advances in Computational Intelligence and Robotics. IGI Global., DOI: 10.4018/978-1-6684-9189-8

Regin, R., Gaayathri, R. S., Paramasivan, P., Rajest, S. S., & Radwan, R. (2024). VehiWalnut: Smart Fuel Management with Real-Time Data and User Interaction. *FMDB Transactions on Sustainable Intelligent Networks*, *1*(1), 56–71. DOI: 10.69888/FTSIN.2024.000157

Saxena, R. R., Sujith, S., & Nelavala, R. (2023). MuscleDrive: A Proof of Concept Describing the Electromyographic Navigation of a Vehicle. FMDB Transactions on Sustainable Health Science Letters, 1(2), 107–117. https://www.fmdbpub.com/user/journals/article_details/FTSHSL/81

Sayedelahl, M. A. (2024). Enabling Intelligent Traffic Systems: A Deep Learning Method for Accurate Arabic License Plate Recognition. *FMDB Transactions on Sustainable Intelligent Networks*, *1*(1), 40–55. DOI: 10.69888/FTSIN.2024.000156

Singaravelan, A., Sujitha, S., Gopikha, S., Karthikeyan, T., & Panakkal, R. (2025). Smart transportation in VANET using a hybrid reptile search algorithm-based infrastructure model with VANET. *AVE Trends in Intelligent Computer Letters*, *1*(3), 104–118. DOI: 10.64091/ATICL.2025.000226

Singh, O. J., Bose, S. R., Jeba, J. A., Flavia, B. J., & Sulthana, M. R. (2025). Real-time identification of traffic violations through deep learning techniques. *AVE Trends in Intelligent Computing Systems*, *2*(2), 99–110. DOI: 10.64091/ATICS.2025.000134

Srilakshmi, U., Sandhya, I., Manikandan, J., Bindu, A. H., Regin, R., & Rajest, S. S. (2024). Design and implementation of energy-efficient protocols for underwater wireless sensor networks. In *Advances in Computer and Electrical Engineering* (pp. 417–430). IGI Global., DOI: 10.4018/979-8-3693-3739-4.ch021

Storani, F., Di Pace, R., Bruno, F., & Fiori, C. (2021). Analysis and comparison of traffic flow models: A new hybrid traffic flow model vs benchmark models. *European Transport Research Review*, *13*(11), 1–16. DOI: 10.1186/s12544-021-00515-0

Sumalee, A., Zhong, R. X., Pan, T. L., & Szeto, W. Y. (2011). Stochastic cell transmission model (SCTM): A stochastic dynamic traffic model for traffic state surveillance and assignment. *Transportation Research Part B: Methodological*, *45*(3), 507–533. DOI: 10.1016/j.trb.2010.09.006

Tan, X., Deng, Q., & Hu, X. (2022). Research on vehicle carrying efficiency of three-lane expressway based on DEA method. *Transportation Letters*, *14*(8), 838–848. DOI: 10.1080/19427867.2021.1950267

Trupthi, Y. N., Chitra, K., Harilakshmi, V. M., Paramasivan, P., Rajest, S. S., Ali, M. M. S., & Christodoss, P. R. (2025). Comparative analysis of Random Forest and K-Nearest Neighbours for traffic volume prediction in smart cities. *AVE Trends in Intelligent Computing Systems*, *2*(2), 111–121. DOI: 10.64091/ATICS.2025.000135

Venkatasubramanian, S., Abirami, A., Kannan, R., & Senthil, S. (2024). Optimizing traffic prediction in continuous data stream in vehicular networks with triplet transfer learning and Dhole's hunting-based optimization. *FMDB Transactions on Sustainable Intelligent Networks*, *1*(3), 165–177. DOI: 10.69888/FTSIN.2024.000286

Waller, S. T., Mouskos, K. C., Kamaryiannis, D., & Ziliaskopoulos, A. K. (2006). A linear model for the continuous network design problem. *Computer-Aided Civil and Infrastructure Engineering*, *21*(5), 334–345. DOI: 10.1111/j.1467-8667.2006.00440.x

Wang, J., Li, S., Lu, Y., & Wang, L. (2020). A division method of determining the early-warning zone on an expressway for automated vehicles. *Discrete Dynamics in Nature and Society*, *2020*(1), 9523819. DOI: 10.1155/2020/9523819

Chapter 14
Topological Efficiency in Digital Twins of Autonomous Vehicles With Synthetic Data and Artificial Intelligence

Jaime Aguilar-Ortiz
http://orcid.org/0009-0003-5302-1454
Universidad Politécnica de Pachuca, Mexico

Ocotlán Diáz-Parra
Universidad Politécnica de Pachuca, Mexico

Jorge A. Ruiz-Vanoye
http://orcid.org/0000-0003-4928-5716
Universidad Politécnica de Pachuca, Mexico

Francisco R. Trejo-Macotela
http://orcid.org/0000-0003-2133-3456
Universidad Politécnica de Pachuca, Mexico

Marco A. Vera-Jiménez
http://orcid.org/0009-0009-3712-1440
Universidad Politécnica de Pachuca, Mexico

Carlos R. Domínguez-Mayorga
http://orcid.org/0009-0007-1018-4412
Universidad Politécnica de Pachuca, Mexico

Víctor M. Zamudio-García
http://orcid.org/0000-0002-4660-8025
Universidad Politécnica Metropolitana de Hidalgo, Mexico

ABSTRACT

Autonomous-vehicle digital twins increasingly rely on synthetic data and AI, yet they often lack formal guarantees of structural fidelity. This article proposes a reproducible framework for "topological efficiency," redefining efficiency as the joint optimization of computational cost, time, and invariant preservation. Real sensor streams are mapped to point clouds, persistent-homology signatures are extracted, and generative models produce diverse scenarios under topological supervision. Synthetic outputs and real-time twin updates are accepted only when bottleneck/Wasserstein deviations remain below calibrated thresholds. Experiments analyze fidelity, downstream learning robustness, and scalability, showing how topology-in-the-loop validation accelerates development while improving trustworthiness and interoperability across complex environments.

DOI: 10.4018/979-8-3373-7785-8.ch014

1. INTRODUCTION

1.1 Structural Fidelity as the Missing Dimension of Efficiency in Autonomous-Vehicle Digital Twins

In autonomous-vehicle digital twins, efficiency is often measured by faster simulation or shorter validation. Yet these gains can mislead if acceleration drifts from the real structural organization. Structural fidelity is essential: the twin must preserve the geometry and topology of the scene–behavior manifold for sensing and control. Although AI-enabled twin pipelines can improve performance and latency (Chen & Lv, 2022), and vehicle-oriented twin programs frame the twin as a scalable platform for experimentation (Bhatti et al., 2021), scaling with synthetic data introduces risks beyond marginal distribution shift. It can distort connectivity, class separability, and hole-like patterns from occlusions, rare events, or road topology, yielding brittle models. Accordingly, synth-data surveys stress evaluation for safety relevance (Song et al., 2024), while twin simulators show how scenarios enable dataset generation (Jang et al., 2024). Structural fidelity thus remains the guardrail for efficiency.

A topological notion of structural fidelity requires a digital twin to preserve the multi-scale shape of representations such as LiDAR/radar point clouds, trajectory embeddings, occupancy grids, and generative-model latent spaces, not just low-order moments. Persistent homology extracts filtration-based invariants summarized as persistence diagrams, with dissimilarity quantified by bottleneck or Wasserstein-type distances (Chazal & Michel, 2021). This enables efficiency by acting as a compact "structural checksum" for fast acceptance/rejection or reweighting of synthetic batches prior to costly training and by using stable summaries such as persistent entropy and Betti-curve descriptors studied for robustness to perturbations and scale effects (Atienza et al., 2020). Topology can further be enforced via persistent-homology losses that preserve structure beyond pointwise error (Clough et al., 2022), and it is increasingly needed because latent-variable generators can fail on data with non-trivial topology (Jin et al., 2024), consistent with broader topological ML surveys (Hensel et al., 2021) and synth-data guidance that frames rigorous evaluation as a prerequisite for safe autonomous-driving deployment (Song et al., 2024). Under this lens, "topological efficiency" is acceleration achieved under explicit bounds on topological divergence between the twin and the real system, making structural fidelity measurable and pipeline-compatible. Figure 1 provides an intuitive contrast between preserved and drifted structure, making the role of connectivity and loop preservation explicit.

Figure 1. Conceptual contrast between a structurally faithful twin and a topologically drifted synthetic scene. The left panel preserves connectivity and a loop structure, whereas the right panel shows broken connectivity and loop collapse

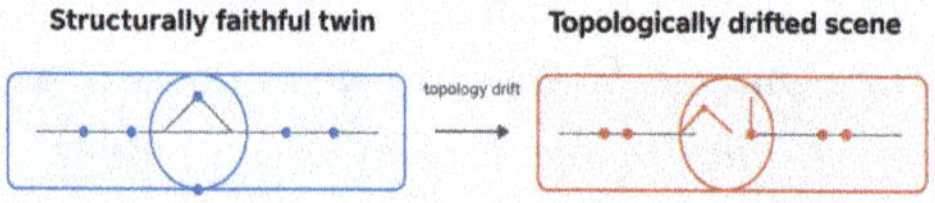

1.2 Research Gap, Objectives, Contributions, and Article Roadmap

A key gap remains in autonomous-vehicle digital twins: many pipelines still lack a mathematically grounded way to certify that large-scale synthetic scenes preserve the structural relations required for safe navigation, even when perception accuracy and simulator realism improve. High visual plausibility may still coexist with safety-relevant topological distortions, so the objective shifts from "more data faster" to "more data faster without structural drift," motivating topological data analysis as a validation and control layer where persistent homology captures relational geometry and persistence-diagram distances measure deviation between real and generated scenarios (Chazal & Michel, 2021). This monitoring is practically feasible because topology-derived summaries such as persistent entropy remain stable under noise and sampling variability in point clouds (Atienza et al., 2020). Thus, structural fidelity determines when synthetic data is trustworthy for training or operational twin updates (Jang et al., 2024).

Accordingly, the article operationalizes "topological efficiency" as a criterion coupling computational efficiency with structural fidelity so synthetic acceleration preserves realism. Its contributions are topology-based signatures to measure deviation between real and synthetic geometries, a reproducible point-cloud pipeline that generates and filters synthetic batches through diagram-consistency thresholds, and an architecture that applies topology to offline validation and online auditing. This supports synthetic-data validation for perception (Jang et al., 2024), translates invariants into practical constraints (Hensel et al., 2021), and preserves reproducible provenance tracking (Leipzig et al., 2021). The remainder of the chapter addresses three linked axes: issues of structural drift and synchronization, problems of acceptance control and evaluation, and trends in topology-aware synthetic generation and online auditing.

2. THEORETICAL FOUNDATIONS

2.1 Digital Twins for Autonomous Vehicles: Concepts, Lifecycle, and Real-Time Synchronization

An autonomous-vehicle digital twin can be formalized as a bidirectionally coupled cyber–physical system in which the physical vehicle P and computational replica D co-evolve through continuous data exchange, keeping the virtual state a decision-grade proxy across the lifecycle rather than a static simulator snapshot (Barricelli et al., 2019; VanDerHorn & Mahadevan, 2021; Boyes & Watson, 2022). This lifecycle is sustained by a digital thread linking requirements, dynamics, sensor models, scenarios, and logs, so the twin supports offline engineering and online services within one artifact (Bhatti et al., 2021; da Silva Mendonça et al., 2022). Let $x(t) \in \mathbb{R}^d$ denote the state, $u(t)$ the control, and $y(t)$ the sensor observations; then the physical evolution and sensing can be written as in Equation (1):

$$\dot{x}(t) = f(x(t), u(t)) + u(t),\ y(t) = h(x(t)) + v(t) \tag{1}$$

and the digital twin implements a computational state $\hat{x}(t)$ that runs the same structural model (or a learned surrogate) while being corrected by streamed observations, so that $\hat{x}(t)$ becomes the operational carrier of synchronized reality, not merely a predictive simulation (Fuller et al., 2020; Chen & Lv, 2022). Within autonomous-vehicle programs, this lifecycle framing is particularly consequential because digital-twin environments are increasingly used to generate controllable synthetic training datasets and to test autonomy stacks under systematically varied conditions, which makes the integrity of the physical–digital coupling a central prerequisite for credible development acceleration (Jang et al., 2024; Sarker et al., 2025).

Real-time synchronization is the operational core of that lifecycle: the twin must continually assimilate fresh measurements under latency, bandwidth limits, and model mismatch, while ensuring that the resulting $\hat{x}$ remains sufficiently close to x to support safety-relevant decisions (Boyes & Watson, 2022; Tan & Matta, 2024). In discrete time (sampling period Δt), a common engineering abstraction is to rewrite the dynamics as $x_{k+1} = Fx_k + Gu_k + w_k$ and $y_k = Hx_k + v_k$, after which the twin performs recursive estimation; before the central update equation, it is natural to introduce the innovation (measurement residual) $r_k = y_k - H\hat{x}_{k|k-1}$, yielding the canonical correction step in Equation (2):

$$\hat{x}_{k|k} = \hat{x}_{k|k-1} + K_k\left(y_k - H\hat{x}_{k|k-1}\right), \tag{2}$$

where K_k (e.g., Kalman-type gain or a learned gain) mediates how aggressively the twin follows incoming data versus its internal model. Synchronization quality is then quantified through an explicit discrepancy; before defining the objective, one defines the synchronization error $e_k = x_k - \hat{x}_{k|k}$, which immediately induces the measurable loss in Equation (3):

$$\mathscr{L}_{sync} = \sum_{k=1}^{T} \|e_k\|_Q^2, \tag{3}$$

but high-rate synchronization is not "free," because frequent updates increase network load and operational costs, while infrequent updates increase bias and decision error; this cost–accuracy tension motivates event-triggered or policy-driven synchronization that updates only when an error proxy (or data-age) exceeds a threshold, a phenomenon analyzed as an explicit synchronization-policy problem (Tan & Matta, 2024). A compact way to express that trade-off is to define an update indicator $\delta_k \in \{0,1\}$ and optimize a combined criterion; before the equation, it is natural to state that c_k represents communication/compute cost per update and $\lambda > 0$ balances fidelity and cost in Equation (4):

$$\min_{\{\delta_k\}} J = \sum_{k=1}^{T}\left(\|e_k\|_Q^2 + \lambda\delta_k c_k\right), \delta_k = 1\left(\|e_k\|_2 \geq \varepsilon\right). \tag{4}$$

This formulation is consistent with real-time intelligent-vehicle settings in which localization, perception, and decision-making must remain timely under constrained resources, and where latency-aware architectures (including vehicular digital-twin networking patterns) explicitly target reduced delay and improved operational reliability (Chen & Lv, 2022; Zia et al., 2025; Sarker et al., 2025).

2.2 Algebraic Topology and Topological Data Analysis for Structural Verification

Algebraic topology provides the formal language to treat a digital-twin perception stream as an object whose structure can be verified independently of superficial realism, because the verification target is not a pixel-level match but the preservation of invariant relational patterns such as connectivity, loops, and higher-dimensional voids that arise from road networks, obstacle fields, and traffic-flow geometries

(Chazal & Michel, 2021; Su et al., 2026). When a real sensor snapshot (e.g., LiDAR/radar fusion) is represented as a point cloud $X = \{x_i\}_{i=1}^{N} \subset \mathbb{R}^d$, the first step is to convert metric proximity into combinatorial structure through a simplicial complex; a widely used choice for scalable verification is the Vietoris–Rips complex, which encodes the multi-scale adjacency relationships that must remain coherent under synthetic generation and real-time twin updates (Bauer, 2021; Zhou et al., 2022). Before the central definition, it is natural to fix a scale $\varepsilon > 0$ and a metric $d(\bullet)$; then the complex is defined as in Equation (5):

$$VR_{\varepsilon}(X) = \left\{\sigma = \{x_{i_0}, \ldots, x_{i_k}\} \subseteq X : d\left(x_{i_p}, x_{i_q}\right) \leq \varepsilon \, \forall p.q\right\}. \tag{5}$$

Once a simplicial complex K is built, algebraic topology formalizes "structural features" through chain groups and boundary maps; before the key relationship, it is natural to define $C_k(K;\mathbb{F})$ as the k - chains over a field $\mathbb{F}$ and $\partial_k : C_k \rightarrow C_{k-1}$ as the boundary operator. Then homology groups are defined by Equation (6):

$$H_k(K;\mathbb{F}) = \ker\frac{(\partial_k)}{im(\partial_{k+1})}, \beta_k = rank\, H_k(K;\mathbb{F}). \tag{6}$$

In an autonomous-driving digital twin, β_0 operationalizes the number of connected components (e.g., fragmented drivable regions), β_1 captures loop-like structures (e.g., roundabouts, block-level cycles, circulation patterns), and β_2 relates to voids/cavities that can emerge in 3D occupancy representations; these quantities can therefore be treated as structural invariants whose preservation is essential for safety-relevant coherence across real and synthetic scenarios (Chazal & Michel, 2021; Hensel et al., 2021). Table 1 summarizes how the principal topological concepts used in this chapter map directly onto autonomous-vehicle interpretation and structural verification tasks.

Table 1. Topology concepts mapped to autonomous-vehicle applications. The table condenses the main invariants and their operational use in validation and auditing

Concept	Structural meaning	AV interpretation	Verification use
H_0	Connected components	Drivable-space continuity and fragmented regions	Detect split or merged traversable areas
H_1	Loops and cyclic structure	Roundabouts, block cycles, repeated circulation	Preserve loop integrity across real and synthetic scenes
Persistence diagram	Birth/death across scales	Scenario-level structural signature	Compare real, synthetic, and updated twin states
Bottleneck/Wasserstein distance	Worst-case or distributed drift	Condition-wise scenario mismatch	Accept, reject, or reweight candidate batches
Persistent entropy	Stable summary statistic	Lightweight online structural checksum	Fast auxiliary audit under noise and sampling variation

Topological Data Analysis turns those invariants into multi-scale verification signals by tracking how homological features appear and disappear along a filtration, thereby distinguishing persistent structural content from noise and sampling artifacts typical of point clouds (Chazal & Michel, 2021; Atienza et al.,

2020). Before introducing persistence, it is natural to consider a nested family of complexes $\{K_\varepsilon\}_{\varepsilon \geq 0}$ such that $K_{\varepsilon_1} \subseteq K_{\varepsilon_2}$ for $\varepsilon_1 \leq \varepsilon_2$; persistent homology records the birth and death of features across ε, yielding a persistence diagram $D_k = \{(b_i, d_i)\}_i$ at dimension k: This can be written succinctly as in Equation (7):

$$D_k(X) = \{(b_i, d_i) \in \mathbb{R}^2 : a\ k - dimensional\ class\ is\ born\ at\ b_i\ and\ dies\ at\ d_i\}. \tag{7}$$

Structural verification between a real stream $X^{(R)}$ and a synthetic or twin-updated stream $X^{(S)}$ becomes a comparison between diagrams $D_k^{(R)}$ and $D_k^{(S)}$ using metrics designed for topological summaries; before the metric formulas, it is natural to define a matching γ that pairs points in one diagram to points in the other (allowing matches to the diagonal). The bottleneck distance and the p-Wasserstein distance are commonly used as complementary checks and are summarized in Equation (8) (Chazal & Michel, 2021):

$$d_B(D, D') = \inf_\gamma \sup_{u \in D} \|u - \gamma(u)\|_\infty,\ W_p(D, D') = \left(\inf_\gamma \sum_{u \in D} \|u - \gamma(u)\|_\infty^p\right)^{1/p}. \tag{8}$$

Because point clouds are noisy and incomplete, stable summary functionals can also be used to strengthen robustness; before defining persistent entropy, it is natural to define bar lengths $\ell = d_i - b_i$ and normalized weights $p_i = \ell_i / \sum_j \ell_j$. Then persistent entropy is given in Equation (9):

$$H_{pers}(D) = -\sum_i p_i \log p_i, \tag{9}$$

which is studied precisely for stability and scale behavior, making it suitable as an auxiliary "structural fingerprint" for acceptance testing (Atienza et al., 2020). From an implementation standpoint, this verification logic is consistent with computing persistence efficiently via optimized Vietoris–Rips algorithms and lightweight software stacks (e.g., Ripser and Ripser.py) when repeated comparisons must be performed across many synthetic batches or streaming updates (Bauer, 2021; Tralie et al., 2018), and it also supports extracting representative cycles when interpretability requires concrete geometric witnesses of detected holes (Čufar & Virk, 2023; Kozlov, 2020; Obayashi, 2018).

With these mathematical objects in place, "structural verification" for an autonomous-vehicle digital twin can be posed as a rigorous gatekeeping rule: synthetic scenes or real-time twin updates are accepted only if their topological divergence from the reference real stream remains below calibrated tolerances across relevant homology dimensions, thereby preventing fast generation or rapid synchronization from silently breaking the invariant geometry of the operational environment (Hensel et al., 2021; Su et al., 2026). Before the acceptance criterion, it is natural to define a weighted divergence that aggregates distances across dimensions $k \in \mathcal{K}$ (typically $k = 0,1,2$) and possibly across multiple modalities or embeddings; one convenient form is given in Equation (10):

$$\Delta_{topo}(X^{(R)}, X^{(S)}) = \sum_{k \in \mathcal{K}} w_k d_B(D_B(X^{(R)}), D_k(X^{(S)})),\ w_k \geq 0. \tag{10}$$

Then a topology-consistency acceptance rule can be stated as in Equation (11):

$$Accept\ X^{(S)} \Longleftrightarrow \Delta_{topo}(X^{(R)}, X^{(S)}) \leq \tau, \tag{11}$$

with τ chosen by calibration on trusted real sequences (e.g., to reflect sensor noise, sampling density, and scenario variability). This is precisely where algebraic topology becomes operational: it provides invariant-preserving constraints that can be used either as an external validator (filtering synthetic datasets before training) or as an internal regularizer inside learning, where a model is trained not only to minimize a task loss but also to respect topological coherence (Clough et al., 2022; Jin et al., 2024). Before the coupled objective, it is natural to denote the downstream task loss by $\mathscr{L}_{task}$ and introduce a topology penalty based on diagram distances; then a topology-aware learning objective can be written as in Equation (12):

$$\mathscr{L} = \mathscr{L}_{task} + \mu \Delta_{topo}(X^{(R)}, X^{(S)}), \mu > 0. \tag{12}$$

In a digital-twin lifecycle, this formulation supports the chapter's core aim: the twin's computational speedups and synthetic-data scaling are treated as valid only when structural invariants remain controlled, turning topology into a measurable "integrity budget" that makes efficiency compatible with trustworthiness rather than antagonistic to it (Chazal & Michel, 2021; Bauer, 2021; Su et al., 2026).

2.3 Synthetic Data and Generative AI in AV Ecosystems: Benefits, Failure Modes, and the Need for Topological Supervision

Synthetic data and generative AI have become central instruments in autonomous-vehicle (AV) ecosystems because they decouple learning progress from the slow, risky, and expensive pace of real-world data collection, while enabling controlled coverage of corner cases (rare lighting, adverse weather, unusual traffic interactions) and perfectly consistent labels when the simulator or generator has full scene knowledge (Song et al., 2024; Jang et al., 2024). In a probabilistic formulation, the technical aim is to learn a generator whose synthetic distribution approximates the real operational distribution; before the core objective is stated, it is natural to denote the real data distribution as $p_{real}(x)$ and the model distribution as $p(x)$, where x may encode multi-modal AV observations (images, LiDAR point clouds, trajectories, maps). Then the distribution-matching target can be written as $\min_{\theta} \mathscr{D}\left(p_{real}(x), p_{\theta}(x)\right)$, where $\mathscr{D}$ is a divergence or discrepancy functional chosen to reflect downstream utility. In practice, many AV-oriented generators are conditional (e.g., conditioned on semantic maps, weather, road topology, or intent), and adversarial training remains a common workhorse for scenario synthesis; before the adversarial objective is given, it is natural to introduce a discriminator D_{ϕ} and a generator G_{θ}. The canonical conditional GAN objective is given in Equation (13):

$$\min_{\theta} \max_{\phi} \mathbb{E}_{x \sim p_{real}}\left[\log D_{\phi}(x|c)\right] + \mathbb{E}_{z \sim p(z)}\left[\log\left(1 - D_{\phi}\left(G_{\theta}(z|c)\middle|c\right)\right)\right]. \tag{13}$$

Yet the same mechanisms that make synthetic data powerful also produce distinctive failure modes: distribution gaps between simulated and real sensor domains, spurious correlations introduced by rendering pipelines, mode collapse or incomplete coverage under adversarial learning, and "plausible-but-wrong" generations that preserve local texture while corrupting global scene structure (Miller et al., 2025; Goyal & Mahmoud, 2024). Diffusion models are frequently adopted to improve training stability and sample quality, but their iterative sampling cost and the possibility of generating structurally inconsistent content under weak constraints remain practical concerns; before the diffusion training surrogate is written, it is natural to denote a forward noising process that produces x_t and a network $\varepsilon_\theta(x_t, t)$ that predicts injected noise. A common denoising objective is given in Equation (14):

$$\min_\theta \mathbb{E}_{t,x,\varepsilon}\left[\left\|\varepsilon - \varepsilon_\theta(x_t, t\right\|_2^2\right], \tag{14}$$

which highlights that high perceptual fidelity does not automatically imply structural correctness in AV-relevant geometry and interaction patterns (Zhu, 2024; Song et al., 2024).

The need for topological supervision arises precisely because AV digital-twin pipelines are judged by safety-relevant structural coherence connectivity of drivable space, persistence of loops in road graphs, separability of obstacle clusters, and stable relational geometry under sensor noise while conventional synthetic-data checks can pass samples that look realistic yet violate those invariants. A particularly deep reason is that many latent-variable generators impose topological limitations on the data manifold they can represent, which can lead to systematic failures in generation and interpolation when the underlying distribution has non-trivial topology (Jin et al., 2024). Topological supervision operationalizes "structural validity" by comparing real and synthetic sensor-derived geometries through persistent-homology signatures computed on point clouds or learned embeddings; before the structural penalty is defined, it is natural to denote a real sample as $X^{(R)}$ and a synthetic one as $X^{(S)}$, with persistence diagrams $D_k(\bullet)$ at dimensions $k = \{0,1,2\}$. A compact topological divergence is given in Equation (15):

$$\Delta_{topo}(X^{(R)}, X^{(S)}) = \sum_{k\in\{0,1,2\}} w_k d\left(D_k(X^{(R)}), D_k\left(X^{(S)}\right)\right), w_k \geq 0, \tag{15}$$

where $d(\bullet,\bullet)$ can be instantiated as bottleneck or Wasserstein-type distances and computed efficiently at scale with modern persistence tooling (Bauer, 2021). This yields a clear acceptance criterion for topology-in-the-loop generation; before stating it, it is natural to introduce a calibrated threshold τ reflecting sensor noise and permissible variability. The gating rule is stated in Equation (16):

$$Accept\ X^{(S)} \iff \Delta_{topo}(X^{(R)}, X^{(S)}) \leq \tau \tag{16}$$

and the same principle can be embedded directly into generative training to prevent "fast but structurally drifting" synthesis. Before writing the coupled objective, it is natural to denote the base generative loss as $\mathscr{L}_{gen}$ and a topological regularizer weight λ. Then the topology-supervised training criterion is given in Equation (17):

$$\mathscr{L} = \mathscr{L}_{gen} + \lambda \Delta_{topo}((X^{(R)}, X^{(S)})). \tag{17}$$

This construction is consistent with established uses of persistent-homology–based losses and regularizers in deep learning, where topology acts as a global constraint that complements local reconstruction or adversarial terms (Clough et al., 2022; Chen et al., 2023). In AV ecosystems, the practical effect is that synthetic data retains its advantages coverage expansion, safer exploration of rare hazards, and accelerated iteration while the digital twin gains an explicit structural "integrity check" that reduces the probability of silently introducing invalid connectivity or interaction geometry into training and evaluation loops (Jang et al., 2024; Jia et al., 2024; Ren et al., 2025).

3. METHODOLOGY

3.1 Topology-in-the-Loop Framework: From Sensor Data to Topological Signatures, Generation, and Acceptance Criteria

The topology-in-the-loop framework treats the autonomous-vehicle digital-twin data stream as a sequence of structured geometric observations that must preserve invariants while being augmented by synthetic generation. Concretely, let the multi-modal sensor packet at time t be denoted by s_t (LiDAR, radar, camera features, and optional HD-map context). A deterministic preprocessing and fusion operator Φ maps the packet into a geometric carrier suitable for topological verification, typically a point cloud (or an embedding whose geometry is interpreted as a point cloud), so that structural properties can be evaluated at scale rather than inferred indirectly from pixels or raw tensors (Chazal & Michel, 2021; Song et al., 2024). Before formalizing signatures, it is natural to define this conversion step as $X_t = \Phi(s_t) \subset \mathbb{R}^d$. From X_t, the framework builds a filtration of simplicial complexes (commonly Vietoris–Rips complexes) that encodes adjacency as a function of scale ε. Before stating the filtration, it is natural to fix a metric $d(\bullet)$ and a scale $\varepsilon > 0$ yielding Equation (18):

$$VR_{\varepsilon}(X_t) = \left\{\sigma \subseteq X_t : d(x_i, x_j) \leq \varepsilon \, \forall x_i, x_j \in \sigma\right\}. \tag{18}$$

Persistent homology then produces persistence diagrams $D_k(X_t)$ for selected dimensions $k \in \{0,1,2\}$, which act as compact, multi-scale "structural fingerprints" of connectivity, loops, and cavities relevant to drivable-space topology and obstacle-field organization (Chazal & Michel, 2021). In practice, high-throughput computation is achieved with optimized implementations such as Ripser and ripser.py, which are designed precisely for repeated Vietoris–Rips persistence computations in applied pipelines (Bauer, 2021; Tralie et al., 2018). To stabilize monitoring under noise and sampling variability, the diagrams can be summarized by stable functionals; for instance, before introducing persistent entropy, it is natural to define bar lengths $\ell_i = d_i - b_i$ and normalized weights $p_i = \ell_i / \sum_j \ell_i$, giving Equation (19):

$$H_{pers}(D_k) = -\sum_i p_i \log p_i, \tag{19}$$

a summary whose stability properties support its use as an auxiliary verification statistic alongside diagram distances (Atienza et al., 2020).

Once topological signatures are available for real streams, synthetic generation is treated as admissible only under explicit structural constraints, because generative realism alone can conceal topological drift, especially when the data manifold has non-trivial topology (Jin et al., 2024; Song et al., 2024). Let a conditional generator G_θ produce synthetic samples under context c (e.g., weather, traffic density, map segment, scenario class), written naturally as in Equation (20):

$$X^{(S)} = G_\theta(zc), \; z \sim p(z), \tag{20}$$

where G_θ may be instantiated by diffusion-based generators or other generative AI approaches commonly used for high-fidelity synthesis (Rombach et al., 2022; Zhu, 2024), and where digital-twin simulators can provide controllable synthetic corpora with labels and scenario coverage (Jang et al., 2024; Jia et al., 2024). The acceptance criterion is formulated directly in the space of topological summaries: synthetic samples (or batches) are compared against real references via persistence-diagram discrepancies computed across dimensions. Before stating the gate, it is natural to define a weighted divergence that aggregates diagram distances across k, for example with bottleneck or Wasserstein-type metrics that are standard for comparing persistence diagrams and are summarized in Equation (21) (Chazal & Michel, 2021; Bauer, 2021):

$$\Delta_{topo}(X^{(R)}, X^{(S)}) = \sum_{k\in\{0,1,2\}} w_k d\left(D_k(X^{(R)}), D_k\left(X^{(S)}\right)\right), \ w_k \geq 0. \tag{21}$$

With a calibrated tolerance τ that reflects sensor noise, sampling density, and permissible scenario variability, the topology-in-the-loop gate is naturally expressed as in Equation (22):

$$Accept\ X^{(S)} \Longleftrightarrow \Delta_{topo}(X^{(R)}, X^{(S)}) \leq \tau. \tag{22}$$

Moreover, the same principle can be integrated into training so that generation is driven toward structural validity, not merely filtered after the fact; before writing the combined loss, it is natural to denote the base generative objective by $\mathscr{L}_{gen}$ and introduce a penalty weight $\lambda > 0$, yielding Equation (23):

$$\mathscr{L}(\theta) = \mathscr{L}_{gen}(\theta) + \lambda \Delta_{topo}(X^{(R)}, X^{(S)}), \tag{23}$$

which is consistent with topological regularization and persistent-homology–based losses used to enforce global structural constraints in deep learning pipelines (Chen et al., 2023; Clough et al., 2022). In the digital-twin context, this closes the loop between sensor-derived structure, synthetic generation, and acceptance: the twin gains scalable scenario coverage while maintaining explicit control over connectivity and relational geometry, thereby aligning computational acceleration with structural fidelity rather than trading one for the other (Jang et al., 2024; Jin et al., 2024). For procedural clarity, Table 2 condenses the topology-in-the-loop workflow into a compact pseudocode sequence, while the full executable implementation remains available in the GitHub repository cited at the end of the chapter.

Table 2. Compact pseudocode for the topology-in-the-loop pipeline. The full executable implementation remains available in the GitHub repository cited at the end of the chapter

Step	Pseudocode summary
1	Acquire synchronized sensor packet x_t and scenario context c_t.
2	Fuse inputs: $X_t \leftarrow \varphi(x_t)$ and build the reference geometric carrier.
3	Compute persistence signatures $D_k(X_t)$ (Persistence diagram in dimension k) and $Pers_k(X_t)$ (Persistent Homology of X_t.
4	Generate candidate batch: $\hat{X}_t \leftarrow G(z\|c_t)$.

continued on following page

Table 2. Continued

Step	Pseudocode summary
5	Compute $D_k(\hat{X}_t)$ and $\Delta_{topo} = d(D_k(X_t), D_k(\hat{X}_t))$.
6	If $\Delta_{topo} \leq \tau$, accept and update the audit or training buffer.
7	Else reject or reweight $\hat{X}_t$, log drift, and retrain or update only with accepted data.

3.2 Experimental Design and Evaluation Metrics: Topological Distances, Consistency Scores, and Downstream Performance

A rigorous experimental design for topology-in-the-loop evaluation begins by treating each real driving sequence as a time-indexed collection of geometric carriers $X_t = \Phi(s_t)$ and by defining three non-overlapping partitions: a calibration set to set thresholds and normalize distances, a development set for model fitting and ablations, and a hold-out operational test set used only for final reporting (Song et al., 2024; Jang et al., 2024). Structural verification is performed per time window (or per scenario) by computing persistence diagrams $D_k(X)$ at dimensional $k \in \{0,1,2\}$, after building a filtration (typically Vietoris–Rips) and extracting multiscale births and deaths (Chazal & Michel, 2021; Bauer, 2021). Before comparing real versus synthetic outputs, it is natural to define a matching γ that pairs off-diagonal points and allows matches to the diagonal (noise), which yields the canonical diagram distances used as primary endpoints; the bottleneck distance is written as in Equation (24):

$$d_B(D,D') = \inf_{\gamma} \sup_{u \in D} \|u - \gamma(u)\|_{\infty}, \tag{24}$$

and the p- Wasserstein distance is written as in Equation (25):

$$W_p(D,D') = \left(\inf_{\gamma} \sum_{u \in D} \|u - \gamma(u)\|_{\infty}^{p} \right)^{1/p}. \tag{25}$$

Because large-scale experimentation requires many diagram comparisons, fast approximation algorithms for the 1-Wasserstein distance can be incorporated to make the metric evaluation itself scalable without changing the conceptual endpoint (Chen & Wang, 2025). Next, a single topological divergence per sample (or per window) is defined by aggregating across dimensions; before stating it, it is natural to introduce weights $w_k \geq 0$ that reflect which invariants are most safety-relevant in the specific AV setting. A compact divergence is then given by Equation (26):

$$\Delta_{topo}(X^{(R)}, X^{(S)}) = \sum_{k \in \{0,1,2\}} w_k d\left(D_k(X^{(R)}), D_k\left(X^{(S)}\right)\right), \tag{26}$$

where $d(\bullet)$ can be instantiated as d_B or W_p depending on sensitivity and computing budget (Chazal & Michel, 2021; Bauer, 2021). Finally, an interpretable consistency score is reported alongside distances; before defining it, it is natural to normalize by a calibrated tolerance τ learned on the calibration partition. One convenient bounded score is given in Equation (27):

$$TCS = 1 - \min\left(1, \frac{\Delta_{topo}}{\tau}\right), \tag{27}$$

and population-level stability across scenarios can be assessed either by reporting distributional summaries of

TCS (e.g., medians and lower quantiles) or by permutation-based hypothesis testing on vectorized functional summaries of diagrams when the design calls for group comparisons (e.g., "real vs. synthetic," or "accepted vs. rejected") (Islambekov & Pathirana, 2024).

Downstream performance evaluation is then constructed as a controlled set of training regimes that differ only in the inclusion and selection rule of synthetic data: a real-only baseline, an unfiltered synthetic-augmented regime, and a topology-gated regime in which synthetic samples are admitted only when $\Delta_{topo} \leq \tau$ (Song et al., 2024; Jin et al., 2024). This produces a direct causal test of whether topological supervision improves generalization and robustness rather than merely increasing sample count. For perception tasks, classification-style outcomes are summarized by precision and recall; before defining the harmonic meaning, it is natural to denote true positives, false positives, and false negatives by *TP*, *FP* and *FN* . The *F*1 score is then given in Equation (28):

$$F1 = \frac{2TP}{2TP + FP + FN}, \tag{28}$$

and for segmentation or occupancy prediction, overlap quality is reported via Intersection-over-Union; before stating it, it is natural to denote predicted and ground-truth regions by *A* y *B*. *IoU* is given in Equation (29):

$$IoU = \frac{|A \cap B|}{|A \cup B|}. \tag{29}$$

For motion forecasting or planning surrogates, Average Displacement Error and Final Displacement Error can quantify trajectory errors; before writing them, it is natural to define predicted and ground-truth positions as $\hat{p}_t$ and p_t over a horizon *T*. *ADE* and *FDE* are given in Equation (30):

$$ADE = \frac{1}{T}\sum_{t=1}^{T}\|\hat{p}_t - p_t\|_2, \; FDE = \|\hat{p}_T - p_T\|_2. \tag{30}$$

These downstream metrics are interpreted jointly with topology metrics through a constrained efficiency lens: performance gains are credited only when structural divergence remains controlled and computational cost does not explode. Before writing the scalar index, it is natural to denote a downstream metric by $\mathcal{M}$ (higher is better) and total compute by *C* A simple "topological efficiency" summary is given in Equation (31):

$$TE = \frac{\mathcal{M}_{gated} - \mathcal{M}_{real}}{C_{gated} - C_{real}} \; subject \; \Delta_{topo} \leq \tau, \tag{31}$$

which operationalizes the section's intent: synthetic generation (including diffusion-based or adversarial generators) is evaluated not only by downstream scores but by the structural validity constraints that prevent plausible-looking yet topologically inconsistent scenarios from contaminating training and evaluation (Rombach et al., 2022; Zhu, 2024; Jia et al., 2024).

4. COMPUTATIONAL ARCHITECTURE

4.1 End-to-End Architecture for Topologically Efficient Digital Twins: Data Pipeline, Topological Module, and AI Training/Update Integration

An end-to-end architecture for topologically efficient autonomous-vehicle digital twins is a cyber–physical pipeline where the vehicle and environment generate multi-modal observations, the twin maintains synchronized state and scenario memory and learning plus simulation are structurally verified. The data plane fuses LiDAR, radar, camera, IMU, map, V2X, and weather signals into geometric representations (Barricelli et al., 2019; Fuller et al., 2020; VanDerHorn & Mahadevan, 2021; Semeraro et al., 2021). Its key element is a topological module before synthetic-data use or updates: persistent-homology signatures compare real and synthetic geometries through structural checksums (Chazal & Michel, 2021; Bauer, 2021). Synthetic outputs are admitted only below calibrated divergence thresholds, preserving benefits without artifacts that weaken autonomy reliability (Song et al., 2024; Jang et al., 2024; Jin et al., 2024; Rombach et al., 2022; Zhu, 2024).

The learning and update plane adds an operations layer that makes topology-in-the-loop scalable: orchestration manages retraining, while registries preserve lineage so changes can be traced to data and validation outcomes (Kreuzberger et al., 2023; Leipzig et al., 2021). The same topological module supports offline governance for batch validation and online auditing for gating updates, synchronizing states only when evidence remains structurally consistent. This fits policies balancing update cost and bias, since topological divergence acts as a risk signal for updates (Tan & Matta, 2024). In AV ecosystems, topological verification constrains synthetic-data ingestion and continuous learning so speedups count only when the twin remains faithful to the world it emulates (Chen & Lv, 2022; Chen et al., 2023; Song et al., 2024).

5. RESULTS AND ANALYSIS

5.1 Topological Fidelity of Synthetic Scenarios: Persistence-Based Comparisons Across Driving Conditions

This subsection establishes the baseline by quantifying how synthetic scenarios preserve the persistence-based topology of driving data across conditions such as clear day, fog, night, and rain. It reports divergence and outcomes to identify where regimes induce topological drift before learning claims are interpreted. Table 3 reports the full persistence-based audit across conditions, allowing the reader to identify which synthetic scenarios remain structurally admissible under the topology gate.

Table 3. Topological fidelity audit of synthetic driving scenarios across conditions. The table lists each synthetic_id, its condition and generator, then reports persistence-based distances (bottleneck and

Wasserstein-1 in H_0 and H_1). These are aggregated into divergence, mapped to consistency_score, and finalized as a binary gate accepted indicating structural admissibility

Synthetic _id	condition	generator	Bottleneck _H0	Bottleneck _H1	Wasserstein 1 _H0	Wasserstein 1 _H1	divergence	Consistency _score	accepted
syn_clear_ day_0000_ benign	clear_ day	synthetic_ transform_ benign	0.1835	0.0855	0.9473	0.1056	0.4844	0.2343	1
syn_clear_ day_0020_ benign	clear_ day	synthetic_ transform_ benign	0.2440	0.1163	1.1464	0.1364	0.5909	0.0659	1
syn_clear_ day_0040_ benign	clear_ day	synthetic_ transform_ benign	0.2095	0.1477	1.0888	0.2290	0.6159	0.0264	1
syn_clear_ day_0060_ benign	clear_ day	synthetic_ transform_ benign	0.2058	0.1728	0.8054	0.1929	0.4685	0.2594	1
syn_fog_0080_ drift_merge_ clusters	fog	synthetic_transform_ drift_merge_ clusters	0.0688	0.0850	0.4756	0.1793	0.3126	0.5058	1
syn_fog_ 0100_benign	fog	synthetic_ transform_benign	0.0603	0.0666	0.7525	0.1398	0.4155	0.3432	1
syn_fog_ 0120_benign	fog	synthetic_ transform_benign	0.0986	0.0850	0.8592	0.1687	0.4795	0.2421	1
syn_fog_ 0140_benign	fog	synthetic_ transform_benign	0.1280	0.0473	0.8155	0.0629	0.4016	0.3652	1
syn_night_ 0160_benign	night	synthetic_ transform_benign	0.0830	0.0674	0.6268	0.1049	0.3398	0.4629	1
syn_night_ 0180_benign	night	synthetic_ transform_benign	0.1005	0.0674	0.9437	0.1143	0.4875	0.2294	1
syn_night_0200_ drift_merge_ clusters	night	synthetic_ transform_drift_ merge_clusters	0.1319	0.0674	0.7876	0.0832	0.4002	0.3674	1
syn_rain_0220_ drift_merge_ clusters	rain	synthetic_ transform_drift_ merge_clusters	0.4452	0.1000	1.3718	0.1300	0.6888	0.0000	0
syn_rain_ 0240_benign	rain	synthetic_ transform_benign	0.2934	0.1354	1.2648	0.1354	0.6436	0.0000	0
syn_rain_ 0260_benign	rain	synthetic_ transform_benign	0.1375	0.1815	0.8060	0.2423	0.4960	0.2160	1
syn_rain_0280_ drift_merge_ clusters	rain	synthetic_ transform_drift_ merge_clusters	0.2221	0.1000	0.9997	0.2144	0.5678	0.1025	1

Reading guide: Read accepted as the gate decision, then use divergence and consistency_score to explain why a scenario passes or fails. The H_0/H_1 split separates connectivity from loop distortion, while bottleneck and Wasserstein distinguish worst-case from distributed drift.

Why it matters: The table anchors the chapter's later claims on structurally admissible synthetics. By auditing topology before training and evaluation, it prevents visually plausible but geometrically invalid scenarios from biasing robustness and safety analyses.

Managerial meaning: Operationally, accepted=1 denotes reusable synthetic assets, whereas rejected cases should inform stress testing and generator refinement. Condition- and metric-specific patterns show where corrective effort should focus. This condition-wise behavior is synthesized visually in Figure 2, which shows how topological divergence varies across the main driving regimes.

Figure 2. Topological divergence (weighted Wasserstein-1) across driving conditions. The figure summarizes, via boxplots, the distribution of persistence-based divergence for synthetic scenarios under clear day, fog, night, and rain, where lower values indicate higher structural fidelity. The dashed horizontal line represents the acceptance tolerance used to operationalize topology-preserving validity within the twin workflow

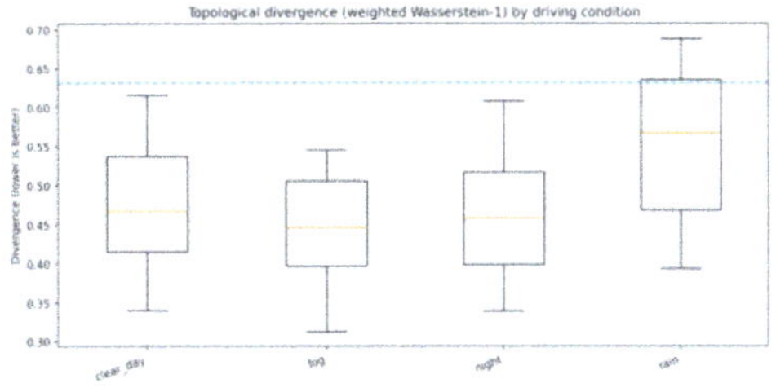

Reading guide: Compare medians and spread across conditions and read the dashed line as the acceptance tolerance. Rain concentrates the largest divergence and dispersion, whereas fog and night remain comparatively stable.

Why it matters: The plot shows that structural drift is condition-dependent, so topology validation cannot rely on global averages alone. It explains why adverse regimes require tighter governance before downstream learning results are trusted.

Managerial meaning: The figure supports prioritizing calibration and mitigation in rain-like regimes. Validation effort can therefore be concentrated where structural drift is most likely to compromise safety.

Complementarily, Figure 3 converts those divergence outcomes into an operational acceptance view by reporting the proportion of synthetic scenarios that pass the topology gate in each condition.

Figure 3. Topology-gate acceptance rate by driving condition. The bar chart reports the fraction of synthetic scenarios that pass the persistence-based structural validity gate in clear day, fog, night, and rain. Higher bars indicate stronger topology preservation relative to the reference constraints enforced in the twin

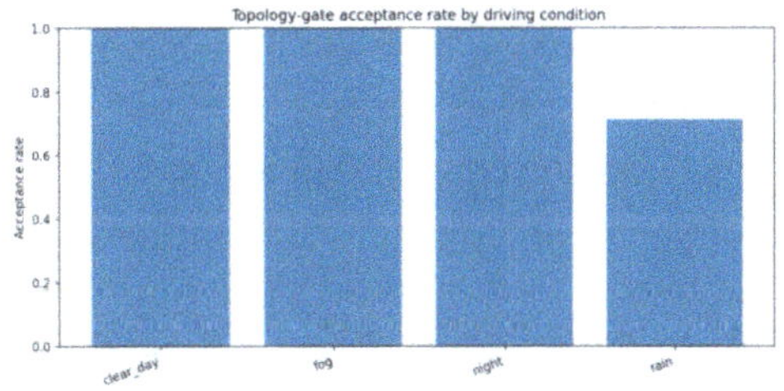

Reading guide: Bar height gives the share of synthetic scenarios that satisfy the topology gate in each condition. The lower rain bar confirms a higher rejection risk under adverse weather.

Why it matters: The acceptance rate translates persistence distances into an operational governance signal. It shows that the gate actively controls what enters training and evaluation instead of remaining a descriptive metric.

Managerial meaning: As a KPI, acceptance rate helps decide where generator refinement or additional calibration is needed. It also supports allocating validation resources to the conditions with the greatest structural risk.

To make the geometric meaning of these persistence-based comparisons more interpretable, Figure 4 presents a representative persistence diagram highlighting the loop structure preserved in a synthetic scenario.

Figure 4. Representative synthetic H_1 persistence diagram for loop structure. The plot places each H_1 feature by its birth and death scales, with the dashed diagonal marking zero persistence. A point far from the diagonal indicates a comparatively persistent loop-like structure in the synthetic scenario

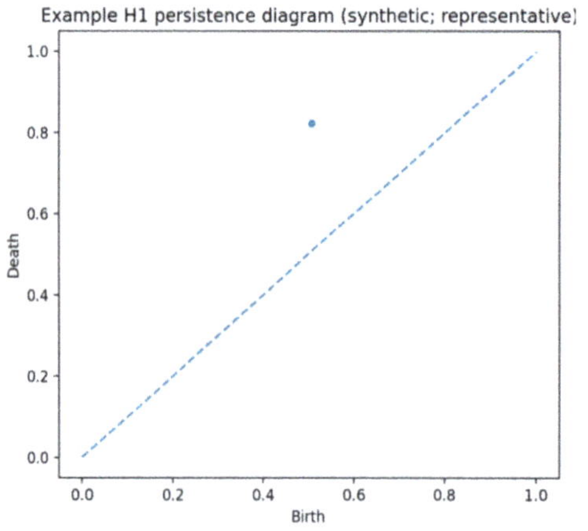

Reading guide: Distance from the diagonal measures loop persistence: points near the diagonal are weak, whereas distant points indicate stable cyclic structure. The diagram therefore visualizes the loop geometry later summarized by the distance metrics.

Why it matters: The figure provides the geometric intuition behind H1-based divergence. It clarifies what is preserved or lost when synthetic generation alters cyclic road structure.

Managerial meaning: Persistent loop structure offers a compact diagnostic for generator quality. Distorted cycles can be flagged early, before they affect training, evaluation, or online auditing.

5.2 Impact on AI Tasks Within The Twin: Robustness, Generalization, and Safety-Relevant Error Patterns

This subsection tests whether topology-governed scenario selection translates into more reliable downstream AI behavior by comparing robustness and generalization under clean versus perturbed evaluations. It emphasizes safety-relevant error patterns, especially hazard-miss tendencies, to link structural validity to operational risk inside the twin. Table 4 presents the downstream task results under the three training regimes, allowing direct comparison of accuracy, F1, ROC-AUC, and hazard false-negative behavior under clean and perturbed tests.

Table 4. Downstream AI task performance under topology-governed synthetic regimes. The table reports accuracy, F1, ROC-AUC, and hazard false-negative rate for three data regimes (real-only, synthetic-unfiltered, synthetic-topology-gated) under clean and perturbed tests. It operationalizes how topology-constrained scenario selection propagates into robustness and safety-relevant error behavior inside the twin

Regime	test_type	accuracy	f1	roc_auc	hazard_false_negative_rate
real_only	clean	0.828	0.286	0.996	0.833
real_only	perturbed	0.793	0.000	0.844	1.000
synthetic_unfiltered	clean	0.897	0.667	0.884	0.500
synthetic_unfiltered	perturbed	0.759	0.222	0.822	0.833
synthetic_topology_gated	clean	0.862	0.500	0.848	0.667
synthetic_topology_gated	perturbed	0.759	0.000	0.783	1.000

Reading guide: Compare rows within each regime from clean to perturbed to evaluate robust degradation, then compare regimes under the same test type to isolate the effect of synthetic augmentation and topology gating. Use F1 and hazard false-negative rate as primary safety-facing indicators when class imbalance is present, with ROC-AUC providing ranking quality. In these results, perturbations reduce F1 sharply and can drive hazard false negatives to 1.000, indicating missed critical events despite moderate accuracy.

Trade-off interpretation: Table 2 and Figure 4 show that clean-set gains, safety behavior, and topological control do not move in lockstep. Unfiltered synthetics lead on clean F1, but that advantage weakens under perturbation and can still coexist with hazardous false negatives, whereas topology gating sacrifices some nominal performance to protect structural validity and provide a more defensible basis for deployment-oriented evaluation. Figure 5 complements Table 4 by visualizing the F1 trade-off between clean and perturbed evaluations across the three regimes.

Managerial meaning: Decision-makers should treat hazard false-negative rate and perturbed-test F1 as go/no-go criteria for deployment validation, because they reflect failure modes with direct safety implications. Comparison across regimes supports policy that synthetic expansion must be coupled with structural gating and explicit robustness testing rather than relying on clean-set performance. The table also guides resource allocation toward reducing perturbation sensitivity and hazard-miss rates before scaling scenario generation or relaxing acceptance thresholds.

Figure 5. Downstream F1 comparison across training regimes under clean and perturbed tests. The bar chart contrasts F1 scores for real-only, synthetic-unfiltered, and synthetic-topology-gated regimes, reporting performance on clean versus perturbed evaluations. It visualizes how topology-constrained scenario selection propagates into task-level robustness within the twin

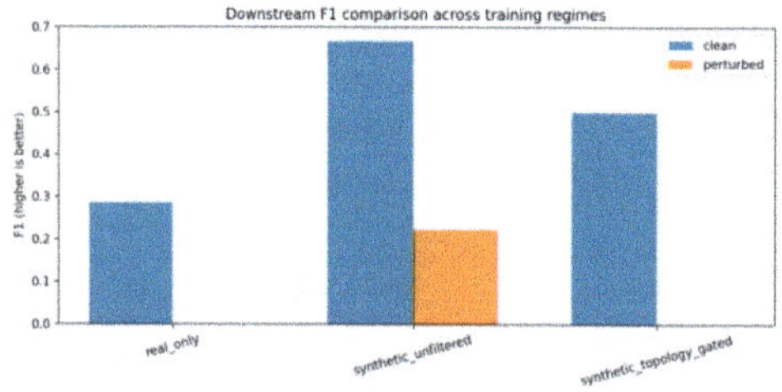

Reading guide: Read blue bars as clean-test F1 and orange bars as perturbed-test F1, then compare regimes at each test type to isolate the effect of synthetic augmentation and gating. The synthetic-unfiltered regime yields the highest clean F1, while perturbed performance collapses across regimes, indicating sensitivity to distributional stress. The topology-gated regime sits between real-only and unfiltered synthetics on clean performance, reflecting a fidelity–performance tradeoff.

Why it matters: The article's objective requires demonstrating that structural validation is not cosmetic but reshapes downstream generalization when the evaluation shifts from clean to stress conditions. This figure makes visible the central risk that clean-set improvements can overstate real-world reliability if perturbations drive F1 toward failure. It therefore motivates coupling synthetic scaling with topology-aware governance and explicit robustness testing aligned with the methodological framework.

Managerial meaning: Managers should interpret clean-test gains as insufficient and prioritize perturbed-test F1 as a deployment-facing criterion, because it reflects operational fragility under adverse conditions. The regime comparison supports using topology-gated synthetics as a controlled compromise that limits structurally risky augmentation while retaining some performance benefits. It also informs investment decisions toward perturbation mitigation and scenario governance before expanding synthetic volume or loosening acceptance thresholds. Because aggregate performance can hide critical safety failures, Figure 6 isolates the hazard false-negative pattern across regimes.

Figure 6. Safety-relevant error pattern: hazard false-negative rate under the clean test. The bar chart reports the proportion of missed hazard events for three training regimes: real-only, synthetic-unfiltered, and synthetic-topology-gated. Lower values indicate better safety performance because fewer hazards are incorrectly predicted as non-hazards

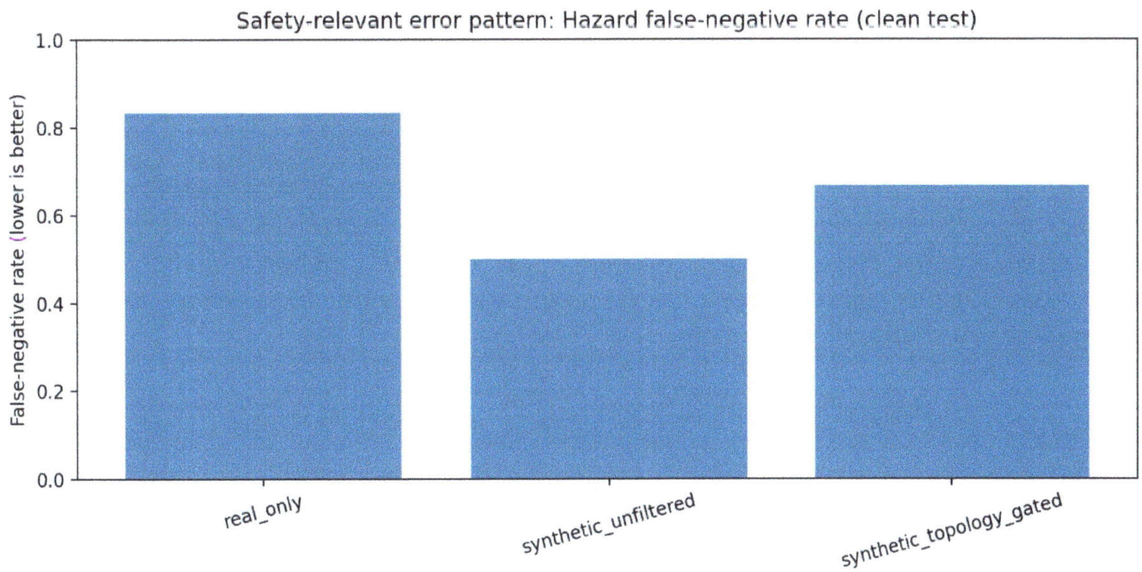

Reading guide: Read each bar as the hazard miss rate for a given regime and compare heights to identify which training strategy reduces safety-critical omissions. A lower bar implies improved detection of rare or critical events even when overall accuracy may appear acceptable. In this figure, synthetic-unfiltered shows the lowest miss rate, while real-only is highest and topology-gated lies in between.

Why it matters: The article's objective emphasizes that topology-aware scenario governance should be evaluated not only with aggregate metrics but with safety-relevant error modes that determine operational risk. This figure makes it explicit that regime choice can change the hazard-miss profile, which is central to robustness and generalization claims in the twin. It also reinforces why structural validation must be paired with downstream safety metrics rather than assumed to translate automatically into safer decisions.

Managerial meaning: Managers should adopt hazard false-negative rate as a primary acceptance criterion for deployment-facing evaluation, because it directly reflects the costliest failure mode in safety contexts. The regime comparison supports controlled use of synthetic data to reduce hazard misses while monitoring whether structural gating alters the safety benefit under different conditions. It also guides investment toward improving hazard coverage and stress testing before scaling scenario generation or relaxing governance thresholds.

5.3 Efficiency Analysis: Cost–Time Tradeoffs, Scalability, and Overhead of Topological Validation

This subsection quantifies the cost–time tradeoffs and scalability of topology-aware governance by reporting validation overhead, runtime, and performance to determine when structural assurance remains operationally feasible.

Table 5 provides the joint cost, runtime, overhead, divergence, and topological-efficiency accounting needed to evaluate whether structural governance remains computationally viable.

Table 5. Efficiency and scalability summary with topology-validation overhead and a topological-efficiency index. The table reports training size, downstream F1 on the clean test, total runtime, topology-validation time, overhead fraction, mean topological divergence, the tolerance τ, and the resulting topological-efficiency index across regimes. It operationalizes efficiency as performance achieved per unit time under explicit structural-fidelity constraints

Regime	n_total_train	f1_clean	total_time_sec	t_topology_sec	Overhead_fraction	mean_divergence	tau	topological_efficiency_index
real_only	29	0.2857	2.5241	1.4367	0.5692	0.0000	0.6326	0.1132
synthetic_unfiltered	58	0.6667	3.6061	1.9925	0.5525	0.4828	0.6326	0.1049
synthetic_topology_gated	56	0.5000	3.6307	1.9925	0.5488	0.4692	0.6326	0.0791
synthetic_unfiltered	30	0.2857	1.9911	1.7242	0.8659	0.4828	0.6326	0.0814
synthetic_topology_gated	30	0.2857	1.9955	1.7242	0.8640	0.4692	0.6326	0.0822
synthetic_unfiltered	58	0.6667	2.2643	1.9925	0.8800	0.4828	0.6326	0.1670
synthetic_topology_gated	56	0.5000	2.2518	1.9734	0.8763	0.4692	0.6326	0.1275
synthetic_unfiltered	58	0.6667	2.2649	1.9925	0.8797	0.4828	0.6326	0.1669
synthetic_topology_gated	56	0.5000	2.2534	1.9734	0.8757	0.4692	0.6326	0.1274

Reading guide: Compare rows by regime to see how increasing training volume affects runtime and whether topology time dominates total time via the overhead fraction. Interpret means divergence relative to as the structural-fidelity burden carried by each regime, then read the topological-efficiency index as the joint outcome of performance, cost, and fidelity. Replicated rows indicate variability across runs and should be summarized by regime-level patterns rather than single best cases.

Why it matters: The article's objective requires demonstrating that topology-aware governance is not only valid but feasible at scale, with quantifiable overhead and transparent tradeoffs. This table provides the accounting layer that connects the structural validation logic and downstream task behavior to computational cost, enabling a defensible "efficiency under constraints" claim. It also clarifies whether improvements in F1 are achieved with acceptable divergence and manageable validation overhead.

Managerial meaning: Managers can use the overhead fraction to budget validation capacity and decide when topology checks should be selective, batched, or condition-prioritized to control runtime. The topological-efficiency index supports regime selection by ranking options that balance safety-facing performance with structural compliance and execution cost. The divergence and columns enable governance policies that tie deployment readiness to explicit fidelity thresholds rather than to accuracy alone. The runtime burden of topology-aware validation is shown more directly in Figure 7, which plots topology overhead against training-set size.

Figure 7. Topology overhead versus training-set size under synthetic training regimes. The plot shows the overhead fraction $t_{topology}/\left(t_{topology} + t_{train}\right)$ *as a function of the number of training scenarios for synthetic-unfiltered and synthetic-topology-gated regimes. It quantifies the share of end-to-end pipeline time devoted to topological validation relative to model training*

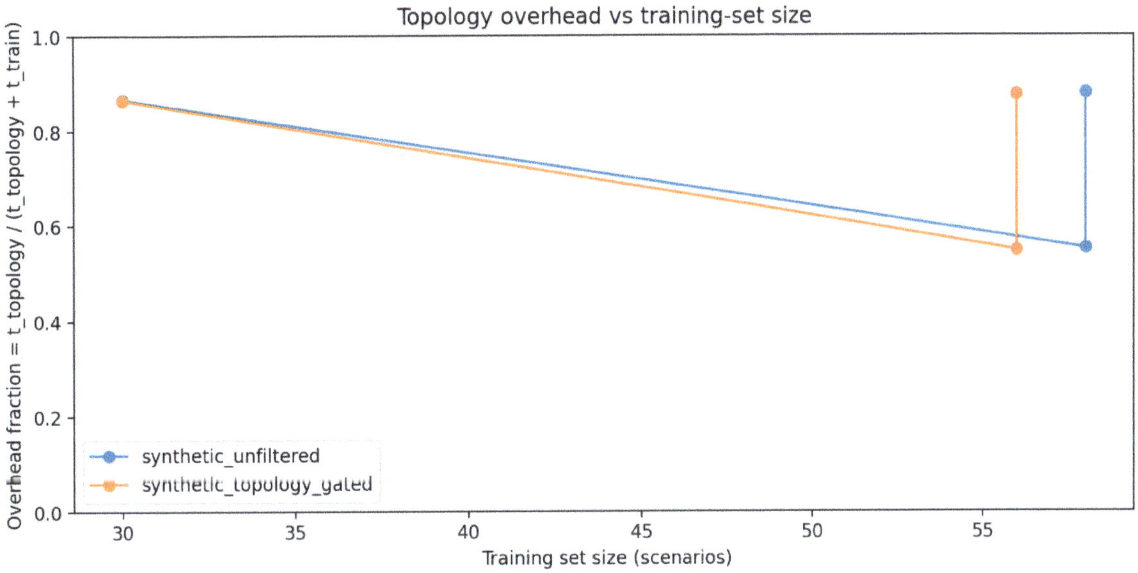

Reading guide: Read the y-axis as the share of runtime attributable to topology computations, where higher values indicate greater validation dominance. Compare curves at the same training size to see whether gating changes overhead and compare sizes to infer scalability trends. In this figure, overhead remains substantial across sizes and does not monotonically decrease, indicating that topology time can stay a primary bottleneck.

Why it matters: The article's objective requires demonstrating that topology-aware governance is operationally feasible, not only methodologically sound, which makes overhead accounting a core result rather than an implementation detail. This figure links the structural validation layer to computational scalability, clarifying whether the twin can sustain condition-aware gating without prohibitive cost. It also contextualizes performance and safety gains by revealing the runtime price paid to enforce topological fidelity.

Managerial meaning: Managers can use this plot to budget validation capacity and decide when to batch topology checks, reduce validation frequency, or prioritize conditions where structural drift risk is highest. The persistent high overhead motivates investment in faster persistence computation or selective gating policies before scaling scenario volume. It also supports governance decisions that explicitly trade time and cost against structural compliance and downstream safety reliability. Figure 8 then summarizes the cost–performance operating point of each regime under the clean test, making the efficiency trade-off visually explicit.

Figure 8. Cost–performance tradeoff under the clean test across training regimes. The scatter plot positions each regime by total pipeline time on the x-axis and downstream F1 on the y-axis, where higher F1 and lower time are preferable. It summarizes how synthetic augmentation and topology gating shift the operating point of the twin under structural-fidelity governance

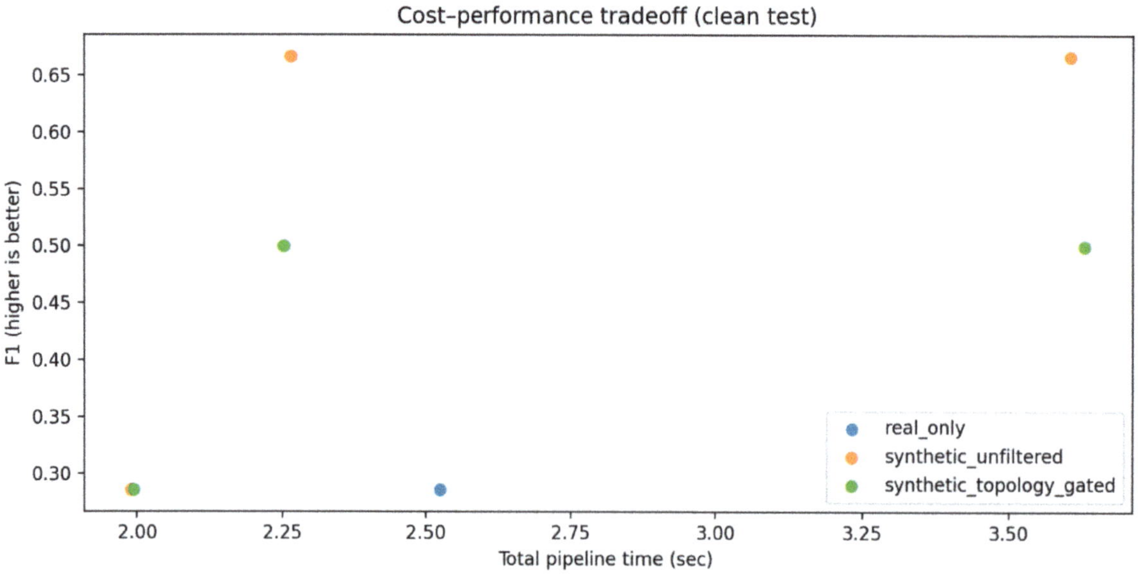

Reading guide: Interpret points closer to the upper-left as more efficient, then compare clusters by color to see which regime achieves higher F1 at a given runtime. Synthetic-unfiltered attains the highest clean-test F1 but at increased time, while topology-gated yields intermediate F1 with comparable costs. The real-only regime sits at lower F1, indicating limited clean-test effectiveness despite moderate runtime.

Why it matters: The article's objective frames efficiency as performance achieved under explicit topology constraints, so this figure makes the tradeoff visible rather than implicit. It connects the structural validation logic and downstream task outcomes to computational cost, supporting a defensible claim about "topological efficiency" rather than raw accuracy. It also provides context for why robustness and safety analyses must be interpreted alongside runtime overhead.

Managerial meaning: Managers can use this plot to select a regime based on operational budgets, choosing whether higher clean-test performance justifies additional pipeline time. The intermediate placement of topology-gated regimes supports a governance strategy that limits structurally risky scenarios while retaining meaningful performance benefits. It also motivates condition- and risk-aware deployment policies where cost allocation follows the marginal safety and validity gains of structural validation.

To illustrate how these efficiency principles extend beyond offline evaluation, Table 6 presents a simulated online topology-audit log with acceptance, latency, and adaptive reference updates.

Table 6. Simulated online topology-audit log with acceptance, latency, and adaptive reference updates. The table tracks an incremental stream of candidate scenarios by step and condition, recording divergence, consistency score, a binary acceptance decision, and per-step latency. It also logs whether the reference was updated and the condition-specific buffer size, operationalizing online auditing within the twin

Step	condition	candidate_id	accepted	divergence	consistency_ score	latency_ ms	reference_ updated	Buffer _size _condition
0	fog	syn_fog_ 0070_benign	1	0.5287	0.1642	9.4029	0	1
1	fog	syn_fog_ 0140_benign	1	0.4016	0.3652	7.8366	0	2
2	rain	syn_rain_ 0250_benign	1	0.4413	0.3024	9.3987	0	1
3	fog	syn_fog_0080_drift_ merge_clusters	1	0.3126	0.5058	9.7274	1	3
4	fog	syn_fog_ 0120_benign	1	0.3519	0.4438	8.0050	1	4
5	night	syn_night_ 0180_benign	1	0.4875	0.2294	11.4991	0	1
6	fog	syn_fog_ 0130_benign	0	0.7159	0.0000	12.9477	0	4
7	night	syn_night_0210_ drift_break_loop	1	0.4591	0.2743	9.8424	0	2
8	fog	syn_fog_ 0110_benign	1	0.3633	0.4257	8.7261	1	5
9	rain	syn_rain_ 0240_benign	0	0.6436	0.0000	10.4750	0	1
10	fog	syn_fog_0090_drift_ merge_clusters	0	0.6442	0.0000	9.6814	0	5
11	clear_day	syn_clear_day_ 0000_benign	1	0.4844	0.2343	8.8638	0	1
12	clear_day	syn_clear_day_ 0030_benign	1	0.3405	0.4617	8.1468	0	2
13	night	syn_night_0190_ benign	1	0.5470	0.1354	10.6433	1	3
14	clear_day	syn_clear_day _0020_benign	1	0.5909	0.0659	8.3908	1	3
15	fog	syn_fog_0100_ benign	1	0.3875	0.3874	9.1337	1	6
16	clear_day	syn_clear_day_ 0040_benign	1	0.5192	0.1792	10.8500	1	4

continued on following page

Table 6. Continued

Step	condition	candidate_id	accepted	divergence	consistency_ score	latency_ ms	reference_ updated	Buffer _size _condition
17	clear_day	syn_clear_day_ 0050_benign	1	0.3723	0.4115	10.4141	1	5
18	night	syn_night_0200_ drift_merge_clusters	1	0.5671	0.1035	9.3253	1	4
19	clear_day	syn_clear_day_ 0060_benign	1	0.4207	0.3349	11.2779	1	6
20	rain	syn_rain_0260_ benign	1	0.4960	0.2160	8.7138	0	2
21	night	syn_night_0160_ benign	1	0.4784	0.2438	9.7714	1	5
22	rain	syn_rain_0230_drift_ merge_clusters	1	0.6288	0.0060	9.0051	1	3
23	rain	syn_rain_0280_drift_ merge_clusters	1	0.5138	0.1878	8.4591	1	4
24	clear_day	syn_clear_day_ 0010_benign	1	0.5596	0.1153	9.2011	1	7
25	rain	syn_rain_0220_drift_ merge_clusters	0	0.6623	0.0000	9.1416	0	4
26	rain	syn_rain_0270_ benign	1	0.4568	0.2779	7.9742	1	5
27	night	syn_night_0150_ benign	0	0.6360	0.0000	9.5842	0	5
28	night	syn_night_0170_ drift_break_loop	0	0.6388	0.0000	10.5412	0	5

Reading guide: Read each row as one audit cycle: a candidate arrives, its divergence is scored, acceptance is decided, and latency_ms records the real-time cost of validation. Consistency_score near zero aligns with rejections, while accepted rows indicate admissible topology under the current reference. The reference_updated and buffer_size_condition columns indicate adaptive behavior, showing when the system refreshes its baseline and how much context it retains per condition.

Why it matters: The article's objective extends topology validation from an offline check to a governance mechanism that can operate in-stream, enabling condition-aware control over what enters downstream learning and evaluation. This log demonstrates that acceptance decisions, drift signals, and computational latency can be jointly monitored, linking the methodological structure of Sections 2–4 to an online-capable workflow. It also provides traceability for when adverse conditions trigger rejections or necessitate reference updates, strengthening auditability.

Managerial meaning: Managers can treat this log as an operational dashboard for compliance and safety governance, using acceptance and latency to balance structural assurance against real-time constraints. Reference updates and buffer sizing offer levers to tune responsiveness versus stability, especially in conditions where drift risk is higher. The step-level trace supports incident analysis and continuous improvement by pinpointing which scenario types and regimes cause structural failures and when corrective adaptation was invoked. Figure 9 complements Table 6 by tracing validation latency and topological divergence step by step over the incremental online audit stream.

Figure 9. Online auditing over an incremental stream: validation latency and topological divergence. The plot tracks per-step latency in milliseconds and the corresponding divergence signal as scenarios are audited sequentially. It summarizes whether topology-aware governance can operate continuously while producing actionable drift diagnostics

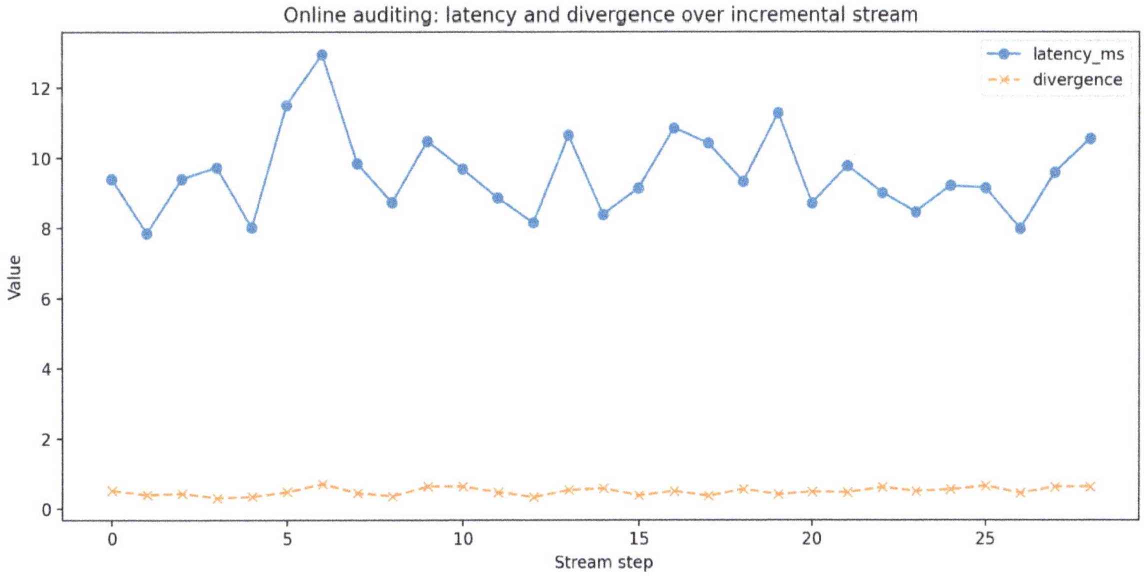

Reading guide: Read the blue curve as the real-time cost of each audit step and the orange curve as the structural drift magnitude for the same step. Stability is indicated when latency stays within a narrow band while divergence remains below the tolerance implied by the validation gate. Spikes in divergence should be interpreted as candidates that are more likely to be rejected or to trigger reference adaptation under the online protocol.

Why it matters: The article's objective requires extending topology validation beyond offline reporting into a deployable auditing mechanism with measurable runtime and interpretable drift signals. This figure demonstrates the joint behavior of computational overhead and structural fidelity over time, linking methodological design to operational feasibility. It also supports robustness and safety analyses by showing that drift can be monitored continuously rather than inferred post hoc.

Managerial meaning: Managers can use the latency trace to set service-level budgets for validation and to decide when to batch, throttle, or prioritize audits under workload constraints. The divergence trace enables early-warning monitoring, supporting escalation or fallback policies when structural drift rises in production-like streams. Together, the curves provide a practical control panel for balancing governance rigor against real-time performance requirements.

6. DISCUSSION AND CONCLUSIONS

6.1 Interpretation and Implications: What "Topological Efficiency" Enables in Digital-Twin Reliability and Interoperability

Topological efficiency redefines digital-twin efficiency as reliability under explicit structural constraints: acceleration counts only when learned representations and synthetic scenario expansions remain consistent with the invariant geometry of real driving data, not simply when simulation is faster or throughput is higher. In this perspective, persistent-homology signatures act as compact, multi-scale integrity markers that capture connectivity and loop-like organization, the very relations most vulnerable to silent degradation when synthetic generation or simulator control is scaled without governance. Calibrated bottleneck and Wasserstein tolerances turn these signatures into an enforceable acceptance rule that filters, reweights, or blocks synthetic batches and incremental updates whenever topological divergence exceeds a risk-sensitive threshold. Evaluation thus becomes structurally grounded, preventing apparent gains from invalid data and showing when clean-test improvements fail under perturbations, stress, or rare events. Efficiency therefore becomes a measurable, auditable, deployment-ready reliability contract for the digital-twin pipeline.

The same mechanism strengthens interoperability by making structural validity portable: topology-based summaries are largely modality- and simulator-agnostic, so they serve as a compact structural checksum across heterogeneous sensors, embeddings, and platforms while preserving a common language for fidelity to real-world geometry. Cross-system comparability therefore depends less on matching rendering artifacts or simulator aesthetics and more on invariant-preserving agreement in the relational structure that governs perception and planning, which matters when consolidating scenario libraries, transferring twins across vendors or environments, or auditing software and model changes. In fast-evolving digital-twin ecosystems, topology-aware validation provides a stable reference for detecting subtle structural drift even when conventional statistics or benchmark scores remain unchanged. By linking fidelity, downstream performance, and computational cost through an accountable gate that also exposes overhead and latency, Topological Efficiency supports offline curation and online auditing under real runtime budgets, offering a deployment-ready reliability contract for scalable, auditable, and safe interoperability in multi-stakeholder autonomous-driving workflows.

6.2 Limitations and Consolidated Conclusions: Validity Boundaries, Practical Constraints, and Final Takeaways

The validity of the proposed Topological Efficiency framework depends on the representativeness of the reference topology, the stability of filtration settings, and the calibration of tolerance thresholds, so the gate certifies fidelity only relative to the structure already observed by the twin. Practical deployment must therefore combine selective topology auditing, condition-prioritized validation, adaptive thresholds, approximate persistence when latency is critical, and scheduled refreshing of the reference buffer for under-represented regimes. Under those conditions, topology-constrained governance remains valuable because it improves auditability, exposes robustness gaps and hazard-miss risks beyond headline metrics, and provides a portable structural criterion for comparing regimes, versions, and updates.

7. FUTURE WORK

7.1 Research Agenda: Differentiable Topology, Multi-Agent/Fleet Extensions, Benchmarking, and Deployment Pathways

Research should move from post hoc topology checks to differentiable topology, enabling end-to-end training in which latent representations and generators preserve persistence signatures under calibrated constraints. This would align structural fidelity with learning, reduce hard rejection gates, and support auditable tolerance learning adapted to condition, risk, and coverage. Multi-agent and fleet twins should model inter-vehicle topology, propagate gates across shared libraries, and audit drift at agent and collective levels. Benchmarking should standardize datasets and topology-aware metrics across simulators, modalities, and budgets. Deployment should prioritize online auditing, accelerated persistence approximations, and governance hooks linking alarms to retraining, rollback, and compliance reporting.

Availability of code: Table A2 provides the compact pseudocode summary of the workflow, while the full Python implementation for data generation, perturbation simulations, autoencoder training, and topological metrics is available at: https://github.com/JAIME6609/TE/blob/main/CODE-ART-1-02.py. It supports reproducibility of the computational pipeline and the resulting figures and tables.

REFERENCES

Atienza, N., González-Díaz, R., & Soriano-Trigueros, M. (2020). On the Stability of Persistent Entropy and new Summary Functions for Topological Data Analysis. *Pattern Recognition, 107*, 107509. DOI: 10.1016/j.patcog.2020.107509

Barricelli, B. R., Casiraghi, E., & Fogli, D. (2019). A Survey on Digital Twin: Definitions, Characteristics, Applications, and Design Implications. *IEEE Access : Practical Innovations, Open Solutions, 7*, 167653–167671. DOI: 10.1109/ACCESS.2019.2953499

Bauer, U. (2021). Ripser: Efficient Computation of Vietoris–Rips Persistence Barcodes. *Journal of Applied and Computational Topology, 5*(3), 391–423. DOI: 10.1007/s41468-021-00071-5

Bhatti, G., Mohan, H., & Raja Singh, R. (2021). Towards the Future of Smart Electric Vehicles: Digital Twin Technology. *Renewable & Sustainable Energy Reviews, 141*, 110801. DOI: 10.1016/j.rser.2021.110801

Boyes, H., & Watson, T. (2022). Digital Twins: An Analysis Framework and Open Issues. *Computers in Industry, 143*, 103763. DOI: 10.1016/j.compind.2022.103763

Chazal, F., & Michel, B. (2021). An Introduction to Topological Data Analysis: Fundamental and Practical Aspects for Data Scientists. *Frontiers in Artificial Intelligence, 4*, 667963. DOI: 10.3389/frai.2021.667963

Chen, D., & Lv, Z. (2022). Artificial Intelligence enabled Digital Twins for Training Autonomous Cars. *Internet of Things and Cyber-Physical Systems, 2*, 31–41. DOI: 10.1016/j.iotcps.2022.05.001

Chen, M., Wang, D., Feng, S., & Zhang, Y. (2023). Topological Regularization for Representation Learning via Persistent Homology. *Mathematics, 11*(4), 1008. DOI: 10.3390/math11041008

Chen, S., & Wang, Y. (2025). Approximation Algorithms for 1-Wasserstein Distance between Persistence Diagrams. *Computational Geometry, 129*, 102190. DOI: 10.1016/j.comgeo.2025.102190

Clough, J. R., Byrne, N., Oksuz, I., Zimmer, V. A., Schnabel, J. A., & King, A. P. (2022). A Topological Loss Function for Deep-Learning Based Image Segmentation Using Persistent Homology. *IEEE Transactions on Pattern Analysis and Machine Intelligence, 44*(12), 8766–8778. DOI: 10.1109/TPAMI.2020.3013679

Čufar, M., & Virk, Ž. (2023). Fast Computation of Persistent Homology Representatives with Involuted Persistent Homology. *Foundations of Data Science (Springfield, Mo.), 5*(4), 466–479. DOI: 10.3934/fods.2023006

da Silva Mendonça, R., de Oliveira Lins, S., de Bessa, I. V., de Carvalho Ayres, F. A.Jr, de Medeiros, R. L. P., & de Lucena, V. F.Jr. (2022). Digital Twin Applications: A Survey of Recent Advances and Challenges. *Processes (Basel, Switzerland), 10*(4), 744. DOI: 10.3390/pr10040744

Fuller, A., Fan, Z., Day, C., & Barlow, C. (2020). Digital Twin: Enabling Technologies, Challenges and Open Research. *IEEE Access : Practical Innovations, Open Solutions, 8*, 108952–108971. DOI: 10.1109/ACCESS.2020.2998358

Goyal, M., & Mahmoud, Q. H. (2024). A Systematic Review of Synthetic Data Generation Techniques using Generative AI. *Electronics (Basel), 13*(17), 3509. DOI: 10.3390/electronics13173509

Hensel, N., Moor, M., & Rieck, B. (2021). A Survey of Topological Machine Learning Methods. *Frontiers in Artificial Intelligence*, *4*, 681108. DOI: 10.3389/frai.2021.681108

Islambekov, U., & Pathirana, H. (2024). Vector Summaries of Persistence Diagrams for Permutation-based Hypothesis Testing. *Foundations of Data Science (Springfield, Mo.)*, *6*(1), 41–61. DOI: 10.3934/fods.2024002

Jang, I. S., Li, B., Kwon, S., & Han, J.-H. (2024). Synthetic Training Dataset Generation Using a Digital Twin-based Autonomous Driving Simulator. *Sensors and Materials*, *36*(9), 4029–4041. DOI: 10.18494/SAM5343

Jia, L., Yang, D., Ren, Y., Qian, C., Feng, Q., Sun, B., & Wang, Z. (2024). A dynamic test scenario generation method for autonomous vehicles based on conditional generative adversarial imitation learning. *Accident; Analysis and Prevention*, *194*, 107279. DOI: 10.1016/j.aap.2023.107279

Jin, Y., McDaniel, R., Tatro, N. J., Catanzaro, M. J., Smith, A. D., Bendich, P., Dwyer, M. B., & Fletcher, P. T. (2024). Implications of Data Topology for Deep Generative Models. *Frontiers of Computer Science*, *6*, 1260604. DOI: 10.3389/fcomp.2024.1260604

Kozlov, D. N. (2020). A Combinatorial Method to Compute Explicit Homology Cycles using Discrete Morse Theory. *Journal of Applied and Computational Topology*, *4*(1), 79–100. DOI: 10.1007/s41468-019-00042-x

Kreuzberger, D., Kühl, N., & Hirschl, S. (2023). Machine Learning Operations (MLOps): Overview, Definition, and Architecture. *IEEE Access : Practical Innovations, Open Solutions*, *11*, 31866–31879. DOI: 10.1109/ACCESS.2023.3262138

Leipzig, J., Nüst, D., Hoyt, C. T., Ram, K., & Greenberg, J. (2021). The Role of Metadata in Reproducible Computational Research. *Patterns (New York, N.Y.)*, *2*(9), 100322. DOI: 10.1016/j.patter.2021.100322

Miller, L., Navarro, P. J., & Rosique, F. (2025). EdgeNet: An end-to-end Deep Neural Network Pre-trained with Synthetic Data for a Real-world Autonomous Driving Application. *Sensors (Basel)*, *25*(1), 89. DOI: 10.3390/s25010089

Obayashi, I. (2018). Volume-optimal cycle: Tightest Representative Cycle of a Generator in Persistent Homology. *SIAM Journal on Applied Algebra and Geometry*, *2*(4), 508–534. DOI: 10.1137/17M1159439

Ren, D., Huang, H., Li, Y., & Jin, J. (2025). High-risk Test Scenario Generation for Autonomous Vehicles at Roundabouts using Naturalistic Driving Data. *Applied Sciences (Basel, Switzerland)*, *15*(8), 4505. DOI: 10.3390/app15084505

Rombach, R., Blattmann, A., Lorenz, D., Esser, P., & Ommer, B. (2022). High-resolution Image Synthesis with Latent Diffusion Models. In *Proceedings of the IEEE/CVF Conference on Computer Vision and Pattern Recognition (CVPR)* (pp. 10684–10695). DOI: 10.1109/CVPR52688.2022.01042

Sarker, M. A. L., Sarker, M. O. F., & Han, D. S. (2025). A Survey on Digital Twin-assisted Intelligent Vehicle Localization. *ICT Express*, *11*(5), 981–992. DOI: 10.1016/j.icte.2025.08.008

Semeraro, C., Lezoche, M., Panetto, H., & Dassisti, M. (2021). Digital Twin Paradigm: A Systematic Literature Review. *Computers in Industry*, *130*, 103469. DOI: 10.1016/j.compind.2021.103469

Song, Z., He, Z., Li, X., Ma, Q., Ming, R., Mao, Z., Pei, H., Peng, L., Hu, J., Yao, D., & Zhang, Y. (2024). Synthetic Datasets for Autonomous Driving: A Survey. *IEEE Transactions on Intelligent Vehicles*, *9*(1), 1847–1864. DOI: 10.1109/TIV.2023.3331024

Su, Z., Liu, X., Bou Hamdan, L., Maroulas, V., Wu, J., Carlsson, G., & Wei, G.-W. (2026). Topological Data Analysis and Topological Deep Learning beyond Persistent Homology: A Review. *Artificial Intelligence Review*, *59*(2), 58. DOI: 10.1007/s10462-025-11462-w

Tan, B., & Matta, A. (2024). The Digital Twin Synchronization Problem: Framework, Formulations, and Analysis. *IISE Transactions*, *56*(6), 652–665. DOI: 10.1080/24725854.2023.2253869

Tralie, C., Saul, N., & Bar-On, R. (2018). Ripser.py: A Lean Persistent Homology Library for Python. *Journal of Open Source Software*, *3*(29), 925. DOI: 10.21105/joss.00925

VanDerHorn, E., & Mahadevan, S. (2021). Digital Twin: Generalization, Characterization and Implementation. *Decision Support Systems*, *145*, 113524. DOI: 10.1016/j.dss.2021.113524

Zhou, C., Dong, Z., & Lin, H. (2022). Learning Persistent Homology of 3D Point Clouds. *Computers & Graphics*, *102*, 269–279. DOI: 10.1016/j.cag.2021.10.022

Zhu, J. (2024). Synthetic Data Generation by Diffusion Models. *National Science Review*, *11*(8), nwae276. Advance online publication. DOI: 10.1093/nsr/nwae276

Zia, Q., Jan, A., Yang, D., Zhang, H., & Li, Y. (2025). Optimized Real-time Decision Making with EfficientNet in Digital Twin-based Vehicular Networks. *Electronics (Basel)*, *14*(6), 1084. DOI: 10.3390/electronics14061084

Compilation of References

3GPP. (2023). *Technical specification group services and system aspects; Study on enhancement of 5G support for V2X services (Release 18)*. 3rd Generation Partnership Project. https://www.3gpp.org

3GPP. (2025). Study on enhancement of 5G and beyond support for V2X services (Release 19). 3rd Generation Partnership Project. https://www.3gpp.org/specifications

Abboush, M., Knieke, C., & Rausch, A. (2024). A Virtual Testing Framework for Real-Time Validation of Automotive Software Systems Based on Hardware in the Loop and Fault Injection. *Sensors (Basel)*, *24*(12), 3733. Advance online publication. DOI: 10.3390/s24123733 PMID: 38931515

Abdullah, S. M. (2025). Inventory Optimization in Global Automotive Manufacturing Supply Chains. *Journal of Procurement and Supply Chain Management*. DOI: 10.58425/jpscm.v4i1.377

Abushaega, M. M., González, A. D., & Moshebah, O. Y. (2024). A fairness-based multi-objective distribution and restoration model for enhanced resilience of supply chain transportation networks. *Reliability Engineering & System Safety*, *251*, 110314. DOI: 10.1016/j.ress.2024.110314

Acharya, S., Khan, A. A., & Päivärinta, T. (2024). Interoperability levels and challenges of digital twins in cyber-physical systems. *Journal of Industrial Information Integration*, *42*, 100714. DOI: 10.1016/j.jii.2024.100714

Achenef, T. B., Abera, S. N., Admas, Y. A., & Tegegne, S. Z. (2025). Latest breakthroughs, research results, and challenges in intelligent control of autonomous vehicles. Proceedings of the Institution of Mechanical Engineers, Part D: Journal of Automobile Engineering. DOI: 10.1177/09544070251327616

Afraj, S., Böhmländer, D., Vaculín, O., & Hynčík, L. (2021). Quantification methodology for crash behavior comparison between virtual crash simulations and real-time crash tests. *FISITA World Congress 2021 - Technical Programme*. DOI: 10.46720/F2021-PIF-072

Aghaabbasi, M., & Sabri, S. (2025). Potentials of digital twin system for analyzing travel behavior decisions. *Travel Behaviour & Society*, *38*, 100902. DOI: 10.1016/j.tbs.2024.100902

Aghaei Anvigh, A., Khavan, Y., & Pourghebleh, B. (2024). Transforming vehicular networks: How 6G can revolutionize intelligent transportation? *Science Engineering and Technology*, *4*(1), 80–93. DOI: 10.54327/set2024/v4.i1.127

Agnusdei, G. P., Elia, V., & Gnoni, M. G. (2021). Is digital Twin technology supporting safety management? A bibliometric and systematic review. *Applied Sciences (Basel, Switzerland)*, *11*(6), 2767. DOI: 10.3390/app11062767

Agrawal, A., Fischer, M., & Singh, V. (2022). Digital twin: From concept to practice. *Journal of Management Engineering, 38*(3), 06022001. Advance online publication. DOI: 10.1061/(ASCE)ME.1943-5479.0001034

Aheleroff, S., Xu, X., Lu, Y., & Aristizabal, M. (2021). Digital twin as a service (DTaaS) in Industry 4.0: An architecture reference model. *Advanced Engineering Informatics, 47*, 101225. DOI: 10.1016/j.aei.2020.101225

Ahmadi, H., Nag, A., Khar, Z., Sayrafian, K., & Rahardja, S. (2021). Networked twins and twins of networks: An overview on the relationship between digital twins and 6G. *IEEE Communications Standards Magazine, 5*(4), 154–160. DOI: 10.1109/MCOMSTD.0001.2000041

Ahmad, Y. A. B., Kolachina, S., Rajest, S. S., Singh, M., Mishra, A., & Sundar, S. S. (2024). Impact of digital HRM on academicians' performance: Exploring the mediating role of organisational commitment. *International Journal of Intelligent Enterprise, 12*(1), 1–21. DOI: 10.1504/IJIE.2025.143439

Ahmed, M., Khan, W. U., Ihsan, A., Li, X., Li, J., & Tsiftsis, T. A. (2022). Backscatter sensors communication for 6G low-powered NOMA-enabled IoT networks under imperfect SIC. *IEEE Systems Journal, 16*(4), 5883–5893. DOI: 10.1109/JSYST.2022.3194705

Al Ridhawi, I., Aloqaily, M., Bany Salameh, H., & Jararweh, Y. (2025). Digital twin-enabled V2X for resilient autonomous transportation systems. *IEEE Communications Magazine, 63*(2), 30–37. DOI: 10.1109/MCOM.001.2500051

Alaba, S. Y., Gurbuz, A. C., & Ball, J. E. (2024). Emerging trends in autonomous vehicle perception: Multimodal fusion for 3D object detection. *World Electric Vehicle Journal, 15*(1), 20. DOI: 10.3390/wevj15010020

Alfaro-Viquez, D., Zamora-Hernandez, M., Fernandez-Vega, M., Garcia-Rodriguez, J., & Azorin-Lopez, J. (2025). A comprehensive review of AI-based digital twin applications in manufacturing: Integration across operator, product, and process dimensions. *Electronics (Basel), 14*(4), 646. DOI: 10.3390/electronics14040646

Alharbi, F., Zakariah, M., Alshahrani, R., Albakri, A., Viriyasitavat, W., & Alghamdi, A. A. (2023). Intelligent transportation using wireless sensor networks, blockchain and license plate recognition. *Sensors (Basel), 23*(5), 2670. DOI: 10.3390/s23052670 PMID: 36904873

Ali, A., Huang, J., Jabbar, A., Ali, M., & Ali, S. (2025). Federated learning for connected autonomous vehicles: Enhancing mobility, safety, and sustainability. *Physica Scripta, 100*(7), 072001. DOI: 10.1088/1402-4896/addca2

Alipour Sormoli, M., Koufos, K., Dianati, M., & Woodman, R. (2024). A survey on hybrid motion planning methods for automated driving systems. https://doi.org//arXiv.2406.05575DOI: 10.48550

Ali, W. A., Fanti, M. P., Roccotelli, M., & Ranieri, L. (2023). A review of digital twin technology for electric and autonomous vehicles. *Applied Sciences (Basel, Switzerland), 13*(10), 5871. DOI: 10.3390/app13105871

Ali, W., Roccotelli, M., & Fanti, M. P. (2022). Digital twin in intelligent transportation systems. *RE:view*, 576–581. Advance online publication. DOI: 10.1109/CoDIT55151.2022.9804017

Almeaibed, S., Al-Rubaye, S., Tsourdos, A., & Avdelidis, N. P. (2021a). Digital twin analysis to promote safety and security in autonomous vehicles. *IEEE Communications Standards Magazine*, *5*(1), 40–46. DOI: 10.1109/MCOMSTD.011.2100004

Amanatidis, P., Lyratzis, E., Angelopoulos, V., Kouloumpris, E., Skaperdas, E., Bassiliades, N., Vlahavas, I., Maris, F., Emmanouloudis, D., & Karampatzakis, D. (2025). Intelligent water management through edge-enabled IoT, AI, and big data technologies. *IoT*, *7*(1), 5. DOI: 10.3390/iot7010005

Amoozad Mahdiraji, H., Yaftiyan, F., Abbasi-Kamardi, A., Vrontis, D., & Gong, Y. (2024). Disentangling the resiliency of international transportation systems under uncertainty by a novel multi-layer spherical fuzzy decision-making framework: Evidence from an emerging economy. *Transportation Research Part A, Policy and Practice*, *186*, 104151. DOI: 10.1016/j.tra.2024.104151

Anandkumar, A., Sambasivam, R., Ashokan, A., Sekar, J. C., & Balu, K. (2025). Digital twin-based condition monitoring and predictive maintenance in transportation systems. *Results in Engineering*, *21*, 106336. DOI: 10.1016/j.rineng.2025.106336

Anusha, M. P., & Department of CSE Hyderabad., G. N. I. of T. (2024). A review of machine learning. INTERANTIONAL JOURNAL OF SCIENTIFIC RESEARCH IN ENGINEERING AND MANAGEMENT, 08(06), 1–5. DOI: 10.55041/IJSREM35355

Anwar, S., Panda, U., & Mohapatra, H. (2024). Legal and ethical issues in IoT based smart city: Data privacy, surveillance, and citizen rights. *Journal of Computer Science Engineering and Software Testing*, *10*(2), 17–26. DOI: 10.46610/JOCSES.2024.v10i02.003

Application of digital twins to improve automotive assembly processes. (2022). In *Truck*. DOI: 10.36652/1684-1298-2022-7-11-17

Arulvendhan, K., Srinivasan, P., & Kabilan, D. (2025). Dynamic wireless power transfer for electric vehicles: A high-frequency converter and battery charging perspective. *AVE Trends in Intelligent Energy Letters*, *1*(2), 61–70. DOI: 10.64091/ATIEL.2025.000186

Ashja-Ardalan, S., Alesheikh, A. A., Sharif, M., & Wittowsky, D. (2025). Resilience of urban road networks to climate change: A spatial-topological approach. *Transportation Research Part D, Transport and Environment*, *148*, 104948. DOI: 10.1016/j.trd.2025.104948

Atienza, N., González-Díaz, R., & Soriano-Trigueros, M. (2020). On the Stability of Persistent Entropy and new Summary Functions for Topological Data Analysis. *Pattern Recognition*, *107*, 107509. DOI: 10.1016/j.patcog.2020.107509

Atmakuri, N. B. (2025). Recent advances in automotive cybersecurity: From secure boot to vehicle-to-Everything communication. *European Modern Studies Journal*, *9*(4), 1085–1098. DOI: 10.59573/emsj.9(4).2025.101

Attaran, M., & Celik, B. G. (2023). Digital twin: Benefits, use cases, challenges, and opportunities. *Decision Analytics Journal*, *6*, 100165. DOI: 10.1016/j.dajour.2023.100165

Auweraer, H., Anthonis, J., De Bruyne, S., & Leuridan, J. (2013). Virtual engineering at work: The challenges for designing mechatronic products. *Engineering with Computers*, *29*(3), 389–408. DOI: 10.1007/s00366-012-0286-6

Avevor, J., Adeniyi, M., Enyejo, L. A., & Aikins, S. A. (2024). Machine Learning-driven predictive modeling for FRP strengthened structural elements: A review of AI-based damage detection, fatigue prediction, and structural health monitoring. International Journal of Scientific Research and Modern Technology, 1–20. DOI: 10.38124/ijsrmt.v3i8.420

Avram, S. (2026). Advancing urban analytics: Geo AI applications in spatial decision-making and sustainable cities. *Urban Science (Basel, Switzerland)*, *10*(3), 148. Advance online publication. DOI: 10.3390/urbansci10030148

Babaei, P., Riahinia, N., Ebadati, E. O. M., & Azimi, A. (2025). Towards a data-driven digital twin AI-based architecture for self-driving vehicles. *IET Intelligent Transport Systems*, *19*(1), e70017. Advance online publication. DOI: 10.1049/itr2.70017

Babu, K. A., Arulvendhan, K., Srinivasan, P., Ahmad, M. A., Prabha, A., Thariq, M. M., Ali, M. M. S., & Angelin, C. C. (2024). Economical infotainment solution augmented with advanced telematics for collision detection, vehicle localization, and real-time health status monitoring. AVE Trends in Intelligent Health Letters, 1(4), 206–216. https://www.avepubs.com/user/journals/article_details/ATIHL/88

Baimukhanov, S., Ali, H., & Yazici, A. (2025). Enhancing ML-based anomaly detection in data management for security through integration of IoT, cloud, and edge computing. *Expert Systems with Applications*, *293*, 128700. DOI: 10.1016/j.eswa.2025.128700

Bajwa, M. U., Saleh, W., & Fountas, G. (2025). Identifying a framework for implementing Vision Zero approach to road safety in low- and middle-income countries: A qualitative perspective. *Safety (Basel, Switzerland)*, *11*(4), 93. Advance online publication. DOI: 10.3390/safety11040093

Balderas, D., Ortiz, A., Méndez, E., Ponce, P., & Molina, A. (2021). Empowering digital twin for Industry 4.0 using metaheuristic optimization algorithms: Case study PCB drilling optimization. *International Journal of Advanced Manufacturing Technology*, *113*(5–6), 1295–1306. DOI: 10.1007/s00170-021-06649-8

Balla, M., Haffner, O., Kučera, E., & Cigánek, J. (2023). Educational Case Studies: Creating a Digital Twin of the Production Line in TIA Portal, Unity, and Game4Automation Framework. *Sensors (Basel)*, *23*(10), 4977. Advance online publication. DOI: 10.3390/s23104977 PMID: 37430895

Bambura, R., Šolc, M., Dado, M., & Kotek, L. (2020). Implementation of Digital Twin for Engine Block Manufacturing Processes. *Applied Sciences (Basel, Switzerland)*, *10*(18), 6578. DOI: 10.3390/app10186578

Bao, J., Guo, D., Li, J., & Zhang, J. (2018). The modelling and operations for the digital twin in the context of manufacturing. *Enterprise Information Systems*, *13*(4), 534–556. DOI: 10.1080/17517575.2018.1526324

Barabás, I., Iclodean, C., Beles, H., Antonya, C., Molea, A., & Scurt, F. B. (2025). An Approach to Modeling and Developing Virtual Sensors Used in the Simulation of Autonomous Vehicles. *Sensors (Basel)*, *25*(11), 3338. Advance online publication. DOI: 10.3390/s25113338 PMID: 40968833

Barbie, A., & Hasselbring, W. (2024). From Digital Twins to Digital Twin Prototypes: Concepts, Formalization, and Applications. *IEEE Access : Practical Innovations, Open Solutions*, *12*, 75337–75365. DOI: 10.1109/ACCESS.2024.3406510

Barricelli, B. R., Casiraghi, E., & Fogli, D. (2019). A survey on digital twin: Definitions, characteristics, applications, and design implications. *IEEE Access : Practical Innovations, Open Solutions*, *7*, 167653–167671. DOI: 10.1109/ACCESS.2019.2953499

Barsi, Á., Potó, V., Lógó, J. M., & Krausz, N. (2020). Creating an OpenDRIVE model of the campus of the Budapest University of technology and Economics for automotive simulations. *Periodica Polytechnica. Civil Engineering*. Advance online publication. DOI: 10.3311/PPci.16768

Bashir, T., Bergantino, A. S., Troiani, G., Henke, I., & Pagliara, F. (2025). Vulnerability and resilience analysis of road network: A systematic literature review using Bibliometric. *Sustainable Futures : An Applied Journal of Technology, Environment and Society*, *10*, 101142. DOI: 10.1016/j.sftr.2025.101142

Bauer, U. (2021). Ripser: Efficient Computation of Vietoris–Rips Persistence Barcodes. *Journal of Applied and Computational Topology*, *5*(3), 391–423. DOI: 10.1007/s41468-021-00071-5

Bednarz, T., Baier, A., & Paprocka, I. (2024). A Framework for Communicating and Building a Digital Twin Model of the Electric Car. *Applied Sciences (Basel, Switzerland)*, *14*(5), 1776. Advance online publication. DOI: 10.3390/app14051776

Bedulli, F., Leite, R., Freitas, F., Murari, T., & Winkler, I. (2024). Optimizing Automotive Product Development: Integration of Electronic Control Units and Virtual Prototypes Using Virtual Reality. *SAE Technical Paper Series*. DOI: 10.4271/2023-36-0111

Behrendt, S., Altenmüller, T., May, M., Kuhnle, A., & Lanza, G. (2025). Real-to-sim: Automatic simulation model generation for a digital twin in semiconductor manufacturing. *Journal of Intelligent Manufacturing*. Advance online publication. DOI: 10.1007/s10845-025-02572-x

Bella, F., Gulisano, F., & Gagliardi, V. (2025). Crash risk of automated vehicles in mixed traffic: A driving simulator study. *Accident; Analysis and Prevention*, *200*, 107809. DOI: 10.1016/j.aap.2024.107809 PMID: 39395369

Bergantino, A. S., Gardelli, A., & Rotaris, L. (2024). Assessing transport network resilience: Empirical insights from real-world data studies. *Transport Reviews*, *44*(4), 834–857. DOI: 10.1080/01441647.2024.2322434

Bhatti, G., Mohan, H., & Raja Singh, R. (2021). Towards the Future of Smart Electric Vehicles: Digital Twin Technology. *Renewable & Sustainable Energy Reviews*, *141*, 110801. DOI: 10.1016/j.rser.2021.110801

Biesinger, F., & Weyrich, M. (2019). The Facets of Digital Twins in Production and the Automotive Industry. *2019 23rd International Conference on Mechatronics Technology (ICMT)*, 1–6. DOI: 10.1109/ICMECT.2019.8932101

Bi, L., Shuai, B., Liu, Z., Sun, Y., & Yang, F. (2026). ODPL: An objective-driven decomposed policy learning framework for urban autonomous driving control. *Applied Soft Computing*, *192*, 114781. DOI: 10.1016/j.asoc.2026.114781

Bisht, L. S., & Tiwari, G. (2023). Identification of road traffic crashes hotspots on an intercity expressway in India using geospatial techniques. *IATSS Research*, *47*(3), 349–356. DOI: 10.1016/j.iatssr.2023.07.003

Biswas, A., & Wang, H.-C. (2023). Autonomous vehicles enabled by the integration of IoT, edge intelligence, 5G, and blockchain. *Sensors (Basel)*, *23*(4), 1963. DOI: 10.3390/s23041963 PMID: 36850560

Bogdevičius, M., Kojis, P., & Skrickij, V. (2025). Digital twin of a vehicle suspension system for ride comfort analysis and optimization. *Applied Sciences (Basel, Switzerland)*, *15*(16), 8933. DOI: 10.3390/app15168933

Boschert, S., & Rosen, R. (2016). Digital twin—The simulation aspect. In *Mechatronic futures* (pp. 59–74). Springer.

Botín-Sanabria, D. M., Mihaita, A.-S., Peimbert-García, R. E., Ramírez-Moreno, M. A., Ramírez-Mendoza, R. A., & Lozoya-Santos, J. de J. (2022). Digital twin technology challenges and applications: A comprehensive review. *Remote Sensing (Basel)*, *14*(6), 1335. DOI: 10.3390/rs14061335

Böttjer, T., Tola, D., Kakavandi, F., Wewer, C., Ramanujan, D., Gomes, C., Larsen, P., & Iosifidis, A. (2023). A review of unit level digital twin applications in the manufacturing industry. *CIRP Journal of Manufacturing Science and Technology*, *45*, 162–189. Advance online publication. DOI: 10.1016/j.cirpj.2023.06.011

Boyes, H., & Watson, T. (2022). Digital Twins: An Analysis Framework and Open Issues. *Computers in Industry*, *143*, 103763. DOI: 10.1016/j.compind.2022.103763

Campolo, C., Genovese, G., Molinaro, A., Pizzimenti, B., Ruggeri, G., & Zappalà, D. M. (2024). An Edge-Based Digital Twin Framework for Connected and Autonomous Vehicles: Design and Evaluation. *IEEE Access : Practical Innovations, Open Solutions*, *12*, 46290–46303. DOI: 10.1109/ACCESS.2024.3382001

Cantas, M. R., & Guvenc, L. (2023). *Customized co-simulation environment for autonomous driving algorithm development and evaluation.*

Cao, Z., Dong, H., Jide, J., & Yi, S. (2024). Research on Intelligent Manufacturing Production Lines for Automobile Wheel Hubs by Digital Twin Models. *2024 3rd International Conference on Data Analytics, Computing and Artificial Intelligence (ICDACAI)*, 825–829. DOI: 10.1109/ICDACAI65086.2024.00155

Cao, J., Leng, S., Xiong, K., & Chen, X. (2025). 6G-enabled autonomous driving: Requirements, challenges, and key technologies. *Tsinghua Science and Technology*, *30*(1), 102–111. DOI: 10.26599/TST.2024.9010076

Cao, X., Yao, M., Zhang, Y., Hu, X., & Wu, C. (2023). Digital Twin Modeling and Simulation Optimization of Transmission Front and Middle Case Assembly Line. *Computer Modeling in Engineering &amp. The Sciences*. Advance online publication. DOI: 10.32604/cmes.2023.030773

Cardoso, E. U., & Ferreira, J. L. A. (2022). Estimation of fatigue life under random multiaxial conditions using the projection-by-projection method. *Journal of the Brazilian Society of Mechanical Sciences and Engineering*, *44*(11), 570. DOI: 10.1007/s40430-022-03869-1

Carvalho, T. P., Soares, F. A. A. M. N., Vita, R., Francisco, R. P., Basto, J. P., & Alcalá, S. G. S. (2019). A systematic literature review of machine learning methods applied to predictive maintenance. *Computers & Industrial Engineering*, *137*, 106024. DOI: 10.1016/j.cie.2019.106024

Chai, X., Yan, J., Zhang, W., Sulowicz, M., & Feng, Y. (2024). Recent progress on digital twins in intelligent connected vehicles: A review. *Elektronika ir Elektrotechnika*, *30*(2), 4–17. DOI: 10.5755/j02.eie.36209

Challoumis, C. (2025b). The impact factor of Tangibles and Intangibles of controlled transactions on economic performance. *Economic Alternatives, 31*(1), 64–76. https://doi.org/https://doi.org/10.37075/EA.2025.1.04

Challoumis, C. (2025c). THE INFLATION ACCORDING TO THE CYCLE OF MONEY (C.M.). *Economic Alternatives, 2025*(2), 324–353. https://doi.org/https://doi.org/10.37075/EA.2025.2.03

Challoumis, C., Eriotis, N., & Vasiliou, D. (2025). Social Movements' Impact on the Greek Economy During the Financial Crisis. *Economies, 13*(9), 269. https://doi.org/https://doi.org/10.3390/economies13090269

Challoumis, C. (2023). FROM SAVINGS TO ESCAPE AND ENFORCEMENT SAVINGS. *Cógito (Salvador)*, *XV*(4), 206–216. https://cogito.ucdc.ro/COGITO_DECEMBER_2023.pdf

Challoumis, C. (2024a). From Economics to Economic Engineering (The Cycle of Money): The case of Romania. *Cógito (Salvador)*, *XVII*(2), 161–170. https://cogito.ucdc.ro/issues/COGITO no.2_27062024_BT.pdf

Challoumis, C. (2024b). The Index of the Cycle of Money: The Case of Switzerland. *Journal of Risk and Financial Management*, *17*(4), 135. https://doi.org/https://doi.org/10.3390/jrfm17040135. DOI: 10.3390/jrfm17040135

Challoumis, C. (2025a). Economocracy: Global Economic Governance. *Economies*, *13*(8), 230. DOI: 10.3390/economies13080230

Challoumis, C., & Eriotis, N. (2025). The Impact of Artificial Intelligence on the Greek Economy. *Journal of Open Innovation*, *11*(3), 1–13. https://doi.org/https://doi.org/10.1016/j.joitmc.2025.100578. DOI: 10.1016/j.joitmc.2025.100578

Changalvala, R., & Malik, H. (2019). LiDAR data integrity verification for autonomous vehicle. *IEEE Access : Practical Innovations, Open Solutions*, *7*, 138018–138031. DOI: 10.1109/ACCESS.2019.2943207

Chataut, R., Nankya, M., & Akl, R. (2024). 6G networks and the AI revolution-exploring technologies, applications, and emerging challenges. *Sensors (Basel)*, *24*(6), 1888. DOI: 10.3390/s24061888 PMID: 38544151

Chaturvedi, M., & Srivastava, S. (2025). *Distributed computing and secure storage framework for intelligent transportation system*. International Journal of Intelligent Transportation Systems Research., DOI: 10.1007/s13177-025-00600-x

Chawla, S., & Singari, R. (2023). Modelling and Simulation of Crankcase Cover Manufacturing in the Automobile Industry. *Journal of Scientific &amp. Journal of Scientific and Industrial Research*, *82*(6). Advance online publication. DOI: 10.56042/jsir.v82i06.1816

Chazal, F., & Michel, B. (2021). An Introduction to Topological Data Analysis: Fundamental and Practical Aspects for Data Scientists. *Frontiers in Artificial Intelligence*, *4*, 667963. DOI: 10.3389/frai.2021.667963

Chen, X., Kang, E., Shiraishi, S., Preciado, V., & Jiang, Z. (2018). Digital behavioral twins for safe connected cars. DOI: 10.1145/3239372.3239401

Chen, D., & Lv, Z. (2022). Artificial intelligence enabled digital twins for training autonomous cars. *Internet of Things and Cyber-Physical Systems*, *2*, 31–41. DOI: 10.1016/j.iotcps.2022.05.001

Chen, H., Liu, N. Y., Yang, Y., Wang, Y., Li, Q., & Shan, Y. (2026). Impact effects of transport structure changes on urban traffic congestion: A case study of core cities in China. *Transportation Research Part E, Logistics and Transportation Review*, *208*, 104676. DOI: 10.1016/j.tre.2026.104676

Chen, M., Wang, D., Feng, S., & Zhang, Y. (2023). Topological Regularization for Representation Learning via Persistent Homology. *Mathematics*, *11*(4), 1008. DOI: 10.3390/math11041008

Chen, S., Hu, X., Zhao, J., Wang, R., & Qiao, M. (2024). A review of decision-making and planning for autonomous vehicles in intersection environments. *World Electric Vehicle Journal*, *15*(3), 99. DOI: 10.3390/wevj15030099

Chen, S., & Wang, Y. (2025). Approximation Algorithms for 1-Wasserstein Distance between Persistence Diagrams. *Computational Geometry*, *129*, 102190. DOI: 10.1016/j.comgeo.2025.102190

Chen, X., Jin, Z., Zhang, Q., Li, P., Zhang, S., Sun, J., Tian, X., Wang, Y., & Zhang, J. (2022). Research on automatic driving simulation test system based on digital twin. *Journal of Physics: Conference Series*, *2170*(1), 012039. DOI: 10.1088/1742-6596/2170/1/012039

Chen, Y., Zhou, M., Zhang, M., & Zha, M. (2025). Research on the Construction of Automobile Wheel Hub Intelligent Production Line Based on Digital Twin. *Applied Sciences (Basel, Switzerland)*, *15*(11), 5871. Advance online publication. DOI: 10.3390/app15115871

Chong, J., Kay, P., & Chang, W.-C. (2020). *The Impact of Virtual Environments for Future Electric Powered-Mobility Development Using Human-in-the-Loop: Part A - Fundamental Design and Modelling*. Intelligent and Efficient Transport Systems - Design, Modelling, Control and Simulation., DOI: 10.5772/intechopen.90375

Choudhury, B., Hota, A., Karmakar, M., Saha, S., & Roy, P. (2025). Blockchain-enabled secure V2X communication framework for intelligent transportation systems. *IEEE Access : Practical Innovations, Open Solutions*, *13*, 20783–20793. DOI: 10.1109/ACCESS.2025.3608623

Cigánek, J., & Choma, M. (2025). Simulation and Optimization of Foaming Cabins Utilization on the Production Line. *2025 Cybernetics & Informatics (K&I)*, 1–6. DOI: 10.1109/KI64036.2025.10916427

Ciriaco, T. G. M., Zehra, S. N., Wambura, V., & Wong, S. D. (2025). Equitable transportation and resilience hubs: Analysis of underserved population needs, usage, and travel behavior. *Transportation Research Interdisciplinary Perspectives*, *29*, 101314. DOI: 10.1016/j.trip.2024.101314

Cirillo, S., Polese, G., Salerno, D., Simone, B., & Solimando, G. (2023). Towards Flexible Voice Assistants: Evaluating Privacy and Security Needs in IoT-enabled Smart Homes. FMDB Transactions on Sustainable Computer Letters, 1(1), 25–32. https://www.fmdbpub.com/user/journals/article_details/FTSCL/38

Ciunel, S., Popa, D. L., Gherghina, G., Bogdan, M. L., & Tutunea, D. (2014). Human head-neck system behavior during virtual impact automotive simulations. *Applied Mechanics and Materials*, *659*, 177–182. . DOI: 10.4028/www.scientific.net/AMM.659.177

Clough, J. R., Byrne, N., Oksuz, I., Zimmer, V. A., Schnabel, J. A., & King, A. P. (2022). A Topological Loss Function for Deep-Learning Based Image Segmentation Using Persistent Homology. *IEEE Transactions on Pattern Analysis and Machine Intelligence*, *44*(12), 8766–8778. DOI: 10.1109/TPAMI.2020.3013679

Coleman, J., Madinni, J., Samak, T., Samak, C., McCane, K., Brault, J., Harber, C., Smereka, J. M., Brudnak, M., Gorsich, D., & Krovi, V. (2025). Model-based system engineering framework for verification and validation of cyber-physical vehicle systems. *ASME Letters in Translational Robotics*, *1*(2), 1–9. DOI: 10.1115/1.4069966

Crespi, N., Drobot, A. T., & Minerva, R. (2023). The Digital Twin. In *The Digital Twin* (2nd ed.). Springer International Publishing., https://doi.org/https://doi.org/10.1007/978-3-031-21343-4 DOI: 10.1007/978-3-031-21343-4_1

Crespo-Aguado, M., Lozano, R., Hernandez-Gobertti, F., Molner, N., & Gomez-Barquero, D. (2024). Flexible hyper-distributed IoT–Edge–Cloud platform for real-time Digital Twin applications on 6G-intended testbeds for logistics and industry. *Future Internet*, *16*(11), 431. DOI: 10.3390/fi16110431

Cruz-Oliver, R., Monzón, L., Ramirez-Laboreo, E., & Rodríguez-Fortún, J.-M. (2023). ROM-based stochastic optimization for a continuous manufacturing process. *ISA Transactions*, •••, 1–8. DOI: 10.1016/j.isatra.2024.08.010 PMID: 39147610

Čufar, M., & Virk, Ž. (2023). Fast Computation of Persistent Homology Representatives with Involuted Persistent Homology. *Foundations of Data Science (Springfield, Mo.)*, *5*(4), 466–479. DOI: 10.3934/fods.2023006

Cui, J., Liu, Y., & Nallanathan, A. (2020). Multi-agent reinforcement learning-based resource allocation for UAV networks. *IEEE Transactions on Wireless Communications*, *19*(2), 729–743. DOI: 10.1109/TWC.2019.2935201

D., M., & T., S. (2025). Features of real-time modeling of steelmaking processes using unreal engine 5. *System Technologies*. DOI: 10.34185/1562-9945-6-155-2024-24

da Silva Mendonça, R., de Oliveira Lins, S., de Bessa, I. V., de Carvalho Ayres, F. A.Jr, de Medeiros, R. L. P., & de Lucena, V. F.Jr. (2022). Digital Twin Applications: A Survey of Recent Advances and Challenges. *Processes (Basel, Switzerland)*, *10*(4), 744. DOI: 10.3390/pr10040744

Daly, N., Manvi, P., Chhatbar, T., Schmid, M., Castanier, M., & Wagner, J. (2024). Modeling & Validation of a Digital Twin Tracked Vehicle. *SAE Technical Paper Series*. DOI: 10.4271/2024-01-2323

Damiri, H., Steinberger, M., Kuchler, L., Azimi, A., Martinuzzi, S., Sagmeister, P., Williams, J., Koch, S., Tranninger, M., Rehrl, J., Celikovic, S., Sacher, S., Kappe, C., & Horn, M. (2024). Model-based real-time optimization in continuous pharmaceutical manufacturing. *Computers & Chemical Engineering, 192*, 108915. DOI: 10.1016/j.compchemeng.2024.108915

Damtew, A. W. (2024). Roles of digital twins on material performances and utilization on upstream industry (The case of automotive industry). *International Journal of Advanced Manufacturing Technology, 130*(7-8), 1–12. DOI: 10.1007/s00170-023-12706-1

Dangi, S. B. (2025). Application of machine learning algorithms in autonomous vehicle navigation systems. *INTERNATIONAL JOURNAL OF SCIENTIFIC RESEARCH IN ENGINEERING AND MANAGEMENT, 09*(04), 1–9. DOI: 10.55041/IJSREM46514

de Albuquerque Damasceno, M. A., Maia, J. A., Espíndola Gonçalo, T. E., Rocha, M. K., Cabral Peixoto, J. K., & Ferreira, E. A. (2025). A GIS-MCDA spatial classification model to support group decision-making in traffic crash risk management. *Case Studies on Transport Policy, 20*, 101450. DOI: 10.1016/j.cstp.2025.101450

de Medeiros, A. S., da Silva, M. A. V., Cardoso, M. H. S. A., Santos, T. F., Toro, C., Rojas, G., & Aprigliano, V. (2025). Evaluating urban mobility resilience in Petrópolis through a multicriteria approach. *Urban Science (Basel, Switzerland), 9*(7), 269. DOI: 10.3390/urbansci9070269

Debevec, M., Šimic, M., & Herakovič, N. (2014). VIRTUAL FACTORY AS AN ADVANCED APPROACH FOR PRODUCTION PROCESS OPTIMIZATION. *International Journal of Simulation Modelling, 13*(1), 66–78. DOI: 10.2507/IJSIMM13(1)6.260

Dempsey, C. (n.d.). *Buffers in GIS*. Geography Realm. https://www.geographyrealm.com/buffers-in-gis/

Dengiz, B., Iç, Y., & Belgin, O. (2016). A meta-model based simulation optimization using hybrid simulation-analytical modeling to increase the productivity in automotive industry. *Mathematics and Computers in Simulation, 120*, 120–128. DOI: 10.1016/j.matcom.2015.07.005

Deng, S., Ling, L., Zhang, C., Li, C., Zeng, T., Zhang, K., & Guo, G. (2023). A systematic review on the current research of digital twin in automotive application. *Internet of Things and Cyber-Physical Systems, 3*, 180–191. Advance online publication. DOI: 10.1016/j.iotcps.2023.04.004

Deniz, S., Barzegar, A., Sagirli, F. Y., Vasiloff, S., & Seibold, B. (2025). Real-time digital twin of freeway traffic for incident prediction and management. *Control Engineering Practice, 151*, 106519. DOI: 10.1016/j.conengprac.2025.106519

Department of Mechanical Engineering Bangalore India, A. S. of E., Reddy, G. J., Sharma, D., & Department of Mechanical Engineering Bangalore India, A. S. of E. (2024). Edge AI in autonomous vehicles: Navigating the road to safe and efficient mobility. INTERANTIONAL JOURNAL OF SCIENTIFIC RESEARCH IN ENGINEERING AND MANAGEMENT, 08(01), 1–13. DOI: 10.55041/IJSREM28427

Dhinakaran, D., Edwin Raja, S., Ramathilagam, A., Vennila, G., & Alagulakshmi, A. (2025). Ethical and legal challenges with IoT in home digital twins. *Methods (San Diego, Calif.), 14*, 103409. DOI: 10.1016/j.mex.2025.103409 PMID: 40852565

Directory, P. C. B. (n.d.). *What is digital twin technology in PCB manufacturing?* https://www.pcbdirectory.com/community/what-is-digital-twin-technology-in-pcb-manufacturing

Doan, K., & Ukkusuri, S. V. (2012). On the holding-back problem in the cell transmission based dynamic traffic assignment models. *Transportation Research Part B: Methodological*, *46*(9), 1218–1238. DOI: 10.1016/j.trb.2012.05.001

Doan, K., & Ukkusuri, S. V. (2015). Dynamic system optimal model for multi-OD traffic networks with an advanced spatial queuing model. *Transportation Research Part C, Emerging Technologies*, *51*(2), 41–65. DOI: 10.1016/j.trc.2014.10.011

Domenteanu, A., Diaconu, P., Florescu, M.-S., & Delcea, C. (2025). The road to autonomy: A systematic review through AI in autonomous vehicles. *Electronics (Basel)*, *14*(21), 4174. DOI: 10.3390/electronics14214174

Dong, L., Wang, J., & Hu, X. (2025). Optimization of Joint Distribution Routes for Automotive Parts Considering Multi-Manufacturer Collaboration. *Sustainability (Basel)*, *17*(14), 6615. Advance online publication. DOI: 10.3390/su17146615

Doumiati, M., Victorino, A., Charara, A., & Lechner, D. (2009). Lateral load transfer and normal forces estimation for vehicle safety: Experimental test. *Vehicle System Dynamics*, *47*(12), 1511–1533. DOI: 10.1080/00423110802673091

Douthwaite, J. A., Lesage, B., Gleirscher, M., Calinescu, R., Aitken, J. M., Alexander, R., & Law, J. (2021). A modular digital twinning framework for safety assurance of collaborative robotics. *Frontiers in Robotics and AI*, *8*, 758099. DOI: 10.3389/frobt.2021.758099 PMID: 34977162

Duan, J., Wang, Z., & Jing, X. (2024). Digital Twin Test Method With LTE-V2X for Autonomous Vehicle Safety Test. *IEEE Internet of Things Journal*, *11*(18), 30161–30171. DOI: 10.1109/JIOT.2024.3409781

Du, H., Leng, S., He, J., Xiong, K., & Zhou, L. (2025). Cooperative perception in vehicular networks: A survey. *Digital Communications and Networks*, *11*(1), 1–26. DOI: 10.1016/j.dcan.2023.06.002

Dui, H., Zhang, H., Wu, S., & Xie, M. (2025). Spatiotemporal resilience of IoT-enabled unmanned system of systems. *Engineering (Beijing)*, *54*, 355–369. DOI: 10.1016/j.eng.2025.06.024

Duyun, T., Duyun, I., Kabalyants, P., & Rybak, L. (2023). Optimization of a 6-DOF Platform for Simulators Based on an Analysis of Structural and Force Parameters. *Machines (Basel)*, *11*(8), 814. Advance online publication. DOI: 10.3390/machines11080814

Ehsan, M. K., Naz, N., Sodhro, A. H., Mumtaz, S., & Rodrigues, J. J. P. C. (2025). Energy-aware resource management in vehicular edge computing for autonomous driving. *IEEE Transactions on Mobile Computing*, *24*(9), 6932–6944. DOI: 10.1109/TMC.2025.3544918

El Marai, O., Taleb, T., & Song, J. (2021). Roads infrastructure digital twin: A step toward smarter cities realization. *IEEE Network*, *35*(2), 136–143. DOI: 10.1109/MNET.011.2000398

El-Agamy, R. F., Sayed, H. A., Al Akhatatneh, A. M., Aljohani, M., & Elhosseini, M. (2024). Comprehensive analysis of digital twins in smart cities: A 4200-paper bibliometric study. *Artificial Intelligence Review*, *57*(6), 154. DOI: 10.1007/s10462-024-10781-8

ElNawawy, A., Lee, J., & Zaki, M. H. (2024). Optimizing smart bike-sharing station placement near public transit stops using GIS: A case study of London, Ontario. In *2024 IEEE International Conference on Smart Mobility (SM)* (pp. 203–208). DOI: 10.1109/SM63044.2024.10733372

Elouadrhiri, I., El Barkany, A., Ramadany, M., & El Ouadrhiri, A. (2025). AI-driven Predictive Maintenance for intelligent tires: A real-time Digital Twin framework. MATEC Web of Conferences, 415, 03005. DOI: 10.1051/matecconf/202541503005

Emmert-Streib, F. (2023). What is the role of AI for digital twins? *AI*, *4*(3), 721–728. DOI: 10.3390/ai4030038

Erdem, U., Sharifi, A., & Ökmen, Z. (2026). Neighborhood-scale assessment of urban flood impacts on transportation network resilience: A case study of Mavişehir, İzmir. *International Journal of Disaster Risk Reduction*, *132*, 105970. DOI: 10.1016/j.ijdrr.2025.105970

Erhan, L., Ndubuaku, M., Di Mauro, M., Song, W., Chen, M., Fortino, G., Bagdasar, O., & Liotta, A. (2021). Smart anomaly detection in sensor systems: A multi-perspective review. *Information Fusion*, *67*, 64–79. DOI: 10.1016/j.inffus.2020.10.001

Eskandarian, A., Mehr, G., Nayak, A., & Shang, X. (2024). Challenges and algorithms for connected and autonomous vehicle safety and mobility in smart cities. DOI: 10.1007/978-3-031-64769-7_9

Esquivel, R. V., López, A. A., & Almaguer, C. A. G. (2025). Design of Virtual and Physical Automotive Concepts for Virtual Assembly Plant. *2025 Institute for the Future of Education Conference (IFE)*, 1–7. DOI: 10.1109/IFE63672.2025.11025112

European Commission. (2024). *Facts and figures: Cyclists. European Road Safety Observatory*. Directorate-General for Transport.

Feizizadeh, B., & Omar Zadeh, D. (2025). A GIS based spatiotemporal modelling approach for cycling risk mapping using crowd-sourced sensor data. *Annals of GIS*, *31*(2), 333–351. DOI: 10.1080/19475683.2025.2453550

Felício, S., Hora, J., Ferreira, M. C., Abrantes, D., Costa, P. D., Dangelo, C., Silva, J., & Galvao, T. (2022). Handling OpenStreetMap georeferenced data for route planning. *Transportation Research Procedia*, *62*, 189–196. DOI: 10.1016/j.trpro.2022.02.024

Ficzere, D., Tihanyi, V., & Varga, P. (2023). Large-scale cellular vehicle-to-everything deployments and challenges. *IEEE Access : Practical Innovations, Open Solutions*, *11*, 98765–98780. DOI: 10.1109/ACCESS.2023.3287456 PMID: 37631567

Florescu, A. (2024). Digital Twin for Flexible Manufacturing Systems and Optimization Through Simulation: A Case Study. *Machines (Basel)*, *12*(11), 785. Advance online publication. DOI: 10.3390/machines12110785

Folorunso, A., Olanipekun, K., Adewumi, T., & Samuel, B. (2024). A policy framework on AI usage in developing countries and its impact. *Global Journal of Engineering and Technology Advances*, *21*(1), 154–166. DOI: 10.30574/gjeta.2024.21.1.0192

Fortune Business Insights. (2024). *Digital twin market size, share and industry analysis, 2024–2032.* Fortune Business Insights Research Report. https://www.fortunebusinessinsights.com/digital-twin-market-106246

Fragner, A., Kreis, A., & Hirz, M. (2020). Virtual Tools to Support Design and Production Engineering: Early detection of stone chips to optimize production processes. *2020 IEEE 7th International Conference on Industrial Engineering and Applications (ICIEA)*, 399–403. DOI: 10.1109/ICIEA49774.2020.9102004

Friederich, J., Francis, D., Lazarova-Molnar, S., & Mohamed, N. (2022). A framework for data-driven digital twins for smart manufacturing. *Computers in Industry, 136*, 103586. Advance online publication. DOI: 10.1016/j.compind.2021.103586

Fuller, A., Fan, Z., Day, C., & Barlow, C. (2020). Digital twin: Enabling technologies, challenges and open research. *IEEE Access : Practical Innovations, Open Solutions, 8*, 108952–108971. DOI: 10.1109/ACCESS.2020.2998358

Future Market Insights. (2025). *Automotive vehicle-to-everything (V2X) market forecast 2025–2035.* Retrieved from https://www.futuremarketinsights.com/reports/automotive-vehicle-to-everything-v2x-market (Future Market Insights)

Gade, S. M., Sumana, S. G., Aarthi, S., Ravikumar, R. N., & Swetha, C. B. (2025). Advancing towards 6G Innovations, Challenges and Future Prospects. In *Advances in Wireless Technologies and Telecommunication* (pp. 1–26). IGI Global. DOI: 10.4018/979-8-3373-2220-9.ch001

Gao, H., Qu, T., Gong, X., Wang, P., & Chen, H. (2025). Driving risk assessment in intelligent vehicles based on dynamic traffic environment modeling. *Accident; Analysis and Prevention, 206*, 108039. DOI: 10.1016/j.aap.2025.108039 PMID: 40280018

Gao, J., Peng, C., Yoshinaga, T., Han, G., Guleng, S., & Wu, C. (2024). Digital twin-enabled internet of vehicles applications. *Electronics (Basel), 13*(7), 1263. Advance online publication. DOI: 10.3390/electronics13071263

Garcia, L. I. B., Villegas, A. T., Moreno, J. C. G., Rivera, L. Y. G., & Rubio, Y. A. F. (2025). Process simulation and optimization in industry 4.0: Redesigning assembly lines in an automotive industry. *Ingeniería, Investigación y Tecnología, 26*(3), 1–12. Advance online publication. DOI: 10.22201/fi.25940732e.2025.26.3.020

Ge, C., & Qin, S. (2024). Digital twin intelligent transportation system (DT-ITS): A systematic review. *IET Intelligent Transport Systems, 18*(12), 2325–2358. DOI: 10.1049/itr2.12539

Ghasemi, A., Farajzadeh, F., Heavey, C., Fowler, J., & Papadopoulos, C. (2024). Simulation optimization applied to production scheduling in the era of industry 4.0: A review and future roadmap. *Journal of Industrial Information Integration, 39*, 100599. DOI: 10.1016/j.jii.2024.100599

Giannopoulos, G. A., & Li, Y. (2025). Transport system resilience in climate crises. In *Human mobility, artificial intelligence and climate change* (pp. 85–107). Springer Nature Switzerland., DOI: 10.1007/978-3-032-08171-1_4

Gilly, K., Filiposka, S., Alcaraz Carrasco, S., & Mishev, A. (2019). Dynamic resource management of real-time edge services for intelligent vehicular networks: A case study. *Elektronika ir Elektrotechnika, 25*(4), 58–61. DOI: 10.5755/j01.eie.25.4.23971

Global Market Insights Inc. (2025). *Vehicle-to-Everything (V2X) communication module market size and forecast.* Retrieved from https://www.gminsights.com/industry-analysis/vehicle-to-everything-v2x-communication-module-market (Global Market Insights Inc.)

Gonzalez Bautista, D., Pérez Rastelli, J., Milanes, V., & Nashashibi, F. (2015). A review of motion planning techniques for automated vehicles. *IEEE Transactions on Intelligent Transportation Systems.* Advance online publication. DOI: 10.1109/TITS.2015.2498841

Göppert, A., Grahn, L., Rachner, J., Grunert, D., Hort, S., & Schmitt, R. (2021). Pipeline for ontology-based modeling and automated deployment of digital twins for planning and control of manufacturing systems. *Journal of Intelligent Manufacturing, 34*(5), 2133–2152. DOI: 10.1007/s10845-021-01860-6

Gorza, D., Saly, G., & Csikor, D. (2025). Simulation of environment recognition systems for autonomous vehicles in CARLA simulator. *Engineering Proceedings, 113*(1), 30. Advance online publication. DOI: 10.3390/engproc2025113030

Goyal, M., & Mahmoud, Q. H. (2024). A Systematic Review of Synthetic Data Generation Techniques using Generative AI. *Electronics (Basel), 13*(17), 3509. DOI: 10.3390/electronics13173509

Grieves, M., & Vickers, J. (2017). Digital twin: Mitigating unpredictable, undesirable emergent behavior in complex systems. In Kahlen, F.-J., Flumerfelt, S., & Alves, A. (Eds.), *Transdisciplinary Perspectives on Complex Systems* (pp. 85–113). Springer., DOI: 10.1007/978-3-319-38756-7_4

Groshev, M., Guimaraes, C., De La Oliva, A., & Gazda, R. (2021). Dissecting the impact of information and communication technologies on digital twins as a service. *IEEE Access : Practical Innovations, Open Solutions, 9*, 102862–102876. DOI: 10.1109/ACCESS.2021.3098109

Groshev, M., Guimarães, C., Martín-Pérez, J., & de la Oliva, A. (2021). Toward intelligent cyber-physical systems: Digital twin meets artificial intelligence. *IEEE Communications Magazine, 59*(8), 14–20. DOI: 10.1109/MCOM.001.2001237

Grznár, P., Gregor, M., Gašo, M., Gabajová, G., Schickerle, M., & Burganová, N. (2021). Dynamic Simulation Tool for Planning and Optimisation of Supply Process. *International Journal of Simulation Modelling, 20*(3), 441–452. Advance online publication. DOI: 10.2507/IJSIMM20-3-552

Guinea-Cabrera, M. A., & Holgado-Terriza, J. A. (2024). Digital twins in software engineering—A systematic literature review and vision. *Applied Sciences (Basel, Switzerland), 14*(3), 977. DOI: 10.3390/app14030977

Gu, L., Cui, M., Xu, L., & Xu, X. (2023). Collaborative offloading method for digital twin empowered cloud edge computing on internet of vehicles. *Tsinghua Science and Technology, 28*(3), 433–451. DOI: 10.26599/TST.2022.9010006

Gunapriya, B., Samanvita, N., Karthikeyan, T., & Venkatasubramanian, S. (2025). Managing the power in smart grid management hybrid model with MRA in electric vehicle system. *AVE Trends in Intelligent Energy Letters*, *1*(2), 100–114. DOI: 10.64091/ATIEL.2025.000189

Guo, J., Zhang, Y., Li, X., & Wang, Z. (2024). Digital twin driven intelligent transportation systems: Architecture and applications. *Transportation Research Part C, Emerging Technologies*, *158*, 104238. DOI: 10.1016/j.trc.2024.104238

Guo, J., Zhang, Y., Li, X., & Wang, Z. (2025). Digital twin–driven intelligent transportation systems: Architecture, applications, and challenges. *Transportation Research Part C, Emerging Technologies*, *160*, 104489. DOI: 10.1016/j.trc.2025.104489

Guo, X., Du, Q., Li, Y., Zhou, Y., Wang, Y., Huang, Y., & Martinez-Pastor, B. (2023). Cascading failure and recovery of metro–bus double-layer network considering recovery propagation. *Transportation Research Part D, Transport and Environment*, *122*, 103861. DOI: 10.1016/j.trd.2023.103861

Guo, Z., Zhou, X., Lu, C., Li, S., Zhu, Y., Liu, Y., & Li, Z. (2025). Urban agglomeration transportation resilience: Evaluation and evolution analysis using a data-driven model. *Environmental and Sustainability Indicators*, *26*, 100714. DOI: 10.1016/j.indic.2025.100714

Gutjahr, T., Kruse, T., & Huber, T. (2024). ADVANCED MODELING AND OPTIMIZATION FOR VIRTUAL CALIBRATION OF INTERNAL COMBUSTION ENGINES. *SAE Technical Paper Series*. DOI: 10.4271/2024-01-3630

Gu, X., Duan, W., Zhang, G., Hou, J., Peng, L., Wen, M., Gao, F., Chen, M., & Ho, P.-H. (2026). Digital twin technology for intelligent vehicles and transportation systems: A survey on applications, challenges and future directions. *IEEE Communications Surveys and Tutorials*, *28*, 3235–3271. DOI: 10.1109/COMST.2025.3581152

Hadi, M. U., & Murtaza, G. (2022). Fibre wireless distributed antenna systems for 5G and 6G services. *Electronics (Basel)*, *12*(1), 64. DOI: 10.3390/electronics12010064

Haghshenas, S. S., Astarita, V., Guido, G., Mobini Seraji, M. H., Aldana Gonzalez, P. A., Haghdadi, A., & Haghshenas, S. S. (2023). Assessment of machine learning techniques and traffic flow: A qualitative and quantitative analysis. *Journal of Computational and Cognitive Engineering*, *3*(2), 119–129. DOI: 10.47852/bonviewJCCE32021062

Han, M., Zhang, J., Huang, Y., Xu, J., Chen, X., & Li, S. (2025). Digital twin-driven construction safety monitoring for autonomous equipment. *Automation in Construction*, *162*, 106108. DOI: 10.1016/j.autcon.2025.106108

Han, Y., Shao, J., Zhou, R., Liao, Y., & Zhong, Y. (2025). Robotic Digital Twin Based Full Lifecycle Decision Framework for Automotive Productions. *IEEE Network*, *39*(4), 173–181. DOI: 10.1109/MNET.2024.3418624

Hardaway, K., & Cai, H. (2026). Reviewing autonomous vehicle simulation literature: Policy insights for transportation. *Transport Reviews*, *46*(1), 1–27. DOI: 10.1080/01441647.2025.2545224

Hasan, S. K. K., & Crawford, C. W. (2025). *A new era for digital twins: Progress and industry adoption*. Digital Twin., DOI: 10.1080/27525783.2025.2555877

Haverkamp, P., Anantheswar, A., May, M., Wadlig, G., Hildebrandt, J., Thiessat, K. A., Wollny, I., Traverso, M., Müller-Mall, S., Kaliske, M., Habich, D., & Lehner, W. (2025). Digital twin road: Value and implications involving data and application. *Discover Applied Sciences*, *7*(6), 510. DOI: 10.1007/s42452-025-07018-w

He, Y., Chen, H., & Shi, W. (2024). *An advanced framework for ultra-realistic simulation and digital twinning for autonomous vehicles.*

He, J., He, Z., Fan, B., & Chen, Y. (2020). Optimal location of lane-changing warning point in a two-lane road considering different traffic flows. *Physica A*, *540*(2), 123000. DOI: 10.1016/j.physa.2019.123000

He, J., Yang, K., & Chen, H.-H. (2021). 6G cellular networks and connected autonomous vehicles. *IEEE Network*, *35*(4), 255–261. DOI: 10.1109/MNET.011.2000541

Hensel, N., Moor, M., & Rieck, B. (2021). A Survey of Topological Machine Learning Methods. *Frontiers in Artificial Intelligence*, *4*, 681108. DOI: 10.3389/frai.2021.681108

Herchlová, M., Važan, P., Burčiar, F., Juhás, M., Juhásová, B., & Čambál, D. (2025). A simulation Approach to Improve the Performance of a Sub-assembly Zone in Automotive Industry. *2025 Cybernetics & Informatics (K&I)*, 1–6. DOI: 10.1109/KI64036.2025.10916456

He, Y., Kong, M., Du, C., Yao, D., & Yu, M. (2022). Communication security analysis of intelligent transportation system using 5G internet of things from the perspective of big data. *IEEE Transactions on Intelligent Transportation Systems*, 1–9. Advance online publication. DOI: 10.1109/TITS.2022.3141788

Hlophe, M. C., & Maharaj, B. T. (2023). From cyber–physical convergence to digital twins: A review on edge computing use case designs. *Applied Sciences (Basel, Switzerland)*, *13*(24), 13262. DOI: 10.3390/app132413262

Hoang, M. L. (2024). *Artificial Intelligence Development in sensors and Computer Vision for Health Care and Automation Application*. BENTHAM SCIENCE PUBLISHERS., DOI: 10.2174/97898153130551240101

Horner, J., Trautrim, T., Ruiz-Martín, C., Borshchev, A., & Robinson, S. (2025). A digital twin of an air transport system for resilience assessment and decision support. *Aerospace (Basel, Switzerland)*, *12*(10), 912. DOI: 10.3390/aerospace12100912

Horr, A., & Drexler, H. (2025). Real-Time Models for Manufacturing Processes: How to Build Predictive Reduced Models. *Processes (Basel, Switzerland)*, *13*(1), 252. Advance online publication. DOI: 10.3390/pr13010252

Hou, G. (2023). Evaluating efficiency and safety of mixed traffic with connected and autonomous vehicles in adverse weather. *Sustainability (Basel)*, *15*(4), 3138. Advance online publication. DOI: 10.3390/su15043138

Hou, Z., Wang, S., Liu, H., Yang, Y., & Zhang, Y. (2024). Twin Scenarios Establishment for Autonomous Vehicle Digital Twin Empowered SOTIF Assessment. *IEEE Transactions on Intelligent Vehicles*, *9*(1), 1965–1976. DOI: 10.1109/TIV.2023.3304353

Hu, X., Li, S., Huang, T., Tang, B., Huai, R., & Chen, L. (2023). *How simulation helps autonomous driving: A survey of sim2real, digital twins, and parallel intelligence.*

Huang, Y., Du, J., Chen, M., Lin, Y., Huang, S., & Cai, Y. (2026). Evaluating the spatial-temporal impact of urban nature on urban vitality in Vancouver: A social media and GPS data approach. *Land Use Policy*, *160*, 107824. DOI: 10.1016/j.landusepol.2025.107824

Huang, Z., Fey, M., Liu, C., Beysel, E., Xu, X., & Brecher, C. (2023). Hybrid learning-based digital twin for manufacturing process: Modeling framework and implementation. *Robotics and Computer-integrated Manufacturing*, *82*, 102545. DOI: 10.1016/j.rcim.2023.102545

Hui, Y., Ma, X., Su, Z., Cheng, N., Yin, Z., Luan, T. H., & Chen, Y. (2022). Collaboration as a Service: Digital-Twin-Enabled Collaborative and Distributed Autonomous Driving. *IEEE Internet of Things Journal*, *9*(19), 18607–18619. DOI: 10.1109/JIOT.2022.3161677

Hu, W., Lim, K. Y. H., & Cai, Y. (2022). Digital twin and Industry 4.0 enablers in building and construction: A survey. *Buildings (Basel, Switzerland)*, *12*(11), 2004. DOI: 10.3390/buildings12112004

Hu, Z., Lou, S., Xing, Y., Wang, X., Cao, D., & Lv, C. (2022). Review and perspectives on driver digital twin and its enabling technologies for intelligent vehicles. *IEEE Transactions on Intelligent Vehicles*, *7*(3), 417–440. Advance online publication. DOI: 10.1109/TIV.2022.3195635

Huzzat, A., Anpalagan, A., Khwaja, A. S., Woungang, I., Alnoman, A. A., & Pillai, A. S. (2025). A comprehensive review of digital twin technologies in smart cities. *Digital Engineering*, *4*, 100040. DOI: 10.1016/j.dte.2025.100040

Ibn-Khedher, H., Laroui, M., Alfaqawi, M., Magnouche, A., Moungla, H., & Afifi, H. (2024). 6G-edge support of Internet of Autonomous Vehicles: A survey. *Transactions on Emerging Telecommunications Technologies*, *35*(1), e4918. Advance online publication. DOI: 10.1002/ett.4918

Ibrahim, M., Rassõlkin, A., Vaimann, T., & Kallaste, A. (2022). Overview on digital Twin for autonomous electrical vehicles propulsion drive system. *Sustainability (Basel)*, *14*(2), 601. DOI: 10.3390/su14020601

Ibrahim, M., Rjabtšikov, V., & Gilbert, R. (2023). Overview of Digital Twin Platforms for EV Applications. *Sensors (Basel)*, *23*(3), 1414. Advance online publication. DOI: 10.3390/s23031414 PMID: 36772453

Ibrahim, M., Rjabtšikov, V., & Rassõlkin, A. (2025). Digital shadow of an electric vehicle-permanent magnet synchronous motor drive for real-time performance monitoring. *Digital Twins and Applications*, *2*(1), e12024. Advance online publication. DOI: 10.1049/dgt2.12024

Iclodean, C., Jurchis, B.-M., Macavei, C.-M., Volosciuc, E.-R., & Iclodean, A.-G. (2025). Optimizing the Energy Efficiency of Electric Vehicles in Urban and Metropolitan Environments According to Various Driving Cycles and Behavioral Conditions. *Electronics (Basel)*, *14*(11), 2224. Advance online publication. DOI: 10.3390/electronics14112224

Ihsan, A., Chen, W., Khan, W. U., Wu, Q., & Wang, K. (2023). Energy-efficient backscatter aided uplink NOMA roadside sensor communications under channel estimation errors. *IEEE Transactions on Intelligent Transportation Systems*, *24*(5), 4962–4974. DOI: 10.1109/TITS.2023.3240159

Inamdar, A., & Patil, S. (2024). Digital twin technology: A review and its applications in smart manufacturing. *Electronics (Basel), 13*(16), 3255. DOI: 10.3390/electronics13163255

Irfan, M. S., Dasgupta, S., & Rahman, M. (2024). Toward transportation digital twin systems for traffic safety and mobility: A review. *IEEE Internet of Things Journal, 11*(14), 24581–24603. DOI: 10.1109/JIOT.2024.3395186

Islambekov, U., & Pathirana, H. (2024). Vector Summaries of Persistence Diagrams for Permutation-based Hypothesis Testing. *Foundations of Data Science (Springfield, Mo.), 6*(1), 41–61. DOI: 10.3934/fods.2024002

Islam, S., & Welch, E. W. (2024). Information technology systems as both contributor to risk perception and adaptive behavior: Public transit agencies' response to extreme weather events. *International Journal of Disaster Risk Reduction, 115*, 105007. DOI: 10.1016/j.ijdrr.2024.105007

Islam, T., Vu, H. L., Hoang, N. H., & Cricenti, A. (2018). A linear bus rapid transit with transit signal priority formulation. *Transportation Research Part E, Logistics and Transportation Review, 114*(6), 163–184. DOI: 10.1016/j.tre.2018.03.009

Itäpelto, T., Elhajj, M., & van Sinderen, M. (2025). Digital twin application in lifecycle security of critical infrastructures: A systematic literature review. *International Journal of Critical Infrastructure Protection, 50*, 100783. DOI: 10.1016/j.ijcip.2025.100783

Jabeen Siddiqi, S., Alobaidi, A. H., Ahmad Jan, M., & Tariq, M. (2025). Securing vehicle-to-Digital twin communications in the Internet of Vehicles. *ACM Transactions on Multimedia Computing Communications and Applications*, (3711863). Advance online publication. DOI: 10.1145/3711863

Jaiswal, B. D. (2025). *The Influence and Application of Digital Twin Technology in Automotive Automation*. International Journal For Multidisciplinary Research., DOI: 10.36948/ijfmr.2025.v07i01.37342

Jaiswal, S., & Mohan, B. C. (2023). Deep learning-based path tracking control using lane detection and traffic sign detection for autonomous driving. *Web Intelligence, 22*(2), 185–207. DOI: 10.3233/WEB-230011

Jang, I. S., Li, B., Kwon, S., & Han, J.-H. (2024). Synthetic Training Dataset Generation Using a Digital Twin-based Autonomous Driving Simulator. *Sensors and Materials, 36*(9), 4029–4041. DOI: 10.18494/SAM5343

Javaid, M., Haleem, P. A., & Suman, R. (2023). Digital Twin applications toward Industry 4.0: A Review. *Cognitive Robotics*. DOI: 10.1016/j.cogr.2023.04.003

Jazar, R. N. (2025). *Vehicle Dynamics: Theory and Application*. Springer Nature. DOI: 10.1007/978-3-031-74458-7

Jeba, J. A., Bose, S. R., Regin, R., Banupriya, P., & Maseleno, A. (2025). A comprehensive real-time traffic monitoring and visualization system with automated vehicle analysis. *FMDB Transactions on Sustainable Computing Systems, 3*(4), 242–252. DOI: 10.69888/FTSCS.2025.000526

Jeon, G., Bellandi, V., Chehri, A., & Damiani, E. (2023). Deep learning approaches for vulnerable road users safety. *Safety Science, 158*, 105964. DOI: 10.1016/j.ssci.2022.105964

Jia, L., Yang, D., Ren, Y., Qian, C., Feng, Q., Sun, B., & Wang, Z. (2024). A dynamic test scenario generation method for autonomous vehicles based on conditional generative adversarial imitation learning. *Accident; Analysis and Prevention*, *194*, 107279. DOI: 10.1016/j.aap.2023.107279

Jia, L., Yang, S., Wang, W., & Zhang, X. (2022). Impact analysis of highways in China under future extreme precipitation. *Natural Hazards*, *110*(2), 1097–1113. DOI: 10.1007/s11069-021-04981-6

Jiang, B., Sharma, N., Liu, Y., Li, C., & Huang, X. (2022). Real-Time FPGA/CPU-Based Simulation of a Full-Electric Vehicle Integrated with a High-Fidelity Electric Drive Model. *Energies*, *15*(5), 1824. Advance online publication. DOI: 10.3390/en15051824

Jiang, C., Blom, H., & Rattanagraikanakorn, B. (2025). Integrated safety and security risk assessment for autonomous transport systems. *Risk Analysis*, *45*(6), 1115–1131. DOI: 10.1111/risa.17649 PMID: 39276027

Jiang, H., Qin, S., Fu, J., & Ding, G. (2020). How to model and implement connections between physical and virtual models for digital twin application. *Journal of Manufacturing Systems*. Advance online publication. DOI: 10.1016/j.jmsy.2020.05.012

Jiang, W., Han, B., Habibi, M. A., & Schotten, H. D. (2021). The road towards 6G: A comprehensive survey. *IEEE Open Journal of the Communications Society*, *2*, 334–366. DOI: 10.1109/OJCOMS.2021.3057679

Jing Yik, C., Zainal Abidin, M. I., Ismail, K., Mohd Zawawi, F., Abdul Keyon, A. S., & Mohd Nor, N. S. (2025). Location and orientation tracking in Autonomous Surface Vehicles: Real world data versus digital twin predictions. *Jurnal Teknologi*, *87*(3), 567–577. Advance online publication. DOI: 10.11113/jurnalteknologi.v87.22992

Jin, Y., McDaniel, R., Tatro, N. J., Catanzaro, M. J., Smith, A. D., Bendich, P., Dwyer, M. B., & Fletcher, P. T. (2024). Implications of Data Topology for Deep Generative Models. *Frontiers of Computer Science*, *6*, 1260604. DOI: 10.3389/fcomp.2024.1260604

Kabashkin, I. (2025). Digital-twin-based ecosystem for aviation maintenance training. *Information (Basel)*, *16*(7), 586. DOI: 10.3390/info16070586

Kabir, M. R., Ravi, B. B. Y., & Ray, S. (2023). A Virtual Prototyping Platform for Exploration of Vehicular Electronics. *IEEE Internet of Things Journal*, *10*(18), 16144–16155. DOI: 10.1109/JIOT.2023.3267339

Kabir, M. R., Ravi, B. B. Y., & Ray, S. (2025). Digital Twin Technologies for Vehicular Prototyping: A Survey. *IEEE Open Journal of Intelligent Transportation Systems*, *6*, 503–521. DOI: 10.1109/OJITS.2025.3562504

Kabir, M. R., & Ray, S. (2025). Digital twin tools for smart manufacturing: Integration with IIoT and cyber-physical systems. *IEEE Open Journal of the Industrial Electronics Society*, *6*, 1–15. DOI: 10.1109/OJIES.2025.3628531

Kabir, R., Watanobe, Y., Ding, D., Islam, M. R., & Naruse, K. (2025). A comprehensive survey on advanced data science platforms for cyber-physical systems, digital twins, and robotics. *IEEE Access : Practical Innovations, Open Solutions*, *13*, 177269–177304. DOI: 10.1109/ACCESS.2025.3619776

Kachhoria, R., Jaiswal, S., Lokhande, M., & Rodge, J. (2023). Lane detection and path prediction in autonomous vehicle using deep learning. In *Intelligent edge computing for cyber physical applications* (pp. 111–127). Academic Press. DOI: 10.1016/B978-0-323-99412-5.00012-5

Kampa, A. (2023). Modeling and Simulation of a Digital Twin of a Production System for Industry 4.0 with Work-in-Process Synchronization. *Applied Sciences (Basel, Switzerland)*, *13*(22), 12261. Advance online publication. DOI: 10.3390/app132212261

Kampker, A., Wessel, S., Lutz, N., Heine, S., Mayr, A., & Kuhn, A. (2021). Model improvement through real data connection for Virtual commissioning in ramp-up management of scalable production systems. *Procedia CIRP*, *99*, 645–649. DOI: 10.1016/j.procir.2021.03.087

Kang, J. (2025). Software Practice and Experience on Smart Mobility Digital Twin in Transportation and Automotive Industry: Toward SDV-empowered Digital Twin through EV Edge-Cloud and AutoML. *Journal of Web Engineering*, *23*, 1155–1180. DOI: 10.13052/jwe1540-9589.2385

Karanjkar, N., Joglekar, A., Mohanty, S., Prabhu, V., Raghunath, D., & Sundaresan, R. (2018). Digital twin for energy optimization in an SMT-PCB assembly line. In *Proceedings of the International Conference on Internet of Things and Intelligence Systems* (pp. 85–90). DOI: 10.1109/IOTAIS.2018.8600830

Karoonsoontawong, A., & Waller, S. T. (2010). Integrated network capacity expansion and traffic signal optimization problem: Robust bi-level dynamic formulation. *Networks and Spatial Economics*, *10*(9), 525–550. DOI: 10.1007/s11067-008-9071-x

Karunaratne, T., Ajiero, I. R., Joseph, R., Farr, E., & Piroozfar, P. (2025). Evaluating the economic impact of digital twinning in the AEC industry: A systematic review. *Buildings (Basel, Switzerland)*, *15*(14), 2583. DOI: 10.3390/buildings15142583

Katsoulakis, E., Wang, Q., Wu, H., Shahriyari, L., Fletcher, R., Liu, J., Achenie, L., Liu, H., Jackson, P., Xiao, Y., Syeda-Mahmood, T., Tuli, R., & Deng, J. (2024). Digital twins for health: A scoping review. *NPJ Digital Medicine*, *7*(1), 77. DOI: 10.1038/s41746-024-01073-0

Ke, G., Zhang, D., Liqin, M., Jing, W., Juan, D., Shubo, L., Huan, Q., & Sun, L. (2023). Intelligent machine plus production line digital twin model construction technology. *Journal of Physics: Conference Series*, *2478*(10), 102011. Advance online publication. DOI: 10.1088/1742-6596/2478/10/102011

Kehoe, G., Jula, H., & Ariaei, F. Developing successful autonomous ground vehicles: Lessons learned from DARPA challenges. DOI: 10.3182/20090902-3-US-2007.0087

Khan, L. U., Yaqoob, I., Imran, M., Han, Z., & Hong, C. S. (2020). 6G wireless systems: A vision, architectural elements, and future directions. *IEEE Access : Practical Innovations, Open Solutions*, *8*, 147029–147044. DOI: 10.1109/ACCESS.2020.3015289

Khan, L. U., Yaqoob, I., Tran, N. H., Han, Z., & Hong, C. S. (2020). Network slicing: Recent advances, taxonomy, requirements, and open research challenges. *IEEE Access : Practical Innovations, Open Solutions*, *8*, 36009–36028. DOI: 10.1109/ACCESS.2020.2975072

Kim, J., Park, S., Kim, J., & Yoo, J. (2023). A deep reinforcement learning strategy for surrounding vehicles-based Lane-keeping control. *Sensors (Basel)*, *23*(24), 9843. DOI: 10.3390/s23249843 PMID: 38139694

Kim, S., & Shim, D. (2024). Validation of speed limit recognition systems for autonomous driving using real-road experiments. *International Journal of Engineering Trends and Technology*, *72*(9), 137–145. DOI: 10.14445/22315381/IJETT-V72I9P137

Kirovskii, O. M., & Gorelov, V. A. (2019). Driver assistance systems: Analysis, tests and the safety case. ISO 26262 and ISO PAS 21448. *IOP Conference Series. Materials Science and Engineering*, *534*(1), 012019. DOI: 10.1088/1757-899X/534/1/012019

Kishore, M. K., Kumar, V. G., & Nancharaiah, B. (2025). Secure lightweight digital twin (DT) technology for seamless wireless communication in vehicular ad hoc network. *Computers & Electrical Engineering*, *123*, 110291. DOI: 10.1016/j.compeleceng.2025.110291

Kousi, N., Gkournelos, C., Aivaliotis, S., Lotsaris, K., Bavelos, A., Baris, P., Michalos, G., & Makris, S. (2021). Digital Twin for Designing and Reconfiguring Human–Robot Collaborative Assembly Lines. *Applied Sciences (Basel, Switzerland)*, *11*(10), 4620. DOI: 10.3390/app11104620

Kozlov, D. N. (2020). A Combinatorial Method to Compute Explicit Homology Cycles using Discrete Morse Theory. *Journal of Applied and Computational Topology*, *4*(1), 79–100. DOI: 10.1007/s41468-019-00042-x

Krenczyk, D. (2022). Dynamic simulation models as digital twins of logistics systems driven by data from multiple sources. *Journal of Physics: Conference Series*, *2198*(1), 012059. Advance online publication. DOI: 10.1088/1742-6596/2198/1/012059

Krenczyk, D., & Paprocka, I. (2023). Integration of Discrete Simulation, Prediction, and Optimization Methods for a Production Line Digital Twin Design. *Materials (Basel)*, *16*(6), 2339. Advance online publication. DOI: 10.3390/ma16062339 PMID: 36984218

Kreuzberger, D., Kühl, N., & Hirschl, S. (2023). Machine Learning Operations (MLOps): Overview, Definition, and Architecture. *IEEE Access : Practical Innovations, Open Solutions*, *11*, 31866–31879. DOI: 10.1109/ACCESS.2023.3262138

Kritzinger, W., Karner, M., Traar, G., Henjes, J., & Sihn, W. (2018). Digital twin in manufacturing: A categorical literature review and classification. *IFAC-PapersOnLine*, *51*(11), 1016–1022. DOI: 10.1016/j.ifacol.2018.08.474

Krynke, M., & Mazur, M. (2024). *Innovative Work Order Planning with Process Optimization Using Computer Simulation in the Automotive Industry, in the Case of Repair Workshops*. Periodica Polytechnica Transportation Engineering., DOI: 10.3311/PPtr.23546

Kshatra, D., & Tjprc. (2019). Development of Virtual Modelling for Optimization and Botttleneck Analysis of an Automotive Stamping using Plant Simulation. *International Journal of Mechanical and Production Engineering Research and Development*. DOI: 10.24247/ijmperdjun2019101

Kumarasamy, V. K., Saroj, A. J., Liang, Y., Wu, D., Hunter, M. P., Guin, A., & Sartipi, M. (2024). Integration of decentralized graph-based multi-agent Reinforcement Learning with Digital Twin for traffic signal optimization. *Symmetry*, *16*(4), 448. DOI: 10.3390/sym16040448

Kumari, S., Rajak, S. K., Siddharth, D., & Kumar, M. (2024). Improving Autonomous Vehicle Technology Through Reinforcement Learning and deep learning models. In *Advances in Computational Intelligence and Robotics* (pp. 461–474). IGI Global., DOI: 10.4018/979-8-3693-4326-5.ch021

Kumar, P., Prasad, S., Patel, D., Gupta, L., Nag, M. B., & Chadha, P. (2022). Production improvement on the assembly line through cycle time optimization. [IJIDeM]. *International Journal on Interactive Design and Manufacturing*, *17*(5), 2617–2630. DOI: 10.1007/s12008-022-01031-8

Kumar, P., Prasad, S., Patel, D., Kumar, K., Dixit, S., & Nikolaevna, S. N. (2023). Optimization of cycle time assembly line for mass manufacturing. [IJIDeM]. *International Journal on Interactive Design and Manufacturing*, •••, 1–12. DOI: 10.1007/s12008-023-01343-3

Kuo, H.-A., Chien, C.-F., & Chan, Y.-L. (2026). Digital twin framework for advanced process time prediction in PCB laser micromachining using AI-driven models. SSRN *Electronic Journal*.

Kušić, K., Schumann, R., & Ivanjko, E. (2023). A digital twin in transportation: Real-time synergy of traffic data streams and simulation for virtualizing motorway dynamics. *Advanced Engineering Informatics*, *55*, 101858. DOI: 10.1016/j.aei.2022.101858

Kuts, V., Rassõlkin, A., Partyshev, A., Jegorov, S., & Rjabtšikov, V. (2021). ROS middle-layer integration to Unity 3D as an interface option for propulsion drive simulations of autonomous vehicles. *IOP Conference Series. Materials Science and Engineering*, *1140*(1), 012008. DOI: 10.1088/1757-899X/1140/1/012008

Kwizera, N., Haidoura, H., & Sudha, P. (2025). Analyzing the causes and impacts of disputes in the Rwanda road construction sector and determining ways of reducing disputes. *AVE Trends in Intelligent Social Letters*, *2*(4), 163–172. DOI: 10.64091/ATISL.2025.000237

Lattanzi, L., Raffaeli, R., Peruzzini, M., & Pellicciari, M. (2021). Digital twin for smart manufacturing: A review of concepts towards a practical industrial implementation. *International Journal of Computer Integrated Manufacturing*, *34*(6), 567–597. DOI: 10.1080/0951192X.2021.1911003

Lawson, G., Salanitri, D., & Waterfield, B. (2016). Future directions for the development of virtual reality within an automotive manufacturer. *Applied Ergonomics, 53 Pt B*, 323–330. DOI: 10.1016/j.apergo.2015.06.024

Lee, C. C., Rajput, A. A., Hsu, C. W., Fan, C., Yuan, F., Dong, S., Esmalian, A., Farahmand, H., Patrascu, F. I., Liu, C.-F., Li, B., Ma, J., & Mostafavi, A. (2022). Quantitative measures for integrating resilience into transportation planning practice: Study in Texas. *Transportation Research Part D, Transport and Environment*, *113*, 103496. DOI: 10.1016/j.trd.2022.103496

Lehner, D., Zhang, J., Pfeiffer, J., Sint, S., Splettstößer, A., Wimmer, M., & Wortmann, A. (2025). Model-driven engineering for digital twins: A systematic mapping study. *Software & Systems Modeling*, *24*(5), 1339–1377. DOI: 10.1007/s10270-025-01264-7

Lei, W., Shen, P., Zhu, J., & Ou, P. (2025). Virtual Simulation Debugging and Optimization of Automotive Connecting Rod Production Line Based on Digital Twin. *2025 IEEE 3rd International Conference on Image Processing and Computer Applications (ICIPCA)*, 320–325. DOI: 10.1109/ICIPCA65645.2025.11139027

Leipzig, J., Nüst, D., Hoyt, C. T., Ram, K., & Greenberg, J. (2021). The Role of Metadata in Reproducible Computational Research. *Patterns (New York, N.Y.)*, *2*(9), 100322. DOI: 10.1016/j.patter.2021.100322

Lei, T., Sellers, T., Luo, C., Cao, L., & Bi, Z. (2024). Digital twin-based multi-objective autonomous vehicle navigation approach as applied in infrastructure construction. *IET Cyber-Systems and Robotics*, *6*(2), e12110. Advance online publication. DOI: 10.1049/csy2.12110

Lei, W. (2025). Design and Development of a Cylinder Head Production Line Virtual Simulation Cognition System Based on Unity3D. *Computer Applications in Engineering Education*, *33*(5), e70078. Advance online publication. DOI: 10.1002/cae.70078

Lei, Y., Li, N., Guo, L., Li, N., Yan, T., & Lin, J. (2018). Machinery health prognostics: A systematic review from data acquisition to RUL prediction. *Mechanical Systems and Signal Processing*, *104*, 799–834. DOI: 10.1016/j.ymssp.2017.11.016

Li, X., Niu, W., & Tian, H. (2024). Application of Digital Twin in Electric Vehicle Powertrain: A Review. *World Electric Vehicle Journal*. DOI: 10.3390/wevj15050208

Liang, S., Wu, H., Zhen, L., Hua, Q., Garg, S., Kaddoum, G., Hassan, M. M., & Yu, K. (2022). Edge YOLO: Real-time intelligent object detection system based on edge-cloud cooperation in autonomous vehicles. IEEE Transactions on Intelligent Transportation Systems: A Publication of the IEEE Intelligent Transportation Systems Council, 23(12), 25345–25360. DOI: 10.1109/TITS.2022.3158253

Liang, K., Wang, Y., Li, Z., Zheng, G., Wong, K., & Xu, S. (2025). Risk-aware trajectory planning for autonomous vehicles in mixed traffic. *IEEE Transactions on Vehicular Technology*, *74*(3), 8457–8471. DOI: 10.1109/TVT.2025.3526198

Liang, Z., Wang, J., Zhang, T., & Yong, X. (2025a). DTTF-Sim: A Digital Twin-based simulation system for continuous autonomous driving testing. *Sensors (Basel)*, *25*(11), 3447. DOI: 10.3390/s25113447 PMID: 40968948

Liao, X., Wang, Z., Zhao, X., Han, K., Tiwari, P., Barth, M., & Wu, G. (2021). Cooperative ramp merging design and field implementation: A digital twin approach based on vehicle-to-cloud communication. *IEEE Transactions on Intelligent Transportation Systems*. Advance online publication. DOI: 10.1109/TITS.2020.3045123

Li, H., & Hong, T. (2025). A digital twin platform for smart parking management in intelligent transport systems. *Building Simulation*, *18*(4), 563–579. DOI: 10.1007/s12273-025-1290-2

Li, T., Bian, Z., Lei, H., Zuo, F., Yang, Y.-T., & Wang, Y. (2025). Digital twin-based evaluation framework for cooperative driving automation in connected vehicle environments. *IEEE Transactions on Intelligent Transportation Systems*, *26*(9), 9080–9090. DOI: 10.1109/TITS.2025.3604569

Littfinski, D., & Verl, A. (2025). Intelligent and autonomous partitioning of real-time simulation models. *2025 The 16th International Conference on Mechanical and Intelligent Manufacturing Technologies (ICMIMT)*, 214–219. DOI: 10.1109/ICMIMT65123.2025.11091903

Liu, H., Zhang, B., Wu, V., Yang, X., & Wang, L. (2025). Review of Digital Twin in the Automotive Industry on Products, Processes and Systems. *International Journal of Automotive Manufacturing and Materials*. DOI: 10.53941/ijamm.2025.100006

Liu, S., Liu, L., Tang, J., Yu, B., Wang, Y., & Shi, W. (2019). Edge computing for autonomous driving: Opportunities and challenges. Proceedings of the IEEE. Institute of Electrical and Electronics Engineers, 107(8), 1697–1716. DOI: 10.1109/JPROC.2019.2915983

Liu, C., Zhang, P., & Xu, X. (2023). Literature review of digital twin technologies for civil infrastructure. *Journal of Infrastructure Intelligence and Resilience*, *2*(3), 100050. DOI: 10.1016/j.iintel.2023.100050

Liu, J., He, M., Schonfeld, P. M., Kato, H., & Li, A. (2022). Measures of accessibility incorporating time reliability for an urban rail transit network: A case study in Wuhan, China. *Transportation Research Part A, Policy and Practice*, *165*, 471–489. DOI: 10.1016/j.tra.2022.09.011

Liu, J., Sheng, X., Tan, L., Zhang, W., Zhang, P., & Wu, Q. (2025). Cooperative perception for autonomous driving: Architecture, challenges, and future directions. *IEEE Transactions on Vehicular Technology*, *74*(2), 3650–3665. DOI: 10.1109/TVT.2024.3485073

Liu, J., Wen, X., Zhou, H., Sheng, S., Zhao, P., Liu, X., Kang, C., & Chen, Y. (2022). Digital twin-enabled machining process modeling. *Advanced Engineering Informatics*, *54*, 101737. DOI: 10.1016/j.aei.2022.101737

Liu, J., & Zhang, K. (2023, April 14). Liu, Jiayan, & Zhang, K.-R. (2023). Design and Simulation Debugging of Automobile Connecting Rod Production Line Based on the Digital Twin. *Applied Sciences (Basel, Switzerland)*, *13*(8), 4919. Advance online publication. DOI: 10.3390/app13084919

Liu, T., Tang, L., Wang, W., He, X., Chen, Q., Zeng, X., & Jiang, H. (2022). Resource allocation in DT-assisted internet of vehicles via edge intelligent cooperation. *IEEE Internet of Things Journal*, *9*(18), 17608–17626. Advance online publication. DOI: 10.1109/JIOT.2022.3156100

Liu, Y., Feng, J., Lu, J., & Zhou, S. (2024). A review of digital twin capabilities, technologies, and applications based on the maturity model. *Advanced Engineering Informatics*, *62*, 102592. DOI: 10.1016/j.aei.2024.102592

Liu, Y., Xia, X., Zhang, J., Wang, K., Yu, B., Wu, M., Shi, J., Ma, C., Liu, Y., Hu, B., Wang, X., Wang, B., Wang, R., & Wang, B. (2025). Optimization of monocrystalline silicon photovoltaic module assembly lines based on simulation model. *PLoS One*, *20*(6), e0325152. Advance online publication. DOI: 10.1371/journal.pone.0325152 PMID: 40498735

Liu, Z., Chen, X., Wu, H., Wang, Z., Chen, X., Niyato, D., & Huang, K. (2026). Integrated sensing and edge AI: Realizing intelligent perception in 6G. *IEEE Communications Surveys and Tutorials*, *28*, 2725–2770. DOI: 10.1109/COMST.2025.3592989

Li, X., Liu, G., Sun, S., Yi, W., & Li, B. (2023). Digital twin model-based smart assembly strategy design and precision evaluation for PCB kit-box build. *Journal of Manufacturing Systems*, *71*, 206–223. DOI: 10.1016/j.jmsy.2023.09.010

Li, Y., Chen, S., Wang, X., & Zhao, L. (2025). Vehicle-to-grid integration for sustainable transportation: Communication, control, and energy management. *Renewable & Sustainable Energy Reviews*, *184*, 113623. DOI: 10.1016/j.rser.2025.113623

Li, Y., Liu, W., Liu, Q., Zheng, X., Sun, K., & Huang, C. (2024). Complying with ISO 26262 and ISO/SAE 21434: A safety and security. *Sensors (Basel)*, *24*(6), 1848. DOI: 10.3390/s24061848 PMID: 38544111

Li, Y., Yabuki, N., & Fukuda, T. (2022). Exploring the association between street built environment and street vitality using deep learning methods. *Sustainable Cities and Society*, *79*, 103656. DOI: 10.1016/j.scs.2021.103656

Llagostera-Brugarola, E., Perez, J., & Molina, J. (2025). A digital twin for intelligent transportation systems using V2X communications. *Applied Sciences (Basel, Switzerland)*, *15*(13), 7454. DOI: 10.3390/app15137454

Loia, F., Perillo, C., & Gravili, G. (2026). Unleashing the power of digital twin and big data as a new frontier for smart mobility: An ecosystem perspective. *Big Data Research*, *43*, 100576. DOI: 10.1016/j.bdr.2025.100576

Lopes, W. A. C., Rusteiko, A. C., Mendes, C. R., Honório, N. V. C., & Okano, M. (2025). Optimization of New Project Validation Protocols in the Automotive Industry: A Simulated Environment for Efficiency and Effectiveness. *Journal of Computational and Cognitive Engineering*, *4*(3), 343–354. Advance online publication. DOI: 10.47852/bonviewJCCE52024627

Lugaresi, G., Alba, V. V., & Matta, A. (2021). Lab-scale Models of Manufacturing Systems for Testing Real-time Simulation and Production Control Technologies. *Journal of Manufacturing Systems*, *58*, 93–108. DOI: 10.1016/j.jmsy.2020.09.003

Lugaresi, G., & Matta, A. (2021). Automated manufacturing system discovery and digital twin generation. *Journal of Manufacturing Systems*, *59*, 51–66. Advance online publication. DOI: 10.1016/j.jmsy.2021.01.005

Lu, Y., Huang, X., Zhang, K., Maharjan, S., & Zhang, Y. (2021). Low-latency federated learning and blockchain for edge association in digital twin empowered 6G networks. *IEEE Transactions on Industrial Informatics*, *17*(7), 5098–5107. DOI: 10.1109/TII.2020.3017668

Lu, Y., Liu, C., Wang, K., Huang, H., & Xu, X. (2019). Digital twin driven smart manufacturing: Connotation, reference model, applications and research issues. *Robotics and Computer-integrated Manufacturing*, *61*, 101837. Advance online publication. DOI: 10.1016/j.rcim.2019.101837

Lv, Z. (2023). Digital Twins in Industry 5.0. *Research*, *6*, 0071. Advance online publication. DOI: 10.34133/research.0071 PMID: 36930777

Lyu, Z., Li, Y., Feng, H., & Lv, H. (2021). Deep learning for security in digital twins of cooperative intelligent transportation systems. *IEEE Transactions on Intelligent Transportation Systems*. Advance online publication. DOI: 10.1109/TITS.2021.3122566

Madni, A. M. (2021). MBSE testbed for rapid, cost-effective prototyping and evaluation of system modeling approaches. *Applied Sciences (Basel, Switzerland)*, *11*(5), 2321. DOI: 10.3390/app11052321

Madni, A. M., Madni, C. C., & Lucero, S. D. (2019). Leveraging digital twin technology in model-based systems engineering. *Systems*, *7*(1), 7. DOI: 10.3390/systems7010007

Magargle, R., Johnson, L., Mandloi, P., Davoudabadi, P., Bhatt, A., Shrivastava, R., & Farber, J. (2017). A simulation-based digital twin for model-driven health monitoring and predictive maintenance of an automotive braking system. *Proceedings of the 12th International Modelica Conference*, Prague, Czech Republic, 35–46. DOI: 10.3384/ecp1713235

Maiwada, U. D., Danyaro, K. U., & Sarlan, A. B. (2024). Enhancing 5G energy efficiency through digital twin networks: A comprehensive review. *Digital Twins and Applications*, *1*(1), 4–25. DOI: 10.1049/dgt2.12008

Malayjerdi, M., Baykara, B. C., Sell, R., & Malayjerdi, E. (2021). Autonomous vehicle safety evaluation through a high-fidelity simulation approach. *Proceedings of the Estonian Academy of Sciences*, *70*(4), 413–421. DOI: 10.3176/proc.2021.4.07

Malega, P., Gazda, V., & Rudy, V. (2021). Optimization of production system in plant simulation. *Simulation*, *98*(4), 295–306. DOI: 10.1177/00375497211038908

Manfredi, K. A., Nervoso, A., Solis, A. O., & Longo, F. (2023). Simulation-driven analyses of performance of PCB assembly operations: A case study. In *Proceedings of the 22nd International Conference on Modelling and Applied Simulation*. DOI: 10.46354/i3m.2023.mas.022

Mansour, I., & Singh, S. (2025). Role of AI in an autonomous vehicle perception systems: Use of convolutional neural network approach to design the vehicle perception system. DOI: 10.4271/2025-01-8012

Mao, R., Li, Y., Li, G., Hildre, H. P., & Zhang, H. (2025). A Systematic Survey of Digital Twin Applications: Transferring Knowledge From Automotive and Aviation to Maritime Industry. *IEEE Transactions on Intelligent Transportation Systems*, *26*(4), 4240–4259. DOI: 10.1109/TITS.2025.3535593

Ma, Q., Huang, G., & Tang, X. (2021). GIS-based analysis of spatial–temporal correlations of urban traffic accidents. *European Transport Research Review*, *13*(1), 50. DOI: 10.1186/s12544-021-00509-y

Marques da Silva, M., & Dinis, R. (2021). Power-ordered NOMA with massive MIMO for 5G systems. *Applied Sciences (Basel, Switzerland)*, *11*(8), 3541. DOI: 10.3390/app11083541

Martínez-Gutiérrez, A., Díez-González, J., Ferrero-Guillén, R., Verde, P., Álvarez, R., & Pérez, H. (2021). Digital Twin for Automatic Transportation in Industry 4.0. *Sensors (Basel)*, *21*(10), 3344. Advance online publication. DOI: 10.3390/s21103344 PMID: 34065011

Martinez, V. M. G., Campelo, D. R., & Ribeiro, M. R. N. (2025). Sustainable intelligent transportation systems via digital twins: A contextualized survey. *IEEE Open Journal of Intelligent Transportation Systems*, *6*, 363–392. DOI: 10.1109/OJITS.2025.3553696

Masaracchia, A., Sharma, V., Canberk, B., Dobre, O. A., & Duong, T. Q. (2022). Digital twin for 6G: Taxonomy, research challenges, and the road ahead. *IEEE Open Journal of the Communications Society*, *3*, 2137–2150. DOI: 10.1109/OJCOMS.2022.3219015

Maulik, S., Riordan, D., & Walsh, J. (2022). Dynamic reduction-based virtual models for digital twins—A comparative study. *Applied Sciences (Basel, Switzerland)*, *12*(14), 7154. DOI: 10.3390/app12147154

Ma, W., Lin, S., Ci, Y., & Li, R. (2024). Resilience evaluation and improvement of post-disaster multimodal transportation networks. *Transportation Research Part A, Policy and Practice*, *189*, 104243. DOI: 10.1016/j.tra.2024.104243

May, M., Finke, A., Theuner, K., & Lanza, G. (2024). Framework for automatic production simulation tuning with machine learning. *Procedia CIRP*, *121*, 49–54. Advance online publication. DOI: 10.1016/j.procir.2023.11.002

Mehta, G., Bose, S. R., & Selva Naveen, R. (2023). Optimizing Lithium-ion Battery Controller Design for Electric Vehicles: A Comprehensive Study. FMDB Transactions on Sustainable Energy Sequence, 1(2), 60–70. https://www.fmdbpub.com/user/journals/article_details/FTSES/132

Melders, L., Smigins, R., & Birkavs, A. (2025). Recent advances in vehicle driver health monitoring systems. *Sensors (Basel)*, *25*(6), 1812. DOI: 10.3390/s25061812 PMID: 40292968

Melo, V., Barbosa, J., Mota, G., De La Prieta Pintado, F., & Leitão, P. (2024). Design of an ISO 23247 Compliant Digital Twin for an Automotive Assembly Line. *2024 IEEE 7th International Conference on Industrial Cyber-Physical Systems (ICPS)*, 1–6. DOI: 10.1109/ICPS59941.2024.10640052

Mendi, A. (2022). A Digital Twin Case Study on Automotive Production Line. *Sensors (Basel)*, *22*(18), 6963. Advance online publication. DOI: 10.3390/s22186963 PMID: 36146313

Meng, K., Zhou, R., Li, Z., & Zhang, K. (2023). A quantitative approach of generating challenging testing scenarios based on functional safety standard. *Applied Sciences (Basel, Switzerland)*, *13*(6), 3494. DOI: 10.3390/app13063494

Meng, Y., Yates, K., Dahiya, A., & Untaroiu, C. D. (2025). Occupant safety assessment in autonomous vehicles using integrated simulation and physical testing. *Computer Methods in Biomechanics and Biomedical Engineering*, *28*(5), 1–13. DOI: 10.1080/10255842.2025.2476184 PMID: 40083123

Meng, Z., Zhao, S., Chen, H., Hu, M., Tang, Y., & Song, Y. (2022). The Vehicle Testing Based on Digital Twins Theory for Autonomous Vehicles. *IEEE Journal of Radio Frequency Identification*, *6*, 710–714. DOI: 10.1109/JRFID.2022.3211565

Miller, L., Navarro, P. J., & Rosique, F. (2025). EdgeNet: An end-to-end Deep Neural Network Pretrained with Synthetic Data for a Real-world Autonomous Driving Application. *Sensors (Basel)*, *25*(1), 89. DOI: 10.3390/s25010089

Milliken, W. F., & Milliken, D. L. (1995). *Race Car Vehicle Dynamics*. Society of Automotive Engineers, Inc.

Milliken, W. F., & Milliken, D. L. (2002). *Chassis Design: Principle and Analysis*. Society of Automotive Engineers, Inc. DOI: 10.4271/R-206

Minerva, R., Lee, G. M., & Crespi, N. (2020). Digital twin in the IoT context: A survey on technical features, scenarios, and architectural models. *Proceedings of the IEEE. Institute of Electrical and Electronics Engineers, 108*(10), 1785–1824. DOI: 10.1109/JPROC.2020.2998530

Mohanraj, E., N, E., S, S., & S, S. (2024). Digital Twins for Automotive Predictive Maintenance. *2024 International Conference on Inventive Computation Technologies (ICICT)*, 1579–1584. DOI: 10.1109/ICICT60155.2024.10544392

Mohd Nor, N., Zakaria, Z., Yano, J., & Mohd Pisal, S. M. (2026). Proposed end-of-life vehicle (ELV) management framework for local government in Klang Valley, Malaysia. *Journal of Material Cycles and Waste Management, 28*(2), 1011–1028. Advance online publication. DOI: 10.1007/s10163-025-02458-3

Moshood, T. D., Rotimi, J. O. B., Shahzad, W., & Bamgbade, J. A. (2024). Infrastructure digital twin technology: A new paradigm for future construction industry. *Technology in Society*, *77*, 102519. DOI: 10.1016/j.techsoc.2024.102519

Moumane, A., Al Karkouri, J., & Batchi, M. (2025). Utilizing GIS, remote sensing, and AHP-multi-criteria decision analysis for optimal landfill site selection in Kenitra Province, Morocco: A step towards sustainable development goals. *Discover Environment*, *3*(1), 4. DOI: 10.1007/s44274-025-00183-0

Mudunuri, L. N. R., & Bhattacharya, P. (2024). Ethical Considerations Balancing Emotion and Autonomy in AI Systems. In Tikadar, S., Liu, H., Bhattacharya, P., & Bhattacharya, S. (Eds.), *Humanizing Technology With Emotional Intelligence* (pp. 443–456). IGI Global Scientific Publishing., DOI: 10.4018/979-8-3693-7011-7.ch023

Müller, A., Klein, P., & Schmid, R. (2024). Data of automated optical inspection of surface-mounted technology. *Data in Brief*, •••, 48. PMID: 38328301

Mun, H., & Jung, J. (2025). Impact of compact city on carbon emission reduction based on urban size: A spatial analysis using satellite imagery. *Sustainable Cities and Society*, *126*, 106326. DOI: 10.1016/j.scs.2025.106326

Munoz Diaz, E., Rubio Hernan, J. M., Jurado Romero, F., Karite, A., Vervisch-Picois, A., & Samama, N. (2023). Advanced smartphone-based identification of transport modes: Resilience under GNSS-based attacks. *Future Transportation*, *3*(2), 568–583. DOI: 10.3390/futuretransp3020033

Musa, S. S., Zennaro, M., Libsie, M., & Pietrosemoli, E. (2022). Mobility-aware proactive edge caching optimization scheme in information-centric IoV networks. *Sensors (Basel)*, *22*(4), 1387. DOI: 10.3390/s22041387 PMID: 35214288

Naseri, F., Gil, S., Barbu, C., Çetkin, E., Yarimca, G., Jensen, A. C., Larsen, P. G., & Gomes, C. (2023). Digital twin of electric vehicle battery systems: Comprehensive review of the use cases, requirements, and platforms. *Renewable & Sustainable Energy Reviews*, *179*, 113280. Advance online publication. DOI: 10.1016/j.rser.2023.113280

Navarro-Ortiz, J., Romero-Diaz, P., Sendra, S., Ameigeiras, P., Ramos-Munoz, J. J., & Lopez-Soler, J. M. (2020). A survey on 5G usage scenarios and traffic models. *IEEE Communications Surveys and Tutorials*, *22*(2), 905–929. DOI: 10.1109/COMST.2020.2971781

Nawaz Khan, M., & Ahmad, I. (2025). Harnessing digital twins: Advancing virtual replicas for optimized system performance and sustainable innovation. *Babylonian Journal of Mechanical Engineering, 2025*, 18–33. DOI: 10.58496/BJME/2025/002

Nayan, K. R. (2025). Digital Manufacturing Transformation in the Automotive Industry: A Technical Analysis. *International Journal of Scientific Research in Computer Science, Engineering and Information Technology*. DOI: 10.32628/CSEIT25112362

Nayyef, Z. T., & Mahmood, I. S. M. (2025). Federated Learning for 6G networks: A comprehensive review of challenges, techniques, and future directions. *Warith Scientific Journal of Engineering and Technology*, *1*(1), 30–44. DOI: 10.57026/wsjet.v1i1.14

Negri, E., Fumagalli, L., & Macchi, M. (2017). A review of the roles of digital twin in CPS-based production systems. *Procedia Manufacturing*, *11*, 939–948. DOI: 10.1016/j.promfg.2017.07.198

Neto, A. A., Da Silva, E. R., Deschamps, F., Do Nascimento, L. A., & De Lima, P. (2023). Modeling production disorder: Procedures for digital twins of flexibility-driven manufacturing systems. *International Journal of Production Economics*, *260*, 108846. Advance online publication. DOI: 10.1016/j.ijpe.2023.108846

Neto, L. N., Reway, F., Poledna, Y., Drechsler, M., & Hanke, T. (2025). Functional safety of automotive SoCs for autonomous driving: Challenges and trends. *International Journal of Vehicle Safety and Mobility Technology*, *15*(2), 55–70. DOI: 10.1504/IJVSMT.2025.147353

Nguyen, H. X., Sun, K., To, D., Vien, Q.-T., & Le, T. A. (2025). Digital twin for O-RAN toward 6G. *IEEE Communications Magazine*, *63*(3), 174–181. DOI: 10.1109/MCOM.003.2400016

Nguyen, H. X., Trestian, R., To, D., & Tatipamula, M. (2021). Digital Twin for 5G and Beyond. *IEEE Communications Magazine*, *59*(2), 10–15. DOI: 10.1109/MCOM.001.2000343

Nonomura, K., Wang, K., Li, Z., Yu, T., & Sakaguchi, K. (2025). *Digital twin-empowered cooperative autonomous car-sharing services: Proof-of-concept.*

Noviati, N. D., Putra, F. E., Sadan, S., Ahsanitaqwim, R., Septiani, N., & Santoso, N. P. L. (2024). Artificial Intelligence in autonomous vehicles: Current innovations and future trends. *International Journal of Cyber and IT Service Management*, *4*(2), 97–104. DOI: 10.34306/ijcitsm.v4i2.161

NVIDIA. (2024a). *Foxconn develops physical AI-enabled smart factories with digital twins*. https://www.nvidia.com/en-us/customer-stories/foxconn-develops-physical-ai-enabled-smart-factories-with-digital-twins/

NVIDIA. (2024b). *Foxconn trains robots, streamlines assembly with NVIDIA AI and digital twins*. https://blogs.nvidia.com/blog/foxconn-digital-twin-ai/

Obaid, L., Alattieh, S. A., Abdallah, M., & Hamad, K. (2023). Environmental impacts of the transition to automated vehicles: A life cycle perspective. *Sustainable Materials and Technologies*, *38*, e00725. DOI: 10.1016/j.susmat.2023.e00725

Obayashi, I. (2018). Volume-optimal cycle: Tightest Representative Cycle of a Generator in Persistent Homology. *SIAM Journal on Applied Algebra and Geometry*, *2*(4), 508–534. DOI: 10.1137/17M1159439

Olayinka, A. (2023). Synergistic integration of Artificial Intelligence and machine learning in smart manufacturing (Industry 4.0). *World Journal of Advanced Engineering Technology and Sciences*, *10*(1), 255–263. DOI: 10.30574/wjaets.2023.10.1.0264

Oliveira-Silva, E., Zamarreño, J., Moraga, C., Navia, D., Marmol, S., & Gonzalez, R. (2023). A virtual environment of an industrial splitter to test Dynamic Real Time Optimization. *Simulation Modelling Practice and Theory*, *129*, 102821. DOI: 10.1016/j.simpat.2023.102821

Onaji, I., Tiwari, D., Soulatiantork, P., Song, B., & Tiwari, A. (2022). Digital twin in manufacturing: Conceptual framework and case studies. *International Journal of Computer Integrated Manufacturing*, *35*(8), 831–858. DOI: 10.1080/0951192X.2022.2027014

Öngir, S., Kaleli, E. C., Konyar, M. Z., & Ertunç, H. M. (2025). Vertical Force Monitoring of Racing Tires: A Novel Deep Neural Network-Based Estimation Method. *Applied Sciences (Basel, Switzerland)*, *15*(1), 123. Advance online publication. DOI: 10.3390/app15010123

OpenStreetMap contributors. (n.d.). *Planet dump*. OpenStreetMap. https://planet.osm.org

Orgován, L., Bécsi, T., & Aradi, S. (2021). Autonomous Drifting using Reinforcement Learning. *Periodica Polytechnica Transportation Engineering*, *49*(3), 292–300. DOI: 10.3311/PPtr.18581

Orlov, S. P., & Susarev, S. V. (2023). Decision Support System for autonomous vehicle maintenance management. *Ontology of Designing*, *13*(3), 424–436. DOI: 10.18287/2223-9537-2023-13-3-424-436

Overbeck, L., Graves, S., & Lanza, G. (2023). Development and analysis of digital twins of production systems. *International Journal of Production Research*, *62*(10), 3544–3558. DOI: 10.1080/00207543.2023.2242525

Panyaram, S. (2024). Enhancing performance and sustainability of electric vehicle technology with advanced energy management. *FMDB Transactions on Sustainable Energy Sequence*, *2*(2), 110–119. DOI: 10.69888/FTSES.2024.000311

Paolini, E., Valcarenghi, L., Maggiani, L., & Andriolli, N. (2024). Real-time network packet classification exploiting computer vision architectures. *IEEE Open Journal of the Communications Society*, *5*, 1155–1166. DOI: 10.1109/OJCOMS.2024.3363082

Papadakis, D. M., Savvides, A., Michael, A., & Michopoulos, A. (2024). Advancing sustainable urban mobility: Insights from best practices and case studies. *Fuel Communications*, *20*, 100125. DOI: 10.1016/j.jfueco.2024.100125

Papanagnou, C. (2019). A Digital Twin Model for Enhancing Performance Measurement in Assembly Lines. *Internet of Things : Engineering Cyber Physical Human Systems*. Advance online publication. DOI: 10.1007/978-3-030-18732-3_4

Paramasivan, P., Rajest, S. S., Chinnusamy, K., Regin, R., & John Joseph, F. J. (2024). *Cross-Industry AI Applications*. Advances in Computational Intelligence and Robotics. IGI., DOI: 10.4018/979-8-3693-5951-8

Parashar, A., & Gameti, N. (2024). Digital twins in manufacturing: A survey of current practices and future trends. *International Journal of Science and Research Archive*, *13*(1), 1240–1250. DOI: 10.30574/ijsra.2024.13.1.1705

Park, N., Park, J., Joo, Y.-J., & Abdel-Aty, M. (2025). Micro-level hotspot identification at intersections using traffic conflict analysis. *Accident; Analysis and Prevention*, *220*, 108167. DOI: 10.1016/j.aap.2025.108167 PMID: 40644754

Parra, A., Rodríguez, A., Zubizarreta, A., & Pérez, J. (2020). Validation of a Real-Time Capable Multibody Vehicle Dynamics Formulation for Automotive Testing Frameworks Based on Simulation. *IEEE Access : Practical Innovations, Open Solutions*, *8*, 213253–213265. DOI: 10.1109/ACCESS.2020.3040232

Pasupuleti, M. K. (2024). *Future networks: AI, IoT, and Sustainable Communications from Earth to orbit*. National Education Services., DOI: 10.62311/nesx/rb978-81-982172-0-2

Patil, Y. J.Yuvaraj J Patil. (2025). Scenario-driven safety verification: A comprehensive framework for autonomous vehicle validation within ISO 26262. International Journal of Scientific Research in Computer Science. *Engineering and Information Technology*, *11*(2), 1047–1056. DOI: 10.32628/CSEIT25112431

Pedon, D., Bani Hashemi, S., LeNguyen, K., & Derrible, S. (2024). Navigating urban complexity: The transformative role of digital twins in smart city development. *Sustainable Cities and Society*, *111*, 105583. DOI: 10.1016/j.scs.2024.105583

Pekarčíková, M., Kliment, M., Kronová, J., Trebuňa, P., & Hovana, A. (2025). Simulation-Based Optimization of Material Supply in Automotive Production Using RTLS Data. *Applied Sciences (Basel, Switzerland)*, *15*(16), 9102. Advance online publication. DOI: 10.3390/app15169102

Peng, P., Wang, Z., Cui, P., Hu, X., Yao, J., & Li, J. (2025). Public health risk assessment of urban air pollution using traffic and mobility data. *Frontiers in Public Health*, *13*, 1686346. DOI: 10.3389/fpubh.2025.1686346 PMID: 41080884

Petit, J., & Shladover, S. (2014). Potential cyberattacks on automated vehicles. *IEEE Transactions on Intelligent Transportation Systems*, 1–11. Advance online publication. DOI: 10.1109/TITS.2014.2342271

Pfeiffer, J., Fuchß, D., Kühn, T., Liebhart, R., Neumann, D., Neimöck, C., Seiler, C., Koziolek, A., & Wortmann, A. (2024). Modeling Languages for Automotive Digital Twins: A Survey Among the German Automotive Industry. *Proceedings of the ACM/IEEE 27th International Conference on Model Driven Engineering Languages and Systems*. DOI: 10.1145/3640310.3674100

Pierre, T. J., Tao, C., Vénant, K., & Erneste, B. (2024). Speed management blueprint: Conception of an IoT-based electric vehicle speed limiter monitoring system for Kigali city vehicles. *FMDB Transactions on Sustainable Energy Sequence*, *2*(1), 33–48. DOI: 10.69888/FTSES.2024.000190

Pikner, H., Malayjerdi, M., Bellone, M., Baykara, B., & Sell, R. (2024). Autonomous driving validation and verification using digital twins. In *Proceedings of the 10th International Conference on Vehicle Technology and Intelligent Transport Systems* (pp. 204–211). SCITEPRESS - Science and Technology Publications. DOI: 10.5220/0012546400003702

Piromalis, D., & Kantaros, A. (2022). Digital Twins in the Automotive Industry: The Road toward Physical-Digital Convergence. *Applied System Innovation*, *5*(4), 65. Advance online publication. DOI: 10.3390/asi5040065

Punia, A., Geetha, C. J., Ramesh, D. B., Nikhila, K., Manjunath, H. R., & Tripathi, R. K. (2025). Implementing Digital Twins for real-time library operations monitoring. *Indian Journal of Information Sources and Services*, *15*(3), 66–75. DOI: 10.51983/ijiss-2025.IJISS.15.3.08

Qi, H. (2025). Microscopic modeling of abnormal driver behavior in mixed traffic with automated vehicles. *IEEE Transactions on Intelligent Transportation Systems*, *26*(5), 1163–1176. DOI: 10.1109/TITS.2024.3485668

Qin, Q., Zhang, Y., & Liu, H. (2026). Robot digital twin systems in manufacturing: Technologies and applications for intelligent production. *Robotics and Computer-integrated Manufacturing*, *89*, 102733.

Qi, Q., & Tao, F. (2018). Digital twin and big data towards smart manufacturing and Industry 4.0: 360 degree comparison. *IEEE Access : Practical Innovations, Open Solutions*, *6*, 3585–3593. DOI: 10.1109/ACCESS.2018.2793265

Qureshi, K., & Abdullah, H. (2014). Sensor based vehicle environment perception information system. DOI: 10.1109/UIC-ATC-ScalCom.2014.60

Rahman, M. A., Shahrior, M. F., Iqbal, K., & Abushaiba, A. A. (2025). Enabling intelligent industrial automation: A review of machine learning applications with digital twin and edge AI integration. *Automation*, *6*(3), 37. DOI: 10.3390/automation6030037

Rajamani, R. (2006). Vehicle Dynamics and Control. In Rajamani, R. (Ed.), *Vehicle Dynamics and Control*. Springer US., DOI: 10.1007/978-1-4614-1433-9_2

Rajan, G., & Li, S. (2024). Smart building Digital Twin for interior water distribution system management. ISPRS - International Archives of the Photogrammetry Remote Sensing and Spatial Information Sciences, XLVIII-4–2024, 373–379. DOI: 10.5194/isprs-archives-XLVIII-4-2024-373-2024

Rajest, S. S., Singh, B. J., Obaid, A., Regin, R., & Chinnusamy, K. (2023). *Recent developments in machine and human intelligence*. Advances in Computational Intelligence and Robotics. IGI Global., DOI: 10.4018/978-1-6684-9189-8

Rakha, H. A., Ahn, K., & Moran, K. Integration framework for modeling eco-routing strategies: Logic and preliminary results. International Journal of Transportation Science and Technology. DOI: 10.1260/2046-0430.1.3.259

Ramesh, G., & Praveen, J. (2021). Artificial Intelligence (AI) framework for multi-modal learning and decision making towards autonomous and electric vehicles. E3S Web of Conferences, 309, 01167. DOI: 10.1051/e3sconf/202130901167

Ravikumar, R. N., & Aarthi, S. (2025b). Real-time IoT, quantum advances, and ethical implications in autonomous AI systems. In *Advances in Computational Intelligence and Robotics* (pp. 185–216). IGI Global Scientific Publishing. DOI: 10.4018/979-8-3373-3146-1.ch007

Ravikumar, R. N., & Aarthi, S. (2025). Digital Twin-driven green energy systems. In *The Future of Green Energy* (pp. 1–28). IGI Global Scientific Publishing., DOI: 10.4018/979-8-3373-3226-0.ch001

Ravikumar, R. N., & Aarthi, S. (2025c). Web-based cybersecurity architectures. In *Impact of Web Technologies on Digital Transformation* (pp. 187–216). IGI Global Scientific Publishing., DOI: 10.4018/979-8-3373-5167-4.ch007

Regin, R., Gaayathri, R. S., Paramasivan, P., Rajest, S. S., & Radwan, R. (2024). VehiWalnut: Smart Fuel Management with Real-Time Data and User Interaction. *FMDB Transactions on Sustainable Intelligent Networks*, *1*(1), 56–71. DOI: 10.69888/FTSIN.2024.000157

Reimpell, J., Stoll, H., & Betzler, J. W. (2001). *The Automotive Chassis: Engineering Principles* (2nd ed.). Butterworth-Heinemann.

Ren, D., Huang, H., Li, Y., & Jin, J. (2025). High-risk Test Scenario Generation for Autonomous Vehicles at Roundabouts using Naturalistic Driving Data. *Applied Sciences (Basel, Switzerland)*, *15*(8), 4505. DOI: 10.3390/app15084505

Richmond, J., Lawal, Y., Rose, C., & Kayali, O. (2026). Security and privacy challenges in vehicle-to-everything (V2X) communications.

Riedmaier, S., Ponn, T., Ludwig, D., Schick, B., & Diermeyer, F. (2020). Survey on scenario-based safety assessment of automated vehicles. *IEEE Access : Practical Innovations, Open Solutions*, *8*, 87456–87477. DOI: 10.1109/ACCESS.2020.2993730

Rios-Torres, J., & Malikopoulos, A. (2016). A survey on the coordination of connected and automated vehicles at intersections and merging at highway on-ramps. *IEEE Transactions on Intelligent Transportation Systems*. Advance online publication. DOI: 10.1109/TITS.2016.2600504

Rjabtšikov, V., Rassõlkin, A., Kudelina, K., Kallaste, A., & Vaimann, T. (2023). Review of electric vehicle testing procedures for digital twin development: A comprehensive analysis. *Energies*, *16*(19), 6952. DOI: 10.3390/en16196952

Robert, O., Iztok, P., & Borut, B. (2019). Real-Time manufacturing optimization with a simulation model and virtual reality. *Procedia Manufacturing*, *38*, 1103–1110. Advance online publication. DOI: 10.1016/j.promfg.2020.01.198

Rokseth, B., Haugen, O. I., & Utne, I. B. (2019). Safety verification for autonomous ships. MATEC Web of Conferences, 273, 02002. DOI: 10.1051/matecconf/201927302002

Rombach, R., Blattmann, A., Lorenz, D., Esser, P., & Ommer, B. (2022). High-resolution Image Synthesis with Latent Diffusion Models. In *Proceedings of the IEEE/CVF Conference on Computer Vision and Pattern Recognition (CVPR)* (pp. 10684–10695). DOI: 10.1109/CVPR52688.2022.01042

Rosen, R., von Wichert, G., Lo, G., & Bettenhausen, K. D. (2015). About the importance of autonomy and digital twins for the future of manufacturing. *IFAC-PapersOnLine*, *48*(3), 567–572. DOI: 10.1016/j.ifacol.2015.06.141

Rosique, F., Navarro, P. J., Fernández, C., & Padilla, A. (2019). A systematic review of perception system and simulators for autonomous vehicles research. *Sensors (Basel), 19*(3), 648. DOI: 10.3390/s19030648 PMID: 30764486

Russo, M. B., Franciosa, P., Greco, A., & Gerbino, S. (2024). Reduced-order modelling for real-time physics-based variation simulation enhanced with adaptive sampling and optimized interpolation. *International Journal of Advanced Manufacturing Technology, 132*(7-8), 3709–3734. DOI: 10.1007/s00170-024-13493-z

Rybak, L., Hurtasenko, A., Skitova, V., & Voloshkin, A. (2023). Numerical Method of Designing an Automotive Driving Simulator for Training Drivers of Motor Vehicles. *E3S Web of Conferences*. DOI: 10.1051/e3sconf/202344606007

Sadaf, M., Iqbal, Z., Javed, A. R., Saba, I., Krichen, M., Majeed, S., & Raza, A. (2023). Connected and automated vehicles: Infrastructure, applications, security, critical challenges, and future aspects. *Technologies, 11*(5), 117. DOI: 10.3390/technologies11050117

Saidi, S., Koutsopoulos, H. N., Wilson, N. H. M., & Zhao, J. (2023). Train following model for urban rail transit performance analysis. *Transportation Research Part C, Emerging Technologies, 148*, 104037. DOI: 10.1016/j.trc.2023.104037

Sajadieh, S. M. M., & Noh, S. D. (2025). From simulation to autonomy: Reviews of the integration of artificial intelligence and digital twins. *International Journal of Precision Engineering and Manufacturing-Green Technology, 12*(5), 1597–1628. DOI: 10.1007/s40684-025-00750-z

Samak, T. V., Samak, C. V., & Krovi, V. N. (2024a). Metaverse for safer roadways: An immersive digital twin framework for exploring human-autonomy coexistence in urban transportation systems. In *2024 IEEE Conference on Telepresence* (pp. 160–165). DOI: 10.1109/Telepresence63209.2024.10841549

Samak, T. V., Samak, C. V., & Krovi, V. N. (2024b). Towards validation of autonomous vehicles across scales using an integrated digital twin framework. In *2024 IEEE International Conference on Advanced Intelligent Mechatronics (AIM)* (pp. 1068–1075). DOI: 10.1109/AIM55361.2024.10637205

Sanz Rodrigo, M., Rivera, D., Moreno, J. I., Àlvarez-Campana, M., & López, D. R. (2023). Digital twins for 5G networks: A modeling and deployment methodology. *IEEE Access : Practical Innovations, Open Solutions, 11*, 38112–38126. DOI: 10.1109/ACCESS.2023.3267548

Sarker, M. A. L., Sarker, M. O. F., & Han, D. S. (2025). A survey on digital twin-assisted intelligent vehicle localization. *ICT Express, 11*(5), 981–992. DOI: 10.1016/j.icte.2025.08.008

Sathish Babu, B., Sandhya, S., & Subramanya, K. N. (2024). Quantum Key Distribution in securing next-generation cyber-physical systems. In *Advances in Information Security, Privacy, and Ethics* (pp. 215–248). IGI Global. DOI: 10.4018/979-8-3693-9220-1.ch008

Saxena, R. R., Sujith, S., & Nelavala, R. (2023). MuscleDrive: A Proof of Concept Describing the Electromyographic Navigation of a Vehicle. FMDB Transactions on Sustainable Health Science Letters, 1(2), 107–117. https://www.fmdbpub.com/user/journals/article_details/FTSHSL/81

Sayedelahl, M. A. (2024). Enabling Intelligent Traffic Systems: A Deep Learning Method for Accurate Arabic License Plate Recognition. *FMDB Transactions on Sustainable Intelligent Networks*, *1*(1), 40–55. DOI: 10.69888/FTSIN.2024.000156

Sayed, S. A., Abdel-Hamid, Y., & Hefny, H. A. (2023). Artificial intelligence-based traffic flow prediction: A comprehensive review. *Journal of Electrical Systems and Information Technology*, *10*(1), 13. Advance online publication. DOI: 10.1186/s43067-023-00081-6

Schmidt, H., Büttner, K., & Prokop, G. (2023). Methods for Virtual Validation of Automotive Powertrain Systems in Terms of Vehicle Drivability—A Systematic Literature Review. *IEEE Access : Practical Innovations, Open Solutions*, *11*, 27043–27065. DOI: 10.1109/ACCESS.2023.3257106

Schroeder, G., Steinmetz, C., Rodrigues, R., Henriques, R., Rettberg, A., & Pereira, C. (2021). A Methodology for Digital Twin Modeling and Deployment for Industry 4.0. *Proceedings of the IEEE*, *109*(4), 556–567. DOI: 10.1109/JPROC.2020.3032444

Schwalb, E. (2021). Analysis of hazards for autonomous driving. *Journal of Autonomous Vehicles and Systems*, *1*(2), 021003. Advance online publication. DOI: 10.1115/1.4049922

Schwarz, C., & Wang, Z. (2022). The Role of Digital Twins in Connected and Automated Vehicles. *IEEE Intelligent Transportation Systems Magazine*, *14*(6), 41–51. DOI: 10.1109/MITS.2021.3129524

Seidel, R., Rachinger, B., Thielen, N., Schmidt, K., Meier, S., & Franke, J. (2023). Development and validation of a digital twin framework for surface mount technology. *Computers in Industry*, *134*, 103831. DOI: 10.1016/j.compind.2022.103831

Semeraro, C., Lezoche, M., Panetto, H., & Dassisti, M. (2021). Digital Twin Paradigm: A Systematic Literature Review. *Computers in Industry*, *130*, 103469. DOI: 10.1016/j.compind.2021.103469

Serdar, M. Z., Koç, M., & Al-Ghamdi, S. G. (2022). Urban transportation networks resilience: Indicators, disturbances, and assessment methods. *Sustainable Cities and Society*, *76*, 103452. DOI: 10.1016/j.scs.2021.103452

Shang, J., Xiao, L., Wu, Z., Yang, J., Xiao, Z., Wang, J., Zhang, Y., Chen, X., Wang, J., & Li, H. (2024). GvdsSQL: Heterogeneous Database Unified Access Technology for Wide-Area Environments. *Electronics (Basel)*, *13*(8), 1521. DOI: 10.3390/electronics13081521

Sharma, S. N. (2026). Urban spatial digital twin (USDT) in sustainability to spur economic growth for TOD-based development. In Ting, D. S.-K., & Awazi, N. P. (Eds.), *Tenable engineering for a sustainable future: Integrating SDGs and natural resource utilization* (1st ed.). Elsevier. DOI: 10.1016/B978-0-443-40576-1.00009-3

Sharma, S. N., & Dehalwar, K. (2025a). A systematic literature review of pedestrian safety in urban transport systems. *Journal of Road Safety*, *36*(4), 55–78. DOI: 10.33492/JRS-D-25-4-2707507

Sharma, S. N., & Dehalwar, K. (2025b). A systematic literature review of transit-oriented development to assess its role in economic development of cities. *Transportation in Developing Economies*, *11*(2), 23. DOI: 10.1007/s40890-025-00245-1

Sharma, S. N., Singh, D., & Dehalwar, K. (2024). Surrogate safety analysis: Leveraging advanced technologies for safer roads. *Warasan Technology Suranaree*, *31*(4), 010320. DOI: 10.55766/sujst-2024-04-e03837

Sheng, J., Zhang, Q., Li, H., Shen, S., Ming, R., Jiang, J., & Wang, J. (2023). Digital twin-driven intelligent manufacturing for flexible printed circuit board production. *Computers & Industrial Engineering*, *183*, 109587.

Sheraz, M., Chuah, T. C., Lee, Y. L., Alam, M. M., Al-Habashna, A., & Han, Z. (2024). A comprehensive survey on revolutionizing connectivity through artificial intelligence-enabled digital twin network in 6G. *IEEE Access : Practical Innovations, Open Solutions*, **•••**, 1–1. DOI: 10.1109/ACCESS.2024.3384272

Shladover, S. (2017). Connected and automated vehicle systems: Introduction and overview. *Journal of Intelligent Transport Systems*. Advance online publication. DOI: 10.1080/15472450.2017.1336053

Shoukat, M. U., Yan, L., Yan, Y., Zhang, F., Zhai, Y., Han, P., Nawaz, S. A., Raza, M. A., Akbar, M. W., & Hussain, A. (2024). Autonomous driving test system under hybrid reality: The role of digital twin technology. *Internet of Things : Engineering Cyber Physical Human Systems*, *27*, 101301. https://doi.org/https://doi.org/10.1016/j.iot.2024.101301. DOI: 10.1016/j.iot.2024.101301

Siemens PLM Software. (2017). *Smart manufacturing for electronics: The foundation of digital twin and digital thread in product and process planning*.

Siemens, A. G. (2024). *Realize your digital enterprise suite* (White paper). https://www.plm.automation.siemens.com/media/global/pl/Digital%20Enterprise%20Suite_tcm83-60580.pdf

Siemens, AG. (2021). *Digital enterprise suite: Realizing the digital twin*.

Singaravelan, A., Sujitha, S., Gopikha, S., Karthikeyan, T., & Panakkal, R. (2025). Smart transportation in VANET using a hybrid reptile search algorithm-based infrastructure model with VANET. *AVE Trends in Intelligent Computer Letters*, *1*(3), 104–118. DOI: 10.64091/ATICL.2025.000226

Singh, M., Fuenmayor, E., Hinchy, E., Qiao, Y., Murray, N., & Devine, D. (2021). Digital Twin: Origin to future. *Applied System Innovation*, *4*(2), 36. DOI: 10.3390/asi4020036

Singh, O. J., Bose, S. R., Jeba, J. A., Flavia, B. J., & Sulthana, M. R. (2025). Real-time identification of traffic violations through deep learning techniques. *AVE Trends in Intelligent Computing Systems*, *2*(2), 99–110. DOI: 10.64091/ATICS.2025.000134

Singh, P. K. (2023). Digital transformation in supply chain management: Artificial Intelligence (AI) and Machine Learning (ML) as catalysts for value creation. *International Journal of Supply Chain Management*, *12*(6), 57–63. DOI: 10.59160/ijscm.v12i6.6216

Smeets, J., Öztürk, K., & Liebich, R. (2023). Digital twins for automotive development: Two wheelers application. *Advanced Engineering Informatics*, *56*, 101982. DOI: 10.1016/j.aei.2023.101982

Song, B. (2024). Review on multisensor SLAM datasets for advanced perception and mapping technologies. *Applied and Computational Engineering*, *97*(1), 170–174. DOI: 10.54254/2755-2721/97/20241270

Song, J., Liu, S., Ma, T., Sun, Y., Tao, F., & Bao, J. (2023). Resilient digital twin modeling: A transferable approach. *Advanced Engineering Informatics*, *58*, 102148. DOI: 10.1016/j.aei.2023.102148

Song, Z., He, Z., Li, X., Ma, Q., Ming, R., Mao, Z., Pei, H., Peng, L., Hu, J., Yao, D., & Zhang, Y. (2024). Synthetic Datasets for Autonomous Driving: A Survey. *IEEE Transactions on Intelligent Vehicles*, *9*(1), 1847–1864. DOI: 10.1109/TIV.2023.3331024

Son, Y. H., Park, K., Lee, D., Jeon, S., & Do Noh, S. (2021). Digital twin–based cyber-physical system for automotive body production lines. *International Journal of Advanced Manufacturing Technology*, *115*(1-2), 291–310. DOI: 10.1007/s00170-021-07183-3

Soori, M., Arezoo, B., & Dastres, R. (2023). Virtual manufacturing in industry 4.0: A review. *Data Science and Management*. DOI: 10.1016/j.dsm.2023.10.006

Sosfenov, D. (2023). Use of digital twins in automotive industry: Russian and foreign experience. *Economics and Management*. DOI: 10.35854/1998-1627-2023-6-662-669

Sosik-Filipiak, K., & Osypchuk, O. (2023). Identification of solutions for vulnerable road users safety in urban transport systems: Grounded theory research. *Sustainability (Basel)*, *15*(13), 10568. Advance online publication. DOI: 10.3390/su151310568

Spiryagin, M., Edelmann, J., Klinger, F., & Cole, C. (2023). Vehicle system dynamics in digital twin studies in rail and road domains. *Vehicle System Dynamics*, *61*(7), 1737–1786. DOI: 10.1080/00423114.2023.2188228

Špitálová, Z. (2023). Vehicle-to-everything communication. Communications – Scientific Letters of the University of Zilina, 25, C24–C35. DOI: 10.26552/com.C.2023.017

Srilakshmi, U., Sandhya, I., Manikandan, J., Bindu, A. H., Regin, R., & Rajest, S. S. (2024). Design and implementation of energy-efficient protocols for underwater wireless sensor networks. In *Advances in Computer and Electrical Engineering* (pp. 417–430). IGI Global., DOI: 10.4018/979-8-3693-3739-4.ch021

Stavdas, A., Kosmatos, E., Maple, C., Hugues-Salas, E., Epiphaniou, G., Fowler, D. S., Razak, S. A., Matrakidis, C., Yuan, H., & Lord, A. (2024). Quantum Key Distribution for V2I communications with software-defined networking. *IET Quantum Communication*, *5*(1), 38–45. DOI: 10.1049/qtc2.12070

Stefko, R., Frajtova-Michalikova, K., Strakova, J., & Novak, A. (2025). Digital twin-based virtual factory and cyber-physical production systems. Equilibrium. *Quarterly Journal of Economics and Economic Policy*, *20*, 389–425. DOI: 10.24136/eq.3557

Stevanov, B., Sremčev, N., Lazarević, M., Anderla, A., Sladojević, S., & Vidicki, P. (2022). Optimization of the Subassembly Production Process Using Simulation. *International Journal of Simulation Modelling*, *21*(4), 663–674. Advance online publication. DOI: 10.2507/IJSIMM21-4-633

Storani, F., Di Pace, R., Bruno, F., & Fiori, C. (2021). Analysis and comparison of traffic flow models: A new hybrid traffic flow model vs benchmark models. *European Transport Research Review*, *13*(11), 1–16. DOI: 10.1186/s12544-021-00515-0

Su, C., Han, Y., Tang, X., Jiang, Q., Wang, T., & He, Q. (2024). Knowledge-based digital twin system: Using a knowlege-driven approach for manufacturing process modeling. *Computers in Industry*, *159-160*, 104101. Advance online publication. DOI: 10.1016/j.compind.2024.104101

Su, C., Tang, X., Jiang, Q., Han, Y., Wang, T., & Jiang, D. (2025). Digital twin system for manufacturing processes based on a multi-layer knowledge graph model. *Scientific Reports*, *15*(1), 12835. Advance online publication. DOI: 10.1038/s41598-024-85053-0 PMID: 40229336

Sujová, E., Bambura, R., Vysloužilová, D., & Koleda, P. (2023). Use of the digital twin concept to optimize the production process of engine blocks manufacturing. *Production Engineering Archives*, *29*(2), 168–174. DOI: 10.30657/pea.2023.29.20

Sujová, E., Čierna, H., & Bambura, R. (2019). *Simulation model of production as tool for industry 4.0 implementation into practice*. Engineering for Rural Development., DOI: 10.22616/ERDev2019.18.N279

Suleiman, R., Maradapu Vera Venkata Sai, A., Yu, W., & Wang, C. (2025). Blockchain for security in digital Twins. *Future Internet*, *17*(9), 385. DOI: 10.3390/fi17090385

Sumalee, A., Zhong, R. X., Pan, T. L., & Szeto, W. Y. (2011). Stochastic cell transmission model (SCTM): A stochastic dynamic traffic model for traffic state surveillance and assignment. *Transportation Research Part B: Methodological*, *45*(3), 507–533. DOI: 10.1016/j.trb.2010.09.006

Su, S., Jiang, L., Wang, W., Wang, W., Chu, C., & Wang, J. (2024). A digital twin modeling method of production lines based on flexible manufacturing. *Flexible Services and Manufacturing Journal*. Advance online publication. DOI: 10.1007/s10696-024-09571-9

Su, Z., Liu, X., Bou Hamdan, L., Maroulas, V., Wu, J., Carlsson, G., & Wei, G.-W. (2026). Topological Data Analysis and Topological Deep Learning beyond Persistent Homology: A Review. *Artificial Intelligence Review*, *59*(2), 58. DOI: 10.1007/s10462-025-11462-w

Szalay, Z. (2021). Next generation X-in-the-loop validation methodology for automated vehicle systems. *IEEE Access : Practical Innovations, Open Solutions*, *9*, 35616–35632. DOI: 10.1109/ACCESS.2021.3061732

Szymonik, A. (2024). Cybersecurity in autonomous vehicles: Threats, challenges and countermeasures. *LogForum*, *20*(3), 455–467. DOI: 10.17270/J.LOG.001099

Tagne, G., Talj, R., & Charara, A. (2015, July). Design and validation of a robust immersion and invariance controller for the lateral dynamics of intelligent vehicles. *Control Engineering Practice*, *40*, 81–92. Advance online publication. DOI: 10.1016/j.conengprac.2015.03.002

Tan, B., & Matta, A. (2024). The Digital Twin Synchronization Problem: Framework, Formulations, and Analysis. *IISE Transactions*, *56*(6), 652–665. DOI: 10.1080/24725854.2023.2253869

Tan, C., Wang, T., Zhang, M., & Yue, T. (2025). Simulation-based safety validation of autonomous driving functions: A systematic mapping study. *Software & Systems Modeling*, *24*(4), 1463–1483. DOI: 10.1007/s10270-024-01261-2

Tang, F., Chen, X., Rodrigues, T. K., Zhao, M., & Kato, N. (2022). Survey on digital twin edge networks (DITEN) toward 6G. *IEEE Open Journal of the Communications Society*, *3*, 1360–1381. DOI: 10.1109/OJCOMS.2022.3197811

Tang, L., Dai, J., Cheng, Z., Zhang, H., & Chen, Q. (2024). A Digital Twins-Assisted Multi-Autonomous Vehicle Distributed Collaborative Path Planning Algorithm With Fidelity Guarantee. *IEEE Transactions on Intelligent Transportation Systems*, *25*(12), 19904–19916. DOI: 10.1109/TITS.2024.3454633

Tang, S., Randhawa, S., Rui, J., Ludwig, C., Knoblauch, S., Hatfield, C., & Zipf, A. (2026). Estimating road speed classes: Integrating OpenStreetMap and Street View imagery for missing data imputation. *Computers, Environment and Urban Systems*, *125*, 102392. DOI: 10.1016/j.compenvurbsys.2025.102392

Tang, Z., He, J., Yang, K., & Chen, H.-H. (2024). Matching 5G connected vehicles to sensed vehicles for safe cooperative autonomous driving. *IEEE Network*, *38*(3), 227–235. DOI: 10.1109/MNET.2023.3321530

Tan, X., Deng, Q., & Hu, X. (2022). Research on vehicle carrying efficiency of three-lane expressway based on DEA method. *Transportation Letters*, *14*(8), 838–848. DOI: 10.1080/19427867.2021.1950267

Tan, Y. R., Hofmeister, M., Phua, S. Z., Brownbridge, G., Rustagi, K., Akroyd, J., Mosbach, S., Bhave, A., & Kraft, M. (2025). Beyond connected digital twins–can digital twins really deliver sustainable cities? *Sustainable Cities and Society*, *131*, 106596. DOI: 10.1016/j.scs.2025.106596

Tao, F., Qi, H., Liu, A., & Kusiak, A. (2024). Digital twin—A review of the evolution from concept to technology. *Applied Sciences (Basel, Switzerland)*, *14*(13), 5454. DOI: 10.3390/app14135454

Tao, F., Qi, Q., Wang, L., & Nee, A. Y. C. (2019). Digital twins and cyber–physical systems toward smart manufacturing. *Engineering (Beijing)*, *5*(4), 653–661. DOI: 10.1016/j.eng.2019.01.014

Tao, F., Zhang, H., Liu, A., & Nee, A. Y. C. (2019). Digital Twin in Industry: State-of-the-Art. *IEEE Transactions on Industrial Informatics*, *15*(4), 2405–2415. DOI: 10.1109/TII.2018.2873186

Tao, F., Zhang, H., Liu, A., & Nee, A. Y. C. (2025). Digital twin–enabled cyber–physical systems: Architecture, technologies, and future trends. *IEEE Transactions on Industrial Informatics*, *21*(2), 1450–1462. DOI: 10.1109/TII.2024.3456789

Tao, M., Zhang, Y., & Liu, L. (2023). Digital twin for smart manufacturing: A review. *Journal of Manufacturing Systems*, *73*, 1–18.

Thrun, S. Winning the DARPA Grand Challenge. IFAC Proceedings Volumes. DOI: 10.3182/20060912-3-DE-2911.00002

Tian, R., Li, N., Kolmanovsky, I., Yildiz, Y., & Girard, A. R. (2022). Game-theoretic modeling of traffic in unsignalized intersection network for autonomous vehicle control verification and validation. IEEE Transactions on Intelligent Transportation Systems: A Publication of the IEEE Intelligent Transportation Systems Council, 23(3), 2211–2226. DOI: 10.1109/TITS.2020.3035363

Tiwari, A., & Farag, H. E. Z. (2025). Responsible AI framework for autonomous vehicles: Addressing bias and fairness risks. *IEEE Access : Practical Innovations, Open Solutions*, *13*, 58800–58822. DOI: 10.1109/ACCESS.2025.3556781

Török, Á., & Pethő, Z. (2020). Introducing safety and security co-engineering related research orientations in the field of automotive security. *Periodica Polytechnica Transportation Engineering*, *48*(4), 349–356. DOI: 10.3311/PPtr.15850

Toth, B., & Szalay, Z. (2023). Development and functional validation method of the Scenario-in-the-Loop simulation control model using co-simulation techniques. *Machines (Basel), 11*(11), 1028. DOI: 10.3390/machines11111028

Tralie, C., Saul, N., & Bar-On, R. (2018). Ripser.py: A Lean Persistent Homology Library for Python. *Journal of Open Source Software, 3*(29), 925. DOI: 10.21105/joss.00925

Trupthi, Y. N., Chitra, K., Harilakshmi, V. M., Paramasivan, P., Rajest, S. S., Ali, M. M. S., & Christodoss, P. R. (2025). Comparative analysis of Random Forest and K-Nearest Neighbours for traffic volume prediction in smart cities. *AVE Trends in Intelligent Computing Systems, 2*(2), 111–121. DOI: 10.64091/ATICS.2025.000135

Tukaram Patil, V. (2025). Autonomous AI vehicle. *Journal of Integrated Engineering Sciences, 1*(2), 10–17. DOI: 10.63686/Jies.v1i2007

Utku, D. H. (2023). The Evaluation and Improvement of the Production Processes of an Automotive Industry Company via Simulation and Optimization. *Sustainability (Basel), 15*(3), 2331. Advance online publication. DOI: 10.3390/su15032331

Vachálek, J., Bartalsky, L., Rovný, O., Šišmišová, D., Morháč, M., & Lokšík, M. (2017). The digital twin of an industrial production line within the industry 4.0 concept. *2017 21st International Conference on Process Control (PC)*, 258–262. DOI: 10.1109/PC.2017.7976223

Valencia, E., Toapanta, F., Oña, G., Carrillo, A., & Herrera, C. (2025). Cooperative control of autonomous ground vehicles using connected infrastructure. *Journal of Intelligent & Robotic Systems, 111*(3), 71. DOI: 10.1007/s10846-025-02276-7

van Dyck, M., Lüttgens, D., Piller, F. T., & Brenk, S. (2023). Interconnected digital twins and the future of digital manufacturing: Insights from a Delphi study. *Journal of Product Innovation Management, 40*(4), 475–505. DOI: 10.1111/jpim.12685

Vanajakshi, J., Renuka, A., Kamath, V., & Adesh, S. (2025). Real-time traffic state estimation using connected vehicles and roadside sensors. *IEEE Access : Practical Innovations, Open Solutions, 13*, 1000–1010. DOI: 10.1109/ACCESS.2025.3544776

VanDerHorn, E., & Mahadevan, S. (2021). Digital Twin: Generalization, Characterization and Implementation. *Decision Support Systems, 145*, 113524. DOI: 10.1016/j.dss.2021.113524

Venkatasubramanian, S., Abirami, A., Kannan, R., & Senthil, S. (2024). Optimizing traffic prediction in continuous data stream in vehicular networks with triplet transfer learning and Dhole's hunting-based optimization. *FMDB Transactions on Sustainable Intelligent Networks, 1*(3), 165–177. DOI: 10.69888/FTSIN.2024.000286

Verreydt, S., Landuyt, D. V., & Joosen, W. (2025). Engineering trustworthy digital twins: A survey on safety, security and verification approaches. *Software & Systems Modeling, 24*(3), 873–901. DOI: 10.1007/s10270-024-01242-5

Vieira, A., Guilherme, E., Oliveira, J. A., Dias, L., & Pereira, G. (2019). *Combining simulation and optimization models on a production line problem: A case study*. THE EUROPEAN MODELING AND SIMULATION SYMPOSIUM., DOI: 10.46354/i3m.2019.emss.026

Visser, R., Basson, A., & Kruger, K. (2024). An Architecture for the Integration of Product and Production Digital Twins in the Automotive Industry. *Proceedings of the ACM/IEEE 27th International Conference on Model Driven Engineering Languages and Systems*. DOI: 10.1145/3652620.3688257

Vogl, G. W., Weiss, B. A., & Helu, M. (2019). A review of diagnostic and prognostic capabilities and best practices for manufacturing. *Journal of Intelligent Manufacturing*, *30*(1), 79–95. DOI: 10.1007/s10845-016-1228-8 PMID: 30820072

Volhonskaya, E. (2023). The problem of optimal assignment of autonomous vehicles in production-logistics system. *Vestnik of Samara State Technical University. Technical Sciences Series*. DOI: 10.14498/tech.2023.2.2

Vy Le, L., Do, S., Paul Lin, B.-S., & Tung, L.-P. (2018). Big data and machine learning driven Open5G-MEC for vehicular communications. *Transactions on Networks and Communications*, *6*(5), 103. Advance online publication. DOI: 10.14738/tnc.65.5410

Wachnicka, J., Jarczewska, A., & Pappalardo, G. (2023). Methods of cyclist training in Europe. *Sustainability (Basel)*, *15*(19), 14345. Advance online publication. DOI: 10.3390/su151914345

Waller, S. T., Mouskos, K. C., Kamaryiannis, D., & Ziliaskopoulos, A. K. (2006). A linear model for the continuous network design problem. *Computer-Aided Civil and Infrastructure Engineering*, *21*(5), 334–345. DOI: 10.1111/j.1467-8667.2006.00440.x

Wang, J., Zhang, Q., & Zhao, D. (2022). Highway Lane change decision-making via attention-based deep reinforcement learning. IEEE/CAA Journal of Automatica Sinica, 9(3), 567–569. DOI: 10.1109/JAS.2021.1004395

Wang, K., Li, Z., Yu, T., & Sakaguchi, K. (2023). Smart mobility digital twin for automated driving: Design and proof-of-concept. DOI: 10.1109/VTC2023-Spring57618.2023.10200728

Wang, C., Storms, K., Zhang, N., & Winner, H. (2024). Runtime unknown unsafe scenarios identification for SOTIF of autonomous vehicles. *Accident; Analysis and Prevention*, *195*, 107410. https://doi.org/https://doi.org/10.1016/j.aap.2023.107410. DOI: 10.1016/j.aap.2023.107410 PMID: 38056026

Wang, H., Shao, W., Sun, C., Yang, K., Cao, D., & Li, J. (2024). A Survey on an Emerging Safety Challenge for Autonomous Vehicles: Safety of the Intended Functionality. *Engineering (Beijing)*, *33*, 17–34. https://doi.org/https://doi.org/10.1016/j.eng.2023.10.011. DOI: 10.1016/j.eng.2023.10.011

Wang, J., Li, H., & Chen, K. (2022). Development and validation of a digital twin framework for surface mount technology assembly. *International Journal of Advanced Manufacturing Technology*, *121*, 1545–1562.

Wang, J., Li, S., Lu, Y., & Wang, L. (2020). A division method of determining the early-warning zone on an expressway for automated vehicles. *Discrete Dynamics in Nature and Society*, *2020*(1), 9523819. DOI: 10.1155/2020/9523819

Wang, K., Chen, C., & Wang, Y. (2022). Edge intelligence for digital twin-based predictive maintenance in autonomous systems. *IEEE Transactions on Industrial Informatics, 18*(7), 4672–4683. DOI: 10.1109/TII.2021.3110218

Wang, K., Dong, J., Wang, S., Yuan, Z., Sha, L., & Chen, X. (2025). Real-time scheduling for safety-critical tasks in autonomous vehicles. *IEEE Transactions on Vehicular Technology, 74*(5), 2335–2346. DOI: 10.1109/TVT.2025.3552481

Wang, K., Li, Z., Nonomura, K., Yu, T., Sakaguchi, K., Hashash, O., & Saad, W. (2024). Smart mobility digital twin based automated vehicle navigation system: A proof of concept. *IEEE Transactions on Intelligent Vehicles, 9*(3), 4348–4361. DOI: 10.1109/TIV.2024.3368109

Wang, Q. (2025). Enhancing Automotive Engineering Education with Interactive Virtual Simulation: A Research Perspective. *Computer Fraud & Security*, 298–312. Advance online publication. DOI: 10.52710/cfs.315

Wang, W., Su, S., Jiang, L., Chu, C., Chen, C., & Liu, M. (2025). Digital twin modeling and simulation method for production line equipment units. *Journal of Mechanical Science and Technology, 39*(2), 805–819. DOI: 10.1007/s12206-025-0125-5

Wang, X., Hao, M., Wu, M., Shang, C., Yu, R., & Kang, Q. (2025). Intelligent fault diagnosis in industrial IoT using digital twin and edge computing. *IEEE Internet of Things Journal, 12*(4), 4471–4487. DOI: 10.1109/JIOT.2024.3464521

Wang, Y., Xue, H., & Zhou, M. (2025). A digital twin-assisted VEC intelligent task offloading approach. *Electronics (Basel), 14*(17), 3444. DOI: 10.3390/electronics14173444

Wang, Z., Gupta, R., Han, K., Wang, H., Ganlath, A., Ammar, N., & Tiwari, P. (2022). Mobility Digital Twin: Concept, Architecture, Case Study, and Future Challenges. *IEEE Internet of Things Journal, 9*(18), 17452–17467. DOI: 10.1109/JIOT.2022.3156028

Wang, Z., Lv, C., & Wang, F.-Y. (2023). A new era of intelligent vehicles and intelligent transportation systems: Digital twins and parallel intelligence. *IEEE Transactions on Intelligent Vehicles, 8*(4), 2619–2627. Advance online publication. DOI: 10.1109/TIV.2023.3264812

Wei, C., Qin, Z., Zhang, Z., Wu, G., & Barth, M. J. (2025). Integrating multi-modal sensors: A review of fusion techniques for intelligent vehicles. DOI: 10.1109/IV64158.2025.11097396

Weingram, A., Cui, C., Lin, S., Munoz, S., Jacob, T., Viers, J., & Lu, X. (2025). A definition and taxonomy of digital twins: Case studies with machine learning and scientific applications. *Frontiers in High Performance Computing, 3*, 1536501. DOI: 10.3389/fhpcp.2025.1536501

Wei, R., McDonald, A. D., Mehta, R. K., & García, A. (2025). Human factors in automated vehicle supervision: Mental workload and trust in high-level driving automation. *Human Factors, 67*(4), 613–634. DOI: 10.1177/00187208241295932 PMID: 39486160

Weissensteiner, P., Stettinger, G., Khastgir, S., & Watzenig, D. (2023). Operational design domain-driven coverage for the safety argumentation of automated vehicles. *IEEE Access : Practical Innovations, Open Solutions, 11*, 12263–12284. DOI: 10.1109/ACCESS.2023.3242127

Wijesinghe, W., & Withanage, W. (2025). A GIS-MCDA based evaluation of the quality of life variations in Anuradhapura Municipal Council: A policy implication road map for human well-being. *Journal of Geospatial Surveying*, *5*(1), 1–10. Advance online publication. DOI: 10.4038/jgs.v5i1.62

Wu, K., Li, P., Cheng, Y., Parker, S. T., Ran, B., Noyce, D. A., & Ye, X. (2025). *A digital twin framework for physical-virtual integration in V2X-enabled connected vehicle corridors.*

Wu, D., Zhao, Q., Xia, X., Liu, C., Xu, Y., & Li, Y. (2025). Road adhesion information estimation of connected autonomous vehicle based on digital twin and vision sensor fusion. *IEEE Internet of Things Journal*, *12*(24), 54284–54303. Advance online publication. DOI: 10.1109/JIOT.2025.3621457

Wu, H., Ji, P., Ma, H., & Xing, L. (2023). A comprehensive review of digital twin from the perspective of total process: Data, models, networks and applications. *Sensors (Basel)*, *23*(19), 8306. DOI: 10.3390/s23198306 PMID: 37837136

Wu, J., Wang, S., Jiang, H., & Xue, W. (2024). Study on intelligent assembly process planning and execution system based on digital twin. *Robotic Intelligence and Automation*, *44*(3), 366–381. DOI: 10.1108/RIA-05-2023-0065

Wu, J., Wang, X., Dang, Y., & Lyu, Z. (2022). Digital twins and artificial intelligence in transportation infrastructure: Classification, application, and future research directions. *Computers & Electrical Engineering*, *101*, 107983. DOI: 10.1016/j.compeleceng.2022.107983

Wu, W., Sivaparthipan, C., & Sanz-Prieto, I. (2021). Application of Automobile Modelling Optimization Design Based on Virtual Reality Technology. *J. Interconnect. Networks*, *22*(Supp02), 2143007. DOI: 10.1142/S0219265921430076

Wu, Y. (2023). Obstacle avoidance control algorithm of self-driving electric vehicle based on DRL. *Applied and Computational Engineering*, *4*(1), 541–547. DOI: 10.54254/2755-2721/4/2023321

Wu, Y., Wang, W., Ding, Q., & Luan, W. (2024). Research on intelligent driving system based on V2X communication. In *Advances in Transdisciplinary Engineering*. IOS Press., DOI: 10.3233/ATDE240388

Xia, F., & Wan, J. (2024). Digital Twins for Discrete Manufacturing Lines: A Review. *Big Data and Cognitive Computing*, *8*(5), 45. DOI: 10.3390/bdcc8050045

Xie, J., & Wan, J. (2023). Digital Twin Four-Dimension Fusion Modeling Method Design and Application to the Discrete Manufacturing Line. *Big Data and Cognitive Computing*, *7*(2), 89. DOI: 10.3390/bdcc7020089

Xing, L., Li, B., Deng, K., Gao, J., Wu, H., Ma, H., & Zhang, X. (2025). Advancing intelligent transportation through digital twin: Challenges, models, and future prospects. *Ad Hoc Networks*, •••, 104077.

Xiong, H., Wang, Z., Wu, G., & Pan, Y. (2022). Design and implementation of digital twin-assisted simulation method for autonomous vehicle in car-following scenario. *Journal of Sensors*, *2022*, 1–12. DOI: 10.1155/2022/4879490

Xu, G., Chen, J., Wang, Z., Zhou, A., Schrader, M., Bittle, J., & Shao, Y. (2025). Enhancing traffic safety analysis with digital twin technology: Integrating vehicle dynamics and environmental factors into microscopic traffic simulation. *Scientific Reports*, *15*(1), 44404. DOI: 10.1038/s41598-025-31930-1 PMID: 41436761

Xu, H., Shao, Y., Chen, J., Wang, C., & Berres, A. (2024). Semi-automatic geographic information system framework for creating photo-realistic digital Twin Cities to support autonomous driving research. *Transportation Research Record: Journal of the Transportation Research Board*, *2678*(6), 1068–1084. DOI: 10.1177/03611981231205884

Yan, D., Sha, W., Wang, D., Yang, J., & Zhang, S. (2022). Digital twin-driven variant design of a 3C electronic product assembly line. *Scientific Reports*, *12*(1), 3846. Advance online publication. DOI: 10.1038/s41598-022-07894-x PMID: 35264664

Yang, J., Son, Y. H., Lee, D., & Noh, S. (2022). Digital Twin-Based Integrated Assessment of Flexible and Reconfigurable Automotive Part Production Lines. *Machines (Basel)*, *10*(2), 75. Advance online publication. DOI: 10.3390/machines10020075

Yang, K., Li, S., Chen, Y., Cao, D., & Tang, X. (2025). Safe reinforcement learning for autonomous driving with risk constraints. *IEEE Transactions on Vehicular Technology*, *74*(3), 3828–3842. DOI: 10.1109/TVT.2024.3488749

Yannis, G., Nikolaou, D., Laiou, A., Stürmer, Y. A., Buttler, I., & Jankowska-Karpa, D. (2020). Vulnerable road users: Cross-cultural perspectives on performance and attitudes. *IATSS Research*, *44*(3), 220–229. DOI: 10.1016/j.iatssr.2020.08.006

Yao, J.-F., Yang, Y., Wang, X.-C., & Zhang, X.-P. (2023). Systematic review of digital twin technology and applications. *Visual Computing for Industry, Biomedicine, and Art*, *6*(1), 10. DOI: 10.1186/s42492-023-00137-4 PMID: 37249731

Yeğin, V. (2025). MATLAB/Simulink based autonomous vehicle collision simulation and energy absorption analysis. *Journal of Materials and Mechatronics: A*, *6*(1), 249–261. DOI: 10.55546/jmm.1650323

Yegul, M., Erenay, F., Striepe, S., & Yavuz, M. (2017). Improving configuration of complex production lines via simulation-based optimization. *Computers & Industrial Engineering*, *109*, 295–312. DOI: 10.1016/j.cie.2017.04.019

Yeong, D. J., Panduru, K., & Walsh, J. (2025). Exploring the unseen: A survey of multi-sensor fusion and the role of explainable AI (XAI) in autonomous vehicles. *Sensors (Basel)*, *25*(3), 856. DOI: 10.3390/s25030856 PMID: 39943496

Ye, Y., Wong, S. C., Li, Y. C., & Choi, K. M. (2023). Crossing behaviors of drunk pedestrians unfamiliar with local traffic rules. *Safety Science*, *157*, 105924. DOI: 10.1016/j.ssci.2022.105924

Yoon, K., Choi, J., & Huh, K. (2023). Adaptive decentralized sensor fusion for autonomous vehicle: Estimating the position of surrounding vehicles. *IEEE Access : Practical Innovations, Open Solutions*, *11*, 90999–91008. DOI: 10.1109/ACCESS.2023.3308152

Yu, G., Zhang, S., Hu, M., & Wang, Y. (2020). Prediction of highway tunnel pavement performance based on digital twin and multiple time series stacking. *Advances in Civil Engineering*, *2020*(1), 1–21. DOI: 10.1155/2020/8824135

Yu, J., & Mei, G. (2025). V2X fusion communication framework based on VANETS collaborative autonomous driving. *Transactions on Emerging Telecommunications Technologies*, *36*(10), e70263. Advance online publication. DOI: 10.1002/ett.70263

Yun, H., & Park, D. (2021). Virtualization of self-driving algorithms by interoperating embedded controllers on a game engine for a digital twining autonomous vehicle. *Electronics (Basel)*, *10*(17), 2102. DOI: 10.3390/electronics10172102

Zambrano, V., Mueller-Roemer, J., Sandberg, M., Talasila, P., Zanin, D., Larsen, P., Loeschner, E., Thronicke, W., Pietraroia, D., Landolfi, G., Fontana, A., Laspalas, M., Antony, J., Poser, V., Kiss, T., Bergweiler, S., Serna, S., Izquierdo, S., Viejo, I., & Stork, A. (2022). Industrial digitalization in the industry 4.0 era: Classification, reuse and authoring of digital models on Digital Twin platforms. *Array (New York, N.Y.)*, *14*, 100176. DOI: 10.1016/j.array.2022.100176

Zapata, N., Pérez-González, G., Bustos, P., Barroso, S., & Núñez, P. (2025). An efficient and versatile digital twin model implementation for autonomous connected vehicles based on distributed, low-latency working memory. *Internet of Things : Engineering Cyber Physical Human Systems*, *32*, 101627. DOI: 10.1016/j.iot.2025.101627

Zhang, Y., & Li, J. (2023). Research on Real-time Simulation of Automobile Production Line based on Discrete Event and Multiagent. *Frontiers in Computing and Intelligent Systems*. DOI: 10.54097/fcis.v4i1.9466

Zhang, H., Liu, Q., Chen, X., Zhang, D., & Leng, J. (2017). A Digital Twin-Based Approach for Designing and Multi-Objective Optimization of Hollow Glass Production Line. *IEEE Access : Practical Innovations, Open Solutions*, *5*, 26901–26911. DOI: 10.1109/ACCESS.2017.2766453

Zhang, H., Liu, Q., Chen, X., Zhang, D., & Leng, J. (2020). A digital twin-based approach for designing and multi-objective optimization of manufacturing systems. *IEEE Access : Practical Innovations, Open Solutions*, *8*, 210354–210367.

Zhang, H., Zheng, Z., Yu, H., Yang, G., & Yuan, S. (2025). Analysis of intelligent and connected vehicles driving system modeling. *Proceedings of the Institution of Mechanical Engineers. Part D, Journal of Automobile Engineering*, *239*(5), 1807–1819. DOI: 10.1177/09544070241228643

Zhang, J., Ding, G., Zou, Y., Qin, S., & Fu, J. (2021). Review of job shop scheduling research and its new perspectives under Industry 4.0. *Journal of Intelligent Manufacturing*, *30*(4), 1809–1830. DOI: 10.1007/s10845-017-1350-2

Zhang, J., Zhao, B., Yang, G., Zhou, X., Huang, Y., & Li, W. (2025). A digital twin framework for intelligent operation and maintenance of highway tunnels. *Building Simulation*, *18*(5), 545–558. DOI: 10.1007/s12273-025-1332-9

Zhang, L., He, R., Liu, Q., & Gardoni, P. (2026). *Resilience in urban transit systems*. Springer Nature Singapore., DOI: 10.1007/978-981-95-4322-9

Zhang, M., Xu, J., Gao, Y., Shen, D., & Xu, Z. (2025). Can combined virtual-real testing speed up autonomous vehicle testing? Findings from AEB field experiments. *Communications in Transportation Research*, *5*, 100216. DOI: 10.1016/j.commtr.2025.100216

Zhang, Q., Shen, S., Li, H., Cao, W., Tang, W., Jiang, J., Deng, M., Zhang, Y., Gu, B., Wu, K.-J., Zhang, K., & Liu, S. (2022). Digital twin-driven intelligent production line for automotive MEMS pressure sensors. *Advanced Engineering Informatics*, *54*, 101779. DOI: 10.1016/j.aei.2022.101779

Zhang, S., Dinavahi, V., & Liang, T. (2025). Towards real-time digital twins of power-electronic traction systems for electric vehicles. *Energy*, *310*, 135451. DOI: 10.1016/j.energy.2025.135451

Zhang, T., Ding, J., Liu, Z., & Zhang, W. (2025). Visualization of industrial big data: State-of-the-art and future perspectives. *Engineering (Beijing)*, *52*, 85–101. DOI: 10.1016/j.eng.2025.08.014

Zhang, X., Lai, C., Li, G., & Zheng, D. (2025). Towards digital-twin-assisted resource management for vehicular networks. *Computer Networks*, *248*, 111514. DOI: 10.1016/j.comnet.2025.111514

Zhang, X., Li, J., Zhou, J., Zhang, S., Wang, J., Yuan, Y., Liu, J., & Li, J. (2025). Vehicle-to-everything communication in intelligent connected vehicles: A survey and taxonomy. *Automotive Innovation*, *8*(1), 13–45. DOI: 10.1007/s42154-024-00310-2

Zhang, Y., & Wang, X. (2025). Advances in digital twin technology in industry: A review. *Journal of Industrial Computing*, *18*(5), 72–89.

Zhao, H., Meng, M., Li, X., Xu, J., Li, L., & Galland, S. (2024). A survey of autonomous driving frameworks and simulators. *Advanced Engineering Informatics*, *62*, 102850. DOI: 10.1016/j.aei.2024.102850

Zhao, J., Wen, Z., Mohanta, K., Subasu, S., Fremoul, A., & Song, Y. (2025). Digital twins and drones for real-time road network inspection and monitoring. *Drones (Basel)*, *9*(9), 621. DOI: 10.3390/drones9090621

Zhou, C., Dong, Z., & Lin, H. (2022). Learning Persistent Homology of 3D Point Clouds. *Computers & Graphics*, *102*, 269–279. DOI: 10.1016/j.cag.2021.10.022

Zhou, J., Li, Z., Zhang, Y., & Dong, S. (2026). Transportation infrastructure resilience and safety under climate risks: A global bibliometric and thematic analysis (1995–2025). *Multimodal Transportation*, *100307*(3), 100307. Advance online publication. DOI: 10.1016/j.multra.2026.100307

Zhu, X., Li, C., Mai, J., Yang, J., & Kuang, Z. (2024). An Empirical Study on the Digital Twin System of Intelligent Production Line. *2024 4th International Conference on Computer Science and Blockchain (CCSB)*, 280–286. DOI: 10.1109/CCSB63463.2024.10735491

Zhuang, C., Miao, T., Liu, J., & Xiong, H. (2021). The connotation of digital twin and the construction and application method of shop-floor digital twin. *Robotics and Computer-integrated Manufacturing*, *68*, 102075. DOI: 10.1016/j.rcim.2020.102075

Zhu, H., Yuen, K., Mihaylova, L., & Leung, H. (2017). Overview of environment perception for intelligent vehicles. *IEEE Transactions on Intelligent Transportation Systems*, *18*(10), 2584–2601. Advance online publication. DOI: 10.1109/TITS.2017.2658662

Zhu, J. (2024). Synthetic Data Generation by Diffusion Models. *National Science Review, 11*(8), nwae276. Advance online publication. DOI: 10.1093/nsr/nwae276

Zhu, L., Yu, F., Wang, Y., Ning, B., & Tang, T. (2018). Big data analytics in intelligent transportation systems: A survey. *IEEE Transactions on Intelligent Transportation Systems*. Advance online publication. DOI: 10.1109/TITS.2018.2815678

Zhu, M., Liu, H., Miao, C., Li, G., Zhang, Y., & Zhao, F. (2025). Digital twin-assisted stability analysis of transportation infrastructure under extreme cold regions. *Cold Regions Science and Technology, 218*, 104395. DOI: 10.1016/j.coldregions.2024.104395

Zia, Q., Jan, A., Yang, D., Zhang, H., & Li, Y. (2025). Optimized Real-time Decision Making with EfficientNet in Digital Twin-based Vehicular Networks. *Electronics (Basel), 14*(6), 1084. DOI: 10.3390/electronics14061084

Židek, K., Pitel', J., Adamek, M., Lazorík, P., & Hošovský, A. (2020). Digital Twin of Experimental Smart Manufacturing Assembly System for Industry 4.0 Concept. *Sustainability (Basel), 12*(9), 3658. Advance online publication. DOI: 10.3390/su12093658

Zöldy, M., Szalay, Z., & Tihanyi, V. (2020). Challenges in homologation process of vehicles with Artificial Intelligence. *Transport, 35*(4), 435–446. DOI: 10.3846/transport.2020.12904

About the Contributors

Mazhar Hussain Shaik is an academician and researcher with 15 years of teaching and research experience at Higher Education Institutions (HEIs), having worked at both undergraduate and postgraduate levels. Previously, he held the position of Senior Lecturer in the Department of Computing and Electronics Engineering, Research Coordinator, and Quality Coordinator for the Centre for Research and Consultancy at Middle East College (MEC), Muscat, Oman. He completed his PhD in Electrical Engineering (Specialized in Artificial Intelligence and Autonomous Navigation) in 2023 from Universiti Teknologi Malaysia (UTM), Johor Bahru, Malaysia. He obtained my Masters in Embedded Systems (ES) in 2012 from Jawaharlal Nehru Technological University, Hyderabad (JNTUH), and his Bachelor's in Electronics and Communication Engineering in 2008 from JNTUH. Further, he earned a Postgraduate Certificate (PGCert) in International Higher Education Practice (IHEP) in December 2017 from Coventry University, UK. He is a member of several professional bodies and a Senior Member of IEEE. He has also obtained certified expert in Digital Circuits and Systems from IIT Madras through National Programme on Technology Enhanced Learning. He has earned several academic certifications and completed multiple training courses from reputed organizations. He has published over 30+ research articles in peer-reviewed journals and contributed more than 20 research works in various conference proceedings. In addition, he has filed patents and registered copyrights. He is the author of several edited books and book chapters. He has successfully attracted research grants from The Research Council (TRC), Oman, as well as internal grants from Middle East College (MEC), Muscat, Oman. He has supervised more than 60 final-year undergraduate projects in Computing, IT, and Electronics and Telecommunication Engineering and he is currently co-supervising 2 PhD candidates. He was nominated for and received the IEEE ComSoc Internet of All Competition Award – Winners, 2022, for "Connecting Underserved Communities to the Internet" in the Europe, Middle East, & Africa Region. In addition to academic responsibilities, he has held several administrative roles contributing to institutional planning, accreditation, and academic development.

Imran Mohd Ibrahim is an Associate Professor at Universiti Teknikal Malaysia Melaka. He received his bachelor, master and doctoral degree from Universiti Teknologi Malaysia, all in electrical engineering, in 2000, 2005, and 2016, respectively. He served as faculty's inaugural Deputy Dean (Research and Post Graduate Study) and contributed to the early development of research activities at faculty and institution. He has lead several grants from industry, government and university in antenna research and wireless communication. He is also a committee member to IMT and Future Networks Working Group under Malaysia Technical Standard Forum Berhad. He also serves as drafter to the Technical Code, Prediction and Measurement of RF-EMF Exposure from Base Station. He has published more than 100 journals and conference papers. His research interests are antenna and microwave device design. He also supervised a PhD and Master students by research in antenna design for beyond 5G and medical application. He was elevated to IEEE Senior Membership in 2021 based on his significant contribution in Electrical and Electronic Engineering field. In January 2023, he has appointed as TVET ambassador for UTeM for the project Knowledge Transfer and Mobile Wifi Router Installation for Rural School Area.

Khaizuran Abdullah is an associate professor, department of Electrical and Computer Engineering at International Islamic University Malaysia. He is currently registered as professional engineer with Board of Engineers Malaysia. He obtained his Ph.D. in Electrical and Computer Engineering from RMIT University, Melbourne, Australia, in 2010. He also obtained his master degree in Electrical Engineering from Universiti Teknologi Malaysia (UTM), Skudai in 2003. In addition, in 1997, he obtained his Bachelor of Science in Electrical Engineering from Ohio University, Athens, USA. Dr. Abdullah's main research interest lies in wireless communication particularly in 5G system, IoT and LTE-A system dealing with an Orthogonal Frequency Division Multiplexing (OFDM) technique. He served as the Vice Chair of IEEE Communication Society and VT (ComSoc/VT) for Malaysia Chapter in 2018, and also as senior member of IEEE. He is also a registered member of Board of Engineers Malaysia.

***

Mallareddy Adudhodla is a Professor in the Department of Information Technology at CVR College of Engineering, with over two decades of academic and research experience. He obtained his B.Tech, M.Tech, and Ph.D. from Jawaharlal Nehru Technological University Hyderabad. His research interests include Network Security, Cloud Security, Artificial Intelligence, Machine Learning, Blockchain, and IoT. He has published numerous papers in reputed journals and conferences and holds multiple Indian patents. He is also an active member of the Computer Society of India and the Indian Society for Technical Education.

Jaime Aguilar-Ortiz holds a Ph.D. in Mathematical Sciences (CINVESTAV–IPN, Mexico) and serves as a professor and researcher in the fields of Mathematics, Artificial Intelligence, and Project Management, with academic involvement also extending to the Universidad Politécnica Metropolitana de Hidalgo. He additionally leads innovation-driven initiatives as Director General of CICAINTE and TEDNOVA GROUP, bridging rigorous academic work with applied technological development and institutional impact. His prior scholarly and editorial contributions include the preparation and/or editing of a substantial body of books and educational resources spanning mathematics education, financial mathematics, programming, and technology-based learning, complemented by the creation of audiovisual materials, educational platforms, and serious-game applications aimed at strengthening learning outcomes. His academic production further includes dozens of peer-reviewed articles and book chapters addressing themes at the intersection of smart cities, education, and AI, together with sustained experience in research mentoring, curriculum development, and interdisciplinary collaboration. These achievements, combined with recognized academic credentials and a consistent record of knowledge dissemination and capacity building, position him as a strong editor for a high-impact scholarly volume with methodological rigor, cross-sector relevance, and measurable educational and societal value.

Anorgul Ashirova is affiliated with the Department of General Professional Sciences at Mamun University, Khiva, Uzbekistan. Her academic interests focus on interdisciplinary education, professional skill development, and the integration of foundational knowledge across multiple academic disciplines. She is actively engaged in teaching and academic activities that aim to strengthen students' theoretical understanding and practical competencies required in modern professional environments. Her work emphasizes innovative teaching approaches, student-centered learning, and the application of academic knowledge to real-world professional contexts. Anorgul Ashirova also contributes to academic discussions related to curriculum development, educational improvement, and professional training. Through her teaching and scholarly engagement, she aims to support the development of well-prepared graduates equipped with the knowledge, critical thinking abilities, and professional skills necessary to succeed in diverse career fields.

Vasavi Bande is an accomplished academic and researcher with over 18 years of teaching experience, currently serving as Sr.Associate Professor in Information Technology at MVSR Engineering College, Hyderabad. She holds a PhD in CSE from JNTUH and has published more than 29 research papers in reputed international journals and conferences. Her expertise spans cloud computing, cybersecurity, artificial intelligence, blockchain, and machine learning. She has also contributed to academia through patents, textbooks, consultancy projects, and active roles as editor, reviewer, and resource person in national and international forums. With a strong record of leadership as HoD and committee member, Dr. Bande is dedicated to advancing research, fostering innovation, and mentoring the next generation of engineers.

Constantinos Challoumis is a Visiting Professor at the National and Kapodistrian University of Athens (NKUA), at AUEB, and at CNAM University (France) via Descartes College, and an Assistant Professor in IT, Law, and Management at Philips University. He holds a PhD in Economics (NKUA), is a Postdoc cand. (NKUA), and has 7 BScs (1 of which is a cand.) and 8 MScs (1 of which is a cand.). His research spans economics, accounting, law, technology, and quantitative modeling.

J. V. P. Udaya Deepika, B.Tech., M.Tech., is having 4 years of experience in teaching. Her area of research includes Computer Networks, Network Security, IOT, ML &AI.

Ocotlán Diaz-Parra is a Professor and Researcher at Universidad Politécnica de Pachuca (UPP), a National Researcher under the Secretaria de Ciencia, Humanidades, Tecnología e Innovación program, and an Adjunct Researcher at the National Laboratory of Autonomous Vehicles and Exoskeletons (LANAVEX). His research interests include Smart Cities, Smart Water, Smart Education, Smart Government, Smart Healthcare, Smart Farming, Smart Energy, Smart Sports, Smart Food, Smart Tourism, Algorithmic Finance, Algorithmic Portfolio Management, Applications and Theory of Algorithms, Bio-inspired Algorithms, Combinatorial Optimization Problems, Compilers, Computational Intelligence, Computational Complexity Theory, Computational Financial Intelligence, Complexity of Algorithms, Complexity of Instances, Computational Statistics, Computer Networks, Computer Science Security, Cybercrimes, Data Mining, Education, Evolutionary Computation, Heuristic Optimization Techniques in Bioinformatics, Hybrid Evolutionary Algorithms, Hybrid Optimization Algorithms, Machine Learning, Meta-heuristics, Operations Research, Operations Management, Parallel & Distributed Computing, Production Planning and Logistics Optimization, Project Scheduling Problems, Software Engineering, and Transgenic Algorithms.

Carlos R. Domínguez-Mayorga holds a Ph.D. in Sciences specializing in Artificial Intelligence, with a foundational background in Physics and Mathematics. His research focuses on Deep Learning, NLP, neural networks, and the development of predictive models. He has an extensive track record in scientific publications and graduate program management, applying cutting-edge data science techniques to engineering and sustainability projects.

Swati Jaiswal is an accomplished academician and researcher with over 16 years of experience in teaching, research, and academic administration in the field of Computer Science and Engineering. She holds a Ph.D. in Computer Science and Engineering from SCOPE, VIT University, Vellore. Her areas of expertise include Artificial Intelligence, Machine Learning, Data Analytics, Cloud Computing, IoT, and emerging intelligent systems. Dr. Jaiswal has made significant research contributions with multiple patents, an authored book, several copyrights, and numerous publications in reputed SCI and Scopus-indexed journals, international conferences, and edited book chapters. She actively serves as a reviewer for leading international journals and conferences and has coordinated national and international academic events, FDPs, and research activities. Her professional interests focus on applying AI-driven solutions to real-world problems, fostering interdisciplinary research, and mentoring students and young researchers. Dr. Jaiswal continues to contribute to academic excellence through research, innovation, and collaborative initiatives.

Prachi Joshi is the Head of School (HOS) at DES Pune University, where she provides academic leadership and strategic direction to foster excellence in teaching, research, and innovation. With extensive experience in higher education administration and curriculum development, she has been instrumental in strengthening interdisciplinary learning, industry collaboration, and outcome-based education. Dr. Joshi is recognized for her commitment to quality assurance, faculty development, and creating an inclusive academic environment that supports student success and institutional growth.

K. S. Sharvanthika serves as an Assistant Professor in the Department of Computer Technology at Kongu Engineering College. With a strong academic foundation in computer science and emerging technologies, she is dedicated to fostering innovative learning environments and promoting technical excellence among students. Her teaching interests include programming, data analytics, and modern computing paradigms. She actively contributes to academic development through curriculum design, mentoring, and participation in research-oriented activities. Committed to continuous professional growth, she engages in workshops, conferences, and collaborative initiatives to stay aligned with advancements in the field of computer technology and education.

Karu Prasada Rao is an Assistant Professor in Computer Science and Engineering at GITAM University with 18+ years of academic experience. His research focuses on Computer Vision, Machine Learning, and Deep Learning, particularly facial expression recognition and object detection.

Sravani M. is working as an Assistant Professor in the department of Information Technology, MVSR Engineering College, Nadergul, Hyderabad and she have 14 years of teaching experience in the field of Computer Science and Information Technology. She completed her M.Tech in Computer Science and Engineering (CSE) and doing research in Deep Learning.Her areas of interest include Big Data Analytics, Machine Learning, and Cyber Security

M. Swapna is an Assistant Professor with over 18 years of teaching experience in IT Department at MVSR Engineering College, Hyderabad. She is currently pursuing a Ph.D. in CSE (AI & ML) at SR University and holds an M.Tech in Digital Systems and Computer Electronics. Her research interests include machine learning, healthcare analytics, and data science. She has published research papers in reputed journals and conferences, holds a patent in deep learning for CKD prediction, and has co-authored books on Artificial Intelligence and Data Science. She is actively involved in academic research, curriculum development, and faculty development programs in emerging technologies

N. Naveena serves as an Assistant Professor in the Department of Computer Technology (UG) at Kongu Engineering College. She possesses a strong academic background in computer science and is actively engaged in teaching, research, and student development. Her areas of interest include data analytics, software engineering, and emerging computing technologies. She is committed to delivering quality education through innovative teaching methodologies, fostering critical thinking, and encouraging practical learning among students. In her academic role, she guides undergraduate students, supports project-based learning, and contributes to curriculum development aligned with current industry requirements. She also participates in academic conferences, workshops, and faculty development programs to enhance her professional knowledge and pedagogical skills. Her dedication to academic excellence and student-centered learning has enabled her to contribute effectively to the development of technical competencies and career readiness among learners in the field of computer technology.

Ravikumar R. Natarajan is an experienced academician with over 12+ years of teaching and research expertise across institutions in India, the UAE, and the Maldives. He currently serves as an Assistant Professor at Marwadi University, Rajkot, specializing in Machine Learning, Recommender Systems, and AI-driven applications in healthcare and security. He holds a Ph.D. in Machine Learning and Recommender Systems from Amity University, Jaipur, a Master of Engineering in CSE from VMRF University, Salem, and a Bachelor of Engineering in CSE from Anna University. He also has a MiniMBA from the Swiss eLearning Institute. Dr. Ravikumar has authored more than 8+ multiple SCIE/Scopus-indexed journal articles, 25+ IEEE/Springer conference papers, and co-authored a book on Artificial Intelligence. He has also published 9 patents and contributed 35+ book chapters in emerging domains such as Federated Learning, Blockchain, and Digital Twins for IGI Global, Wiley and Springer publisher. He actively mentors students through initiatives like the Research Activities Club (RAC) and Student Research Internship Training (SRIT), promoting innovation and research culture.

Mahfujur Rahman is an Assistant Professor in the Department of Computer Science at American International University-Bangladesh (AIUB). He received his B.Sc. in Computer Science and M.Sc. in Computer Science with a specialization in Intelligent Systems from AIUB. He began his academic career at AIUB as a Teaching Assistant and later served as an Instructor and Lecturer before being promoted to Assistant Professor in 2023. In addition to his academic experience, he has industry exposure as a Web Application Developer at RF Builder Ltd., where he was involved in web application development and maintenance. He has over five years of experience supervising undergraduate thesis projects and actively contributes to research and academic activities. His research interests include Intelligent Systems, Natural Language Processing, Machine Learning, Data Science, Medical Image Processing, Internet of Things (IoT), and Big Data Analytics. He also serves as a reviewer for several local and international peer-reviewed journals and conferences.

Jorge A. Ruiz-Vanoye is a Professor and Researcher at Universidad Politécnica de Pachuca (UPP), a National Researcher under the Secretaria de Ciencia, Humanidades, Tecnología e Innovación program, and an Adjunct Researcher at the National Laboratory of Autonomous Vehicles and Exoskeletons (LANAVEX). Additionally, he holds the title of Lecturer-level Researcher for the Agency for the Quality of the University System of Catalonia (Generalitat de Catalunya). His research interests include Smart Cities, Smart Water, Smart Education, Smart Government, Smart Healthcare, Smart Farming, Smart Energy, Smart Sports, Smart Food, Smart Tourism, Algorithmic Finance, Algorithmic Portfolio Management, Applications and Theory of Algorithms, Bio-inspired Algorithms, Combinatorial Optimization Problems, Compilers, Computational Intelligence, Computational Complexity Theory, Computational Financial Intelligence, Complexity of Algorithms, Complexity of Instances, Computational Statistics, Computer Networks, Computer Science Security, Cybercrimes, Data Mining, Education, Evolutionary Computation, Heuristic Optimization Techniques in Bioinformatics, Hybrid Evolutionary Algorithms, Hybrid Optimization Algorithms, Machine Learning, Meta-heuristics, Operations Research, Operations Management, Parallel & Distributed Computing, Production Planning and Logistics Optimization, Project Scheduling Problems, Software Engineering, and Transgenic Algorithms.

Aarthi S is a dedicated Assistant Professor in Computer Science with over six years of teaching experience. She is currently pursuing her Ph.D. at Marwadi University, Gujarat, and holds an M.Phil. and MCA from Bharathiar University, Tamil Nadu. Throughout her academic career, Aarthi has specialized in programming languages such as C++, Java, and C, and contributed to research in recommender systems and AI-related data privacy. She has published journal articles, contributed to book chapters, and actively participated in technical workshops. Known for her student mentorship and engagement in academic events, Aarthi remains committed to fostering innovation and excellence in computer science education.

Prakruti Shah is an experienced academician and researcher with over two decades of teaching experience in Electrical Engineering. She completed her Ph.D. in microgrid optimal scheduling with renewable energy sources. Her research interests include Electric Vehicles, Microgrids, Power Systems, and Battery Energy Storage Systems. She is actively engaged in teaching, research, and mentoring, with a focus on sustainable energy technologies and modern power systems.

Venkataprasad Thaneeru is a B.Tech student in Computer Science with research interests in Machine Learning, Deep Learning, and cybersecurity. He is particularly interested in applying intelligent systems to areas such as cyber threat detection, data analysis, and real-world security challenges.

Francisco R. Trejo-Macotela holds a Ph.D. in Electronics from INAOE and is Professor and Senior Researcher at Universidad Politécnica de Pachuca (UPP). He is a National Researcher of the Secretariat of Science, Humanities, Technology and Innovation (SECIHTI) of Mexico and adjunct member of LANAVEX. His prolific academic output comprises slightly more than 60 publications in domains including smart cities, embedded IoT systems, telecommunications, electronics, aquaculture, artificial intelligence, bio-inspired algorithms, combinatorial optimisation, and educational technologies.

Dilmurod Turaev is affiliated with the Department of Information Technology and Exact Sciences at Termez University of Economics and Service, Termez, Uzbekistan. His academic interests focus on information technology, computer science, and the application of computational methods in scientific and educational environments. He is actively involved in teaching and academic activities that aim to strengthen students' knowledge in programming, data analysis, and modern computing technologies. His work emphasizes the integration of digital technologies, problem-solving skills, and analytical approaches to address real-world technological challenges. Dilmurod Turaev also contributes to academic discussions related to emerging technologies, information systems, and the advancement of IT education. Through his teaching and scholarly engagement, he seeks to promote innovation in technology education and support the development of skilled professionals capable of contributing to modern digital and scientific advancements.

Amit Kumar Tyagi is working as an Assistant Professor, at National Forensic Sciences University, Gandhinagar, Gujarat, India. He received his Ph.D. Degree (Full-Time) in 2018 from Pondicherry Central University, 605014, Puducherry, India. About his academic experience, he has worked as an assistant professor at several institutes like Lord Krishna College of Engineering (LKCE), Ghaziabad (for the periods of July 2009- July 2010, and October 2012- October 2013), Lingaya's Vidyapeeth (formerly known as Lingaya's University), Faridabad (September 2018- May 2019), VIT Chennai (June 2019- November 2022) and NIFT New Delhi (November 2022- September 2025). His supervision experience includes more than 10 Masters' dissertations and one PhD thesis. He has contributed to several projects such as "AARIN" and "P3- Block" to address some of the open issues related to the privacy breaches in Vehicular Applications (such as Parking) and Medical Cyber Physical Systems (MCPS). He has published over 350 research articles in refereed high impact journals, conferences and books, and some of his articles has been awarded as best paper awards. Also, he has filed more than 15 patents (Nationally and Inte

Khayrulla Urozboev is affiliated with the Department of International Scientific Journals and Ratings at Alfraganus University, Tashkent, Uzbekistan. His professional interests focus on scholarly publishing, academic journal management, research evaluation systems, and international research visibility. He is actively involved in initiatives that support the development and quality improvement of scientific journals, including strengthening editorial standards and promoting best practices in publication ethics. His work also emphasizes enhancing the global visibility of research through international indexing platforms and academic collaboration. Khayrulla Urozboev contributes to activities related to journal ranking systems, research dissemination, and the advancement of high-quality scientific publications. Through his professional engagement, he aims to support researchers and academic institutions in improving research impact, publication standards, and international academic recognition.

Saavanth Veerumneni is a research-oriented undergraduate student with strong interests in artificial intelligence, machine learning, IoT, cybersecurity, bioinformatics, and intelligent systems. He has contributed to research in adaptive and secure IoT design through the paper Adaptive Network Architectures for Scalable, Resilient and Secure IoT Systems and in smart-agriculture automation through Cognitive IoT-Enabled Soft Telerobotics for Precision Smart Agriculture in Remote Villages. These works reflect his interest in building scalable, resilient, and application-driven systems that combine sensing, edge intelligence, secure communication, and real-world deployment considerations. He has also worked on eDNA-based classification for deep-sea biology, showing his growing interest in applying computational methods to interdisciplinary scientific problems. His broader academic focus lies at the intersection of AI and domain-centered research, where intelligent systems can support scientific discovery and address practical challenges in emerging fields. He aspires to pursue advanced research and contribute to impactful innovations in interdisciplinary computing, with long-term goals in both research and academia.

Index

S

T

U

V

W

Y

www.ingramcontent.com/pod-product-compliance
Lightning Source LLC
LaVergne TN
LVHW081415021026
849161LV00011BA/2732